FATHERS, BROTHERS, AND SONS

BY LARRY GRAY

Larry Gray

15.02.05

Printed in Victoria, Canada

A cataloguing record for this book that includes the U.S. Library of Congress Classification number, the Library of Congress Call number and the Dewey Decimal cataloguing code is available from the National Library of Canada. The complete cataloguing record can be obtained from the National Library's online database at: www.nlc-bnc.ca/amicus/index-e.html
ISBN: 1-4120-1901-X

TRAFFORD

This book was published on-demand in cooperation with Trafford Publishing. On-demand publishing is a unique process and service of making a book available for retail sale to the public taking advantage of on-demand manufacturing and Internet marketing. **On-demand publishing** includes promotions, retail sales, manufacturing, order fulfilment, accounting and collecting royalties on behalf of the author.

Suite 6E, 2333 Government St., Victoria, B.C. V8T 4P4, CANADA

Phone	250-383-6864	Toll-free	1-888-232-4444 (Canada & US)
Fax	250-383-6804	E-mail	sales@trafford.com
Web site	www.trafford.com	TRAFFORD PUBLISHING IS A DIVISION OF TRAFFORD HOLDINGS LTD.	
Trafford Catalogue #03-2279		www.trafford.com/robots/03-2279.html	

10   9   8   7   6

DEDICATION:

To my three sons,

Scott, Kevin and Chris.

That they may read and learn;

never to be conscripted for education by experience.

FOREWORD

WE WILL REMEMBER THEM

Before embarking for overseas in 1940 I was a student at Queen's University. I remember the cubicles in the Memorial Union with portraits of young people in service uniforms who never made it home from the Great War. I was intrigued by the earnest faces wishing I could discover somehow their individual stories. We all owe each of them so much!

Larry Gray knows exactly what I mean. Coming from Carleton Place, conveniently close to the National Capital, – a proud old town with rich traditions of military heroism, Larry too has served his Queen and Country throughout an adventurous and productive life. He has 'paid his dues,' Now, as an established historian, he is summoning a parade of these dead, the people who perished in World War II. He is restoring them to life. Please take time to know each of them and say a prayer of thankfulness for their sacrifices. Enjoy this great read and be glad.

John.

The Hon. Col. John Ross Matheson, OC.
CD, QC, BA, MA, LLM, KStJ, KCIJ, FRES.

ACKNOWLEDGEMENTS

Books are not written in a vacuum. I owe a great deal to many people, especially for their help during the research prior to any writing. My heart-felt thanks to all the following:

First and foremost, my wife Gloria continues to be my spiritual and temporal inspiration. Her patience is much appreciated for the days and nights I spent typing and formatting on the computer instead of paying due attention to her. As well as forebearance, she also exercised her language skills by proof-reading and suggesting improvements to the text.

Robert Mullan, a talented cartoonist, provided the original artwork that prefaces several sections.

Brian Costello who provided constant encouragement.

Larry Richer and Marilyn Caillier, Access to Information co-ordinators at the National Archives, Personnel Records, steered me towards raw material of inestimable value. Janet Baril and her librarians at the Carleton Place Library gave advice and assistance in locating research material. The staff of *The Carleton Place Canadian*, especially Jeff Maguire, Theresa Fritz and Liz Bardawill for their indulgence while I rooted around in the paper's archives. Liz did double duty in providing scanning of articles and pictures plus she is the designer responsible for the splendid cover illustration; husband Rick sorted out my many computer problems.

Many, many people agreed to be interviewed and loaned me personal family photographs that have proven invaluable to the telling of these stories. They are: Allan Barker, Aileen Brouse (sister of Ross MacFarlane), Doug Brown for collaborating on research and gathering valuable family photographs, Kevin and Mervyn Camelon, Glady Dowdall (sister of Fred Ryan (Dray), Art Evoy (friend of Lloyd Scott), Dave Findlay, Ron Irvine, Marion LeClair (Joe Borland's daughter) and Janice Gibson (grandaughter of Joe Borland), Orm Giles, Wally Mace (friend of Wilson Costello), Ron & Joyce MacFarlane, Ilene MacIntosh and her sister Brenda Schaller(sisters of Boyne Dunphy), Alice (Mrs. Murray) McRae (sister of Cedric Cameron), Audrey (Babe) Morphy-Kennedy (fiancée of Maurice Fieldhouse), Tex Morris, Isobel Robertson (sister of Jimmy Warren), David Patterson, Bernard Pye, Bob Richter (curator–Comox Air Force Museum), Marj

Whyte, The Royal Canadian Legion Branch 92, Carleton Place (Garry Pond, President), Branch 240, Almonte (Joe LeBlanc, President), Sandy Walker (nephew of Andy Porterfield) and Morley & Joan Whalen.

Both my editor, Susan Code-MacDougall and Leanne Enright, layout and design, are thanked for their professionalism, patience and perseverance in preparing the rough manuscript for publication

CONTENTS

INTRODUCTION

On November 11, 1985, commemorating the sixty-sixth anniversary of the end of the Great War, the President of the United States, Ronald Reagan, spoke these words at Arlington National Cemetery:

> It is, in a way, an odd thing to honour those who died in defence of our country in wars far away. The imagination plays a trick. We see these soldiers in our mind as old and wise. We see them as something like the Founding Fathers, grave and grey-haired. But most of them were boys when they died, they gave up two lives—the one they were living and the one they would have lived. When they died, they gave up their chance to be husbands and fathers and grandfathers. They gave up their chance to be revered old men. They gave up everything for their country, for us. All we can do is remember.

For the second time in the twentieth century, the town of Carleton Place gave its men—fathers, brothers, and sons—as grist to the mills of the war gods. Grinding the century's second generation of world youth into the dust of Europe, death did not exempt Carleton Place. Forty-six of her young men lay dead before their time, an ocean away from home.

Historian Terry Copp has written that history signifies three very different things: "The actual events that took place, the surviving memories and written evidence about those events, and the attempts of historians to construct a narrative account of some part of the story." This book records the biographies of men from a small eastern Ontario town who fought in World War II. They gave their lives just as those in my earlier book, *We Are The Dead*, perished in Flanders during World War I. Both books attempt to recover personal experiences almost completely lost in the sands of time. Again the purpose is to put faces to the names engraved on the town's war memorial.

Story telling about people whose names are recognized by a reader is an excellent method of interesting young Canadians in their long-neglected military history. With any luck a national pride may also be instilled. The stories of those who went overseas to risk life and limb for King and Country; real people from real communities, is much more compelling than dry political history. There is no fiction in this book. It records in detail the life experience of each man from Carleton Place who died in the defence of freedom. Yet not one of these soldiers expected to die! Would they have gone if they did?

I have filled in details only where I could confirm their accuracy, and those few conversations that do appear were recorded verbatim from military files.

The greatest challenge to the historical storyteller is to learn the protagonist's train of thought without deviating from the established historical record. Dead soldiers have phenomenal stories that are untold and unrecorded. I have tried to see the world as these men saw it, to stand where they stood. I have used my imagination and military experience to get inside their heads. I stand by the historical accuracy of the events but readily take ownership of any errors in interpretation.

LEST WE FORGET! 1939

During the early dawn of September 1, 1939, the town of Carleton Place slept blissfully as the sun rose over eastern Europe. German armies were massed, poised for action on their eastern border. In a rumble of engines, armoured Panzer divisions, with lightning speed, crossed the Polish frontier. In mere hours they destroyed defences that were barely equipped to fight World War I, let alone the modern mechanized military might of the resurrected Germany. A new word entered the military lexicon—*blitzkreig*—the lightning war.

Russian troops, as agreed in a previous pact with Germany, pushed west. Futile Polish resistance was crushed between two quickly advancing armies. With no options left, Poland surrendered.

Britain and France had a pact with Poland that demanded their assistance should the Balkan state be attacked. On September 3, 1939, they declared war on Germany.

In 1914, Canada had been automatically committed to following Britain's lead in foreign affairs. Now, although there was little doubt but that she would follow, Canada's independent action, delineated in the 1931 Statute of Westminster, dictated no such automatism. Still, Parliament purposely dithered until it met in special session on September 7. Support of British and French action was approved on September 9, and on September 10, 1939, George VI was able to announce that the Dominion of Canada had declared war on Nazi Germany.

Canadians were especially fond of this king and his queen. The Royal Couple had toured the Dominion that summer of 1939. "For King and Country" was no idle slogan in an age that now seems so naive. That naïveté was soon, once again, to be dissolved on the battlefields of Europe, as well as on the seas, in the air, and on the bloody ground.

THEY SHALL GROW NOT OLD

With courage, with a sense of duty, they have laid at their country's feet the most glorious contribution they could offer. 'They have met danger face to face, and, after one brief moment while at the summit of their fortune, left behind them not their fear, but their glory.' This is the way the Athenian warriors who fell in the war against Sparta were described 2,500 years ago. This is the way we can describe these four men who, by offering their lives, have ensured that they will be remembered by us.

—The Right Honourable Adrienne Clarkson, Governor General of Canada, in reference to soldiers of the Third Battalion, Princess Patricia's Canadian Light Infantry, killed in the war against terror in Afghanistan.

April 28, 2002.

There are many narratives recording conversations with World War II veterans. Veterans who are only now ready to share their stories. It has taken more than half a century for their personal agonies to fade sufficiently to allow these men and women to talk about their wartime experiences. However, the stories that follow here are those of veterans who cannot tell their own tales, and their stories have remained largely untold. So it is for their survivors, curious children, grandchildren, weeping wives and lovers, that these biographies are recorded. When veterans gather in community veterans' clubs, over a beer or a gingerale, conversation inevitably turns to memories of war–some terrifying, some humourous. Just as inevitable is their remembrance of those who did not make it back and the tacit recognition of their own and their dead comrades' contribution to the victory over the most evil of tyrannies. These are the stories that many men took to their graves.

In a small town, everyone knows everyone else, all joys and every sorrow is shared. So, while this book is about Carleton Place boys, similar stories played out in every community across Canada. These were real people. They "lived, felt dawn, saw sunset glow."

They were soldiers, airmen, and sailors. They did not cause the war in which they died. The men and women who donned uniforms to serve their nation knew only that they were needed. It was not a call they could ignore. So they went: to England, to Italy, to Normandy, to the Far East, and to the furthest reaches of the British Empire. Be grateful that they did. They got there in time to ensure that this world is a better place for those they left behind.

PART 1—ANCHORS AWAY

CHAPTER 1—DOWN TO THE SEA IN SHIPS

Oh God, Thy sea is so great,
And my boat is so small.[1]

This title was not chosen capriciously. It has no relation to the song "Anchors Aweigh," which refers to the raising of an anchor so a ship may freely sail away. Rather, it recognizes that each sailor Carleton Place lost is, in fact, the loss of an anchor.

V6408 Able Telegrapher Horace Garner Stark
Royal Canadian Navy Volunteer Reserve

Canadian warships flew the same ensign
as that of the Royal Navy.

A week after his nation declared war on Germany, in September 1939, Horace Stark joined the Royal Canadian Navy Volunteer Reserve (RCNVR). He was nineteen years old when he had his medical examination for enlistment on September 15. He was officially sworn into the Navy on September 30.

Horace was not totally unfamiliar with things military. During his graduating year at Carleton Place High School (CPHS) in 1939, he held the rank of cadet lieutenant in command of No. 1 Platoon, No. 435 Cadet Corps. (Among those marching in the platoon behind him were: Boyne Dunphy, Lloyd Scott, Arthur Prime, and Wilson Costello.) During that spring inspection, Horace also directed the physical training exercise.

Horace was born on March 19, 1920, in Finch, Stormont County.

C.P.H.S. photo taken 1937 or 1938.

[1] Author unknown. Prayer of Breton fishermen.

His parents, James and Laura, were staunch Presbyterians, and they raised him and his younger brother, Bevis, according to the tenets of their faith. Horace was an active member of the Young People's Society of St. Andrew's Presbyterian Church in Carleton Place.

The family moved to Carleton Place in 1929 when his father was hired to instruct mathematics and history at CPHS, where he gained the nickname "Picky" from his students because of his insistence upon precision in their written work.

Although Horace went directly from high school into the naval service, he quickly qualified as a telegraphist. He was already a ham[2]-radio operator and had his own amateur radio station using Morse code[3] to "talk" to other operators worldwide. His radio call sign, which identified him when he was on the air, was VE3UH[4].

After his induction, Horace travelled by train to Halifax, reporting for basic training to HMCS *Stadacona*, a shore-based installation on the edge of Halifax harbour. His indoctrination in navy life and customs lasted two months, from October 2 to November 27, 1939, before he was drafted to the destroyer, HMCS *Fraser*. An accomplished musician, he still found time to play piano in navy musicales broadcast by the CBC. During his teen years Horace had played with a Carleton Place orchestra, and he and his brother Bevis had often played duets in local concerts.

The Royal Canadian Navy (RCN) was mobilizing, although its entire force comprised only six destroyers, five minesweepers, and two training ships, one of which was powered by sail. The total active strength of 145 officers and 1,674 seamen had, however, been well trained during exchange service on Royal Navy vessels. Also, at war's outbreak, the Volunteer Reserve claimed twenty-one divisions based in the larger Canadian cities, which boosted the total to 366 officers and 3,477 men. These amateur sailors, as a rule, had spent only two or three fortnights a year aboard floating, as opposed to shore-based naval vessels.

Between the Great War of 1914–18 and this conflict, the Canadian government had accepted the fact that it had to support its own navy. Although it could no longer rely on the Royal Navy for protection, it could look to them for support. The first two men-of-war built in the U.K. specifically for the Canadian Navy were 1,500-ton displacement destroyers, the *Saguenay* and the *Skeena*. They arrived in 1931. *Fraser*[5] and the *St. Laurent* followed in 1937, and in 1938, Canada acquired the *Ottawa* and the *Restigouche*.

[2] An informal term for the operator of an amateur radio station.
[3] An alphabet or code in which letters and numbers are represented by combinations of long and short sound (or light) signals. Samuel Morse, a pioneer in the use of electric telegraph systems, developed it.
[4] Each operator was assigned a distinct call sign that was only to be used by him (or her). In Canada call signs were assigned regionally with the prefix VE1 for the Maritime Provinces, VE2 for Quebec, VE3 for Ontario, etc. Horace's call sign identified him as operator"UH" registered in the province of Ontario.
[5] These ships were "River" class destroyers, each named for a Canadian river. Fraser's name is for the river honouring Simon Fraser. The ships' company was known as "the Frasers."

HMCS Fraser in the Panama Canal in 1937 enroute for Esqimault. (National Archives of Canada).

At the time, Germany had two almost-completed 45,000-ton battleships, the *Bismarck* and the *Tirpitz*, an uncompleted aircraft carrier, two 26,000-ton battleships, three 10,000-ton "pocket battleships," eight cruisers, twenty-two destroyers, twenty-six armed merchant cruisers, and fifty-seven submarines. Germany was also building two submarines a month and gearing up for greater production. The security of Canada's east and west coasts was tenuous at best.

In late August, the destroyers *Fraser* and *St. Laurent* arrived in Vancouver for the 1939 Pacific Exhibition. For a few days the public was welcomed aboard. In the afternoon of August 31, their civilian guests were hurriedly but politely put ashore and within two hours the ships were steaming at twenty-five knots[6] for the Panama Canal with orders to be "in all respects ready for action." On September 10, the day Canada officially declared war, they were transiting the canal, and on September 15, they arrived in Halifax. The next day, the *St. Laurent* headed back to sea with the *Saguenay* to escort eighteen merchant ships in the first convoy bound for England. On September 17, the *Fraser* was outward bound with a convoy of fast ships capable of maintaining fifteen knots.

Burdened with ceaseless zigzagging, the little ships' limited fuel supply could not hope to be sufficient for a crossing. Therefore, they were relegated to shepherd duties from the coast to the mid-Atlantic where larger Royal Navy ships would take over.

Even the most audacious merchant ship soon learned that safety lay only in the convoys, as by September's end, the Germans had sunk forty ships.

[6] A knot is the speed of a ship (or an aircraft) over a nautical mile. A nautical mile is approximately 1,852 meters (2,025 yards).

The Canadian destroyers settled in to a schedule of two convoys a week leaving Halifax, each usually lasting two to three days at sea. Interspersed  were anti-submarine patrols in the port approaches, as well as orders to escort damaged ships to harbour and to maintain an ever-vigilant watch against attack from any source at any time.

On November 28, Ordinary Seaman H. G. Stark hoisted his kit bag, buttoned his dufflecoat to his neck against a bitterly cold wind sweeping the shores of Halifax harbour, and made his way up the  gangway of the HMCS *Fraser*. Saluting the quarterdeck, he stepped onto the main deck, wiped salt spray from his glasses, and was sent to stow his gear in cramped quarters with the other telegraphists. At 5' 10" tall, it was going to be a tight fit for him in his hammock, but at a slight137 pounds, he navigated the ship's confined passageways with ease.

Horace had studied handbooks about his first ship and knew she was originally built by Vickers-Armstrong and commissioned into the Royal Navy as HMS *Crescent* in 1931; she had been given to Canada and commissioned into the RCN in February 1937 as HMCS *Fraser*, carrying a crew of fourteen officers and 158 seamen.

Convoy escort proved immensely boring, and the Atlantic became a familiar tableau as they endlessly zigzagged, protecting their flock of freshly painted dun-coloured merchantmen. The weary and fed-up sailors were sure, as their fathers had been two decades before, that the war was passing them by. For by year's end, no Canadian ship had even sighted the enemy, let alone made an attack.

The routine changed on December 10. The *Fraser*, the *Ottawa* (the command ship), the *Restigouche*, and the *St. Laurent* led convoy TC-1 out of Bedford Basin into the Halifax approaches. Aboard the escorted ocean liners *Aquitania*, *Empress of Britain*, *Duchess of Bedford*, *Monarch of Bermuda*, and *Empress of Australia* were 7,400 men of the First Canadian Division. It was the inaugural troop convoy and, due to the liners' speed, a straight-line crossing was ordered.

That same month, Stark was certified by the Navy as a qualified telegraphist and was promoted to the rank of ordinary telegrapher. He was a luxury aboard his ship—a telegrapher who was fully trained and familiar with radio equipment and procedures—as during the first days of the war, there was a serious shortage of trained men. On January 2, 1940, he was elevated to the rank of able telegrapher.

Horace did not enjoy perfect vision, usually a prerequisite for naval service. When he joined the Navy, his grey eyes tested at 6/30 in the right eye and 6/20 in the left. With glasses, his vision was improved to 6/10. But in the dark recesses of the radio rooms, it was his ears, not his eyes, that guaranteed success.

In March, Horace, who had now picked up the nickname "Sparks," standard for any radio operator, was able to get leave from his convoy duties. He took this opportunity to visit his parents and brother at their Victoria Street home in Carleton Place from March 7 to 14. It would be the last time they saw him.

In April 1940, German troops seized Denmark and launched an offensive against Norway. On May 10, Winston Churchill was named Prime Minister of Great Britain and Germany unleashed her *blitzkrieg* against Holland, Luxembourg, Belgium, and France. Working with well-honed precision, the Wehrmacht reached the English Channel ports in ten days. On May 27, Belgium surrendered and the Allied troops had their backs to the sea.

On May 24, with no convoy in evidence, the destroyers *Restigouche*, *Skeena*, and *St. Laurent* nosed out to sea. Victoria Day weekend celebrations were forgotten. The *Assiniboine*, *Ottawa*, and *Saguenay* stayed in Halifax for much-needed refit, while the *Fraser*, en route for duties in the West Indies, was ordered to Bermuda for refuelling then direct to the U.K. Invasion of the British Isles seemed imminent, and every ship that Canada could send was needed in England's waters.

The first three ships reached Plymouth on June 1, and the Fraser followed her sisters into harbour on June 3. The "Miracle of Dunkirk" was at its height, when, from May 27 to June 4, approximately 350,000 men, mostly from the British Expeditionary Force, were evacuated to England in almost every kind of vessel that could float. Most of their weapons and equipment, however, were abandoned on French shores[7].

---

[7] The 1st Canadian Brigade Group had been sent to France to reinforce the retreating B.E.F. forces. The 1st Regiment, Royal Canadian Horse Artillery, 48th Highlanders, Royal Canadian Regiment and the Hastings and Prince Edward Regiment were aboard trains heading inland. With considerable difficulty they were turned around and sent back to Brest. Ordered to leave their heavy equipment behind as they embarked for Plymouth, Lt.Col. J.H. Roberts, commanding 1 RCHA, ignored two orders to destroy his guns and fought hard to get them loaded for evacuation. His perseverance ensured that an important stock of guns was saved.

The four Canadian war ships, after replacing one torpedo mount on each ship with anti-aircraft guns, went to sea to salvage whatever remained of the defeat. On June 11, near Dieppe, the *St. Laurent* and *Restigouche* traded shots with a German artillery battery situated behind the town of St-Valèry. These were the first shots fired in anger between Canadian ships and the enemy.

On June 21, France capitulated. That day, the *Fraser* was sent to station off the town of St-Jean-de-Luz, on the border of France and Spain and one of the last remaining exit points for refugees. That night, she carried out an anti-submarine patrol, and at dawn, was ordered to rendezvous with the British cruiser, HMS *Galatea*. The *Fraser* was given a secret message to be delivered by hand to the British ambassador to France and was sent at full speed for Arachon, the French port where the ambassador was believed to be. As she approached the harbour in a furious rainstorm, a small sardine fishing boat, tossing and bobbing alongside, hailed the *Fraser*. From this tiny vessel, the warship took the British ambassador and the Canadian minister to France, Lieutenant Colonel Georges Vanier (as he then was)[8]. Transferring them to the *Galatea*, she returned to duty off St-Jean-de-Luz.

The *Restigouche* joined the *Fraser* and several British destroyers engaged in shepherding all manner of craft overloaded with evacuees into a convoy for return to England. In forty-eight hours, 16,000 soldiers and a multitude of civilians made their escape over rough and dangerous waters. The two Canadian ships entered the French harbour to take off their own evacuation shore parties and hurry along the last ships. Their men got aboard just as a tank and an armoured car pulling a field gun appeared on a hill overlooking the town and trained their guns at the Canadians. The message was clear. The two ships sped for the open sea where they joined and came under the control of the British light cruiser *Calcutta*. The *Fraser* was carrying forty-four members of the British, French and Polish forces.

The ships headed for Bordeaux and after a brief and fruitless patrol, the *Calcutta* ordered a new course for the U.K.

It was now about ten o'clock in the evening with a fresh breeze, a moderate swell and visibility of about one and a half miles. *Fraser* was off the starboard bow of *Calcutta*, a mile and a half distant. *Restigouche* was on the cruiser's port quarter, a mile and a half to the left of her and slightly astern. The ships were travelling at high speed, with the probability of attack by submarine or from the air at any time. They had been in continuous action for nearly a week, carrying on rescue work and embarking troops and refugees under threat of submarine attack, air attack and the harassment of

---

[8] Following service at the front in World War I, Vanier entered the diplomatic service. After escaping France he stayed on in London as minister to all allied governments in exile and returned as ambassador to France in 1944. From 1959 to 1967 he was Canada's Governor General.

a general evacuation. *Fraser's* commanding officer had had one night's sleep in the preceding ten and there is little likelihood that the captain of *Calcutta* had had more[9].

Abeam of the Pointe de Coubre lighthouse, *Calcutta* signalled the ships to form a "single line ahead." *Fraser* altered her course to the left to get in line. The Canadian commander, Wallace B. Creery, was on the bridge and intended to turn towards *Calcutta*, then slip down her right side to take up a position astern of the British cruiser. In the darkness the two ships were barely visible to each other. The officer on watch on *Calcutta's* bridge saw *Fraser* change to port and assumed that the destroyer would cross in front and pass down the British ship's port side. At their high speed, the manoeuvre would be close, so the *Calcutta's* watch officer ordered a turn to starboard and sounded a single blast on the siren. That signal was *Fraser's* first indication of impending disaster. The two ships were converging at a combined speed of thirty-four knots, and although engines were put hard astern and the wheels spun, nothing could be done to avoid the collision.

The ships covered the last two hundred yards intervening between them in less than eleven seconds and *Calcutta*, still swinging to starboard, sheared her way through the forward part of *Fraser*. The destroyer's forepart broke clean off and floated away bottom up. Her entire bridge, with the captain and bridge personnel, was lifted onto *Calcutta's* bow and remained there, swaying and groaning above the cruiser's forecastle[10].

Restigouche reacted swiftly. Fighting the heavy swell, she worked around until her stern touched that of *Fraser's*. Sixty of *Fraser's* crew and one stretcher case safely crossed as the two ships ground their hulls together. Both *Calcutta* and *Restigouche* had dropped scramble-nets from their rails to assist the men in the water to climb to safety.

Fraser's bow had disappeared into the darkness with some of the crew clinging to the guardrails. Just as *Restigouche* approached, the bow capsized and *Fraser's* men were thrown into the water. *Restigouche* lowered her boats and in spite of the black night and a heavy swell, rescued fourteen officers and about 100 men. Lost were forty-five Canadian and thirteen English seamen. One of the survivors who was plucked from the sea after spending a number of dark hours treading frigid water clutching a lifebelt, was Able Telegrapher Horace Stark.

The stern portion could not be salvaged so a scuttling party was put aboard. One of those was *Restigouche's* radio officer, thirty-year-old C. L. Carroll. His job was to retrieve the radio log and confidential code books. The scene in *Fraser's* radio cabin never left his mind. Writing for *Legion* magazine many years later he recalled:

[9] Joseph Schull, "The Far Distant Ships" (Ottawa: King's Printer, 1950) p. 36
[10] ibid, p. 37

The radio officer, a friend of mine, lay decapitated on the floor. Another buddy lay close by, his body skewered by a spike of steel. He was breathing his last and all I could do was fulfil his last request for a cigarette and leave him to go down with the ship. He couldn't be moved and there wasn't time to get rescue equipment. We had to open the seacocks to sink the ship, and then get on with the convoy[11].

The last trace of *Fraser* slipped below the surface a few minutes past midnight on June 25, 1940. As the two remaining ships steamed for home, *Fraser*'s bridge rode sadly on *Calcutta*'s forecastle. The captain and other bridge personnel had been able to step aboard the cruiser. Canada's small navy acutely felt the loss of the destroyer and her sailors.

Horace, on leave in London, wrote home describing his narrow escape. Part of his letter was published in an article in the Carleton Place Canadian on July 18, 1940:

'I galloped from the lower deck mess room and crawled through an opening onto the part of the ship that remained afloat.' Horace wrote. . . He states that he was asleep in his berth about 10:30 p.m. when he was startled into full wakefulness by a terrific 'bang' as another ship collided with the *Fraser*, cutting the latter completely in two. He further adds that one half sank almost immediately, leaving the other half floating on the port side. He crawled through an opening and remained there for a time until the other portion of the hull began to go down, when he was forced to the sea. Here he swam about for some 30 minutes before a floating lifebelt came his way. This he grasped and it served to keep him afloat until he was picked up an hour later, almost numbed from exposure and suffering from shock. During the sinking and afterwards the survivors never lost heart, members of the crew singing 'Roll Out the Barrel' to hearten their comrades.

Stark lost all his possessions so hurried was his departure from his berth, and when rescued was without money, spectacles or clothing except those he was wearing at the time. He also lost several souvenirs gathered during a visit to the tropics last Fall.

Horace's claim for lost items was not settled until after his death. He had claimed $33 for his Bulova wrist watch, $10 for a "wash kit," $15 for his Packard electric razor, $15 for his Kodak camera, $17.50 for his Burberry

[11] Jane Dewar, Ed. True Canadian War Stories (Lester & Orpen Dennys Limited, 1990) p. 109.

(a waterproof coat), $5 for a pair of shoes, $22.50 for his glasses, and $10 for a pen and pencil set, for a total claim of $128. The Navy, however, approved compensation only in the amount of $47.50.

Stark's luck with ships and collisions at sea turned from bad to worse.

After a summer's recuperation in England, during which he attended a gathering of radio operators in London[12], he and most of the rest of *Fraser*'s surviving crew were assigned to HMCS *Margaree* on September 6, 1940, the day she entered Canadian service. To replace *Fraser*, the Royal Canadian Navy had purchased the Royal Navy destroyer, HMS *Diana*. After re-commissioning, the ship was refitted at London's Albert Docks during the heavy air raids of September. Fire bombs and shrapnel damaged the ship on the night of September 17, but she was soon repaired and declared seaworthy.

Safely afloat and away from the targeted dockyard, she sailed for Londonderry, Ireland, after making short stops in Liverpool and Greenock. On October 20, with Horace Stark on duty in the telegraph room, *Margaree*, as the sole escort, led a convoy of five merchantmen, designated OL-8, from 'Derry to the open Atlantic and Canada. *Margaree* had a complement of ten officers and 166 crew, all of whom were keenly anticipating a return home. In fact, Horace had advised his family that, upon his return, he had been granted leave and was looking forward to visiting them

In the North Atlantic, death came from many directions. Navigation was hazardous at the best and men died from exposure to the extreme elements and accidents in the fog and winter gales. Rescued once, Horace's accident was repeated four months later.

In mid-Atlantic, two days after sailing and during a night of rough seas and frequent squalls, *Margaree*'s first lieutenant ordered reduced speed in order to maintain visual contact with her small herd of merchant ships. At about 0100 hours, a particularly ferocious rain squall, lasting about twenty-five minutes, caused visibility to be reduced to zero. When the storm lifted, *Port Fairy*, an 8,300-ton motor vessel leading the left-hand column, found *Margaree* directly ahead to starboard and dangerously close. The convoy was travelling without zigzagging at the relatively high speed of fourteen and a half knots.

Port Fairy threw her engines into emergency stop and then full astern, sounding three blasts to warn her escort. Just then *Margaree* inexplicably

[12] Horace was the sole Canadian representative at this meeting of "hams" and "sparkers" of the Empire. Radio operators of the British army, air force and navy, as well as civilian operators were in attendance. A magazine commemorating the gathering was published with Horace's picture as the only Canadian representative. It arrived at his parent's home two days after his death. (The Carleton Place Canadian, October 24 & 31, 1940)

Survivors at Sea (War Museum).

turned left and rode directly across *Port Fairy*'s course. The merchantman could not move to the right, away from the warship, because she was too close to other ships in the convoy. Disaster could not be prevented. *Port Fairy*'s bow sliced *Margaree* in half at the bridge. Horace, who undoubtedly appreciated that his ship had once again been rammed, must have recognized the shriek of rending metal.

The destroyer's bow drifted clear, rolled over, and sank within a minute. No sailor in the forward part of the ship—mostly off-duty men in their hammocks—or any of the officers and men on the bridge could be saved. Horace Stark and all his telegrapher mates were gone, as well as Commander J. W. R. Roy and 140 other seamen of the ship's company. This was the second ship to have been cut in two beneath them within four months.

Port Fairy threw flares into the water to aid in the rescue of sailors floundering in the brine and then put herself further in danger by coming alongside *Margaree*. Heavy swells ground the two ships together and then flung them apart. The scream of grinding metal reminded Irish seamen of their grandmothers' descriptions of wailing banshees. Meanwhile, thirty men managed to cross the heaving decks to safety. Three officers and a seaman[13] left on the quarterdeck let down a raft and stayed afloat long enough for *Port Fairy* to come round and pick them up.

With no survivors from *Margaree*'s bridge, no one knew what had happened on the destroyer leading up to impact. *Margaree* had diminished speed and fallen back rapidly, and the heavy rain squalls had reduced visi-

---

[13] The officers were the First Lieutenant, P.F.X. Russell, Lt. William M. Landymore, SLt. Robert W. Timbrell and Surg. Lt. T.B."Scotty" McLean. The seaman was AB V.H. Holman, duty watchkeeper at the switchboard. Both Landymore and Timbrell achieved the rank of Rear Admiral and the job of Commander, Maritime Command, Landymore from 1964 to 1966 and Timbrell from 1971 to 1973. (Fraser McKee and Robert Darlington, The Canadian Naval Chronicle, p.24.)

bility such that her last movements went unseen. Such risks had to be accepted when large numbers of ships had to sail in close company. Fledgling radar equipment would later reduce the risk, but during storms, collisions at sea could not be eliminated.

The ship was operating under blackout conditions in rough seas. The telegraph room behind the bridge would have been closed down with watertight doors and heavy blackout curtains in place to prevent any stray beam of light alerting a vigilant enemy. Able Seaman Stark's first indication of impending doom would have been the horrendous noise of the ship being torn apart as *Port Fairy* cut through it. At the same time, he was undoubtedly hurled against the bulkhead as power was lost and the ship thrown into darkness. Locked in his small steel cabin, Stark and his mates would have had no chance for escape.

On October 26, James Stark received a telegram from the Naval Department advising that "the Minister of National Defence deeply regrets to inform you that your son, H. G. Stark, telegraphist, R.C.N.V.R. (V6408), is missing and believed killed." Horace Stark became the first young man from Carleton Place and Lanark County to give his life in World War II.

Lost at sea at age twenty, Horace Stark's name is inscribed on the Halifax Memorial in Point Pleasant Park. The Memorial was erected by the Commonwealth War Graves Commission and was unveiled by Lieutenant Governor H. P. McKeen in November 1967; the great granite Cross of Sacrifice is clearly visible to all ships approaching Halifax harbour. It stands on an octagonal podium upon which twenty-three bronze panels bear the names of 3,257 men and women of the RCN and Merchant Navy who were lost at sea, as well as some soldiers who were buried at sea. Horace's name is on panel seven. The monument is inscribed:

IN HONOUR OF THE MEN AND WOMEN OF THE
NAVY, ARMY AND MERCHANT NAVY OF CANADA
WHOSE NAMES ARE INSCRIBED HERE.

THEIR GRAVES ARE UNKNOWN
BUT THEIR MEMORY SHALL ENDURE.

The *Carleton Place Canadian*, on January 28, 1941, carried the following item:

THEIR MAJESTIES' TRIBUTE

Mr. and Mrs. J. S. Stark have received from Buckingham Palace a letter from Their Majesties, King George and Queen Elizabeth, expressing to them their heartfelt sympathy in the great sorrow occasioned by the loss of their son, Horace Garner Stark. Their Majesties expressed the sincere hope that the country's gratitude for a young life so nobly given in service may bring them some measure of consolation.

Horace had served in the RCN as a wireless operator on H.M.C.S. Fraser and Margaree, and was on his way home to Canada after five months overseas when the destroyer Margaree was sunk in collision in the North Atlantic, October 22nd last, when 142 officers and ratings were lost.

The form letter from the king and queen remained the same throughout the war. It came on fine vellum paper with the crest of Buckingham Palace at the top. The original read:

The Queen and I offer you our heartfelt sympathy in your great sorrow. We pray that your country's Gratitude for a life so nobly Given in its service may bring You some measure of consolation.

Signed: George R. I.

Because he died without a will, Horace's estate, as proscribed by Ontario law, was divided equally among his mother, father, and brother. However, by the time his estate was settled, the family had moved to Somerset Street in Ottawa and it was there that his medals—the Canadian Volunteer Service Medal, the 1939–45 Star, the Atlantic Star, the War Medal, and the Memorial Cross[14]—were delivered to his mother. His War Service Gratuity[15] was paid to his estate for his 387 days of service, 303 days on the high seas at an additional 25¢ a day plus his last pay of $45.83. This included his "grog money" of $1.32 a month[16].

This being Carleton Place's first casualty, the town's flags were lowered to half-mast, a nicety that was ignored when the death toll began to mount. *The Canadian* eulogized:

The early passing of this brilliant young Canadian closes a life which had a most promising future and citizens of the town were stunned when the tragic news was announced.

[14] The Memorial Cross, also know as the Silver Cross, was issued to the widows or mothers of those killed on Active Service, or who died as a result of Active Service. The Cross is cast in dull silver, surmounted by a crown and is hung from a ribbon of purple satin. The monarch's royal cipher is in the centre. World War I Crosses bear George V's cipher and World War II Crosses that of George VI. A wreath of laurel appears between the arms of the Cross. The Cross is registered and a serial number is engraved upon it.
[15] The War Service Gratuity, along with a re-establishment program passed by Parliament in 1944, was intended to provide members of the services with assistance after their discharge when they were deciding on their future as civilians. The Gratuity provided a basic payment of $7.50 for each bloc of 30 days' service in the Western Hemisphere and $15.00 for each 30 days' service overseas. A supplementary gratuity of seven days' pay and allowances, plus Canadian subsistence allowance, was paid for each six months overseas service. Aircrew, flying outside Canadian waters and naval personnel in sea-going ships of war were regarded as on overseas service.
[16] Payment in lieu of the daily issue of rum and water to which he was entitled by Navy custom dating back at least as far as the mid-1700s.

On November 10, a memorial service was held in St. Andrew's, officiated by the Reverend James Foote[17], who paid high tribute. The large congregation placed many floral tributes upon the altar, and representatives of the Board of Education and the town council attended in a group.

A regular contributor to the *Canadian*, Mr. Richard P. Dunphy, wrote a tribute to Horace, commenting:

He was only a little boy when I came to Carleton Place. A quiet, unassuming little boy, whom I used to meet, on his way to and from school. Horace was a friendly boy, and I like friendly boys. We soon had chats nearly every time we met. He grew up under my eyes. He began to be heard of in Carleton Place. People knew he was musical. They knew he was clever. They knew he was a levelheaded little chap whose boyish successes in every effort he made did not make him cocky and self-conceited. We liked him for those qualities.

Over night he became a man, accepting a man's responsibilities and going forth to meet them in the quiet way that he had. We learned only after he had gone that he had been one of the first to join the Canadian Forces when war broke out. It seemed from the first that Horace was to be the hometown boy of this war who was perhaps the most often thought of, by all of us. We heard of the disaster to the Fraser, and our hearts slowed with the sickening realization that one of our own boys was in the gallant roll of heroes who manned that craft. And many of us sent post haste to find from his parents if there were news of Horace. We were a little happier when we learned that he had cabled of his safety to his loved ones at home. We were proud when we learned in the stories that came from England of the fine heroism in danger shown by the men on board the Fraser, for one of our boys was one of the crew.

And Horace became more than ever one of our very own. We loved all those boys who had gone from us, just a little

---

[17] The Reverend James Foote was a brother to Honourary Captain John W. Foote, Chaplain of the Royal Hamilton Light Infantry, who landed with his regiment on the stony beach of Dieppe on August 19, 1941. He cared for the wounded, carrying many to the boats for return to England. When it came time for him to embark and withdraw he chose to stay amongst his soldiers, believing that he would be of far better use to them in captivity than to those heading back to England. He became the first Canadian Chaplain to receive the Victoria Cross for valour.

more dearly because of the youth they were giving so generously in the battle to fight back the barbarism that threatened the world. We watched and we still watch for news of each one. But Horace had his baptism of danger and escape, and he became our charmed figure.

For very much like a Galahad was this slender boy. Very much a Joyce Kilmer, who left his songs and laughter and beauty to play his part in grim warfare in the last war. Horace Stark had won recognition as a musician. He would have become known as a composer of no mean order. But, like all lovers of beauty, he quickly reacted to the hideousness that was being forced on Europe. His poetic imagination could conceive of no better place to do his part than above the deck of a wave-tossed ship-of-war. And so he went to face a relentless foe, eager and unafraid.

And when death came to him, we may be sure that he stepped a pace to meet it, with a smile in his heart. For a heart such as his was filled with the cleanliness which keeps it always far from fear and close to God.

James and Laura Stark moved to Ottawa in January 1944, where Mr. Stark went to work for the Dominion government. Horace's younger brother, Bevis, left his science courses at Queen's University in 1943 to join the RCN, where he also trained as a telegraphist. He survived the war.

Apart from his immediate family, Horace left his grandparents, Mr. and Mrs. W. J. Brownlee of Finch and the late Dr. and Mrs. A. Stark of Berwick, Ontario.

CHAPTER 2—THE BATTLE OF THE ATLANTIC

The Battle of the Atlantic lasted six years along the ocean's convoy routes and was the longest continuous campaign of the Second World War. Had the ocean lanes been lost, supplies, troops, and equipment from North America—almost everything required to keep England from starvation and invasion—would certainly not have arrived in Britain. The RCN and Canada's merchant navy played significant roles in this battle against German marine technology, U-boat commanders' wit and wile, and most dangerous of all, the whimsy of weather on the North Atlantic.

After the fall of France in 1940, the RCN's four destroyers were working to protect the southwestern approaches of Great Britain from submarine attack. During the summer of 1940, all trans-Atlantic shipping was re-routed around the north coast of Ireland and down the Irish Sea. But relentless U-boat incursions threatened both this route and any surface ship traffic in the English Channel. The Canadian vessels were kept busy trying to fend off U-boat attacks and rescuing sailors from torpedoed merchant ships.

At the end of 1940, under the *Lend-Lease Act*, the U.S. traded fifty American four-funnelled destroyers, which had been built in 1919–20, to the Royal Navy in exchange for the lease of several bases, in places such as Bermuda, British Guyana, the West Indies, and Argentia, Newfoundland. Six of these ships were assigned to the RCN, so by February 1941, Canada was able to contribute a total of ten destroyers to Britain's Home Fleet. But by that spring, German submarines were sinking Allied merchant ships faster than they could be replaced. In June, more than 500,000 tons of shipping were lost and three or four merchant ships with their crews and cargoes were going down every day.

Following World War I, most of Canada's fleet of uneconomical and slow, coal-fired merchant ships were sold or scrapped. In September 1939, Canada had only thirty-nine ocean-going ships and approximately 1,450 merchant seamen to man them. Yet the war's outcome would depend upon the successful and unrestricted flow of material. The ships carrying this trade were terribly vulnerable.

The war at sea heated up quickly. On September 5, two days after the declaration of war, the first Canadian merchant seaman, stewardess Hannah Baird, lost her life when the unarmed Cunard liner, *SS Athenia*, sailing west towards Montreal, was torpedoed and sunk. *Athenia* carried 1,000 civilian passengers; 118, including twenty-two Americans, went down with her.

Hannah Baird was the first of eight women to lose her life aboard civilian ships during this war[18].

There was a Carleton Place connection to the sinking of the *Athenia*. Many citizens feared for the life of Mrs. Charles W. McGregor, of Ramsay, who was reputed to have sailed for home on the ill-fated ship. She had, however, sailed just ahead of the *Athenia*, on the *SS Montrose*, and landed safely in Montreal.

Obviously, the ships providing the material for war needed substantial protection. But the RCN had no ships that could cross the Atlantic in the required zigzag sailing pattern used to deter U-boat attacks. They were too small, too lightly armed, and did not have the fuel capacity for such a crossing. Nor was air cover available. The best the Canadian navy could do was provide coastal escort to a point about 300 miles out to sea where the convoy would be met by larger and better armed British cruisers. The first convoy sailed on September 16, 1939.

Life aboard a merchant ship, even in the best of times, left much to be desired. The merchant navy was far from being, in any sense, a navy. Few merchant sailors wore uniforms, there was no pride of service, seamen were ill paid, and the service conditions were wretched. Ashore, merchant sailors had none of the navy's amenities and were often objects of scorn simply for not being in uniform. Consequently, merchant seamen became a very independent lot—which became an attraction in itself.

Initially, convoys sailed from Halifax and included only ships that could maintain nine knots. But as older vessels were pressed into service, slower convoys were organized, usually departing from Sydney, Cape Breton Island. Faster ships—those capable of at least fifteen knots—were allowed to sail, and were routed, independently.

But they had to be armed, and defensive equipment for merchant ships (DEMS) evolved. For their own protection, ships sailing unescorted were provided with guns and gunners, initially a 4-inch gun that dated before the Great War that was possibly augmented with a Lewis machine gun of similar vintage. The *Vancouver Island* was fitted with four Mark VII guns and two machine guns on the bridge. Shells were scarce. Her gunners were trained by RCN gunners seconded for that purpose and who became known as DEMS gunners. However, as the war progressed, a better range of arma-

[18] The German commander of U-30, Fritz Lemp, was severely reprimanded when his boat returned to base even though he claimed to have considered his target to be an armed merchant cruiser. Although Germany had warned all shipping of neutral nations to keep out of British waters they had also exempted them from attack without warning. The overexcited U-boat captain had acted contrary to Hitler's orders causing great concern to both Grosadmiral Erich Raeder, Commander-in-Chief of the German Navy and Grosadmiral Karl Doenitz, the Admiral Commanding U-boats. At this early stage of the war the Fuhrer had no desire to provoke neutral nations, least of all the United States.
Fritz Lemp's second wartime mistake was to allow his boat to surface and be boarded early in 1941 after Royal Navy ships attacked with depth charges. The boarders seized his Enigma cypher machine that finally gave the Allies access to the Kriegsmarine's codes and to the positioning and routing of the U-boat fleet. The boarding party shot Captain Lemp.

ment became available and more than 1,600 Canadian sailors eventually could claim DEMS service.

It has been estimated that a Canadian merchant ship of 10,000 tonnes dwt[19] could carry enough food stuffs to feed 225,000 people for a week. Cargo could also include clothing, fuel, steel, aluminium, lumber, aircraft, tanks, jeeps, trucks, guns, munitions, and whatever else was required for the war effort. Not surprisingly, they became the prized targets for enemy surface raiders and U-boats[20].

The independent life of a merchant sailor was soon lost and there was little attraction to being herded into a convoy escorted by weakly armed destroyers. Regulations forbade them from making smoke, pumping their bilges overboard, or showing lights at night—all actions that could attract an enemy.

Once torpedoed, there was not much hope of rescue. The icy sea would be covered with their own bunker oil and often the navy escort, "for the good of the whole," would not stop to pick up survivors. A man floating or clinging to a bit or wreckage in the North Atlantic had a life expectancy of about five minutes maximum. It rarely took longer for the frigid sea to paralyse and kill him.

Into this morass the *Vancouver Island* sailed from Victoria to Montreal, arriving in April 1941.

House flag of the Canadian Steamship Line.

Vancouver Island sailed under the flag of the Canadian National Steamship Line with a crew of seventy-six, including eight DEMS gunners. The ship had a top speed of seventeen knots, but her master, Mr. Eric L. Roper, found she was most efficient at a constant speed of fourteen knots. While her main payload was cargo, she had room for twenty-four paying passengers, of which the Department of Defence took full advantage. Her cabin facilities were rated first class, therefore she carried only those holding a rank of sergeant and above. She was in constant use.

During the summer of 1941, faced with strengthened defences in English waters, the German navy developed techniques for intercepting convoys in mid-ocean. Far from any help, with no air cover, U-boat tactics became highly successful. These submarines were much faster on the surface than submerged, and operating in a "wolf pack," they attacked at night, moving quickly through a convoy to make numerous attacks.

[19] Dwt refers to deadweight, the capacity of a merchant ship. It is the difference between the weight of water displaced when a ship is empty (but with all the fuel and supplies aboard for a voyage) and the weight of the water displaced when the cargo bays are fully loaded.
[20] Patricia Geisler, *Valour At Sea*, (Ottawa: Veterans Affairs Canada, 1998), p8n

In July Malcolm Forbes was promoted to the civilian rank of "junior engineer"[21]. He had just completed a voyage from June 26 to July 4 arriving in Liverpool with 1,400 tons of war stores and 10 aircraft. On September 1, *Vancouver Island* was fully loaded at Huskisson Dock in Liverpool, preparing to sail for Canada, when, at 1950 hours, a fire was discovered between decks in the No. 3 lower hold. With assistance from the Liverpool Fire Brigade and using the ship's own firefighting equipment and hoses, the fire was extinguished by 0145 hours on September 2. The cargo was then completely unloaded, inspected, and reloaded, and although there was water and fire damage and extensive charring on the woodworks in the hold, it was determined that more substantial repairs could be delayed. *Vancouver Island* sailed on September 4, safely arriving in Montreal on September 14.

On September 24, with the assigned number E292[22], she slipped away from Shed 14 at the Montreal docks, carrying nineteen RAF civilian technicians—all radio operators—and two RCAF pilot officers and two sergeants. One day out, everyone on board suddenly was thrown off his feet as the ship, sailing quickly up the St. Lawrence River, abruptly came to a full stop. She had run aground.

The captain docked at Quebec City for an inspection and repairs to the hull, if necessary. For the passengers, this was an enjoyable and unexpected break in their ocean voyage. Granted leave by the ship's captain, they had a few days to enjoy the city's sights and delights. In fact, the four air force men and some of the civilians, having enjoyed many libations, were tottering back to the ship one evening when one man, by the name of Mitchell, stepped off a curb and broke his ankle. The air force men carried him to a hospital and then returned to the ship to inform the captain that he would leave with one less passenger. His injury proved to be his lucky break.

At 1320 hours on October 13, *Vancouver Island* cleared Quebec City harbour and again headed upstream. Her destination, and therefore her routing, had been changed. She was now headed for Belfast instead of Liverpool, to her misfortune. A floating target, very lightly armed, she was sunk on the high seas by *U 558* on October 15, 1941. The last message received from her was "QRM[23]. Received two torpedoes. Bearing impossible." It was a very weak signal and it was thought, but could not be confirmed, that she also sent "on fire."

How interesting the vagaries of fate! Had the ship not gone aground and proceeded on her original schedule, had the routing been a bit further south

---

[21] The lowest rank in the engineering officer's rank structure, roughly equivalent to a sub-lieutenant in the navy.
[22] The "E" refers to the fact that the voyage was eastbound. A "W" would have indicated a westbound trip. The number was simply a sequential tracking number allotted by the convoy control authorities in either Canada or Great Britain depending upon the origin of the trip.
[23] A code used to get the attention of all listening radio operators. It was universally used before "SOS" became the usual signal of distress after the Titanic disaster in April 1912.

to Liverpool instead of to Belfast, chances are that she and *U 558* would not have met in mid-Atlantic. A few days earlier, and they would have been miles apart. But because she went aground in the St. Lawrence, all crew—including the eight RCN DEMS gunners—and passengers lost their lives.

A cablegram from England informed the Canadian authorities:

> Ministry of War Transport reports SS 'Vancouver Island' torpedoed Oct. 15. Two escort vessels sent to her assistance, but no news yet received regarding vessel or crew.

The crew of *Vancouver Island* had little hope of rescue. Because of her speed, she was sailing alone.

That same morning, 400 miles south of Iceland and not far from the Vancouver Island, convoy SC-48[24] was attacked. During the day and that night the convoy lost nine merchantmen and the escorting British corvette, *Gladiolus*. An American destroyer, USS *Kearney*, one of four that had joined the escorting force, was hit with a torpedo, nudging the U.S. even closer to war with Germany. The Canadian corvette, HMCS *Pictou*, dropped depth charges causing the U-boat to surface. *Pictou* tried to ram her but she crash-dived[25]. More depth charges were dropped on the German's bubbling swirl, but *Pictou* was only credited with a "probable."

HMCS Pictou had been tasked to assist convoy SC-48 after searching for *Vancouver Island* survivors. Escorting a west-bound convoy, *Pictou* was three days out of St. John's when the convoy commander received the following from the Commander-in-Chief Western Approaches: "Detach one escort to stand by SS Vancouver Island torpedoed and drifting 57E 37" north, 25E 37" west."

HMS *Dianthus*, HMS *Aconity*, and HMCS *Pictou* were sent to search and assist. The weather was good and *Pictou*'s navigator was able to take star and sun sights by sextant to determine position. They arrived at *Vancouver Island*'s position in a day and a half and spent the remaining half day and night searching. On October 16 they reported to the commander-in-chief that there was no trace of survivors or the ship. They were then ordered "at best prudent speed" to rejoin convoy SC-48. *HMCS Pictou* left the search area at 1516 (3:16 p.m.).[26]

The Book of Remembrance for the Merchant Navy's war dead, housed in the Memorial Chamber of the Centre Block of Parliament, contains 1,629

---

[24] An "SC" convoy consisted of slow ships, sailing from six to nine knots, which originated in Sydney, Nova Scotia.

[25] A crash-dive took a U-boat to periscope depth, about 20 feet below the surface, in a little over 30 seconds. Within another minute, driving forward and downward at a speed of about 8 knots, twisting away on a sharp alteration of course, it would be 120 feet below and some 700 feet distant from the swirl that marked its dive. Joseph Schull, The Far Distant Ships (Ottawa: King's Printer, 1950), p.73.

[26] Anthony Griffin. A Naval Officer's War (www. naval.ca/article, 2001) p. 2

names—one in eight of the 12,000 of those who served—of those Canadian merchant seamen who lost their lives at sea during World War II. Eight are women. On page 136 are the names of two men named Forbes who went down with the *Vancouver Island*. One is Harry Malcolm Forbes, Engineer, whose name also appears on the Carleton Place War Memorial.

Harry Malcolm Forbes
Engineer
Canadian Merchant Navy

Malcolm Forbes, son of Mr. and Mrs. Harry Stewart Forbes of Vancouver (later Nelson, British Columbia), joined the engine room crew of the SS

The Merchant Navy flew the Red Ensign with the Canadian Coat of Arms in the fly.

Vancouver Island on January 11, 1941. Malcolm signed on in Victoria as a wiper. It was his job, using a rag soaked in oil, to keep the moving parts of the ship's engines well lubricated. The *Vancouver* was twenty-three-year-old Malcolm's first ship and marked the first time he had been to sea. From Montreal, Malcolm Forbes signed on four times during 1941. After his first voyage, he was promoted to "oiler[27]" and sailed twice in this job, from April 26 to June 17 and from June 18 to July 27. He took six weeks off in May and June, returning to the ship with the rank of junior engineer. However, each time they slipped away from the jetty it would have been in lonely silence. It would have been unlikely that any wives, family, friends or girl-friends were there to wave farewell and wish "God speed!"

Harry Forbes' name is etched on Panel 17 of the Halifax Memorial in Point Pleasant Park.

To secure the Atlantic supply route and to ensure protection, it had become necessary as early as 1939 to run ships in convoys. Canadian sea-men and airmen, flying coastal patrols, played an ever-increasing role in maintaining the lifeline to Britain.

In December 1941, the U.S. entry into the war allowed Admiral Karl Dönitz, commander of the elite U-boat fleet, to extend the German area of operations to the entire North American eastern seaboard. Their success reached its highest level of the war, as U.S. Navy protection of shipping was "pitifully inadequate" without aircraft or escorts available for coastal con-voys. American seaboard cities took no defensive actions such as dimming their waterfront lights, so as not to ruin the tourist season. As late as April 1942, four months after Pearl Harbor, Miami was still lighting up six miles of coast with neon lights, which illuminated shipping for the U-boat com-

[27] An oiler is responsible for the lubrication of all moving parts of s ship's engine

manders. Fortunately, of Dönitz' ninety-one operational U-boats, only five were deployed off the east coast of North America[28].

Convoy escorts were now required for the entire voyage from Canada to Britain, and Newfoundland became key to filling the mid-ocean gap. Local escorts took convoys from Halifax to a point somewhere off St. John's where mid-ocean escorts would take over for the run to Iceland. There they would meet British escorts, and after refuelling, would pick up a west-bound convoy for the return to St. John's. Only by using such a relay system could Allied destroyers and small escorts provide protection for the entire voyage.

To secure the Atlantic supply route and to ensure protection, it had become necessary as early as 1939 to run ships in convoys. Canadian seamen and airmen, flying coastal patrols, played an ever-increasing role in maintaining the lifeline to Britain.

William Henry Porter
V 33072 Chief Engine Room Artificer
Royal Canadian Navy Volunteer Reserve

In the midst of all the carnage at sea, Harry Porter, a machinist foreman with the Canadian Pacific Railroad, decided to join the Royal Canadian Navy. On June 5, 1940, he wrote the following to Engineering Lieutenant Commander Harrison at the RCNVR Barracks on Mountain Road in Montreal:

> I am thirty-six years old and have eighteen years service with the Canadian Pacific Railway. I served an apprenticeship as a machinist and worked nine years at the trade and for the past nine years have been in charge of a shop, which includes machine shop, electric and acetylene welding and complete charge of repairs, maintenance and testing of locomotive boilers and machinery assigned to the terminal.
>
> I have no extensive experience on diesels, my work being steam boilers and engines and plant equipment.
>
> I have a little experience afloat and feel possibly I could readily be of use and quickly adapt myself to the service . . .

On June 14, he received a reply stating that there was nothing available for him in the navy. Not to be deterred, and in spite of the fact that he was making a very good wage with the railroad ($280 a month), he believed his

[28] David A. Thomas. The Atlantic Star 1939-45 (London: W.H. Allen & Co Plc, 1990) p. 116

skills could be put to better use in service to the country, so he applied twice more. Navy bureaucrats moved slowly, and it was not until a year later that a navy commander noted Harry's most anxious pleas to serve. The commander wrote to headquarters: "This man will (be) very useful for one of the base repair shops. Therefore (I) would be willing to accept him as a C.E.R.A. (V.R.)"[29]

Harry enlisted in Montreal on July 7, 1941. Ten days later, he and his oldest son, Donald, were in Carleton Place visiting one of Harry's aunts, Miss Eva Tetlock, and in McCullough's Landing visiting his uncle and aunt, Mr. and Mrs. L. M. Tetlock. He and all three of his sons—Donald Lyon, Kenneth Bruce, and David Ross—had visited in Carleton Place earlier in May for a weekend with his sister Laura (Mrs. Mel Cummings) and his aunt Eva. Harry was soon due to leave his job as a foreman in the Farnham, Quebec CPR shops to report for duty with the RCN.

Harry had married Goldie Juanita McKerracher in Arnprior on July 15, 1928. Both his parents were dead; his father, William J. Porter, having died in 1932, and his mother, Edith Tetlock, in 1938. Harry was their oldest child, born on May 22, 1904. One brother had died at birth and his sister Laura was one year younger. He also had a brother, Ralph, living in Sorel, Quebec, and another sister Doris (Mrs. William White) in Toronto. Educated at Carleton Place public and high schools, Harry then took employment in the town's CPR shops. When the company promoted him to locomotive foreman, he was moved to Farnham, where he soon became an active member of the Montreal Masonic Order.

Although older than most recruits at age thirty-seven, his specialized skills were in demand, and Harry was found "in all respects fit for His Majesty's service." He was immediately granted the rank of chief petty officer. He was not a big man, standing only 5' 5" tall and weighing 137 pounds. Like the rest of his siblings, he had a fair complexion, brown hair, and blue eyes. On August 14, 1941, Chief ERA Harry Porter reported to his first RCN base, HMCS *Stadacona*.[30] He had never been to sea and now had weeks, instead of months, to learn the discipline, nautical customs, and distinct language of a warship. Although he had run a machine shop in civilian life, he was ill-prepared for the duties and responsibilities of a senior non-commissioned officer upon whose decisions and expertise the very lives of his men depended. He would have to conquer seasickness, profound fatigue, bitter cold and extreme heat, all in the confines of a small ship that a hostile sea was doing its best to tear apart. And, although railway steam engines were

[29] Harry was being offered enlistment in the rank of Chief Engine Room Artificer, equivalent to a Chief Petty Officer, the highest non-commissioned rank in the Navy.
[30] Stadacona is a shore-based navy unit in Halifax. It houses the dockyards for all Atlantic based war-ships, maintenance and repair facilities and all the command, training and administrative structure of the navy.

similar, he would still have to become intimately familiar with the range of steam engines, boilers, and plumbing that powered the navy's vessels.

It finally came time for Harry to put his training and skill into practice, and on January 25, 1942, he was posted to HMCS *Niobe*, the Canadian naval establishment in the U.K. To get there, he "hitchhiked" aboard HMS *Belmont*, a Royal Navy destroyer assigned to escort troop convoy NA 2.[31]

Sailing the North Atlantic in winter leaves a great deal to be desired. Winter storms are relentless and as the sea broke over the *Belmont*, the entire upper decks and rigging soon carried a very thick and heavy coat of ice. Sailors were well aware that, if torpedoed and if they got clear of their sinking ship, they had little chance of survival and rescue. Many tales were told of lifeboats found full of ice-sheathed corpses.

Seven days after he joined HMS *Belmont*, the ship was sunk:

> (Chief ERA W. Henry Porter) Reported missing on 31 Jan 1942 when the ship in which he was serving, H.M.S. *Belmont*, was torpedoed and sunk by enemy action while on operational duty at sea, and no further information concerning him having become available he is, for official purposes, presumed to have died on that date.

According to the ship's log of *U-82*, a U-boat commanded by Siegfried Rollman, the British destroyer *Belmont* was torpedoed in position 4202N 5718W at 2212 hours on January 31.

Belmont and another destroyer, HMS *Firedrake*, were the only two escorts for the troop convoy NA2. At 2322Z[32] on January 31, *Firedrake* signalled to navy headquarters that *Belmont* had been torpedoed and presumed sunk. Both the German and British navigators were in accord about the position of the sinking.

Harry's wife, Goldie, was informed that he was declared lost at sea and presumed dead. She was given the date, but officials informed her that "in the public interest" no details were available, not even the name of the ship he was on! It was not until August 1942, when *The Carleton Place Canadian* printed an RCN press release stating that Harry Porter was declared "Officially Reported Dead." A year after Harry's death, on February 17, 1943, Goldie wrote to Navy Headquarters in Ottawa seeking more information. Her sons were "asking about their daddie and how his ship was hit and what he did." A naval officer replied:

---

[31] The appellation "NA" signified that the convoy was a military convoy (all the ships were carrying troops or military cargo) out of a North American port bound for the United Kingdom. These were later combined with "AT" convoys, carrying military cargo from New York for the United Kingdom.
[32] Z is the symbol used to denote Greenwich Mean Time (GMT) which was (and is) the time all ships and aircraft use when operational. Z is spoken as "Zulu" in compliance with the phonetic alphabet.

Your husband was serving on loan in *HMS Belmont*, a Royal Navy ship which, while escorting a troop Convoy, was torpedoed and sunk by enemy action on the 31st of January 1942. For reasons of security the location of the sinking of this ship cannot be given.

She was paid his war service gratuity which amounted to $45 for 200 days service, paid at $7.50 a day, nothing for overseas service even though he had served seven days at sea, plus a dependant's allowance of $1.94 per day for a total of $46.94.

Almost three years later, in October 1944, Goldie remarried in Montreal. Harry's medals and a Memorial Cross were mailed to her new address.

The name of Chief ERA William Henry Porter is inscribed on Panel 9 below the great granite Cross of Sacrifice of the Halifax Memorial in Point Pleasant Park.

THEIR GRAVES ARE UNKNOWN BUT
THEIR MEMORY SHALL ENDURE.

CHAPTER 3—CONVOY DUTY

One of the seven over-age destroyers given to the RCN by the U.S. Navy (USN), as part of the US/UK Lend Lease agreement, was the USS *McCook*, which was re-christened HMCS *St. Croix*. These four-funnelled ships had

HMCS St. Croix, August 1943. (Ken Macpherson collection)

been built in haste at the end of World War I, and their handling in rough weather and manoeuverability against submarines left much to be desired. But when they arrived in Canada, they came crammed with USN luxuries: food stuffs, navigation instruments, blank log books, pens, pencil sharpeners, bunks instead of hammocks, mattresses, sheets, pillows and even pillowcases, typewriters, radios, and coffee-making machines.

On September 9, 1940, American sailors hauled down the Stars and Stripes and marched off the ship for the long train ride from Halifax to Boston. Royal Navy crews swarmed aboard and raised the White Ensign, made needed improvements, and then handed the ships over to the RCN, few of whose sailors had any real sea experience.

Early in December 1940, *St. Croix*, accompanied by *Niagara* and *St. Clair*, sailed from Halifax for England. Fighting a North Atlantic gale, *St. Croix* experienced a fuel line problem that caused her to turn about and make for Newfoundland. The ship pitched and rolled dangerously in the terrible weather making the 180° turn extremely hazardous. As well, the wind-whipped sea spray had built a thick coat of ice on the super-structure. The destroyer was already top heavy so the thick ice had to be chipped and hacked away by men wielding axes while clinging to any hand hold on the deck. The ships' radio frequencies did not allow ship-to-ship communication so *St. Croix* was unable to inform her sister ships of her intentions to return.

In the black wee hours of December 8, in waves more than sixty feet high and in the teeth of a gale-force wind, heavy seas crashed over *St. Croix*'s foredeck, carrying away most of the rigging and smashing lifeboats and floats into slivers. It was not until December 15 that the battered warship limped into the calm of St John's harbour. After completing emergency repairs, *St. Croix* departed and turned south for Halifax where, for the next three months, she sat in dry dock while an extensive refit repaired the most severe damage. Almost her entire crew and some of her officers were reassigned to other ships.

Finally, in April 1941, she headed once more to sea. For several months she seemed doomed to fight her war on the Halifax to Newfoundland run as part of the Newfoundland Escort Force. She became known as a hard-luck ship in that every time she put to sea, something untoward happened. Either she experienced damaging bad weather or crippling equipment malfunctions. Running out of Halifax harbour one grey morning at fourteen knots, a somewhat excessive speed, a small fleet auxiliary vessel lost sight of *St. Croix*'s grey hull and scraped all along her starboard side.

St. Croix was assigned to Escort Group 21, operating out of St. John's, in August 1941. She got a new coat of white, blue, and green camouflage paint and headed into dangerous waters on August 26 to join convoy SC41. Stopping in Iceland, after handing the convoy over to Royal Navy mid-ocean escorts, *St. Croix* was almost immediately ordered to sea again to help protect the beleaguered convoy SC42 that had taken considerable pounding from U-boats.

The bright clear afternoon of September 13 provided maximum visibility. One of the bridge lookouts spotted a surfaced raider five miles away and *St. Croix* changed route to intercept. The boat submerged and although an asdic[33] contact was made, lost, and made again, the depth charges bubbled no proof of success to the surface. The destroyer completed her first trans-Atlantic trip with a frustrated and exhausted crew and nagging mechanical problems. Finally, in mid-November, she was ordered into dry dock at Saint John, New Brunswick, for a long-overdue refit. Her commander for the trying year, Harry Kingsley, was posted to command a new ship, HMCS *Skeena*.

In May 1942, with a new commander on the bridge, Lieutenant Commander Arthur Hedley Dobson, *St. Croix* sailed from the flooded dry dock into the Bay of Fundy, rounding Nova Scotia for Halifax. After the Japanese attack on Pearl Harbor on December 7, 1941, the U.S. Navy had shifted the bulk of its forces to the Pacific, leaving the RCN to fill the gap. Royal Navy and RCN escorts were tasked to herd their convoys all the way across the Atlantic to Londonderry, where the scenery was green and placid and the people, especially the girls, welcomed Canadian sailors to shore.

[33] Allied Submarine Detection Investigation Committee. An early form of sonar used to detect submarines by bouncing sound waves off the target's hull.

On July 24, 1942, *St. Croix*, sailing in the Second Canadian Escort Group, enjoyed Canada's first success against a U-boat. Escorting the thirty-three-ship convoy ON113, the masthead lookout spotted a submarine on the surface several miles ahead. The captain ordered his crew to action stations and the engine room to apply "full speed ahead." The old destroyer raced for her target. At a range of three nautical miles, the U-boat dived and should have made good her escape. However, the asdic operators on *St. Croix* were good. They gained contact and stubbornly tracked the twisting sub.

Three times *St. Croix* dropped ten depth charges in a set pattern. Although some oil and wreckage appeared after the third drop, often released from the sub's torpedo tubes as a ruse, the tenacious destroyer pressed home a fourth attack. This time there was no doubt. Bits of clothing, human flesh, books, cigarettes, food, and a flimsy brassiere (labelled "Triumph, Paris"[34]) were fished from the oily waters. The gulls quickly disposed of the detritus.

The U-boat, under K. K. Oldörp, an inexperienced captain, had not made a single attack before its demise. Dobson received the Distinguished Service Cross for the kill and *St. Croix* traded the term "hard-luck ship" for "sub killer." She was an old ship, but she was a good ship.

Navy crews called the area in mid-ocean that could not be covered by anti-submarine or surveillance aircraft as the Black Pit. It was in this "Pit" that *St. Croix* next demonstrated her skills. C4, the fourth Canadian Escort Group, was escorting convoy ON-127 with two destroyers, *St. Croix* in the lead and *Ottawa* following the merchantmen accompanied by four corvettes. None could have guessed that thirteen submarines lay directly in their path. On September 13, *Ottawa* hurried ahead to meet a relief destroyer from St. John's, so she was ten miles in front of the convoy when a torpedo tore off her bow. She had stumbled into the U-boat pack.

While carrying out damage control a second torpedo hit, the ship broke up and sank quickly. *St. Croix*, busy assisting a sinking merchantman, completed that task then steamed quickly for her mortally wounded sister ship. The convoy continued ahead, but the *St. Croix* stayed. She circled, throwing life jackets and floats to the stricken men while two corvettes picked up the survivors. On a wind-driven rising sea, in freezing waters, men struggled to stay afloat. But by the time help arrived, most had been in the ocean for about five hours. Five officers and 109 men were lost, but among the officers saved was First Lieutenant Tom Pullen of Ottawa who would prove his bravery several times over in this war and leave a distinguished navy career to become an expert in arctic marine operations.

The winter of 1942–43 brought the worst weather North Atlantic mariners had witnessed in more than thirty years. While Canadian sailors in their little

---

[34] "Triumph" is a brand name of a Paris-based lingerie manufacturer

ships endured great misery, the bad weather proved favourable for U-boat operations. Air cover was curtailed while navy and merchant crews were preoccupied with their personal safety and that of their ships in the ferocious gales.

St. Croix gained a little respite between January and April 1943, as she
and her sister ships in the First Canadian Escort Group (C1) were kept in the
eastern Atlantic, sailing, training, and re-equipping from ports in England
and Scotland. During this hiatus, Commander Dobson was able to ensure
that both *St. Croix* and her crew were in top shape. Two modern 20-mm
Oerlikon guns replaced her ancient 4-inch beam guns, and additional 50-cal-
ibre machine guns were mounted.

In February, the Escort Group C1 sailed to protect a "Torch"[35] convoy
bound for Algeria. En route, off Portugal, three submarines stalked them. On
March 4, all guns in the convoy opened up against two Luftwaffe Folke-
Wulf Condors. Neither the aircraft bombs nor the ships' guns contributed
more to the war effort than a deafening noise, but, suddenly, HMCS *Shediac*
gained an underwater contact and *St. Croix* closed in to assist. They each
dropped ten depth charges. Asdic operators were convinced that they had
scored a hit and sunk a U-boat homeward bound from the Azores. It was a
victorious return to the U.K. for C1. *Shediac* and *St. Croix* were confident
even if the Admiralty only granted a conclusion of "probable, slightly damaged." The evidence later showed that *U-87*, under Kriegsmarine Leutnant
Joachim Berger, had disappeared without a trace and could only have been
the sub sunk by the combined efforts of *Shediac* and *St. Croix*.

In early April, *St. Croix* returned to the North Atlantic and the Iceland-
Halifax run.

On April 17, 1943, Able Seaman F. H. Savage joined the crew in Halifax.
He made two crossings with his ship in April and May, escorting SC127 and
ON184, before the ship was again in need of rest and refit in Halifax.

V 6676 Able Seaman Francis Herbert Savage
Royal Canadian Navy

Herb Savage joined the navy on November 22, 1940. But it was not until
June 1, 1941, that he started his basic training at HMCS *Bytown*, a land-
based unit in Ottawa. In the meantime, he was held on divisional strength
and allowed to live at home and continue with his civilian employment. The
navy had, however, assumed responsibility for his health and treated him for
a head cold on May 15.

Herb was born in Ashton on September 1, 1922, into a family that suffered more than its share of tragedy. His father, Thomas Miller Savage, had
died on January 7, 1922. Three brothers—Weldon, age eight; John, age six;

---

[35] This convoy was delivering supplies to the Allied forces that had landed in November in North Africa
(Operation Torch). Re-provisioning could only be carried out by sea through Algerian and Moroccan ports
and was essential to the next planned landings in Sicily.

and James, age one—and one sister, Florence, age four, all died within a span of eleven days from scarlet fever. His only remaining sibling, his older brother Albert Oliver, lived and worked in Ottawa.

After completing his schooling in Carleton Place, Herb became an "office clerk Grade I," working in the Hunter Building with the Department of National Defence. Florence Matilda Savage, Herb's mother, was living in Ashton when he joined the navy, but later moved to Bronson Street in Ottawa to live with her sister-in-law, Florence Elsie Savage. Herb lived alone in a small apartment at 424 Bank Street and was a regular attendee at Church of England services. He stood 5' 8" tall, was a thin 138 pounds, and had fair complexion with brown hair and blue eyes. Somehow in his earlier days he had suffered the traumatic amputation of the distal phalanx[36] of his left thumb.

Herb's first posting was to HMCS *Stadacona*, the navy's land base in Halifax, where he was duly introduced to the idiosyncrasies and customs of the Royal Canadian Navy. He arrived on August 8, 1941, to begin his training as a seaman and learn his duties as a navy deckhand. It was during this time that he was hit in the right eye with a bit of flying debris. Unable to clear the fragment himself, he reported to sickbay to have it removed.

With his training completed, Able Seaman Savage was transferred, on September 26, 1941, to HMCS *Avalon*, the shore base in St. John's, Newfoundland, where the Newfoundland Force was headquartered. His office duties were uneventful except that he spent much of the Christmas and New Year's holidays of 1942–43 being treated for mumps at St. John's Lester Field Military Hospital.

The last known photograph of the St. Croix ship's company taken in St. John's Newfoundland on May 30, 1943. (NAC PA 192997)

[36] The end of the thumb, severed at the knuckle.

His first sea-going ship was HMCS *St. Croix*, joining her on April 17, 1943.

For one week, July 16 to 24, AB Savage was posted to the frigate HMCS *Montreal*, while *St. Croix* was undergoing her refit in Halifax. He returned to *St. Croix* on July 27 and they sailed for St. John's. Part of Escort Group C5, the Barber-Pole Brigade, she sailed with new red and white stripes painted on her funnel[37]. Going east on August 5 with convoy HX-250, they experienced a very dull passage with no U-boat contacts or any other signs of the enemy.

The crossing took only six days. After re-fuelling off Moville, Ireland, in the entrance to the Foyle River, they steamed up to Londonderry. As well as the warm Irish hospitality, orders awaited them to join the new Canadian group, EG9, to serve as a hunter-killer. Led by the HMS *Itchen*, they practised daily in the Irish Sea.

On September 12, a slow convoy, ONS-18, set out from the U.K. It was followed on September 15 by ON-202, a much faster convoy. At 1600 hours that same day, *St. Croix* weighed anchor and steamed down river from her new base in Plymouth. It was a calm day with a slight wind but a fairly heavy swell. Those crew members not on watch enjoyed the sun on deck and speculated about their destination. Among several new officers on board was Surgeon Lieutenant William Lyon Mackenzie King, namesake and nephew of the prime minister. Just as the sky was darkening, HMS *Itchen* and the rest of Escort Group EG9 joined the *St. Croix*.

Two days later, EG9 was ordered to assist convoy HX-256 heading for the U.K. They determined that all was well with the heavily laden merchantmen and were ordered to continue westwards to support convoy ONS-18 and ON-202. Intelligence had ascertained that the German navy was sending a considerable force to intercept the two convoys.

By the 18th, ON-202 had easily caught the slower group of ships. The two were ordered to join, and EG9, following an evasive route to confuse German trackers, changed course to take up defensive positions. The escorts, the British frigate *Itchen*, and the Canadians *St. Croix*, *St. Francis*, *Chambly*, *Sackville*, and *Morden* slipped seamlessly into line. An increased number of U-boat radio transmissions indicated that an attack was imminent on the now-very-large eighty-eight-ship convoy. Counting the original escorts, the addition of EG9 gave the defenders fifteen warships.

Radio messages during the night of September 15–16, from the Commander-in-Chief of the Kriegsmarine, Karl Dönitz, ordered twenty-eight submarines to

[37] In both World Wars, the usual funnel painting for the grey-coated Canadian warships was a green maple leaf. This was to distinguish them from ships of the Royal Navy since both navies flew the same White Ensign from the stern. The RCN did fly the Canadian Red Ensign from the masthead as the national flag until 1965 when the now familiar Red Maple Leaf was adopted. The red and white "barber pole" stripe is still painted on the mast structure or radar pedestals of ships of the Fifth Canadian Destroyer Squadron.

U 305 *in the Battle of the Atlanti*

form Gruppe Leuthen in a ten-mile line across the proposed track of the converging convoys. In the middle of the line was *U-305*, commanded by twenty-seven-year-old Oberleutnant Rudolf Robert Bahr. Nine of the U-boats, including *U-305*, were equipped with the German navy's latest weapon, an acoustic homing torpedo, nicknamed by the Allies the GNAT (German Navy Acoustic Torpedo). Bahr had already been credited with sinking two British ships from convoy SC-122 on March 17, the SS *Zouave*, carrying 7,000 tons of iron filings, and the SS *Port Auckland*, an 8,789-ton refrigerator ship.

On September 20, at approximately 1500 hours, *St. Croix* acquired an asdic contact on a sub, dropped a few depth charges but lost contact. Shortly after 1600 hours, six U-boats on the surface attacked the convoy in an attempt to get inside the anti-submarine screen of ships and aircraft. Suddenly *U-305* was driven to crash dive to avoid the attentions of a shadowing Liberator VLR (very long range) aircraft. The aircraft, from 120 Squadron in Reykjavik, Iceland, had already been airborne some eleven hours. Bahr heard no depth charges exploding near him so ordered his ship to re-surface. Minutes later, the Liberator spotted him again and the two opened fire on each other with cannon and flak, but neither scored a hit. *U-305* submerged and in thirty seconds was at periscope depth. This required the new VIIC-class boat to run on its twin 750-horsepower battery-powered electric motors. At this depth her best speed was slightly more than seven knots, whereas on the surface her best speed was seventeen knots.

Oberleutnant Bahr glued his eyeball to the periscope and swept the horizon. He was rewarded by sighting a destroyer about three to four miles ahead. The Liberator was circling the roiling water marking the spot where *U-305* submerged. The aircraft signalled for assistance by aldis lamp and *St.*

Croix turned hard to get into position. After losing the previous contact, activity had quieted and most of *St. Croix'* crew were at supper. The old four-stack destroyer built up a speed of twenty-four knots in her race to get to the U-boat before darkness fell. The wind had now become quite cold, and the sea had risen to the point that green waves occasionally broke over the side. Now began the game of tactical wit as the surface and U-boat captains matched their stamina and nerve. An old Great War destroyer was tangled in a death struggle with a brand new state-of-the-art submarine.

As *St. Croix* reached the spot marked by the aircraft's smoke float, Savage felt the ship slow as the captain ordered reduced speed and began to zigzag. The asdic operators obtained an immediate contact, and Savage had to hold on as the ship began to heel over in a hard port turn. Suddenly, he was thrown violently against the bulkhead and was deafened by a terrible explosion. Seconds later, the ship's stern heaved upwards when a deck-mounted depth charge exploded, blowing many of Savage's mates on the quarterdeck into the water. The first torpedo had hit them in the stern, homing in on the noise of the ship's propellers. The ship stopped and began to list.

Through the periscope, Lieutenant Bahr sighted the destroyer listing to port and smoking considerably and the crew attempting to lower the warship's lifeboats. He decided another torpedo was needed to finish her off. He fired and called for the time to be recorded—202151.

The second strike took out the engine and boiler rooms. Stokers and engine-room artificers, scalded by escaping steam or crushed by the blast, had no time to get clear. *St. Croix* was dying, and Dobson gave the order to abandon ship. Surgeon Lieutenant King and his sickbay attendant were at the destroyed stern bandaging and treating the injured sailors. However, as *St. Croix* heeled over, those who could dove into the cold sea that by now

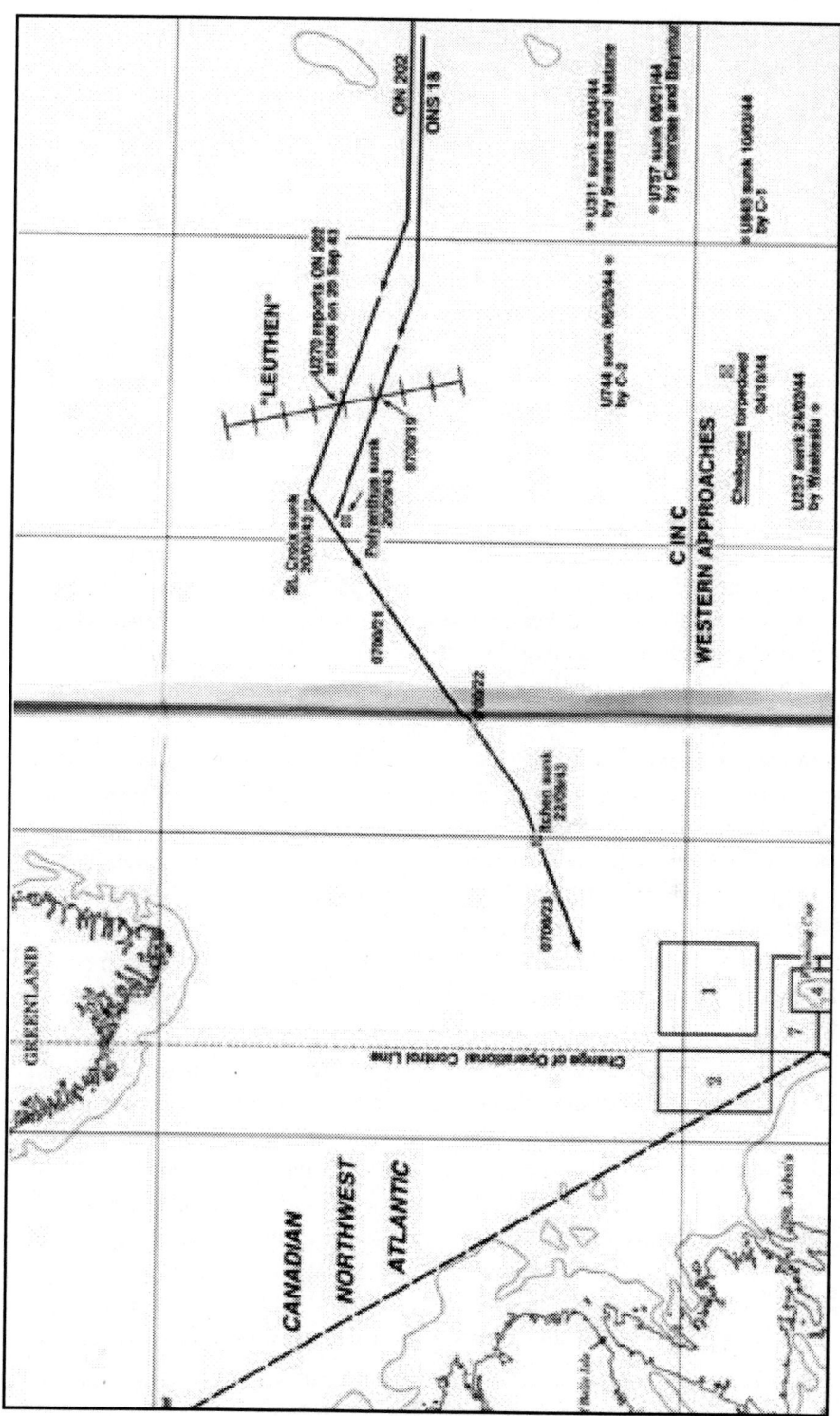

was layered with thick bunker oil and debris. *Itchen* sent the following message to B-2, the British escort group:

> ST. CROIX TORPEDOED AND BLOWN UP. FORECASTLE STILL AFLOAT. SURVIVORS IN RAFTS AND BOATS. TORPEDOES FIRED AT ME. DOING FULL SPEED IN VICINITY. WILL NOT ATTEMPT TO P.U. SURVIVORS UNTIL POLYANTHUS ARRIVES.

Bahr, attacked by another destroyer and an aircraft, dove deep to make his escape and record his second victory over a destroyer[38]. His log shows that *St. Croix* did not sink immediately and that an hour later he fired a third torpedo into her, the *coup de grace*. The stern disappeared quickly, but the section from amidships forward stayed afloat for about five minutes. Then, with a long sigh of escaping steam, the bow rose high into the air before sliding below the waves.

It is not known whether Savage was killed in the explosions that ripped the bowels out of *St. Croix* or whether he survived the sinking only to die cold and alone in the merciless sea. If he did, he would have clung to one of the Carley floats or have been crowded in the almost submerged whaler. Bailing furiously, the survivors would get most of the water out of the boat only to have a wave come over the side. Most were dressed only in sweaters and dungarees and few wore any footwear.

Some survivors were fished out of the brine by the Royal Navy corvette *Polyanthus*, which was in turn torpedoed in the stern by an acoustic torpedo. She went down in about thirty seconds. *Itchen* had picked up the only survivor from *Polyanthus*, a man originally from *St. Croix*. At dawn, *Itchen* spotted a little flotilla of eighty-two survivors and changed course to rescue them, including the commander, Lieutenant Commander Dobson. These men had been adrift for over twelve hours. They were provided with showers, clean clothes, hot black coffee, and food. *Itchen*'s coxswain even liberated a few tots of rum.

Itchen remained in the thick of the battle with the submarine wolfpack. On September 20, U-boat contacts and depth charge attacks were continuous. RCAF Liberators from Newfoundland joined in the melee making several attacks miles ahead of the convoy, while *U-666* penetrated the head of the convoy and positioned herself for attacks. At midnight on September 22, a searchlight from *Itchen* pierced the blackness to light up the submarine. The call to action stations was sounded, and the destroyer's forward gunners opened fire. They missed. In retaliation, *U-666* fired two torpedoes, one homing on the destroyer's amidships. Before the gun crew could load anoth-

---

[38] Most of the information on the last moments of H.M.C.S. St. Croix and her battle with U-305 has been taken from the book Deadly Seas written by David Bercuson and Holger Herwig; published by Random House of Canada Limited, Toronto, in 1997.

er round, the torpedo scored, touching off a holocaust of flame and flying metal. The frigate's ammunition magazine had taken a direct hit.

No one could stand on the rapidly slanting deck as the ship convulsed with multiple explosions. At 0200 hours, she was a sinking wreck.

At 0300, Stoker William Fisher of Victoria, British Columbia, the sole surviving sailor from *Polyanthus*, plus one crewman from the *Itchen*, were dragged aboard the Polish freighter *Waleha*. Fisher was also the only *St. Croix* survivor.

U-305 sank one more warship, the Royal Navy frigate, *Tweed*, on January 7, 1944, and then ten days later went to her own watery grave with all hands.

The last entry in Able Seaman Herbert Savage's military file is that he was "lost at sea with *H.M.C.S. St. Croix* 20.9.43 while on convoy duty in the Atlantic due to enemy action. Discharge dead."

His mother received Herb's War Service Grant of $277.85, which comprised his 907 days' service paid at $225, 137 days at sea paid at 25¢ a day, and a supplemental grant of $18.60. She was also sent the Memorial Cross on January 12, 1944. Francis Herbert Savage's name is cast on Panel 10 of the Halifax Memorial in Point Pleasant Park. He was twenty-one years old.

CHAPTER 4—AMONG THE SHROUDS

V 49510 Able Seaman Earl Franklin Lancaster
Royal Canadian Navy Volunteer Reserve

Earl Franklin Lancaster was nineteen years old when he joined the Royal Canadian Navy on October 27, 1942. Earl was named for his father, Franklin (Frank), who had a painting and wallpapering business in Carleton Place. Earl was the sixth child and the fourth son of twelve children born to Frank and Sarah Lancaster.

Growing up in Carleton Place, Earl enjoyed swimming and hockey, playing on the CPHS hockey team. He completed his education in the town's public and high schools, finishing what was known as "second form," roughly equivalent to grade ten. For the last two years of his schooling, he worked with his father as a painter and then as a "bobbin boy"[39] at the Bates and Innes Limited textile plant.

Officially enlisted into the navy on October 27, Earl was able to continue working at the Bates factory until December 4 when he was called to active service. During the interim, he was carried on the navy rolls as "divisional strength" with HMCS *Bytown*, the navy nomenclature for Naval Service Headquarters in Ottawa, and HMCS *Carleton*, the Royal Canadian Navy Volunteer Reserve division in Ottawa.

On December 14, Ordinary Seaman Earl Lancaster was sent to HMCS *York*, the divisional training centre in Toronto to learn how to dress, eat, talk, and think like a sailor. As he was close enough to Carleton Place to visit during leave, on February 6, he brought one of his new navy friends, Melvin McIntyre, home with him for the weekend. During the spring of 1943, Earl was usually able to get home every second weekend, and he took great pleasure in walking the streets of town in his navy-blue uniform with its jaunty white cap. The bell-bottomed trousers fit his 5' 10", 147-pound frame very well. With a dark complexion, black hair and sparkling walnut eyes, he caught the admiring glance of many a female eye.

The last weekend in April he was home with his parents for the Easter holiday, and at the Anglican church services, they beamed with pride in their sailor son.

From Toronto he was sent, on Monday, May 11, 1943, to HMCS *Cornwallis*, a navy training base at Deep Brook, near Digby, Nova Scotia, for basic training in one of the various trades he would need to master as a sailor aboard His Majesty's Canadian ships. At *Cornwallis*, he could see and smell the sea, or at least the Bay of Fundy. As part of their final training and

[39] A bobbin boy was responsible for keeping the machines' bobbins full of yarn or thread to quickly replace the bobbins in use, as they became empty.

to test what they had learned, Earl and his mates went to sea for two days in July on the armed yacht HMCS *Husky* out of Halifax. Under the watchful eyes of the commander, Lieutenant J. P. Kieran, RCNR, they were exposed to all of the manpower needs of a navy vessel and were able to use the skills they had learned on shore.

Earl proceeded to the second, advanced phase of his training at *Cornwallis* before being posted to HMCS *Stadacona*, the RCN's main shore base on the Atlantic coast at Halifax. He arrived at his new posting on the August 25, and was given leave in November, which he took with his parents in Carleton Place. When he returned, he learned of his advancement, on December 4, to acting able seaman. Earl was home for the last time on the weekend of March 5 and 6, 1944.

The summer of 1944, Lancaster spent at HMCS *Scotian*. On September 28, he was sent to the naval base at Montreal, HMCS *Hochelaga*, and a month later HMCS *Chaleur II*, at Quebec City, for an immediate posting to the frigate HMCS *Fort Erie*. This was Earl's first transfer to a fighting ship.

Each time Earl was posted, his commanding officer had rated Earl's character as consistently "very good."

The *Fort Erie* went to sea from October 28 to November 7. These eleven days, combined with the two days aboard HMCS *Husky*, comprised Earl's total service on the high seas.

On Wednesday morning, November 8, Sarah Lancaster responded to a knock on her front door. She was alone. Frank was at work and the remaining children living at home—James Stanley, seventeen; Grace Dorene, fifteen; and Mary Sadie, thirteen—were at school. Standing forlornly on the step was their rector, the Reverend Canon T. H. Iveson. The war had been going on long enough that she suspected Canon Iveson's visit pertained to one of her sons in uniform. Her mind quickly reviewed them: William Douglas, twenty-nine, her third oldest, was overseas; Earl was in Quebec City; and the next youngest boy, Leslie Stewart, nineteen, was also in the navy, but he was downtown in Carleton Place, home on sick leave from HMCS *Naden* stationed on the Pacific coast.

Canon Iveson soon realized that Sarah had not received the customary, "We regret to inform you . . ." telegram from the navy. The family had been notified about an hour before the minister's arrival that Earl was in hospital and dangerously ill, but Canon Iveson would be the first to inform her that she had lost a son. It was not a completely new experience for her. In 1923 she had lost two-year-old George Duncan and, in 1936, Alexander McDonald had died at age twenty-three. But there was nothing to still

Sarah's breaking heart on learning the news that it was Earl who had tragically died. He had accidentally fallen from the mast of his ship while it was docked in Quebec City and subsequently passed away, never regaining consciousness.

On November 7, HMCS *Fort Erie* was berthed at Shed 29 at the Quebec City docks. Leading Seaman Peter J. Clements was in charge of a working party of six men, oiling the guardrails along the ship's side as well as the rigging leading from the mast to the deck. At 1315 hours, Clements sent three men to work on the rails and three others, Seamen Lancaster, Johnson and Stewart, up the mast. Johnson and Lancaster went up the mast immediately while Stewart stayed below to rig a bosun's chair.

There are four short guylines leading from the mast of a frigate to the upper bridge; two run forward and two run to each wing of the bridge. They are short enough that the sailors can slide down them from the crow's nest to the bridge. It was these lines that Johnson and Lancaster began sliding down, oiling with a linseed oil-soaked rag as they went. The rest of the lines, running to the deck from above the yardarm, were too long to slide down so Stewart was rigging the bosun's chair for use on them. After a walk around the ship, Clements climbed the mast to check that Johnson and Lancaster were finished oiling the four short lines and preparing to do the longer lines. He warned them to be careful then climbed down and went below decks.

About 1400 hours, the men climbed down to the deck for a break. When it was time to return to work, Johnson climbed back up the mast by the ladder. His oil can was at the yardarm, leaving him in position to attach the line holding the bosun's chair[40] to a pulley on the mast. A sailor sits in the chair with lines around him while it is hauled[41] up and down the stays leading from the mast to the deck. He is therefore able to go up and down the stay with both hands free to work. Another seaman on deck hauls the chair up and down.

Lancaster joined a group of his mates who had been oiling the rails on the stern deck. He looked up along the stay running from the port side of the deck to the yardarm, about twenty-five to thirty feet in the air.

"Betch'a buck I can shinny up that stay," he challenged Able Seaman Maybee.

"I doubt it. But you're on!" Maybee replied and reached into his wallet to produce his dollar bill.

---

[40] A boatswain (pronounced bo'sun) is the non-commissioned officer in charge of the equipment and the duties of the ship's crew on the upper deck. He is the seamanship expert of a crew. A boatswain's chair is a seat suspended from ropes for work aloft or on the side of a ship in which a sailor may securely sit and have both hands free to perform his task. It could be as rudimentary as a bowline knot tied in a rope. A bowline forms a non-slip bow in the line.
[41] In the navy a seaman does not "pull" on ropes or lines. "Pulling" is what one does in a small boat using oars. If one is using a rope/line, one is "hauling" or "hauling up."

"Ah! I don't want to take your money," retorted Earl and walked away. "But I think I'll see if I can do it anyway."

Again he looked up the stay, calculating his chances. He knew he was in excellent condition due to his physical training. Earl was confident that he could climb the stay, so he pulled on his leather gloves and began hoisting himself up the cable, hand-over-hand using his feet to hold his position. At first he ascended quite easily. Then, about three-quarters of the way up, he had to make his way around a radio antenna. He had some trouble getting past but finally made it. An officer on deck had now noticed Lancaster's proximity to the aerial and sent a sailor to the telegraph cabin to ensure that all the power was turned off.

Earl was above the funnel, but still some distance from the top where Able Seaman Johnson was clinging to the mast, when he found himself tiring more quickly than he thought he would.

"Allan," he called, "give me your hand. I need some help."

Extending his arm as far as he could reach, Johnson replied, "I can't quite reach you, can you get a little higher?"

Slowly, ever so slowly, Earl began to slide down the stay. There were two insulators built into the stay. On the way up they made fine handholds, but on the way down they were a hazard, especially as he picked up speed sliding down towards the deck. As he slid past the uppermost insulator, his feet cleared it, but it appeared to knock his hands off the cable and he began a fifty-foot fall. It was about 1440 hours.

Earl landed on the flag deck, a small deck elevated from the main stern deck, on his back shoulders, but his head hit a small step. Terrified, Seaman Johnson clung to the mast for a couple of minutes until he was able to start down. The men on deck and the officer of the day, gunnery officer, Lieutenant D. A. Woodcroft, saw and heard the sickening thump as Lancaster hit the deck. They rushed to him. He was unconscious and bleeding from the nose and ears. Woodcroft ordered a seaman to call an ambulance and had Earl taken to a small cabin. The lieutenant removed some of Earl's clothes and was making a cursory examination when a jeep pulled up to the ship. Lancaster was put on a stretcher, loaded into the jeep, and rushed to the sickbay, where Surgeon Lieutenant Paul Levesque provided first aid. Diagnosing a fractured skull, the medical officer transferred his patient to Jeffrey Hale Hospital in the city.

He was admitted to hospital at 1600 hours. Still unconscious, his breathing was loud and deep, almost as if he was snoring. He had two small cuts, one behind his left ear and one on his left ankle. His face, hands, and feet were turning blue, and the left side of his head was considerably swollen.

Blood was seeping from his nose and left ear. An X-ray of his skull revealed a fracture from the left ear to the top of his head. His pulse slowly became very weak and rapid. Two hours later he stopped breathing and was pronounced dead. He was twenty-one years old.

Two officers from HMCS *Fort Erie*, the first lieutenant and the gunnery officer, positively identified the body of Earl Franklin Lancaster. A coroner's inquest ruled that the death was from accidental events, so no autopsy was considered necessary. Earl's commanding officer, Lieutenant Commander Aubrey Winston Ford, RCNR, wrote his condolences to Mrs. Lancaster on November 9, explaining that Earl met his death carrying out his duties in a seamanlike manner, working aloft in the rigging. The Board of Enquiry, which convened on November 22 to investigate the circumstances of Lancaster's death, determined that Lieutenant Commander Ford's letter to Mrs. Lancaster might mislead her into believing that Earl was killed by accident in the line of duty and so concluded that his death should be considered a service casualty.

Leading Seaman Peter Clements accompanied Earl's body from Quebec City to Carleton Place, where it lay in his parents' home on Clayton Street until Saturday, November 12, when it was moved to St. James Anglican Church for the funeral. Earl's brothers, Raymond, John Gordon, Stewart and Stanley, his sisters Irene (Mrs. Fred Toop), Gladys (Mrs. Orville Brydges), Dorene, and Mary, together with their families, stood before the church doors with the Legion guard of honour.

Reverend Canon Iveson conducted the hour-long service during which all town businesses closed their doors out of respect for the young serviceman. Six navy ratings carried the flag-draped coffin to its grave, Earl's white flat-topped hat perched precariously on top. A sole trumpeter sounded a mournful "Last Post" into the cold November air.

Sarah received Earl's Memorial Cross on March 17, 1945. His parents also received a total of $174.11 constituting the War Service Grant. It provided compensation for 705 days service, nothing for service on the high seas (Earl only had thirteen days at sea and a minimum of fifteen days were required), and subsistence pay of $1.61. The navy also credited Earl's account with $4.14 for "kit upkeep and grog money." In keeping with a very ancient military tradition, the bulk of Earl's personal effects were auctioned off among his mates[42].

The body of V 49510 Able Seaman Franklin Earl Lancaster is buried in the St. James Anglican Cemetery in Carleton Place, Ontario.

---

[42] In the days before pensions were provided to dependants of fallen service men it became customary, in order to provide aid for his dependants, for the dead man's comrades to auction his personal belongings. His mates were encouraged to bid very generously and the proceeds were given to the deceased's widow or mother.

PART 2—FROM WORKERS TO WARRIORS

THE ROYAL CANADIAN AIR FORCE
1941–1942

In 1938, the British government made an informal request for Canada to train aircrew in Canada. On September 26, 1939, Britain renewed that request to Prime Minister MacKenzie King. The Canadian parliament agreed, and on October 10, Britain's Air Minister, Sir Kingsley Wood, announced the creation of the British Commonwealth Air Training Plan (BCATP). The U.K., Australia, New Zealand, and Canada all agreed that Canada would establish air-training centres for pilots and airmen from all parts of the British Empire.

The responsibility shouldered by the dominion was enormous. The previous year, the RCAF had graduated only forty-five pilots. Total strength of the service was 4,000 all ranks in both the regular and auxiliary squadrons. It was forecast that 40,000 trained people would be needed to instruct, administer, and provide ground crews for the proposed fifty-five aviation training schools. The first school was planned to open in May 1940, and by 1942, the scheme was to be turning out 20,000 pilots, navigators/bomb-aimers, air gunners, and wireless operators each year.

After the Great War, many pilots took their aeroplanes "barnstorming" to earn a living. They travelled from town to town, often following the fall fair schedule, to awe the crowd with their mastery of flight and offer rides to those citizens with nerve and money. Missions over France had turned aviators like A. Roy Brown, D. Douglas Findlay, and Murray Galbraith into heroes. Decorated by King and Empire, they were described in reverential tones as medieval knights and avenging angels. There was an aura of mystique and poetry surrounding them. "In an age of modern weapons, the aviator had the power to turn back the clock to a time when combat was clean, clear and simple. Free of the suffocating constraints of the trenches, he sailed aloft in a realm of clarity, cleanliness and order.[1]"

The Second World War removed that cloak of awesome respectability. Aircraft became far more common and had lost their mystery. The blitz of London, night raids on Berlin, the total destruction of the city of Dresden[2] and the dropping of atomic bombs on Hiroshima and Nagasaki took all the

[1] Jonathan F. Vance, High Flight (Toronto: Penguin Press Canada) 2002
[2] A once-beautiful Baroque city in eastern Germany, Dresden has since become synonymous with civilian suffering under the barrage of total war.

poetry out of pilots and aeroplanes. The Allied bombing campaign destroyed towns that were a thousand years old and ravaged the countryside. The German state had triggered a maelstrom, and the hot winds blew back into its face.

Not every recruit was destined to wear wings. For every airman, there was a host of ground-bound technicians who provided training instruction, administration, maintenance, and repairs, as well as the provision of food, quarters, clothing, and personal equipment. Many flying instructors came from commercial flying schools throughout the Commonwealth and even the U.S., while technicians came from the pre-war auxiliary squadrons and the militia. Ultimately, Canadian men and women were trained in some sixty-five trades, from clerks to technicians in the fields of airframe, aero-engine, radar and radio.

The R.C.A.F. comes to
CARLETON PLACE
MEN! WOMEN! OPPORTUNITY comes to your door!
YOUNG MEN, age 18 to 33 years, are needed for Flying Duties in Air Crew and a few specialized trades. Educational requirements, High School Entrance or better.
WOMEN are required for such trades as Stenographers, Typists, General Duties, Drivers, Teleprinter Operators and Accountants.
Interviews will be welcomed by the R.C.A.F. Recruiting Officer and an Officer of the Women's Division at the Post Office, on Friday, September 18th, from 4 p.m. to 9 p.m.
Serve Your Country In The
ROYAL CANADIAN
AIR FORCE

Chapter 5—NON-OPERATIONAL LOSSES

Duncan Cedric Cameron
R 82457 Aircraftsman 2nd Class
Royal Canadian Air Force

Duncan Cedric Cameron, oldest son of Duncan Stewart and Eva Gertrude Bole, had been involved in military organisations since his days in high school. He enjoyed three years in the Army Cadet Corps, rising to the rank of cadet lieutenant, and he enlisted with the Lanark and Renfrew Scottish Regiment (militia) in Smiths Falls on June 28, 1935. He attended annual training exercises in 1935, '36 and '37, while pursuing his civilian occupation as a blacksmith, motor mechanic, and welder in his father's Carleton Place blacksmith shop located between his brick home, at 297 Bridge Street, and the Maple Leaf Dairy. He was described as being 5' 9" tall and weighing 172 pounds.

When he was struck off strength (SOS) on February 5, 1940, to join the RCAF, Cedric was an acting sergeant in the Lanark and Renfrew Scottish. Two brothers were already in active force uniform: Byron, a staff sergeant, was serving in the army "somewhere in England," while Victor, a flying officer, was in the RCAF in Dartmouth, Nova Scotia.

In spite of the fact that the need for men was great, it was not easy to join the RCAF early in the war. The RCAF had a high tradition from the Great War to be maintained, and it was particular about those it allowed into its ranks. Alert, physically fit young men of good

Cedric in his 1921 school photo. (Courtesy Mrs. Alice McRae)

character, with intelligence and personality, who were observant, self-reliant, and keen on flying were the standards set by the air service.

Reporting to the recruiting centre in Ottawa, Cedric Cameron found himself waiting in a hallway where a strange man looked him over very carefully. The intensity of the examination made Cedric wonder if a large pimple had suddenly broken out on the end of his nose. In fact, he was being examined by a "character expert" to see if he had augmented his courage with a few drinks or otherwise displayed characteristics unsuitable for admittance to this elite service.

Every applicant had to produce proof of age and education and have at least two letters of recommendation specifically mentioning his character. It was preferable for one of those letters to be from his present or recent employer. Accordingly, Cedric provided letters from his employer, Charles Bates, and his high school principal, Mr. A. D. Lamont. He also had a reference from Major W. H. Hooper[3] of the Canadian Legion of the British Empire Service League:

> This will serve to introduce Mr. D. Cedric Cameron. This man has two brothers in the service but has stayed behind to help out in his father's business. Now he is free to enlist, and on my recommendation is first making application to the Air Service branch.
>
> My reasons for this are that this man is well qualified to take a trade test in Welding of all sorts, he is also a qualified black-smith and is especially good at ignition and motor mechanics.
>
> At camp with the regiment he was quite good with Lewis Machine Gun. He also received a diploma for First Aid, from the St. Johns Ambulance Assn.

For proof of birth, his mother added further information. She wrote on the proof of age certificate, "he was born on October 23, 1912—I am his mother and remember said date." He was also armed with his militia discharge papers and a letter from his commanding officer, Major J. A. B. Dulmage.

Nearly every applicant to the RCAF wanted to be a pilot. The romance of soaring through the sky in sole control of a flying machine was the dream of most young boys between the wars. But for every flying aircraft, there is a large crew needed to keep it serviceable and airworthy. Experienced men in one of the required trades were preferred, but inexperienced men could be trained. And, as the war ground on, it became harder to find men with experience.

All potential recruits for a trade had to pass a "trades test" even before they had a medical examination. As well as the well-known trades related to aircraft and flying, the RCAF also offered training to become diesel oilers, pigeon loftmen, masseurs, or interpreters. Every skill was needed.

Every recruit had to complete an "attestation paper," with the admonishment to print clearly and legibly. On it were the typical questions, such as name, age, place of birth. As well, recruits had to answer: "Have you ever been convicted of an indictable offence? Are you in debt? [If the answer was yes then specific information was required.] Sports and hobbies? Flying experience?"

On August 2, 1940, Cedric submitted to an enlistment medical examination for enrolment into the RCAF. He gave his date of birth as October 23, 1916, and the place as Pembroke. The family lived in Carleton Place but Eva traveled to her mother's family home in Pembroke for the birth. He admitted to measles as his only childhood illness and declared that his tonsils had been removed.

---

[3] Major Hooper, a veteran of the Boer War, was the postmaster and well known for his World War I service. He led the first contingent of World War I recruits from Carleton Place overseas and into battle on April 22, 1915, near Ypres. Most did not survive. Hooper was wounded and taken prisoner of war. See We Are The Dead also authored by Larry Gray.

This examination was very thorough with particular attention paid to vision and hearing acuity. One's eyes had to have perfect muscular co-ordination in order to accurately judge distances, especially helpful when landing an aircraft. Useless as aircrew or technical tradesmen were those with colour blindness. This was tested by having the candidate look at a coloured mosaic pattern. A person with normal vision would see one pair of numbers whereas a person suffering from colour blindness would see a totally different set of numbers.

Following this examination, Cedric was declared unfit for service and awarded a medical category of "D" (temporarily unfit). He was found to be overweight; at age twenty-seven, Cedric weighed 198 pounds, carried on a 5' 8½"frame. He had gained twenty-six pounds since enlisting in the militia five years earlier. He was also dentally unfit, and with a blood pressure of 144/86,[4] was considered to have hypertension (this probably accounted for his ruddy complexion). His physical development was recorded as being only "fair." In spite of this "temporary" medical category, and the air force's much-vaunted insistence upon only physically and mentally fit specimens, his processing for enlistment was continued.

The final process was the taking of fingerprints and a photograph for an identity card. The photographer had a single one-size-fits-all, too large uniform tunic, shirt, and tie that each man donned. This "official" photograph would follow him for most of his career and would be the butt of many jokes.

Cedric was assigned to the air force trade of aero-engine mechanic. He told the interviewer that he had worked for the previous year as a weaver for the Bates and Innes Renfrew Woollens Mill, glossing over his experience with motors in his father's shop.

Cedric had attended Carleton Place Public School from 1916 until 1927 and Carleton Place High School from 1927 to 1933 where he earned his junior matriculation. As well, he had credits for his senior matriculation in Latin, English literature and composition, algebra, geometry, trigonometry, physics, and zoology. He claimed to have participated extensively in rugby, moderately in hockey, and occasionally in basketball.

Although still medically categorized "D,"after swearing an oath of allegiance, Cedric was sent by train to the Manning Depot in Toronto, reporting on January 7, 1941. The next day he was re-examined and this time, although his weight had increased to 210 pounds, his category was raised to "A," fit for general service.

Within hours, he traded his civilian clothes for the Air Force blue[5] uni-

---

[4] A reading of 140/90 is considered by medical authority to be the baseline for a diagnosis of hypertension.
[5] The particular shade of air force blue adopted by the RAF, and subsequently the RCAF, is the colour of the old Tsarist Russian uniforms. England had supplied Russia with uniforms for years but when the October Revolution occurred, a large quantity of this cloth remained on hand and unused. It seemed perfect for this new service that came into being in World War I. J. Douglas Harvey, The Tumbling Mirth (Toronto: McClelland and Stewart, 1983), p.16.

form of an aircraftsman, second class, which meant that he wore no rank badges. With a host of other recruits, and with his brown hair shorn to within millimetres of his scalp, he took his place on the drill square of the Exhibition Grounds as one of the oldest men on parade, at age twenty-eight.

The drill sergeant now took total control of the mens' lives, acting as mother, father, priest, and confessor for the next three weeks of their existence. He would mold these recruits into first rate military men.

But first it was imperative that Cedric keep his blue eyes focussed straight ahead, neither to left or right, when on parade. After participating in the most arduous physical training he had ever experienced, applying the art of spit-and-polish to his military boots, and rushing through institutional but nutritional meals, he was allowed to fall exhausted into one of the bunks, upper or lower, arranged in never-ending rows in a cattle barn.

Six weeks later, his uniform appeared to fit, including the unaccustomed wedge cap that never seemed to stay in place. He was given a few days' leave to strut before family and friends before reporting, on February 22, 1941, to No. 1 Technical Training School (TTS) in St. Thomas, Ontario, to begin learning the intricacies of an aircraft engine. The weekend of March 20, he was again a welcome visitor in his parents' home.

At the beginning of the war, the RCAF had technical schools at air bases in Trenton and Borden, but it soon became obvious that these facilities were not large enough to handle the influx of trainees. In order to produce enough technicians, a much larger school was required. After an intensive search, buildings in St. Thomas, recently constructed for a mental hospital, were obtained. After some renovation and the construction of suitable hangars, it became, on November 1, 1939, No. 1, TTS. A month later, the St. Thomas school was humming with its first class.[6] It eventually became the largest technical training school in the BCATP.

On March 31, Cedric reported sick with a sore throat and was admitted to the St. Thomas RCAF Station Hospital. By eight o'clock that night, he was having difficulty breathing. Examination showed extremely large tonsils, and he was diagnosed as suffering acute follicular tonsillitis, which was curious in view of the fact that at enlistment he had claimed to have had his tonsils removed. With a temperature of 101°F and the appearance of an abscess around his tonsils (a condition called quinsy), he was kept under observation until morning. On April 1, Cedric was breathing hard and his throat was swelling. He was transferred to the intensive care ward so more immediate action, if required, could be readily available.

By 2100 hours on April 2, Cedric was feeling miserable. He had thick mucous in his throat, his breath was foul, and he had a temperature of 102°F.

⁶ Paul Ozorak, Abandoned Military Installations of Canada, Vol I: Ontario (privately published, 1991) p.204.

At 0500 the next morning, he was having great difficulty breathing due to the accumulation of fluid around his larynx. At 0220, he was put on oxygen and administered atropine in an attempt to give him some relief. Forty-five minutes later, the attending medical staff became alarmed and called the medical officer from his home. Cedric was rushed to the operating room and a tracheotomy to clear the obstructive tissue was carried out at 0630.

At 0700 on April 3, Cameron's breathing had slowed and he was looking much better. At 1430, his lungs seemed clear but his colour was poor, and cyanosis, a bluish discolouration of his skin, was moderate. His heart action was very rapid but steady. By 1600, his heart was racing and was impossible to hear because of bubbling respiration and wheezing. At 1730, Cedric's pulse was imperceptible, his heart beat was very faint and rapid, and his breathing sounded like snores. The doctors determined that he was in the final stages of life.

A CN telegram to the family, sent on April 3, advised that Cedric had had an emergency tracheotomy performed for Ludwig's angina and that he was critically ill. Ludwig's angina is a severe inflammation of the tissue below the tongue and beneath the chin usually from a penetrating injury to the floor of the mouth.

At 1800 hours, Cedric Duncan Cameron was pronounced dead from cardiac failure with pulmonary oedema. From his septic sore throat, the toxic streptococci had spread quickly throughout his bloodstream and to his heart.

The RCAF released Cedric's body to the care of Dr. Bews in Carleton Place who was making funeral arrangements for the family. The group captain commanding the school wrote to Dr. Bews asking that he convey to "Mrs Cameron that her son was highly thought of here both by his fellow airmen and his instructors, and will be a loss to the service of which he was such a promising member." The regulations for service financial arrangements were explained. The RCAF would pay $75 for the funeral service and $25 for graveside services and transportation charges to the place of burial.

The body of Aircraftsman Second Class Cedric Cameron arrived by CPR train in Carleton Place at 9:50 a.m. on April 5, 1941, and was taken to the home of his parents. The C. A. Towers funeral home took charge of the remains and dressed him for burial in the RCAF uniform of which he was so proud. Flags on local buildings were lowered to half-mast, and he was laid to rest on Easter Weekend in the Carleton Place United Cemeteries (Pine Grove). The entire parade marched out of town and gathered at the grave with his brothers John B., Victor S., and Robert J. and his sister Alice K. Cameron[7].

The Canadian reported the funeral procession from the Cameron home to Zion Church, the largest ever seen in town at well over a mile in length. The cortege was headed by the Carleton Place Band playing Elgar's "At Rest"

[7] Lilies covered one entire wall of the family home where Cedric lay. To this day their smell causes Alice to remember that poignant Easter.

with drums muffled. Following was a detachment from the RCAF, the Carleton Place platoon of the Lanark and Renfrew Scottish, members of the Canadian Legion, and the Volunteer Civil Guard led by its bugle band under the direction of Kerry Dunphy. At the graveside, a salute was fired by the twelve-man firing squad of the Civil Guard; Horace Sedman played "Last Post" and "Reveille."

Cedric, a quiet and sincere young man who made many friends easily, was very popular and had been active in the church's Young People's Society and choir.

The Minister of National Defence, the Honourable Norman Rogers, and King George VI sent the family cards of condolence. On May 31, 1941, Cedric's mother was sent the Memorial Cross.

A tribute was written for the *Canadian* by local man of letters, Richard P. Dunphy. It was printed in the April 10, 1941 edition. An excerpt:

> Cedric Cameron had lived for all but a few brief months in Carleton Place. He was known by nearly all our citizens and well loved by all who knew him. He was possessed of talents which might well have sent him seeking for wider opportunities than those offered in a small town. He chose rather to work in affectionate companionship beside his father. He went about his work, and in his leisure hours, quietly. He had the lovely attribute of being able to strictly mind his own affairs. He was a man's man in the very finest sense of the word. He loved his home and his town.
>
> As did we all, he knew the growing seriousness of the struggle which is raging for the very existence of the peaceful, simple life such as he loved. And being a brave man, he offered the strength of his youth and his fine physique to the service of his country. Death came to him in that service, death just as glorious as if he had been flying over England, because Cedric Cameron, by his manly spirit, gave something that was fine and clean to the air force and to the fighting men with whom he came in contact. He will live in their hearts, helping them to become braver men for having known such a companion.

As the war ground on, it became evident to Cedric's mother that a support group for bereaved parents was necessary. On the 1944 Victoria Day weekend, she organized a meeting of twelve mothers at her cottage on Mississippi Lake. All had sons who had been killed, or who had died on active service, in Canada or overseas. She planned the event so that the women could become better acquainted in their common bereavement.

CHAPTER 6—IN PURSUIT OF WINGS

In December 1939, the Government of Canada announced that it would begin recruiting for the BCATP in an effort to enlist 45,000 airmen. The air forces of Britain, Canada, Australia, and New Zealand would all be sending men to train in Canada.

The joint training program was to begin at the earliest possible opportunity. By the end of the first year, it was expected to have 5,000 or more pilots, observers, and air gunners graduated to "wings standard" and proceeding to a theatre of war. Ten thousand aircrew were expected to train in the second year, and by year three, as the BCATP reached its peak, as many as 20,000 fliers would be added to the rolls of the RAF from the sixty-seven training schools in Canada. The three-year plan was to be "a remarkable effort" concluded Department of Defence authorities.

Canadian authorities and civilians were woefully ignorant of the strength and capabilities of the German Luftwaffe. In November, the *Canadian* published the following editorial:

GERMANY'S AIR FORCE MYSTERY

One of the greatest mysteries of this war of mystery has been the failure of the German air force to prove its striking power. It has failed to stop the British planes showering leaflets on German industrial centres, even on Berlin itself. It has failed to stop the allied machines from photographing the Seigfried line. Its pilots have avoided conflict with allied machines over the Western front unless assured of a large numerical superiority, and it has failed dismally to carry out its attempted raids on British soil.

Apart from subduing the hopelessly outnumbered Polish Air Force, it has, in fact, accomplished nothing.

Have we expected too much? The Nazis have boasted too hard and too often of the might of their air fleet and the picture they have painted of wave after wave of German bombers raining down fire and destruction on British and French cities is turning out to be a bogey intended to scare us.

Two months of fighting have revealed that far from possessing an air force capable of sweeping allied machines from the skies, Germany cannot hold her own. Her invincible armada is not so invincible after all.

We must not overlook the fact that the German air force is still a powerful factor. It is as dangerous to belittle it as it is foolish to overestimate its strength.

After lifting of the United States embargo the Allies now have an unlimited supply of air war craft. We shall be able, in the not too distant future to sing that old music hall song; *"There'll be a hot time in the old town tonight."*

One has to wonder if the editorial writer changed his tune at all a year later, after the British Expeditionary Force, including Canadian troops, had been ignominiously thrown out of France at Dunkirk and when the Battle of Britain was in full swing. There was no assurance then that British skies would remain under the control of the RAF.

R 54048 Sergeant James Francis Cranston

Pilot

Royal Canadian Air Force Special Reserve

After the tests at the recruiting centre, a prospective airman's next challenge was Manning Depot, the first step in the training process. James Cranston, a Bank of Nova Scotia employee in Carleton Place, breezed through the recruit screening and joined the RCAF Special Reserve on June 2, 1940. (James had been working for the bank since 1935, and, most recently had passed the practical banking course through Shaw's Correspondence School.) On June 20, he travelled by train from Ottawa to Toronto to attend No. 1 Manning Depot.

Cranston left Ottawa with high recommendations. Both Lieutenant Colonel R. Lorne Gardner of the RCAMC and Mr. C. F. Lindsay of the Bank of Nova Scotia in Ottawa wrote glowing letters of recommendation, so much so that the interviewer at the recruiting centre suggested that James was of officer calibre and recommended that he train as a pilot. The interviewer also found James, "courteous, neat, well set up and intelligent. He comes from a good family background, is frank, honest, well behaved and trustworthy. He is excellent officer material. As an alternative, he would make a good gunner."

In Toronto, James made his way to the Manning Depot in the Coliseum building on the CNE grounds. At the Orderly Room his papers were processed and a personal record was begun. He was then photographed, fingerprinted, and presented with an identification card, which, he was warned, he must have in his possession at all times. Without it he could neither leave nor re-enter the depot. Then he was given his regimental number and shown to his bed.

How overwhelming that must have been when he first saw it—a bunk amongst seemingly endless rows of double-deck bunks. Yet a system was in place such that a runner could find him within minutes. However, it is unlikely he would have been awestruck by the white sheets and pillowcases that adorned each bunk; some of the recruits from more remote parts of the country had never used such items and kept them folded under their mattresses for their entire stay at Manning Depot[8].

James' day at Manning Depot began at 0600 with physical training—mainly callisthenics—for half an hour before breakfast. At 0830 there was the first parade followed by foot drill until 1130. An hour and a quarter was allotted for lunch, then more drill until 1630. By 1800, supper was completed. Evenings were free except for those who were taking lectures to brush up on their mathematics, algebra and trigonometry, all subjects aircrew candidates would soon be using quite extensively.

The dining hall emphasized the sheer size of the Coliseum. It could seat five thousand men at a time at row upon row of long tables stretched across the hall. A skylight provided some natural light, and on one wall was painted a great albatross emblem[9]. The mechanized kitchen was capable of feeding all five thousand within one hour. In this modern war, the state-of-the-art kitchen contained huge electric food mixers, stainless steel bowls large enough to mash a bushel-and-a-half of potatoes at a time, and machines that automatically washed and peeled potatoes using a hose and whirling discs of sandpaper. World War I veterans, used to a large group of men individually peeling spuds from a never-ending mountain of potatoes, would only shake their heads in wonder at these machines.

The men of this war, at least those in the air force, ate very well. Fresh bread and cakes lined pantry shelves, and big bowls of Canadian apples usually graced the dining hall tables.

In the north corner of the Coliseum was a theatre equipped with thousands of seats in front of the stage with curtains emblazoned with the letters RCAF. An electric organ provided music and the men could watch the latest movies several times a week.

Over in the horse show arena, there was enough room for games of soccer, volleyball, and badminton—all at the same time. Tanbark—crushed tree bark used in the riding rings—had been left on the floor, but when an epidemic of

[8] Most of the information regarding the British Commonwealth Air Training Plan flying schools came from a series of articles printed in the 1940/41 editions of The Canadian. Mr. Hugh Templin wrote them for the Ontario weekly newspapers.

[9] Often mistaken for an eagle, the bird representing the Air Force and used on its emblems, badges and buttons is, in fact, an albatross.

colds broke out, the medical officer soon replaced it with asphalt and the colds ceased. The RCAF firmly believed in *mens sana in corpore sano*[10].

James' personal favourite sports had been rugby, golf, swimming, and skiing. At the Manning Depot he would get his fill of team sports.

During the first week of training, there were never ending lectures on general service procedures and language. Learning air force acronyms was especially tedious.

The first drills included identifying the right foot and how to make a smart salute. Drill 'till you drop was the drill instructors' credo, then pass the recruit on for some intense physical training.

Men slated to be ground crew stayed three or four weeks before moving on to trade schools. In turn, future pilots and gunners were sent to various schools for guard duty while they awaited openings at the Initial Training School (ITS).

James' turn at ITS came rather quickly. On June 30, he was sent to Regina to join Course No. 4 at No. 2 ITS and be initiated into the intricacies of flying an airplane. When he enlisted, James had stated that he had flown for a half-hour as a passenger, but this would be his first experience in a cockpit. His evaluation at the end of this training concluded that he was "excellent material-potential officer."

Undoubtedly, James was now starting to look like an airman. He had learned the secret of keeping one's boots and buttons shiny and keeping a razor sharp crease in one's tunic and trousers. His tie would be knotted to perfection and the wedge cap would have found a jaunty angle on his head where it would stay. A good looking man of twenty-five years, standing 5' 10 ½" tall and weighing a trim 165 pounds, with a dark complexion, dark brown hair and brown flashing eyes, he could turn many a head when striding confidently down a street.

James was born in Arnprior on January 21, 1915, the youngest of five sons of Dr. James Goldie Cranston and his wife Mary Frances Toller. James and his four brothers all attended Arnprior schools and the Church of England. James had participated in the high school cadet signal corps and left school just one subject short of attaining his senior matriculation. His father, a prominent physician in Arnprior, died of a blood clot at age sixty-three, so when James joined the RCAF, he listed his brother Monty (Montague), then living in Noranda, Quebec, as his next of kin. He later changed his records to make his mother next of kin.

At his enlistment medical examination, James was found to be in excellent health; his hearing, vision, and teeth were all good. Although his nose had a deviated septum to the left with about a fifty per cent blockage of the

[10] A clean mind in a clean body.

airway—a concern for aircrew breathing through an oxygen mask—he was declared fit for service and given the air force medical category of A1B A3B (fit for full flying and full ground duties anywhere and under any conditions). Identifying features recorded were a birthmark on his left thigh, a scar on the tip of his left fifth finger, and a scar on his left shin. He told the examiner that he liked hunting and fishing, working in the home and machine shop, and model building. He claimed canoeing as a hobby, and admitted to drinking the occasional beer and to smoking three or four cigarettes a day.

Following ITS, James was sent to London, Ontario, to attend Course No. 5 at No. 3 Elementary Flying Training School (EFTS). He left Regina on August 30 and, after leave and travel time, reported to London to begin the course on October 21. In the meantime, he became eligible for flying pay, and on September 23, he was reclassified to the rank of leading aircraftsman.

For two-and-a-half weeks he was subjected to intense flying training on the Finch II aircraft, at the end of which he had logged thirty-three hours and fifty minutes dual (flying with an instructor) and thirty-two hours and fifteen minutes flying solo. On landing after his first solo flight, his fellow students would, in the grandest tradition, douse him with a pail of water and cut off the bottom part of his tie. He left No. 3 EFTS with the evaluation that he was "slightly above average but this is mostly due to self confidence. Has showed good progress . . . posted to Camp Borden."

With six square miles of flat, sandy land, Camp Borden was Canada's largest flying training school. In fact, everything at Borden was large. The landing strips alone were 3,300 feet long and 600 feet wide—larger than most commercial airfields and paved to boot. Auxiliary fields were maintained at Edenville and Alliston.

Students arrived at Camp Borden with the ability to fly an aircraft at about 100 mph. Here, however, they would fly the sleek, yellow, and noisy, single-engine Harvard at more than 200 mph. A control tower was necessary to sort out the swarms of aircraft rising from the ground.

The Camp Borden tower was three storeys high with roofs and walls covered by asphalt shingles. Above the roof spun an anemometer, giving the controllers an instant and continuous reading of wind speed and direction, necessary information for a pilot desiring to take off or land. The entire top floor was all glass inside, which housed a crew of three or four controllers, surrounded by instruments, radios, and signalling equipment. The powerful, narrow beam of an aldis lamp signalled the pilots permission to land or take off; it could also be used to send Morse code signals. The control tower also

managed, by an elaborate switchboard, all lighting on the airfield, including runways, taxi strips, hangars, and radio towers.

Verey pistols were also used for signalling. They fired coloured flares, like Roman candles: green for "go," red for "stop," and a white flare recalled all flying aircraft to the field. A system of flags, balls, and cans indicated weather conditions and the runway in use.

The last ten weeks of a pilot's training were spent at a Service Flying Training School (SFTS). Flying took the majority of their time, but the student pilots still attended lectures on subjects such as flight theory and armaments and RCAF regulations, history, and customs.

At Camp Borden, James joined No. 1 Squadron at No. 1 SFTS, the largest and finest air school in North America. He trained here from November 4, 1940, to January 25, 1941, learning to fly Yales and Harvards. His total flying time by the end of the course was thirty-five hours ten minutes dual time and thirty-seven hours thirty-five minutes solo. This included his first night flying of three hours twenty minutes solo and two hours five minutes dual. In his logbook, he had recorded a total of sixty-six hours five minutes on the Fleet Finch II, sixty-seven hours ten minutes on the Yale, and three hours twenty minutes on the Harvard.

The absolute highlight of any aviator's career was his Wings Parade. On that night, all graduates were paraded before those family and friends invited to witness the presentation of air force wings to the fortunate few. Each graduate was called forward, saluted the presenting officer and then had his pilot's badge pinned to his left chest. The Canadian pilot's wing was a pair of wings with the letters RCAF in the central globe, surmounted by a crown. James was awarded his pilot's badge on January 30, 1941. The wings told the world that he was a pilot and that he would soon be flying missions from some airbase in England.

That same day, James was also appointed to the rank of sergeant and assigned to Overseas Pool No. 1 to await sea transport to the U.K. He embarked from Canada on February 21 and landed in England on March 6, headed to his first posting at No. 9 Bombing and Gunnery (B&G) School, in Penhros, Caernarvonshire, Wales, where he would be attached to the RAF flying Fairey Battle aircraft. After a thorough checkout on the new machine, James was put to work towing target drogues for gunnery firing exercises.

The Fairey Battle was a docile and rugged aircraft, but had been a notable failure at operational roles. It had been designed as a light-day bomber in 1932 and, although seventeen RAF squadrons were equipped with the Battle in 1939, its obsolescence was quickly apparent in 1940, when it was pressed into action. It was

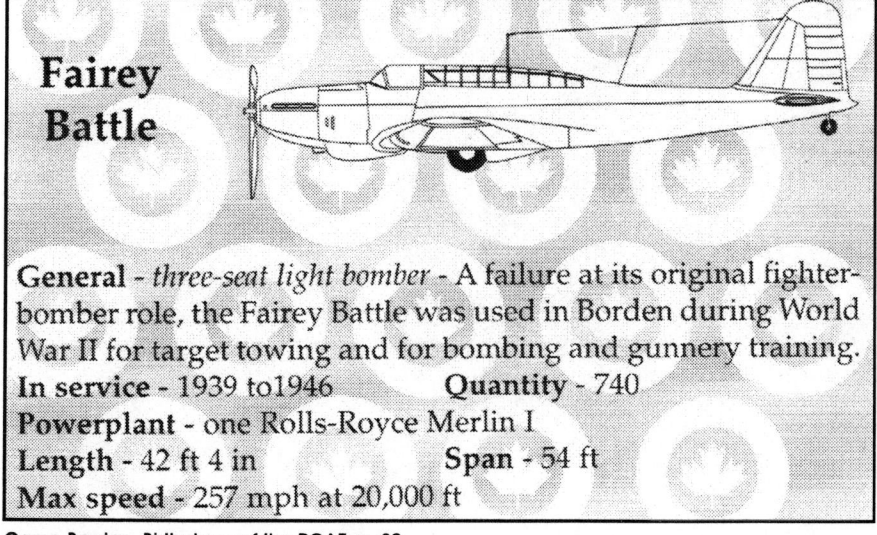

Fairey Battle

General - *three-seat light bomber* - A failure at its original fighter-bomber role, the Fairey Battle was used in Borden during World War II for target towing and for bombing and gunnery training.
In service - 1939 to 1946   **Quantity** - 740
Powerplant - one Rolls-Royce Merlin I
Length - 42 ft 4 in   **Span** - 54 ft
Max speed - 257 mph at 20,000 ft

Camp Borden, Birthplace of the RCAF, p. 80.

then used as a night bomber against the Channel ports and then as a trainer, for the BCATP in Canada, Australia, and England.

Sergeant James Cranston was piloting aircraft L 5004 towing a target during the afternoon of May 31, 1941. (Pilots would take turns flying the tow plane for another aircraft to practise firing at the target.) On board were tow cable operators Leading Aircraftsman F. Froggart and Leading Aircraftsman O. Cumins. Suddenly, just off Gimlet Rock, two miles south of Pwllheli, the aircraft suddenly went into a spin then hurtled into the ocean. Boats raced to the rescue, but all three occupants had been killed on impact. James had been overseas one hundred days.

James had left specific instructions that his older brother was to be notified of any accidents prior to his mother. Besides Monty, who was also now in uniform, James' brothers were Captain Fred Cranston, serving with the Royal Canadian Ordnance Corps (RCOC); Philip, on the engineering staff of Bell Telephone; and Hugh T. living in Arnprior. The first message received by the family stated that James was "missing, believed killed."

Sergeant Cranston was buried by his mates, with full military honours, in the Pwllheliborough cemetery adjoining the Delio churchyard. His mother was sent James' last pay, which amounted to $114.70 (thirty-one days at $3.70 per day); additional pay from the RAF of $30.40; the balance in James' savings account at the British Post Office of $90.61; and £2 15s 5p ($12.39) cash found in his effects. As well, she was sent his War Service Gratuity of $82.50 representing his total of 346 days service, $21.00 for his 100 days overseas, and a $17.40 supplement for overseas service. The Minister of Defence sent a card of condolence and Buckingham Palace sent a Royal Message. Mrs. Cranston received a Memorial Cross on October 10, 1941.

The Memorial Cross is also known as the Silver Cross presented to mothers and/or wives of servicepersons killed on duty.

Chapter 7—Love Stories

When men go off to war they never consider their own mortality. Never theirs is the fate of no return. Mothers, fathers, and siblings put on brave faces when their soldiers depart for foreign fields. As young men, they are caught up in the romance of combat, filled with raging hormones, and more often than not, are inspired by patriotic fervour. Often they leave behind lovers and wives. When they fail to return, left behind are young women with a lost future. Some even had a young child, which only added to their grief and difficulties in making a new life.

FRIENDLY FIRE

R 54197 Sergeant James Snedden Warren
Air Observer
Royal Canadian Air Force

Until he joined the RCAF, Jimmy Warren had centred his entire life on Carleton Place. Even when he was teaching in outlying areas he came home at every opportunity.

James Snedden Warren was born in Carleton Place on May 25, 1913, to William James Warren and Isobel Snedden. He had one sister, Isobel, and two living brothers, Jack and William. Another brother, David, had drowned in the Mississippi River at age eight.

Jim attended Memorial Park United Church and received his education from local public and high schools. At church, he was actively involved with the Trail Rangers and the Tuxes Boys. Jim was well known throughout the Ottawa Valley for his participation in sports, including football, rugby, baseball, and hockey. He was an excellent badminton player, served as the president of the local club and continued playing after leaving school. In April 1939, only one month before joining the forces, he and G. E. Findlay won a district doubles badminton tournament by defeating the Almonte team.

He suffered through the normal childhood diseases (measles, chicken pox) and when he was twelve years old, caught scarlet fever. Then at age fifteen, he spent about a week in bed with pneumonia. In 1929, when Jim was sixteen, his father, a commercial traveller[11], died of pneumonia at age forty-five. Isobel now struggled to make ends meet as a single parent with four children to raise.

After high school Jim wanted to study forestry. This would have meant an expensive couple of years away at school, which his mother could not afford[12]. So, being at loose ends, and to help ease the family's financial bur-

[11] A travelling salesman .
[12] Much of the family information came during an interview with Jim's sister, Isobel Robertson on April 3, 2001.

den, Jim joined the militia and spent his summer at the militia camp. Jim, an easy-going fellow, soon befriended another soldier named "Whips" MacLaughlan. After camp closed, Jim went with "Whips" to his cottage. "Whips" spent his winters teaching school and inspired Jim to become a teacher, too. Not wanting him to rush into anything, his mother told him to think about it for a week or two and if he still thought that was what he wanted to do, they would send for the application papers.

He eventually applied to and was accepted by the Ontario Provincial Normal School in Ottawa. On April 21, 1932, he received a certificate of qualification as an instructor in elementary manual training with a grade B qualification in physical training. On July 15, Jim graduated with his Interim First Class Certificate and his Elementary Physical Culture Diploma. He then took and passed an extra course in History 3 from Queen's University.

James' first teaching job was at the Middleville Public School, near Lanark, from 1933 to 1935. Because he had his First Class certificate, he was paid $500 a year. Jim came home every weekend; during the winter months, he made the twelve-mile trip across the fields on cross-country skis leaving Friday evening and returning early Monday morning. Once he arrived at the two-room school, he would have to start the fire in the stove, and when it was going well, he would ski on to his boarding house to dress in a suit, vest, and tie in time to return to teach his classes.

In 1935, he transferred to the James Settlement Public School to be closer to Carleton Place, and that same summer, he re-joined the Lanark and Renfrew Scottish (42nd Regiment). At the time, he stood 5' 10½" tall and weighed 168 pounds. He attended summer camps again in 1936, then, in 1937, he was offered a position at a higher salary with School Section No. 3 Howland District, at the Little Current School on

Manitoulin Island. He only stayed the year before returning to Carleton Place to teach at Prince of Wales in 1938.

Jim's sister Isobel recalled that Jim loved teaching and loved working with the town's young people and, until the Air Force called, would have been content to devote his life to teaching.

When he returned to Carleton Place, Jim also renewed his militia connections. With the coming war, he spent his summers on duty, and 1939 found him employed as a guard at the St. Hubert airport in Montreal. He returned to his classes that fall, but his sense of loyalty and duty beckoned and, as soon as the school year finished the following spring, he applied to the RCAF as a pilot.

In 1939, the local board of education decided that it would hold a teaching position and make superannuation payments for any teacher who volunteered for active service. It made this guarantee to Jim in August when he joined up.[13]

Jim thought that his application was taking an inordinately long time to process. He felt that if he re-applied as an observer he would be accepted sooner. At the recruiting centre his interviewer wrote:

> Suitable for pilot or observer. Well-built athletic type of very good appearance, quiet manner and personality, not assertive but appears to be dependable. Good officer type with above average intelligence and useful NPAM[14] training. Holds first aid and PT (Normal) certificates, with seven years public school teaching experience. Keen and anxious for early call.

Possibly Canada's most important contribution to victory in World War II was the training of more than 131,000 aircrew through the BCATP. From the ground up, Canada built, equipped, and staffed schools for pilots, air observers, navigators, wireless operators, air gunners, and bomb-aimers. The schools reflected the various stages of an airman's progress and the specializations for particular trades. Flying instructors, civilian and RCAF, were soon busy in ITS's, EFTS's, SFTS's, Flying Instructor Schools (FIS), General Reconnaissance Schools, Air Observers Schools (AOS), Air Navigation Schools (ANS), Wireless Schools, B&G Schools, Naval Air Gunners Schools, Flight Engineers Schools, Operational Training Units (OTU), and an Instrument Flying School.[15]

---

[13] Miss Leita Anderson was appointed to fill the vacancy. She would later stay on to become the principal of the school.

[14] Non Permanent Active Militia

[15] Rachel Lea Heide, "The Politics of British Commonwealth Air Training Plan Base Selection in Western Canada," (Ottawa: an unpublished Master's thesis submitted to Carleton University, 2000)

On July 19, 1940, James Warren boarded the CNR train from Ottawa bound for Toronto. He had enlisted as an "aircrewman (Standard)." Following his basic training at the Manning Depot, he was sent for the month of August to the Equipment Depot in Montreal, and in September to a training school in Regina, to fulfill guard duties while he waited for an opening at Observer School.

Unless a pilot is flying a single-seat fighter, he is accompanied by other aircrew trades. In fact, in bomber aircraft, the pilot is not necessarily the most important member of the crew. Although the pilot is often the crew commander in the air (regardless of rank), there are other aircrew on board without whom the mission could not be successfully completed. One of these is the observer.

The name observer is somewhat of a misnomer held over from World War I when there were only two men in an aircraft, the pilot and the observer; the former to fly the plane, the latter to do everything else. A more accurate term would be navigator.

Jim started his training as an observer at No. 1 AOS at Malton airport[16] airport near Toronto. The school was formed under the auspices of Messrs. W. W. Woolett and C. R. Troup, bush pilots and owners of Dominion Skyways Limited, which flew in Canada's north. Both men were veteran pilots of the Great War.

These older pilots were invaluable in bringing the BCATP up to speed, and the RCAF used the knowledge and expertise offered by companies such as Dominion Skyways to great effect. The company's pilots and repairmen maintained the aircraft, buildings and airfield and provided flying instruction. The RCAF had sole jurisdiction over ground training and discipline.

An AOS course lasted twelve weeks and every month graduated one course and welcomed another. There were always three courses in residence. Although the educational requirements for an observer were higher than for pilots, often pilots who "washed out" were sent to an AOS. Understandably, they were at first quite disappointed, but it did not take long for them to change their minds and be pleased with their new prospects.

The observer had to master several tasks to the point that he could execute them perfectly; there was no room for error. He had to learn how to lay out an exact course, taking into consideration the effect of wind and weather. He had to master the optics of a tricky bombsight so that the bombs dropped on the target. He also had to know how to operate the airplane's machine guns. And finally, he had to get the aircraft back to base and, just as importantly, especially in bad weather, know when they had arrived.

[16] This airport would become Pearson International.

Jim trained at Malton from October 12, 1940, to January 1941. On arrival he received the rank of leading aircraftsman, which increased his pay to $1.50 per day, plus 75¢ a day flying pay. He was taught to chart a course and to communicate to the pilot where the aircraft, an Avro Anson was to go. The pilot would follow his instructions to the letter, unless, of course, the airplane became endangered. At the end of the trip, the pilot submitted a detailed report, including whether the student navigator became airsick and whether he was capable of carrying out his duties in spite of becoming ill.

When the students reported to the briefing room each morning, they would find a large map of Ontario laid out on a table. Coloured pins were scattered across the map, some connected with lengths of black thread marking out routes the fledgling navigators were to fly that day. The routes could be triangular, rectangular, or have no discernible shape at all. The student had to learn to navigate the course accurately, and before take-off, be able to tell, to the minute, when their aircraft would arrive back at base. The total length of the trip could be several hundred miles and take several hours to complete. When he became reasonably proficient at this task during daylight hours, the student would be assigned similar exercises at night.

Everywhere there was evidence of wartime economies. Oil was filtered and reclaimed. Spare parts were manufactured in small workshops. Each of the Anson's two Armstrong-Siddley engines was overhauled at a predetermined interval. At top speed they could pull the aircraft to 200 miles an hour.

All the amenities of a small community were on base, including an ambulance and a twenty-five-bed hospital, with two beds always kept warm with hot water bottles in the event of a crash. Officers, civilians, and lower ranks had separate eating halls, but the food came from a large central kitchen. In the men's mess was hung a full-sized propeller backed by a large square piece of blue carpet, which had been used in Westminster Abbey during George VI's coronation. On the hub of the propeller was a silver model of an Anson and on each blade was a silver replica of the observer's wing. Each wing carried the name of the highest-ranking graduate of a class.

On a typical flight, Jim would plan his exercise in the map room, load all his equipment into a large leather case and then strap on his parachute harness. (The parachute was on his seat in the aircraft.) Sitting behind the pilot, Jim would automatically connect his seat belt across his lap.

Once in the air, Jim would lay out his instruments on the navigator's table in front of him. He had a chart, bearing no landmarks except the outline of the Great Lakes, and various hieroglyphics, understandable only to a navigator: circles with arrows pointing out compass variations, lines forming squares marking latitude and longitude, a scale for measuring nautical miles, and numbers representing heights of land beneath him. Not much help to anyone familiar only with road maps! His personal tools were a triangular ruler, a circular slide rule, and a few pencils.

In front of him were mounted a compass and two dials, one showing airspeed and the other indicating his altitude above sea level. The drift indicator, showing how far the aircraft was being blown off course by the wind, was located in the nose of the plane. To get to it, Jim had to crawl through a hole beside the pilot and lie flat on his stomach to adjust and read the instrument.

The Anson's main cabin had splendid visibility through many Plexiglas windows. But over Ontario on a summer day, the air was hazy and the ground visibility was probably not much more than ten miles. It was important for the navigator to be able to identify geographical landmarks to accurately "fix" his position. However, once above 5,000 feet, the plane would probably be in the lower layer of cloud and the navigator would then have to rely on his calculations to determine his position. Often navigation was reduced to "dead reckoning," (DR) timed runs on a specific course.

After successfully completing this twelve-week course, Jim was posted to No. 1 B&G School in Jarvis, Ontario, where he joined Course No. 9 on January 6, 1941. Here, the curriculum focussed on mathematics, comparable to a university engineering course, except compressed into six weeks.

Bomb-aimer students[17] had to learn the theory of bombing using trajectory angles and how to use a vector attachment for the bombsight when aiming at moving targets. There were several types of bombs, each for a different purpose. Some exploded on impact; others went through the roof of a building or a ship and exploded inside. There were armour-piercing bombs and bombs that had adjustable detonators for various purposes. Bombs were released electrically from either the under-wing mounts or from the fuselage bomb-bay of larger aircraft.

The bombsight was a most ingenious device, covered with knobs, dials, and scales. All had to be adjusted to ensure that the bomb landed on target. The sight had to be set for high- or low-level bombing, wind drift, height of the plane above ground, aircraft speed, wind velocity and direction, and even for the temperature. Through an eyepiece, the bomber watched his target apparently move down between two pairs of wires and coloured beads spaced at intervals to indicate distance ahead. When the desired target

[17] Navigators usually carried out the duties of bomb- aimers, especially early in the war before bomb aiming became a specialty itself.

appeared between two tiny pointers, the bomb-aimer pulled a lever and the bombs were released. Depending upon altitude, it probably took twenty seconds for the bomb to hit and another ten seconds for it to explode.

Jim spent hours in the "bombing teacher," a gallery three storeys up in a specially constructed building. He adjusted the sight according to a given set of conditions and then would lie on his stomach to peer through the eyepiece. Above him, intricate projectors, adjusted for altitude, speed and wind, projected a landscape on the ground below. The bomb-aimer would see towns, cities, farms, and factories going past, then pick his target, watch it come down the wires, and pull the trigger. The scenery below stopped and a small white light came on twenty seconds later to show where the bombs had landed.

Actual bombing was done with practice bombs fitted to the wings of a Fairey Battle airplane. They would climb to at least 5,000 feet over Lake Erie and try to hit a red-painted raft. The practice bomb would emit a puff of white smoke when it hit the water. The student then marked his chart where he thought the bombs had hit, while on shore, observers used simple trigonometry to plot the hits. The best target hung in a conference room under a sign: "Beat this and yours will hang here instead." The best bomb-aimer would also lead his class as they received their coveted wings during the graduation parade.

During training, students wore a wedge cap tilted to one side of their heads. Tucked into the front "pocket" of this cap was a starched, spotlessly white insert, which marked the trainee as aircrew. New recruits wearing the white flash would wonder why the local girls avoided them, until they learned that the boys in ground crew had spread the rumour that the white flash marked those diagnosed with a venereal disease.

Jim ended his bombing course with twenty-two hours and fifteen minutes flying time on the Fairey Battle. That included fifteen hours and thirty minutes devoted to bombing, and five hours and five minutes to gunnery. His instructors assessed Jim as an "aggressive average student. Neat and energetic. Will be a good NCO."

On February 15, 1941, Jim Warren had his Wings Parade as an air bomber. As well as sporting the Air Observers Badge prominently on his chest, he wore on both sleeves the three chevrons of a sergeant. His pay jumped to $2.70 a day and $1 a day extra for flying. Flying pay was colloquially known as "risk allowance."

Jim was now sent to No. 1 ANS in Rivers, Manitoba, for advanced navigator training in eleven flights on Ansons. The school had moved from Trenton in November 1940, so Jim was in one of the first courses at Rivers.

Jim in winter flying suit standing before an Avro Anson.

But before going, he had some personal business to attend to.

When he was sixteen, Jim met and fell in love with Ordelia Giles West. She was from Almonte but attended high school in Carleton Place. They were inseparable until Jim left for the air force. While he was away, Orrie went to work as a stenographer for the Principal Protestant Chaplain of the Armed Forces in Ottawa.

As soon as Jim arrived in Rivers, on February 16, 1941, he made application to his commanding officer for permission to get married. No one, especially those in the aircrew trades, could marry without air force permission. The school commandant granted Jim permission to marry, but only after he had proven that he was debt-free. Plus, the RCAF had to be assured that the prospective bride was "suitable." Honorary Captain, the Reverend J. Logan-Venta, Orrie's boss in the Chaplain Service, wrote on March 8 that:

> She comes of good, honest, industrious parents, and she is of high moral character, and I feel certain she is well acquainted with the increased responsibility that may be placed on her after marriage.

Jim completed his training in Rivers, racking up ninety-one hours and forty minutes on the Anson. However, en route to report to the Embarkation Pool in Debert, Nova Scotia, for shipment overseas, Jim was given a few days' leave at home. On March 18, he married Orrie at 33 Butternut Terrace in Ottawa, the home of her sister, Edith, who was married to an army doctor. Orrie had moved there when she began working in Ottawa. Her father, Wesley West, gave the bride away. Orrie's mother had died some years earlier. She wore a blue crepe dress and matching hat and a corsage bouquet of Johanna Hill roses. Five-foot-eight-inch Jim, whose sister remembers him as a "pretty good looking guy," looked very smart in uniform. His brown hair was slicked into place and his sparkling blue eyes saw only the lovely Orrie. For a honeymoon, the couple travelled to the East Coast to await his sailing to England.

The last week of March, Jim and Orrie came back to Carleton Place for his embarkation leave. His sister, Isobel, remembers the evening he left for overseas:

> We lived in the big house on the corner of George and Edmund, kitty-corner from the present museum. Mother was sick in bed and after Jim bade her farewell, I walked with him to the train station. We walked down George Street and when we got to the corner at Bridge Street, we saw Earl Rathwell sitting on a veranda.
>
> Earl came over to shake Jim's hand and asked me, "Isobel, could I walk over with you?" We walked to the station and that is the last time I saw Jim. Earl walked home with me and by the time I got to the house I started to get teary because now I had to see mother and Jim was gone. Earl walked me around and around the block until I finally dragged up enough courage to go in the house.

Both Earl and Isobel worked at the local branch of the Royal Bank. Later, Earl also went into the air force and he, too, never came home.

On April 19, 1941, Jim disembarked in England. He was sent to the RAF OTU in Chivenor, Devonshire, to hone his skills on the Bristol Beaufort.

Bristol Beaufort Mk I N1030 aircraft "N" at Pat Bay, B.C., on June 18, 1943. (Photo – RCAF Squadrons and Aircraft, p.66)

It was a fairly new aircraft, entering production in 1939, and was intended as a torpedo bomber and for general reconnaissance. Its twin engines gave it a speed of 225 mph at 5,000 feet, although it could climb as high as 16,500 feet. It carried two .303 Vickers machine-guns in the dorsal turret and one in the port wing and could carry a bomb load of 1,000 pounds in the bomb bay and one 500-pound bomb under the wing or a 1,605-pound torpedo. The first aircraft went to Coastal Command.

After dinner on June 17, Jim and his crew went flying on a coastal patrol in Beaufort No. L 9809. Suddenly, although they were still over the coast of England, they found themselves in an operational flying battle. It was later learned that a Polish pilot, flying with the RAF and unfamiliar with the fairly new Beaufort, mistakenly identified it as enemy and attacked with all guns blazing. According to a witness, Jim's aircraft went into a nosedive, then levelled out at treetop height, but a wing caught a wire and it crashed and burned. The tail-gunner survived and reported that the pilot was immediately shot and that Jim had taken the controls to try to get it down on the ground safely. Killed instantly, by "friendly fire," were the pilot and the mid-upper-gunner. The navigator, Jim Warren, survived the crash, but died of multiple injuries in the station hospital at Chivenor. The aircraft crashed at 2100 near Exeter in Devonshire. Jim had been in England two months.

A devastated Orrie received the following telegram:

> Regret to inform you that your husband, Sergeant Warren, killed in flying accident 17 June. Aircraft, of which he was an observer, crashed at Woodend Farm, Shoute, Devonshire. Funeral expected to take place June 20.

Orrie returned to Almonte. She never re-married. She did, however, join the RCAF Women's Division and volunteered for overseas duty so she could visit Jim's grave. His brother Bill also went to find the grave in England. He met the owner of the farm who showed him the exact site of the crash. The farmer had witnessed the accident and provided Bill with the details. He said that the tail-gunner got out, ran around the field, and collapsed. Jim and his comrades were buried on June 21, 1941.

Because he and his crew were killed by friendly fire during a training exercise, the RAF held a court of enquiry, but its results were never published. Orrie received his War Service Gratuity of $82.50 for 334 days' service, $17.50 at 25¢ a day for his 70 days overseas service and a supplement of $16.16 for overseas service including a dependant's allowance of $35 a month. A message from the Minister of Defence and the King arrived in due course, and both Orrie and Jim's mother, Isobel, received the Memorial Cross.

Following the war, Orrie went with her sister Edith and her husband, Lieutenant Colonel G. L. Morgan-Smith to Australia where the doctor attended the Australian army's staff college. When she returned in 1951, she settled in Toronto where she died

The first (temporary) grave marker.

of cancer in Sunnybrook Hospital on March 28, 1989. Jim's sister, Isobel Robertson, mourned Orrie as the sister she never had.

Isobel became philosophical about her brother's early death. "He had a lot of fun in life. Jim lived a lot in his twenty-eight years. He had a good time no matter where he went."

Sergeant James Snedden Warren, Air Observer, RCAF, is buried in Exeter Higher Cemetery, Devon, U.K. The cemetery belongs to the corporation of Heavitree and contains 400 military bodies, mostly from local hospitals, in its two war plots.

On Wednesday, September 17, 1941, Miss Hilda Cram's class held a remembrance service in Memorial Park in Carleton Place. They gathered after 4:00 p.m. and conducted a short but impressive service in memory of the late James Warren. All of the pupils placed flowers at the base of the cenotaph's single shaft. Prayers were said and the oath of remembrance prayer was recited. Leonard Baird sounded "Last Post" and "Reveille." on the trumpet. This class was the students taught by Jimmy Warren before his enlistment for overseas service.

War separated Jim and Orrie by distance and time, but with a love like theirs, neither war nor death kept them apart. When Orrie died in Toronto, her body was cremated, and a family friend carried a small vial of her ashes to England. On a beautiful, quiet, sunny afternoon, Orrie's ashes were scattered on Jim's grave. Together forever.

R 54312 Sergeant Maurice Fieldhouse
Pilot
Royal Canadian Air Force

Maurice Fieldhouse was born in Farsley, Leeds, England, on July 11, 1915, to Mr. and Mrs. James Fieldhouse. He did his elementary schooling there, graduating with a senior matriculation from Pudsey Grammar School. He went on to study textile design, winning ten scholarships for further academic study. In the U.K., he worked from 1931 to 1935 at Leigh Mills Co. Ltd. as a clerk in the weaving office, then he took a position as an assistant designer and manager with O. A. Jewett & Co. where he stayed a year before emigrating to Canada.

He worked in Montreal, where he learned to speak acceptable French. He was a designer with the Victoria W & H Mills for a year, then spent 1937–38 as an assistant designer with Slingsy Manufacturing Company. In 1938, Maurice accepted the position of designer and superintendent with Bates & Innes Ltd., and moved to Carleton Place.

Fieldhouse quickly became active in his new community. He was a regular attendee at the United Church, sang in the choir, took charge of the church's boys' work, and became a member of Stella Lodge, No. 125, of the Imperial Order of Odd Fellows. He was very athletic and did not smoke or drink alcohol. He stood 5' 7¾" tall and weighed 153 pounds, but was very well developed, especially in the chest area, due to his great fondness for weightlifting. He was well known for this hobby and taught it to the boys of the church. In 1940 he won the weightlifting middleweight championship for the province of Quebec.

Maurice met the girl of his dreams in Carleton Place—Audrey Morphy (known to her friends as "Babe"), daughter of Mr. and Mrs. Charles Morphy. Babe was working as a telephone operator for Bell Telephone, when the two were introduced at a house party given by one of Maurice's colleagues from Bates and Innes, a Mr. Ritchie. Babe shared Maurice's enthusiasm for sports, especially badminton at which she was quite proficient. The two also spent many quiet hours drifting in Babe's father's boat to the family cottage on Dinky Dooley Island in Mississippi Lake.

He was twenty-four and Babe twenty-two when he asked her to marry him. There was no hesitation in her reply, and he presented her with a diamond solitaire ring set in gold with two smaller diamonds on each side[18].

[18] Audrey provided much of the personal information in an interview with the author on November 6, 2001.

They would have been married before Maurice went overseas but, when he left England, Maurice had promised his mother he would not marry without returning home to consult her.[19]

When Maurice went to apply to the RCAF, he carried the following letter of recommendation from Mr. William King, the managing editor of the *Canadian Textile Journal*:

> May 17, 1940
>
> ... he is a man of good character, although in various positions in textile mills he has perhaps been a little over ambitious and dogmatic.
>
> There is no doubt that in textiles at least, particularly in wool goods manufacturing, he has outstanding ability and his drawback in Canada has been the quality mentioned above.
>
> It may be that the aggressive qualities he has shown in industry can be used to greater advantage in the RCAF where discipline and routine should direct him into the proper channels.

Maurice enlisted on August 14, 1940. The interviewer at the recruiting office found him intelligent, thoughtful, deliberate, and determined. He wrote, "This is a very determined ambitious man who aught [*sic*] to go a long way as an Airman Pilot. He is officer material, a 'British Bulldog Yorkshireman' and is recommended to be enlisted in the rank of Provisional Pilot Officer."

Maurice did, however, admit to having a debt: "Yes, I am buying a car from Industrial Finance Corp owing $97 paying $11 per month. I can pay this off immediately if advisable since I have a credit note balance." When he left, he parked this car in Audrey Morphy's backyard. Babe did not have a driver's licence, nor did she know how to drive an automobile, but she had watched her father start and drive his inboard motor launch many times and was not about to let a minor thing like experience keep her from using Maurice's car. She got it going, and by trial and error, undoubtedly accompanied by a great noise of clashing gears, got the relationship of clutch and transmission sorted out. Thereafter, Babe could often be seen taking a spin around town.

This 1941 photo was taken the last day that Babe saw Maurice. (Photos from Audrey Morphy-Kennedy)

[19] Maurice had a married sister who, when she gave birth to her first child, a daughter, named her Audrey.

The enrolment medical examiner found a man, albeit small, in good physical shape (Babe Morphy described him as "well built—all muscle."). He had scars on his left shin and on the outside of his left thigh, and reported that his only illness had been measles when he was a child. He was described as being of medium complexion with dark brown hair and hazel eyes. Maurice Fieldhouse, with an A1B medical category, was declared fit for flying duties anywhere, but he had made it quite clear to the recruiter that he was "particularly desirous of learning to fly and to qualify for and obtain a commission in the Permanent Air Force and possible subsequent promotion."

Maurice was immediately given the rank of aircraftsman second class and was selected to train as a pilot. With the great influx of volunteers, courses at the Manning Depot in Toronto were full so Maurice was posted to Brandon, Manitoba, to attend No. 2 Manning Depot. After ten days leave, he left town, sharing the train with many other young men heading west to participate in the grain harvest.

Following basic training, he had to wait a month to get course-loaded for flying training, which he spent doing guard duty at Prince Rupert, British Columbia.

On October 22, 1940, Maurice reported to No. 2 ITS in Regina for early testing. It was easy to understand why the air force wanted matriculation from high school or better for entry into aircrew. At an ITS, the students had a stiff course load of higher mathematics, armament, signals, and navigation.

A routine day at ITS began at 0600 with the ringing of the fire alarm. Morning parade was at 0715, and in the meantime, the cadets had to wash, shave, fold their sheets and blankets, neatly placing them at the foot of their cots in a prescribed air force way with no deviation allowed, polish their boots and hat and tunic buttons, clean and dust the room so that no inspecting officer wearing white gloves would find a trace of dust above the door ledge, hustle to the mess hall to stand in line for breakfast, return to pick up their books, and march to the parade square for inspection. Inspecting officers were merciless in looking for the slightest uniform or personal hygiene defect.

Morning classes lasted from 0800 to 1230. One half hour was allotted for lunch after which lectures resumed until 1700. In case they found themselves at loose ends during the evening, they were given about three hours homework to complete for the next day when it would all start again. But morale was high. If they cleared this course they were off to flying training.

All aircrew were easily identifiable now by the white flash they wore in their wedge caps. Regardless of rank (most were LACs) they were known as "flight cadets." ITS was six weeks long and designed primarily to determine the aptitude of the cadets and whether or not they could become pilots or navigators. Students who had difficulty with the academics were offered the opportunity to remain aircrew as wireless operators or gunners.

The flight cadets studied navigation (their most difficult course), the theory of flight, airmanship, engines and aerodynamics, and LDAO (law, discipline, administration, and organization of the RCAF). They practised Morse code on buzzers and with Aldis lamps, studied armament and war gasses, and took a rudimentary course in meteorology. Every day they had PT and drill on the parade square. Usually they were dismissed Saturday at noon and had the rest of the weekend to themselves.

They were also tested mentally and physically to determine if they could take the pressure of flying and fighting five miles above the earth. A second medical examination, lasting four hours, tested colour vision, depth of vision, and such abilities as being able to stand on one leg with eyes shut. This would undoubtedly prove invaluable if they were ever subjected to a sobriety test by the local constabulary.

Each man was also wired up like some kind of robot and put through an electroencephalogram (EEG) test. Wires were attached to the top of the head, the back of the neck, and to the left ear. The two on the head measured the part of the brain controlling muscular co-ordination; the two on the neck measured the optic nerve; and the one on the ear was just a ground. The candidate had to lie on a bed and try to think of nothing, but still stay awake. Although no one flunked on the basis of one test alone, an abnormal test certainly hindered the aircraftman's chances of successfully completing flight training.

The men were also given HAI (high altitude indoctrination) tests in a huge cylindrical tank in which ten persons could be tested at once. The tank looked very much like a miniature submarine, with its Plexiglass portholes. In fact, it had a very similar function. It could be pressurized to simulate conditions at very high altitudes, where the air gets thin and the oxygen scarce. Pressurized aircraft were still a pipe dream, but this procedure highlighted the physical and mental effects of high-altitude flying.

A doctor sat outside, watching through a porthole. Another officer was in the tank with the class taking the test. By manipulating the outside valves, the air in the tank was drawn out to duplicate the air pressure at 5,000 feet, 10,000 feet, and more. As the participants sat, waiting for goodness-knows-what, they noticed no particular sensation except a fullness in their ears. Above 10,000 feet they noticed their fingernails had a bluish tinge. They also felt that their brains were functioning normally and became quite annoyed that they could not do simple mathematics and language tests. To someone looking in, they seemed to demonstrate the effects of a few alcoholic drinks.

At that point each man was provided with a rubber oxygen mask and hose to plug into a supply of raw oxygen and air. With the oxygen, the men could function normally, no matter how little air remained in the tank (i.e. no matter what altitude was simulated).

Even a winter flying suit over layers of uniform clothing did not keep out bone-chilling cold.

The trainees were also exposed to extremely low temperatures. They were taken into giant refrigerators where temperatures were constant at 20° F above zero in one, zero in the next and 20° F below zero in a third. Dressed in their usual uniforms, they rapidly felt the changes and did not stay long, exiting through thick insulated doors. In a final chamber, a cold wind blew constantly and the thermometer registered 43° F below zero. A quick in and out was sufficient to convince aircrew to wear appropriate survival dress when flying. That last room was a similar temperature to what would be encountered five miles up. The point was made when they were reminded that most of their bombing would be done at altitudes of 15,000 feet (about three miles) and higher.

When he finished the ITS course on November 27, Maurice was promoted to leading aircraftsman and his pay was increased from $1.30 to $1.50 a day. After passing the physical and psychological testing at ITS, plus demonstrating at least some aptitude for flying in a ground-based simulator, Maurice was sent to No. 3 EFTS at London, Ontario. He arrived on January 16, 1941, about three months after Jim Warren's training there.

Maurice had some time to wait for his course to begin and he was given leave. The furlough was a great opportunity to spend some time, including Christmas, with Babe and her family on Frank Street. Maurice was very well regarded by Babe's parents, and he was a welcome guest in their home.

No. 3 EFTS was operated by the London Flying Club and flew the two-seater Fleet Finches and Tiger Moth biplanes. All ground and air training at the thirty-six EFTS's was conducted by local civilian flying clubs, except the school at Davidson, Saskatchewan (later moved to Yorkton), which was operated

by the RCAF. The use of civilian instructors allowed the utilization of older men, freeing many RCAF pilot instructors for operational duty.

Up until now, the students had all been aircrew, regardless of trade; pilots, navigators, and gunners were all lumped in together. EFTS was the first time that training was devoted strictly to flying, and LAC Fieldhouse did well at his first attempts to fly an airplane. He experienced the greatest thrill of any airman when he soloed in the minimum amount of time. At EFTS, he added fifty hours flying time to his logbook, and when he graduated, his instructor rated him as an average pilot, but noted that he was quite a hard worker. It was time for him to move on to advanced pilot training.

Dunnville, Ontario, was the home of No. 6 SFTS, the final posting en route to earning his pilot's wings. Up until now, students had flown only at speeds of about 100 mph. Here, experienced RCAF pilots taught them in the sleek, yellow Harvard aircraft that was capable of speeds in excess of 200 mph. Night flying was also introduced for the first time.

Only experience can make you appreciate the difference between day and night flying. On very dark nights, with no moon and few stars, there is no discernible horizon. Once the pilot cleared the runway, marked every one hundred yards by a kerosene flare pot, the pilot was totally dependent upon his instruments. Night flying, especially solo night flying, often had a cadet making deals with his God. There was no one else around to help. Of the eighty-two hours and ten minutes flying Maurice completed at SFTS, nine hours and fifty-five minutes were at night.

By March 29, 1941, the air force considered Maurice Fieldhouse sufficiently trained to be sent overseas. He was appointed temporary sergeant, with a raise in pay to $3.70 a day, but more importantly, he was awarded his pilot's flying badge, his "wings"! Maurice was ordered to report to Debert, Nova Scotia, by April 14 for embarkation instructions. In the meantime he was on leave. Stopping only long enough to sew on the three sergeant's chevrons and throw away his flight cadet white flash, he hurried to Carleton Place to spend the first week of April with Audrey.

Sergeant pilot Maurice Fieldhouse.
(Photo Audrey Morphy-Kennedy)

On April 18, Sergeant Fieldhouse arrived in the U.K. The first order of business was to report to No. 3 (RCAF) Personnel Reception Centre (PRC) in Bournemouth for posting instructions. Few went immediately to their new units, but the PRC had ingenious ways to keep them busy. They would often be sent out on field exercises, harvesting, fruit picking, or inter-section games. Leave was usually generous, so it is quite likely that Maurice had the opportunity to visit his family in Farsley. Finally, on May 26, he reported to No. 55 OTU to fly Hurricanes.

The OTU had a critical role to play in a pilot's training. It was here that he learned to fly the machine and use the tactics he would employ in combat.

When war broke out, there were nineteen RAF squadrons equipped with Hurricanes, a fast, single-seat aircraft. The Hurricane first flew in 1935 and was used as a fighter-bomber, night-fighter; it even flew off ships as a fighter. A Hurricane claimed the first RAF victory over a German by shooting down a Dornier 17 on October 30, 1939. Early in the air war, Hurricanes were also used on offensive sweeps over the Channel ports and northern France. For the duration of the war, the Hurricane fought on more fronts than any other RAF airplane. It proved to be an extremely adaptable aircraft and was able to withstand severe punishment.

Hawker Hurricane Mk IIB, BE 485, coded AE-W with No. 402(F) Squadron, crossing the Channel with two 250-pound bombs beneath the wings, on an intruder sortie into occupied France. (Photo – RCAF Squadrons and Aircraft, p. 85)

In flight, the aircraft had a very distinctive sound when the pilot ran the 1,300-hp Merlin engine to its upper limits. Its forty-foot wing span could carry its 7,000-pound load up to 29,500 feet easily and, if necessary, up to 36,000 feet. With auxiliary wing tanks, it could fly 1,351 miles at a maximum speed of 295 to 340 mph. It could be armed with either eight or twelve .303 machine-guns, or two 40-mm or 20-mm cannon, or two 250-pound or one 500-pound bomb, or eight rockets slung under the wings.

No. 55 OTU was formed at Aston Down on November 1, 1940. It was a fighter-training unit that taught pilots the intricacies of flying Hurricanes,

Blenheims, Defiants, and Masters. As well as the field at Aston Down, the unit maintained a satellite field at Ouston that could be used by pilots in difficulty or when a crash or equipment blocked the primary field's runways.

Audrey's greatest fear came true early in July. A cable was delivered to her from Mr. and Mrs. Fieldhouse. "Regret to inform you," it read "that Maurice was killed while flying. [20]" Late afternoon on July 1, Maurice had taken off in Hurricane number V 6868 to fly a low-level cross-country exercise. Suddenly, his aircraft was seen to spin into the ground at the Rothbury Golf Course at Rothbury Morpeth, Northumberland. It was 1720 on a bright, cloudless summer day. It was believed that he was killed instantly from multiple injuries, including fractured legs and skull and severe burns to his face and hands.

A memorial service was held at St. James Anglican Church in Carleton Place on Sunday, July 27, 1941. Many friends in Carleton Place and former colleagues from Bates and Innes were present to pay homage to the young man who gave his life in the cause of freedom and democracy. The altar was covered with attractive floral tokens of sympathy. Once again Horace Sedman's trumpet sounded "Last Post" and "Reveille[21]."

The body of Sergeant Maurice Fieldhouse was taken to his parents' home in Farsley, where he was interred in the Farsley Baptist Burial Ground adjoining the old chapel. He was twenty-six years old.

An interesting accounting of his finances resulted in his father receiving £21 3s 10d as the balance of Maurice's service estate. There was his pay of £12 11s 6d, cash found in his effects of £6 4s 4d, and an income tax refund of £8. However, his expenses had to be deducted from that. He owed a mess bill at RAF Aston Down, No. 55 OTU's home station, of 1s 8d and another mess bill at RAF Oundle of 2s 7d. There was a regulation funeral grant of £11 5s 6d, but deducted from that was the £7 10s spent by the unit for a coffin in which to ship his body home. That left a balance of £3 15s 6d in the funeral grant, plus his service estate of £17 8s 4d totalling £21 3s 10d paid to Mr. James Fieldhouse. That would be roughly about $50 Canadian.

The Canadian government computed his War Service Grant to be $75 plus the overseas allowance of $13.75. A supplement of $13.05 was owed for a total grant of $101.30. However, Maurice had been sending his mother Eliza an assignment of $23 a month. The pay section had continued to

[20] Audrey was in the same uncomfortable position as a number of young women who became involved with servicemen. Even engaged women were seldom listed on the man's service record as his next of kin. It usually remained as one of his parents. Thus when any accident happened or when he became ill, or when he was killed, the immediate notice went to the next-of-kin of record. It was then left to that person to ensure that others who knew the man were informed. Sometimes they were not; often the man's parents were unaware of the fiancée.

[21] The grim reaper was not done with the Morphy family. Shortly after losing Maurice, Babe lost her two sisters, Helene and Hilda, both killed in an automobile accident in August 1941 at Granby, Quebec.

send her that assignment from August 1941 to January 1942, creating an overpayment of $138. Therefore, although the governmenty did not take total recovery action, they also refused to pay any gratuity.

C 1179 Flying Officer Hugh John Findlay
Pilot
Royal Canadian Air Force Special Reserve

Hugh John Findlay, known as "Jock," or among the family as "Joke," was born on June 6, 1913, to David Findlay and Effie May Hamilton. His father

was president of Findlays Limited, a well-known stove manufacturer, until his death in 1934 from stomach cancer at age 74. Jock was the fifth son in the family, which also included three daughters. He attended school in Carleton Place until 1929, when he followed his brother Ken, who was one year older, to Aurora, Ontario, to attend St. Andrew's College. While at the prep school, Jock excelled at hockey, rugby, and cricket. Both brothers then went to McGill University in Montreal, Ken taking his Bachelor of Commerce and Jock his Bachelor of Arts. At university, Jock was a member of the university boxing team and was captain of the varsity golf team, but he could never beat his brother Ken, who played a championship game.

Ken and Jock Findlay in militia uniform, likely at McGill.(Photo courtesy David Findlay)

While at McGill, the handsome brown-eyed Jock won the heart of co-ed Jessie Carroll. Jessie and Jock spent a great deal of time with each other and graduated together in 1936. When Jock went to Toronto, to continue his education in law at Osgoode Hall, Jessie remained at home in Westmont, but they stayed in constant touch.

Jock graduated with his Bachelor of Laws in 1939, was admitted to the Ontario Bar, and came home to Carleton Place to practise law in his uncles' firm, Findlay and Findlay, Barristers and Solicitors. However, with war threatening Europe and remembered stories of his uncle, David Douglas Findlay, who had been a noted pilot with the RAF during World War I, Jock found the practice of law not very exciting. Therefore, shortly after the declaration of war in September 1939, both Jock and Ken applied to the RCAF. They received a telegram on October 2, advising them to report as soon as possible to RCAF Headquarters in Ottawa for interviews, and on October 6, Jock accepted an appointment to the Special Reserve. Undoubtedly because of his law degree, combined with the recruiter's recommendation, Jock was immediately granted a short service commission and appointed to the rank of provisional pilot officer.

However, he first had to pass an aircrew medical examination to assess his vision, hearing, and reflexes. After being poked, prodded, and measured, he was recorded as being 5' 11½" tall, weighing 140 pounds, with a chest measurement of thirty-four inches (this expanded to thirty-seven when he took a deep breath). He was described as having a dark complexion, brown hair and eyes, and being of fair development. Visible scars included an appendectomy scar and an oval scar on the right knee. He told the examiner that he had had his tonsils and adenoids removed in 1919 and his appendix in 1934. He smoked ten to twelve cigarettes daily and drank moderately,

usually only beer. Having proved to be a medically fit, the twenty-six-year-old was sent to London, Ontario, on October 9, to begin his training.

Since it appeared that Jock was definitely committed to going into the air force, he also made a commitment to Jessie. In the November 23 edition of *The Canadian* was the following announcement:

> Miss Jessie Maud Salmon Carroll and Mr. Hugh John Findlay, RCAF, engagement is announced. Miss Carroll is the daughter of Mr. and Mrs. J. M. S. Carroll of Westmount, and Mr. Findlay is the youngest son of the late David Findlay and Mrs. Findlay of Carleton Place. Both Miss Carroll and Mr. Findlay are graduates of McGill University and Mr. Findlay is a graduate of Osgoode Hall, Toronto.

On December 14, having been found to have a satisfactory aptitude for flying as an air force aviator, Jock was sworn in to the RCAF with the rank of pilot officer. He completed his initial flying training in London and was then sent to Camp Borden for intermediate flying training at No. 1 SFTS. Most of the students training to be pilots were wearing the rank of LAC, so Jock was a rarity, being an officer.

No 1 SFTS was the first of twenty-nine training schools to be opened during the war, and Jock was on one of the first courses. Camp Borden had been an air training camp during the Great War, and while many original structures remained, the build-up for the BCATP meant there was always construction in progress. In addition to new brick buildings and three paved runways, a three-storey-high control tower was erected, a rarity at most of the early airfields.

At Camp Borden, pilots-in-training attended lectures in the intricacies of the Harvard or Yale aircraft, acrobatic flying tactics, and such mundane topics as meteorology and armaments. Very experienced pilots taught advanced flying, as managing the noisy, sleek, fast, single-engine Harvard was not for a neophyte.

Once in February and once for the Easter weekend, Jock was given leave, which he spent with his mother in Carleton Place. The long Easter weekend he also went to Montreal to visit Jessie.

Jock had a very close call during training. He was a member of "D" Flight on the Intermediate Training Squadron when, on April 10, 1940, he was "bounced" by another aircraft. He wrote the following report to his commanding officer:

> I taxied out at 16:05 hrs. and took off. I had climbed to a thousand feet and was flying at 110 M.P.H. along the crosswind leg of the windward end of the field. I saw a flash of yellow through the sides and roof of my aircraft, and almost simultaneously there was quite a loud bang. Momentarily I caught a glimpse of the plane that had hit me. It was yellow and I believed at the time that it was an Anson. My plane continued to fly without loss of height so I looked around for the other plane. I saw a "Battle" about 45° off my port bow, which as far as I could judge should be the approximate position of the other plane. I continued on with my circuit, landed at 16:25 hrs. I reported the accident to the Flying Control Officer.

A careful search did not reveal the pilot or aircraft involved. All yellow aircraft that were in the air at that time were examined but no trace of a collision could be discovered. All pilots were reminded of the importance of "flying discipline," and a lecture was given to all instructors and students drawing attention to the results of carelessness.

Jock finished twenty-first in a class of forty-four, with a grade average of 69.1%. *The Canadian* observed on May 23 that "H. J. 'Jock' Findlay, who has been training in the RCAF at Camp Borden for some months was given his 'wings' last week. He is now in advanced training there preparatory to service overseas." The advanced training lasted from April 27 to June 8, 1940.

When he graduated from advanced training school, Jock was promoted to the rank of temporary flying officer[22]. It was recommended that he be posted to twin-engine bombers, probably on a reconnaissance squadron. Most graduates were single-seater fighter-pilots, having trained on Harvards. They had been taught to find their way across country alone in all kinds of weather, how to use advanced gun-sights, and how to fire machine guns. After further training in England, most were destined to fly Hurricanes or Spitfires, but a few would be trained as bomber pilots on the Avro Ansons. Jock was warned to prepare for overseas service.

1940 was a year of emotional peaks and valleys for Jock and the Findlay family. It began with the tragic death of Jock's closest brother, Kenneth. On December 29, 1939, Ken and his wife Betty were visiting his invalid mother at the family home on High Street in Carleton Place. The young Findlays were leaving to go to their home in Almonte when, walking to the car across the icy lawn, Ken fell. Ken, as a bond salesman, was in the habit of carrying a loaded pistol. When Ken hit the ground, the pistol fired a bullet that lodged in Ken's head, killing him instantly.

While January was an extreme low point for the family, June turned out to be Jock's high. He completed his flying training and on June 8 was promoted to flying officer. Then, on June 13, Jock and Jessie were married at the Carleton Place United Church. After a lengthy leave to enjoy their honeymoon, Jock reported[23] on July 23 to the School of Army Co-Operation at Camp Borden to learn flying tactical support of ground units and air firing. He knew that upon arrival overseas, he was being sent to an army co-operation squadron, No. 112, based at the High Post aerodrome near Old Sarum, the base for the RAF's School of Army Co-Operation.

Jock and Jessie at the family home on High Street on the day of their wedding. (Photo courtesy David Findlay)

---

[22] Equivalent to the army rank of lieutenant.

[23] Jessie went home to live with her parents on Landsdowne Ave. in Westmont until Jock came home from the war.

However, before he sailed from Montreal on September 27, Jock's mother passed away. Effie May Findlay had suffered a stroke seven years before and had been an invalid ever since. On September 23 she suffered another severe stroke and died the next day. Two days after her funeral, Jock bade his bride farewell and sailed for England. Neither knew then that she was carrying their first child.

Jock arrived in Liverpool on October 5 and had time to spend a few days in London before reporting to No. 112 Squadron. Jock found it especially exhilarating to walk through the city in the early morning, after the sirens had wailed an all-clear and the anti-aircraft guns had stopped firing. In Trafalgar Square, he was thrilled with Nelson's Column, and through the throng of pigeons recognized Canada House and the Royal Bank Building. He meandered down Whitehall, past the Horse Guards, the Cenotaph, and Parliament Square and stood in awe before the House of Lords guarded by Richard the Lion-Heart, riding tall but with a bent sword. He walked out along Westminster Bridge to get the best view of the Parliament Buildings stretched magnificently along the banks of the Thames. He came to the Duke of York's steps and stood at the top looking over the Mall. This was storybook England, the heart of the Empire. He murmured "City of London, I am here!"

No. 112 (Winnipeg) Squadron was the second RCAF Army Co-Operation Squadron to land in England, having sailed from Montreal on the *Duchess of Athol* on June 11, 1940, which dockeding in Liverpool. No. 112 was

A 112 Squadron Westland Lysander Mk. II in April 1940. (Photo Credit: RCAF Squadrons and Aircraft. P.45)

equipped with Canadian-built Westland Lysander, a two-seat aircraft with a maximum speed of 230 mph at 10,000 feet that made it far too slow for action against modern fighters. Its only armament was two fixed .303 machine guns aimed forward and another operated manually from the rear cockpit. The squadron used the aircraft in air/sea rescue and to carry agents and supplies to resistance forces on the continent. The spring before Jock arrived, in May and June 1940, the Westland Lysanders had dropped supplies to the beleaguered troops defending Calais and evacuating from Dunkirk. The squadron, and its combat role, was only of use if the British Isles were invaded. Meanwhile, Jock was occupied with army co-operation training.

The Battle of Britain dominated English skies from July 10 to September 15, 1940. Jock arrived in the U.K. just as the fighter air war was winding down. On December 11, No. 112 Squadron became No. 2 Canadian Squadron, to be equipped with fighters and based at Digby. In keeping with the practice of numbering Canadian squadrons in the "400 series," it was renumbered on March 1, 1941, as No. 402 (Winnipeg Bears) Squadron.

At the same time the squadron was re-equipped with the Hawker Hurricane I fighter aircraft. Jock had been flying with No. 112 for two months when he was checked out on the new fighter aircraft, much to his delight after having flown the lumbering Lysander.

On December 18, 1940, No. 402 Squadron war diary noted that Jock made his first solo flight in the new Hurricane. His confidential personal report of December 1940 described a "completely reliable and conscientious officer."

(Credit There Shall Be Wings)

On January 10, 1941, the Canadian Chief of the Air Staff, Air Vice Marshall L. Breadner, DSC, visited the squadron. Prior to lunch in the Officers' Mess, each officer was presented to Breadner. As the air vice marshall was also from Carleton Place, he took great interest in Jock Findlay, having flown with his uncle David Findlay during World War I.

In January 1941, Jock and several other Carleton Place boys became the first recipients of *The Canadian* newspaper's Overseas Cigarette Fund. Approximately thirty "banks" had been placed in strategic locations in stores about town, soliciting donations for the fund. As well, under the direction of Major Will Hooper, a Great War veteran, the Canadian Legion solicited donations. The object was to ship free cigarettes to every Carleton Place boy overseas. One of the first donations was for $40, a significant amount in those days, from Clayton McMullen of Passaic, New Jersey. Mr. McMullen was a Carleton Place boy who had fought in the Great War and was aware "of the value of such a fund and the resultant happiness and contentment it will bring to those boys thousands of miles from home and in strange surroundings, fighting for democracy-the lifeblood of the British Empire."

January brought a month of bad flying weather, alternating between snow and rain and sleet, and always with low cloud. The pilots were spending a great deal of time in lectures and such activities as learning to strip and assemble the Browning machine guns. On February 13, the CBC set up microphones in the mess billiard room for officers to record messages to be sent to Canada for broadcast on February 17.

Somewhere along the road, Jock suffered a broken nose. Whether from boxing or from any of the other contact sports he so thoroughly enjoyed, it is unknown, but during a routine medical examination on February 21, 1941, the medical officer commented on Jock's septal deviation and chronic rhinitis. The doctor found that Jock had no difficulty clearing his ears on climbing or descending in a high-powered aircraft, but warned that, if difficulty developed, he would have to undergo a sub-mucous resection. However the doctor allowed Jock to keep his A1B medical status so that he could remain fit for full flying duties. Jock was now flying with "B" Flight under Flight Lieutenant E. M. Reyno, who would later become an air vice marshall.

With flying conditions improved, and after many training flights, Jock was declared "day operationally trained" on February 25, 1941, meaning he could fly daylight operations. He practised formation flying on March 1, and on March 3, flew his first operational patrol in a Hurricane. On April 14, a JU 88 slipped out of low-hanging cloud over the station and dropped four bombs, barely missing the wireless office and the post office. However, the German plane flew away before the squadron could scramble its planes to mount an attack.

From a letter from his brother Dave, on May 15, 1941, it is learned that Jock had made a trip to Scotland, quite likely to visit Stirling in search of his Scottish ancestors. In any event he took some photographs that were sent home to Jessie. She showed them to members of his family, apologizing for

At the outbreak of World War II, Canadians still fulfilled their need for news almost solely from newspapers. Radio, however, was gaining audiences and influence, and in 1940, the CBC created a news department that broadcast news at noon and 2 p.m., the later broadcast known as The National. At the government's request, the 2 o'clock broadcast was moved to 10 p.m. Eastern time to encourage people to go to bed earlier so as to save power and fuel for the war effort. Lorne Greene (later to be known as Pa Cartwright on the 1960s television show, Bonanza) was the last voice many Canadians heard before trundling off to bed. His sonorous tones and grim news stories soon had him known as the Voice of Doom.

A hastily organized CBC Overseas Unit scrounged whatever equipment they could and travelled to Halifax to sail for Britain with the First Canadian Division in December 1939. They would have been left on the dock but for the direct intervention of General A. G. L. MacNaughton. After embarking on the Aquitania, they started recording shipboard interviews with the troops. In London, they recorded sounds of the Blitz and broadcast programs home to Canada, including "Messages Home," brief communications recorded by sailors, soldiers, and airmen that became enormously popular. CBC London received many cables from Canada, which typically read: "Bless you. Tonight I heard my son[24]."

the poor quality. Jock claimed to have dropped his camera on the floor, so his brother Hamilton arranged to have a new Kodak Bantam camera, which could take both colour and black and white photographs, delivered to him in England.

David wrote that they had heard Jock talking on the radio in April and how clear and natural his voice sounded. The announcer had made reference to Jock's trip to Scotland, making a wise crack about a golfer like Jock going to Scotland without his golf clubs. David reported that brother Geordie had visited in Montreal and had seen Jess, who seemed in fine spirits. He wrote that, of course by the time Jock received his letter he would know all about it. "It" was the daughter—Mary Hamilton—Jessie delivered on May 23, 1941.

No. 2 Squadron was first employed in sinking small enemy ships and in attacking small vital ground objectives from a low height in enemy-occupied territory. On a blustery, rainy June 10, Jock was flying Hurricane IIB Number Z-3233 on a morning patrol. He had taken off from auxiliary landing field WC 2 (Coleby) and was returning after the operation when the Hurricane's Merlin 29 engine

[24] Bill Twatio, Radio Days, Airforce, The Magazine of Canada's Air Force Heritage (Ottawa: Spring 2002, Vol 26/No.1) pp.22/23.

started to sputter and run roughly. With only one engine, there were not a lot of options, so Jock headed for an emergency landing at WC 2. Just as he was on approach to the grass strip, the engine quit, dropping the Hurricane to earth considerably short of the airstrip. He bounced onto a field about a thousand yards from the edge of the aerodrome, crashed through a hedge, making a ground loop and ended up with his machine poised on its nose. The aircraft suffered a bent propeller, wheels, and wing, while Jock suffered an abrasion on his right shin and a bruised ego.

On June 15, Jock's commanding officer wrote a report recommending that he be employed "as a night fighter pilot on twin-engined aircraft. (He is) a good steady pilot (and) will go far if he develops his initiative."

On June 23, the same day that No. 402 Squadron moved to RAF Stapleford Tawney, Jock reported to No. 406 Squadron at RAF Station Acklington,

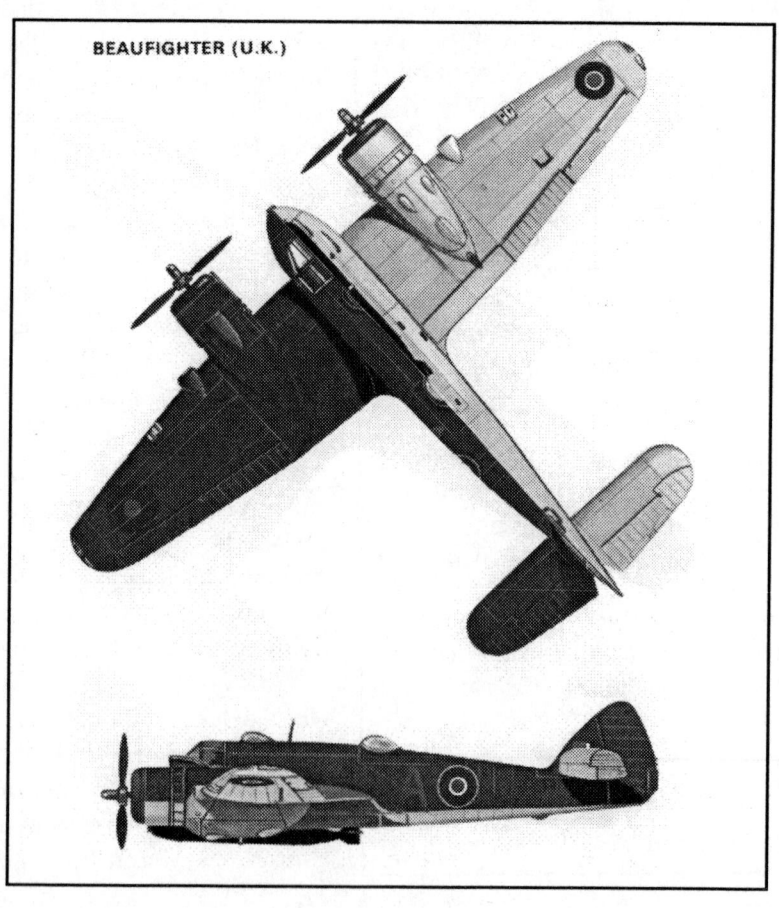

BEAUFIGHTER (U.K.)

Northumberland. 406 "Lynx" Squadron was formed on May 10 as the RCAF's first night-fighter squadron and adopted the motto "We Kill By Night." It was initially equipped with Blenheims, but two days before Jock's arrival, it had taken delivery of its first Beaufighter II. This twin-engine aircraft was deadly with its four cannon and six machine guns, and it became the mainstay of Fighter Command in defending Britain against German night-fighters. Its normal crew was two—a pilot and a navigator/observer. It could be configured to carry a torpedo, eight rockets, or two bombs slung under the wings. 406 Squadron's main role for the remainder of 1941 was to provide defensive air cover over northeast England.

With the training required to master yet another airplane, plus some leave, Jock did not become operational on the Beaufighter II until August 19.

Inside the hut where pilots await orders. LtoR: Sgt Trask, Sgt Handley, F/O H.J. "Joke" Findlay, F/O R.E. Morrow, F/L E.M. "Pop" Reyno, F/O C.T. "Chuck" Cantrill.

Night flying was an entirely different world for aircrew. In the soft summer darkness, while waiting to take off, the pilot could make out the rounded humps of hangars only as a deeper shade of black. Runways were outlined by dim red flares that looked like a long string of double beads, converging as they grew distant. At night, the pilot had to fight the urge to look out of the cockpit and instead concentrate on the instruments or the nose would rise and the aircraft would stall, dropping like a dart to earth.

However, once the pilot reached cruise speed, he could throttle back and relax. Still climbing, he could behold the stars and marvel at these signposts in the sky. Polaris, the Big Dipper, and Cassiopeia would guide him through the night.

On the dark, clear night of September 14, Jock and his observer, Sergeant E. K. Vickers, took off at 2135 hours in Beaufighter II, number R-2473, in company with another Beaufighter piloted flown by Pilot Officer J. Robert Browning Firth. The 406 Squadron "B" flight commander, Squadron Leader J. A. Leathart, had authorized the two to go night flying and carry out Ground Controlled Intercept and Airborne Intercept Exercises. This entailed one of the two aircraft being vectored to intercept the other. The interception was controlled first by the ground controllers and then by the observers in the aircraft, who were able to follow the target aircraft's movements on a rudimentary radar screen. Such exercises enabled pilots and observers to develop the skills required to intercept enemy bombers at night. The two crews took turns trying to find and intercept each other.

Both aircraft entered the overcast cloud layer at 2,800 feet, but broke out into clear skies at 5,000 feet. Firth and Findlay flew several exercises over the next two and a half hours. Feeling they had accomplished a good night's practice, they separated and turned for home. Firth landed first and had just got clear of the runway when he heard Findlay request permission to land.

F/O Findlay & Sgt Vickers 1941 - Acklington (photos–D. Findlay)

At 0004 hours, Osram 21[25] requested permission to land. The aerodrome control officer on duty in the tower, Pilot Officer G. A. Hornblower, acknowledged the call with the standard reply, "Roger," meaning that the message had been received and was understood.

Findlay replied, "Osram 21 calling Herring[26] Control, understand I may pancake."

Nothing further was heard from Osram 21. At 0010 hours, a pilot standing on the control tower roof and LAC Berry, the controller's assistant inside the tower, reported that they had seen the navigation lights on the airplane disappear[27].

The control tower immediately alerted the crash tender and ambulance. They, along with a search party, were sent to Crowther's Farm, which had been identified as the likely crash site by a gunner manning a light machine gun post at the end of the runway.

Squadron Leader Leathart and his second-in-command, Flight Lieutenant F. W. Hillock, were

---

[25] Osram was the codeword of the day for 406 Squadron and 21 was the identifier of F/O Findlay in Beaufighter R-2473.

[26] Herring was the codeword of the day for the Acklington aerodrome.

[27] The two small lights attached to each end of the main wing. The port (left) light is green and the starboard (right) light is red. It is the same navigation lighting system as is used on boats.

driving from the officers' mess to the dispersal point when they saw the two aircraft approaching. They stopped near the end of the flare path to watch. Leathart thought the second plane was approaching normally, if somewhat low. Suddenly the aircraft "dropped like a stone" below the horizon. Leathart was first on the scene and later testified during the crash investigation:

> (The aircraft) had struck the ground at a steep angle, nose first, and facing away from the aerodrome, from which I concluded that it had spun. I then looked for the flaps and found that the port one was down and the starboard one up. This would have induced a spin, but I am not qualified to say whether or not the starboard flap was pushed up on impact.

Hillock testified that the second aircraft:

> . . . waited until the runway was clear and made a normal approach. . . . Then it appeared to climb slightly and finally dived at 60° towards the ground.

The duty medical officer was Flying Officer E. W. Miles. He recalled being called out at 2355 hours to go to a crashed Beaufighter. He was with the first group to arrive at the scene and immediately began a search for bodies.

> One body [that of the pilot] was partially buried in the ground with the body of the radio operator directly on top of it. The two bodies were covered by metal fragments of the aircraft . . . . Death in both cases was instantaneous.

The officer in charge of the investigation wrote the following conclusion:

> Inspection of the wreckage left no doubts in my mind that the aircraft had spun into the ground. The starboard wing tip struck the ground first and both engines and the nose of the aircraft were buried to a depth of four or five feet, The leading edge and main spars of the main plane had broken off and the remainder of the airframe apparently cartwheeled. The tail broke away and the remainder finished on its back 50 yds away from the engines. Other pieces of wreckage were strewn over a wide area. The port flap was fully down and the starboard flap was almost fully up. The jack of the starboard flap was broken and it had the appearance of having been bent and broken in the crash itself. The condition of the wreckage made it impossible to say whether any mechanical defect had developed before the accident. In the absence of any such evidence it is not possible to say whether the spin was caused by mechanical defect or error

of judgement. The pilot had a very sound record but had been airborne fully 2½ hours, and may have failed to distinguish the lights at the approach end of the runway. It seems probable that during his final approach he failed to maintain a sufficiently high speed and this resulted in a stall which he was unable to correct. The possibility of some mechanical trouble or failure cannot be entirely excluded.

Wing Commander D. G. Morris weighed all the evidence and concluded:

I consider the pilot lost flying speed in his approach and crashed as a result. Although obstructions to leeward of the flare path were marked by Red Glim lamps these should not have confused the pilot as he crashed approx. 2 miles from the aerodrome and the angle of the glide lamp would be brighter that [sic] a Glim lamp, F/O Findlay was moderately experienced having done 24 hours of night flying on Beaufighters.

Indeed, Jock's flying logbook showed that he had flown 748 hours in the air force on a variety of aircraft. Most recently he had flown thirty-seven hours on the Blenheim and eighty-eight hours on the Beaufighter. In terms of World War II pilots, he was very experienced.

On September 17, the squadron war diary recorded that the weather was unfit for flying. Flying Officer H. J. Findlay and Sergeant E. K. Vickers were given a full military funeral and were interred at Chevington cemetery, which is located on the east coast of England, 100 miles south of Edinburgh. A full turn-out of officers and men attended, and the escorts, pallbearers, and firing party were all squadron members.

Jock was survived by his wife and baby daughter in Westmount, his brothers David, Hamilton, and George, all of Carleton Place, and his sisters Helen and Jean (McColl) of Toronto, and Margaret (Phillips) of Nanaimo, British Columbia.

The Minister for Air sent a card of condolence, the King sent a message on behalf of himself and the Queen, and a Memorial Cross was delivered to Jessie on October 14, 1941. Jessie also received a letter from Air Vice Marshall L. S. Breadner, a Carleton Place boy who had flown with the town's World War I eagles and had met Jock at No. 2 Squadron in December 1940:

It is indeed unfortunate that so promising a career should be thus terminated and I would like you to know that his loss is greatly deplored by all those with whom your husband was serving.

War Correspondent

David K. Findlay, one of Jock's brothers and a subsequent noted author with the publication of his wartime novel Search for Amelia, spent four months in England as a war correspondent for Canadian newspapers and magazines.

He journeyed across the North Atlantic on a Norwegian mail boat that sailed unescorted through U-Boat infested waters. Fortunately, the crossing was without incident and he landed safely, making his way to London. Locating living quarters was a challenge, but he eventually found lodging in one of the city's suburbs.

After the brightness of Canadian towns and cities, he was totally unaccustomed to blacked-out England. Over every window hung heavy black curtains, and over the doors were two spaced slightly apart so no light escaped as one entered. The streets were like being at the bottom of a pit. No stray beam of light sneaked through. Walking was done at one's peril and usually by keeping one hand on the walls and fences, turning corners by touch and memory. Rough cobblestones only added to the difficulty.

Living and working in this metropolis gave Findlay a great appreciation of the added duties assumed by the citizenry. Everyone took on the additional responsibilities, such as fire watching and block watching. He found the unique humour of the Londoners kept them cheerful and only added to their heroism. They took comfort in making jokes about the German blitz.

On several occasions he watched bombing raids from the rooftops of London. He could see the light of distant fires and hear the sound of not-so-distant aircraft. He saw incendiaries scattered all over the place and thought that one of the scarier jobs in London was driving a fire truck through black streets. On the ground, people were rushing about through the streets and among the trees, beating at fires with shovels and soaking them with stirrup pumps. The sound of fires hissing and the stench of phosphorous wafted to the roofs. After what seemed like hours, the air raid siren wailed an "All Clear."

With his war correspondent's credentials, he visited several RAF airfields. He became familiar with many of the types of combat aircraft and was privileged to see much of England. He also received a rare invitation from the navy to visit a number of warships harboured along England's south coast.

When it was time to return to Canada, David's navy contacts were put to good use. With three days' warning, he was granted permission to sail home on a destroyer. Making his way to an Irish port, with the stamp of approval from the Chief Censor on all his notes and writings, he found he had been bumped by another official. He secured a berth on another destroyer a short time later and spent a miserable passage sailing through one of the worst November gales in recent memory. His was the only spare bunk, and part way into the voyage, he had to give it up to a sick sailor that the destroyer had taken off a corvette.

He had visited Jock's grave in Chevrington often, mourning his lost brother and the life that might have been.

CHAPTER 8-FIGHTER PILOT

A Pilot's Prayer
Almighty and all present power,
Short is the prayer I make to Thee;
I do not ask in battle hour
For any shield to cover me.

The vast unalterable way
From which the stars do not depart
May not be turned aside to stay
The bullet flying to my heart.

I ask no help to strike my foe,
I seek no petty victory here;
The Enemy I hate, I know
To Thee is dear.

But this I pray be at my side,
When death is drawing through the sky;
Almighty Lord who also died
Teach me the way that I should die.

Flight Officer E. R. Davey
London, Ontario
RCAF Pilot
Killed in Action

R 77143 / J 5483 Pilot Officer William Robert Hughes
Pilot
Royal Canadian Air Force Special Reserve

Robert (Bob) Hughes was born in 1916 and grew up in Carleton Place. He was the eldest son of William James, a druggist and optician who owned the Rexall Drug Store in town, and Mabel Vaughan Strong, a prominent member of the local Imperial Order of the Daughters of the Empire (IODE). The family lived on Emily Street and attended St. Andrew's Anglican Church. Bob went to the Central Public school from 1922 to 1929, then attended CPHS from 1929 to 1934, graduating with his junior matriculation. As well as being an honours student, he was active in the school army cadet corps, participating in all training sessions and qualifying as a first-class marksman on the rifle.

He was also an excellent athlete, participating in baseball, badminton, basketball, swimming, and tennis. He played baseball for Carleton Place in the St. Lawrence League, and in track and field, he captured the high school junior championship in 1931, intermediate championship twice, in 1932 and 1933, and the senior championship in 1934. He played an outstanding out-side wing for the school rugby team from 1930 to 1934, which defeated Kingston in 1934 for the Eastern Ontario Secondary School Association (EOSSA) title. But his first love was hockey.

Bob Hughes was the net-minder for the Carleton Place Red Wings in the Upper Ottawa Valley Senior League, and with Bob in between the posts, the Wings had several successful seasons. In 1938, following high school, Bob went to work as a teller for the Royal Bank and was soon transferred to the village of Newboro, between Smiths Falls and Westport. He continued his hockey career, but with the Smiths Falls Mic-Macs. There was an especial-ly notable game played in Carleton Place that *The Canadian* reported on:

Hughes Brilliant

The (Carleton Place Red Wings) swarmed in the Smiths Falls' blue line only to be robbed by Goalie Bob Hughes, ex-Carleton guardian, who repeated his sensational display of his last appearance. . .

Hughes was immense in his flopping and kicking style and, when the final whistle blew, was showered with congratula-tions from both teams and supporters. From the outset of the last session the Red Wings closeted themselves in the visi-tors' defence area but were turned back at every turn by the invincible Hughes.

However, Bob's hockey career tapered off the following year when the bank transferred him to the St. Catherine and McGill College branch in Montreal. This was soon followed by his enlistment into the RCAF Special Reserve on October 11, 1940.

No matter where he lived, Bob was a regular visitor at his parents' home. His sister Freda, who worked at the Ontario Hospital in Toronto, and he often went home together, especially for the holidays. He was home at least once a month, in addition to three weeks in May 1940, and in July, arrived with a colleague from the bank, Douglas Moffatt. They spent the weekend at Mi-Chemin camp on Mississippi Lake.

Almost immediately afterwards, Bob went to the Manning Depot in Brandon, Manitoba, where he passed the requirements for aircrew training. While waiting for his first flying course, he went to Vancouver for a couple of days' guard duty, before reporting to No. 2 ITS in Regina. From December 1, 1940, to January 2, 1941, Bob attended ground school classes where his aptitude for further aircrew training was rated.

Bob told his examiner that he had flown two hours previously as a passenger and that he had suffered double pneumonia at age seven that had taken three months to clear. He reported that he smoked about ten cigarettes a day and would sometimes drink about two quarts of beer a week. He stood 5' 9" tall, weighed 138 pounds, and had a chest measurement of 36½". He was found fit for the air force medical category A1B A3B, meaning fit for aircrew anywhere.

Bob Hughes in flight training.

Bob graduated from ITS with a 71% average and was assessed as an "Average pilot and a good instrument pilot, keen and willing," although he had yet to leave the ground in an aircraft. He was appointed to the rank of leading aircraftsman.

Would-be pilots were first exposed to flying in the Link trainer, a plane with a shortened body and miniature wings firmly anchored to the ground in one of the school's many training buildings. Inside the cockpit, everything looked and operated normally: a "stick" to operate the "elevators" or wings; pedals to control the rudder; and an instrument panel with compass, altimeter, engine speed indicator, "turn and bank" indicator, and other gauges to simulate flight. Adding to the illusion was a circle of celluloid mounted on the nose that was supposed to look like a spinning propeller, and murals on the walls of mountains, lakes, farms, and towns. One portion was painted to resemble a large bank of grey cloud.

The Canadian trainers were made in Gananoque, Ontario, and at first were not much more than toys—attractions for amusement parks and local community fairs. But without such a device, it would have been difficult to produce wartime pilots in the short space of a few months. Advanced trainers were also available, with much more sophisticated systems, more instruments, and a hood that fitted over the cockpit so that the trainee had no visual references.

When the student could handle the Link, he was ready to move on to his first taste of actual flight. For Bob, this meant a posting to Mount Hope, near Hamilton, Ontario, and No. 10 EFTS. There, in a class of forty students, he started a new ground school course more directly related to flying. His instructors were all civilians, employed by the Hamilton Aero Club under the guidance of RCAF officers and NCOs. The aircraft in which Bob would learn to fly was the Fleet Finch.

The primary trainer for RCAF and BCATP pilots.

The Finch was a two-seater biplane that the RCAF used, along with the Tiger Moth, for pilot training. The student sat in the forward seat with his instructor in tandem behind him. The Finch had a single 125 hp engine and would cruise at 98 mph, but with the throttle wide open, it could hit 113 mph and climb as high as 15,000 feet.

At EFTS, pilots would become proficient in straight and level flying, medium turns, straight climbs, glides, climbing turns and gliding turns, recovery from stalls, and spins. The time was now ripe to be introduced to aerobatics, including the loop and roll. Such aerial dances were to become Bob's delight and joy.

Bob finished EFTS on February 19, 1941, with an academic and flying average of 78.5% and a total flying time of sixty-three hours and fifty minutes. But he had yet to earn those coveted wings and there were no course openings for the next stage, forcing him to cool his heels for a couple of weeks at the Auxiliary Manning Depot in Picton, Ontario. Leave, however, was generous and he spent most of the time at home.

Bob Hughes was sent to No. 6 SFTS in Dunnville, Ontario, reporting on March 6, 1941. This school provided more realistic training for those pilots destined to fly fighters.

The students wasted no time in becoming familiar with the Yale and Harvard aircraft they would be flying. Yales were low-wing, single-engine monoplanes, closely resembling the Harvard with the exception that the Harvard had retractable landing gear.

The Harvards were the primary advanced trainers at Dunnville. They were purchased from the U.S. and, to preserve that country's neutrality, were flown to flat open spaces on the international border then pushed or towed across to Canada.

The student had to remember which aircraft he was flying because to land a Harvard with the wheels retracted could be forgiven once, but a second infraction meant a train trip to Trenton and a change of career. Men in a little hut at the end of the runway were watching. If a Harvard came below 500 feet on approach without the wheels showing, they would fire a red flare to warn the pilot and they would report the aircraft numbers to the chief flying instructor. A very stern lecture and the likelihood of some punitive duties would result.

The SFTS emphasised daylight cross-country navigational flights, instrument flying, and reconnaissance flying. Opportunities to fly at night abounded, and the students were tested on two or three night cross-country flights. The advanced curriculum meant that more time was spent in the cockpit than the classroom.

The Wings Test consisted of a joyless flight of forty-five minutes, during which the hapless student had to demonstrate everything he had ever learned about flying. Afterwards, the emotionless air force test officer let no hint of result escape, leaving the student to sweat for a day or two.

Wings Parties, to which almost everyone at the station was invited, preceded a Wings Parade. Each graduate was required to contribute to the cost of booze and food, but as most were poor drinkers, they were very short parties. Just as well—the parade was usually next morning.

Friends and family would gather in a hangar to witness this momentous occasion. The reviewing officer was usually a senior officer of air rank[28] who had had a distinguished career, most likely beginning in World War I. Following the customary congratulatory speech, each cadet was called for-

[28] Equivalent to the army's general rank.

ward by name to have the officer pin his wings onto the left breast of a care-fully pressed blue serge uniform.

Bob Hughes' Wings Parade was on May 16, 1941. He graduated with an average of 73.7% and had flown eighty-four hours and fifty minutes on this last training course. His final evaluation, dated April 28, 1941, read: "high average pilot, navigation good, no serious faults, good effort shown through-out." At last he was a sergeant pilot, and he was sent home on leave to await instructions to proceed to the east coast for transportation to the U.K.

The 24th of May, Queen Victoria's birthday, was a very special day for Bob Hughes—he was made a pilot officer. Usually, the air force awarded commissions to the top third of the graduating SFTS class, making the rest sergeant pilots, and usually such news was announced the same day as their wings were presented. For some reason, the communication from Ottawa did not reach Bob's class until most had departed on leave. So, it was not until the following week, on the holiday weekend, that Bob received the news that he had been awarded a commission, effective May 17, 1941. His happiness and confidence took a quantum leap, and his father promptly marched Bob to a military tailor to have an officer's uniform made for him.

As an officer, Pilot Officer Hughes was entitled, to travel first class by train to Halifax for embarkation to England. He sailed on June 20, 1941, and landed in Britain on July 2, with orders to report to No. 53 OTU to begin fight-er pilot training on Spitfires, the queen of RAF air fighters. Imbued with the adventure of solitary flying

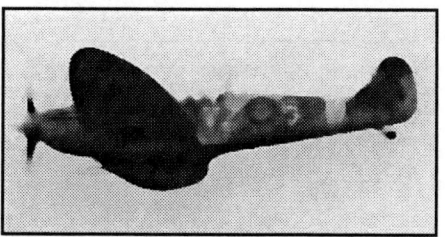

Submarine Spitfire Mk VB, in the markings of 412 (F) Squadron, makes a low pass over the field. (Photo credit RAF Squadrons and Aircraft.)

and the challenge of personal combat in the air, these pilots enthusiastically embraced their lessons.

The Spit was incredibly fast, cruising at 657 kph at 25,000 feet with a maximum permissible speed of 735 kph,[29] and could climb to 15,000 feet in six minutes and ten seconds. It was a single-seat fighter with a 36-foot wing span, and she carried two 22-mm cannon and four .303 machine guns mounted in the wings. There was no more distinctive sound in the air than her Merlin engine boring holes in the sky.

[29] There is one recorded case of a Spitfire reaching "unintentionally" the speed of 965 km per hour — Mach 0.96 — very close to the speed of sound. At that speed, rudders and ailerons became stiff or even "rock solid."

On November 29, 1940, at the Carleton Place home of Miss Dorothy Findlay, a tea was held. Thirty-nine ladies named Dorothy attended, and each brought a friend. Miss Dorothy Edwards and Miss Dorothy Wilson poured tea from 4 to 6 p.m at a table decorated with red, white, and blue candles in silver candlesticks, toy red Spitfire aeroplanes, and models of air force men. Every Dorothy at the two local schools and most of them from the surrounding countryside were present. Some who were unable to attend sent donations, for the object of the tea was to raise money for the Spitfire Fund. A sum of $210.45 was sent to the factory in Montreal. An official receipt, along with gratitude for "a great deal of hard work and most generous giving" was returned to the Honorary Secretary, Dorothy Christie.

Bob Hughes flew forty-five hours and twenty minutes at the OTU and was rated "An average pilot. A keen type but improves slowly. All his flying is satisfactory but [he] could afford a little spirit in it." Whether or not he was overwhelmed by the speed of the new aircraft remains unknown, but he was deemed good enough to be posted for operational flying at No. 412 Squadron at Wellingore near Digby in Lincolnshire.

Bob reported to No. 412 on August 26, 1941. The squadron had been in operation for only two months and was equipped with Spitfire II A's, the first two aircraft arriving on July 7. On August 27 and 28, squadron pilots practised scrambles, aerobatics, and attacks with camera guns. During the morning of August 29, Pilot Officer Hughes, assigned to "A" Flight, took aircraft P 8086 up twice for local flying. At 0940, he was airborne for familiarization and at 1055 was aloft again for reconnaissance flying.

At dawn on August 30, No. 412 Squadron became officially operational and was scrambled to meet the enemy. That afternoon, Pilot Officer Hughes, flying airplane P 7856 in formation with the rest of the squadron aircraft, climbed to 25,000 feet to complete an exercise in cloud flying and camera-gun practices. They were airborne only twenty-five minutes.

The weather during the Sunday morning of August 31 prohibited any flying; visibility was poor. In the afternoon the weather improved greatly, although it remained very cloudy. The squadron was scrambled three times during the day, but no enemy aircraft were intercepted. At 1125, Pilot Officer Hughes again took P 7876 up for local flying. Forty five minutes later he was dead.

At 1210, Hughes' Spitfire collided over Waddington with a Hampton bomber. Both aircraft crashed and burned, killing Hughes and the three bomber-crew members. Five days into operational flying, Bob Hughes died of a fractured skull, multiple injuries, and burns[30]. At twenty-five years of age, he was six weeks short of a year in the RCAF, and had been flying operationally for only five days.

On September 1, Bob's parents received a cable from the Air Ministry announcing that he was "reported to have lost his life on active service." The following day, the casualties officer in London sent a further cable advising them that Bob's funeral would take place at Scopwick cemetery on September 3.

Flying conditions were unfavourable on the morning of the funeral. The ground mist and overcast skies matched the attitude of the squadron pilots, and there was no flying that afternoon as all squadron pilots went to Scopwick Cemetery for Bob Hughes' funeral.

There was a pathetic cheapness about the light-coloured, plain coffin. But the lack of ostentation was sadly appropriate in keeping with the simplicity of a military ceremony. Officers stood to attention, smartly saluting as the coffin was lowered and the firing party volleys echoed over the graveyard. They had been together only a short time, but Bob was a comrade-in-arms during a time when friends were quickly made and just as quickly lost. As they said their goodbyes, many thought of grieving parents an ocean away and wished to be able to help ease the pain.

The military police accompanied the padre to Bob's quarters to collect and sort through his belongings before sending them home[31]. The clerks processed the necessary papers, and the squadron commander wrote a letter to the next of kin, valiantly searching his brain for a personal anecdote about their lost son.

William C. Pollock, KC, a barrister and solicitor in Carleton Place, was tasked with the probating of Bob Hughes' will. Bob's War Service Grant was calculated at 325 days service for a total of $75.00; 49 days overseas at $12.25, and an overseas supplement of $22.50, for a grand total of $109.75. The estate was also sent the proceeds from Bob's savings account at Lloyd's Bank in Pall Mall, London—£26. 1. 0 ($116.44). A uniform allowance of $150 was ignored until Bob's father wrote to Ottawa reminding them of the debt.

In addition to a card of condolence from the Minister of Air, Air Vice Marshall L. S. Breadner, Chief of the Air Staff and a native of Carleton Place, sent his personal condolences to the family. A Royal Message arrived,

---

[30] The squadron information is taken from the 412 Squadron War Diary at the National Archives.
[31] When the belongings arrived in Carleton Place, Bob's father was dismayed that there was no sign of his wristwatch, an ID disc on a chain, a ring and Bob's wallet, all gifts from his father. He wrote to Air Force Headquarters but the missing items never showed up.

and some months later on October 14, 1941, the Memorial Cross was dispatched to Bob's mother.

Pilot Officer William Robert Hughes lies buried in the Scopwick Church Burial Ground, in the village of Scopwick, approximately eight miles from Sleaford and eleven miles from Lincoln. A lane about 500 yards north of Holy Cross Church reaches the burial ground. All of the war graves are in a special plot in the top half of the cemetery over which a Commonwealth War Graves Commission Cross of Sacrifice stands.

In *The Canadian* of September 3, 1942, the following "In Memoriam" notice appeared:

> HUGHES—In fond and loving memory of a dear son and brother, Pilot Officer Robert Hughes, who was killed on active service overseas August 31, 1941.
>
> He is gone but not forgotten;
>
> And, as dawns another year,
>
> In our lonely hours of thinking,
>
> Thoughts of him are always near.
>
> Days of sadness will come o'er us;
>
> Friends may think the wound is healed;
>
> But they little know the sorrow
>
> That lies within the heart concealed.
>
> —Father, Mother, Sister and Brothers.

And in the August 29, 1946 edition:

> HUGHES—In loving memory of a dear son and brother, P.O. Robert Hughes, killed on active service overseas on August 31, 1941.
>
> Years are swiftly passing.
>
> Still we don't forget;
>
> For in the hearts that loved you,
>
> Your memory lingers yet.
>
> —Mother, Father, Sister and Brother.

There was only one brother left, Morley; Cyril had lost his life overseas on September 17, 1944.

In 1950, the Hughes family were advised that the Odeon and J. Arthur Rank theatres would be screening the British Film Corporation newsreel No. 73. It included pictures of Scopwick Churchyard Cemetery and Pilot Officer Hughes' headstone.

Hawker Hurricane Mk. IIB

R 82227 Flight Sergeant Edward Earl Rathwell
Royal Canadian Air Force
Pilot

Earl Rathwell was born in Carleton Place to Thomas E. Rathwell, a farmer, and his wife, Alice Ellen Dowdall on January 12, 1921. The family lived in Innisville, and it was there that Earl grew up.

Earl was educated at McCreary's School and CPHS, where he was a very active athlete, playing on almost every team. He played guard on the CPHS basketball team, and after graduation, with the CPHS Grads team. He was especially good at rugby. Often he could be seen tramping the local woods hunting with his friends, but he also enjoyed the solitude of fishing Mississippi's waters.

Earl was active in the CPHS Army Cadet Corps No. 435, and at its annual inspection in May 1939, he and his friends, Murray McEwen and Donnie Knox, were the colour party cadets.

On the farm, Earl learned to drive on his father's Model "A" Ford. He often drove into Carleton Place from Innisville during his last year at high school, and usually gave lifts to other Innisville students.

When he joined the RCAF, Earl claimed that he had been consistently in the upper third of his senior matriculation class. The principal of CPHS, Mr. A. D. Lamont, wrote a letter of recommendation on August 30, 1940, stating that Earl had completed his junior matriculation and had English Composition, Literature, Geometry, Trigonometry, Botany, Chemistry, Latin Authors and Composition, and French Authors and Composition towards his

senior matriculation. Examination results listed in *The Canadian* in August 1939 showed Earl as having attained an "F" in Modern History, Physics and Zoology; "Cs" in Geometry, Botany and Chemistry, and a "2" in Trigonometry.

After school, Earl first worked as a short-order cook and clerk in Mr. Dan Miller's general store. Then, on September 5, 1939, the Carleton Place branch of the Royal Bank hired Earl as a ledger keeper; he also worked for a time at the Kemptville branch. Isobel Robertson, sister of Jim Warren who also lost his life in the RCAF,[32] was working with Earl in the bank when he left to join the air force:

> I can remember the day he came into the bank as if it was yesterday. He walked into the bank with his uniform on looking quite smart, and went around to the manager and to the accountant shaking hands, and I was in the stenographer's corner and he just took one look at me and said 'Goodbye Isobel, I'll never see you again!' And he just took off. I can still see Earl; he was so brave until he got to me.

> It must have been a year later that the accountant got a notice wondering after the whereabouts of Edward Earl Rathwell, because he hadn't turned up for his military call. Well, was our accountant mad! He was furious! Because Earl had joined up, taken his training and gone overseas and was killed. And they wanted to know his whereabouts! [33]

Having spent all five years of high school in the cadet corps, it was only natural that Earl would continue this military association by joining "D" Company of the Lanark and Renfrew Scottish in Perth. He was assigned regimental number C-416917 and, although he was found to have a slightly fallen right arch, he was accepted on July 26, 1940. The army medical examiner recorded Earl as a youth of 19 years 215 days, of good development if somewhat short at 5' tall, weighing 156 pounds, and with a fair complexion, fair hair, and blue eyes. There was a visible scar on the back of his right wrist. Earl was found fit for medical category "A" and was enrolled into the militia. He attended the annual summer training in August 1940, but then was discharged to join the RCAF.

---

[32] See Part Two, Chapter Three.
[33] Interview with Isobel Robertson April 2, 2001.

When Earl went into the recruiting office in Ottawa, he did so with the intentions of signing on as a ledger keeper. He had with him a letter of recommendation from Major W. H. Hooper, a World War I veteran and the Carleton Place postmaster as well as first vice president of the Carleton Place Branch of the Red Cross Society. However, the interviewer recommended that Earl be trained as a pilot or observer and wrote:

> Fine clean cut young man with a good education. Intelligent, deliberate, strong will power but not obstinate. Pleasant, good manners, good talker. Not very keen to fly, would prefer to serve as Acct. clerk. Had to be convinced to consent to take medical test.

At his medical examination, Earl reported that he had occasional tonsillitis but had no problems for the past year, that he had had developed scarlet fever at age sixteen, that he drank no alcohol at all, and smoked only four cigarettes a day. He reported that he had "some discomfort at heights." The medical officer concluded that Earl was a "Splendid candidate. Stable. Alert. Good education. A1B A3B. Should be good pilot material." And Earl's fate in the Royal Canadian Air Force was sealed.

Earl took the train to Toronto and the Manning Depot and, on December 11, 1940, he was outfitted in air force blue and told he was an aircraftsman second class. Following basic training, Earl did guard duty at No. 31 ANS in Port Albert, on Lake Huron just north of Goderich, Ontario, then returned to Toronto to attend Course No. 22 at No.1 ITS.

This was Earl's introduction to flight and a test of his aptitude for flying. However, the toughest subject at ITS was navigation, which consisted of ninety hours attending lectures and 150 hours solving navigation problems. Whether a man was destined to become a pilot or a navigator, it was essential that he have a good working knowledge of navigation.

At ITS, the students learned the basic advantages of each type of cartographic map and chart; how to plot a rhumb line, references in latitude and longitude, and the requirement to fly a "great circle route."

Earl managed to get home to his parents near Innisville for a weekend in April, before graduating thirty-ninth out of sixty-four students. His course report read: "Co-operative, keen and smart. This man is conscientious and has worked well on his Initial Training Course. Recommended pilot or secondly, WAG."

He started flying as a member of Course No. 27 at No. 7 EFTS in Windsor, Ontario, where he met and fell in love with Ellen Smith, who was added to his list of next-of-kin in his records. This ensured that, in the event that anything happened to him, the RCAF would notify her in accordance with his wishes.

Every moment that Earl could spare from his flying lessons he spent with Ellen, and at least once, some hours he couldn't spare. Earl was awarded six days confined to barracks and lost one day's pay for being absent without leave (AWL) from 2359 hours (bed check) on May 20 to 0730 hrs (first class) on May 21, 1941[34]. It was a costly seven hours and thirty minutes, but most likely time Earl found very well spent.

When Earl arrived on course, on May 4, 1941, he was promoted to leading aircraftsman and was allowed to wear the appropriate insignia—a single propeller blade—on the upper arm of his tunic sleeves. And as the RCAF wasted no time in putting its students into the air, Earl's familiarizsation flight in the Fleet Finch came the very next day, and his first solo flight fifteen days later, on May 20, during which he spent fifteen minutes of solitude over Essex County's flat fields.

By graduation day, Earl had logged sixty-one hours and twenty minutes in the Finch. One of his instructors rated Earl as "slightly over-confident. His instrument flying is fair, but aerobatics definitely weak." However, by his final parade on June 21, he passed sixteenth out of twenty-nine pilots and was rated "Aerobatics weak. Needs more practice in steep turns and climbing turns. Slow to learn but tries hard." It was trusted that the instructors at the advanced flying school could correct any minor problems.

After a short leave, Earl reported to No. 6 SFTS at Dunnville, Ontario. The school was quite new, having been opened in November 1940, and its role was to train fighter pilots on Yales and Harvards. Students arrived with some flying time, but the SFTS would provide more realistic training on faster, more complex machines during the ten-week course. Earl was on Course No. 32, from July 3 to September 13, 1941.

Dunnville was a completely self-sustaining air station. It had its own barracks, messes, lecture huts, infirmary, and control tower, which overlooked its two paved runways and five large hangars. There were two emergency relief landing fields, one at Kohler and one at Welland. More than 2,400 pilots were trained during the war at No. 6 SFTS, and while most went overseas, a few did return to haunt other students.

Earl was medically grounded for four days, from July 30 to August 2, when he fell victim to a summer cold. Two weeks later, he was hospitalized again for a short time to treat multiple lacerations on his forehead just over his eyes. At midnight on August 15, Earl and four other airmen were driving on Highway 7 when another car entered the intersection at Highway 41 and

---

[34] Civilian instructors from the Windsor Flying Club did all flying training but RCAF personnel controlled administration and discipline.

slammed into their vehicle. The automobile Earl was in rolled over three times, but luckily, he suffered only minor injuries.

On September 13, Earl Rathwell proudly paraded in front of his fellow aviators, and Ellen, to have his RCAF pilot's wings pinned to his left breast. The same day, he sewed sergeant's chevrons on his sleeve and became a sergeant pilot ready for overseas service as a fighter pilot. He graduated with an average of 73.3%, twenty-sixth out of a class of sixty-six. His final evaluation was: "Progress good. Skids on all manoeuvres (heavy on rudder). Very satisfactory. Good effort shown throughout." He was ordered to report, after two weeks leave, to No. 1 "Y" Depot in Halifax to await sailing for Britain. The first week of his leave he spent with his parents at Scotch Corners.

Wartime Halifax was a dismal, squalid town. The weather was always bleak, drenching the city in cold, wet fog. It was overcrowded, the streets teeming with sailors. However, while there, the airmen's schedule was quite relaxed. If they had not experienced an exercise in the decompression tank, they took the opportunity now. The usual objective was to get clearance to fly to 35,000 feet, the basic certification that all aircrew had to have stamped on the inside front cover of their flying logbooks. "Needle parades" re-inoculated them for everything they had been inoculated for before plus a few extras, leaving arms (and bums) throbbing for several hours. Night vision acuity was tested and another endorsement entered in red ink into the flyer's logbook. "Y" Depot also had a Link trainer for those pilots who felt their skills may get rusty before they arrived overseas on an operational squadron. Finally the day came and the group was warned to pack all their possessions and load themselves on trucks for the docks.

Having safely crossed the Atlantic, Earl travelled by train to No. 3 PRC in Bournemouth, a holding unit to prepare aircrew for more flying training until openings became available at the advanced training units. Everyone at the PRC was issued new, top-quality flying equipment: flying suits, fleece-lined boots, leather gloves so soft they had to be chamois, helmets and goggles. The Canadians would also hear their first eerie wail of air raid sirens at Bournemouth, while Spitfires wheeled high overhead.

Bournemouth is just eighty miles southwest of London and had been a popular coastal resort in happier days. By the time Earl arrived, the beaches had been mined and barbed wire strung to keep errant servicemen away. The elegant hotels that lined the oceanfront were mostly filled with boisterous young Canadians, where breakfast consisted of powdered eggs scattered on dry toast adorned with a greasy bit of Spam. Earl thought the food couldn't get much worse, then he was served Brussels sprouts.

Earl went to No. 9 SFTS at Hallavington on November 3 where he learned the difference between training in peaceful Canada and training in a war zone. Both defensive and offensive measures were now paramount. The following month, on December 30, he reported to No. 30 OTU, where he trained on various Spitfire models, which he would soon fly in combat. He flew the Spitfire I, II, and IV before being introduced to the Hurricane, all of which were single-seat aircraft. In addition to the Hurricane I, a fighter, Earl also learned to fly the IIB, a bomber.

Earl was posted to No. 175 RAF Squadron, whose motto was "Stop At Nothing." It was formed on March 3, 1942, as a fighter unit and was equipped with the Hurricane IIB's left behind by No. 402 Squadron when it moved. The squadron, based at RAF Station Warmwell, was tasked with maritime patrol in support of convoys and often operated as dive-bombers, carrying out attacks on enemy shipping with two 250-pound bombs or eight rockets slung beneath their wings. Earl arrived as one of the first pilots on March 10, 1942, in time to fly with the squadron's first operational mission on April 16, when six Hurricanes attacked Luftwaffe airfield at Maupertus airfield. For the next two months, the squadron's role was attack enemy shipping and carry out local and convoy protection patrols.

On June 22, 1942, Sergeant Rathwell took off as "Red 2" flying Hurricane IIB number HL 723 in a section of four aircraft to practicse dive-bombing. Next to low flying, there is nothing as dangerous, or more seductive to a pilot, than formation flying. Flying with another airplane seemingly suspended in air only twenty feet away is quite exhilarating. While it is the leader's job to ensure that his formation is kept safe, each pilot must keep all attention rivetted on his leader's aircraft. If any teammate disappears from sight, the pilot must fight the urge to move for fear of moving into the aircraft he cannot see. Only experienced pilots fly formation.

The formation was carrying out dummy attacks on four high-speed navy motor-gun boats that were travelling in echelon. They flew to 3,200 feet and then commenced to dive at a 45° angle. The leader, "Red 1," would initiate the pull out and his wing mates would follow. On one of the attacks, Earl did not pull out with his leader. He continued for another 300 feet before attempting to climb, but he was far too low. His radiator hit the sea, he bounced, hit a wing tip, cartwheeled and exploded, completely destroying the aircraft, which sank immediately.

The squadron commander's report concluded:

> The sea was ruffled and as he was diving in the vicinity of boats the pilot should have had no difficulty in judging distance, particularly as the flight had been carrying out similar attacks previously.
>
> In my opinion the pilot misjudged his height over the water and pulling out, struck the sea.

The station commander concurred and added: "I can only assume that the pilot determined to go lower than the rest of the section for some reason, and failed to pull out in time."

Earl's body was recovered from the sea for burial on June 27 in Brookwood Military Cemetery in Surrey. Brookwood is thirty miles from London.

On July 4, 1942, W. W. "Dit" Bittle, a Carleton Place lad serving with the RCAF, wrote to *The Canadian* thanking them for the gift of cigarettes and writing about Earl:

> I've heard the dreadful news of Earl Rathwell. It shook me up terribly for I looked on him as a dear friend and pal. A better man could not be found.
>
> He had a very tough job but smiling he went ahead to do his bit. . . . His body was recovered and buried in Tarnborough with full R.C.A.F. honours. The cemetery is for Canadians.
>
> I'm sure Mrs. Rathwell must be in great sorrow over the loss of her son. Perhaps if you print the enclosed poem it may help to cheer her and many other mothers who have lost their sons.
>
> Thanks again for the cigarettes. I shall not forget your kindness.

Faithful Unto Death

He was our son, bright-eyed and strong.
Pride of our years, our hope and joy.
Crown and completion of our love.
Our darling boy
Yet in his country's hour of need,
Gladly he left us.

Who would blame?
Was he not also England's son?
She had the first and greater claim.

She had his heart.
And we are proud,
He served her to his dying breath.
He loved her with a love supreme.
And he was faithful unto death.

Another writer was Mrs. Rupert (Lila Lemieux) Cooke, Convenor of the Canadian Red Cross Society to the Aldershot Command:

> I represented the Society at the funeral of your son. . . I wish to express to you the deep sympathy of the Society in your sad bereavement.

> My heart ached for you during the beautiful service. The Padre prayed that those mourning the loss of their young son at home might be comforted. I said a prayer for you as I placed a lovely spray of flowers on the casket draped in the Union Jack. The service was very touching.

On Tuesday, August 25, 1942, President John Steele and members of the Carleton Place branch of the Royal Canadian Legion visited Tom and Alice Rathwell at their home in Scotch Corners. Mr. Steele read an address from the Minister of National Defence expressing his sympathy for their bereavement. He also presented Alice with the silver cross of sacrifice, the Memorial Cross.

On October 1, 1942, the assistant private secretary to the Minister of the Department of National War Services, Mr. George Deas, wrote a personal letter to Tom Rathwell:

> I have a sister who lives at 9 Almondbank Terrace, Edinburgh, Scotland, her name being Mrs. A. Aitken.

> I received a letter from her dated August 19 from Edinburgh, wherein she states as follows:

> 'Do you remember my writing and telling you that Drucival Wescott, that is Harry Gilder's sister's boy, came to stay a leave with us and brought another boy with him. He came from Ottawa. His name was Earl Rathwell. Well he was

killed just after his leave. I was glad he had had a good time while he was staying with me, and I made him feel just like my own boys.'

I thought it would be of interest to you to know that your boy, before he met his death, had enjoyed a visit with my sister and her family in Edinburgh. I never met your boy, but I am quite sure that Mrs. Aitken and the girls, my nieces, did everything possible to make his stay in Edinburgh enjoyable.

Earl Rathwell had been twenty-one.

In November, the Rathwells were informed that Earl had been promoted to the rank of flight sergeant effective March 13, 1942. The RCAF had a policy that all aircrew members, if recommended by their commanding officer, should at the end of proscribed time from their last promotion be promoted to a higher rank. The policy was made retroactive to extend the same recognition to those who had lost their lives.

CHAPTER 9—WOAG

There was a wartime poster with the following information for prospective air force recruits:

> Why argue who is most important? Without the pilot you're grounded. Without the WAG you're deaf . . . without the air bomber you're harmless . . . without the navigator you're blind . . . without the air gunner you're defenceless. Each job is vitally important. . . . It's the *team* that counts!

R 54187 Flight Sergeant Robert Joseph O'Leary
Royal Canadian Air Force
Wireless Operator/Air Gunner

Robert "Bob" O'Leary journeyed to Carleton Place from Ottawa after he completed high school searching for work. He worked as a general labourer for Mr. L. Goldstein for four months in the winter of 1939–40, then as David Thompson's Esso service station attendant for four months until he finally landed a position with Findlay's Foundry as a welder. He only stayed with Findlay's for another four months before he enlisted in the RCAF in Ottawa.

While in Carleton Place, Bob boarded at 3 Sarah Street. He made his presence known in town as an exceptionally good hockey player with the Carleton Place junior team during the 1939–40 season. He also took up paddling and came to thoroughly enjoy skimming the Mississippi River becoming, in July 1940, a member of the Carleton Place Canoe Club War Canoe team.

Bob was born in Ottawa to Michael Joseph O'Leary and Bernice Chouinard on September 22, 1921. He was raised a Roman Catholic and received his first schooling at St. Joseph's Separate School from 1927 to 1935,

GANANOQUE – 0
VISITORS – 0

Carleton Place Red Wings circa 1940.

before attending the University of Ottawa High School for two years, from 1935 to 1937. He suffered the normal childhood diseases, such as measles, and in 1933 had his tonsils and adenoids removed. Robert had three brothers, but two had died as infants and the third, Edward, lived at home on Nelson Street. He also had two sisters.

From 1937 to 1939, Bob attended Ottawa Technical High School where he took his matriculation course and became trade-skilled in machine shop, electricity, draughting, aeronautics, and related ship work. It was here that he acquired the welding proficiency necessary to work at Findlay's. At high school, he played on the football and hockey teams, playing with the EOSSA hockey championship team in 1939.

On June 17, 1940, Bob was interviewed for enrolment into the RCAF. The interviewing officer wrote in typical cryptic military language that Bob was an "Outstanding athlete. Short on education, but very fine type of air-crew. Serious, determined, aggressive and with training should prove excellent air gunner."

On July 1, he had a medical to determine his fitness for air force duties, and the doctor found his left foot to be slightly flat and that he had a scar on his left forearm. He was 5' 8¾" tall, weighed 157 pounds, and was described as being of dark complexion with hazel eyes and black hair. The medical officer awarded a category "A", A1B A3B fit for all air force duties. His evaluation ultimately noted that Bob was a "Young man, quiet and well balanced physically and can improve with training."

Bob was given the rank aircraftsman second class and a train ticket from Ottawa to Toronto, where was to report on July 18 to the Manning Depot.

The wireless-operator/air gunner was a specialist as soon as he marched off the drill square for the last time at Manning Depot and into wireless school. But in the fall of 1940 the flow of recruits was becoming a flood that the BCATP was having difficulties handling. Consequently many men, after learning the basics at the Manning Depot, had to wait months for an opening in a trades course. In the meantime, they were posted to various other units for guard duties. For Robert O'Leary this meant transfers to No. 5 Bombing and Reconnaissance (BR) Squadron in Dartmouth, Nova Scotia, and from there to 8 BR Squadron in North Sydney. On October 11 he returned to Toronto for duties at No. 1 ITS and then, on November 8, 1940, he was assigned to Course No. 7 at No. 1 Wireless School in Montreal.

At No. 1 Wireless School, Bob toiled long hours in classrooms and practised transmitting Morse code for weeks on end. When he could handle basic communications on the ground, he was sent flying where turbulence and aircraft noise would garble transmissions and jostle his sending hand. Most wireless operators had far less trouble sending than receiving. When this phase of training was over, he would have mastered the various techniques of two-way communication involving aircraft and have reached a standard of fifteen five-letter words per minute, both receiving and sending.

While at the Wireless School, Bob found more to do than study. He decided that he needed longer to celebrate Christmas and New Year's than the allotted days the air force gave him, so he just took the time off. He was AWL from December 21 to 30, 1940, which cost him ten days' pay. In addition he was sentenced to 168 hours (seven days) detention from December 30 to January 5, 1941. Then, from February 11 to 13, he was hospitalized in Ste-Anne-de-Bellevue veterans' hospital with a sore throat and fever and was diagnosed with acute naso-pharagitis.

In spite of the extra-curricular activities, Bob completed thirteen hours and thirty minutes flying in a Fairey Battle, graduating thirty-sixth in a class of ninety. Next, he went for gunnery training at No. 4 B&G School at Fingal, Ontario.

Prior to November 1940, when the RCAF's 4 B&G School opened, Fingal was a small, quiet Elgin County town within short flying distance of Lake Erie. The base was opened to train WAGs, air gunners, and air observers. The gunners took four to six weeks of intense training on weapons, in-flight firing, drill, PT, and lectures on current affairs. Fingal had fifty-eight Fairey Battles in which the trainees flew and fired machine guns and aerial cannon. The air gunner learned about ammunition, how to operate the gun turret, the theory of range estimation and sighting, and aircraft recognition to ensure he fired at an enemy target.

Bob fired a Vickers machine gun for the first time at a twenty-five-yard range. He would not get to fire a Browning, the guns actually mounted in the aircraft, until he reached advanced training. At this stage, he stood in a long building, open along one side, and fired at targets in a sand-filled concrete buttress in bursts of eight to fifteen bullets at a time. When he felt comfortable using the Vickers, he moved on to another building in which there were power-operated machine-gun turrets. The guns had been modified to fire a ray of light towards a tiny German airplane that moved across a painted sky. Every time he scored a hit a bell would ring, exactly like the firing ranges set up for local fairs and exhibitions.

Live firing was done over Lake Erie. Flying in the school's Fairey Battles, the gunners fired at moored buoys and at drogues towed 1,000 feet behind a plane vividly painted with black and yellow stripes. Two gunners sat side by side near the rear of the aircraft while an experienced pilot sat up front. Over Lake Erie, in the summer especially, the sky became very bumpy and more than a few young men tossed their breakfasts on the aircraft floor. (One was obligated to clean up after oneself.)

The two aircraft flew pre-arranged patterns and schedules, meeting over the lake. Each gunner's ammunition belt of bullets was dipped in paint, one ammunition belt in red, the other in blue, so that an accurate tally could be made afterwards. The drogue aircraft did not have to land but would fly back over the field, release the target drogue and allow another to slide out to the end of the cable.

At the end of this course the gunner was awarded a badge with an AG in a laurel wreath on a half wing. Bob received his wing on April 14, 1941, and, at the same time, was promoted to temporary sergeant. His graduating mark was a respectable 73%.

Bob was now ready for embarkation overseas to train with a bomber crew before going into action. The first step was a posting to the RAF trainee's pool in Debert, Nova Scotia, which was basically a holding point until ship transportation could be arranged. He was

Sgt Robert O'Leary

granted embarkation leave and it was noted in *The Canadian* of April 24 that "Sergeant Gunner Robert O'Leary, RCAF, who played brilliant hockey with the Carleton Place Junior Hockey team during the season of 1939–40 visited in town this week."

Bob arrived in Debert on April 25, but did not get overseas until July. He went AWL again—June 8 and 9—which cost him another day's pay. When he arrived in Britain, he was posted to No. 1 Signal School to polish his wartime communications and gunnery skills.

On August 1, Bob was arrested in the nearby town of Sleaford for being drunk and disorderly. The local constable took a dim view of "colonial" NCOs who drank a little more English ale than was good for them, so Bob was taken before a magistrate and fined 30 shillings, which he paid on the spot. He was released and returned to the school a much more sober airman.

On October 21, he proceeded to No. 16 OTU to learn the procedures and tactics of the aircraft he would fly on operations and to join an air crew. Within ten days of the men's arrival, they were organized into crews of five persons each: a pilot, a bombaimer, a navigator, a wireless operator, and an air gunner. The men could "crew up" amongst themselves if they liked, but at the end of the ten-day familiarisation, those not yet in a group would be arbitrarily assigned to a crew. Trying to choose crewmembers, or a crew, to which you wanted to belong, was basically an exercise in self-preservation. You wanted people who were good at their jobs and who could perform under the untold stress of wartime flying. And you had only ten days in which to make these decisions.

No. 16 OTU was located at Upper Heyford, and its primary role was to train night fighter crews on Hampden and Hereford aircraft. Bob was assigned to a Hampden crew and found the new Handley-Page Hampdens a revelation. Twin-engine bombers with attractive lines, they seemed to be the epitome of modernity and efficiency in that they were surprisingly agile, posing no serious handling problems. Their most serious deficiencies were a lack of room to move about in the exceptionally narrow fuselage and their rather feeble defensive armament. They had only one fixed and one moveable .303 gun forward and twin .303 guns in the dorsal and ventral positions and a a maximum bomb-load of 4,000 pounds.

Bob was promoted to the rank of flight sergeant on December 1, 1941, which elevated his pay to $3.75 a day plus an additional $1 per day for rations and quarters.

His flying was briefly interrupted by an attack of scabies, a contagious skin disease causing severe itching, so he spent January 26 to February 12, 1942, in sick quarters at Upper Heyford. Very irritating lesions on his trunk,

Hampdens in action.

arms and legs plagued him, so the medical staff treated and tried to clear the condition with a routine of benzyl benzole applications.

When Bob returned to flying, his crew found additional obstacles to taxi around as, in March, construction had begun on upgrading and paving the runways. They were often sent out on raids to drop leaflets, which was a standard part of OTU crew training.

On March 25, the crew took Hampden IP 1221 on a night training exercise. However, shortly after midnight, the aircraft crashed and burned near the Polebrook airfield. No reason for the crash was discovered, and the crew was carbonized. Robert O'Leary, dead at age twenty, was buried in the Old Weston (St. Swithun) Churchyard in Huntingdonshire.

Bob's mother received the standard card of condolence from the Minister of Defence, a royal message of sorrow from the king and queen, and a Memorial Cross, which was delivered on April 21, 1941. His war service gratuity came to $150 for 600 days service, $70.50 for his 282 days service overseas, and a supplement of $51.24 for a grand total of $271.74.

PART THREE—CALL TO ARMS!

CHAPTER TEN–WAR

The only thing necessary for the triumph of evil
is for good people to do nothing

In early 1939, Britons felt secure from any threat from Germany. Prime Minister Neville Chamberlain, in concert with the French government, had appeased Hitler's desire for *lebensraum* by standing silently by while the Fuehrer annexed Austria and moved against Czechoslovakia. But this was tantamount to stoking the boilers at the Findlay Foundry in Carleton Place without providing an escape valve for the steam. Something was sure to blow.

On May 11, the CPHS Cadet Corps held its annual inspection. Little did many of these boys know that by year's end they would be trading cadet uniforms for khaki and webbing, air force and navy blue. High school students on parade included signallers Cyril Hughes and Ross Stanzel, with colour party members Murray McEwen, Earl Rathwell, and Donnie Knox. In Platoon No. 1 marched Boyne Dunphy, Lloyd Scott, Arthur Prime, and Wilson Costello, and in Platoon No. 2, Earl Lancaster, Ross Stanzel, and Ross MacFarlane. The bugle band with drummer Andrew Porterfield and bugler Bob Irvine led the corps on parade. Had they marched past and saluted the cenotaph with an "eyes right," none would have believed that their own names would be engraved on new wings of stone in the near future.

During the long Victoria Day weekend, many Carleton Place residents travelled by automobile and train to Ottawa to see George VI and Queen Elizabeth on their Canadian tour. Eight local boy scouts, including Cyril Hughes and Lloyd Scott, were chosen to go to Ottawa for four days during the Royal Visit. Having passed their first aid and ambulance badges, they were placed at first aid stations along the parade route.

Meanwhile, the Reverend Stoddert Kennedy expressed his thoughts on the impending war in poetry and had them published in the *Carleton Place Herald*:

WAR!

Waste of muscle, waste of brain,
Waste of patience, waste of pain,
Waste of manhood, waste of health,
Waste of beauty, waste of health.

Waste of blood and waste of tears,
Waste of youth's most precious years.
Waste of ways the Saints have trod,
Waste of glory, waste of God.

WAR!

On September 1, 1939, German armies swept into Poland. That April, Britain had pledged to defend Poland against any German incursion, so with the advent of war with Germany, George VI took to the airwaves to address his subjects in all parts of the Commonwealth:

> In this grave hour, perhaps the most fateful in history, I send to every household of my peoples, both at home and overseas, this message, spoken with the same depth of feeling for each one of you as if I were able to cross your threshold and speak to you myself.
>
> For the second time in the lives of most of us, we are at war.
>
> Over and over again, we have tried to find a peaceful way out of the differences between ourselves and those who are now our enemies; but it has been in vain.
>
> We have been forced into a conflict, for we are called, with our allies to meet the challenge of a principle which, if it were to prevail, would be fatal to any civilized order in the world.
>
> It is a principle which permits a state in the selfish pursuit of power to disregard its treaties and its solemn pledges, which sanctions the use of force or threat of force against the sovereignty and independence of other states.

Such a principle, stripped of all disguise, is surely the mere primitive doctrine that might is right, and if this principle were established through the world, the freedom of our own country and of the whole British Commonwealth of nations would be in danger.

But far more than this, the peoples of the world would be kept in bondage of fear, and all hopes of settled peace and of security, of justice and liberty, among nations, would be ended.

This is the ultimate issue which confronts us. For the sake of all that we ourselves hold dear, and of the world order and peace, it is unthinkable that we should refuse to meet the challenge.

It is to this high purpose that I now call my people at home and my peoples across the seas, who will make our cause their own.

I ask them to stand calm and firm and united in this time of trial.

The task will be hard. There may be dark days ahead, and war can no longer be confined to the battlefield, but we can only do the right as we see the right, and reverently commit our cause to God. If one and all we keep resolutely faithful to it, ready for whatever service or sacrifice it may demand, then with God's help, we shall prevail.

May He bless and keep us all.

On September 10, the Canadian Parliament proclaimed that Canada was in a state of war with the German Reich. A week later, on September 13, the *Carleton Place Herald* reported that "Recruiting [is] Progressing Favorably." Lieutenant Harold Murfitt, a weaver with the Hawthorn Woolen Mills in Carleton Place, also opened a recruiting office for the Lanark and Renfrew Scottish Militia in the Legion rooms on September 7. An officer recruiting for the Cameron Highlanders of Ottawa, which had been mobilized to full wartime strength, he represented the active force. He was seeking "only men of good physique and character," luring them with the promise that the machine gun battalion would be mechanized, eliminating the "foot slogging" of the Great War. He expected training with the machine gun to be of great interest for Ottawa Valley boys and "a fine response is expected from young men with the fire of the Scottish clans in their blood." Within a week, twenty-two Carleton Place men had joined, including Roy McKittrick, William Loney, the Nerons (father Leo and son Rene), and two West boys (Wilfred and George).

Word was received in October that Constable W. R. Phillips RCMP, son of Mr. J. R. Phillips of McArthur Avenue, had been selected from his post at Weyburn. Saskatchewan, to be one of the 106 Mounties to be attached to the First Division for overseas service.

In June 1940, the *National Resources Mobilization Act* (NRMA) was passed by parliament. Hotly debated and vigorously opposed by the French-speaking citizens of Quebec, it required every male in Canada, over the age of sixteen, to register for national service. Those who voluntarily enlisted in the armed forces could be sent overseas. Men who were called up under the NRMA could not.

In July 1940, it was officially announced that the Lanark and Renfrew Scottish Regiment was to be immediately brought up to wartime strength of 800 men. This meant recruiting sixty men from Carleton Place for "D" Company in Perth, under the command of Captain J. Briggs. Uniforms were issued, and the men were paid on the basis of the time they spent in training. However, until the regiment was called to active duty, the recruits would continue in their local jobs and would be required to drill with the company every Tuesday and Thursday, where they were instructed on the use of the rifle and the machine gun. Each recruit had to have a medical examination to determine his fitness for general service (Category A), service abroad, not general service (B1 or B2), or Canada service only (C1 or C2). The regiment accepted all three categories.

Many men joined their local unit with their friends, and many had been in the militia regiment for some years. In March 1942, George E. Findlay, managing director of Findlay's Limited, offered an incentive to help recruiting in Carleton Place. Findlay's would pay any of their men who enlisted and were sent to the mandatory two-week camp the difference between their army pay and the men's regular pay at the factory. This was a very generous offer.

Findlay's would pay up to fifty men $3 each per day, over and above their army pay when the plant was in operation and they were called to camp. If the call out came during the factory's regular shutdown period, it would pay each man $2 per day. (Normally, Findlay's did not pay its workers during the regular shutdown period.) Enlisted Findlay's men would then draw more pay than if they declined enlistment.

Getting their first taste of army life were Lanark and Renfrew Scottish soldiers Jim McKittrick, Gerald Lewis, and Bob Irvine. A large number of Carleton Place men, like Wilmer Camelon and Jim Pye, had already volunteered with other units. All these men met their deaths in Italy.

In March 1943, under Lieutenant Colonel J. McL. Beatty, the Lanark and Renfrew Scottish Regiment was mobilized for active service. It had already sent seventy-three officers and approximately 2,000 men to other active units, but it could now recruit for an overseas battalion that would stay together under its own name. This marked the first time the Scottish had been mobilized as a unit for wartime duties. During World War I, the 130th and 240th were recruited in Lanark and Renfrew counties, but both were broken up when they arrived overseas. Beatty would not accompany the regiment overseas. For medical reasons Colonel Percy H. Gardner, MC, VD, of Arnprior replaced him.

A recruiting office was opened in Carleton Place, seeking men of medical category "A" between the ages of nineteen and forty-five. A few local militiamen were at a four-day senior NCO school at the Pembroke armouries when news of the mobilization reached them. They were all appointed as NCOs in the active battalion.

Until 1943, World War II, as far as Carleton Place was concerned, was very much an air war. There had been three losses at sea — Horace Stark, Harry Porter, and Malcolm Forbes — but the rest of the men lost between 1941 and July 1943 had been air force. At the cenotaph on Remembrance Day 1942, as reported in *The Canadian*, Captain McBride of the local Salvation Army Corps read the names of the fallen. There were eleven names: Horace Stark, Cedric Cameron, J. F. Cranston, James Warren, Morris (*sic*) Fieldhouse, W. Robert Hughes, H. J. Findlay, Malcolm Forbes, R. J. O'Leary, E. E. Rothwell (*sic*), and A. E. Prendergast. Many of them had been killed in training accidents, although by 1943, both the navy and the air force had considerable battle experience. The army had not yet been involved in any operations, and there was a growing public demand for the Canadian army to see action and gain much needed battle experience.

The men in the army trained, trained, and trained again in England. The disaster in Hong Kong occurred at Christmas 1941, and the raid on Dieppe was mounted in August 1942. Thankfully, no Carleton Place soldiers were involved.

By 1941, there were three Canadian infantry divisions in England, augmented by two armoured divisions and two armoured brigades. With this number of troops, re-organization was required, and in 1942, the First Canadian Army was formed with two corps. The Canadians had prepared for an imminent German invasion of Britain that, fortunately, never happened. So they trained, and waited, hoping to spearhead any invasion of the continent.

Long stretches of inactivity and aimless activity are not good for morale. The Canadians marched miles in full wartime kit, dug World War I-type trenches, and manned coastal defences where they watched high-flying tiny aircraft locked in the Battle of Britain. Many wondered, privately and aloud, why they had left families, farms, schools, and jobs to sit around idly in England.

The First Division had arrived during the worst winter in fifty years. A serious influenza epidemic reminded them of the pandemic that signalled the end of their fathers' war in 1918.

Soldiers were sometimes billeted in comfortable British homes, but more often were stuck in primitive barracks without indoor plumbing and electricity. Some spent months in tents in remote locales. Some made the best of their situation, marrying local women and settling into local communities, but the Canadian was a reluctant soldier at best. While he was fearless and unmatched on the field of battle, he would become rapidly contemptuous of indifferent leadership and routine without object when deployed.

Disciplinary problems were widespread. Sit-down strikes occurred over the quality of food (British rations prepared by bored and untrained cooks) and military policemen had their hands full retrieving servicemen who were AWL. Canadians had a homing instinct for livelier surroundings. They quickly cleaved to the traditional British pub, and periodically brawls would erupt, spurred on by taunts from other units or from locals with the epithet that the Canadians were not "real fighting" soldiers, but only home guardsmen.

Chapter Eleven — Italy
Sicily — 1943

The great divide between waiting and action was July 10, 1943. On that day, soldiers of the 1st Canadian Division and the 1st Canadian Army Tank Brigade waded ashore, in neck-deep water, near Pachino on the island of Sicily. Since the previous April, Canadians had been training on the beaches and in the fields of Scotland for this moment. They went ashore as part of the 30th British Corps in the famous 8th Army led by General Sir Bernard Montgomery. Two task forces were to carry out the landings. The British Task Force mounted their assault between Syracuse and Pozzalo, while the American Task Force, led by Lieutenant General George S. Patton Jr., attacked the beachhead between Pozallo to Licata.

Sicily's main strategic importance was its airfields, which could be used to launch strikes at the mainland. The Strait of Messina, which is only eight to ten kilometres wide, separates Sicily from the "boot" of Italy, and located ninety kilometres north of Malta, it dominated Mediterranean shipping routes. In 1943, Sicily had a population of about four million, mostly living in the cities of Palermo, Syracuse, Catania, and Messina. The mountainous interior boasts the 3,000-metre-high Mount Etna, a volcano in the northeast leading down to a coastline of steep cliffs. Coastal roads were generally good, but the interior roads were narrow and twisting, usually with sharp switchbacks as they climbed the hilltops. Troop landings could best be made on the southern coastal plains.

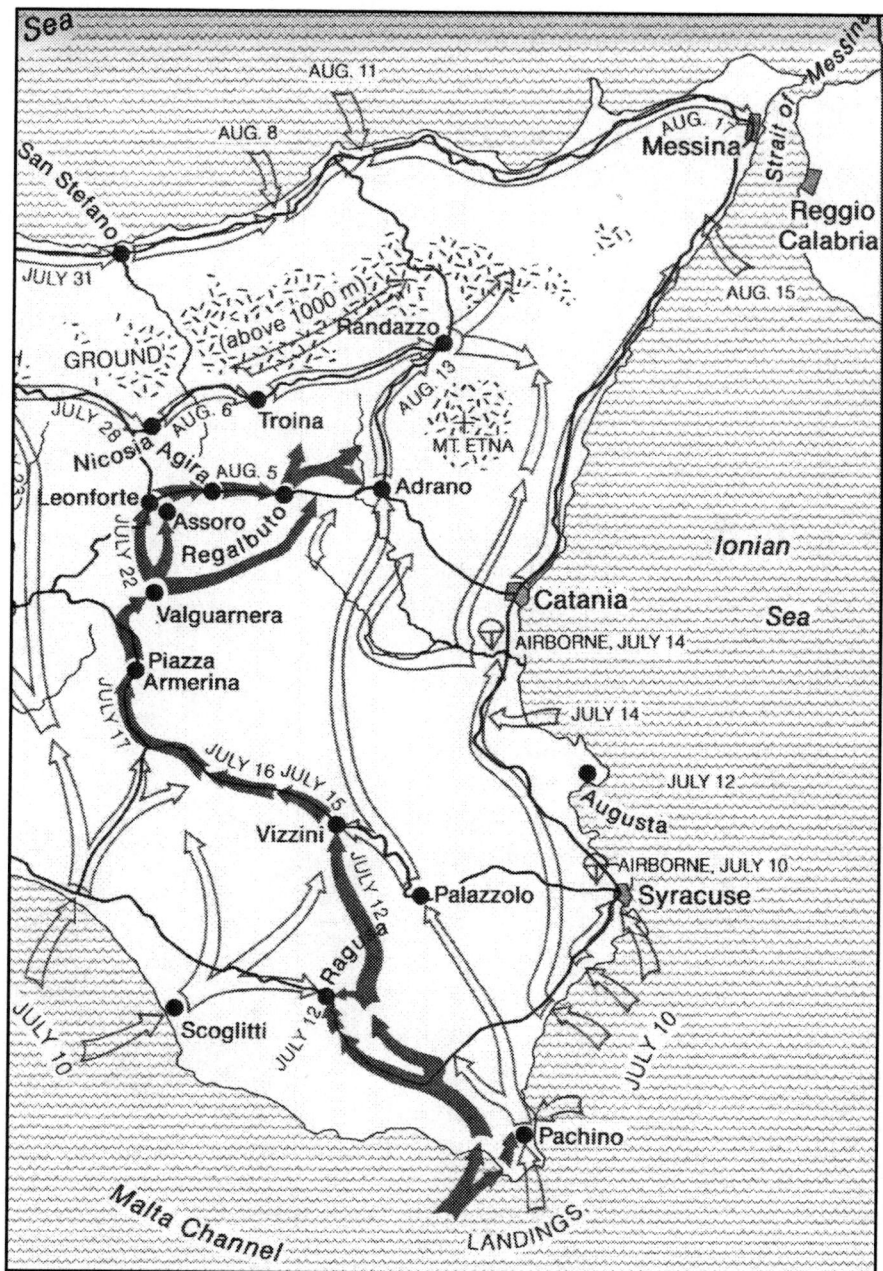

Showing the route of advance of Canadian troops from July 10 to August 17, 1943.

Code-named "Husky," the invasion was intended to take Italy out of the war and keep German troops occupied there so they could not be deployed to northwest Europe.

H 16455 Private Wilmer Camelon
Princess Patricia's Canadian Light Infantry

Wilmer Camelon's parents, David Camelon and Katherine E. C. McNab, were married in the United Church in Pakenham on December 15, 1896. They moved to Clayton where David took up mixed farming, growing mostly wheat. There they raised their children, David L., Mary B, and Wilmer. Two older sisters, one David's twin, died in infancy.

Wilmer was born on July 23, 1904, and took his early education at the rural school near Clayton. At age sixteen, having completed Grade 7, he left home to go west in search of work. He stopped in Manitoba and settled into employment as a farm labourer.

On November 27, 1939, Wilmer left his Alexander Street residence in Winnipeg and made his way to the recruiting office of the Princess Patricia's Canadian Light Infantry (PPCLI). Wilmer had barely time enough to be issued the new battle dress uniform, which had just replaced the First World War service uniform, when the battalion left, on December 17, for Halifax. With the Edmonton Regiment and the Seaforth Highlanders, they would form the 2nd Canadian Infantry Brigade as part of General A. G. L. McNaughton's 1st Canadian Division.

Aboard HMT *Orana*, the battalion left Halifax on December 21, spent Christmas at sea, and landed in Greenock on the Clyde on December 30. On a bitterly cold New Year's Eve, they arrived by train at the frozen Morval Barracks at Cove. The battalion settled in to a very busy time of training the new soldiers and receiving and issuing new equipment. Training with weaponry was only interspersed by hours of drill and miles of route marches. On January 17, 1940, Wilmer reported to sick parade with extremely sore feet. He was given a chit excusing him from wearing boots until his feet recovered.

In his early thirties, Wilmer was one of the oldest men in his section. He stood 5' 7" tall and weighed 131 pounds. His years of farm labour ensured that he was physically fit and could meet the conditions of medical category "A." The sun had left him with a permanently tanned and ruddy complexion, and he was described as having blue eyes and brown hair. His only visible mark was a scar on his left thumb.

Training was interrupted twice during this period. On January 24, George VI inspected the Patricias, and on February 10, for the first time in twenty-one years, the Colonel-in-Chief, Lady Patricia Ramsay, inspected her regiment.

The battalion moved to Scotland on April 18 and was issued equipment for operations in the north, in preparation for a planned assault on the Norwegian port of Trondheim. A week later, the raid was called off and the men were ordered to turn in their special equipment and return to barracks.

After the evacuation of the British Expeditionary Force from Dunkirk, the 1st Canadian Division was the only fighting unit in Britain equipped and ready to do battle. It was given the role of a mobile force to repel any invaders, and the Patricias were moved to Wotten Park near Oxford. On July 2, they were moved again to the Kentish Downs on the southern outskirts of London, and by the end of the month were re-located to Godstone, where they were to stay the better part of a year practising almost every facet of war operations.

Preparing for an exercise called "Heather" in August 1941 seemed to the troops to be too realistic for just an exercise. Wilmer was posted to a special "Force III" on August 3 and travelled by train to Glasgow where he and the others boarded the HMT *Empress of Canada*. The ship sailed that same day with none of the Patricias any wiser of their destination or their job when they arrived. On August 9, they were landed and marched to a camp at Inverary where they carried out mountain climbing and beach exercises. Four days later they returned to ship, went back to Glasgow, and by rail, back to Surrey. Exercise "Heather" was over.

It later became known that the Patricias and the Edmontons, who had also taken part in this "exercise," were in fact intended to carry out a raid on Spitzbergen. They were recalled when a much smaller expedition carried out the raid. Wilmer's records show that he was attached to "Duke's Camp" August 9 to 13 and then returned to the PPCLI.

By 1942, field exercises were much more frequent and the training was tougher and more realistic. It was often done with live ammunition. Mental and physical endurance were pushed to the limits. Medical records were updated, and the men were given the requisite large number of inoculations. On January 4, 1942, Wilmer reacted to the shots he had received and had to report to the aid station where he received a hot pack for his sore arm.

Pte. Camelon in England. Photos courtesy Merv Camelon."

The battalion was frequently bombed and strafed as the Battle of Britain raged overhead. During the summer of 1941, air raids occurred almost daily, and in August 1942, the battalion scored a victory by bringing down a Folke-Wolfe 190 with machine-gun fire, a feat the machine gunners repeated in February 1943.

Three months later, the battalion departed for Scotland for advanced amphibious training. A three-week period of mountain training preceded practice landings from the transport ship *Llangibby Castle*. Forced marches, hill climbing, and special weapons handling alternated with training on scramble nets and landing craft. Thompson sub-machine guns replaced the Sten gun, and the small two-pound antitank gun was replaced with seventeen- and six-pounders. A new, still secret hand-held antitank weapon, the projector infantry anti-tank (PIAT), was introduced.

On the evening of June 28, they sailed from the Clyde and joined a convoy heading south. The next day they learned they were going to the Mediterranean. Major General Guy Simonds, General Officer Commanding (GOC) the 1st Canadian Division, issued his Special Order of the Day:

> The new 1 Canadian Division will enter its first battle beside formations of the Eighth Army which have already had in this war the opportunity to add to great fighting traditions inherited from the past.
>
> We too have inherited a fighting tradition equal to that of any division in all the Armies of the British Empire. To enhance that record by a decisive success in our allotted task will require the full courage and skill of each one of us.
>
> Neither our friends nor our enemies doubt the courage of the Canadian soldier—our skill will be suspect until it has been proven in battle.
>
> We have spent over three years training for this meeting with our enemies. No formation going into its first battle has been more thoroughly prepared. With the cooperating naval

and air forces we form part of the best-found (sic) expedition that has ever set sail to invade a hostile country. We fight under commanders who have led the Eighth Army and 30 Corps through a succession of great victories.

It remains only to apply the lessons of our training under the stress of actual operations. I am not trying to tell you the task will be easy. War is not easy—it is a hard and bitter struggle—the ultimate test of moral and physical courage and skill at arms.

I do tell you that you will be launched into battle on a good plan which has been carefully rehearsed and that if you coolly apply what you have been taught during three years of preparation, success will be ours.

We are honoured in having units of the Royal Navy, the British Army and Royal Air Force cooperating with us in this, our first adventure, and I welcome them on behalf of all the 1 Canadian Division.

I wish each one of you good luck in the business of smashing the Italians.

By July 1, the troops were enjoying hot weather with pleasant breezes cooling the decks of the *Llangibby Castle*. The Patricias were enjoying their "summer cruise" and becoming quite accustomed to life aboard ship. Each day the sun dawned brighter and hotter as they travelled south. On July 4, they passed Gibraltar, hugging the north coast of Africa, and on July 9, Major D. Brain who, as a captain, led "B" Company ashore recorded the following:

... we R.V'd[1] with a great armada off Malta. Ships of every description were there:—former luxury liners, freighters, coasters, specially constructed M.T[2]. ships, cruisers, monitors, destroyers, motor launches, and assault craft of every description. The sea, which for ten days had been very calm, had now developed quite a swell under a strong offshore wind and everyone looked rather apprehensively at the assault craft, which were disappearing completely from sight behind high waves.

To take uneasy minds off the sea, most people went below ...

Following dinner, the decks were again crowded with people. As we moved closer to land, the sea became calmer as the wind had less chance to exert its full effect. The night

[1] Rendezvoused
[2] Motor Torpedo

was beautifully clear and one could make out quite clearly the other ships of the convoy in the moonlight. From the decks we could watch bombing on shore and the sparks as A.A[3]. shells burst above the target areas. Down below, fully half of the men were watching the display, while on the mess-decks men were making final adjustments to the fit and comfort of their equipment. All were confident and cheerful and I can honestly say that I did not meet a man who showed conscious signs of nerves. In one corner, the inevitable 'crap' game was in full swing.

Around 2300 . . . Groups were called to their assembly areas where a final roll call was taken before they moved off to their craft. Here the loading proceeded in a quiet and orderly fashion, and everyone sat quietly waiting until the ship reached her anchorage. At last the time came and out clattered the anchor with what seemed to us like far too much noise and much too many sparks. Then the order 'lower away.'

Despite a slight swell, we cast off without trouble and made our way to join the M.L. and the assault companies of other units at the R.V. When all were assembled there was a shout from the naval commander on the M.L.[4] and we got under way. From this time until comparatively close to shore, the men were allowed to stand to relieve the pressure in the cramped quarters of the L.C.A[5].

As we approached closer to shore, flares could be seen being put up by an enemy even more uncertain than ourselves as to what to expect. Machine gun tracer made very attractive patterns against the sky in the distance while on the shore every once in a while would appear a bright flash followed by quite a loud report as though someone were tossing grenades about.

The shore gradually became more clearly defined and the order was given for the craft to deploy. From this time on small arms fire was almost negligible but on touchdown the doors of the craft were let down (and) the men were disembarked into water well above their waist. In a few instances men landed in water six feet deep and had to abandon weapons and equipment and swim for it. Certain platoons were landed in a different order from that planned and

[3] Anti Aircraft
[4] Motor Launch
[5] Most likely an L.C.I, Landing Craft Infantry.

expected, while the S. of C[6]. who were to have been on our left, appeared later in the morning from well off to the right.

From our craft we made our way up a very sandy beach until we encountered wire, which held us up for some time. In the meanwhile, the enemy were tossing grenades amongst us. Fortunately the effect was almost entirely blast and no one came to grief, while a couple of 36 grenades tossed at the enemy succeeded in killing them. Finally the wire was cut and we made our way forward to find an M.G[7] post with two sentries whom we wiped out. A search of the huts near the post brought to light another Italian obviously just awakened by the noise as he had not yet had time to put on his uniform.

From this point we reorganized and made contact with 'D' Coy in the process of doing the same thing. The confusion of landing on strange country in the middle of the night against unknown opposition is almost impossible to describe. If, in addition you do not land at the intended spot or in the order that had been planned, you have a definite problem on your hands. However, after some time we did achieve a reasonable degree of order and commenced to advance to the initial objective that was reached without further opposition.

A short time later, Bn. H.Q. and the other two rifle coys who had had a somewhat more difficult trip ashore under shell-fire joined us. Once again all escaped without any casualties. On completion of the reorganization the coys moved off. The invasion for us had begun!

Private Wilmer Camelon landed in Sicily with "A" Company. The Italian defenders had no stomach for face-to-face combat, and the coastal positions were breached in a few hours. Marching inland through heat and dust was unusual for troops fresh from England, "A" Company encountered only weak resistance. After being cooped up on ship for the previous month, they were exhausted by the long marches that bothered them far more than the enemy. They also became burdened with an inordinate number of prisoners.

The 2nd Brigade was halfway across Sicily in a week when they ran into the efficient and motivated Panzer Grenadiers in the mountains. The Canadians, in the centre of the island and moving north, were ordered to take the town of Leonforte and then turn towards Mount Etna, the main concentration of German defences.

[6] Seaforths of Canada (The Seaforth Highlanders of Canada)
[7] Machine Gun

Leonforte is a typical Italian hill-town. The only approach was from a switchback road to the south, which angled down the face of a ravine, crossed a narrow bridge, then climbed the opposite side to the town's gates. Its entire length was in full view of the defenders who had, of course, blown up the bridge.[8]

By 2000 hours on July 21, "A," "B," and "D" Companies were in the low ground south of Leonforte, astride the junction of the roads from Valguenera to Leonforte and Enna to Leonforte. They were to provide a firm base from which the Edmonton and the Seaforth battalions would attack the town at 2100 hours.

The two battalions found the 15th Panzer Grenadier and Hermann Göering Divisions holding the town. In fierce street fighting, the Canadians became widely separated and finally lost all contact with their headquarters. No.3 Field Company of the Engineers was trying to build a thirteen-metre Bailey bridge across the ravine so tanks and anti-tank guns could be brought in. They needed infantry protection and at 0300 on July 22, "C" Company, which had been held in reserve, was ordered up to give covering fire to the Engineers. The road was swept by German machine-gun and mortar fire, but by 0430 the temporary bridge was intact.

At 0900, four Sherman tanks and four six-pounder guns, with men of "C" Company mounted on the tanks and guns and another platoon on foot, moved at high speed into the town. The mobile column came under machine-gun fire, but because of their speed suffered only one casualty. The tanks entered the town and the machine guns surrendered to the platoon on foot. The men were in high spirits when they discovered the headquarters unit of the Edmontons hunkered down in a wine cellar in the centre of town. They had been out of contact since the previous night.

About 0945, one of the Sherman tanks came nose to nose with a German Mk. III. The Sherman got the first shot away. However, the dead German tank now blocked the main street to any further advance by vehicles. "C" Company pushed on by foot until enemy machine-gun fire halted their advance. They seized the railway station, but their position was precarious since the Panzer Grenadiers held the high ground east and west of the railway. The rest of the battalion had begun moving forward.

Private Camelon with "A" Company rode up on the Sherman tanks and then went by route march into town. They halted on the south edge of Leonforte while "B" Company passed through them up the main street until they made contact with the pinned down "C" Company. At approximately 1330, Captain Brain, commanding "B" Company, ordered two of his platoons to take high ground held by the enemy and overlooking "C" Company.

[8] Jeffrey Williams, Princess Patricia's Canadian Light Infantry, 1914—1984, Seventy Years Service (London: Leo Cooper, 1972), p.46

They were hit by fire from heavy mortars, a tank, and a dual-purpose gun that caused seventeen casualties. "A" Company, with two three-inch mortars, moved up behind "B" Company.

The wreckage of the enemy tank had been removed, and Canadian tanks started forward. The leading tank just got abreast of "C" Company when the dual-purpose gun was hit. The two mortar detachments of "A" Company put this gun out of action while "A" Company prepared to attack. At 1520, supported by machine-gun fire, "A" Company made a spirited attack to the left of the hill. No. 7 Platoon surprised and cleaned out three machine-gun nests with grenades. No. 8 Platoon came under heavy machine-gun fire.

Private S. J. Cousins and two other men worked forward with a light machine gun to neutralize the German gunners. One Canadian was killed and another badly wounded. Private Cousins picked up the gun, charged the German post firing from the hip, and killed the five German crewmen. He dove to the ground, changed magazines, and repeated his performance on another machine gun, also killing its five gunners. With this, the entire enemy line collapsed. They retired and "A" Company took the ridge. Cousins was recommended for the Victoria Cross, but later that evening, while at his machine gun, friendly artillery fire made a direct hit on his position. He was subsequently Mentioned in Dispatches.

Leonforte was in Canadian hands, and by 1730 hours, their positions were secure. A regimental aid post was set up in the Leonforte hospital. The War Diary of No. 2 Canadian Field Surgical Unit records the following for July 22:

> We worked all night-until 1000 hours getting through six cases—most of them large ones—an abdomen, a compound femur and several multiple wounds, including a penetrating wound of knee joint and a sucking chest. It was very hot working but not nearly as hot as the following morning when we were trying to get our sleep.

During the night there was sporadic shelling but no counter attack was attempted. At first light, "B" Company moved forward to the left of "A" Company, and battalion headquarters moved into position behind "A" Company. Leonforte was won. The Patricias lost sixty-four soldiers killed and wounded.

Private D. Sinclair, Private S. J. Cousins, Private J. R. Scholey, and Private W. Camelon were buried just north of Leonforte on July 23. Subsequently, Private Camelon and his comrades in death were disinterred and reburied in the Canadian War Cemetery, which is located between Regalbuto and Agira, in the Commune of Agira. The graves of all Canadians

who fell in Sicily have been concentrated there. There are nearly 500 graves.

Along with the usual royal message of condolence, Wilmer's parents were sent his medals: the 1939–45 Star, the Italy Star, the Defence Medal, the War Medal, and the Canadian Volunteer Service Medal and Clasp. His War Service Gratuity amounted to $791.70 for his 1,296 days service.

The Canadian capture of Leonforte at the end of July marked the beginning of the end of resistance in Sicily. It took thirty-eight days to conquer Sicily. The Allies now had a base for air power to assist in an attack on the mainland, and they had also freed the Mediterranean from Axis dominance. In fact, the success in Sicily contributed to the downfall of Mussolini, meaning the Axis coalition had been broken.

Although the Italians capitulated on September 3, 1943—four years to the day after Britain went to war against Germany—the Allies did not have control of the country. The Germans seized power, so it was their troops the Allies would have to chase over mountain peaks and across swift flowing rivers. Flush with their first success in battle, the Canadian amateur soldiers were enthusiastic for invasion.

CHAPTER TWELVE — MORO RIVER 1943

The German troops began retreating across the Strait of Messina during the night of August 10-11, 1943. Similar to the British experience at Dunkirk, they had to use anything that floated—ferries, landing craft, motor launches, and barges—all were all put into service. That same day, August 10, L/Sergeant Jack Romanuke wrote to his parents in Carleton Place:

> . . . We have just finished another week of action in which we captured Regalbuto and Aderno. . . .We are at present resting in a lovely orange grove at the base of Mount Etna. We are surrounded by hills on all sides and one can get a marvellous view of Mount Etna in the distance. My only complaint is the heat, but we manage to have a swim in the Simets river not too far from camp. As I said before we are in an orange grove, but the fruit is very green and will not be ripe for some time yet. I did have a few oranges, pears and some grapes, but too much fruit is not good in the hot climate.
>
> Well, Mom, I have lost a little weight . . . [in] the hottest time you will find me reclining under an orange tree trying to rest but this I am unable to do on account of the flies. The evenings are nice and cool, but we are again pestered by mosquitoes.
>
> Cecil Whyte was around to see me the other day . . .
>
> Your loving son
> Jack

It was an orderly withdrawal, and three mobile German divisions managed to make good their escape to the mainland. They withdrew, essentially unhindered by the Allies, more than 55,000 men and all of their equipment. These troops got away to bitterly contest another day, every foot of ground as the Allied forces backed them up the boot of Italy. It remains a mystery why British and American commanders did not use their superior resources to trap and immobilize the Germans.

At 0430 hours on Friday, September 3, the day the Italians surrendered, the Canadians crossed the Strait of Messina in an operation named "Baytown." The 1st Canadian Division's objective was the town of Reggio di Calabria where they met even less resistance than they had on the beaches of Sicily. The Italians were out of the picture, and the Germans had taken the tactical decision that the area below Naples–Salerno was not to be defended. The Germans withdrew and established their defence in the mountainous, narrow central part of the country.

The Canadian advance was rapid. Within a week they were seventy-five miles inland. They captured Potenza on September 20, and then the 1st Canadian Infantry Brigade headed east to link up with the 1st British Airborne Division, which had landed at Taranto and was pushing up the east coast. So far, the Canadians had suffered relatively light casualties: 32 men killed, 146 wounded, and only 3 captured. But sickness was rampant. More than 1,500 men were suffering from malaria or jaundice (infectious hepatitis).[9]

On September 12, the Germans rescued Mussolini from prison and re-established him as leader of the northern Italian state controlled by German forces. However, by the beginning of October, the Allies had won Naples and Foggia, giving them a front line stretching the entire width of the peninsula. They continued their advance towards Rome on the west coast and Ortona on the east. But the Germans now decided to fight to hold Italy. They took their stand on a line from Gaeta to Ortona, cities about eighty-five miles apart. Known as the Bernhard Line to the Germans, the Allies dubbed the defensive position as the Winter Line.

An Anglo-American rift in command and control was developing. The British preoccupation with an invasion in Europe caused a lack of commitment to the Italian campaign. Without direction, General Montgomery despaired of the "haphazard and untidy" planning. His relations with the American commander, General Mark Clark, deteriorated rapidly after Monty claimed to have "saved the bacon" of Clark's Fifth Army at Salerno. Fortunately, Hitler and his crew were equals at dithering. It was not until November that the German General Staff decided to make a concerted stand.

The Eighth Army hit the German line hard at the Sangro River. As the attack went in the first snow was beginning to fall, but it soon turned to rain and the dust turned to mud. Several deep river valleys making defence far easier than offense cut the Adriatic coast. As soon as the Canadians fighting their way up the coast crossed a river, another deep gorge lay a few miles ahead.

North of the Sangro was the Moro River. The Germans repeatedly counter-attacked any advance made by the Canadians and some of the toughest fighting of the war occurred along the Moro. Often the Canadians were engaged in hand-to-hand fighting as they crept up towards Ortona.

[9] Daniel G. Dancocks, The D-Day Dodgers (Toronto: McClelland and Stewart, 1991), p.124.

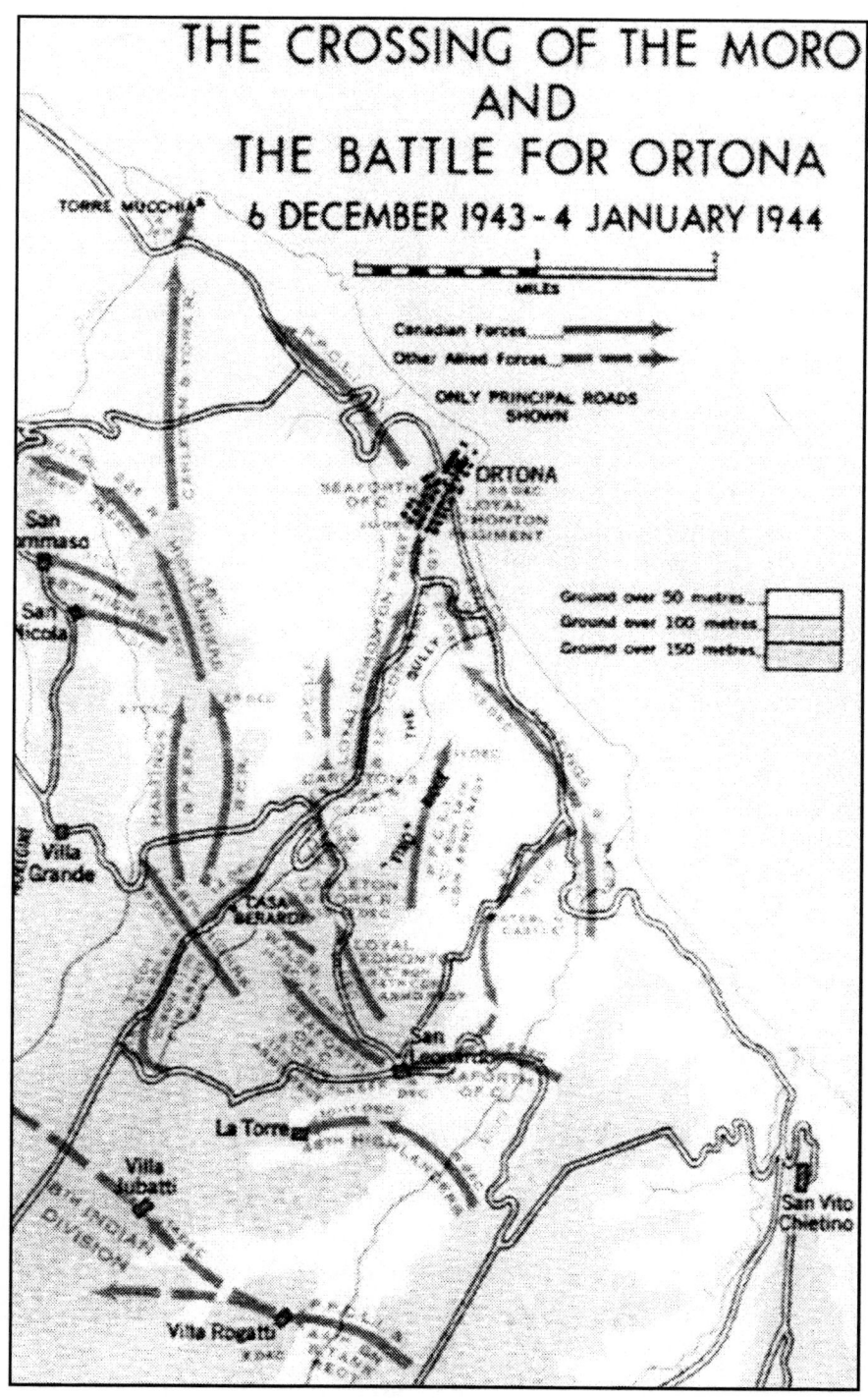

THE CROSSING OF THE MORO
AND
THE BATTLE FOR ORTONA
6 DECEMBER 1943 - 4 JANUARY 1944

C 79330 Private James Herbert McKittrick
The Seaforth Highlanders of Canada

Jimmy McKittrick was the third son born to Mr. and Mrs. John McKittrick. John worked in Kazabazua, Quebec, for the CPR, and Jimmy was born in Aylmer, Quebec, on April 4, 1906. In 1913, when Jim was seven, the family moved to 45 Moffatt Street in Carleton Place. He received his education at Carleton Place schools and then went to work in Findlay's Foundry.

While in school, Jimmy developed an interest in sport that he maintained throughout his life. He joined the Canadian Pacific Recreation Club and was an active member of the town's baseball and hockey teams. He also coached the Carleton Place Canoe Club paddlers during 1941. However, like many other young men in town, he responded to the call for militia recruits and enlisted into the Lanark and Renfrew Scottish. On May 21, 1942, he was taken on strength of "C" Company and accompanied the regiment to the Connaught Ranges for training. It was there that his attestation was formalized and he was accepted into the Active Force.

The Lanark and Renfrew Scottish was called to active service as a unit for the first time in its history on March 17, 1942. All recruits between the ages of nineteen and forty-five who could meet the medical standard of "A" were accepted.

Jimmy McKittrick in his hockey gear.

From the outbreak of World War II, the regiment had been employed as guards at county armouries; at the ammunition magazine, pump house and main gate of Camp Petawawa; and, since 1939, at an internment camp. In May 1939, it provided a personal bodyguard for Queen Elizabeth during the Royal Visit to Ottawa.

At age twenty-nine, McKittrick was found to be in excellent physical condition and was awarded medical category "A". He had a medium complexion, brown hair, and hazel eyes, and stood 5' 8" tall. The only visible mark on his body was a mole on his left hip.

Just prior to following his brothers into the forces, Jimmy was working from February to May at the National Steel Car and Aircraft plant in Malton, Ontario, as an enamel (paint) sprayer. He was near his sisters, Mildred (Mrs. Lyn Munshaw), Kathleen (Dolly), and Agnes (Mrs. Leonard Ashmore) who all lived in Weston.

The McKittrick family set a record for enlistments in this war with six of their seven sons donning the nation's uniform. Corporal Wallace (Wally) D. McKittrick was in the 1st Army Tank AWS RCOC; Trooper Edward (Eddie) R. McKittrick was in "A" Squadron, 11th Army Tank Battalion; Sergeant Roy N. McKittrick served in the ChofO (MG); Corporal John (Harry) McKittrick in the Royal Canadian Army Service Corps (RCASC); and LAC Kenneth (Bob) McKittrick served in the RCAF. Stanley, the seventh and youngest brother, lived and worked in Toronto. Defying all the odds, the family only lost Jimmy.

The Lanark and Renfrew Scottish trained in Ottawa and at Porter Lake near Sussex, New Brunswick. Jim McKittrick rose quickly through the ranks, being promoted to acting lance corporal three months after enlisting, on September 4, 1942. A month later, on October 9, he was promoted to acting corporal. Then, on November 29 while on sentry duty at Porter Lake, he "left his post without leave or permission from 0545 to 0808." He was charged with conduct to the prejudice of good order and discipline, a catch-all charge that would stick if nothing else would, and he was demoted to private.

Early in 1943, the battalion was sent to Halifax to await deployment overseas. Preparatory to sailing, everyone was given a number of immunization shots to ward off foreign sicknesses, and from January 16 to 18, Jim was sent on guard duty with a very sore and swollen arm due to a reaction to the diphtheria injection. Standing guard in the damp maritime climate gave Jim a case of chronic rhinitis that sent him to the Hazelhurst regimental aid post

in Dartmouth for a couple of days. He recovered and was attached to the 15th Coast Battery, Royal Canadian Artillery, for a week of guard duties from February 15 to 22, and then attached to the Halifax Military Hospital at Lawlor's Island from March 8 to 15. Finally, well trained in guard duties, he boarded his ship for England on March 27.

Jim McKittrick arrived in England on April 4, 1943, with the Lanark and Renfrew Scottish. After spending the summer in training, Jim was posted to the Seaforth Highlanders who were already in Italy. Jim sailed from England on September 12 and arrived at the port of Naples twelve days later. By the end of the month, he had caught up with the battalion near Foggia and moved with them into the hills on a push towards Volturara. German resistance stiffened as the battle moved into the narrowest and most rugged part of the peninsula. A particularly tough fight, and Jimmy McKittrick's introduction to the Italian war, came on October 6 when the Seaforth's fought a fierce and costly battle for the crossroads at Decorata.

Jimmie in his Seaforth's tropical uniform.

In July 1943 in another area of Italy, "A" troop of a Canadian Light Anti-Tank Regiment was moving towards Gratta Calda in support of the Royal 22nd Regiment. Light enemy machine-gun fire from two pillboxes set up a crossfire. Sergeant Elmer "Chip" Evoy, son of Milton Evoy of Carleton Place, was commanding No. 3 Gun. He immediately began counter-fire with alternate high-explosive and armour-piercing rounds. As the enemy concentrated on his gun, Evoy coolly and skilfully directed return fire. He never wavered in the face of unrelenting enemy action. For his valour under fire, Chip Evoy was awarded the Military Medal.[10]

---

[10] This was his first Military Medal. He was to win another for valour in action in Korea

The 2nd Brigade, composed of the Seaforth's, the PPCLI and the Loyal Edmonton infantry battalions, spent early November pushing the Germans across the Biferno River, which enabled the Canadians to set up a base in Campobasso. The city was secure and beyond the reach of the enemy's guns, so short leave was given to as many men as could be spared to enjoy the clubs and theatres that had been established in "Maple Leaf City."

With winter came heavy rains, which turned the area into a sea of mud. During the middle of November, so much rain fell that the Trigno and Sangro Rivers became quite swollen just as the Eighth Army attacked across from them. Normally placid, these rivers, which were almost as wide as Carleton Place's Mississippi, became raging torrents.

On the first of December, the heavy rain stopped and the skies cleared. At 0030 hours, the stars were brightly shining when the Seaforths moved across the Sangro River on footbridges that had been built by the engineers. The Seaforths were in the centre of the advance, attacking astride the road to San Leonardo. Facing stiff German resistance, their progress was very slow.

By December 4, under constant heavy shelling from the enemy, they moved towards the Moro River with the PPCLI on their right and the Edmonton Regiment on their left. They were able to consolidate the area they took in their advance, but were not able to stay for long. The battalion was then ordered to cross the Moro River to attack and take the town of San Leonardo. As if on cue, the heavy rain began again, raising the Sangro some eight feet and putting all the bridges either under water or washing them away. The Canadians were embarking on the bloodiest month in the Italian campaign.

Movement began about midnight on December 5/6. The Seaforths were supposed to clear Vino Ridge and then join the PPCLI for the advance to Ortona. The tanks of the 14th Armoured Regiment (The Calgary Tanks) carried the Seaforth platoons to the river on the back decks of the vehicles. The Germans spotted them going into the valley and increased artillery fire, meaning the Seaforths had a vicious fight to secure San Leonardo. A few tanks and small groups of men made their way into the town: the Calgary squadron commander, Major E. A. C. Amy, lost all but four tanks, while platoons only made it half way across the ridge before being forced to ground under murderous fire.

At 0100, "C" Company reported that they were slowly advancing under heavy enemy machine-gun and mortar fire. Runners from "A" Company reached battalion headquarters at 0200 with the news that they had suffered a number of casualties from the intense German opposition. They had lost their company commander and company sergeant major, while two of their platoons remained back on the southeast side of the river. Contact with the enemy continued throughout the night. Machine-gun bullets were constantly raking "C" and "A" Companies, and at 0715, "B" company reported that it, too, was receiving heavy enemy machine-gun opposition. At 0800, five prisoners arrived at battalion headquarters with a message that "B" Company was sending back many more prisoners. They had found a weak spot in the German defence and had made it as far as the hamlet of La Torre, but were unable to communicate with battalion headquarters.

The PPCLI moved up to the left flank of the Seaforths and by 0900 reported that they were making steady progress. There seemed to be no sign of any enemy counter-attack from the town of San Caldari, but a tank battle was being furiously waged. At 1000, "B" Company, under heavy enemy fire and mortar shelling, was in the process of cleaning up enemy opposition on their front. The battle was intense for both infantry and armour, but the Canadians continued to make a very slow but steady advance.

By 1400, the Seaforths' commanding officer ordered "D" Company, battalion headquarters, and the second platoon of "A" Company over the river to join the two companies already across. Just as they were preparing to move, a pitched tank battle developed and they had to hold their positions. "B" and "C" Companies formed a tenuous bridgehead across the river, then moved to their left to assist the PPCLI who were facing enemy concentration in the vicinity of Villa Roatti. They were promised that, during the night, mules would take up rations, including a rum ration. At 1900, "A" Company moved out to escort the muleteers transporting the rations to "B" and "C" Companies. It was dangerous work with the enemy watching their every move from the heights of the northern escarpment.

At 2000 hours, "B" and "C" Companies were ordered to withdraw to the south side of the river. They had killed many Germans, and "B" Company took prisoners back with them. During the night, the entire battalion moved to the right behind the Loyal Edmonton Regiment to try to exploit the bridgehead still held by the PPCLI.

Early the next morning, under relentless enemy shelling, the two companies were sent further back to the battalion headquarters area. "B" Company arrived by 1000 hours and reported having wiped out fourteen machine-gun posts and captured thirty-five prisoners. They also suffered one killed (Private James Herbert McKittrick), two wounded, and six missing.

The Seaforths were constantly shelled the entire day. By 1500 they were relieved by the 7th Punjab Battalion of the 8th Indian Division, and they moved off cross-country because the roads were so heavily shelled. That night they were issued rations, blankets, and their personal small packs;

Jimmy McKittrick's pay book.

however, their comfortable night's rest was disturbed when enemy shell fire hit another unit's vehicles causing them to burn brightly, giving the German gunners good targets to shoot at all night long.

Thirty-one-year-old James McKittrick was left behind on December 8, buried in Lanciano by the Presbyterian padre. His body was later exhumed and reburied in the Moro River Canadian War Cemetery, in the locality of San Donato, commune of Ortona, province of Chieti. The burial ground is situated on high ground overlooking the Adriatic coast. The Canadian Corps chose the site in January 1944, and it contains the graves of those who lost their lives in the fight to cross the Moro River and the street battle to take Ortona. There are more than 1,600 graves with fifty of them containing unidentified soldiers.

In its edition of December 23, 1943, *The Canadian* carried the news of Jim McKittrick's death:

> [He] was a young man with a keen sense of humor which made him very popular with all who knew him and it will be with deep regret that citizens of this town and district learn of his death.

On February 2, 1944, Jim's mother received a message from the king and queen expressing their sorrow. The next week, members of the Canadian Legion and the Mayor of Carleton Place, M. P. Morris, visited the McKittrick home on Moffatt Street. The mayor expressed sympathy on behalf of the Minister of National Defence, and President Kerr of the Legion presented Mary McKittrick with the Memorial Cross, offered by a grateful Dominion in remembrance of her lost son.

Jim's parents were sent a War Service Gratuity of $218.86, representing 564 days of service with 229 of them overseas. In a letter dated July 24, 1944, acknowledging receipt of the gratuity, Mrs. McKittrick wrote: "It sure is a sad loss to us as he was the life of our home."

Chapter Thirteen—The Fall of Rimini 1944

Following the Allied landings in France on June 6, 1944, it became even more important that the troops fighting in Italy continue to pin down German forces. In July, after two months' rest and recuperation in central Italy, the men wearing the red shoulder patches of the 1st Canadian Division were moved back to the Adriatic coast. As part of the re-organization of the Eighth Army, and to reflect the fact that the Italian campaign was more an infantryman's war than a tankman's war, the 5th Canadian Armoured Division was authorized to increase its infantry to two brigades. One of the battalions to be converted to infantry in the 12th Infantry Brigade was the 1st Light Anti-Aircraft Regiment, RCA, which was later designated the Lanark and Renfrew Scottish Regiment.

During the last week in August 1944, the entire Canadian corps attacked the eastern end of the Gothic Line, on the Adriatic coast just above the Foglia River and slightly north of Pesaro. Their objective was the town of Rimini.

Crossing the Foglia required many days of bitter fighting after the Allied air forces had "softened up" the concentrated German defensive positions. The river was crossed on Wednesday afternoon, August 30, but the German defenders opposed every step of the Canadian advance north.

The Foglia was just the first of a score of rivers to be crossed, and once over, the Canadians faced reinforced dugouts and trenches, Panther tank turrets embedded in concrete gun emplacements, anti-tank ditches, and belts of barbed wire. Flat areas north of the many rivers were thickly strewn with mines. Signboards sprouted everywhere with the deadly admonition *"ACHTUNG MINEN."* Stubbornly holding ground against the Canadians was the tough 1st Parachute and 71st Infantry Divisions.

In September, the long hot Italian summer ended with torrents of heavy rain. Within hours, roads rutted and choked with powdery dust became thick impassable quagmires, lazy steams became raging rivers, and tank progress became virtually impossible. All of which slowed the Allied offensive to almost a standstill. But on September 12, the weather moderated and the offensive was re-opened with renewed vigour.

On September 14, in an extraordinary display of courage, the Royal 22nd Regiment (R22Re) — the "Van Doos"— captured a 700-room mansion, the

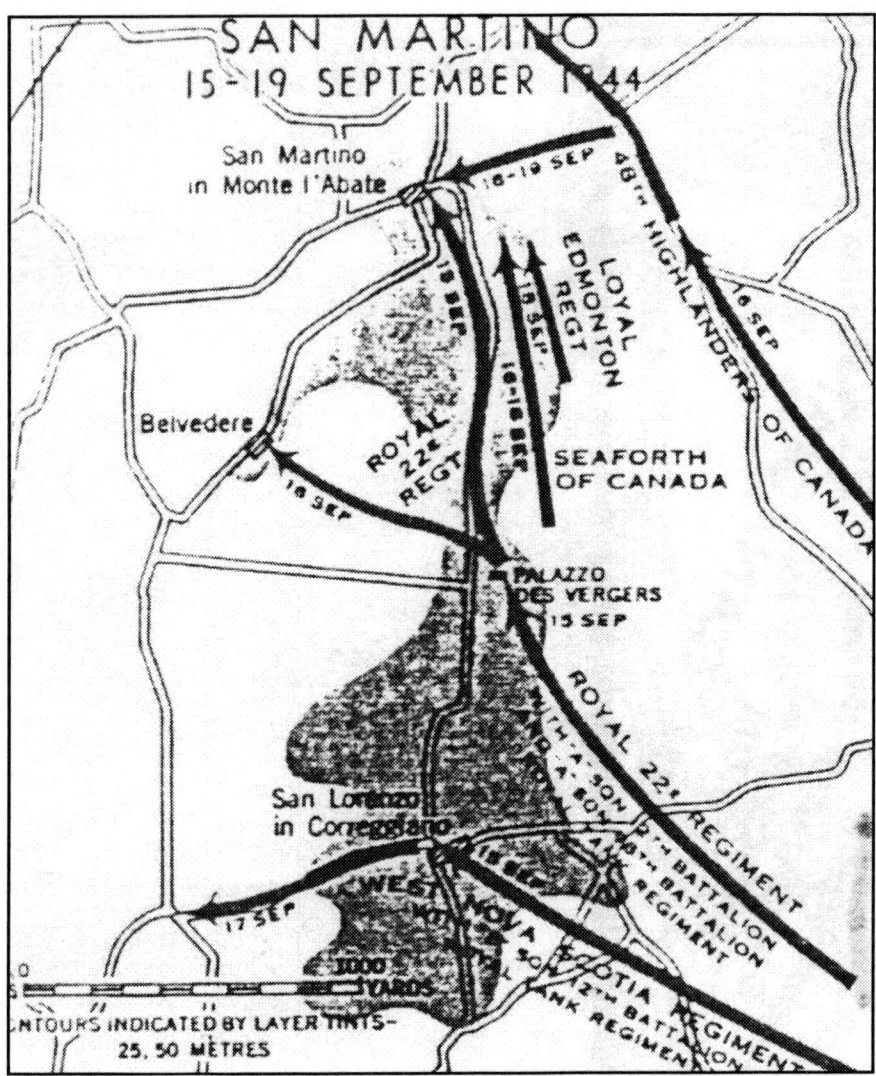

Palazzo des Vergers, in less than an hour and started for the town of San Martino. Braving heavy enemy machine-gun fire, they captured the town shortly after 1700 hours, and the Seaforth Highlanders of the Second Brigade were ordered to relieve the beleaguered French-Canadians. During the brief hiatus of the relief, approximately fifty German paratroopers moved back into the town. It took the Seaforths three days to recapture San Martino from Germans prepared to fight to the bitter end.

It was three more weeks of hard fighting before Allied troops entered a deserted Rimini.

C 100922 Private James William Pye
Seaforth Highlanders of Canada

Jim Pye was born in Appleton, the second son of Hilton Pye and Blanche Stringer, on July 6, 1922. Hilton worked at the Collies' Mill and the family lived in one of the company houses in Appleton. In 1934, the family moved the short distance into Carleton Place, where Jim was educated, but he left high school at age seventeen to help support the family of nine children. He completed Grade 10 except for French and Latin. While at CPHS, Jim was active in the Cadet Corps (1937-39) and participated in Boy Scouts (1936-38). He enjoyed playing ball in the summer and hockey in the winter.

After leaving school, Jim worked as a farmhand for a year and then was hired by the Collie Woolen Mill in Appleton. His older brother, Bernard, also worked in the mill[11], but began having trouble breathing due to the accumulation of lint in his respiratory system, so he, and about seven other employees, decided to join the army together. They were attracted to the pitch "Join the Army. Get a trade." The mill foreman was very upset, as this would severely handicap the mill's production, but Bernard brought Jim in as his replacement. Bernard spent the war in 3 Field Company, Royal Canadian Engineers (RCE).

Jim was trained as a weaver and worked at that job for two years, for $25 a week. Then, a month after his twentieth birthday, he joined the army. At his medical examination, he was found to be in very good health and fit for medical category A1, meaning he could serve anywhere he was required. The examining doctor noted that Jim was 5' 10" tall and weighed 151½ pounds. He was described as having grey eyes and brown hair with a medium complexion, and he exhibited a visible scar on the back of his left knee and one at the base of his left thumb. He reported that he had fractured his right wrist in 1938, but no residual disability appeared that would affect his army training.

[11] Bernard recalled that, when working in the mill, they were making army blankets adorned with an insignia of a circle with an arrow through it. He had no idea what that meant until he joined the army and was issued with one of those blankets. It was the mark of the War Department.

When Jim Pye enlisted on August 3, 1942, the interviewer described him as a pleasant, confident young man, if a bit reserved; he was subsequently sent on the Canadian Army Basic Training Course at Landsdowne Park in Ottawa. Jim originally joined to serve in the Royal Canadian Army Medical Corps, but there was nothing in his background to suggest he was suitable for becoming a medical orderly.

In October, after he completed his basic training, his officers suggested that he be reallocated to the RCE. However, the commandant of basic training,  after a review of Jim's qualifications, recommended that he should be employed as an infantryman with the Stormont, Dundas, and Glengarry Highlanders. He noted that Jim was an active young man whose previous employment in farming and as a weaver provided no background for engineering trades. The infantry, however, needed fit young men, so Jim was ordered to begin his infantry advanced training in Camp Borden on October 14.

But first Jim had other plans. He had applied to the commandant in Ottawa for permission to marry Jean Anne Morrison Cruickshank of Almonte. However, before they would grant permission, the army authorities wanted to know what he planned to do after the war (return to work at Collies), if he was in debt (no), if both sets of parents agreed to the wedding (yes), did his mother, who was receiv-ing his dependent's allowance, agree to the marriage knowing that her allowance would cease (yes), and did both the bride and the groom have written references attesting to their good character (yes). With all these criteria filled, Jim was allowed to get married on his next long weekend pass before leaving for Camp Borden.

On October 13, in the Presbyterian manse in Almonte, Jim and his best man, Lester Dowdall, waited with the Reverend Fowlie for Jean to appear. The pretty young girl, wearing a "poudre" blue suit with navy accessories and carrying a corsage bouquet of Talisman roses, hesitantly stepped forward. A lovely autumn afternoon greeted the newlyweds as they departed for a small reception at the home of the bride's parents, Mr. and Mrs. John Cruickshank. Since Jim only had a pass for the long weekend, the honeymoon was very short.

A month later, on November 16, Jim's mother, Blanche, passed away at the Ottawa Civic Hospital. She had been ill with cancer for over a year, and Jim was just glad that she had witnessed his marriage. Her oldest son, Bernard, a corporal in the army overseas, could not make it home, but the remaining seven children in addition to Jim (Lawrence, John, Constance, Phyllis, Margaret, Marjorie, and Edna May, all at home) stood silently at the gravesite and shivered in the cold, cheerless November afternoon.

Jim was granted fourteen days furlough and an additional three days New Year's furlough for the Christmas holidays in December 1942. He was also paid an additional 50¢ per day while on leave for a meal allowance. On December 6 he had been appointed acting lance corporal, and by February 1943, he had completed six months' satisfactory service so was awarded an increase in pay plus the promotion, on February 6, to acting corporal.

Jim was now training with his battalion, the Glengarrys, at Camp Borden, waiting to go overseas. He passed the unit first aid course in early March, but it appeared that the soldiers in Borden would have a long wait to join the battalion in Britain. Jim was being held as an  instructor at the infantry school, so in order to be closer to his now very pregnant wife, he moved Jean to the Birchcliffe area of Toronto. On April 12, a darling daughter, Carol Anne, was born.

After a long, hot summer of instructional duties at Camp Borden, Jim was warned that he would be going overseas in the fall. He was granted annual leave from September 13 to 26 and then an additional special leave from September 30 to October 4. (He used this time to get his affairs in order prior to embarkation.) On November 25, Jim was given four days special leave and notification of his posting to No. 1 Training Brigade at Debert, Nova Scotia, to await shipment overseas. To get overseas he had had to revert to his original rank of private.

In less than a year, the wilderness area of Debert had been turned into an army city housing some 12,000 men. The Engineers had cleared the forest, built roads, and installed electrical and water systems. And while the soldiers waited, their training continued. They learned to drive the Universal, or Bren Gun, Carrier, a small, tracked, lightly armoured vehicle that could travel cross-country and had a multitude of military uses. They learned the art of camouflage and practised firing Bren guns and the 3" mortars.

The Canadian Volunteer Service Medal awarded for eighteen months' service.

Jim was awarded his Canadian Volunteer Service Medal on February 3, 1944 (he received the clasp to this medal when he arrived overseas), and on February 16, he embarked at Halifax for England. He landed on February 24 and was assigned to the Canadian Infantry Reinforcement Unit (CIRU). Meanwhile, Jean and Carol Anne moved back to Carleton Street in Almonte to live with her parents and wait for Jim's return.

A month later, on March 27, Jim was sailing for the Mediterranean theatre and a posting to a new regiment, the Seaforth Highlanders of Canada. He arrived in Italy on April 9 and was sent to join his unit at Avellino. Brother Bernard had been in Italy with the Engineers for some time, and when he heard of Jim's arrival, he borrowed a motorcycle and went to Avellino to find him. The infantry were living in slit trenches, Bernard recalled, because they were constantly being strafed and bombed by German Stuka dive-bombers. Although Bernard's 3 Field Engineers worked close to the Seaforths, building bridges for the infantry and tanks to cross the many rivers in their paths, this was the last time he would see Jimmy.

The 1st Canadian Corps, with the 1st Canadian Division and the 5th Canadian Armoured Division, began fighting their way north up the eastern coast of Italy. The object was to rid the Gothic Line of its German defenders. On August 30-31, the Division began moving across the Foglia River and picking its way through the minefields. By 1730 hours on the 30th, "B" and "D" Companies had gone down the slope to the river and forded it easily. Once across, "D" Company mounted the tanks of the Royal Tank Regiment and was taken over the shell-torn, littered battlefield to Osteria Nuova. They dismounted and, in concert with the armour, pushed over the hilly secondary roads until heavy German artillery checked their advance.

"B" Company swung too far right after crossing the river valley, ending up in the small town of Borgo Santa Maria. The Germans still held the town, and the Seaforths found themselves under intense opposition from them in addition to a severe pounding from their own mortars and artillery.

Entering the town with their tanks, "B" Company was engaged in very close fighting, but by the end of the day, they had taken twenty-one prisoners.

The Royal Tanks led "D" Company's slow advance, the tanks softening up the Germans for the following infantry. One troop swung right between Pozzo Alto and Borgo Santa Maria where they found and put an enemy anti-tank gun out of action causing some fifty casualties among the enemy's 1st Parachute Division.

There was little sleep for this group of infantrymen and their supporting tanks. They had managed to get behind the enemy's main defences, and their own front and right flanks were under continuous fire from a shaken and disorganized, but very obstinate, enemy. The Seaforths continued their advance under cover of darkness to take the town and the high ground just to the northeast. Opposition lessened and at 0900 on September 1, the Seaforths took the village. "D" Company and its tanks immediately set off to capture the hill beyond. By noon, "A" and "C" Companies came up to Pozzo Alto where Lieutenant Colonel Thomson, the battalion commander, established his tactical headquarters.

The 1st Division, reinforced by a Greek Mountain Brigade, continued to fight their way across the Marano River towards Rimini. Tenacious German paratroopers held one final hill, a finger of high ground crested by the village of San Fortunato. Just over five miles inland lay the tiny independent republic of San Marino. It occupied the top of a mountain, the sole remaining vestige of mediaeval Italy's sovereign cities.

Half way between the Canadians' position on the Marano River and their objective of Rimini was the village of San Martino, on the northern slope of a low hill. The village was held by German troops deeply dug in and protected by artillery situated on the heights of San Fortunato. From this elevation, the gunners rained a torrent of high explosives on the village and its attackers.

The Seaforths had enjoyed a twelve-day rest at Cattolica[12]. On September 15, racing ahead under fierce fire, the Van Doos captured San Martino. That same afternoon, the Seaforths set up battalion headquarters across the Conca River near the partly destroyed village of Santa Maria, so that, the next day, the Seaforths could relieve the Van Doos in San Martino prior to attacking the heights of San Fortunato. They had been told that the enemy infantry was fairly thin on the ground, but the artillery put up harassing fire that was more sustained and heavier than any the Canadians had previously encountered. Fortunately, despite the heavy shellfire that lasted during the all-night advance, casualties were reported as light.

[12] Much of the information regarding this attack was taken from a report "The Action Which Led To The Fall of Rimini, Sept 16/20 Incl." found in the battalion War Diary at the National Archives. The author is unknown but it was likely a report by the Intelligence Officer.

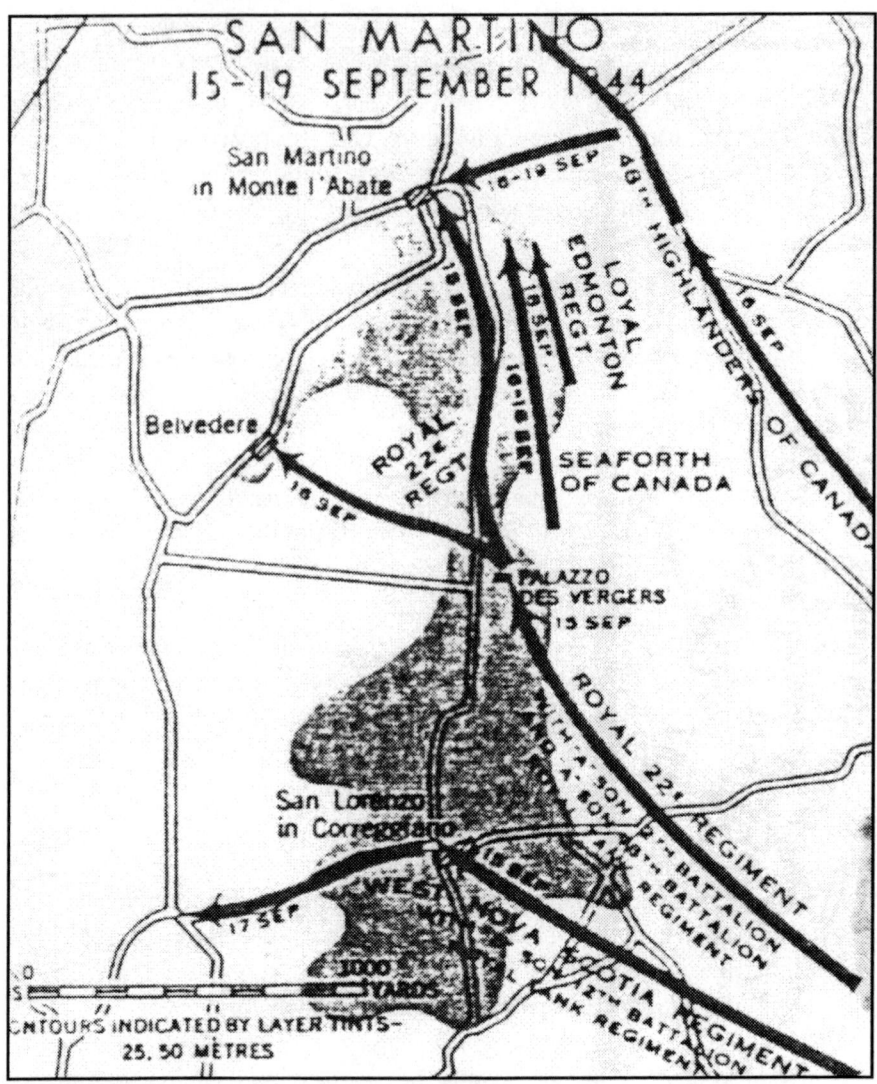

At 0600 on September 16, "B" and "D" companies moved through Santa Maria towards San Martino, followed by "A" and "C" companies. They expected San Martino to have been cleared by the Van Doos, but through an error, either the French-Canadian battalion withdrew too quickly or the Seaforths went to the wrong positions. Subsequently, San Martino was left vacant long enough for fifty German paratroopers, with eight to ten mortars, to move back into their positions. "B" Company came under totally unexpected enemy fire and had to go to ground on a small ridge overlooking the town. "C" Company followed. Both had to dig in as they came under heavy shellfire.

San Martino only had about a dozen houses, but the Germans had transformed each into a pillbox. Concrete cellars provided shelters that only a direct heavy artillery shell could penetrate. Most of the Canadian tanks were knocked out and only a handful of Seaforths made it into town.

"D" Company had contacted a guide from the R22eR and was directed to a large house with very thick walls. It had so far proven impervious, even from many direct hits by enemy artillery. This was the Palazzo des Vergers, in the deep cellar of which the Van Doos had set up their headquarters.

"A" Company took up a nearby position and with them came the 3-inch mortar platoon. By 0900, battalion headquarters had moved forward to a damaged powerhouse. This building was in full view of the enemy and was severely shelled. Minor casualties were suffered, but the commanding officer's jeep took a direct hit. By 1600, the Seaforths, after a bitter battle in which they learned the paratroopers had no thoughts of surrender or retreat, were driven back.

2 Canadian Infantry Brigade headquarters urged the Seaforths to proceed with their attack on San Fortunato. The battalion's commanding officer made it known to brigade that any further advance was impossible until San Martino was neutralized. Battalion headquarters and the regimental aid post were established in the Palazzo for the night. Four soldiers were killed and seventeen wounded in the day's operations. Early next morning, while out on reconnaissance, the machine-gun platoon's captain was killed by a mine.

During the night, patrols were sent out by each company. "D" Company patrols tried twice to bypass the town, but were unsuccessful both times. "A" Company penetrated a short distance and located two enemy machine-gun posts that they could not get past. "B" Company discovered San Martino was held in force with the assistance of Tiger tanks. A patrol of infantry scouts, tank representatives, and engineers went looking for a suitable place to cross the river but found none. It seemed the Germans had assembled the greatest artillery strength in Italy, and with a seemingly unlimited supply of shells, they kept up a barrage causing a steady stream of casualties to flow through the aid post. In the flickering red and yellow light of burning buildings and haystacks, stretcher parties collected the dead and wounded. Many support vehicles were damaged, but replacements for the mortars and anti-tank guns were readily available.

At 1330 on September 17, Allied artillery opened up concentrated fire on the German strong point of San Martino. After twenty-five minutes, the barrage lifted and "A" and "C" Companies moved off for an assault. Supporting them were two troops of Churchill tanks and two troops of Shermans. As soon as they moved, they invited heavy machine-gun fire. The tanks could

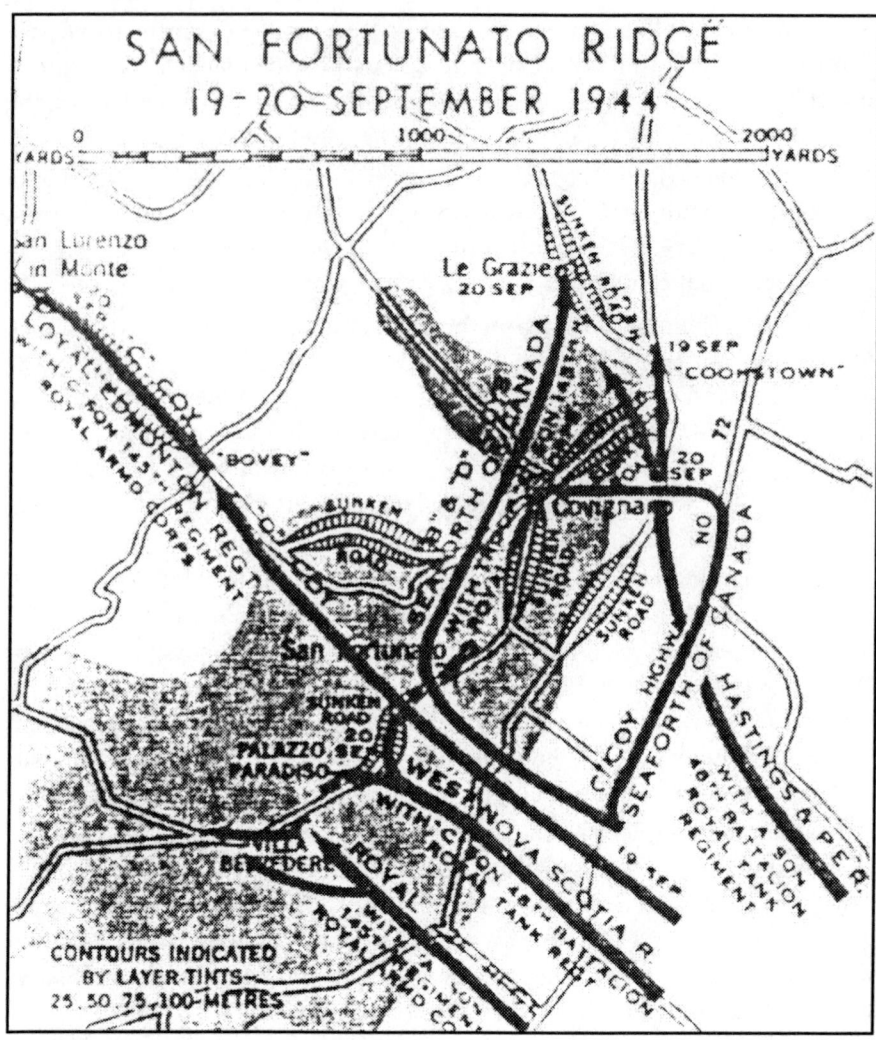

not locate the machine-gun nests and themselves took heavy casualties from anti-tank guns and *faustpatrones*.[13] Infantry casualties were heavy.

"A" Company managed to get within fifty yards of the village, but their losses, including the company commander, forced their withdrawal. The Germans were calling in their artillery on their own well dug-in positions. This was a very effective tactic and by 1600 the attack had to be abandoned.

The Seaforths' forward fighting strength had deteriorated considerably. The supporting armour had taken such losses that they were no longer an effective fighting force. The position was grim, and as a counter-attack seemed certain, a tank squadron attached to the PPCLI was brought up to aid

[13] Literally an "armoured fist," a "faustpatrone" was the German 88-mm anti-tank rocket launcher. It was their version of a bazooka, a lethal anti-tank weapon that could be carried and fired by a single soldier. A simple steel tube, the trigger operated an electrical firing mechanism that propelled a hollow charge rocket up to 130 yards.

in the defence of the Palazzo. "B," "C" and "D" Companies consolidated positions on the slight crest while "A" Company returned to its previous position on low ground behind the Palazzo. Once again, stretcher parties combed the battlefield for the wounded that were taken to the aid post of the 48th Highlanders.

At midnight, "B" and "D" Companies were ordered in for a further attack. However, they came under such murderous machine-gun crossfire that they had to retire. They tried another approach, but it too met the same fate.

The following day, September 18, the enemy continued heavy and sustained shellfire. No one could approach or leave the battalion area without drawing attention from the German gunners. The companies held their positions all day, and at 1800, were ordered to withdraw and regroup. They had taken so many losses that companies were organized with only two platoons[14].

During the night, the paratroopers withdrew, and the next morning, the 48th Highlanders walked into a deserted village where they discovered an underground strong point with five-foot-thick concrete walls. Three tunnels led to observation points where the Germans, using high-powered telescopes had a perfect view of the entire Canadian sector of operations.

On September 20, the Loyal Edmonton Regiment led the attack against San Fortunato. The Seaforths then moved through the Edmontons to exploit their success. However, as they moved forward, they were frequently pinned down by enemy fire, but by noon, it became evident that the Germans had decided to abandon this commanding feature. The Seaforths began to collect prisoners, the abundance of which soon became an embarrassment as they affected the battalion's mobility. Canadian artillery caught many retreating Germans in the gullies running down to the Marecchia River. Ultimately, three companies turned in 214 prisoners of war and estimated at least that number of enemy dead.

That evening, the Hastings and Prince Edward Regiment (H&PE) relieved the Seaforths. Heavy rain had set in, but they found houses for shelter. On September 21, the PPCLI exploited the Seaforths' success and crossed the Marecchia, consolidating their hold on the junction of Highways 9 and 16. The evening of September 22, Lieutenant Colonel S. W. Thomson, DSO, MC, the commanding officer of the Seaforth Highlanders, received the following personal message from 8th Army Commander, General Sir Oliver Leese:

> My congratulations to you and all ranks of your battalion on your hard fighting at Pozzo Alto and S. Fortunato. The regiment may be proud of its part in a great and hard-fought victory. With my thanks and best wishes to you all. Well Done Canada!

[14] Three platoons of 33 men each is the normal strength of a company.

On the morning of September 23, the battalion's personnel carriers were brought up and they retired to rest billets in Cattolica. However, they left buried in Italian mud four officers and thirty-seven other ranks; twenty-two other ranks were missing, mostly two sections of 15 Platoon that were cut off during the attack of September 17. Five officers and eighty-four other ranks were out of the line with wounds.

Bernard Pye was busy building a bridge near San Martino when a comrade stopped to tell him that there was a plain wooden cross a short distance back with the name "Pye" on it, but no other details. Bernard went back and found Jimmy's dog tag hung from the arm.

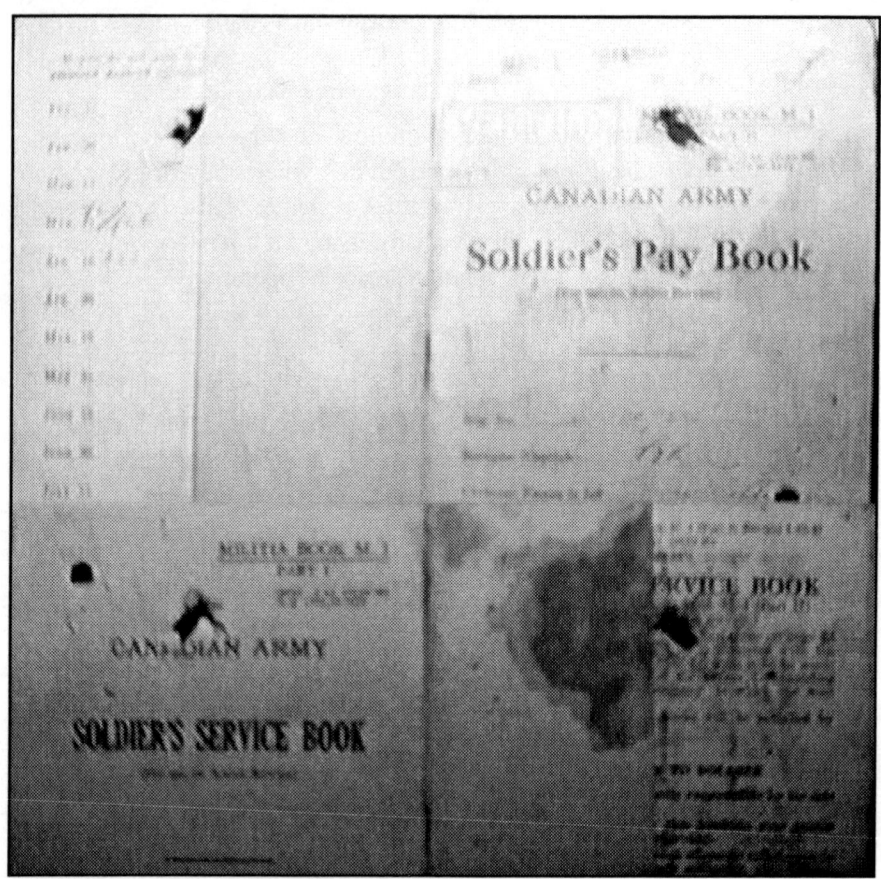

Jim Pye was first listed as missing and then killed in action. His wife, Jean, received his War Service Gratuity of $270.68, a Memorial Cross, and a letter of condolence from the king. He had served 777 days in the army, 214 of them overseas. Among Jim's effects were his gold signet ring, a penknife, his Ronson lighter, and two harmonicas. Jim's mother Blanche, whose death was unknown to the army, was also sent a Memorial Cross.

Private James William Pye is buried in Coriano Ridge War Cemetery, 3.5 kilometres west of Riccione, a seaside resort on the Adriatic coast. The ridge was the last important feature barring the autumn 1944 Allied advance up the Adriatic coast. Its capture was the key to Rimini and eventually the Po River. The fighting for this ridge, on which sits San Fortunato, was the heaviest since Cassino. Nearly 2,000 World War II casualties are commemorated at this site.

r.mullan@sympatico.ca

CHAPTER FOURTEEN—MURDER MOST FOUL

Is it possible for murder to occur during wartime? How does murder differ from killing the enemy? If one kills in the pursuit of illegal activity or for personal reasons, how does that equate to one who kills in the heat of combat?

D 117248 Craftsman Gerald Lewis
Acetylene Welder
Royal Canadian Electrical and Mechanical Engineers

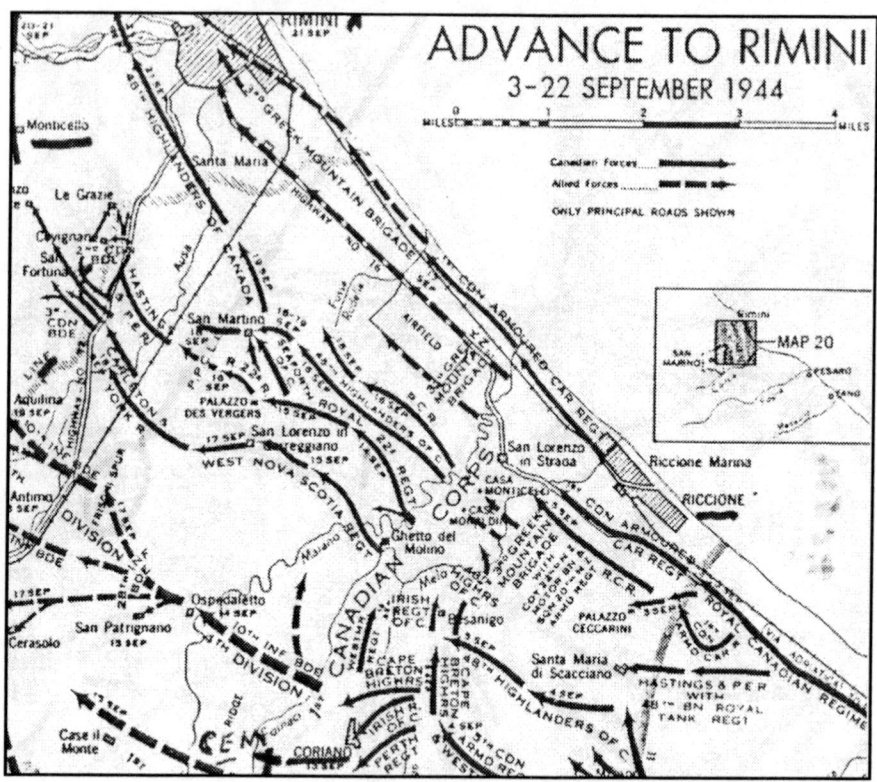

When Gerald Lewis went off to war, his mother must have suffered more than the usual anguish and trepidation. For Jane Lewis it was *déjà vu*. She had sent two sons to the Great War and now had to suffer another son's departure. Robert was wounded in World War I and then, on August 10, 1918, at the age of seventeen, Walter was killed during the battle for Amiens[15]. Gerald, who was born in Carleton Place on January 13, 1920, never knew his older brother.

---

[15] See Larry Gray, "Canada's Hundred Days" We Are The Dead (Burnstown: General Store Publishing House, 2000), pp 223 to 228, for details of Walter's life and death.

Gerald was baptised in the Church of England, received his education at Carleton Place schools, and was trained as a welder, a trade he pursued at the Findlay Foundry. Known as Gerry to his friends, he was an active athlete and a bit of a scrapper with the scars to show for it: a small one on his left cheek, one on his right ear, and another on the right knee. He had also suffered the normal childhood measles and chicken pox.

Just prior to enlisting in the active army, Gerald spent two weeks training with the militia, so at his enlistment medical examination, he was recorded as being 5' 8" tall, weighing 137 pounds, and with good physical development, which resulted in an "A" classification. He was also described as having a medium complexion, dark blue eyes, and brown hair.

On March 19, 1941, Gerald joined No. 4 Army Field Workshop of the Royal Canadian Ordnance Corps (RCOC) at their Westmount (Montreal) recruiting depot. He was twenty-one years old. A skilled acetylene welder, he was transferred to the Light Aid Detachment (LAD) and sent to Camp Borden for basic army training. His trade as a welder meant that he had only to complete basic military training to be posted to an operational unit.

One of Gerald's first considerations was his widowed mother. His father, John Edwin, died four months before Gerald enlisted. He assigned $20 from his pay to her in April 1941 and increased the assignment to $30 in February 1943.

By the end of July, Gerry was considered trained and ready for duty overseas. He was given six weeks embarkation leave—a considerable amount—and was ordered to report to Halifax early in September. He departed for England on September 15, and after an uneventful crossing, disembarked at Liverpool on September 29. He was given a few days "landing leave" and told to report to his new unit, No. 65 LAD at Bordon.

In January, Gerry was sent on an advanced welding course, and graduated on February 5, 1942, as a Group B acetylene and electrical welder, which also meant a pay increase. On February 12, he was posted to the 2 Canadian Armoured Brigade Ordnance Company to use his skills in repairing and modifying tanks. But it was not until October that he was sent on course to learn armoured plate welding.

During the summer of 1942, boredom with the army and army life in England began to set in among all the Canadian troops stationed there. They had been training for years to no visible purpose, so Gerry decided to take some unauthorized leave. He went to London on November 18, and after only two hours away, was apprehended on Trafalgar Street by the military police. Since he had been AWL such a short time, he received only an admonishment from his commanding officer and a notation on his conduct sheet.

Gerry tried again on December 1, failing to show up for the 1300 daily parade; he was caught again, this time being AWL for three and a half hours. Although it was still a minor charge, the fact that it was a second offence meant he was confined to the lock-up in the guard room. However, after three hours, Gerry escaped. He was quickly captured and charged with "escape from confinement," and sentenced to twenty-eight days field punishment and twenty-eight days forfeiture of pay, including his Group B trades pay. His commanding officer ultimately reduced the sentence to twenty-one days for each penalty, and Gerry spent Christmas 1942 restricted to camp and performing field punishment duties.

Reinstated as a Group B welder, Gerry was transferred to 5 Armoured Brigade Workshop on January 29, 1943, where he soon got into trouble again. On February 26, Gerry found himself in a war of words with a corporal. He then grabbed the corporal as he was getting out of a vehicle and drove his fist into the corporal's face. This cost him another twenty-one days field punishment and loss of pay. But he still didn't learn his lesson.

On May 29, 1943, Gerry was sent to a Royal Engineers' drill hall to participate in a welding demonstration. He overstayed his return to his base by thirty-one hours so was sentenced to seven days confinement to barracks and loss of pay. Outwitting the Provost must have become a game because on July 11 he went "over the hill" for thirteen hours for which he was fined one day's pay and seven more days confined to quarters.

In August, Gerry went to the brigade workshop for a welders' refresher course, and in early October, he was warned to prepare to go Italy. Granted embarkation leave, Gerry took it in London. Although he had sprained his ankle on October 14, it did not prohibit his pre-departure partying, which caused him to overstay his leave by nearly two hours, so he was charged again for being AWL and, to add to his misery, with conduct prejudice to good order and military discipline (i.e. he was drunk when apprehended in Trafalgar Street). On the first charge he lost three days pay and on the second he received an admonishment from his commanding officer, as he had no previous charges of drunkenness and he was scheduled to depart the area.

Three days later, on October 23, Gerald sailed for Italy. He landed on November 10 and reported to his new unit. However, by Christmas, Gerald was sentenced by a general court martial to 120 days detention and 129 days loss of pay. His record is mute as to the charges, but they had to have been severe to merit the convening of a court martial. On March 10, Gerry was released from custody at the detention barracks with a remission of forty days from his sentence.

On May 15, Gerald was transferred from the RCOC to the Royal Canadian Electrical and Mechanical Engineers (RCEME) and reinstated as a welder Group B with his trade's pay of $2 a day. He was posted to the 70 Light Aid Detachment, which was attached to the 8th New Brunswick Hussars of the 5th Canadian Armoured Regiment.

During the night of July 3, 1943, Corporal Greenham of 71 Company Military Police was on patrol along Route 6 about 9.5 kilometres south of Rome when he saw a body lying face down on the right hand side of the road. It wore the uniform of a Canadian soldier so Greenham radioed for an ambulance. Examination of the man's identity discs and sleeve patches revealed that it was Private Gerald Lewis of the 5th Canadian Infantry Division. There was no money or other identification in the man's pockets, but the military policeman did find a sandbag containing a quantity of .303 calibre ammunition about fifty yards north of the body.

The ambulance quickly took the body to No. 48 (British) General Hospital, where the medical officer confirmed that the Canadian soldier was dead. Suspecting that Lewis had been the victim of a vehicle accident, the military policeman canvassed all units in the area, but none had any reports of an accident during the night. He also returned to the scene but discovered no marks on the road near the body.

An autopsy revealed a fractured skull with abrasions to the left temple, cheek, and side of nose. The right eyelid was bruised and the right frontal area depressed; the right forearm and the back of the right hand were bruised, probably when he tried to defend himself; and the right thigh and left knee had abrasions. The examiner recorded a grossly fractured skull with widespread contusions and haemorrhage, typical of a crush injury. These findings were recorded on July 4, the date entered as Gerald's date of death.

Gerald Lewis had been on leave in Rome at the time of his death. There were no other members of his unit with him so there was no one who could shed any light on the fatality. At the hospital, a search of his effects uncovered 140 Italian lire, a cigarette lighter, and two packages of cigarettes, while Lewis was wearing a souvenir bone signet ring and his identity discs. His mother later claimed that he should also have been wearing a gold wrist watch attached by a leather band with his name and service number engraved on it. With this attractive watch and most of his money missing, and no evidence of a vehicle accident, it was widely believed that Gerald Lewis had been the victim of a mugging.

Craftsman Gerald Lewis is buried in the Rome War Cemetery beside the Aurelian Wall of the ancient city of Rome. The cemetery was started short-ly after the occupation of Rome in June 1944, and the graves are mainly those from the city garrison, but a few bodies were brought in from the surrounding countryside. The cemetery has more than 400 graves, including soldiers and airmen who died in Rome as prisoners of war.

Gerald's mother, Jane, received the Memorial Cross on October 11, 1944. She was paid his War Service Gratuity of $616.31 representing pay and all allowances for 1,056 days service, of which 869 were spent overseas. Gerald was survived by his brothers, Robert, who was wounded in World War I and was living in Vancouver; John Wilfred, in Victoria; Harold Cummings, serving at Barriefield in the RCOC; and his five sisters: Hilda Ethel (Mrs R. E. Keays) in Carleton Place; Ellen Jane "Nellie" Lewis, a registered nurse in Greenwich, Connecticut; Bessie May (Mrs. J. D. Stone) of Niantic, Connecticut; Marjorie Isobel (Mrs. H. W. Smallwood) of Toronto; and Grace Gertrude (Mrs. William Prendergast) of Malton, Ontario.

C41324 Sergeant Robert David Irvine
Canadian Provost Corps
1st Line of Communications Provost Section

It seems only appropriate that Bobby Irvine served his country in the Provost Corps. He was the son of Christopher R. Irvine, who was the Chief of Police and indeed the only policeman for many years for the town of Carleton Place, and his wife Maude. But Robert did not join the armed forces to be a military policeman.

Robert David Irvine was born in Carp (South March), Ontario, on June 21, 1922, however, he was baptised David Russell Robert Irvine. "Robert" was his father's middle name, and "David Russell" was for his maternal grandfather, David Russell Walters.

When Robert's father was named to the Carleton Place police force, the family moved to 30 Frank Street where Robert and his younger brother Ronald grew up. Robert suffered the usual childhood diseases, had his tonsils and adenoids removed, and at one point was treated for "punctured ear drums."

During his studies at CPHS, Bob was active in the school cadet corps (1936–38) and, being a fine athlete, was involved in all sports, playing inside right on the rugby team and defence on the hockey team. He

Bob and his brother Ron in Scouting uniform.

was especially fond of football, at which he excelled as a place kicker, and is remembered as a "big lad" (he stood 5' 9½" tall and weighed 181 pounds). Coach "Picky" Stark[16], a math teacher and physical education instructor, always had Bobby as one of his first choices for the team.

A group of football players would sometimes gather outside the west end of the high school where there was a wall with a large window facing the sports field. They collected a few pennies and then someone set a ball for Bobby to kick. Bob never missed the window and the crash of glass caused much merriment among his teammates. Sheepishly, they would then troop to the principal's office and offer their meagre collection, often no more than 15 cents, to pay for the window.

In high school, Bob exhibited a love of drawing by filling his schoolbooks with cartoons.

After school, he and his brother Ronald after him had a newspaper route for the *Toronto Daily Star* and delivered groceries for local grocer Bill Bailey whose store was on Bridge Street. In summer they made their deliveries on a bicycle with a large metal carrier mounted on front, and in winter they did their rounds with a toboggan. Meanwhile, the newspapers arrived each night on the 9:15 p.m. train, which Chief Irvine met to ensure the boys got on their way delivering the news.

Following school, Bob joined "B" Company of the Lanark and Renfrew Scottish Regiment (Militia). Two days before his seventeenth birthday, on June 19, 1938, he enlisted as a private soldier and attended the weekly meetings at the armouries in Perth. On December 4, 1939, he was taken on strength of "D" Company and was posted to Petawawa for guard duties at the internment camp on Centre Lake. For all intents and purposes, Bob was now in the wartime active force.

When he was a young lad, Bob's father introduced him to hunting. They often went north to Wildwoods Hunting Camp, which was owned and maintained by a group of local enthusiasts. Bob was a good shot and had many racks of antlers as proof of his prowess. He took these to the internment camp where the inmates made them into bone handles for knives and letter openers. The guards never perceived any danger in allowing their charges such latitude. In exchange they often received cigarettes, which they brought home, but

---

[16] "Picky" Stark was the father of Horace Stark. He got his nickname from his students, never used within his hearing, because he demanded precision in all their written work.

rarely smoked more than one. Even today, German cigarettes are considered especially harsh and acrid.

Clear Lake was close enough to Carleton Place that throughout the winter and spring of 1939–40 Bob was able to spend nearly every other weekend at home. However, the Victoria Day weekend, he overstayed his leave and was charged with being AWL, which cost him one day's pay.

On June 15, 1940, Bob, along with Kenny O'Meara who was also from Carleton Place, was transferred to the H&PE as an infantryman and posted to the regimental depot in Picton, Ontario, before going to Camp Borden. In July, because of their previous militia experience, the army decided to send the two Carleton Place boys directly overseas as replacements for the H&PE in England. Ken went in early August, however Bob was kept back in Canada.

1940 was not a particularly good year in Bob's military career. While the army dithered and changed its orders, Bob was spending more and more time away from his military duties, without authorization. He was legally home in June 1940, but didn't bother returning on time in August and was arrested as being AWL. He did not take kindly to the arrest and took off. His charge then included "breaking arrest," and he was sentenced to seven days detention and six days' pay. His brother Ronald recalls that this was Bob's way of drawing attention to the fact that he wanted to get overseas. If he became a big enough pain in the army's rear then they could get rid of him by sending him to Britain.

Bob went AWL again on August 24, which cost him twenty day's pay, and again on September 11, which cost him twelve day's pay. Between his self-granted furloughs, Bob was in the Camp Borden hospital with myositis (a muscle inflammation) of his left arm and impetigo on his face. His arm cleared rapidly with rest, but the skin infection took some time to heal. He then took fourteen more days off in October for which he forfeited twenty-two day's pay and another fourteen days in November for which he paid twenty-three day's pay. In December, Bob came home for a visit, and while in Carleton Place, he became ill and was confined to his home until he was well enough to return to Camp Borden.

In February 1941, Bob was warned that he had to complete basic infantry training before joining the regiment. He was given furlough from February 17 to March 2, which he spent at home with his family, before starting Course No. 23 Basic Training in Newmarket, Ontario. He completed the five-month course with high standing by the end of August and was given two weeks' leave in September.

Due to Bob's performance in basic training, he was offered a choice of postings. Therefore, on August 14, Bob requested transfer to the Provost

Corps. Although the request would not be approved until December 5, he was ordered to Camp Borden to join No. 12A Provost Company for on-the-job training; he was promoted to acting lance corporal on February 15, 1942.

As a young man, Bob was considered "very dapper." He took pride in his clothes and wore them well. He enjoyed dressing in a suit and tie and was reputed to have at least seven or eight pairs of black oxford shoes, a couple of pairs of which his mother later sent overseas at his request.

In April, Bob was sent to Long Branch, near Toronto, to attend Course No. 421 for training as a PT instructor. After this three-week course, he returned to his unit and was named the Provost Company's physical training instructor.

On June 7, Bob was transferred No. 11 Company, Canadian Provost Corps, and posted to Aldershot, near Kentville, Nova Scotia. He was also promoted to acting corporal. Aldershot was just a way station en route to overseas; on September 9 he was given embarkation leave, on the 29th, he boarded his ship, and on October 8 he arrived in England.

On December 1, 1942, Bob was notified that he was considered a qualified military police officer and that he had been confirmed a corporal. In October 1943, Corporal Irvine was sent to the Central Mediterranean Force in Italy where he joined the 1st Line of Communications Provost Section. (Since his arrival overseas, he had been employed at Canadian Army Headquarters.) He sailed on October 27 and landed in Italy on November 10.

Although Bob and his brother grew up close to a river, neither ever learned to swim. Yet despite this oversight, Bob managed to survive two shipwrecks: one while sailing to England and another to Italy. A review of the dates shows that he was ten days at sea crossing to England and fourteen days sailing to Italy. Neither sailing should have been longer than four or five days. Apparently his first ship to the U.K. was sunk just outside Halifax harbour; however, the survivors were retrieved, loaded onto another troop transport, and sent on their way. Then enroute to the Mediterranean, the ship was sunk just off Gibraltar. The rescued soldiers were then taken to the British base at Gibralter to await another ship so as to complete their voyage.

While Robert was sailing for the Mediterranean, his father was busy at home rounding up German prisoners-of-war. Chief Irvine had learned that

The Uniform Club

While many of Carleton Place's men were signing up and shipping out, there was still no shortage of men on the town's streets. Carleton Place was an east-west hub of the CPR, especially for anything or anyone going to or leaving Ottawa for Petawawa or other western destinations. Soldiers, sailors, and airmen from all parts of Canada would find themselves at the Carleton Place station throughout the day and night awaiting train connections that could take hours to arrive.

With the increase in transient traffic, local businessmen and town officials discussed the need of some place for weary soldiers to relax-a place where young men and women in uniform could find rest, entertainment, and a warm welcome when travelling through Carleton Place. In November 1942, an enthusiastic meeting was held in the town council chambers to establish an organization to operate such a club in rooms the Masonic Lodge had offered, free of charge, in a vacant store below the Masonic temple.

The following were elected to see this scheme through: Mrs. W. K. White, president; Mrs. W. F. Findlay, first vice-president; Captain N. McBride, second vice-president; and Miss Eileen Muff, secretary-treasurer. The intention was to have representation from every interested organization in town with each one taking responsibility for one month at a time. The duties were to ensure that the rooms were open at certain times, were kept clean and friendly, and perhaps even to offer light refreshments for a small fee.

Almost immediately various organizations and service clubs threw their weight into the project. And very shortly, the Carleton Place Uniform Club became a welcome rest stop for military travellers.

Contributions took care of the heating and lighting, and gifts of furniture gave the rooms a "homey" atmosphere. The club was open every evening, and members of the committee were always on hand to welcome the visitors.

Thousands of men who trained or served in Petawawa, and who would have had a long, dull wait, found the time waiting for a connection to be actually quite pleasant. The average soldier passing through Carleton Place came to know the town's friendly atmosphere and unselfish service to the troops. One officer wrote to The Canadian to express the thanks of himself and his men: "Consideration of the man in uniform seems to be inbred in Carleton Place, because both at the Movie Theatre and the Rink I have been told 'Oh, it's pretty late-we won't charge you-come right in.'"

When news of the Uniform Club's closing was announced in June 1945, it garnered letters from many military sources expressing thanks and regret. The president even received one letter from 24 Sussex Drive, signed by Prime Minister Mackenzie King. He wrote that the club had done a great deal to assist members of the armed forces with a place where they could drop in and be welcomed. He stated that the efforts put forth by the club during the war years were greatly appreciated by many Canadians.

two suspicious men were walking on the highway to Smiths Falls. After a short search, he found two men wearing prison clothing, took them into custody without resistance, and locked them up in the town jail. One man was a captured German soldier and the other a captured merchant seaman. Both had been in the Hull internment camp, but had been released to Kingston officials and sent to Chantry to cut wood. They had simply walked away, which launched a widespread search by the RCMP and the Ontario Provincial Police. However, after spending a cold November night wandering the countryside, they were quite happy to be back in custody.

Then, one month later, a contingent of RCMP officers visited Carleton Place, and with the help of its police chief, rounded up some fourteen draft evaders. It was not until January 1946 that town council decided a second police constable should be hired to assist Chief Irvine.

By May 1944, Bob Irvine had proven to be an efficient and conscientious military policeman and was assigned as the NCO in charge of his own detachment. He had personally apprehended many Allied deserters, recovered a number of stolen vehicles, suppressed many black market activities, and assisted in many successful prosecutions.

But it wasn't all work and no play for Corporal Irvine. In August he met a pretty young Italian girl, Ellina (Elena) Falconieri, who lived with her family in the small town of Atripalda, just east of Avellino, where the Provost Company was stationed.

That summer, Bob was on patrol near the Adriatic coast when he stopped to watch some engineers building a bridge across a river. He recognized a face and shouted: "Hey, what are you doing here?" It was Bernard Pye. They spent some time catching up on Carleton Place news before both resumed their respective duties.

In October 1944, Bob was awarded his Canadian Volunteer Service Medal and Clasp for overseas service and was promoted to acting sergeant. He served on the Morals Squad apprehending prostitutes and those involved in prostitution. At times, he was assigned to Area Patrol when he would be charged with apprehending military people who were AWL and civilians in illegal possession of War Department material. Sergeant Irvine was also in charge of radio-equipped vehicles used for running down armed gangs. His activities, especially under war conditions, always contained an element of serious danger.

On January 4, 1945, Sergeant Irvine signed out the jeep that he normally used for duty travel. He carried out some routine maintenance and then left for the rest of the afternoon. Although he was not detailed for any specific duties, it was common practice for the men of his section to continue investigations in their off-duty hours. Bob Irvine was well known for his tenacious pursuit of criminal activity, and at 1730 hours, accompanied by Lance Corporals Booth and Neilson, both of his Provost Company, he drove to Atripalda. Bob parked and locked the jeep in an army building, and all three went their separate ways, with Bob walking the few blocks to Via Roma and up one flight of narrow stairs to the home of his girlfriend, Elena.

Bob often visited Elena when he was not working, and at 1800, they went across the street to the small store to do some shopping for their evening meal. Thirty minutes later, they returned to the apartment. Elena made a small dinner for them and her sister, and they remained there for the rest of the evening. Elena did some housework while they talked until about 2100, when Bob decided it was time to return to base. He went to get the jeep, and Elena followed him down to the street. She waited five minutes until he drove past so they could wave farewell. That was the last time she saw Bobby alive.

When questioned later, Elena could think of no reason or of any person that would want to harm the Canadian sergeant. She testified, through an interpreter, that there were many people in the village who were quite fond of him and were very shocked to learn of his demise.

Next morning, Volpe Silvestro, a farmer from Montello, was urging his old truck along the road from Lacedonia to Atripalda. Near Tavernola, about half a kilometre from the junction to Volturara, he saw what appeared to be a fairly large pool of blood staining the snow in the centre of the road. On the side of the road lay a body. Knowing something was wrong, he was too scared to stop until he arrived at the junction and spotted another farmer, Nariallo Alberico, standing there.

Silvestro told Alberico there was a soldier's body lying back up the road and asked him to notify the police. Alberico, together with his cousin Tomazzo Edmondo who lived about 100 metres from the scene, walked the three kilometres into Volturara where they told the Carabinieri of their find. At 0930, the Italian police informed the Canadian Provost, and Corporal D. Sugarman and Private J. W. Missen of the Regimental Police took Alberico and Edmondo to guide them to the scene. There they found Sergeant Robert Irvine, apparently dead of bullet wounds.

A medical officer was summoned. He arrived at 1000 hours, and after a cursory examination, declared that Sergeant Irvine had been dead for about twelve hours. The Regimental Police placed the body in the back of their truck and took it to the Provost office; it was later forwarded to No. 1 Canadian Field Hospital for a post mortem. Captain W. Dick, Commandant of No. 2 Canadian Field Punishment Camp, was ordered to conduct a thorough investigation into the matter.

There will ever be speculation as to who killed Bob Irvine.

There was a small group of Canadian deserters in Rome named the Sailor Gang, which ran a flourishing racket in black-market goods. Among them was Private Harold Joseph Pringle from Flinton, Ontario, near Napanee, who had joined the H&PE after giving a false date of birth. He was just sixteen when he went overseas.

Harold was described as a "good soldier" but with a fierce temper, and he repeatedly went AWL, often to visit girlfriends. He served six months in prison then, as was the usual practice, was released to his battalion heading into a theatre of operations-in his case, Italy.

Shortly after arriving in Italy, he deserted and joined fellow deserters in the Sailor Gang in Rome. By this time he was exhibiting the all-too-familiar signs of shell shock.

These black-market profiteers were exactly the people on Bob Irvine's list of "bad guys" to be pursued and stopped. As well as hindering Mafia criminal activities, Bob would have been quite anxious to curtail the prosperous trade in black-market goods.

Pringle's problems reached their zenith when he was arrested for the murder of a fellow Canadian deserter and gang member. After serving five years in the army overseas, on July 5, 1945, Private Harold Pringle was executed by his fellow soldiers. The war had been over for some months and all Canadians in Italy had gone home, except for thirty-one men kept at Avellino to form a firing squad for Pringle.

Eight other Canadian soldiers had been convicted of murder during the Second World War, but all of them had their death sentences commuted. But in order to please the British, who had executed English deserters in the Sailor Gang, Pringle was also executed, albeit in secret, but with Prime Minister Mackenzie King's blessing. Pringle was the only Canadian killed by a firing squad in World War II, a fact the Canadian army and government conveniently forgot about for years. The cover-up began in Mackenzie King's office and made its way down to Pringle's firing squad, who had no wish to talk about their actions.[17]

Did Bob Irvine get too close to members of this, or similar gangs of Allied deserters, or was he a victim of a Mafia hit? The records reveal no leads in his case.

[17] Andrew Clark, "The Secret Execution of Private Pringle" A Keen Soldier: The Execution of Second World War Private Harold Pringle (The Ottawa Citizen: Thursday, November 7, 2002), p. A2.

There was snow on the ground; however, as the day warmed, the snow melted and obliterated any vehicle tracks or footprints that may have been left. There was a small amount of blood on the right-hand verge where the snow had been packed down. Fifteen to twenty feet further down the road was a large pool of blood and enough traces of tracks to indicate that Sergeant Irvine had probably died there and then had his body dragged to the side of the road where he was found. Opposite the small spot of blood were found two empty cartridges of .311 calibre, apparently of German manufacture and suitable for a Mauser rifle. Further away another used cartridge was found. There was no trace of the jeep.

From the evidence amassed, Captain Dick deduced that Sergeant Irvine had been shot at the spot where the empty cartridges were found, been rolled over the bank, and left for dead. Irvine had managed to crawl back up to the roadway and along it some sixty yards to where the large blood spot formed before collapsing and dying. Someone had then moved him to the side of the road where he was found the next morning.

The autopsy revealed that multiple gunshot wounds killed Bob Irvine. One went through his left upper arm smashing the bone four inches below his shoulder, then into his chest, fracturing a rib before passing into his diaphragm. Another was found just below where it had entered his stomach and intestines. The third had gone through the left hip, rupturing his spleen. The surgeon concluded that any one of the wounds would have been fatal.

With these results, and the doctor's opinion that Irvine could have walked after being shot, Captain Dick was able to conclude that Sergeant Irvine had been sitting behind the wheel of the jeep when he was shot the first time. He then fell to the right and was shot again before being dragged from the vehicle and rolled over the edge of the road. Although dying, Irvine then dragged himself to the spot where he died.

An intense investigation was carried out over the following weeks by both the Canadian Provost and the Italian Carabinieri, with as many as twelve police officers assigned full time to the investigation. Several hundred people were taken into custody and questioned, but there were no leads that would implicate anyone in the sergeant's death. He had had no quarrels with comrades and was well liked by the Italian civilians with whom he was in contact. No trace of the weapon or the missing jeep was ever found, and no motive for Sergeant Irvine's murder has ever been unearthed.

The body of Robert David Irvine, son of Christopher and Maude Irvine, was laid to rest in the Caserta War Cemetery, near the Communal Cemetery on the eastern edge of the Royal Gardens of the Royal Palace at Caserta. The palace served as headquarters for the Allied armies during the Italian campaign, and the cemetery contains 750 World War II casualties, only ten of which are unidentified. A royal message of condolence was sent to Bob's parents on January 31, 1945, and then early in March, his mother received the Memorial Cross. His War Service Gratuity, for 1,860 days service (including 831 days overseas) came to $782.41. When his effects arrived, his mother was dismayed to find Bob's good ring and his gold watch, for which they had paid $85, were missing. All that was sent to them were a combined cigarette case and lighter, a damaged Eberhard wristwatch without a crystal, and a small ring with a stone set in it. The family was Anglican but included in Bob's possessions was a rosary and

Elena kneels in prayer at Sgt. Bob Irvine's grave. (photos courtesy Ron Irvine)

some small religious medals, probably gifts from Elena. He also had had 5,360 lire on his person.

Bob owned a .45 Colt automatic, but it was illegal to send weapons home to Canada, so it was sold for $44.70 to a Provost friend. That amount was unaccounted for in his effects.

In spring 1946 a comrade of Bob's visited his parents in Carleton Place. He claimed to have seen Bob's body and that it was wearing his gold watch. They made inquiries to the Estates Branch of the Army but no trace of the watch was found.

Elena stayed in touch with the Irvine family for a while, in spite of her lack of English. Photographs of her family and of Bobby's grave made their way to Canada and are treasured to this day by the Irvine family.

After the D-Day landings shifted the world's attention to northwest Europe, some persons in high places were reputed to have remarked that the soldiers fighting in the Mediterranean theatre were "getting off lightly in the sunny vineyards of Italy." The response was a popular and ironic wartime song referring to the men in Italy as "D-Day Dodgers."

> *Looking 'round the mountains, in the mud and rain,*
> *There's lots of little crosses, some which bear no name.*
> *Blood, sweat and tears and toil are gone,*
> *The boys beneath them slumber on,*
> *These are your D-Day Dodgers, who'll stay in Italy.*

—Last verse of "The D-Day Dodgers" sung to the tune of "Lilli Marlene"

An RCAF recruiting advertisement that appeared early in the 1940s in The Canadian.

PART FOUR—IN HOSTILE SKIES

CHAPTER FIFTEEN—COMING IN ON A WING AND A PRAYER

We're coming in on a wing and a prayer
We're coming in on a wing and a prayer
Tho' there's one motor gone we will still carry on
We're coming in on a wing and a prayer

What a show, what a fight
Yes we really hit our target for tonight
How we sing as we fly through the air
Look below there's our field over there
With a full crew aboard and our trust in the Lord
We're coming in on a wing and a prayer

—Popular World War II Song

Many Canadian aviators journeyed to England to fly in the RAF and many more RCAF airmen were posted to RAF squadrons upon their arrival there. In fact, of the 59,000 RCAF airmen overseas in 1944, nearly half were serving in RAF squadrons. Part of the reason for the scattering of Canadian aircrew among RAF squadrons was that Canada, until late 1942, paid only a portion of RCAF costs overseas. The majority expense was borne by Britain who then claimed the right to use the airmen as she saw fit.

Distinct RCAF squadrons were formed only after the tremendous influx of Canadian aircrew graduated from the training schools in Canada. At first the few Canadian squadrons flew in formation with RAF squadrons, but as they grew in numbers, all-Canadian wings were formed. In August 1942, for the raid on Dieppe, eight Canadian squadrons flew supporting missions; and in 1943, at the insistence of Prime Minister Mackenzie King that the RCAF have its own bomber group, eleven RCAF bomber squadrons were brought together into the all-Canadian No. 6 Bomber Group.

Canada's largest air commitment was to Bomber Command under Air Vice Marshall "Bomber" Harris. Young fliers, trained by the BCATP in Canada, and large numbers of new aircraft from Canadian factories were rushed into service as the Luftwaffe ravaged Britain in 1940. Through 1941 and 1942, waves of Canadian bombers, flown by Canadian aircrews, made ever-increasing forays into Nazi Germany, battering industrial, military, and transportation targets. In 1943, saturation bombing subjected German cities to appalling losses, and Canada's participation in these expanded bomber operations increased commensurately. On the night of May 30–31, 1942, sixty-eight RCAF bombers took part in the first thousand-aircraft raid on Germany; 1,045 bombers dropped more than 2,000 tons of bombs in ninety minutes.

By war's end, the RCAF was launching more than 200 heavy bombers each day on nighttime raids, delivering 900 tons of bombs to the enemy.

It took a special kind of courage to board an aircraft, night after terrible night. Roaring down a darkened runway, the airmen would sever earthly ties to rise into pitch-black skies. Men, barely past puberty, flew deafening, frigid machines into enemy territory to face horrendous anti-aircraft fire, searchlights, and night-fighters.

Losses were high: 9,980 Canadian airmen lost their lives while serving in Bomber Command[1]. However, the RAF adopted a strange way of accounting for their operational losses. Partly because they did not wish to alarm the populace, and partly just for propaganda purposes, the air staff only counted a loss as operational if the aircraft was lost over Europe. If a bomber was shot up and many of its crew killed, but the pilot was skilful, or lucky, enough to get the plane back to an airfield in Britain, it was not counted as an "operational" loss. Often the pilot fought a crippled machine through flak over the English Channel, only to lose control on landing and crash. The crew had flown a successful mission, but their loss was attributed to "non-operational" factors!

Two Carleton Place aviators lost their lives under such circumstances.

R 82744 Flight Sergeant Albert Edward Prendergast
Wireless Operator/Air Gunner
Royal Canadian Air Force

Albert Edward "Bert" Prendergast was born to James Henry Prendergast and Sarah Anne Beach on July 9, 1915, the oldest son in a family of five boys and four girls. Bert's parents were born and raised in Woolwich, England, and married there before emigrating to Canada. However, James died at a relatively young age of "stomach problems," leaving Sarah to raise their brood alone.

Wireless Operator/Air Gunner Badge

[1] Proportionately the RCAF had the most losses in World War II. They enlisted 280,000 and lost 17,000. The army also lost 17,000 soldiers but their enlistments totaled 330,000. The Royal Canadian Navy lost 2,024 sailors out of an enrolment of 106,000.

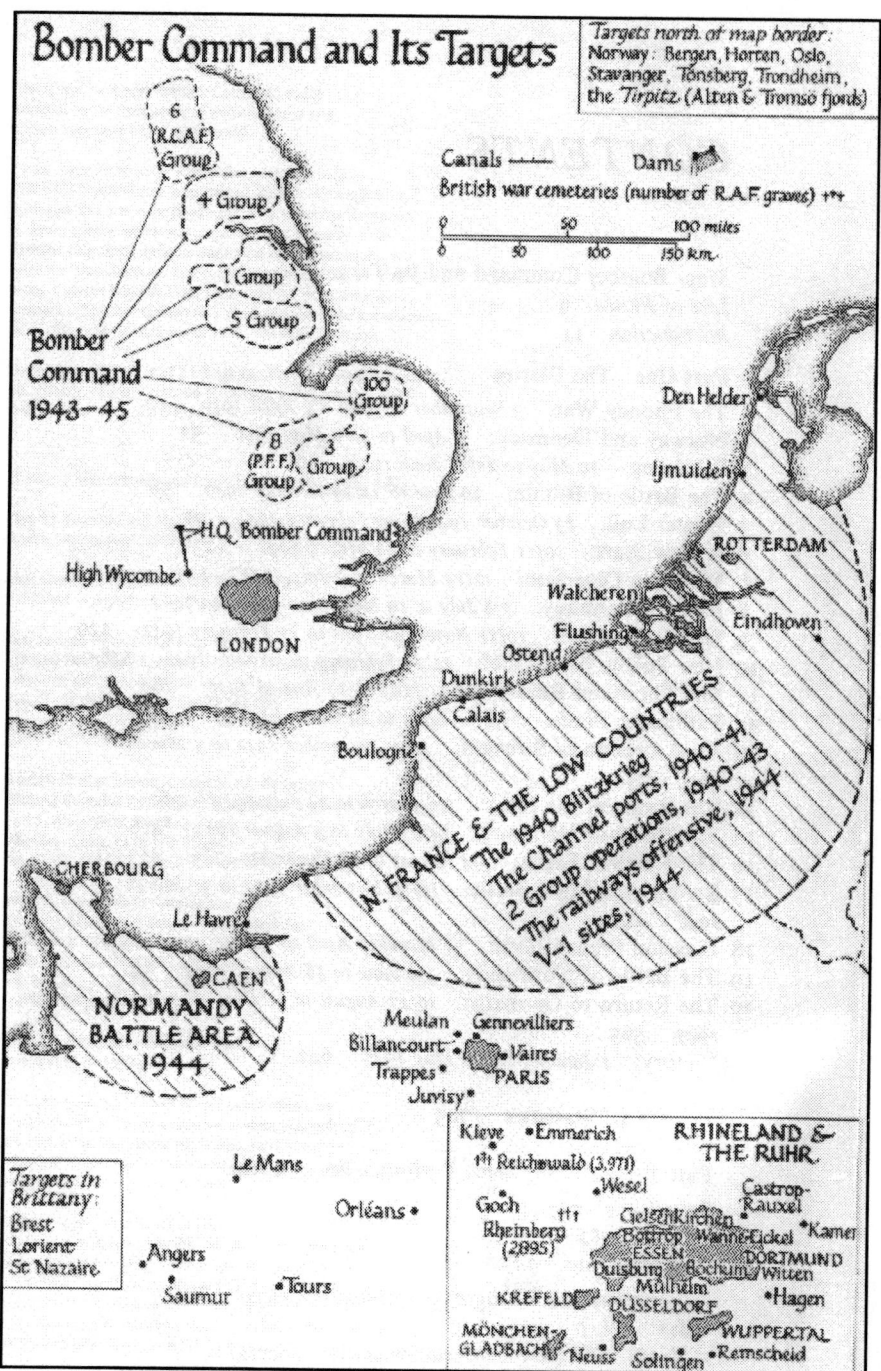

Bomber Command and Its Targets

Targets north of map border:
Norway: Bergen, Horten, Oslo,
Stavanger, Tonsberg, Trondheim,
the *Tirpitz* (Alten & Tromsö fjords)

Canals ——— Dams ◤
British war cemeteries (number of R.A.F. graves) †††

0   50   100 miles
0   50   100   150 km.

6
(R.C.A.F.)
Group

4 Group

1 Group

5 Group

Bomber
Command
1943–45

100
Group

8
(P.F.F.)
Group

3
Group

H.Q. Bomber Command

High Wycombe

LONDON

Den Helder

Ijmuiden

ROTTERDAM

Walcheren

Flushing   Eindhoven

Ostend

Dunkirk

Calais

Boulogne

N. FRANCE & THE LOW COUNTRIES
The 1940 Blitzkrieg, 1940–41
The Channel ports, 1940–43
2 Group operations, 1940–43
The railways offensive, 1944
V–1 sites, 1944

CHERBOURG

Le Havre

CAEN

NORMANDY
BATTLE AREA
1944

Meulan   Gennevilliers
Billancourt
Trappes   Vaires
Juvisy   PARIS

Le Mans

Targets in
Brittany:
Brest
Lorient
St Nazaire

Orléans

Angers

Saumur   Tours

Kleve   •Emmerich   RHINELAND &
††† Reichswald (3,971)   THE RUHR
          •Wesel
Goch   †††   Castrop-
Rheinberg   Gelsenkirchen   Rauxel
(2,895)   Bottrop Wanne-Eickel   •Kamen
          Duisburg ESSEN Bochum DORTMUND
KREFELD   Mülheim Witten
          DÜSSELDORF   •Hagen
MÖNCHEN-   WUPPERTAL
GLADBACH Neuss Solingen •Remscheid

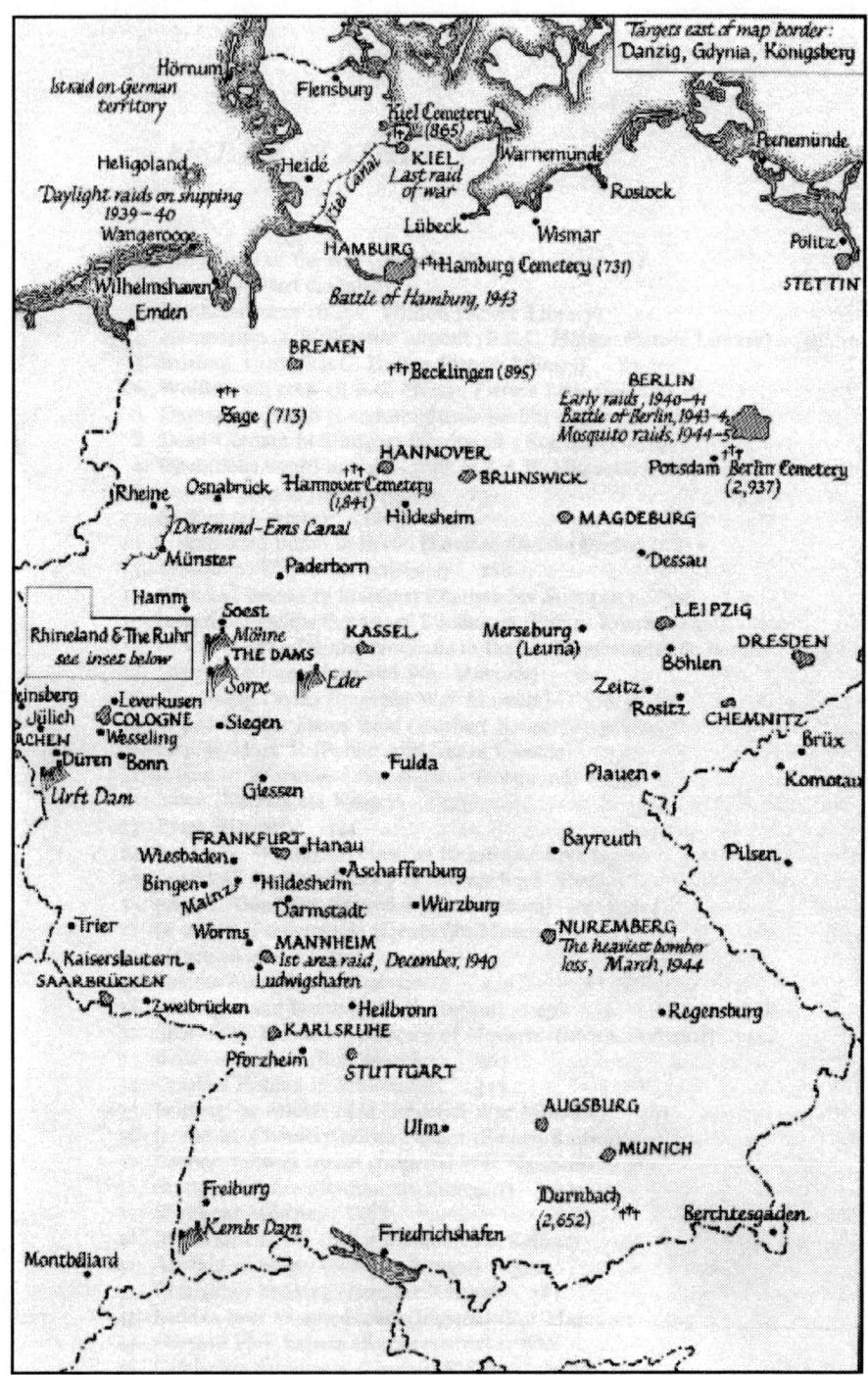

Bomber Command and its targets

Bert was blessed with the fiery red hair and flashing green eyes that were prominent features in his family. He was a wiry, but somewhat short, youth, standing 5' 3" and weighing 115 pounds.

He received his education at Carleton Place schools, attending CPHS for three years and completing the commercial course in 1930. He joined the school cadet corps, paddled with the Canoe Club for five seasons and, as an active young man, participated in most athletic endeavours.

Following school, Bert went to work for the Hawthorne Woollen Mills as a weaver (1931–38) and the Renfrew Woollen Mills as a percher[2] (1938–40) in Carleton Place. In 1940, Bert moved to Ottawa where he was employed as a salesman for Wonder Bakeries.

On October 28, 1940, at age twenty-five, he applied to join the RCAF. The interviewing officer wrote that Bert was a "Keen, clean cut, intelligent, courteous, calm type, eager to fly and fight. Should make a good air-gunner." At his preliminary medical examination, on October 31, he stated that he drank about a quart of beer a week and smoked twenty cigarettes a day. His only distinguishing mark was a one-half-inch scar on his left inner thigh.

It undoubtedly came as a big surprise to him that he was unfit to be a pilot. With legs only thirty-seven inches long, he was too short to reach the rudder pedals in a cockpit, so he was awarded a medical category of A3B, suitable for any air or ground trade except pilot, anywhere required. The interviewer's observation became a recommendation, and Bert was told to go home and wait for an opening for training as an air-gunner.

In January, Bert got his call, and early in February 1941, he left for No. 2 Manning Depot in Brandon, Manitoba. Mr. A. E. Prendergast had now become Aircraftsman Second Class Prendergast. So with a warrant for a rail ticket in his pocket, he boarded a CN train in Ottawa going west.

Soon after receiving their uniforms, some of which fit and some of which didn't, the new recruits were paraded for inoculations. Long lines of airmen filled the drill hall where they rolled up both sleeves and followed each other to tables where sat doctors and nurses and medical assis-

Airman Bert Prendergast

tants. Each recruit was injected with five shots in about two minutes, then shooed on his way. Bert remained standing and was surprised to see about one in five keel over after the second or third needle. Not that it made much difference. Friends carried their unconscious mates through the line and the rest of the inoculations were administered anyway.

[2] A percher was the person responsible for inspecting the finished cloth for any defects

Bert Prendergast at No. 2
Wireless School, May, 1941.

Bert met other aspiring airmen from every part of the Dominion along with a sprinkling of Americans who had come north to join the RCAF. They ate together, slept together, drilled together, and studied together. But at graduation most went their separate ways, depending on the trade to which they were allotted. Not all were aircrew and not all were pilots. Bert was selected as a wireless operator/air gunner and sent to No. 2 Wireless School in Calgary.

Most of his training was conducted in the classroom or in ground-bound trainers; however, he did accumulate ten hours and five minutes flying in a Norseman. The Norseman was a true bush plane. A single-engine, high-wing monoplane built by Noorduyn Aviation of Montreal, it first flew in 1938 with the RCMP. It could cruise at 150 mph for 1,150 miles, and reach an altitude of 17,000 feet. It was a light transport aircraft adapted specifically for the wireless schools.

On July 8, Bert was playing softball with other course members. Running to catch a fly ball, he tripped in a gopher hole, hurting his left hand. An X-ray at the station hospital revealed that he had fractured his fifth finger at the knuckle.

On June 26, a month after reporting to Course No. 18 for training as a radio operator, Bert was promoted to the rank of leading aircraftsman. On October 12, Bert received his wireless operator's badge[3] and was posted directly to No. 3 B&G School at MacDonald, Manitoba. Here he flew in the Tiger Moth, a single-engine biplane, usually used for pilot training, but with the student and instructor flying in tandem it was also quite suitable for gunnery instruction. Aircrew enjoyed flying in this graceful aircraft. Its seats were covered with a perspex coupe top and, being a training aircraft, she was painted a particularly beautiful brilliant shade of yellow.

[3] At the same time, his brother Wilfred, in training at the Technical Training School in St. Thomas, Ontario, won the gold medal as the honour student of Course # 13. Wilfred went on to become an Air Gunner.

Also used at the BCATP gunnery schools was the Fairey Battle. Although operationally obsolete when the war began, the RCAF used many of them as gunnery trainers as because they could cruise at 210 mph and climb to 23,500 feet. Bert flew a total of twelve hours and forty minutes on these two trainers.

With a mark of 74.1%, Bert graduated a respectable ninth out of twenty-six students from his gunnery course, and on November 8, 1941, was promoted to acting sergeant. He received two weeks embarkation leave before reporting to Halifax for shipment overseas, which he chose to spend with his family in Carleton Place. His brothers, including Wilfred who was also training to be a gunner with the RCAF, and two sisters were all at home to see him off to war. In mid-November, after a two-day train trip, he reported to No. 1 "Y" Depot, "somewhere on the east coast," to await a ship for England. He embarked on December 13 for the nine-day trip across the stormy North Atlantic.

Halifax during World War II was a rough and tumble place, only recently freed from the strictures of prohibition, of which the thousands of service personnel passing through the city took full advantage of. The city's peacetime population of 60,000 reeled under the influx of sailors, which alone quickly doubled the number of people living there. The civilian population was unprepared and received no help for the drastic, and unwelcome, changes that war in the Atlantic brought to their town.

Halifax was also the only Canadian city to have a direct line of contact to the front lines. East Coast admirals worked from the "war room," in Navy headquarters. One entire wall which was dominated by a gigantic map of the Atlantic Ocean that covered one entire wall. Sailors and WRENS[4] pushed markers along designated routes showing the progress of convoys; locations were marked showing designating where "wolf packs" or single German submarines were thought to be operating; and areas were highlighted to show where coastal command aircraft were deployed to combat the U-boats.

During the voyage overseas, aircrew, especially gunners, were called upon to stand watch and to man the ship-mounted Oerlikon guns. The weather was frigid, and the aircrew, in their parade greatcoats and black leather gloves, were woefully ill-equipped for the howling winds that keened across the deck. Mercifully, their watches were usually only two hours long.

Bert spent Christmas Day aboard ship and landed in England on the December 26. The gunners were sent immediately to No. 3 (Overseas) Advanced Flying Unit, where they would be introduced to the realities of wartime flying. By making them better aviators, instructors hoped to give

[4] The acronymic nickname for members of the Navy's Womens' auxiliary service (originally Womens' Royal Navy Service–WRNS)

them an increased better chance of survival. The average rate of survival for flight crews was only eight missions.

Canadian aircrews, most of whom had never been very far from home before, also had a lot great deal to learn about English customs and idiosyncrasies. RAF jargon was an entirely new language that, combined with the accent, made many Canadians wonder if it was indeed English that was being spoken. They no longer made bad landings, but "ropey" landings. New aircrew were called "sprogs." Talkative people were told to quit "nattering." Aircraft didn't crash, they "pranged." Information was called "gen," good information was "pukka gen," and bad information was "duff gen." (They soon learned that most news reports were full of "duff gen.") "Wizard" described any good or exceptional thing or event, like planes, the best girls, interesting stories, and great meals[5].

On March 6, 1942, Bert qualified as a wireless operator/air gunner Grade II, and on the 28th, he was sent to No. 14 OTU in Cottesmore. It was equipped with thirty-nine Hampden and Hereford aircraft for training night-flying bomber crews and an additional thirty-nine Ansons for navigation training. Bert trained on the Handley-Page Hampden, which accommodated a crew of four so one pilot could take three gunners aloftup for training. The aircraft had flown as an operational bomber and night fighter and was equipped with three gun turrets, each armed with twin .303 guns-one in the nose, one in the dorsal, and one in the ventral (rear) position. These attractive twin-engine bombers had sleek, rakish lines. They were very agile but the narrow fuselage left little room to move about, and the .303 guns were not very intimidating armament.

It was at the OTU that the mating ritual of "crewing-up" occurred. Heavy-bomber crews usually comprised two pilots, an observer, a wireless operator, and an air gunner; wisely, the air force left crew formation to the men themselves. But they were doing it with little information and only recent acquaintance. For example, how could one tell if a man wearing a gunner's badge was any good at his new profession? A gunner's psychological stability was especially important. Could he respond to a night fighter pouring fiery bullets and cannon shells at the gunner's face? The lives of his crew depended upon his control to return fire and drive off or shoot down the attacker.

In his book, *Above and Beyond*, Spencer Dunmore, a wartime bomber pilot, compared the crewing-up process to "young men asking for first dates[6]." They sized each other up, all the while shyly mingling and chatting. They looked for connections (e.g. hometowns or provinces, schools, relatives or friends), but first impressions were the usual motivating factors.

[5] Murray Peden, A Thousand Shall Fall (Toronto: Canada's Wings, 1979) p.238.
[6] Spencer Dunmore, Above and Beyond, The Canadians' War in the Air, 1939—45 (Toronto: McClelland and Stewart Inc., 1996), p. 245.

Bert and his crew completed OTU training on May 19, 1942 (he had been promoted to flight sergeant on May 8), and were then sent to RAF Station Kinloss, Scotland, to join 115 Squadron. The squadron was on temporary detachment to Coastal Command for operations at sea with their Wellingtons. In September 1942, the squadron moved to Mildenhall and back to Bomber Command No. 3 Group.

Like most Canadian airmen, at least early in the war, Bert was posted to an RAF squadron for operational flying. No. 115 Squadron had a history dating back to the Royal Flying Corps in the Great War, when it was formed in 1917 as a strategic night-bombing squadron. It was disbanded in 1919, was reformed on June 28, 1937, and began receiving Wellington bombers in April 1939; it completed its first bombing mission on December 3, 1939, when seven Wellingtons bombed German warships off Heligoland. In April 1940, 115 Squadron became the first to make a bombing raid on continental Europe, on the enemy-held airfield at Stavanger-Sola in Norway.

After the Germans attacked France, 115 Squadron began raids on German targets and later on enemy-occupied sites in Europe. In August 1941, the squadron undertook the initial trials of "Gee," the first airborne radar to provide navigational and bombing aid. The first trial over enemy territory occurred during the night of August 11–12, 1941, when two Gee-equipped aircraft found their target, Monchengladbach in the Ruhr Valley, without any searching. The bombs were released on Gee information and the town was hit. The following night, the squadron sent out two Gee-equipped Wellingtons to Hanover. One failed to return.

115 Squadron placed great importance on navigation and this is reflected in its badge, which depicts a right hand holding a sailing vessel's tiller bar, and its motto: Despite the Elements. In March 1943, the squadron converted to Lancasters.

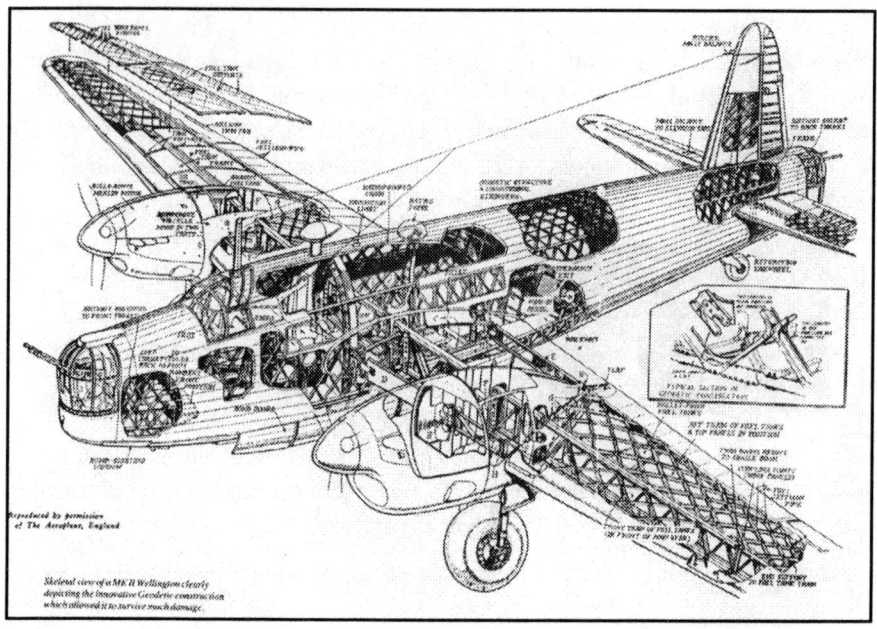

Skeletal view of a Mk II Wellington clearly depicting the innovative Geodetic construction which allowed it to survive much damage.

The first task of Bert's crew was to convert their flying skills to the idio-syncrasies of the Wellington bomber, affectionately known as the "Wimpy." Built by Vickers and famed for its geodetic framework, the aircraft was used for bombing, minesweeping, anti-shipping, air/sea rescue, and transport, and as well as a glider tug. 115 Squadron used it as a long-range night bomber with a crew of six. Its two powerful engines could drive it at a speed of 235 mph at 15,500 feet, and the two automatic .303 guns could be operated in either the nose or tail positions while the manually operated .303 gun could be fired from either waist position.

In the tails of the Lancaster and Wellington bombers were mounted the Nash and Thompson (Parnall) turret carrying four .303 Browning Mk II guns. Each carried 2,500 rounds of ammunition. Once seated in position, the gunner closed the metal doors behind him and strapped himself in. He had a field of fire of 94° to each beam and an elevation of 60°, and he could depress the guns to 45°. To abandon the aircraft, he had to open the doors, grab his parachute, and clip it to the chest hooks on his harness, traverse the turret 90° by hydraulic motor, pull a pin from his seat harness, and fall out backwards. If the gunner was injured, another crewmember could release the door catch. Due to the number of injured gunners who became trapped inside on crash landings, with fatal consequences, the manufacturer later added a hydraulic valve that could turn the turret from the outside.

The Wellington offered very little in crew comfort. Numbing cold, ear-splitting noise, and freezing air streamed from nose to tail through gaps in the fuselage. Sunshine filled the cockpit, but at altitude, its rays offered no warmth. Coffee in Thermos jugs turned into brown ice chunks, and machine guns often refused to fire, being frozen solid. Meanwhile, aircrew wiggled their toes in fleece-lined flying boots and wrapped their scarves tighter above the couple of layers of sweaters they wore. Later came the sheepskin-lined "teddy-bear suits," equipped with electrically heated gloves and socks, made by the Irvine Parachute Company. Still, the cold was so pervasive that the men continued to wear several layers of woollen underwear and civilian clothes underneath.

Bert and his crew spent much of the summer of 1942 familiarizing themselves with each other and the Wellington. After passing a battery of tests, the crew was declared "operational" and allowed to fly bombing missions.

115 Squadron holds one of the finest records of operational service in Bomber Command. Its Wellingtons flew 3,075 sorties, losing 98 aircraft (3.2%). This represented the most raids, the most sorties, and the most losses of any Wellington squadron in Bomber Command. Counting both the Wellington losses and its later Lancaster losses, 115 was the only squadron to lose more than 200 aircraft during the war. Its aircrew flew the third highest number of bombing raids in Bomber Command and the most raids in 3 Group, and its aircrew dropped more bombs than any other squadron in 3 Group.

On Saturday, October 24, 1942, Sarah Prendergast was visiting with her daughters in Toronto when a telegram was delivered informing her of the loss of her son. Flight Sergeant Wireless Air Gunner Albert "Bert" Prendergast had been killed by enemy action two days before.

A letter followed soon after from 115 Squadron Wing Commander A. Cousens. He wrote:

> Your son . . . was comparatively a newcomer to this Squadron, but was becoming very popular, and his loss will be felt by all. He was a member of my best operational crew, and had taken part in several raids over enemy territory. He carried out his duties as Wireless Operator Air Gunner on all occasions in a highly efficient manner.
>
> He was buried with full military honors in the cemetery of St. John church, Beck Row, Mildenhall. The funeral was attended by myself and officers of the squadron and his personal friends acted as pallbearers. I can assure you that his grave will always be well cared for.
>
> I should like to mention how much his comrades in the Royal Force admired the unselfish and gallant sacrifice your son has made so far from home in the service of his country and in the cause of freedom.

Bert had been on a daylight operational sortie. They had taken off from Mildenhall at 1445 hours, and while over the target, were attacked by a fighter aircraft. As the hail of bullets and cannon shells riddled the fabric-covered Wellington, Bert returned fire with his guns. Bert was hit in the forehead and left shoulder. The shoulder wound was insignificant, but his head wound proved fatal. The hit caused a compound fracture of the frontal region that resulted in gross cranial damage. Death was probably instantaneous. He was twenty-seven years old.

In Carleton Place, friends throughout the community mourned Bert Prendergast's death. He was a well-known, popular young man, highly regarded by those who knew him. *The Canadian* wrote:

> He was a fine type of young Canadian manhood, honest and upright, pleasant and courteous, and highly respected by his elders. When the call for duty came Bert gave his services voluntarily to his King and country and last week gave his life for freedom.

As well as his mother, Bert left his brothers (James and William of Toronto, Wilfred in the RCAF at Calgary taking the gunner's course, and Harold at home in Carleton Place) and his sisters (Helen [Mrs Harold Freakley], Ivy [Mrs. R. Morell] both of Carleton Place, Norah [Mrs. R. Eyers] of Ottawa, and Margaret [Mrs. Herb Armstrong] of Toronto).

In November, Sarah received a sympathy card from the Minister of Defence, and in January 1943, a message of condolence from the king along with the Memorial Cross. The government sent her $289.95 for Bert's War Service Gratuity, which was calculated from the 628 days he had served, including 287 days overseas.

In *The Canadian* of October 19, 1944, the following "In Memoriam" appeared:

> PRENDERGAST—In fond and loving memory of a dearly beloved son and brother, Sergeant Albert "Bert" Prendergast, son of Mrs. James Prendergast and the late Mr. Prendergast, who was killed by enemy action overseas with the R.C.A.F., October 22, 1942.
>
> *Boy of my heart we miss you so,*
>
> *Often my darling our tears will flow*
>
> *Dimming your picture before our eyes,*
>
> *But never the one in our heart that lies.*
>
> *We who loved you, sadly miss you,*
>
> *As it dawns another year,*

In our lonely hours of thinking,
Thoughts of you are ever near.

Sadly missed by Mother, Sisters and Brothers

R 143973 Warrant Officer II William Allan Valley
Navigator
Royal Canadian Air Force

Airmen's Prayer
Pilot divine, and Lord of all on high
Thine are the starry squadrons of the sky!
Lead us whose wings for freedom's sake now soar,
Into our hearts thy faith and courage pour
Oh hear our prayer.

Set Thou our course whose trust is laid in Thee!
Oh Thou who chartest all eternity!
Through cloud and sunshine, through darkest night
Guide Thou our wings who battle for the right
Oh hear our prayer.

Father and friend, in whose almighty name
We dedicate our lives to freedom's flame,
Bless now our wings as through space we wend.
Bless us who to Thy care our souls commend
Oh hear our prayer.

—By W/C G. L. Creed

William "Will" or "Bill" Allan Valley was born on May 26, 1916, to Emery Edward and Christena "Tena" Valley in Vankleek Hill, Ontario, where he attended elementary school and began his high school education. In 1931, the family moved to Carleton Place and took up residence at 41

Moore Street. His father was employed as a baker and was known around town as "Cookie." Will enrolled at CPHS, where he was remembered as a good student and very precise in his studies and his actions.

Will brought his considerable athletic abilities to several activities at CPHS. He excelled at tennis, taking a leadership role as president (Tennis Division) of the CPR Recreation Club, and enjoyed badminton, playing for both the St. James Anglican and the Memorial Park United badminton clubs. Swimming and skating rounded out his recreation agenda.

Will's other devotion was to St Andrew's Presbyterian Church, where he volunteered as superintendent of the St. Andrew's Sunday School, president of the local Young People's Society, secretary of the Lanark and Renfrew Young People's Society, and member and secretary of the church choir. He was also active in the Burning Bush Boys' Club, a Bible study group. The Reverend James Foote remembered Will as spiritually minded, ever ready to do good works.

On occasion, Will even occupied the pulpit in the absence of the minister and was recognized as giving a "nicely worded address" in September 1940 on the occasion of a reception for Miss Anna Robertson held in the church manse on Moffatt Street. Teachers and officers of St. Andrew's Presbyterian Sunday School had gathered to present Miss Robertson, who was to marry the next week, with a silver tray.

Following graduation in 1934, Will went to work for Mr. J. Laskaris in the Olympia Restaurant in Carleton Place. He learned to dispense soft drinks, make ice cream sundaes, and whip up milk shakes and was expected to do anything and everything the boss required of him to earn his salary of $36 a month. In 1936, Will then took a sales position with Mr. Elmer D. Robertson, owner of Baird and Riddell Gent's Furnishings on Bridge Street. He stayed with Mr. Robertson for five years, earning $80 a month, at which time he enlisted in the RCAF. Typical of Will's Christian faith, and of his devotion to his family, most of his earnings went to help support the family home.

In the autumn of 1941, Will journeyed to the RCAF recruiting office in Ottawa, intending to enlist as a pilot or for instructional duties. The interviewing officer saw him as an "underweight but wiry lad, deliberate and talkative who wants to please." It was also recorded that, while Will himself was intent upon becoming aircrew, his family did not want him in a flying trade. Therefore, he was instructed to talk things over with his family before coming to a definite conclusion.

It was only logical for Will to be attracted to the air force. Growing up, he had filled his bookshelves and window ledges with hand-built model planes. Will was able to convince his parents that democracy demanded his involvement. To him the issues were clear: a peaceful world was worth the struggle; therefore, on January 5, 1942, he boarded the train for Toronto and the CNE grounds to begin his training at No. 1 Manning Depot.

From Toronto, Will wrote of his experiences in becoming an airman:

> Well since my arrival here I have enjoyed every minute of the time (that is except of the time I had my inoculations). I have met up with some splendid types of chaps, . . .

> Since my arrival here, January 6, every day seems to bring new changes. Here is yesterday's program. Reveille and lights being turned on greeted me at 6:00 a.m. Imagine me getting up every morning at that hour, or can you? However, I feel better for it, I think. The first thing is folding one's sheets and blankets, military style, go for a wash and shave, (we MUST shave EVERY morning here,) then after that task we head for the mess hall and so to breakfast, and royally too. Yesterday's breakfast consisted of scrambled eggs, two strips of bacon, toast, jam or marmalade and coffee. Oh yes! I forgot we start off with a steaming bowl of oatmeal porridge with lots of milk. After breakfast we head back for our bunks; polish our boots, shine our buttons, and at 8:00 a.m. we stand at attention for bunk inspection by one of the senior officers. At 8:15 we are assembled on the parade ground, have roll call; march to another one of the buildings and practice 'about turn' and many other items of drill. Then about 10:15 to 11:15 we have physical training, and immediately following are marched back to barracks and were dismissed till 11:55 and so the next thing after dismissal was dinner. It consisted of homemade vegetable soup, lovely roast pork (lots of lean meat) apple sauce, creamed potatoes, mashed turnips, brown or white bread and tea along with a generous helping of apple pie[7].

[7] Food seemed to occupy a great deal of the recruits' thoughts. Most wrote home in some detail of the grand meals they were given. Once they reached England they would pine for the food they had consumed in Canada.

I next went for my mail, eagerly looking for a letter. At five to one we formed on the parade ground, had roll call, then went on a long route march, right downtown as far as Sunnyside. We came back between 3:30 and 4:00 and were dismissed for supper. It was certainly a long hike but we are all glad of the opportunity to get the exercise and the fresh air.

It gave us a fine appetite for supper, which consisted of sliced cold meat, sliced beets, scalloped potatoes (and were they good!) tapioca pudding with strawberry jello over the top. I went for a second helping of that, which with bread and butter and tea completed a very good meal . . . [A] lecture on Mathematics for our squadron that we had to attend [in the evening] is being given by one of the professors of the University of Toronto, and is the beginning of several such lectures, so I guess from now on there will be less spare time to do as we wish . . . [We] are posted to squadron 5, which means we will take a week's training in rifle drill, present arms, etc.; and all phases of sentry duty. Then I understand we are posted back to squadron 1, which means we will take at least two weeks and maybe six weeks of guard duty.

We had our first rifle drill this a.m. and went on another route march this afternoon, dropping off at the 'Sally Ann' [Salvation Army Canteen] where we rested for about half an hour and had coffee and doughnuts. They have a fine place near here, tables for checkers, croquinole, and even a library, and off to one side there is a theatre where they have movies almost every evening [free to all men of the services]. We were over there a week ago and saw a good movie.

As well as the theatre over there, we have a theatre of our own in this building, in fact it is to one side of the lounge. There is a movie on tonight: they usually have some very good pictures. Last night there was a wrestling match on in the arena. I just saw about ten or fifteen minutes of it. Say, it was rough! Tomorrow night there is a girls' softball game, and on Friday night, of course, there is the CBC broadcast which takes place from the theatre here. No doubt you have listened in to this program often and have heard the airmen sing and also heard Woodhouse and Hawkins put on their comedy act . . .

After four weeks of basic training Will was sent to No. 6 SFTS at Dunnville, Ontario, to determine his fitness for aircrew, to be selected for a particular trade, and to begin flight training. He arrived at Dunnville on February 1, 1942.

Dunnville aerodrome was built in 1940 specifically for training fighter pilots. Aircrew training took a minimum of ten weeks.

Will was fortunate enough to get home on weekend leave once in March and again in April after completing his course. When he was home in April, a group of the St. Andrew's choir members and Sunday School staff surprised him at home with a duffel bag and money belt. Will was commended for his irrepressible cheerfulness, unselfishness, and his way of giving encouragement in times of difficulty. "We wish for you a secure and successful career with the airmen of our forces, and that your return to the work here at home, and in Carleton Place, and to St. Andrew's church, and to us, will not be long delayed, but hastened by a good and desirable turn in the circumstances of the world."

Will was then enrolled in Air Navigators' Course No. 51 at No. 1 ITS in Toronto[8], and upon graduation, on June 5, was promoted to leading aircraftsman with a pay increase to $1.50 per day, plus 75¢ per day flying pay. Will graduated thirteenth in a course of eighteen students and his evaluation read: "A steady dependable unassuming airman. Methodical in habit, with a fine Service spirit." He was becoming an excellent airman and would soon make a good navigator.

After another short leave at home, Will reported, on July 5, to No. 1 AOS, Air Navigation Course No. 54, at Malton airport near Toronto, where it would be determined whether he could safely navigate an aircraft under all weather conditions.

During his course Will flew a total of seventy-two hours, fifteen minutes in daylight and twenty-nine hours, forty-five minutes at night. His air work was fairly good (he received a mark of 72%), but in his final DR plotting examination, he became confused. However, he was able to write a supplemental examination in which he achieved a score of 76%. His course instructor thought he would "Improve with practice."

His proudest moment came in early November when he was paraded and presented with his wings. (He was also promoted to sergeant.) Nothing was more valuable to an airman than a wings badge on his left breast that told the world "I fly airplanes!" Present in Malton to witness Will receiving his wing as an air observer/navigator were his two brothers,

[8] For a further detailed description of navigator, or air observer, training see Part Two, Chapter Seven, the section on James Warren.

Hugh and Cameron and Cameron's wife. Cameron was a corporal in the air force serving in Brantford at the time.

Will got some leave at home, before embarking from Halifax on November 22. Sergeant Navigator Valley cabled his parents that he had arrived safely in England on November 30.

Will was assigned to fly with an RAF squadron, which required that he take more training. The British had their own training system to make fledgling aviators familiar with the type of aircraft they would fly on operations and map reading over England and to expose them to the wartime environment, so Will trudged off to No. 9 EFTS.

Map reading in England was considerably different from that in Canada. In Canada the weather was such that the navigator usually had unlimited visibility in which to see miles of uncluttered countryside neatly divided by section roads and railway lines. In the U.K., there was almost always a low overcast of cloud mixed with industrial haze. Staying below the cloud meant flying at 2,000 feet, which reluctantly gave up five miles of visibility on a good day. Then, on the ground, was overwhelming detail. Railway lines and roads ran in every direction like spider webs, towns and villages melted into one another, and fields and forests presented a great jigsaw puzzle of various shades of green, making it almost impossible to pick out any landmark. However, with great concentration, the navigators from Canada were able to direct the aircraft from point A to point B and back again without becoming hopelessly lost—and without asking the pilot for directions.

On April 23, 1943, Will was promoted to the rank of flight sergeant, with a basic rate of pay of $2.50 a day. Then, within a month, Will was sent to No. 1 Air Fighting Unit (AFU), where he learned to hold on for dear life as his bomber was pitched through the air in corkscrew turns to evade an enemy fighter. After a week of ground school, the navigators flew on long-range map-reading missions while their pilots practised instrument flying without reference to the ground.

To locate themselves, navigators learned to plot radio bearings from ground stations; but these could easily be distorted by bad weather or jammed by enemy interference. A fail-safe alternative was astro-navigation. Every bomber had a Plexiglas dome in the roof where the navigator could use his sextant to take sightings using the sun, moon, or stars. But it took a skilled and experienced navigator to take an accurate sighting and then calculate his position. The mathematics involved took time, so often by the time the calculations were complete and the sighting lines plotted, the aircraft could be fifty to a hundred miles from where the astro sighting was taken. Navigators prefer to work ahead of the aircraft, not behind it.

A remarkable number of navigators suffered airsickness. There was no comparison between plotting courses in a classroom and in a bouncing, deafening, plummeting, freezing aircraft. Many never managed to overcome their nausea. Yet, night after night they flew on operational missions, quietly vomiting into wax-lined paper bags, before returning to their calculations, never complaining.

On June 8, Will Valley was sent to No. 10 OTU. He spent all summer learning how to navigate four-engine bombers then, on September 2, he went to No. 1658 Conversion Unit (CU) to convert his training and navigating techniques to meet the needs of the Halifax.

Handley-Page built the Halifax in 1939, and the aircraft became operational in 1941. When it first came on line, it was dangerously underpowered and had a fatally flawed tail section that over-responded to the rudder controls, which resulted in the deaths of many crews. However, with new engines and a redesigned tail section, the Halifax was destined to become a most effective bomber. The aircraft carried a crew of seven and the Mark III[9] was powered by four 1,615 hp Bristol Hercules

engines. The fuselage was seventy-four feet long, with a wingspan of 104 feet. Its altitude ceiling was 24,000 feet, and at 22,000 feet, its usual cruising altitude, it could travel 3,000 miles at a speed of 312 mph. One .303 manually operated machine gun was in the nose and four were in each of the dorsal and tail turrets. It could carry a maximum of 13,000 pounds of bombs.

On October 20, 1943, Will Valley joined No. 78 "Preston" Squadron (RAF), a World War I squadron that had been disbanded then reformed at Dishforth on November 1, 1936, as a heavy-bomber squadron. It served with the Yorkshire-based No. 4 Group. Initially equipped with Armstrong Whitworth Whitley bombers, 78 Squadron had been converted to the Handley-Page Halifax II aircraft in March 1942 and flew them for the duration of the war. On the night of May 30–31, 1942, the squadron participated in the historic thousand-bomber raid on Cologne; on August 17–18, 1943, on the flying bomb base at Peenemunde; and on June 5–6, 1944, in direct support of the Normandy invasion, it attacked the coastal gun battery at Mont Fleury.

The squadron's motto was *Nemo non paratus* (Nobody unprepared), and its badge displayed a heraldic tiger, rampant and double queued to represent

[9] As improvements were made to airframes and engines they were produced as new versions of the same equipment and given a "Mark" designation. Therefore the Mark III referred to here was the third version of the same basic engine design.

the squadron's aircraft at the time (Whitleys), which had two rudders and two Tiger engines.

No. 78 Squadron flew the most sorties in 4 Group and suffered the most losses of any Halifax squadron and of 4 Group. It had the third highest overall losses in Bomber Command. Their bombers dropped 16,900 tons, believed to be the greatest tonnage of bombs in 4 Group.

In June 1943, just a few months before Will joined, the squadron moved from Linton-on-Ouse to its new base at RAF Station Breighton, near Selby in Yorkshire. Three days after joining 78 Squadron, Will was promoted to the rank of warrant officer II (second class).

On Monday, November 22, 1943, a telegram boy rode his bicycle to the Valley's Moore Street home. "Deeply regret," the message read, "that your son, R 143973 W. A. Valley was killed on active service overseas, November 19th." The death of this young man, who was held in such high esteem by his many friends in the town and at St. Andrew's Presbyterian Church, caused widespread grief.

On November 18, Will had written a newsy letter to his mother on the happenings at his squadron and the flying he was doing. He closed by expressing his thoughts about the coming Christmas season. "Now mother," he wrote, "by this time you really know the three of us [he and his two brothers who were also overseas in the RCAF] won't be home for Xmas so try hard & carry on and don't have Dad work too hard." Unbeknownst to Will, his father, Emery, had undergone surgery at the Ottawa Civic Hospital and did not return home until the week of Will's death. Will offered wartime optimism that "next year we three will be home & how happy we will be to be together again and we will have two turkeys for Xmas and invite all our friends."

On the night of November 19–20, 266 aircraft were ordered to bomb the industrial city of Leverkusen. The majority (170) were Halifaxes. Valley's seven-man crew, under crew captain, Flight Sergeant W. Hrynkiw, took off from RAF Station Breighton in a Halifax II number JP 118 at 1616 hours. It was already dark in miserable weather, and low-lying cloud shrouded the south England airfields, soaking them with cold rain or drizzle. Climbing above the clouds, Will gave the captain a heading to steer for Germany.

The bomber group was being led by ten Mosquitoes, flying at 28,000 feet, working as Pathfinders. Their job was to mark the target for the following bomber crews. Very few German fighters were operating, probably because the bad weather extended well over the continent. As well as the difficult weather conditions, *Oboe*[10] equipment failures prevented the Mosquitoes from marking the target properly. Consequently bombs were scattered over a very wide area. Twenty-seven towns well to the north of Leverkusen recorded bomb strikes while the city itself recorded only one high explosive bomb hitting the town.

However, to add to the challenges caused by the poor weather, Oboe equipment failures prevented the Mosquitoes from marking the target properly, resulting in bombs being scattered over a wide area. Twenty-seven towns well to the north of Leverkusen recorded bomb strikes, while the city itself recorded only one high-explosive bomb hitting the town.

Approaching the target, bombardier Flight Sergeant L. Preece settled over his sight in the Plexiglas nose of the aircraft. Skipper Hrynkiw ordered the gunners to watch vigilantly for enemy fighters. Preece passed directions to the pilot: "Steady . . . right . . . left . . . left . . . steady . . . bombs gone!" Relieved of thousands of pounds the aircraft leapt upward. As Hrynkiw wrestled the machine in a large arc for home, the crew watched wide-eyed as "their" bombs exploded in dull red eruptions, starting a rash of fires. Valley took directional control and passed a course to Hrynkiw for England and home.

Among the more unpleasant surprises for RAF squadrons over Europe was the efficient German flak batteries gathered around every target. They had 20-mm and 37-mm light flak and 88-mm heavy flak guns. They could virtually fill the sky with a solid curtain of steel and fire into which the bombers flew. German night fighters also took their toll. Hurricanes tried to provide escorts, but there were just too many flak batteries and Messerschmitts. The Luftwaffe controlled the skies, and RAF losses mounted at an alarming rate.

Towering search lights swept beams across the night sky, bouncing back off the low clouds, while German defensive flak looked like a mass of white Christmas bulbs flashing on and off. Over the roar of engines the crew heard only a dull "woof" and smelt the acrid cordite as the machine manoeuvred through the black bursts. They could hear spent fragments pattering like rain

[10] Oboe was a radar device installed in Mosquitoes to counter the industrial haze that hung perpetually over the Ruhr valley. It worked in conjunction with two transmitting stations in England. The first station directed the Mosquito in a straight north-south line over the Ruhr. If the aircraft deviated from this preset path a series of dots (for westerly deviations) or dashes (for easterly deviations), heard in their radio head sets, advised the crew of the error.

The second station, sited one hundred miles from the first, measured the Mosquito's progress. Both the air craft's pre-determined altitude and ground speed were to be rigidly maintained by the aircrew. When the airplane reached the target the second station sent a signal. The pilot and navigator had to be skilled experienced crewmen. For the last ten-mile run-in to the release point they had to fly a perfectly straight and level course. At 28,000 feet they were out of range of most flak and few fighters could reach them. In 1943 the Mosquito was the only fighter aircraft to be able to fly at such height.

on the fuselage. Suddenly, Halifax JP 118 lurched sickly to the right. The starboard wing had taken at least one direct hit and the aileron was responding slowly to the controls. Wind whistled through the many holes that appeared suddenly in the fuselage. Braced against his seat straps, Hrynkiw fought to regain control of the plummeting machine.

He was finally able to level out, and found that in straight and level flight, he had decent control of the aircraft. He called for a roll call over the intercom and all crew members responded. None was injured, but all were frightened. Will gave the pilot a new heading for home, and crossing the channel they started a slow and cautious descent. Over the airfield, the pilot began a turn to line up on the runway. Suddenly the airplane bucked and dove. At 2220 hours, it crash-landed at Eastrington, only a few miles from the runway threshold, one of only four Halifaxes lost that night.

All but three of the crew escaped and ran for their lives. The mid-upper gunner, Sergeant G. Creer, and the wireless operator, Sergeant W. Jones, lay injured in the wreckage. Fortunately the airframe did not explode or burn and they were rescued. Warrant Officer II Will Valley was pulled dead from the fuselage. The medical officer arrived twenty-five minutes after midnight to examine the body. Death had almost certainly been instantaneous from a broken neck. His pelvis was also fractured, and he had suffered minor lacerations to the right side of his forehead. His identity disc positively identified him.

Next morning the sad little routines began. The air force police, and the base chaplain went to Will's room to sort through his belongings before sending them home. They arranged for the sale of his bicycle; it brought $8.94. Clerks processed the necessary paperwork and the squadron commander wrote to Will's mother. As the war lingered, and casualties mounted, it was difficult for the commanding officer to keep such letters from becoming formulaic.

> During the time your son had been with us, he had completed several successful flights over Germany. His keenness and enthusiasm for his job proved him one of our most capable navigators. His death has left a sad gap in the Squadron, and his loss we can ill afford. The circumstances in which he met his death are as follows. Their aircraft was badly damaged by enemy anti-aircraft fire over Germany and although the captain, a fellow Canadian, managed to reach this country they crashed only a few miles from Base. Your son was killed instantly and can have suffered no pain. I saw his brother who is stationed only a few miles away and gave him what information I could regarding the accident.

Will's brothers, Cameron, then a sergeant in the RCAF undergoing flight training at 1659 CU, Topcliffe, and Hugh James, a leading aircraftsman in the RCAF, attended the funeral on November 24. Will was buried by his squadron mates in Harrogate (Stonefall) Cemetery in Yorkshire. Although there are graves from both world wars, the majority are from World War II and nearly all are airmen. The Air Forces Section had opened in July 1943, on two acres in the northeastern corner. It is entered through a pair of wrought-iron gates on Forest Lane. On the lintel above the entrance to the shelter containing the grave registry is carved the RAF motto (which is also the RCAF motto) *Per Ardua Ad Astra* (Through Adversity to the Stars).

"There is no room for despair in any church which has among its members such devout, sincere, spiritual-minded young men as Will Valley," intoned the Reverend James Foote at an 11:00 a.m. memorial service held on Sunday, December 12, 1943, in St. Andrew's Presbyterian Church in Carleton Place. The congregation was quite large. Joining Will's friends and family were the mayor and town councillors, an officer representing the Chief of the Air Staff, the Rockcliffe air base chaplain, and a number of other local airmen. Reverend Foote told the audience:

WOII William Allan Valley, Navigator.

> [Will] gave his life in a great cause and a noble consecration. . . . He sought no sheltered place but one of hazard near the pilot. As a navigator he had before him two landscapes-those of earth and heaven. And that night as his plane returned to the landscape of earth, Will's spirit entered the landscape of a new world, with whose spiritual geography he was familiar. He entered it with his Spiritual Pilot, who had vanquished death. It was not merely a stream of flak that overtook the young airman that night, but a streaming of light and goodness of God, opening fresh fields to a pure and lovely spirit. He gave his life in unbroken allegiance to those things which he held dear. He has gone to God's future house, where, if our faith be strong enough, we may still walk with him.

At the end of April 1944, Mayor M. P. Morris and Mr. Gemmil W. Comba, president of the local Legion branch, visited the Valley residence to present Will's mother with the Memorial Cross. The family had been paid his War Service Gratuity of $330.98, representing his 684 days of service, 339 overseas. In October 1945, his mother applied for a pension, writing, "We sure lost a wonderful son he was sure a great help to us in every way. He knew we were in need of his help and he left fifty dollars to be sent home a month." In spite of the family's obvious financial dependency on their

sons, a pension was denied because Emery was earning a monthly salary of $88. Instead, on July 20, 1946, the grateful government sent Mrs. Valley a small silver wing. It was Will's "ops wing," presented in recognition of a tour of operations completed.

CHAPTER SIXTEEN—COASTAL COMMAND

Bombers operated over water as well as land. In 1939, before the war, the RCAF established Eastern and Western Air Commands to patrol Canadian waters in the Pacific and Atlantic Oceans and to protect convoys carrying vital supplies to Europe. The RCAF had also been flying patrols from Newfoundland since 1939, and early in 1940, sent a maritime patrol squadron to Gander to provide air support for the Newfoundland Escort Force. As the Battle of the Atlantic intensified, air bases were developed all along both Canadian coasts.

Western Air Command saw comparatively little action, although one of its fighters had the distinction of shooting down the only enemy plane, a Japanese Zero, destroyed by an aircraft based in Canada. Instead, Western aircraft flew reconnaissance patrols and strafing missions over the Aleutian Islands and established an air supply route to Alaska and on to Russia.

RAF Coastal Command included RCAF squadrons, but the Canadians, with eight squadrons and seventy-eight aircraft on the Atlantic coast, had no long-range aircraft. Coastal Command RAF squadrons were stationed on both sides of the Atlantic and in Iceland to cover the mid-ocean gap where wolf packs of U-boats roamed freely. Then, in May 1943, the RCAF acquired some long-range Liberator bombers that greatly assisted in their surveillance of the North Atlantic.

Interestingly, the only two Carleton Place aviators lost in maritime operations were lost in March and April 1943, exactly one month apart.

R 97637 Warrant Officer II Robert Franklin Cavers
Wireless Operator/Air Gunner
Royal Canadian Air Force

A weak but warming sun broke through cloud-covered skies over Yarmouth, Nova Scotia, on March 23, 1943. It was a good day for flying operations. Cloud cover was no lower than 2,000 to 3,000 feet, and visibility was unlimited. During the morning, the fifteen- to twenty-five-knot wind out of the north-northwest whisked the occasional light snow shower across the runways. During the squalls, horizontal visibility was reduced to five miles. The temperature gradually warmed from a low of 26°F to 32°F as the sun rose to its zenith. It was a super day to be an aviator.

West Camp of RCAF Station Yarmouth was one of the first east-coast bases. Built during 1938–40, it played an important role in protecting Allied convoys. Aircraft made daily patrols off the coast of Nova Scotia protecting ships from enemy submarines. The base was the home for Eastern Air Command and home war establishment bomber reconnaissance squadrons.

No. 113 RCAF Squadron, after previous lives as an army co-operation squadron in 1937 and as a fighter squadron in 1939, was re-formed in Yarmouth on February 15, 1942, for anti-submarine duty flying Hudsons and Venturas. Yarmouth's wartime airbase, with West Camp and East Camp, a BCATP training base, comprised two complete little cities, each with a large work force employed to keep hundreds of aircrew and many types of aircraft flying.

The 113 Squadron Operations Officer briefed five aircrews on March 23, 1942. Three were detailed to fly convoy patrols and one to conduct an exercise with a Royal Navy submarine transiting up the Nova Scotia coast towards Halifax. The last crew was scheduled to carry out an air test on an aircraft that had just finished having some repair work done on its engines. Flying Officer C. L. Tripp was pilot and crew commander of one of the crews briefed for a convoy patrol.

Shortly after lunch in the NCO's mess, the navigator and two air gunners joined Tripp in the briefing room. They were ordered to be airborne at 1500 hours to fly an antisubmarine patrol over the *Princess Helene*, a ferry sailing on regularly scheduled service in the Bay of Fundy from Digby, Nova Scotia, to Saint John, New Brunswick. Their assigned aircraft was a Hudson III, serial number BW 620[11].

Lockheed Hudson Mk I 764 at Dartmouth, N.S, on February 17, 1941, with the markings of No. 11 (BR) Squadron. (Photo–RCAF Squadrons and Aircraft, P.33)

The crew was taken by jeep to the aircraft sitting on the tarmac in front of Yarmouth's hangars. The pilot walked around the airplane as his expert eye checked the control surfaces, the wheels, and the engines. He noted that it had a full fuel load of 3,780 pounds of high-octane aviation gasoline. Satisfied, he climbed into the pilot's seat to prepare for start-up. He was an experienced maritime pilot. In the last six months, he had flown 227 hours and 40 minutes with 106 hours and 5 minutes on the Lysander, and 121 hours, 35 minutes on the Hudson.

[11] Hudson BW 620 flew 113 Squadron's first operational mission on March 25, 1942.

The navigator's pre-flight duties included arming the four 250-pound depth charges carried in the bomb bays and checking the two smoke floats, four flame floats, four sea markers, three flares, and two BM 8A1 flares. He carried his case of maps and charts on board and took his take-off position in the co-pilot's seat. The two gunners checked the two forward Browning .303 guns for ammunition and serviceability. Both gunners were also qualified wireless operators. One climbed into the wireless/telegrapher's seat behind the pilots to prepare the radios, while the other took his position in the plane's main cabin. With the crew (average weight 180 pounds each), full fuel and ammunition, the Wright Cyclone engines would be hauling 19,337 pounds into the air.

Tripp radioed the Yarmouth control tower for take-off instructions. He incorrectly identified his aircraft as BW (Bravo Whiskey) 625 instead of 620. However, with no other airplanes taxiing or over the aerodrome, Tripp was given immediate clearance for take-off. His gloved left hand tightened on the control wheel and his right steadily moved the two throttles forward. His feet were braced on the brakes as the engines gained enough power to begin the take-off roll. His crew confirmed through the intercom that they were seated and strapped in. Tripp released the brakes, and the Hudson gathered speed to break the bonds of gravity.

At 1458 hours, BW 620 went airborne. Observers noticed that the aircraft was in a tail-down attitude and seemed to be "mushing" into the air. It was in a steep climb. Too steep for the engines. The aircraft appeared to stall. The port wing was high, and it swerved sharply to the right. Agonizingly slowly, as if in slow motion, the aircraft began a roll, which was almost completed when it nosed into the ground between No. 3 Runway and Starr's Road at the northeast end of the aerodrome. A horrendous ball of flame enveloped the crash site, incinerating the four crewmen. Flying Officer Charles Leroy Tripp, navigator Sergeant Alexander John Baillie, and wireless air gunners Flight Sergeant Mervin Elwood Tarrant in the radio seat and Flight Sergeant Robert Franklin Cavers in the cabin, were instantly killed.

The tower controller immediately sent the crash truck and ambulance. However, because he thought the airplane was BW 625, as reported by the pilot, instead of BW 620, he told the crash crew they were responding to an unarmed aircraft. Many other airmen raced the truck towards the pillar of black smoke and flame that marked the crash. The crash crew began fighting the fire, standing much closer to the aircraft than they would have if they had known its armament load. Then, after five minutes of pouring foam onto the flames, the entire scene went skyward in a spectacular explosion. The fuel tanks and two of the four depth charges, along with unburnt flares, blew up. Crash truck crew members Leading Aircraftsman L. E. Briggs was killed instantly, and his mate, AC1 F. Halleck, died ten minutes later in the hospital. Three other members of the crash crew were seriously injured.

R. Frank Cavers was born on April 23, 1916, to Bessie May McNabb and Thomas Edgar Franklin at their home in Appleton. He was their first child. Frank went to school in the village, later attending high school in Almonte and Carleton Place. At the Appleton Public School, according to senior teacher Miss Ida Paul, Frank usually headed his class. He took grades seven and eight in one year and won the scholarship ($5) for attaining the highest marks amongst rural schools. He attended high school for two years.

Upon leaving, he worked on his father's farm at RR 4, Almonte. Frank also farmed with his neighbour, J. V. Kellough, Appleton farmers J. A. Turner and P. N. Fumerton, and on the Ashton farm of H. S. McArton. For five years, he took a correspondence course in diesel mechanics from the Hemphill School; then, in January 1941, he borrowed $50 from Miss Paul, his Appleton teacher, to cover expenses so he could go to Vancouver to complete his diesel-engine course. When he applied to join the air force in Vancouver on February 12, 1941, this was his only debt, which he had promised to repay by May 7, 1941.

Frank wanted to join as an aero-engine mechanic. However, despite his interest, experience, and qualifications, the recruiter recommended that he be trained as a wireless air gunner. There was a war on and aircrews were badly needed. The recruiter described Frank as follows:

> A very shy quiet retiring lad. Seems to have his head screwed on the right way. Put himself through Diesel Course after considerable sacrifice and seems to be the type who would wear well. Training in RCAF will doubtless improve him. Observant. Suitable for WAG.

Frank listed his religion as United Church and his interests as hiking, snowshoeing, softball, engines, and cadets. Frank returned to his home at 1007 Pacific Street in Vancouver to await an opening for basic training. A month later, on March 14, he was called in for another interview, a medical examination, and his formal enlistment into the RCAF. At that time, Frank claimed a very slight knowledge of the French language, affiliation with St. Andrew's United Church, Appleton, and that he had been president of the Young Peoples' Union of that church. The medial officer recorded that he stood 5' 10¼" tall, weighed 150 pounds, and had a scar from appendectomy surgery in 1924. He also had a visible scar in his left medial malleolus (ankle). Physically, he was recorded as having brown hair, grey eyes, and a medium complexion.

With the official rank of aircraftsman second class, Frank was given a ticket east and told to report to No. 2 Manning Depot in Brandon, Manitoba, to begin his training. He was told to take a minimum of clothing, as he would be issued everything he needed, even underwear; few men arrived at the depot with much more than one small suitcase containing a toothbrush and basic essentials.

In the classroom and on the parade square, Frank was taught to revere the RCAF and wear his uniform with pride.

Every airman, regardless of trade, had to learn some "soldierly" attributes. He had to know when and how to salute his officers, to stand still and erect on the parade square, and to keep in step on the march. He learned to become a team member amongst an almost seamless body of blue, called a "flight."

From April 7 to 14, 1942, Frank was hospitalized in Brandon with acute tonsillitis. But that did not affect the progress of his training, and on April 30, 1941, his name appeared on the Posting List for a transfer to Medicine Hat, Alberta, where he was assigned for guard duties at No. 34 SFTS. While these schools were the final step in a pilot's training, most airmen just starting their training were sent to them to provide mundane perimeter guard duties as they waited for the next phase of their own training. It was also good for their morale to watch fledgling aircrew take to the skies.

Frank was TOS (taken on strength) of No. 2 Wireless Training School (WTS) in Calgary on June 23, 1941, where he learned the intricacies of ground and aircraft radios, electronic and transmission theory, and perfected his prowess with a Morse code key to the extent that he could send and receive fifteen words per minute. He also learned to identify the bewildering display of flashing lights so that in times of imposed radio silence, he could "talk" to operators on the ground or on ships. While on course, Frank became a basically trained airman and was promoted to the rank of leading aircraftsman on July 24.

On September 8, Frank reported to the base hospital with a high temperature and a red rash covering his entire body. Diagnosed with scarlet fever, a highly infectious disease, he was sent to the Calgary Isolation Hospital, where he stayed until October 6. After two weeks' sick leave, he returned to No. 2 WTS and resumed his studies by joining Course No. 24. Flying was an integral part of the curriculum, and he logged a total of eleven hours, thirty-five minutes practising airborne communications. Frank graduated just before Christmas with an average of 80.6%, eighth in a class of 162 students.

Frank had his wings parade on January 31, 1942, when he was awarded the air gunner's badge. Trained as an airborne radio operator, Frank proceeded, in

February 1942 (he was promoted on February 2 to temporary sergeant) to RCAF Station MacDonald in Manitoba and No. 3 B&G School to learn the fine art of aircraft gunnery, especially the precise skill of leading (aiming ahead of a speeding airborne target) to ensure it was hit. During this course, he flew a total of nine hours in the Fairey Battle training aircraft. Graduating fourth out of twenty-five gunnery students and with a 75.6% average, he was evaluated as a "Good student and [with an] excellent memory." He was now entitled to wear the wings of a wireless operator/air gunner.

Posted to "Y" Depot in Halifax, Frank was sure that he was headed to England and a bomber squadron. However, to his surprise, he was transferred to newly reformed No. 113 Bombing and Reconnaissance Squadron, based in Yarmouth, Nova Scotia. No. 113 was one of the patrol squadrons of Eastern Air Command under Fleet Air Arm Bomber Command.

No. 113 had been given the Lockheed Hudson Mark III aircraft, which had evolved from the American Lockheed 14 airliner, and at the time, was the most modern aircraft in Coastal Command's inventory. Pilots, however, at first considered the machine dangerous and not nearly as genteel as the biplanes they had flown before. The Hudson had high-wing loading and unusually powerful flaps; the pilot had to really work to land it. They also viewed with suspicion the Hudson's modern features, including the Sperry Gyropilot, the propellor and wing de-icers, and the fuel-jettisoning system. However, as they became more comfortable with repeated flying, most pilots developed an intense affection for the aircraft[12.]

On March 25, , 1942, shortly after Frank's arrival, Hudson BW 620 flew the squadron's first operational mission and made the squadron's first operational kill. Frank flew his first operational patrol out to sea in April and was promoted, on August 2, to the temporary rank of flight sergeant.

1942 was a busy flying year for 113 Squadron and Frank Cavers. Air protection of the northwest Atlantic was the responsibility of Eastern Air Command, and its long-range aircraft could extend protection to surface vessels many hundreds of miles out to sea. Antisubmarine action was also at its heaviest in 1942 and in the spring of 1943 when the enemy moved more U-boats into the western Atlantic to harass British-bound convoys. The threat reached into Canadian waters, and the Command's sea and air resources were fully extended. Thousands of hours were flown from isolated air bases, often in foggy weather. After the war, this abuse meant that most Hudsons were scrapped. One, however, remains. Aircraft T 9422 is mounted on a pedestal at the airfield gates in Gander, Newfoundland, commemorating the work of Eastern Air Command and Ferry Command.

[12] Spencer Dumore, Above and Beyond (Toronto: McClelland and Stewart Inc., 1996), p.83.

Flying Officer Tripp was a relative newcomer with only 121 hours on the Hudson, but he had more than 700 total flying hours, making him an experienced pilot, and the investigation after the fatal accident of Hudson 620 determined that the cause was obscure. Therefore, after interviewing many witnesses, it was concluded that the aircraft was improperly trimmed after take-off. The short take-off run, tail down and mushing attitude in the air, steep climb and resulting stall all supported this opinion. As well, all of the propellor blades were bent in a way that indicated the aircraft was under full power when it hit the ground. It was also determined that the improper aircraft identification and inadequate training led to the loss of the crash crew airmen.

On March 25, 1943, one year to the day after Frank reported to the squadron, under overcast skies, a funeral parade was formed at Sweeney's Funeral Home to escort the four bodies to the Dominion Atlantic Railway station to be shipped to their respective homes. Warrant Officer Gibbs, a friend of Frank's since basic training, accompanied his body to Carleton Place, where it was taken to his parents' home near Appleton.

On Tuesday, March 29, Reverend Thomas McCord of Carleton Place conducted a short service in the Cavers' home before the funeral cortege proceeded to the village church where Flight Lieutenant P. H. Ellis, RCAF chaplain in Arnprior, conducted the service with full military honours. Members of the Carleton Place and Almonte Legions attended along with friends and family and RCAF members stationed in Arnprior. The cortege then moved to St. James cemetery where, following the firing of a rifle volley, the coffin was placed in the vault to await interment in the spring in St. Filans, Carleton Place United Cemeteries.

Surviving Frank were his parents, his brother Harold of Appleton, his brother Melville, a private at Camp Borden, and his sister Agnes, at home. On April 23 he would have been twenty-nine years old. His parents were sent the obligatory condolences from the Minister of Defence and the Royal Family, and his mother, Bessie, was presented with a Memorial Cross on May 18, 1943. For his 740 days service his gratuity amounted to $354.18. Mr. and Mrs. Cavers received the following letter dated October 6, 1944, on behalf of the Chief of the Air Staff:

> I am directed to advise you that your son, Robert Franklin Cavers, has been promoted to the rank of Warrant Officer Second Class, with effect from February 2nd, 1943.
>
> This promotion is based on a policy inaugurated by the Royal Canadian Air Force, whereby aircrew members of the service who had been recommended previously by their Commanding Officer for the next higher rank and would

have received the promotion but for the intervention of untimely death, are promoted to that rank effective six months from their last promotion.

It is my sincere hope that you may find sustaining comfort in the knowledge that the qualities of your gallant son are thus recognized, and it is regretted that this information could not be passed to you at an earlier date, but the delay in notifying you was unavoidable.

May I express to you and the members of your family my profound sympathy.

In *The Canadian* of March 22, 1945, appeared the following "In Memoriam":

CAVERS—In fond and loving memory of a dear son and brother WO2 R. Frank Cavers, of the R.C.A.F., killed on active service at Yarmouth, N.S., March 23, 1943.

> *Remembrance is a golden chain*
> *Death tries to break, but all in vain;*
> *To have, to love, and then to part*
> *Is the greatest sorrow of one's heart.*
> *The years may wipe out many things,*
> *But this they wipe out never —*
> *The memory of those happy days*
> *When we were all together.*

—Lovingly remembered by his parents, Mr. and Mrs. Edgar Cavers,
sister and brothers.

And on March 21, 1946, the following appeared:

CAVERS—In fond and loving memory of a dearly beloved son and brother WO2 R Frank, of the RCAF, who was killed at Yarmouth NS Mar 23, 1943.

> *Sunshine passes, shadows fall,*
> *Love's remembrance outlasts all.*
> *And though the years be many or few,*
> *They are filled with remembrance of you.*

Mom, Dad, sister and brothers.

CHAPTER SEVENTEEN—GARDENING

Sea mining (laying mines in harbours and their approaches and code-named "gardening") was a major task for Bomber Command. Bombers "planted" some one thousand "vegetables" every month, and Canada's 6 Group was considered the most experienced and advanced in this endeavour. In 1943 alone, 6 Group flew 911 sorties, laying close to 1,500 mines, and losing nineteen aircraft doing it. In 1944, Bomber Command laid 22,000 mines.

Gardening never dominated the headlines like those written for Bomber Command raids, but mining was an excellent investment. Some claimed that the airdropped mines sank more German ships than the Royal Navy. Spencer Dunmore, in *Reap The Whirlwind*, wrote that possibly the greatest contribution mine-laying operations made to victory was the formidable task they presented to German sailors. Minesweeping duties occupied at least forty per cent of German sailors on a full-time basis.

The laying of mines was a precise art. Accuracy was vital. Crews were instructed to drop from between 500 and 1,000 feet on a timed run from a prominent landmark at exactly 200 mph. The low altitude was necessary because the mines, if they fell too far, had a tendency to break up in the air. And if the crew did not find their aiming point to begin their run, they were ordered to return to base with the load.

Working along the coast, the crews rarely encountered enemy fighters, but ground and ship-based flak were an ever-present deadly hazard. For every 111 mines laid, Bomber Command lost one aircraft. Some flew into the sea because the aneroid altimeters deteriorated rapidly and provided incorrect readings[13]. In the blackness of night, aircrews could discern no horizon and depended upon their altimeters to keep them above the waves.

R 111832 Warrant Officer II Arthur Esmond Prime
Wireless Operator/Air Gunner
Royal Canadian Air Force

Arthur Prime was the only Carleton Place boy lost on "gardening" operations.

Arthur was very fond of hunting and fishing and was an avid duck hunter. On November 9, 1940, he left his home at 59 Moffatt Street to paddle his homemade canoe out to his duck blind on Mississippi Lake. He had his shotgun, a supply of shells, and decoys. He had dressed warmly, pulling his knee-high rubber boots up over woollen socks. It was a clear day with only

[13] Spencer Dunmore and William Carter, Reap the Whirlwind (Toronto: McClelland and Stewart Inc., 1991), p.24

a light south wind blowing, and Arthur had no problem paddling to his blind, which was about a mile off shore, just opposite Lake Park. He was an accomplished canoeist, an active member of the Carleton Place Canoe Club. He never considered the danger of being out alone on the cold, November waters. At nineteen, he had the confidence of youth.

Late in the afternoon, John McCann, home on weekend leave from the RCOC in Ottawa, was loading his canoe at Thackaberry's shore for some duck shooting of his own. Hearing an unfamiliar noise, he immediately determined that someone was in trouble on the lake and quickly pushed off from shore, paddling towards the sound. About one mile out, he found an exhausted Arthur Prime feebly clinging to his duck blind. His flimsy canoe was upside down ten feet away.

McCann tied his canoe to the blind and grabbed Prime's jacket. Arthur was moaning and almost unconscious, and John struggled to drag him aboard, a task made much more difficult by Arthur's soaked clothing and water-filled boots. But Arthur had enough wits to help himself by rolling into his rescuer's boat. However, paddling back to shore, John had trouble keeping his canoe balanced because of Arthur's shivering and shaking. Grounding the canoe, with the help of a nearby farmhand, John carried and dragged Arthur to Stanley Thackaberry's nearby farmhouse. He was in very bad condition, due to shock and exposure, but given dry clothing and a "stimulant," Arthur slowly regained his senses. He had had a very narrow escape from death. Ironically, only a year or so before, Arthur had helped rescue a young girl from drowning in the Mississippi River close to his Moffatt Street home.

Arthur was born and grew up in Carleton Place, the youngest of six children. His parents, David Prime, a steelworker, and Agnes Fishenden had met and married in England before emigrating to Canada. Born in 1923, Arthur attended CPHS for two years, leaving at the end of the school year in 1939. He had joined the school cadet corps, and in May of that year, had participated in the annual inspection. He was in Platoon No. 1 with, among others, Boyne Dunphy, Lloyd Scott, and Wilson Costello.

Although Arthur professed a lack of interest in sports, he played right wing on the Church of England's hockey team, played softball and rugby at school, and enjoyed cross-country skiing and swimming.

When he left school, Arthur followed his father, brothers, and a sister into employment at the Findlay Foundry. His brothers were pattern makers and stove mounters, and his sister was a stenographer. Arthur learned the trade of a sheet metal workering and started at a wage of $50 a month, which rose to $90 a month by 1941, the year he heard the siren call "to serve his country" and joined the air force.

Arthur reported to the recruiting centre on May 3, 1941. The interviewing officer described Arthur as a young man with brown eyes and dark brown hair with slight tracings of a dark moustache on his upper lip. He was a thin but athletic lad, standing 5' 6" tall and weighing a slim 146 pounds. The interviewer also noted that Arthur was "very quiet and reserved. Would make a fair W.O. [wireless operator] Gunner." After suffering the indignity of an aircrew medical examination, Arthur was told to go home and wait for a call to start his service.

That call came on July 28, at which time he was informed that he was now an aircraftsman second class and that he was to go to No. 2 Manning Depot in Brandon, Manitoba, for basic training. (He was a few courses behind Frank Cavers who left Brandon in April.)

Travelling by train half way across the country was an adventure in itself. CN had patched up all the old passenger cars that could still ride the rails, but they were drafty—a good thing in July, but not so welcome in the winter months. Plus, the run west was overnight, a long time for men sprawled in upright wooden seats of ancient day-coaches. However, the blue air force meal ticket each recruit was given bought the recruits an excellent meal in the dining car.

The Manning Depots served to transform raw recruits into smart young men who could be considered suitable for further training as aircrew. As aircraftsmen second class they were the lowest ranking people on the station, a status made no better by their ill-fitting uniforms. And, until they were able to visit a civilian tailor in town and spend their own money for alterations, they were fair game for harassment from all manner of higher ranks.

After four weeks at Manning Depot, Arthur, looking every inch the airman, went to nearby Dauphin for twenty days to guard the base perimeter. On October 29, he reported to No. 3 WTS, in Winnipeg, and was promoted to the rank of leading aircraftsman. Christmas must have been a joyous occasion, for Arthur overstayed his leave by two days, three hours, and fifty-five minutes. For this infraction, he was CBd (confined to barracks), and from December 29 until January 5, he was allowed out of his room only to attend class and parade, and to eat.

From Winnipeg, Arthur was sent to Paulson, Manitoba, to attend No. 7 B&G School. Deflection shooting was the trickiest art to learn. The gunner had to determine that part of the sky ahead of the target in which his bullets and the target would meet. With aircraft twisting quickly and violently, the gunner needed almost-magical marksmanship and judgement. Arthur's experience hunting ducks and other birds was of great use to him at gunnery school, and on April 13, 1942, he proudly paraded and was awarded his air gunner's badge and a promotion to temporary sergeant.

Sergeant Arthur Prime wears his new wings and rank chevrons. (Photo National Archives)

Arthur was then sent to Patricia Bay, an airfield near Sidney, British Columbia, where he joined course No. 8A at No. 32 OTU and was introduced to advanced aerial gunnery, flying twenty-three hours and thirty-five minutes on the Anson and graduating to the Hampden in which he flew another forty-three hours and twenty-five minutes. His course evaluation determined that he was, "An average pupil, [who] should become very efficient with practice."

After spending most of the summer in British Columbia, Arthur was posted to "Y" Depot in Halifax to await sea transport to England. En route, he took some embarkation leave in Carleton Place for a few goodbyes, then sailed for England on October 30 proudly displaying the crown of a flight sergeant above his three sergeant's chevrons. The promotion and increased pay came into effect on October 13.

Arthur arrived in England on November 5 and was sent immediately to Thornaby and No. 6 OTU. Dutifully, he sent a cable to his parents announcing his safe arrival.

No. 6 had been formed in July 1941 as a coastal OTU flying Ansons and Hudsons (the month before Arthur's arrival, they had traded the Hudsons for Mark VIII Wellingtons.), and on December 1, the Canadians joined other Commonwealth airmen and RAF crewmen to train for wartime coastal patrol duties. Arthur accumulated thirteen hours and fifty-five minutes on the Anson and thirty-six hours and fifty-five minutes on the Wellington. When they were considered worthy, the student gunners were passed on to No. 7 OTU, based in Limavady, where all their flying was on the Wellington, the aircraft they would be using in operations.

Most OTU aircraft had many flying hours on them when they were given to the training units. At No. 7, the students were operationally trained on the

Wellington and learned how to drop torpedoes instead of bombs. They were also pressed into service laying mines (the Wellington was easily adapted to carrying two Mark IV, 1,500-pound mines). The last test of a crew was an operational mission flown by a combination of students and instructors. Often they flew leaflet raids, but if their war-weary aircraft was capable of getting airborne, carrying a crew and a bombload, they were sent on the multi-aircraft raids devised by Air Chief Marshall Arthur "Bomber" Harris of Bomber Command.

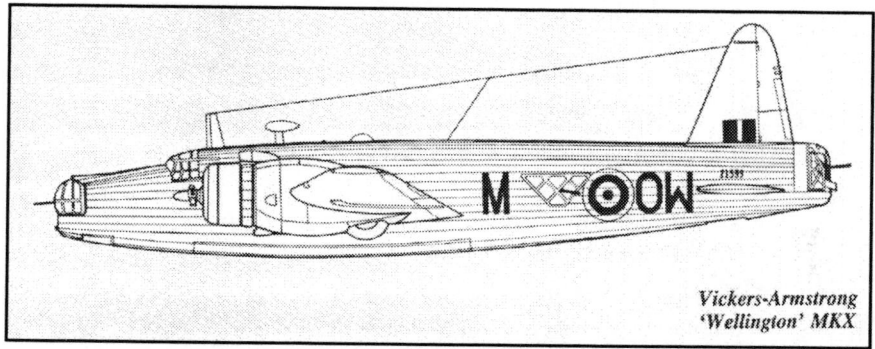

Vickers-Armstrong
'Wellington' MKX

Flight Sergeant Arthur Prime was posted for operational flying to 547 Squadron at RAF Station Chivenor, Barnstaple, North Devon. The squadron had been formed in October 1942 for torpedo bombing and was equipped with Wellington G.R. II bombers. They were later converted to Halifaxes and Liberators which had the Leigh Light (a powerful searchlight) installed. When Arthur arrived on March 19, 1943, nightly bombing missions were being carried out on German industrial targets in what would become known as the Battle of the Ruhr. Letters from home informed Arthur that his brother Harry had also enlisted and was also training to be an air gunner[14].

On the night of April 22–23, in addition to bombing missions, Bomber Command ordered thirty-two aircraft on what they called "Minor Operations." Five aircraft were to fly from the OTUs, and 547 Squadron provided Mark VIII Wellingtons; among them aircraft number HX 743, captained by Flying Officer D. B. Henderson. The remaining crew were: Second Pilot Sergeant R. Ronald, Navigator/Bomb-Aimer Flying Officer R. Deere, and Wireless Operators/Air Gunners Sergeants A. E. Prime, B. Y. Ginn and T. H. Hornbrook.

The Bomber Command War Diaries record that one Lancaster and one Wellington never returned from this sortie. None of the other crews saw them go down, nor was any trace of either aircraft found. The air force informed Arthur's parents that their son was listed as missing on active service.

Although officially listed as missing, after a short time, the administration

---

[14] Harry went overseas in May 1943, after Arthur was lost. He completed a full tour of operations (32 missions), achieved promotion to the commissioned rank of Pilot Officer and was awarded the Distinguished Flying Cross.

accepted the fact the men were gone. On April 26, the officer commanding RAF Chivenor sent his condolences and a gunner's flying badge to Arthur's parents, and on May 7, the Canadian Minister of Defence sent a card of condolence. A telegram from George VI and Queen Elizabeth arrived on March 1, during the same week the mayor, Mr. M. P. Morris, accompanied by Ashley Kerr, president of the Carleton Place Legion, visited the Prime home to present Arthur's mother, Agnes, with a Memorial Cross.

At the end of November 1944, a letter arrived for Agnes informing her that Arthur:

> . . . has been promoted to the rank of Warrant Officer Class II with effect from April 13th, 1943.
>
> This promotion follows a procedure adopted by the Royal Canadian Air Force, that all aircrew members of the service if recommended by their Commanding Officer should at the end of the required lapse of time from their last promotion be promoted to higher rank. This promotion procedure has been made retroactive in order to extend the same recognition to those who have unhappily lost their lives.
>
> It is my sincere hope that you may find sustaining comfort in the knowledge that the qualities of your gallant son are thus recognized, and it is regretted that this information could not be passed to you at an earlier date but the delay in notifying you was unavoidable.

It was never definitively learned whether or not this exercise in bureaucratese eased the grieving parent's pain.

The Primes were paid Arthur's War Service Gratuity of $240.56, repre-

senting his 632 days service, 178 of them overseas. Arthur left three brothers, Harry, D. A., and William, and two sisters, Mrs. R. W. Lloyd and Mildred. On July 31, 1946, a set of operational wings was sent to Arthur's mother "in memory of a young life offered on the altar of Freedom."

No scrap of the lost Wellington nor of the six airmen was ever found. And, although his family could always pray that somehow, somewhere, Arthur had survived, the final blow to this hope arrived by mail on June 25, 1952:

It is with reluctance that after so long an interval, I must refer to the loss of your son, Warrant Officer Class II Arthur Esmond Prime. A report has, however, been received from our Missing research and Enquiry Service, which states that their efforts to locate your son's grave have been unsuccessful. Under the circumstances, therefore, it must be regretfully accepted and officially recorded that he does not have a 'known' grave.

Due to the extreme hazards attending air operations there are, unhappily, many thousands of British aircrew boys who do not have 'known' graves and all will be commemorated on General memorials that will be erected at a number of locations by the Imperial War Graves Commission (of which Canada is a member), each memorial representative of a theatre of operations. One of these Memorials will be erected at Runnymede, England, and the name of your son will appear on that memorial.

Arthur's name appears on The Air Forces Memorial at Runnymede in Surrey. It is situated four miles from Windsor on Cooper's Hill at Englefield Green overlooking the river Thames.

Chapter Eighteen—The Battle of the Ruhr, March to July 1943

Walking the darkness, far from home, at midnight,
Sometimes I see them, lighted at the wing-tips,
The cockpits winking with the spark of signals,
The outbound bombers.

My thought perceives them switch away the sidelights
And cease to signal as they drive to danger,
From England, over sea, to blackened Europe
Where fire awaits them.

I say 'O come home safely, midnight darers,
And may a day dawn when the youths of nations
Will hold like purpose, striving to make perfect
The life that binds us.

—John Masefield

The greatest commitment of the RAF, and the rest of the Commonwealth air forces, was the bombing offensive against Germany. Early in March 1943, bomber crews, aiming at crippling Germany's industrial production, began flying into the impenetrable maze of flak and searchlights guarding the Ruhr Valley. Every night, heavy bombers streamed through the sky for Germany.

Although they flew in unnerving closeness, there was no attempt to fly in any formal formation. However, each navigator was responsible for getting his own machine to the target and home again through a sky full of bombers and protective fighters, led by Pathfinders, flak, searchlight beams, and night fighters. The Ruhr more than lived up to its nickname of "Happy Valley."

Poor visibility through ground haze typically obscured a Ruhr target. But Oboe, a radar device installed in the Pathfinder Mosquitoes, ensured that any target was accurately marked.

Early in the war, bombs were notoriously unreliable. They often failed to detonate and their weight was prohibitive. However, by 1943, the situation had improved. A 4,000-pound steel tube into which molten explosive had

The fast, manoeuvrable deHavilland Mosquito was an excellent aircraft for the Pathfinders.

been poured was introduced. Nicknamed "cookie," it became Bomber Command's main weapon. It had a tremendous blast and was ideal for area bombing in concert with incendiaries.

There were two main incendiaries: four-pound bombs packed into containers that broke open after drop and a phosphorous-filled thirty-pound incendiary. Both high-explosive bombs and incendiaries could have time-delay fuses. Designed to discourage rescue work and demoralize the citizenry, the fuses could be set for any time from an hour or up to a week later.

Bombing could be as dangerous for the aircrews as for the targets. Early reports stated that aircraft had been lost because their bomb loads exploded soon after release. Investigators determined that 500-pound bombs released from the rear bomb bays of Lancasters, under certain circumstances, could collide with the 2,000- or 4,000-pound bombs dropped from the forward bays. After dropping two or three hundred feet, the 500-pound bombs would become "armed" and explode if they were touched. The slightest rub would set them off, causing the heavier bombs to blow up.

The average life of a bomber airman was six weeks: 125,000 men flew in Bomber Command in the Second World War and 55,500 died, 9,919 of them Canadians. Squadrons suffered losses daily. While the death of friends and comrades was hard to take, surviving airmen swallowed their fears with their pre-flight meals and returned each night to the starlit sky. Young men with the unbridled optimism of youth and an absolute conviction that, although the possibility of being shot down was always present, it would not happen to them. They girded themselves with camaraderie and the rare resiliency of youth.

Throughout Bomber Command, crews were under no illusions as to the magnitude of the task and the risks involved. With the number of losses rising steeply, the fortitude and determination of the aircrews cannot be overemphasized. A special brand of courage was necessary to continue flying against such formidable odds.

On January 1, 1943, the all-Canadian 6 Group of Bomber Command came into being. It had eight hastily assembled squadrons: 408 (Goose

Squadron) at Leeming, 424 at Topcliffe, 425 and 426 (Thunderbird) at Dishforth, 428 at Dalton, 419 (Moose) and 420 at Middleton St. George, and 417 at Croft. Canadian in name only, the squadrons' aircrew was a motley collection of British, Australian, New Zealand, South African, Rhodesian, and American airmen. As ships landed fresh young faces at Liverpool and Greenock, Canadian airmen slowly replaced their RAF and Commonwealth brothers.

R 125618 Flight Sergeant David Chester Maxwell
Air Bomber
Royal Canadian Air Force

Chester Maxwell began his aircrew service in the RCAF as a navigator; however, after almost a year of training, he failed the navigation courses at No. 1 Central Navigation School in Rivers, Manitoba. But, Chester wanted to stay in aircrew, so, because he had taken the bombing and gunnery course and done well, he was selected for further training as an air bomber.

He was killed on his first mission over Europe.

Chester was born to Chester Phelan Maxwell and his wife, Mary Ellen Adzaoff, in Montreal on March 19, 1920. He was twenty years old when he walked into the recruiting centre in Ottawa on August 8, 1940, after having lived in Ontario for only two years. His family moved to Carleton Place (57 Lake Avenue then later to 8 Mary Street) when the CPR transferred his father there. Chester senior worked in the signal section, periodically checking the bells on the road-crossing alarms. Later, he became a town councilor. Chester attended Holy Family School in Montreal, then St. Patrick's College in Quebec City.

In school, Chester was an active participant in the cadet corps. A week after he turned eighteen, he joined the militia, The Royal Rifles of Canada, and stayed with the regiment until July 11, 1940.

His hobby was building model airplanes, and he enrolled in ground school, studying the theory of flight and navigation at McGill. He even got two hours dual-control flying. Later, he told the RCAF recruiter that he enjoyed rugby, hockey, baseball, swimming, and target shooting.

After the battery of tests that preceded every enlistment, he was found to be especially good in mathematics and to be bilingual in French and English. The officer wrote that Chester was a "Solid type of boy-quietly spoken, has had 3 years experience as a rifleman in NPAM. Neatly dressed, alert and confident, should make a good aircrew member. Recommend for pilot-air crew." Chester then had to wait over a year to be called for training.

He reported for basic training on August 28, 1941, at Exhibition Grounds in Toronto and No. 1 Manning Depot, leaving behind his job working under Mr. E. Giles in the shipping department of Findlay's Foundry.

His enlistment medical examination on September 4 revealed a youth of twenty years standing 5' 7" tall, weighing 147 pounds. For the record, he was listed as having a fair complexion, brown hair and eyes, and with a chest measurement of 36" was considered well developed. His blood pressure, at 136/88[15], was considered "borderline," but he was declared "fit in every way" and given an A1B A3B[16] medical category. He had sprained his ankle six months previously, but there were no lasting effects. On his personal history form, he wrote that he was unemployed and although he took the "odd social drink," he was a non-smoker. He was an only child, a sister having died at age twenty-seven.

Following the usual training, Chester was graduated on September 12. He returned to Ottawa and the Rockcliffe air base to put in time on guard duties while he awaited an opening at an ITS.

On October 26, Chester travelled back to Toronto and reported to Course No. 39 at No. 1 ITS. Students here never saw the inside of an aircraft, but spent their time in a classroom studying mundane subjects such as mathematics and being introduced to air navigation and air force rules and regulations.

Their flying skills, meanwhile, were tested in the Link trainer. Basically a mock-up of an aircraft cockpit, it could climb, dive, turn, and respond to controls handled by the student. In the Link, the greatest danger was to invoke the scorn of the officer instructor.

Although he had to write a supplemental examination in mathematics (70%), Chester graduated, on December 19, fifteenth in a class of twenty. His course report stated that he was a "Quiet, determined, cautious trainee with leadership qualities. A very dependable type." He was promoted on graduation day to the rank of leading aircraftsman, and because he was in aircrew training, he was granted flying pay of 75¢ a day. But he was not to become a pilot. Chester was sent to No. 3 AOS operated by Prairie Airways, a division of Canadian Pacific Airlines, in Regina, Saskatchewan, for observer training.

Following Christmas leave at home in Carleton Place, Chester travelled west by train to report for Course No. 42, which began on January 5, 1942. There, the intricacies of navigation eluded Chester. At the end of three

[15] A blood pressure of 140/90 was considered the base line indicator of hypertension.
[16] Fit for all aircrew duties anywhere.

Chester Maxwell is shown wearing his observer wing and the rank stripes braid of a sergeant. He was killed before his bomb-aimer wings became available. Photo National Archives C148152.

months, and after thirty-one hours and fifty-five minutes trying to navigate a Fairey Battle through clear western skies, Chester's air work was found to be below average. He was rated twenty-first out of twenty-two students. Although co-operative and conscientious, he tried to do too much at once and could not keep up with the airplane. However, to further evaluate his capabilities, Chester was sent to No. 2 B&G School at Mossbank, Saskatchewan, where he proved to be a poor gunner, but an average bomber. Overall, he was an average student, steady and reliable, and at the end of the course, on May 23, he was awarded his air observer's badge and promoted to the rank of temporary sergeant.

After flying another thirty-three hours and forty-five minutes at the B&G School, Chester complained to the medical officer that he was having trouble with his "stuffy" nose and was experiencing dizziness and bi-temporal headaches that came on during descents. He had fractured his nose some time prior to joining the air force and had a marked deviation of the septum to the right. He said that he had suffered right-sided coryza and some occasional fullness in his right ear ever since the accident, so he was sent to the RCAF hospital in Regina. Surgeons straightened and cleared his nostrils with a submucous resection.

Chester returned to the ANS where the instructors felt that, although he was a very slow and inaccurate worker, he could be brought up to school standards with a further two weeks of concentrated training.

On June 8 he reported to Course No. 42 in Rivers, Manitoba, and the very next day, on his very first training flight, the aircraft made a forced landing about one mile south of the airport. Pilot Officer Cook was flying Chester and two other students in an Anson. At 1758 hours, the ailerons locked, making control of the aircraft impossible during an approach to land. The wheels were down, but they did not make the runway. Fortunately, no one was hurt, but Chester had pulled his seatbelt extra tight in fear of damaging his newly re-set nose.

In spite of all his efforts, and those of his instructors, Chester failed his navigation course. He had to write supplemental examinations and obtained only a "fair" mark (66%). He was thoroughly examined, and his psychological profile, covering such things as "service spirit, keenness and determination," was found to be "average." But he was a very slow and inaccurate navigator. He seemed to know what was required, but he could not produce the desired result. It was especially noted that his plotting of the aircraft's progress was "lacking in neatness." Therefore, after another thirty-one hours and forty minutes flying, he "ceased training as an observer." His final evaluation read:

> Air Training—An average navigator inclined to let the work accumulate and fails to make use of the information in hand. Lacks drive, and initiative in air work. Lacks neatness.

> Ground training—Very slow and inaccurate worker, seems to know what to do but fails to produce the desired results. Lacks neatness in plotting. Made a fair mark in supp. Exam. Officer qualities.

> General—Inclined to be easy going, seems to be well liked, lacks drive, initiative and confidence.

Chester, rated an "Average, rather stolid type," wanted to remain aircrew, and the only option left open to him was as an air-bomber. On the B&G course, his gunnery was too erratic for him to be a gunner, but his bombing was not bad. His instructors concluded that he "Should make a good Air Bomber if he gets down to work." He was reclassified on August 14, and on August 20, was awarded his air-bomber's badge. But this trade was so new that the badges were not yet available, so Chester continued to wear his air observer's badge until the new insignia was issued.

Sergeant Observer Maxwell visited his parents en route to Trenton to await posting overseas. But before he left Canada, an infraction caught up with him. While at Rivers, when his fate in aircrew was being determined, Chester went AWL from midnight on August 5 to 2000 hours on the 7th. The authorities at Trenton put a reprimand on his records, and he was fined two days' pay.

Warned that he would be posted overseas at any time, Chester was allowed embarkation leave to go home over the Labour Day weekend. Chester left Canada on October 27 and landed in England on November 4, 1942, then was sent immediately to Bomber Command's No. 22 OTU, where airmen were gathered together for crew training. When he arrived, Chester was told that his promotion to flight sergeant had come through, effective from November 23. Beginning the next day, he was enrolled in Course No. 34, which he completed on March 13, 1943, and during which

he flew twenty-one hours and thirty minutes daytime and twenty-three hours nighttime on map-reading exercises. Ten hours and fifteen minutes of day flying and ten hours and five minutes of night flying were devoted to bomb-aimer training. However, at the end of the course, he was judged an "average bomb aimer" and transferred to 426 "Thunderbird" Squadron, one of the new Canadian squadrons with 6 Group.

426 Squadron had been formed at Dishforth on October 15, 1942, as a night-bomber unit with No. 4 Group. It was equipped with twin-engine Wellington IIIs, and on January 1, 1943, was attached to the new all-Canadian 6 Group. They flew their first operational mission on January 14, and in March 1943, they began to take receipt of the newer Wellington Mark X aircraft. This airplane had a new engine, the Hercules VI, which was much improved and more powerful than its predecessor. The Wellington IIIs made their last sortie on 426 Squadron on April 16.

At the OTU, Chester was crewed with air gunners Flying Officer H. R. Drake of Winnipeg and RAF Sergeant E. W. Betts; navigator Flying Officer G. MacMillan of Toronto; and pilot Sergeant. K. F. Fighter of Vernon, British Columbia.

Following their crew training, they all reported to Dishforth and 426 Squadron late in March. Chester was feeling confident. The crew had flown many training/bombing flights. They had dropped practice bombs on the range and flown simulated bomb runs, using a camera that gave the bomb-aimer practice that was as close to the real thing as they could get. They practised night flying and flew cross-country navigation and air firing exercises. They joined the squadron full of anticipation of flying the missions for which they had trained so long and hard.

High-level bombing was an art, calling for absolute co-operation between the pilot and the bomb-aimer.

Having built up the same velocity as the aircraft carrying it, a bomb, once released, continued at the same speed. As it dropped, it developed a terminal speed dependant upon the individual bomb, its shape and weight. The bomb-aimer had to take all these variables into consideration and set his bombsight accordingly. Due to the forward speed and the length of time the bomb took to fall, the bomb-aimer often dropped as far as a mile ahead of his target.

For the bombsight to work with reasonable accuracy, the pilot had to keep the aircraft absolutely level, at a constant speed and altitude as set into the sight. However, for the final minutes of a bomb run, they were sitting ducks for night fighters, unable to manoeuvre and evade the fighter's fire. During those last thirty seconds, the pilot would struggle to maintain half a dozen variables as the bomb-aimer opened the bomb doors and issued a stream of minute variations in course.

On May 11, 426 Squadron was told that they would be moving from Dishforth to Linton-on-Ouse the first week of June to join up with 408 Squadron. The two RAF squadrons that had to vacate the station for the Canadians in 408 and 426 were none too happy, and a great deal of animosity arose. Pre-war stations like Linton-on-Ouse were quite comfortable. It had brick buildings close together and well-planned roads and paths. Most of 6 Group's Canadian squadrons occupied bases built since the outbreak of the war. They were cheerless, windswept places apparently chosen for their distance from any decent pubs and their tendency to remain damp and muddy even in dry weather. They attracted ground fog at the most inconvenient times, like at landing and take-off.

The men lived in Nissen huts with stoves; washrooms and toilets were in Nissen huts without stoves. Nissen huts were utilitarian buildings used as offices, medical quarters, operations rooms, briefing rooms, and any other use required by a bomber base. Cinder paths and duckboards, often washed out, connected them, and a concrete perimeter road circled the field, which the aircraft used to taxi to and from dispersal points.

After several training trips on squadron aircraft, Maxwell's crew was warned of their first operational mission, which would occur on the night of May 12–13. May 12 dawned bleak and overcast. The weather did not improve all day, with intermittent rain and only moderate visibility at best. At the briefing, The Right Honourable Malcolm MacDonald, His Majesty's Secretary of State for the Dominions, was present. He heard the ten crews briefed for a fourth attack on Duisberg. The previous three had been only partially successful.

They were told that the centre of the city and the port area, just off the Rhine River, had suffered severe damage: 1,596 buildings had been destroyed and 273 people killed; four of the August Thyssen steel factories had been damaged; and nearly 2,000 prisoners of war and forced workers had been brought in to repair windows, roofs, and other bomb damage. In the port area, twenty-one barges and thirteen other ships had been sunk with another sixty ships damaged. This would be the last raid on Duisberg during the Battle of the Ruhr.

One of the advantages to joining the operational airmen's fraternity was that aircrews got fresh milk to drink every day and enjoyed a pre-flight meal consisting of a real fried egg, bacon, and toast.

But it wasn't just aircrews who had to prepare for the night raids. Gasoline trucks, called bowsers, pumped thousands of gallons of aviation gas into the empty wing tanks, oxygen cylinders were loaded into each aircraft, and tractors towed long lines of trolleys laden with a great variety of lethal canisters. Gunners polished the perspex of their turrets so no speck of grime would impede their vision, while armourers draped long belts of ammunition into the turrets. Chester would ensure that his load was secure. He had two 500-pounds bombs, 420 four-pound incendiaries, 30 Type X, and 32 thirty-pound incendiaries in the bomb-bays

The crew would return for a final briefing about the course, speed, and altitude to fly to the target. They would receive a briefing on the weather at various altitudes and radio and visual codes, while the navigators prepared their maps and charts. Finally, the crews would board the open-sided truck for the drive to the aircraft.

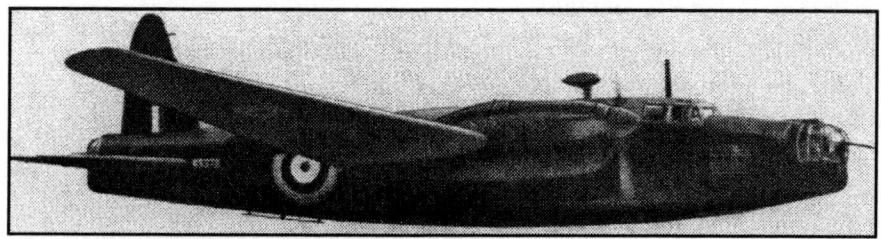

The fabled "Wimpy" Wellington bomber.

On this night, of the 572 aircraft flying, Chester and his crew were aboard one of the newer Wellington X's, side number HE 157. The other aircraft consisted of 238 Lancasters, 142 Halifaxes, 112 Wellingtons, 70 Stirlings, and 10 Mosquitoes. The Mosquitoes with the Pathfinder Force would be marking the target with various red, green, and yellow flares. 426, 428, and 429 Squadrons contributed forty-one Wellingtons.

It was still raining when Sergeant Fighter started each of the Wellington's 1,500- hp Bristol Hercules XI engines. Both sputtered into life and settled down to a dull, continuous roar, and the dials on the instrument panel indicated all was well with each power plant. The wireless operator tested his radios, but made no transmission under strict radio silence for security, and the gunners loaded their weapons, including the two guns in the nose that the bomb-aimer could use to fend off frontal attacks. The pilot, Sergeant Fighter, called for an intercom check before take-off and each man responded: "Nav checks, skipper!" "Gunner here!" "Wireless OK!" "Bomber!" All were strapped into their seats as the brakes were released and the ship trundled into line for take-off. They were in the air at 2349 hours.

Three of the squadron's ten aircraft were forced by mechanical malfunctions to turn back. The rest pressed on over the English Channel and across the Dutch coast. Sergeant Fighter did his best to sound confident as he ordered his gunners to keep a sharp watch for enemy fighters. All new crews (sprogs) were racked with nervousness and eagerness, including Bomb-Aimer Chester Maxwell, who hunkered down in the cold, shuddering nose of the Wellington and settled down to his sights, getting his eyes used to the dark and rolling ground about 12,000 feet below.

Visibility was reasonably good that night, and Chester finally got his sights fixed on Duisberg. Then the defences opened fire, sending up with deadly accuracy copious flak over Duisberg. Like a hundred light bulbs flashing on and off, the flak rose into the bombers' path, making a barely audible "whomp" as it just missed the aircraft. Fragments, like metal rain, spattered off the fuselage.

Eighty per cent of the red target indicators fell within two miles of the aiming point, and most bombs were dropped within three miles of the aiming point with excellent results. The city took a terrible pounding, and no further raids were considered necessary in the immediate future. The old town, suburbs, town centre, and port areas were all badly hit.

On board HE 157 all was quiet as the pilot settled onto the final run. Chester, with his right eye glued to the target in his bombsight, called course corrections: "Right five degrees . . . steady . . . steady . . . left . . . left . . . doors open . . . steady . . . bombs gone!" Suddenly, relieved of a thousand pounds of weight, the bomber leapt upward, and the crew watched *their* bombs erupt in dull red explosions. To this sprog crew the scene resemble images of hell. One large explosion threw reddish-orange flames and black smoke high into the sky, while just below them and to their right, a Wellington was locked in the glare of several German searchlights. It was hit and spiralled downward. No parachutes were seen.

Turning for home, they all started breathing again, none realizing they had stopped. Six hours after leaving Dishforth, the wireless operator called base to advise they were turning for home. That was at 0205 hours and was the last anyone heard from them.

Fighter manoeuvred the Wellington left and right, ducking, diving, and sliding between bursts of flak and the red lines of tracer fire. Suddenly the anti-aircraft fire stopped, and the crew knew that an unseen night-fighter was closing on them. Without warning, the outside blackness was slashed with white tracers. Gunner Drake screamed, "Corkscrew starboard," and Pilot Fighter threw the Wellington into a steep, starboard dive. Navigation instruments, parachute packs, and any other loose piece of gear flew wildly inside the fuselage. A Messerschmitt 210 raked withering cannonfire into the airframe. Gas tanks in the wings burst into a flaming cauldron.

In the night's operational report to Bomber Command, "No. 426 (RCAF) Squadron reported that Wellington aircraft No. 157 with a crew of five failed to return from an operational attack on Duisberg. It left base at 23:45 hours on 12 May 1943, after which no further news was received."

On May 17, Wing Commander Leslie Crooks, DSO, DFC, of 426 Squadron, wrote to Mrs. Maxwell:

> You will have received a telegram informing you that your son Sergeant David Chester Maxwell is 'missing' as a result of air operations, . . . I regret that I have not been able to write sooner to give you such details as are available, for I know how great must be your anxiety.
>
> On the night of May 13th [sic] the squadron took part in an attack on enemy installations at Duisberg, Germany. Your son and his crew, who were all considered to be capable men, took off at 11.50 P.M., and set course for the target, together with other aircraft of the Squadron. Unfortunately nothing further has been heard from any member of the crew. That nothing has been heard is not unusual as wireless silence is always maintained on such sorties.
>
> There is always the possibility that the crew are [sic] prisoners of war, in which case you will either hear from your son direct or from the Air Ministry who will have been notified by the International Red Cross Society.
>
> In the meantime your son's effects have been gathered together and forwarded to the Royal Air Force Central Depository, where they will be held until better news is received, or in any event, for a period of at least six months before being forwarded to you through the Administrator of Estates, Ottawa.
>
> The loss of your son was sustained with great regret by the Squadron as a whole and especially by his many personal friends here. He was a fine chap and a very good Air Bomber. He was very popular with his brother Sergeants and with the members of his own crew. All of us had complete confidence in his ability and respect for his manly character. I can personally say that he set a fine example for all ranks in every way and his loss is being felt very keenly.

I wish to take this opportunity, on behalf of the entire
Squadron, to tender to you our sincere sympathy in your
great anxiety. We join with you in the heartfelt hope that
better news will be forthcoming soon.

A telegram from the International Red Cross Committee, quoting German
information, stated that Pilot Officer Drake and three unknown were killed
on May 13, 1943.

When the box of effects arrived, Chester's mother Mary acknowledged
receipt, but pointed out that Chester's electric iron, two watches, and two
rings were missing. Among the contents were a harmonica, a pipe, a diary
and a rosary.

In a report dated October 3, 1945, German records show that Wellington
X HE 157 crashed at 0330 hours on May 13 at Klundert in the province of
Northern Brabant, Holland, after being shot down by a night-fighter. The
crew was buried in the German Military Cemetery at Bergen Op Zoom. A
cross marked the grave bearing the information: "English Flyer 1.3.43 (sic)
RAF buried beside B. H. Drake and one RCAF unknown and two RAF
unknowns. Remains consist of a body partially burned and in advanced state
of decomposition."

As the Graves Registration team went through the area in 1946, they
exhumed an unknown body from Grave No. 43 in order to identify it. On
March 9, RCAF Headquarters identified it by dental records as that of
Chester Maxwell. Only the lower plate was recovered from the grave along
with pieces of burnt battle dress having an observer's wing on the breast and
an RCAF button on the tunic.

Flight Sergeant David Chester Maxwell was re-buried in the Canadian War
Cemetery in Bergen-Op-Zoom, some forty kilometres northwest of Antwerp.
There are more than 1,100 World War II casualties buried at this site.

R 111837 Flight Sergeant Dalton Arnold Turner
Air Gunner
Royal Canadian Air Force

In the autumn of 1941, hockey officials expressed doubts that the Upper
Ottawa Valley Hockey League would be able to continue. Enlistments into
the army and air force had decimated hockey teams in most Ottawa Valley
towns, and in Carleton Place, the senior team had only one defenceman and
two forwards left at home. The intermediate team, which should have provided replacements, also lost players: Arnie Turner and Jerry Townend had
enlisted in the air force; Peter Valley, "Fat" Bigras, and Wally McKittrick
were already overseas; and Eddie McKittrick and Ron Hastie were in the
army. It was a real possibility that, for the first time in many years, the town
would not be represented in a hockey league.

Arnold Turner, eldest son of Mr. John Steven Turner and Zephir (Zephyr) Victoria Weir, was born at the Turners' Morphy Street residence in Carleton Place on November 13, 1920. Both parents had been born in Ramsay Township, and John was employed as a paymaster.

Arnie attended town schools: the primary and public school from 1926 to 1934 and CPHS from 1934 to 1938. With his education complete, Arnie worked as a clerk for the Cecil McCann and A. McDaniel General Store, but after one year, he left to work at Findlay's Foundry where he learned the trade of electric welding alongside Gerry Lewis. Two years later, he joined the RCAF.

Arnie was an outstanding athlete. Although he was not very big (5' 6" tall and 130 pounds), he was fast, especially on skates. He was well known in sporting circles throughout the Valley, starring in both junior and senior hockey, and in the summer, was a mainstay of the baseball team. He was also a good golfer, and in the fall, he enjoyed hunting. With all his athletic pursuits, he had no time to give to the militia.

When Arnie walked in to the recruiter's office on July 16, 1941, he was twenty years old. He was a good-looking young man, with blue eyes, brown hair, and a medium complexion. He had fractured his left arm in childhood, but had suffered no after-effects and was found medically fit for aircrew training. Arnie made sure the recruiter knew that he wanted to fly; however, with only three-and-a-half years of high school, he was not sure he could "make the grade" as a pilot or observer, so he indicated that he would be quite satisfied to join as a wireless operator or air gunner. He was taken on almost immediately and sent to No. 2 Manning Depot in Brandon, Manitoba.

Because of growth in the RAF and RCAF during 1940, volunteers to serve as pilots, machine-gunners, and radio-operators were in great demand. The age limit for pilots had been raised from twenty-eight to thirty and for the other aircrew classifications to thirty-two. The number of recruiting centres and examination boards had also been increased to speed the selection of candidates, and with the increase in flying training facilities, it was possible to offer new opportunities in aircrew training. Candidates, however, "had to be fit and intelligent and possess dash and initiative," according to the recruiting posters.

On July 28, 1941, Aircraftsman Second Class D. Arnold Turner reported to the Manning Depot in Brandon. He survived the basic training ritual, learned air force regulations, passed the medical examinations, suffered the requisite inoculations, and muddled through the fitting of uniforms. The time fairly whizzed by, and before he knew it, he had become a proud airman. However, before going to wireless school, Arnie spent six weeks, from September 10 to October 27, 1941, on the RCAF base at Claresholm, Alberta, fulfilling guard duties.

Arnie reported to No. 3 WTS in Winnipeg on October 27, and on November 27, he was promoted to leading aircraftsman. That Christmas he went home to Carleton Place to spend the holidays with his family, but on Boxing Day, he was feeling decidedly unhealthy and the doctor was called. The left side of his face had a pronounced swelling. Three days later the right side was also swollen. The doctor diagnosed mumps and, according to board of health regulations, isolated him into his home for at least three weeks, or until the swelling had completely disappeared. Arnie's confinement ended on January 18, 1942, when he was permitted to travel back to Winnipeg.

Because of all the time spent away from the school, Arnie was re-coursed to Course No. 29, which meant he would be staying in Winnipeg and wireless school longer than usual.

On February 10, Arnie was playing poker with some of his new course mates when an officer walked into the room. All of them were found guilty of gambling in the barracks and sentenced to three days confined to quarters. During this time, they all walked the "Primrose Path," which meant they had to report every hour on the hour to the guardhouse, about a kilometre from the barracks, and present themselves in full uniform to the military police. Sleep, or any other activity (like eating) was greatly curtailed.

By March, it was becoming obvious that Arnie was having trouble with the course, especially in sending and receiving Morse code. He could not attain the desired speed, a minimum of fifteen words a minute. Therefore, in consultation with his instructors, it was decided that he would cease training at the wireless school and remuster to the trade of air gunner. He did this on March 15, but it was not until April 30 before his remuster came through, when he was told he was to go to Fingal, Ontario, for Course No. 34 at No. 4 B&G School. As this course did not begin until June 22, he was sent to Trenton for "general duties."

Air gunners endured four to six weeks' gunnery training. This included not only weapons and in-flight instruction, but also a liberal dose of drill and lectures. Being located close to Lake Erie was a distinct advantage, as training would not endanger civilians. However, any accident over water made it difficult to rescue the crash victims.

During his training at Fingal, Arnie flew twelve hours and fifty minutes in the Fairey Battle and six hours and forty-five minutes in the Bolingbroke. His training included air-to-ground and air-to-air firing.

On July 31, Arnold Turner graduated sixteenth out of twenty-nine students and was presented with his air gunner's badge and a promotion to the rank of temporary sergeant. His course evaluation read:

This man started slow but improved as he became more famil-iar with the work. His air firing results are good after firing 500 ground rounds, 200 air-to-ground and 3,387 air-to-air.

Sergeant Air Gunner Turner was given leave to go home before proceeding to Halifax and overseas. He was feted at two grand parties given by friends in Carleton Place who wished to see him off in fine style. Monday evening, August 10, friends gathered at a cottage among the pines on the shores of Mississippi Lake. As well as best wishes for a safe journey and a safe return, Arnie accepted a leather wallet containing a sum of money. On August 11, Mr. and Mrs. Arnold McDaniel, a previous employer, entertained at a six o'clock lunch-eon, held in the Wave's Inn on

Prior to going overseas Sergeant Arnie Turner posed with his family at home. Note the RCAF T-shirt worn by his brother. Such a shirt would only be worn by airmen during PT classes.

Franktown Road. As going away presents, Arnie received a large carton of cigarettes and a case of toiletry articles.

On August 20, Arnie arrived in Halifax and, the next day, boarded a troop-ship for England. He disembarked on September 1, and was sent directly to No. 14 OTU at RAF Station Cottesmore. However, as he had been bothered by a series of sore throats for several months, he did not report until October 8. Then, four days after his arrival on the station, he went on sick parade with another particularly bad sore throat. He was diagnosed with acute follicular tonsillitis and admitted to Station Sick Quarters until the infection cleared; he was discharged on October 20.

There is no indication in his records to account for his sudden absence from duty on that day. He left the station without authorization after classes, about 1700 hours, and was not seen again until he appeared on pupils' parade at 0745 on November 4. He was charged with being AWL for four days, eighteen hours and forty-five minutes. Found guilty, Arnie got a severe reprimand recorded on his personal documents and was fined five-days' pay.

After completing the courses at the OTU, Arnie went to 1654 CU on February 16, 1943, where crews intend-

Arnie with his sister before leaving for Halifax.

ed for four-engine aircraft were trained on the airplane. Slated to a squadron flying Lancasters, on March 25, as a fully trained four-engined bomber air gunner, Sergeant Arnold Turner reported to 106 Squadron based at RAF Station Syerston in Nottinghamshire. The squadron had been flying the Avro Lancaster BI and BIII models since May 1942.

106 Squadron was originally formed for service in the Royal Flying Corps during World War I. It was disbanded in 1919 and re-formed from "A" Flight of No. 15 Squadron as a bomber unit on June 1, 1938, and in 1941, it began regular night-flying operations against Fortress Europe. The squadron motto was *Pro libertate* ("For Freedom"). The squadron flew Lancasters for 5 Group and was the first squadron to use the Mk 14 bombsight.

When Arnie joined 106 Squadron, it was participating in "shuttle bombing" raids on Friedrichshafen and Spezia. The Lancasters would fly over the English Channel and down the Rhine River in bright moonlight to Friedrichshafen on the northern shore of Lake Constance. There, they would drop their loads on the Zeppelin works, but instead of turning back for England, they would continue over lightly defended Italy to North Africa. They landed at either the U.S. Army base at Maison Blanche or the RAF station at Blida, although neither base was equipped for, or knew how to handle, heavy bombers. Two or three nights later, they would load up again to bomb the oil refineries and naval docks at La Spezia, Italy, on their way home. The squadron also took part in the famous raid on Peenemunde, bombing the heavily fortified sites for the V-1 flying bombs.

During the war, 106 Squadron flew on 496 nights and 46 days, for a total of 5,834 operational missions. It lost 187 aircraft, its gunners claimed 20 enemy aircraft destroyed, a further three probably destroyed, and 29 damaged.

Lanc Tail Guns. The flying position of Lancaster "Tail-end Charlies." It was usually the primary target of fighters. (The Lancaster at War p.55)

Lancaster gunners did not lead particularly comfortable lives. Their aircraft flew at high altitudes, there was no heat in the turrets, and they suffered numbing cold. Many suffered as well from airsickness. The miserable conditions demanded that the crew wear several bulky layers of clothing under a flying suit that had electrical wires woven into the cloth which provided some comfort when connected to the aircraft's electrical system. Only men of physical endurance and mental toughness had a chance of surviving. Fire was an ever-present danger in the Lancaster, and hydraulic lines, electrical wiring, oxygen, and ammunition surrounded the gunner. Fire blew backwards through the airframe, and the tail gunner's parachute was stowed outside the turret. Inside, the gunner sat behind turret doors, which would jam shut in excessive heat. There was little chance another crew member would reach the gunner in time, meaning the chances of survival in a burning aircraft were minimal.

In the Lancaster were ten .303 guns in four turrets, and the rate of fire of each gun was 1,200 rounds per minute. As a result, the tail gunner, with four guns, could let loose 4,800 rounds a minute. However, it was rare for a gunner to initiate fire as that would give away the bomber's position.

The Lancasters often flew bombing runs at low level (500 feet), carrying 500-pound bombs. On one memorable raid, on the Schneider-Creusot works, the squadron was tasked to hit the main transformer and switching station at Montchanin, which supplied all the power for the Schneider works. It was also the connecting link between the French Alps and Paris, making it one of the most vital and vulnerable points in the entire electrical system. During the bombing, one aircraft from 106 Squadron was damaged by the blast of its own bombs, and one aircraft was lost, but not to enemy action. It had released its load at very low level and then crashed into the building it was bombing.

After the drop, the Lancasters flew around the target while the gunners fired at the transformer. Each time a bullet hit a vital spot there was a brilliant flash of blue light.

On July 8, 1943, squadrons from 1, 5, and 8 Groups were called to a briefing for a night raid on Cologne. 5 Group called for 106 Squadron, and 282 Lancasters led by six Mosquitoes from the Pathfinder Force penetrated the night sky.

Over the ever-present industrial haze of the Ruhr Valley, it is doubtful that Bomber Command would have enjoyed much success without the Pathfinders. They used a radar device named Oboe to find the target and mark it with flares to signal the bombers' drop point. Only the Mosquitoes could operate at a height (28,000 feet) that would be within the 270-mile range of the Oboe transmitting stations.

The Pathfinders' accuracy made for a very successful raid. The original markers, and those laid by follow-up Pathfinders, were deposited in such a way that the flares created a "bullseye." Several pilots reported that all of Cologne was going up like a torch-two or three square miles of solid flame. The glow was visible from over a hundred miles away, and smoke drifted up to 10,000 feet.

The raid was the third that the week. The northwestern and southwestern sections of the city were the hardest hit, destroying nineteen industrial and 2,381 domestic buildings in areas that had not previously been severely bombed. Killed civilians numbered 502, but fatalities at a POW camp and artillery barracks, both heavily bombed, were not known. A further 48,000 people were bombed out making a total of 350,000 civilians who were made homeless during the three raids made that week.

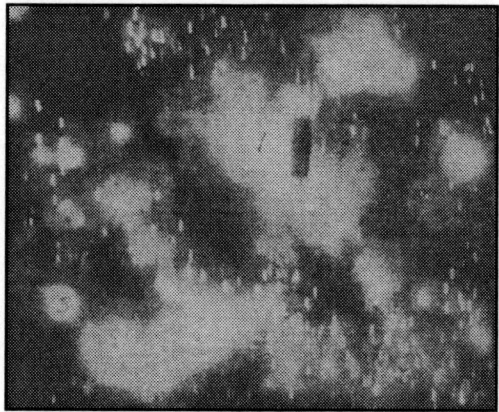

A newspaper clipping from Sergeant Ross MacFarlane's scrapbook, which he described as "very realistic." He explained that No. 1 (centre) showed a 4,000-pound bomb dropping through large smears of light that are photo flashes used to illuminate the film; No. 2 (lower right) shows small white patches that are fires on the ground; and No. 3 (lower left) shows bigger white flashes that are flak.

Seven Lancasters were also lost, and John and Zephyr Turner were informed that Arnie was missing in action. But on September 28, the RCAF Casualties Officer wrote that the International Red Cross had confirmed that, according to German sources, Arnie and his entire crew had been killed. However, until Canadian authorities could make their own confirmation, the RCAF would consider Arnie to be "missing, believed killed."

In a recent letter to his parents, Arnie had stated that "if the worst came he would proudly die for Canada and a good cause." Yet, in Carleton Place, Arnie's death was greeted with grief. The Anglican Church sent condolences, and the flag at CPHS was flown at half-mast. Ironically, the day word arrived that Arnie was believed killed, his youngest brother Allan (Jo) was in Ottawa enlisting for aircrew service.

In August 1944, members of the Canadian Legion, led by President Gemmil Comba, and Reeve W. A. Roe, visited the Turner home on Morphy Street. Reeve Roe extended a message of sympathy from the Minister of National Defence, and Mr. Comba presented Mrs. Turner with the Memorial Cross, on behalf of a grateful Dominion. Then, on November 17, the family received notice that Arnold had been buried on July 11, 1943, in the municipal cemetery in Cambrai, France.

Cambrai is a town about thirty-two kilometres southeast of Arras. In November 1917, British forces enjoyed a spectacular success on a battlefield there employing tanks for the first time. Cambrai Communal cemetery is just west of the Cambrai East Military Cemetery, a mainly German burial ground from the First World War. It has more than seventy Second World War casualties within its walls.

CHAPTER NINETEEN—SOUTHEAST ASIA COMMAND, 1944

Born of the sun they travelled a short while towards the sun
And left the vivid air signed with their honour.

—Stephen Spender

True to its name, World War II was a global war. Canadian aviators flew on air operations in all hemispheres, and RCAF Squadron 413 served in Southeast Asia Command (SEAC) from 1941 to 1944. One of its Catalinas, flown by Squadron Leader Leonard J. Birchall, first noticed the Japanese fleet stealthily approaching Ceylon. The RCAF aircraft was shot down and the crew captured, but not before transmitting information that prevented a surprise attack. The airmen spent the rest of the war suffering in horrendous conditions as Japanese prisoners of war.

Two Canadian transport squadrons, 435 and 424, flying unarmed aircraft, were in Southeast Asia in 1944, dropping supplies by parachute to allied ground forces in dense jungles and moving freight and casualties about the region.

Many Canadian airmen also flew with RAF squadrons in this theatre, including 354 and 357. Andy Porterfield flew on 354 (RAF) Squadron and Lorne "Pat" Patterson flew for 357 (RAF) Squadron. Both Carleton Place men were wireless operators/air gunners, and both achieved commissioned rank.

357 Squadron was formed at Digri, India, in February 1944 from No. 1576 Special Duties Flight. It was equipped with Hudson IIIs until January 1945, when the squadron converted to Liberators, and maintained detachments at Dum Dum (Calcutta) and China Bay.

Consolidated Liberator G.R. Mk VI aircraft "W" on December 9, 1944 following complete stripping of the camouflage finish including serial numbers. (Photo – RCAF Squadrons and Aircraft, p.32)

No. 354 was formed on May 10, 1943, at Drigh Road, Karachi, for long-range general reconnaissance in SEAC, and it was equipped with Liberator IIIs until April 1944 when it converted to Liberator VIs. The squadron kept detachments at St. Thomas Mount and Sigiriya.

J 8624 Flight Lieutenant Lorne Patterson
Wireless Operator/Air Gunner
Royal Canadian Air Force

Flight Lieutenant Lorne Patterson

Lorne Patterson was twenty-eight years old and married when he joined the RCAF on December 26, 1940, transferring from the Lanark and Renfrew Scottish, which he had joined just four months earlier in Perth.

Born on October 8, 1912, the fifth of eight children of David "Patti" Patterson and Annie Margaret Dorou, Lorne was raised in Carleton Place. His parents owned the Patterson Furniture Store and Funeral Business in the large brick building south of the bridge over the Mississippi River, across Bridge Street from the new town hall. Lorne and his large family regularly attended St. Andrew's Presbyterian Church, and in good weather, they would walk the few blocks from their residence at 24 High Street.

Lorne attended Victoria Public School until 1926 when he went to CPHS, where he matriculated in 1929 with extra commercial courses. Lorne was active in school sports, mostly hockey, swimming and softball, and he also learned to play and enjoy golf.

Immediately following high school, at age seventeen, Lorne moved to Perth and began working at the Perth Shoe Company. His education and qualifications were better than most of the company's employees, but still he started at the bottom, in the Cutting Department. With perseverance and a good work ethic, he progressed over the next ten years to become, in the general manager's opinion, one of the company's most skilled and efficient shoe cutters. In a letter of recommendation to the RCAF in 1940, E. M. Sabiston, Vice-President of Perth Shoe, described Lorne as "of the very best character, absolutely dependable, diligent in his work . . . with no bad habits."

When Lorne applied to the militia, he easily passed the medical examination for category "A," being physically fit at 5' 9½" tall and 150 pounds.

He marched in his first parade with the Carleton Place company on August 15, 1940, along with about sixty others in the ranks behind the regimental band. *The Canadian* reported, "The men presented a very smart appearance the great majority of whom were in their new uniforms." Lorne was promoted to acting corporal on September 2.

In the meantime, Lorne met and fell in love with young Dorothy Laura Barber from Buckingham, Quebec, who was pursuing a nursing career at the Great War Memorial Hospital in Perth.

Lorne's brothers (James, Grant, and Elmer) had all joined the air force, so on October 7, 1940, Lorne travelled to Ottawa to undergo the preliminary RCAF medical examination for enlistment. He told the recruiter that his only previous hospitalization had been for a tonsillectomy in May 1940, that he never smoked, but that he would usually drink a glass of beer each day. The doctor found a scar on the lateral side of his right knee and that he had lost five pounds since enlisting in the Lanark and Renfrew Scottish. He was described as having fair hair and blue eyes in a fair complexion.

However, despite this glowing report, he was almost disqualified for medical reasons. His first blood pressure reading was very high, registering 146/100. A reading of 140/90 was the base line for hypertension and eligibility for aircrew. Lorne went back for a re-check on November 11, but it was still 140/90. On speculation that it was excitement causing the high readings, the medical officer sent him for basic training, and on December 26, he was checked again and found to have a reading of 135/85. This was good enough for the air force, and he was given a category of A1B A3B, acceptable for aircrew service anywhere.

The last reading was taken the day Lorne arrived at No. 1 Manning Depot in Toronto, and had it not been within acceptable limits, his flying career would have ended the day it began.

After a month's basic training in Toronto, Lorne moved to No. 1 Auxiliary Manning Depot at Picton, Ontario, for more specialized training, and then on to Moncton, New Brunswick, for guard duties at No. 5 Equipment Depot, while he waited for an opening at a wireless school. However, before his departure from Ontario, Lorne went home to Carleton Place to help bury his father. David Patterson had died on March 11, 1941, at age forty-five. Lorne arrived in Moncton on March 26, 1941, and three months later, on May 26, left for Montreal and wireless school.

During his training, Lorne spent every leave in Perth with Dorothy. They made plans for their future together, hoping to be married before he went overseas, and Lorne applied for permission to wed from the authorities at No. 1 WTS. His application was favourably received, but the soonest they could allow him leave was August. So, with permission in hand, the couple made arrangements to be married on August 2, 1941, in the Anglican Church Rectory in Dorothy's hometown of Buckingham.

There was little time for a honeymoon before Lorne went back to Course No. 18 in Montreal. He was not with Dorothy when their son, James Lorne, was born on August 27. He graduated on October 12, thirty-fourth of 107 students, with a course average of 76.4%. His evaluation read:

> He is a very conscientious and reliable man. He achieved a very high position in class through hard work. He has shown considerable qualities as a leader and is recommended for Commissioned Rank.

The wireless portion of the course completed, Lorne went to No.6 B&G School at Mountain View (near Trenton), where he completed his gunnery training on November 7, 1941, fifth in a class of thirty-five. He did his air-to-air gunnery flying in a Fairey Battle, putting in eleven hours and fifty-five minutes in the air. "His air firing results show him to be a steady and reliable Air Gunner" and he was again recommended for commissioned rank[17].

Canadian policy was that aircrew should be at least the rank of sergeant, so Lorne was guaranteed a promotion to temporary sergeant when he graduated from gunnery school. In addition to receiving his wireless operator's badge (October 12) and air gunner's wing (November 7), Lorne was discharged from the Special Force so that he could accept a commission in the regular RCAF as a pilot officer. *The Canadian* noted, on November 13, that "Lorne Patterson, son of the late Mr. and Mrs. David Patterson, of Carleton Place, graduated at No. 6 B and G School, Mountain View, Ontario, on Nov 7th as a Sergeant Wireless Operator and Air Gunner." News of his commission had not reached the paper.

Pilot Officer Lorne Patterson was given embarkation leave and put on strength of "Y" Depot in Halifax to await shipment overseas. He left Canada on December 7 and arrived in England just before Christmas. On Christmas Day he reported to the PRC at Bournemouth.

This lovely city, a south-coast resort catering, in quieter times, to the middle-aged, presented a rude but genteel introduction to wartime England. The heavily mined beaches, barred by rusty coils of barbed wire, held little appeal, and the many elegant hotels had been taken over by the Air Ministry for transient Canadian airmen. But the city's beauty, breath-taking headlands

---

[17] It is interesting to note that a study recently (2002) revealed that bright boys are more likely to die in war. The Scottish Council for Research in Education, in 1932, tested the IQs of 87,500 schoolchildren born in 1921. The results were reviewed in 1997. While children with low IQs grew up less able to avoid disease or get help, more of the boys with higher IQs were dead. This was entirely due to the Second World War. Boys with higher IQs were more likely to die because boys with lower scores were more likely to be rejected for military service. Because of the war the link between IQ and survival was much weaker in men than women.

(now guarded by anti-aircraft Bofors guns), stately gardens and parks, and music pavilion remained. These attractions, however, were tempered after an airman's first meal in the officers' mess, located in the Royal Bath Hotel. There, the Canadians were introduced to powdered eggs, served on a slice of dry toast along with a greasy slice of Spam. Their next culinary experience was Brussels sprouts—in plentiful quantities.

Pilot Officer Lorne Patterson somewhere in England.

The PRC was a holding unit responsible for equipping the new airmen for flying training under wartime conditions. Here, the airmen were issued with battle dress, photographed for new identification cards, and issued with clothing coupons (all civilian clothing was rationed). They were also issued with the finest quality flying equipment: chamois leather gloves, helmets, goggles, and fleece-lined zippered flying boots. But flying training would not commence until after the Christmas season, so until then, their only duty was to parade twice a day, at 0900 hours and at 1330 hours, after which they were promptly dismissed. The relaxed schedule allowed plenty of time to sample the city's attractions.

The RAF was not entirely satisfied with the training airmen received at BCATP schools. In Lorne's case, he was sent to the WTS at Cranwell, Lincolnshire, until February 25, 1942, and then to No. 3 Radio School at Prestwick, Scotland, on April 21, where he stayed until May 27, 1942.

Lorne already knew that he was going to be flying on a Hudson squadron when he was sent, on June 30, 1942, to No. 6 OTU, a Hudson training unit at Thornaby. He satisfied the instructors of his proficiency on the machine, but was kept at the OTU in a supernumerary position until his posting came through on September 29, when he learned that he was going to SEAC, attached to Air Headquarters in India.

When travelling in England to attend No. 7 (Coastal) OTU, Lorne tripped in his cabin and fell, twisting his right knee. Quite possibly he was celebrating his recent promotion to the rank of flying officer on October 1. He reported sick, to the "Quick Troop" hospital on October 4 and was diagnosed with fluid on the patella (kneecap). He was ordered to bed and kept there until October 14. He arrived at the OTU, attached to 217 Squadron, on November 16.

In SEAC, two RAF squadrons were involved in dropping supplies, arms, and agents into enemy-occupied territory. The flying was low-level, following the contours of the earth. They dropped agents who helped organize resistance action and supplies of food, clothing, medical supplies, weapons, and ammunition where they could be used most effectively to kill or interrupt enemy operations. About 250,000 pounds of supplies were delivered to clandestine forces every month on mostly single sorties by a single aircraft flying on its own. No fighter cover was available, and weather was always a determining factor in the success of the mission. In winter it was usually quite good, but during the monsoon season, it varied from very bad to utterly wretched. Therefore, most flying losses were a result of inclement weather.

The U.S. Office of Strategic Services (OSS), forerunner of the Central Intelligence Agency, was one of the foremost supporting services. For the China–Burma–India (CBI) Theatre it was based in southern China and drew upon the RAF clandestine squadrons for much of its work[18]. Most military services divulge information only on a "need to know" basis. Therefore, if an operative was captured and tortured, he had very little knowledge of use to the enemy. There are grades of security classification from "official use only" through "secret" to "top secret." RAF wags thought there was one more: "frightfully hush-hush, burn before reading." Clandestine operations went one step further and simply put no information on paper.

The two RAF clandestine operations squadrons were 357 and 358. No. 357, with which Lorne was destined to fly, was formed at Digri, India, on February 1, 1944. The central image on the squadron's badge was a crocodile and it adopted the motto: *Mortem hostibus* (We bring death to the enemy). "A" Flight was formed from the former No. 1576 Special Duties Flight, and they were equipped with three Mark III Liberators and seven Mark VI Hudsons. "B" Flight had four Catalinas. The Hudsons were used for shorter-range operations into Burma, and the Liberators and Catalinas were flown on the longer flights to Malaya and Sumatra where they could land to off-load supplies and agents. The crews were from all parts of the Commonwealth—RAF, RCAF, RAAF, and RNZAF.

Lorne arrived in India on December 11, 1942, after a long and rather circuitous trip. He stopped for a few months' flying duties in West

[18] John R.W. Gwyne-Timothy, Burma Liberators, Vol II (Toronto: Next Level Press, 1991), p.823.

Africa, then flew across Africa to Egypt where he stopped again for a short stay before going on to Iraq and undergoing a perilous experience. Flying over the desert at night, engine malfunction caused a forced landing, "a shaky do." No one was hurt, and after spending a night among the Arabs, the crew repaired the fault and took off to India.

Before flying operational missions, Lorne had to be trained for the special circumstances of the squadron's missions and to learn the vagaries of the weather and terrain over which he would be flying. For this he had to go to another OTU.

Lorne was not impressed with India. He especially deplored travel by over-crowded, antiquated trains, and in January 1943 he wrote from Ceylon to his brother Bill and his wife Ida, describing conditions at his base.

> I have travelled far and wide since leaving the U.K., and of all the desolate spots we have seen, this is the worst. We are stuck away in the middle of the jungle, miles away from any inhabitation [sic] and as there isn't any form of entertainment on the camp we are having a time keeping the morale up. Even our beer ration of one bottle per week has been taken from us, pretty grim eh!!

> This place abounds with snakes, reptiles and bugs of all kinds, but our worst pest is the mosquito, if they have a go at you it is into the hospital with malaria for sure, but so far I have been lucky.

> It is very hot here and I often think of all the folks at home, tramping around in the snow and almost freezing but I would gladly change places. All this travelling is O.K. but for me I would give it up any time, I am too lonesome for Dorothy and the baby[19].

On March 18, 1943, Lorne was transferred to 217 Squadron (India), but attended No. 21 OTU. By April 27, he was attached to Middle East Ferry Command, delivering airplanes to many airfields all over the Asian theatre. This flying familiarized him with the local area and conditions. On May 10 he wrote again to Ida and Bill:

> To date I have dropped sixteen pounds in weight since coming out here, from a nice fat, one seventy when I left England to a mere one, fifty four, must be the lack of that good English beer! Our ration of same is nil, if we are lucky enough to have a chance to buy one costs us upwards of three rupees ($1.00) per bottle.

---

[19] David Patterson of Vancouver, a nephew, provided these copies of Lorne's letters.

There has been a few changes made lately, I have been separated from my pilot, really hated to leave him as we did have some exciting times together, but our crew wasn't the same after our observer left us to join the American forces. Our new crew is an all-Canuck one, pilot and gunner coming from up Toronto way, the observer from Alberta, good fellows, so we should have a good crew.

Have just had a letter from a sergeant friend of mine in England. The Perth boys seem to be catching a packet lately, several of my best friends are missing lately. The news from Tunisia is very heartening, let's hope this is the beginning of the end for the Axis, then we'll be able to return to all the things we have missed so much the past few years. . . For myself, I think I have had plenty of this business, I am missing my wife and son very much, he will be all grown up by the time I return, but I guess I can stick it out till this business is over. . .

We had a grand job to do a few weeks ago, we took some important people to a coral isle in the Indian Ocean, crossed the equator for the first time and spent several days on the island. It was very interesting . . . that will be something else we can talk over when I come home, we have a re-union to look forward to, haven't we?

. . . P.S. Address my mail in care of R.A.F. Base P.O. India

On May 29 he went to Squadron headquarters in Chaklala.

During July, Lorne went on leave in Srinagar, Kashmir. On July 18, he woke during the night with severe stomach cramps and barely made his way to the toilet before his bowels exploded with a watery gush and a horrid smell. He could barely stand, but with the help of a friend, he made his way back to Chaklala base. Lorne had contracted bacillary dysentery. While not fatal in usual circumstances, in the Far East medical attention was immediately required. Lorne was admitted to the British Military Hospital in Rawalpindi on July 30, and on August 8, he was feeling considerably better. However, because of his extremely weakened condition, he was sent on compulsory sick leave to the RAF rest camp at Lower Toba.

On August 20, a medical board reviewed his condition and decided that he was not yet fully recovered, so sent him on sick leave to No. 1 Hill Depot. On September 13, another medical board reviewed Lorne's progress and he was declared fit to return to flying duties. He was ordered to 223 Group for flying with 1576 Special Duties Flight at Chaklala.

From October 19 to 22, Lorne's crew operated from Dum Dum, the RAF base at Calcutta, and from Bombay. On November 4, 1943, he was promoted to flight lieutenant, and returned to Dum Dum on temporary assignment from December 3 to 18.

Although Lorne was with a new squadron, he was still flying the same clandestine operations. The squadron did not report through the normal channels, that is via a wing or a group, but was directly responsible to Air Command, Southeast Asia.

On March 14, 1944, Lorne's crew was briefed for a flight to a drop zone northeast of Lashio on the Burma Road near the Salween River. They were again flying from Dum Dum in support of Operation "Spiers" to the district of Kokang on the Burma–China border. Chosen for this sortie were the pilot, Flying Officer R. B. Palmer, RCAF; second pilot, Flight Lieutenant J. C. S. Ponsford, RAF; navigator, Flying Officer W. P. Prosser, RCAF; wireless operator/air gunners, Flight Lieutenant L. Patterson and Wireless Operator Sgt. B. A. Ogilvie, both RCAF; and parachute training instructor, Flight Sergeant J. Wilkinson, RAF.

Although all flying operations were considered secret, this evening's flight was quite routine. This crew, as well as others, had successfully made the trip several times in the previous months. In fact Lorne had flown to this area when he was previously flying from Dum Dum.

Years later, from his home in Alberta, Wallace Prosser recalled the night's flight:

> On the night of March 14–15, 1944 we went to a drop area well known to us . . . about 80 miles N.E. of Lashio. The drop zone was in a long narrow valley. We came in over a range of hills from the east, went down to 500' to make the drop then had to climb sharply to get over the hills at the other end. On this trip, as we approached the drop area at approx. 500' altitude our starboard engine burst into flames, the pilot cut the motor and killed the fire with the governor.[20]
>
> The old Hudson could not climb on one engine. We dumped all supplies and most of the fuel in hopes of climbing high enough to jump. We crashed into a hillside 4 miles from our drop area. Two of us thrown clear lived thru (*sic*) the crash. Ponsford, the other survivor, died a few hours later.
>
> The next two or three weeks are pretty foggy for me. The other 4 boys died instantly.

[20] The regulation method for dealing with a burning engine was to pull the throttle completely off then cut the flow of fuel to the engine by use of the governor.

Air Force Headquarters was informed by message:

> HUDSON AM949 TOOK OFF ON SECRET OPERATION
> LOCATION TARGET CANNOT BE DISCLOSED AIR-
> CRAFT FAILED TO RETURN INFORMATION
> RECEIVED AIRCRAFT CRASHED 98 DEGREES 30
> MINUTES EAST 24 DEGREES NORTH MEDICAL
> OFFICER ORDERED TO CRASH FOUND FIVE DEAD
> TWO ONLY SERIOUSLY INJURED IMPOSSIBLE TO
> REMOVE BODIES OF DEAD STOP

The remarkable story of Prosser's rescue and survival in the jungle was written in an Indian English-language newspaper in May 1944:

> An RAF doctor [F/L G. D. Graham] and a F/Sgt parachute training instructor [F/Sgt T. E. White] who dropped [on March 17] far behind the Jap lines in Burma to look after an injured flyer and stayed with him 14 days in a cave, have trekked back to an Allied base. . .

> F/Lt. Graham, who had never parachuted, volunteered for the rescue because the crashed crew were from his squadron. He took a quick lesson or two from F/Sgt. White, who also volunteered for the trip[21].

> Then they were flown to a mountainous area and at dawn dropped down on to the side of a 5,000-foot mountain. They found F/O W. P. Prosser, of Edmonton, Alberta, lying unconscious in a cattle shed. They had been told before they set off that there were only two survivors. The other had died in the meantime.

> For 14 days they stayed in this rough shelter. Its ceiling was only five feet high.

> A primitive oil lamp was their only light. It was made from a piece of twisted cotton dipped in a warm pig fat, or in poppy seed oil. Water was brought in hollow bamboo from a stream.

> **Watch for Patrols**

> Bees swarmed in the thatched roof, but a smoky fire in an improvised hearth helped to keep them outside.

> 'By day under the hot sun we kept watch for any enemy patrols, and at night we were always on the alert,' said F/Lt

---

[21] This took more courage than just for the parachute jump. In Burma the weather, especially during monsoon season, caused everything to be covered in mildew. This was very hard on parachutes as the mildew glued the parachute pack and the folds in the silk together. Many a fighter pilot in the theatre successfully bailed out but died when his 'chute failed to open.

Graham. 'There was plenty to do to take our minds off worrying about the enemy.

'We said a simple funeral service over the graves of the dead. They lie in a clearing on a misty ridge.'

The rescuers tore their parachutes to pieces so that they could be made into sheets and pyjamas for F/O Prosser.

Their kit was stacked ready to get away within a few minutes for it was known that the Japanese were all the time approaching. When the Japanese were across all the roads but one, the party left.

They got 12 coolies to carry a litter with F/O Prosser lying on it, and seven mules to go with them. They covered nine miles the first day.

Food was scarce, and the party were wet and covered in mud.

In Opium Den

'The most unforgettable part of this stage of the trip was when we sheltered for a night in a den of opium smokers,' said F/Lt Graham.

'Wizened old men pulled away at their narcotics in a small dirty room till four a.m., while in an earthen-floored room alongside we tried to sleep.

'That day we persuaded the bearers to go on only by offering them gifts of rum and aspirin. They rubbed the aspirins on their foreheads till I showed them what to do with them.[22]'

As they dropped into the valleys there was danger of the patient dying from heat exhaustion. He grew very weak but after five days became rational again. He could not remember anything of the experience.

They marched for another six days until they reached an Allied outpost.

Back at base one of the first to greet them was F/Lt. J. A. King, DFC . . . who flew them into Burma.

---

[22] A squadron mate, Tony Day, recalled that the coolies refused to go further for fear they would be conscripted into the Chinese Army. The higher pay, rum and aspirins persuaded them to go on. They reached an American outpost on April 5th. The Americans hired new coolies but paid them in advance. They promptly absconded. The survivors rested while replacements were found. After struggling through terrible weather across several mountain passes they reached, on April 11, a dirt road that led to Yunnanni airfield, a U.S. base. The U.S. Army made plans to fly them to India. On take-off the landing gear failed to retract and they had to return to Yunnanni. The next day, April 17, the flight went off with no problems and the team was delivered to Calcutta.

Prosser wrote that they came out through China where an American "Y Force" helped them. He got back to Calcutta thirty-three days after the crash, and after five months in hospital, he was sent back to England. He recalls being "pretty badly busted up, head, foot, ribs, and eyes." Over the years he has had four eye operations, but considers himself in "pretty good condition." It was his fractured skull that dictated the group wait for two weeks before trying to carry him out.

Prosser recalled that, deep in enemy territory, they could not mark the graves at the time, but he was sure a search party could easily find them. He confirmed that all were given a decent burial.

A search party, after a four-day march to the site, reported that they had located the wreckage of the Hudson, but could find no graves. They had spoken with the headmen of the nearby villages of Hsaihkao and Phangma Sang, but neither had seen nor heard about any crashed aircraft in the area. By contrast, a Burial Report, dated August 8, 1944, reported that the casualties were buried at the place of the crash.

The commanding officer of 357 Squadron wrote a personal letter on June 23, 1944, to Lorne's wife Dorothy, who had moved to Masson, Quebec:

> Dear Mrs. Patterson,
>
> Before you receive this letter you will have been informed by the Air Ministry of the very sad loss of your husband, F/Lt. Patterson.
>
> It is not possible for various service reasons for me to give you exact details of the operations in which your husband was connected, but I can say that he, along with four other members of his crew were, and had been doing a very fine job of work calling for the highest category of skill and courage.
>
> Information has been received by me that your husband, along with four other members of his crew, were decently interred, the service being conducted by a Christian priest, and Military Honours afforded them. The graves were properly marked and fenced off. Should any photographs be obtained (of which I have high expectations) they will be duly sent on to you.
>
> Your husband's execution of his duties was of the highest order, and his popularity was such, that the whole Squadron joins me, in tendering my deepest sympathy in your sad loss.

The squadron leader sent Lorne's operations wing badge to Dorothy in September 1946. His personal belongings, along with those of Flying

Officer Palmer and Wireless Operator Ogilvie, were sent back to England aboard the SS *Mount Revelstoke Park*, a Canadian merchantman, but were lost in transit.

Dorothy received the proceeds of an insurance policy that had cost Lorne $5 a month. The government paid Lorne's War Service Gratuity for 1,176 days service, including 826 days overseas. It came to $893.63, from which the grateful government withheld $1.81 for arrears in his 1939 income taxes.

Lorne was also survived by his brothers David Harold of Texas, William Glen of Brockville, LAC James Archibald in the RCAF at No. 9 Repair Depot in St. John's (St-Jean), Quebec, Grant with the RCAF in Trenton, and Elmer (Sandy) with the RCAF overseas[23], and sisters Margaret (wife of Major George Hepburn who was also overseas) of Picton and Jean (Mrs. Russell Clarke) of Belleville. His mother had died on November 1, 1939, at age fifty-seven, of cancer.

Flight Lieutenant Lorne Patterson's name is engraved on the Singapore Memorial which bears the names of 24,000 soldiers and airmen of the British Commonwealth and Empire who have no known graves. The memorial stands in the Kranji War Cemetery, twenty-two kilometres north of Singapore. Behind the Cross of Sacrifice, flights of steps lead to a terrace on the top of a hill upon which the Memorial stands. Twelve wide columns hold the panels and support a flat roof. Rising through the centre of the roof is a great pylon, twenty-four metres high, surmounted by a star. On a curved panel at the foot of this pylon is inscribed the following:

1939–1945

On the walls of this memorial are recorded the names of twenty-four thousand soldiers and airmen of many races united in service to the British crown who gave their lives in Malaya and neighbouring lands and seas in the air over southern and eastern Asia and the Pacific but to whom the fortune of war denied the customary rites accorded to their comrades in death.

---

[23] F/O Elmer Patterson, also a Wop/AG, was awarded the Distinguished Flying Cross for courage in facing and dealing with enemy attacks. The citation reads: "This officer has completed a number of sorties against heavily defended targets such as Kiel, Starkrade, Duisburg, Essen and Leipzig. In October 1944, he was detailed to attack Duisburg. Shortly before reaching the target, he sighted an enemy fighter closing in to attack; with great calm he directed his captain in evasive action and the enemy was shaken off. A short time later heavy anti-aircraft fire was encountered. Again FO. (Sic) Patterson gave his pilot accurate and precise directions and the mission was completed successfully. This officer has proved to be a keen and intrepid air gunner who has fulfilled his duties as deputy gunnery leader with excellent results. His tenacity, efficiency and courage have been responsible for the safe return of his crew on many occasions." Elmer's wife is credited with having opened Patterson's Restaurant in Perth (still thriving in 2001)

An additional inscription, "They Died for All Free Men," is engraved in Hindi, Urdu, Gurmukhi, Chinese, and Malay.

J 23150 Flying Officer Wilbert Andrew Porterfield
Wireless Operator/Air Gunner
Royal Canadian Air Force

Wilbert Andrew Porterfield was born on March 6, 1921, the youngest son of Wilbert J. Porterfield and Ethel Agnes "Annie" Dunlop. George McIntosh (Mac), Margaret (Peg), and Jean made up the rest of family. They lived in a white clapboard home at 16 Lake Avenue, which in 2002 was still occupied by Peg, and attended the United Church. Andy's father worked in the textile industry as a cloth finisher, but he was also an automobile salesman and the local examiner of candidates for drivers' licences.

Andy Porterfield's name shares space on the Singapore Memorial with Lorne Patterson.

Andy went to the Victoria School for his elementary education from 1926 to 1934 and CPHS from 1934 to 1939, but he did not complete his junior matriculation. During the last year and a half of high school, when he was taking the commercial course, Andy took on most of the administrative duties in the principal's office. He handled correspondence and mimeographing, and kept the attendance and financial records. After leaving school he worked as a clerk for Mr. E. Doyle for a year then, in 1940, went to clerk for Mr. C. McCann[24].

During school, Andy was an active athlete, participating in hockey, rugby, and baseball. He played on the Ottawa District Championship ball team his last year at school, and in 1938, while playing hockey, he took an especially hard check into the boards and fell to the ice unconscious. Hockey equipment was poor in those days: shin pads, knee, shoulder and elbow pads, and gloves were worn only if the player could afford them. Helmets were unheard of, so Andy was fortunate that he suffered no skull fracture or other side effects. His other sports included basketball and a little golf. When he joined the air force, he listed his hobbies as reading and building model airplanes.

He had been active in the CPHS Cadet Corps, and at the annual inspection on May 11, 1939, Andy was one of the drummers in the cadet bugle band.

Andy Porterfield at the 1939 inspection of the CPHS Cadet Corps.

[24] Mr. Elmer Doyle operated the Blue Spot Lunch restaurant beside the Queen's Hotel. Cecil McCann's establishment was a billiards hall where the present day magazine shop is located. McCann's wife, Laurel, was the sister of Wilson Costello.

Finding that he enjoyed working in an office, Andy enrolled in the short clerk's course at Taber Business School. For two months, from August to October 1940, he studied typing and the complexities of the mimeograph and adding machines. On completion of this course, he accepted a position in the civil service as a clerk for the Department of National Defence in the printing and stationary branch and moved to an apartment at 170 Florence Street in Ottawa.

Brother Mac was also living in Ottawa and both boys spent most weekends in Carleton Place with their parents. Mac subsequently joined the navy and was sent to the east coast, and on February 3,1941, Andy visited an RCAF recruiting office to take a medical examination for enlistment. At nineteen, he was a tall (5' 11½"), thin (148 pounds.) youth, but in very good physical shape. He had a medium complexion, hazel eyes, and hair so dark it was almost black.

Andy had aspirations for aircrew. However, an eye examination found his colour vision slightly defective. He was also found to have flat feet, but he exhibited no symptoms nor any problems so was judged fit for enlistment. He was enrolled as a "clerk standard" with the rank of aircraftsman second class and sent to No. 1 Manning Depot in Toronto for basic training. He arrived on May 23, 1941. Being already trades-trained, his basic was limited to a week's intensive indoctrination into air force life and customs. To learn the specific duties of an air force clerk, Andy was sent, on May 31, to RCAF Station Trenton and the Composite Training School (KTS).

The thousands of administrative people who were required to keep the BCATP functioning smoothly learned their skills at the School of Administration in Trenton. Early in 1941 this school became the KTS, which was organized to teach airmen and airwomen to become mechanics, disciplinarians, service police, clerks, and physical training instructors. After six weeks, Andy was posted, on July 13, to duties at Rockcliffe, where he was employed with the headquarters' disciplinarian section, but was attached to the repatriation pool.

At Rockcliffe, on August 19, he had another medical examination and this time his colour vision was found to be normal. He was awarded a medical category A1B A3B, fit for full flying duties anywhere, in Canada or overseas. Armed with this, he applied again, on August 23, for remuster to aircrew standard, either as a pilot or an observer. Coincidentally, he was promoted to aircraftsman first class that same day. In the memorandum he wrote to his commander requesting consideration, he expressed the following opinion: "I feel that I will serve in this capacity in a far greater manner than that of a clerk." A Daily Routine Order was published on January 2, 1942, indicating that Aircraftsman Porterfield was "Clerk Gen 'C' remustered to aircrew O or O Std eff 3.1.42"—air force language indicating that his application was accepted.

Andy spent the Christmas and New Year's holidays on leave in Carleton Place, and on January 4, 1942, he returned to Toronto to No. 6 ITS where his aptitude for flying was tested and he was demoted to aircraftsman second class. But air force life must have been agreeing with him, for a medical for aircrew training found that he had put on weight, and now topped the scales at 155 pounds.

At ITS he received classroom instruction in higher mathematics and navigation and his flying reactions were tested in the Link Trainer. He graduated on January 25, forty-fifth of eighty-five students in Course No. 44. He was found to be "Studious; serious; keen; trying hard; has always given his best," and was recommended for training, first as a pilot and second as a wireless operator. Now that he was in flight training he was elevated to the rank of leading aircraftsman.

AC2 Andy Porterfield

The first step towards pilot's wings was taken at an EFTS; however, waiting for a course opening, he spent the next few weeks attached to the Manning Depot in Toronto. He was granted 14 days' special leave so went home to Carleton Place from February 28 to March 14, and on March 29, Andy travelled to Windsor, Ontario, to join Course No. 52 at No. 7 EFTS. Here he took more Link trainer instruction and was taken into the air for the first time. Although when he joined, Andy had reported that he had six hours flying experience as a passenger, air force flying bore no resemblance to his earlier experience. At EFTS under the guidance of a qualified training pilot, he actually got to take the controls for the first time.

Under the watchful eye of his flying instructor, Sergeant Bradford, Andy was learning to fly the Fleet Finch aircraft. They gathered seventeen hours and fifty-five minutes dual before Sergeant Bradford let him go solo.

Andy's flying ability left much to be desired. He was slow and seemed to lack air sense, and early in his solo flying, he did a minor ground loop on landing. It was a very windy day, late in the afternoon, and as Andy testified for the accident report: "While landing the aircraft bounced once and started to turn right. I gave it a right rudder but it did not check the turn, which continued until the aircraft came to rest. I was not injured." After the mandatory medical check following any accident, Andy was grounded for one-and-a-half days with obstructed ears. The chief instructor evaluated the accident: "Landed wheels first usually. Seemed unable to judge distance and get control column back in time. Poor airmanship."

Once a pilot had soloed, he did five hours practising airfield circuits and landings. As well, with his instructor aboard, he branched out to try steep turns, spins with the power backed off, forced landings, and crosswind landings and take-offs.

In ground school, Andy was proving to be a "fair" student. In class he was quiet and tried hard on all assigned work. He obtained average marks, but his flying was rated as low average. However, before he could continue, he had to pass a "20-hour check," a test flown with a testing officer while his instructor watched from the ground.

As they taxied out and turned into wind, Andy called out the required items from the checklist that he had to perform before take-off: oil pressure, oil temperatures, control settings, radios. However, a favourite trick pulled by test officers was, just as they became airborne, to pull the throttle completely off and call out "Power failure—what're you goin' to do?" The correct answer was "Land straight ahead." But many a novice pilot gave in to the dangerous temptation to turn back towards the field, and at low altitude with no power they would not have made it.

Once over this hurdle, the pair flew on. The test pilot demanded the student perform several standard manoeuvres: straight and level flying, medium turns, straight climbs and gliding while maintaining a constant airspeed, climbing turns, gliding turns, recovery from stalls, and recovery from spins. Finally, they re-joined the circuit and landed.

Sergeant Bradford met Andy and his tester and learned that Andy had failed the check due to extremely poor airmanship and poor flying ability. He could not go on. It was judged that further training would not turn him into a service pilot. The report for his cessation of training summarized:

> Lacks air sense. Judgement poor. Forgets details and is lax
> on manoeuves. Landings poor. Lands wheels first frequent-
> ly. Airmanship poor, Progress unsatisfactory to warrant fur-
> ther training.

Andy then wanted to be trained as an air observer, but the officials went back to his second recommendation at ITS and sent him for training as a wireless air gunner. He left Windsor on May 6, 1942.

After thirteen days' leave, Andy returned to the KTS in Trenton for more waiting. On June 6, he reported to No. 4 WTSs located in Guelph to joined Course No. 45.

Andy spent August 18 to 27 in the RCAF Station hospital in Guelph, and on admission, he had to sign a pledge that he would not gamble or bring alcohol into his room, and if he lost any of his linens, he would be charged for them. He had to be shaved by 0800 hours, take his meals at prescribed times, and have his lights out by 2230 hours, after which any talking was prohibited.

Early in 1942, the RAF attacked the problem of half-trained aircrew arriving at operational squadrons. It had been mandatory that each aircraft carry two pilots, and in a bold stroke, this was reduced to one, thus halving the pilot-training requirement. The second pilot position was now designated as navigator, a new position. To assist the lone pilot, flight engineers were trained, and bomb dropping was taken from the navigator and performed by an air bomber. Air gunners and wireless operators were separated, wireless operators were trained to man the guns in an emergency, but air gunners were no longer required to take the wireless courses. Thus each crewmember became more specialised, and more thorough and specific training was adopted.

The wireless operator's "sparks" badge worn on the shoulder sleeve.

Andy Porterfield graduated and was presented with his wireless operator's badge on December 21, 1942. In *The Canadian* it was reported, "LAC Andrew Porterfield of the RCAF Guelph arrived home to spend Christmas. He recently graduated from the Wireless School No. 4, Guelph and will report to No. 6 Bombing and Gunnery School, Mountain View, to complete his training."

Course No. 45 for air gunners was in residence from December 29, 1942, to January 25, 1943.

Attaining nine hours and forty-five minutes air-to-air gunnery in a Bolingbroke, Andy completed the course with the assessment: "This airman is a keen and enthusiastic student. His classroom work was above average. He has given excellent co-operation both with his instructor, and with his fellow students. He is recommended for commissioned rank."

At the United Nations' Air Training Conference in Ottawa in May 1942, Canada raised the contentious issue of commissioning all aircrew. They argued, "there was no justification for the commissioning of certain individuals while others were required to perform identical duties in NCO rank." They suggested that all aircrew members were of equal importance and all had an equal claim to a commission. The RAF countered that commissions did not necessarily attract men of the "right stuff" with officer qualities. Besides, it was not an officer function in the RAF to lead other ranks into battle. The function of aircrew was battle. The RAF maintained that the only criteria for a commission had to be the capacity to lead, command, and set a worthy example. Aircrew rarely had the opportunity to display such qualities. Once airborne, each crew was on its own; any leading was done entirely in the aircraft. Each crew had its "skipper," usually the pilot, who had to be obeyed implicitly while in the air. The RAF had no problem with junior ranks actually commanding senior ranks in these circumstances, so long as it did not extend to the ground. Thus multi-rank crews continued throughout the war, and long afterwards.

On January 25, 1943, Porterfield was discharged from the air force as an airman and appointed to a commission as a pilot officer. He remained at Mountain View until February 24; however, most of that time was spent on leave. He was given five days' annual leave and a further fourteen days' embarkation leave from February 6 to 24. He went home to Carleton Place wearing his new officer's uniform, sporting the hard-won WOAG wing, and on February 25, he reported to No. 31 Personnel Depot in Moncton, New Brunswick, to await an overseas assignment. On March 19 he was sent to RAF Station Nassau, British West Indies (Bahamas), to attend No. 111 OTU, where his first duty was to cable his parents announcing his safe arrival.

Andy left Ottawa with a cloud over his head. On February 19, at 0120, he had boarded the Ottawa to North Bay train to go home to Carleton Place. However, he had neglected to buy a ticket. When confronted by the conductor shortly after leaving the station, Andy could not show a ticket and swore at the man. Patrolling the train were two members of the Provost Corps who were requested to place the pilot officer under arrest. Sergeant Esty and Private Ireland noted the time as 0135 and proceeded to interview the officer.

> When first asked his name he said 'P/O W. A. Carson,' but upon being asked for identification revealed his name was P/O W. A. Porterfield. When asked where his home station was he replied 'I'm from all over!' Asked for his ticket he acknowledged that he had none but he did pay his fare in cash. The Provost advised him that a report would be made. A contrite young pilot officer asked if it would help if he apologized to conductor Riddell. 'Probably.' Replied Sgt. Esty, 'but a report is going in all the same.'

By the time the report was acted upon in headquarters, it was mid April and Andy was with the RAF in Nassau. Because he was outside Canada it would have been difficult to obtain evidence, so it was recommended that no disciplinary action be taken. But the commander of RAF Nassau was not so lenient. The report arrived on his desk on April 20, and he called Porterfield in to his office. It was probably a memorable tongue-lashing by an RAF senior officer to an upstart colonial wearing an officer's uniform, and it ended with Andy being severely admonished and given extra duties for seven days.

The training unit at RAF Nassau was to prepare students for Liberators and flying in Southeast Asia. The course included flying exercises, over-ocean navigational exercises, bombing practice, and both air-to-air and air-to-ground gunnery practice. The curriculum called for the airman to fly at least thirty-five hours on the North American "Mitchell" (B-25), a twin-engine medium bomber, before converting to the Liberators. Andy logged forty-one hours and fifty minutes day time and nine hours and forty-five minutes night time on the Mitchell. To complete the course, a further seventy hours training was required on the Liberator. Andy's logbook showed that he flew forty-four hours and ten minutes day and twelve hours and five minutes night. At the end of Course No. 4, he was rated as "Average A/G, above average W/Op."

The Consolidated Liberator

The Consolidated Aircraft Corporation in San Diego built the Liberator. The head of the company had an English governess for his children and it is said that she suggested the name. Nearly 20,000 were manufactured, mostly for the European Theater of Operations, but all Commonwealth air forces used them. The RAF, RAAF, RNZAF, and USAAF flew them in the Pacific. It had a tricycle landing gear, which greatly enhanced the pilot's area of vision on the ground, but it did not fly well when heavily loaded, at high altitude, or in unfavourable weather.

If all went well, flying the aircraft was a "piece of cake," but if anything went wrong it usually spelled disaster. Escape hatches for bailing out were poorly placed and difficult to get to. In a crash-landing, the shoulder placement of the wings crushed people in the fuselage. Worst scenario was ditching at sea. On impact the bomb bay broke open and flooded, causing the fuselage to sink like a stone.

On June 30, Pilot Officer Porterfield, with a new crew captained by Flying Officer R. E. Banks, RCAF, was posted to No. 45 Group RAF Ferry

Command at Dorval, near Montreal. They were to take a new Liberator directly to their theatre of operations. The first leg was to Gander, Newfoundland, and the second across the Atlantic to Lajes in the Azores. From there, the route touched down in Rabat, Morocco; Castel Benito, Libya; Cairo, Egypt; Lydda, Palestine; Shaibah, Iraq; and finally their base at Drigh Road, at Karachi. Sometimes the crew could make minor variations to the route so they could arrange stopovers to play tourist. It was a much better way to travel than the terrible troop ships, and the flying experience was a perfect introduction to flying in the Far East.

Andy and his crew arrived in India on August 21, 1943, and again his first task was to send a cable to his folks announcing his safe arrival. The airmen then had to spend a week at No. 30 Canadian General Hospital for medical examinations and lectures on tropical medicine.

Andy had already been awarded his Canada Volunteer Service Medal and with his arrival in India he became eligible for the 1939–45 Star. They were posted to 159 Squadron to deliver the new airplane to their operational squadron, 354 Squadron, on September 11.

354 Squadron was formed at Drigh Road, Karachi, on May 10, 1943. It had no aircraft initially, but the squadron moved to Cuttack, India, on August 17 and began to take delivery of their Liberators, the first of which arrived on August 28. The aircraft Andy and his crew brought from Canada went with them to the squadron.

Initially, the squadron was to be a long-range photographic reconnaissance unit, but its role was changed to convoy escort and anti-submarine patrol and flew its first patrol on September 22. In December 1943, anti-submarine patrols were augmented by attacks on enemy shipping off Burma. Both types of operations continued until the squadron was disbanded on May 18, 1945.

354 Squadron had the usual complement of twelve aircraft and aircrews, the latter of which were drawn from all over the Commonwealth. At one time, of the fifty-six officers, eight were Australian, twenty-six British, twenty Canadian, one Indian, and one New Zealander. The ground crews were equally diverse.

Throughout the last months of the year, as the weather improved with summer approaching, they flew uneventful patrols. From November 7 to 11, they were sent to the RAF rest camp at Puri, from December 4 to 17, the entire crew took leave in India. Then, from January 12 to 25, the crew was attached to No. 8 Hill Depot in Wellington, New Zealand, flying their patrols from there.

They were back at Drigh Road on April 6 when the crew took Liberator "M" on patrol and sighted two dinghies containing eight survivors of a ditched USAAF Liberator off the Arakan coast. The crew circled and radioed the position to home base, then stayed until a Catalina came to pick up the downed aviators making them instrumental in saving the men's lives.

On the evening of May 6, 1944, Banks and his crew were warned for an early morning patrol. They would be flying the squadron's daily "Maxim Green 1A" anti-shipping patrol. These were flown off the Arakan coast from the Mayu River to the mouth of the Irrawaddy and played a large role in preventing the Japanese from supplying their forces on Arakan. Many of the smaller vessels used by the enemy were sunk or damaged by squadron aircraft.

The crew of eight included five RCAF: Flying Officer R. E. Banks, Flying Officer W. H. Pedlar, Flying Officer W. A. Porterfield, Pilot Officer J. Smith, and Wireless Operator II D. W. Vaughan; one RNZAF: Pilot Officer C. C. McCormack, and two RAF: Flight Sergeant W. A. Baker and Sergeant J. F. Clements. They were flying Liberator Mark G.R. VI, side number VE 848, but with the squadron identification of "M" for "Mike." The four Twin Wasp engines were still fairly new and in excellent condition, as was the airframe. A completely serviceable aircraft took off at 0753 on the morning of May 7.

"M" for "Mike" was scheduled to return at 1850 hours. At 1623, the wireless operator, Flying Officer Porterfield, signalled that they were amending their return ETA[25] to base as 1820. An RAF base to the south of Drigh Road, RAF Cuttack, picked up this signal by their radio direction finder (D/F) and recorded the bearing to the aircraft as 074 degrees east. At 1724, the aircraft acknowledged a message from base and this transmission was D/F'd at 075 degrees. At 1744, the radio tracking stations plotted "M" for "Mike" circling Shortt's Island lighthouse, on track for the return flight. The plot faded shortly afterwards.

Two Royal Indian Navy telegraphers manned the Shortt's Island wireless telegraphy station. They were interviewed by the group captain commanding 173 Wing who found their story completely reliable:

> 354 Squadron Liberator "M" circled Shortt's Island at about 071800 [6:00 p.m. on the 7th], it was flying at a reasonable altitude although they were unable to compute the actual height. Nothing abnormal was noted. After circling, it flew over an island about 2 miles to the south of Shortt's Island and lost height gradually. When over the island, it turned towards the East and when at a comparatively low altitude, flashes of fire were seen to come from the windows. Almost immediately afterwards, the aircraft hit the sea in a shallow glide and appeared to explode on impact.

The group captain ordered a court of inquiry to attempt to determine the cause of the crash. With no survivors and no radio communication with the aircraft, the court could not come to any conclusion as to the cause.

[25] Estimated Time of Arrival

At daybreak on May 8, two squadron aircraft searched over land and sea where the airplane went down. After searching all day with no results they returned home. During the morning of May 8, the officer commanding 173 Wing piloted a small aircraft from Dringh Road and landed on the island. The port officer came over in a launch and gave the officer commanding various small articles of the aircraft's equipment, which had washed ashore. He also gave up a wallet that a native had taken from a body found washed up in the surf. The body had not been recovered. The wallet belonged to the New Zealand officer, Pilot Officer C. C. McCormack. Nothing further was seen of the rest of the crew.

All persons in the aircraft were declared missing believed killed.

On May 14, *The Canadian* printed the message sent to the Porterfields: "Regret to advise that your son, Flying Officer Wilbert Andrew Porterfield . . . is reported missing after air operations overseas. Letter follows." *The Canadian* then wrote:

> 'Andy' as he was popularly known to many friends in town and district was born in Carleton Place and is a graduate of the high school, where he took part in various sports and was well liked by teachers and fellow students.

> The young man recently celebrated his birthday in India.

Squadron Leader R. L. Manson wrote to Mrs. Porterfield on May 10:

> By now you will have received my airgraph which was sent at the request of the whole Squadron to convey our sympathy in the loss of your son, Flying Officer Wilbert Porterfield who was posted 'Missing' from an operation against the enemy. Let me assure you that all ranks feel very deeply regarding his loss and that all of us have the memory of a fine Wireless Operator Air Gunner and keen airman.

> I had particular occasion to know your son because he was a young Wireless Operator Air Gunner of my own Flight when we all arrived on the Squadron. As his Flight Commander I had the chance of observing him at work and play and I know well the sterling qualities he possessed. As you may know he had done the major part of his operational work and I had hoped soon to be able to send him to teach others the fine job he had been doing. Had your son lived, I know that he would have made a worthy contribution to the cause for which all of us out here are fighting. Unfortunately the aircraft was lost over the sea and although the greatest efforts have been made by us in searching the locality I cannot hold out great hope for a chance of survival. . .

Would you please convey my personal sympathy to all his relatives as I realise only too well what the loss of such a fine son must mean to you all.

Andy's personal effects were sent back on the SS *Chinese Prince*. His War Gratuity for 1,081 days' service, 417 overseas, was paid to his mother, Ethel. Unfortunately, she died on August 1, 1945, and since she was listed as Andy's next-of-kin, his effects went to her estate. At the time of his going missing, his brother Mac was serving in the RCNVR at HMCS *Stadacona* in Halifax, his sister Mrs. Margaret Walker was living in Belleville, and his sister Mrs. Jean Buffam was living on High Street in Carleton Place.

On May 3, 1945, *The Canadian* published the following In Memoriam:

Porterfield-In proud and loving memory of J-23150 Flying Officer Wilbert Andrew Porterfield, who presumably lost his life over the Bay of Bengal, India, on May 7th, 1944.

He has solved it, life's wonderful problem,

The deepest, the strangest, the last.

And into the school of the angels

With the answer forever has passed.

How strange he should sleep so profoundly,

So young, so unworn by the strife,

While beside him brimful of hope's nectar

Untouched stood the goblet of life.

God knew all about it, how noble,

How gentle he was and how brave,

How bright his possible future,

Yet put him to sleep in his grave.

God knew all about those who love Him,

How bitter the trial must be,

And right through it all God is loving

And knows so much better than we.

Sadly missed by the family.

PART FIVE—FLIGHT INTO DARKNESS

In 1940, Prime Minister Winston Churchill told his Cabinet colleagues and the Chiefs of Staff:

> (Only) the Air Force can win [the war]. Therefore our supreme effort must be to gain overwhelming mastery of the air. The Fighters are our salvation, but the Bombers alone provide the means of victory.

CHAPTER TWENTY—SMOKE AND FIRE

As the air war winged its weary way into history, Canadian involvement increased dramatically. New radar devices enabled heavy bombers to make more accurate hits on their targets, and by 1943, saturation bombing reached a new high. German cities with industrial centres were subject to massive bombing attacks, and at the time, with their backs to the wall, the Allies felt totally justified in carrying out such mass destruction. Their aim was to destroy military and industrial installations and thus the enemy's means for war. The hope was to force Germany's surrender.

But the losses in Bomber Command were tragically high. In the first half of 1943, No. 6 (Canadian) Group lost more than 100 aircraft, seven per cent of their total strength. However, with better equipment, training and experience, plus fighter protection to the target, by the end of 1944, No. 6 Group claimed the lowest casualties in the Command.

In researching the events of Bomber Command's war, the historian is greatly assisted by excellent records kept by the RAF. For every operational flight, forms were completed for each aircraft, recording the aircraft's serial number, its crew, its bomb load, and its take-off time. If the flight returned safely, its landing time and a short history of the crew's experiences were also written into the record.

By the end of May 1943, well before the Battle of the Ruhr ended, Sir Arthur Harris had ordered his commanders to ready their Groups for heavy raids on Hamburg. It was the second largest city in Germany and Europe's largest port; 1.75 million people lived there. Hamburg had escaped the thousand-bomber raids of 1942 and was now ripe for Bomber Command's full attention.

The city was easily identifiable on H2S (radar) screens by a distinctive coastline only sixty miles away and docks and turning basins on the wide river Elbe. This famous shipbuilding city had produced the *Bismarck*, now sunk, and at least 200 U-boats. These shipyard targets were on the south bank of the Elbe but were not primary sites; the intent was to slow production by crippling the general life of the city.

Bomber Command chief, Air Marshall Harris, planned four raids over a period of ten nights. During the day, while the RAF rested, the U.S. Eighth Air Force struck. This would be the first time the bombers of both air forces would combine forces to destroy a German city. The Americans' main targets were the Blohm and Voss U-boat construction yard and the Klöckner aero-engine manufacturing plant. Although they flew 245 sorties and lost only seventeen Fortresses, after this combined operation the USAAF was less than enthusiastic to join Bomber Command for the later advance to Berlin.

The first raid on Hamburg was launched on the night of July 24–25, 1943. Flying on that mission was Flight Sergeant Armour "Joe" Garland of Carleton Place. Later, in August, Sergeant Russell James of Almonte joined the squadron. Both men were air gunners, and both served on 419 "Moose" Squadron, but there was a thirteen-year age difference: Garland was thirty-three and James was twenty. James joined the RCAF fourteen months after Garland, and although they took very different training routes, they both started operationally flying Halifax bombers within three weeks of each other, Garland as a rear gunner and James as a second (waist) gunner. The similarities unfortunately continued. Garland died on September 1, on a raid to Berlin, and James was killed on September 6 flying a bombing sortie to Mannheim. Garland's body was never found while James was buried in a war cemetery in Bavaria, Germany.

R 111417

Flight Sergeant Douglas Haig Armour Garland
Air Gunner
Royal Canadian Air Force

Armour Garland was born to Mr. and Mrs. William James Garland of 25 Franklin Street, Carleton Place, on November 15, 1918. The Great War Armistice had occurred only four days previously, and Armour's mother, Mary Rebecca, named him in honour of Sir Douglas Haig, the famous World War I commander. Known as Armie, while growing up, he was one of four brothers, James, Walter, and William Jr. being the others. He also had two sisters: Mrs. Gertrude Girth of Kitchener and Mrs. Beatrice H. Wisenpas (Wiseman?) of Smiths Falls. The family was raised in the Anglican faith and all attended Carleton Place schools. Armour went to Carleton Place public school from 1924 to 1932 and then moved on to CPHS, which he attended for only two years, completing first form. During his childhood he was afflicted with the usual diseases, including measles and chicken pox.

Armie Garland in CPHS school picture, circa 1933–34.

In the autumn of 1934, at age sixteen, Armour went to work at the Bates and Innes Woollen Mill, and over the next six years he learned the trade of textile spinner, advancing accordingly in the mill. For recreation he played baseball on the town team, enjoyed swimming in the Mississippi, and occasionally boating (not canoeing). Armour also liked to go to the weekly town dances.

On September 28, 1940, Armour married Miss Vivien Genevieve Manion, the daughter of Mr. and Mrs. John Manion of North Bay, at St. Alban's the Martyr Anglican Church in Ottawa. Attending Vivien were Misses Lou Whitworth and Catherine Stafford, both from Carleton Place. *The Canadian* reported: "The bride was becomingly gowned in a street length model of baby blue wool crepe with matching accessories and wore a corsage of roses." The couple made their home in Carleton Place.

On November 7, Armour joined the Lanark and Renfrew Scottish Militia and began attending weekly training sessions. His medical examination, completed on September 19, recorded his physique as 5' 9½" tall, weighing 143 pounds; a great deal of acne dotted his face. Like many Carleton Place boys before him, Armour was drawn to the air force. He was fascinated with airplanes and flying, still considered a bit of a novelty, and expressed a desire to serve in the air force. Plus, with a wife and hopes of starting a family, he also realized the need to get a usable trade that he could pursue after the war.

In July 1941, he joined the RCAF with the intention of becoming an instrument-maker[1], and the paperwork was begun to transfer him from the Lanark and Renfrew Scottish. Vivien was four months pregnant when Armour left, on July 10, to report to No. 1 Manning Depot in Toronto.

After basic training and qualifying as a basic instrument-maker, Armour was sent to No. 17 Equipment Depot in Ottawa for advanced training. He reported on August 12, 1941, and by November 15, he had completed the aircraft instrument course. Three weeks later, on December 5, his first son, Armour Garfield "Garry" was born. Armie had moved his family to Ottawa to 53 Balsam Street, but the young family made regular visits to Carleton Place throughout the early months of 1942.

On March 6, 1942, Armie was promoted to aircraftsman first class, and on April 1, he completed all the qualifying tests to become an instrument repairer. On June 26 a bout of appendicitis interrupted his training, but after a successful appendectomy at the Ottawa Civic Hospital, he was released to resume full duties on July 7.

Armour soon developed a yearning to transfer to aircrew. He knew that aircrew received higher pay, not to mention an automatic promotion to sergeant upon completion of air trades training, with the possibility of gaining an officer's commission. Although this transfer to a potentially dangerous trade caused Vivien considerable concern for herself and her baby son, she supported his pursuit of his dreams. Subsequently, on September 4, he had a medical examination to determine his suitability for aircrew, confessing that he smoked fifteen cigarettes a day and drank about twelve quarts of beer weekly, and the A4B medical category he had as a technician was upgraded to A1B A3B, making him eligible for aircrew. The interviewer wrote that he was a "Good type. Anxious to remuster. Has the stuff and should succeed in aircrew."

On October 11, Armour was sent to No. 9 B&G School, Mont Joli, Quebec, for training as an air gunner. He was promoted to the rank of leading aircraftsman on November 21 and received the promised raise in pay.

[1] A technician whose job was to build and repair various aircraft instruments.

A student gunner's first air exercises were simple, merely a question of flying in Blenheim V's alongside a drogue towed by Westland Lysanders and learning to "lead," so as to compensate for the relative speeds of target and gunner. The drogue was puffed-out and firm like a windsock in a gale, and although it appeared to be an easy target, it wasn't! Vast quantities of ammunition streaked around the sky until the student gunners learned to compensate for the shifting and skidding, the swooping and soaring of the target and their own aircraft. Every student gunner used his own ammunition (each was issued 200 rounds), the rounds having been dipped in blue or red wax for identification purposes. After target practice, ground staff examined the drogue bits, checking colour smudges and counting each man's hits. Student air gunners were frequently dismayed at how few hits they scored[2].

The Bristol Blenheim trainer.

Air gunners were lookouts as much as defenders of their aircraft. Many flew entire tours without firing a single shot in anger. It was their sharp eyes that kept the aircraft free from trouble. At gunnery schools they learned to develop and deliver a running commentary to keep the pilot informed of happenings to the side, rear, above, and below the plane. They became experts in aircraft recognition, and classroom instruction included peering through regulation gun sights at moving scale models of Heinkels, Junkers, Messerschmitts, and other enemy aircraft. They were expected to instantly identify the target with an estimate of range and position relative to their own.[3]

At Mont Joli, Armour flew fourteen hours on the Fairey Battle aircraft (somewhere along the line he also picked up the nickname "Joe" that stayed with him during his time as aircrew). In the Battle, student gunners were positioned at gun doors near the rear of the fuselage. Carbon monoxide and glycol fumes swept over them constantly, driven by the slipstream. When their guns jammed, a common occurrence, they had to strip and reassemble the Vickers gun on the aircraft floor. Bored with waiting for this process, the pilots frequently indulged in a few steep aerobatic turns and dives, and consequently, many of the smaller gun pieces would float around inside the fuselage. Few gunners were impressed with these manoeuvres.

[2] Spencer Dunmore, Wings for Victory (Toronto: McClelland and Stewart, 1994) p. 200.
[3] This was done in reference to a clock face – i.e. – directly in front of the gunner's aircraft was 12 o'clock, 90° right was three o'clock, directly behind six o'clock, etc.

Wings Day for air gunners was just as important an event as for any other aircrew trade, and the gunners on parade were just as tense. For "Joe" Garland that day was officially December 30, 1942, but because of the Christmas holidays, the parade was held early and the graduates were allowed to take a combination of holiday and embarkation leave, since they were all going overseas immediately. Sergeant Garland, wearing his new air gunner's wing, with his wife and baby son, spent some days with his parents in Carleton Place for Christmas.

On January 14, 1943, Joe reported to the "Y" Depot in Halifax to await a berth on a ship headed overseas. He embarked on January 26 and arrived in England on February 4. While Armour was at sea Vivien gave birth to their second son, John, on February 1.

After processing at the PRC, Armie was sent, on March 3, to No. 7 Air Gunnery Training School (AGTS) for refresher training. To receive training as a member of night-bomber crew flying Halifax bombers he was sent to RAF Pershope and No. 23 OTU.

It was at the OTU that Joe "crewed up"with Flying Officer R. Stewart (pilot) RCAF, Pilot Officer S. E. James (navigator) RCAF, Sergeant V. A. F. Cleveland (bomb-aimer) RCAF, Sergeant A. Embley (wireless operator / air gunner) RAF, Sergeants H. R. Tenny (flight engineer) RAF, and L. Northcliffe (second gunner) RCAF. Garland took the position of tail gunner. In training, the crew accumulated fifty-seven hours and forty minutes day flying and forty-one hours and twenty minutes night flying. Joe Garland's final training report read: "Seems a little weak on all gunnery subjects, but should improve with more experience." He volunteered, and was recommended, for Pathfinder duties, and on June 30, 1943, Garland was promoted to flight sergeant.

After training on the Halifax bomber at 1659 HCU at Topcliffe, Yorkshire, the crew moved to Middleton St. George on July 5, 1943, to their new assignment with 419 Squadron. However, two days later Garland was in hospital with influenza, so did not begin squadron duties until July 11.

No. 419 Squadron was part of the new all-Canadian No. 6 Bomber Group, which had been formed as a night-bomber unit at Mildenhall, Suffolk, on December 15, 1941. The squadron was initially equipped with Wellington I

C bombers, but in November 1942, it moved to Middleton St. George and began flying Halifax II's. The squadron became known as the "Moose" squadron, and its badge depicted, in natural colours, an attacking moose and its motto Moosa aswayita, Cree for "Beware of the moose."

For the first few days, Joe Garland and his crew flew familiarization flights on squadron aircraft. On July 18 the squadron enjoyed a "stand-down" from flying operations, and the gunners sharpened their aim with skeet shooting. A highlight of the day was a softball game pitting the officers against the NCO's. The NCO's won by a big margin.

The squadron was then briefed that they would be participating in the opening attack on Hamburg; the first wave would fly on the night of July 24–25. At a flight briefing, the bomber crews were provided with explicit instructions regarding the night's operations, including information on alternate targets in case circumstances prevented proceeding to the primary target. Earlier in the day, armourers selected bombs according to the type of target, transported them to the aircraft, and loaded the bomb bays; the meteorological officer prepared weather forecasts for the target and en route; the medical officer and signals officer were warned of the coming operation; and the intelligence officer gathered specific information about the target. Ground defences were described and vulnerable points marked, including power stations, a group of factories, bridges, and rail facilities. Ground crews prepared the aircraft, but the aircrew carried out the last pre-flight inspection just prior to boarding.

Some 800 aircraft hit Hamburg, the majority of which were Lancasters, Stirlings, and Halifaxes, and flying their first operational mission, in aircraft DT 798 "P for Papa," was Flying Officer Stewart's crew with Flight Sergeant Garland riding the rear gun turret. None of the crews had any illusions about Hamburg. It was a well-defended city and would be a tough target. Flak gunners and night fighters would defend it with vigour and courage, but Bomber Command had a major tactical innovation—Window.

Window was an anti-radar device, consisting of strips of coarse black paper, each precisely two centimetres wide and twenty-seven centimetres long, with aluminium foil stuck to one side. Dropped from attacking aircraft, the foil would swamp German radar sets with false echoes which would prohibit the controllers from vectoring fighters to the bomber stream.

Window had been around since 1942, but Bomber Command had been denied its use for fear that the Luftwaffe might copy it for raids on Britain. Keeping it from Bomber Command was another in a long list of disastrous bureaucratic decisions. During the embargo, Bomber Command lost 2,200 aircraft to German radar-assisted defences.

But on this night, the drop over Hamburg created a nightmare for the city's radar operators. Their screens were suddenly filled with millions of targets and no one could sort the real ones from the false. In one fell swoop the German radar defence was rendered obsolete.

Weather over the city was clear with only a gentle wind. In fifty minutes, 728 aircraft dropped 2,284 tons of bombs on the city. Less than half dropped within three miles of the city centre, but Hamburg was so huge, that severe damage was caused, especially in the central and northwestern districts. The Rathaus (city hall), Nikolaikirche (St. Nicholas Church), main police station, main telephone exchange, and Hagenbeck Zoo were all hit, killing approximately 1,500 people and 140 animals.

Flying Officer Stewart took DT 798 airborne at 2203 hours. The visibility was good, apart from some haze. They saw six fires blazing well all over the town and a great deal of black smoke pluming up to 15,000 feet. The crew felt that the attack appeared to have been well concentrated, and they reported their sortie as successful. At 0500 hours on July 25, they landed, debriefed, ate breakfast, and rolled into bed. They were flying again that night.

The Handley Page Halifax bomber was a potent weapon. Credit "...OF MEN AND PLANES," P. 80.

The tremendous amount of smoke lingering over Hamburg may well be the reason bombers were sent to Essen on the night of July 25–26. The eastern area of the city had been hit, with the Krupp's steel complex suffering particularly heavy damage.

Joe Garland's crew took off at 2201 hours in aircraft JD 270. Over the target they found the visibility to be only fair with much smoke from previous waves of bombers. On their run-in, when the aircraft had to be kept straight and level on a constant heading and altitude, they were flying between two lines of thirty to forty searchlight cones. That and the very heavy barrage made for a harrowing time over the target. On the return flight, just after crossing the French coast, they were attacked by an FW-190.

Flying at 19,000 feet, Garland saw a Junkers 88 "with a large white light in the nose." For a few moments, the fighter flew 300 yards to port and level with the bomber. Then it turned to attack. Garland "opened fire at 250 yards and continued" to blaze away until the fighter dived to the left. The Junkers 88 did not fire a shot,[4] but the hail of bullets from the Halifax's guns put paid to the attack and sent the German spinning to ground on fire. They arrived back at base at 0259 hours.

A total of 705 aircraft struck Essen, and Bomber Command wanted to get in another good raid while the effects of Window were still fresh. Again it was successful in the industrial areas, with the Krupps works taking its most damaging punishment of the war. Fifty-one industrial buildings were destroyed and eighty-three were seriously damaged; 2,852 houses were destroyed and 500 people killed, including forty-two prisoners of war. Next morning, when the extent of the damage was known, Herr Doktor Gustav Krupps, owner of the Krupps Steel Works, suffered a stroke from which he never recovered.

Credit for the Junkers 88 kill was bantered back and forth between Garland, the rear gunner, and Northcliffe, the second. Finally the crew settled on Northcliffe as having most probably fired the fatal shot. The crew had completed two successful sorties and had already shot down one enemy. To note this success, a single swastika was painted on the fuselage just below the pilot's left side window.

Their adrenaline was running high. They had one night off before being sent on their third mission, the night of July 27–28, a night of pure hell for Hamburg. Nearly 800 bombers delivered the devil's handiwork.

It had been an uncommonly hot, dry day in the city, and at six o'clock in the evening, the temperature was still at 30° Celsius and the humidity was only thirty per cent. There had been no rain for some time. People sat in doorways or at open windows, dabbing their foreheads with handkerchiefs. Shortly after midnight, the air raid sirens began to wail, and about an hour later, Pathfinders marked an area about two miles east of the city cente. The bombing proved to be well concentrated and "crept back"[5] only very slightly.

[4] Spencer Dunmore, Reap The Whirlwind (Toronto: McClelland & Stewart, 1991) p.126.
[5] "Creep back" is the phenomenon during which each aircraft bombs a little shorter than the preceeding bomber, making it appear that the target is creeping back along the approach of the bomber stream. This is caused by head winds or more probably the bombaimer on each aircraft dropping a second earlier than the aircraft ahead of him.

Garland's crew took off at 2156 hours, again in Halifax DT 789 "P". Their transit was uneventful, but once they reached the target, things got very hot indeed. Visibility in heavy smoke was hazy at best, and by the time they arrived, the whole town seemed to be in flames. They reported the flak (*Fliegerabwehrkanonen*, anti-aircraft gun fire) as exceptionally heavy, and their airplane was hit with one engine catching fire and the hydraulic system being damaged. Skipper Stewart and the flight engineer, Sergeant Tenny, managed to put out the fire and keep the aircraft under reasonable control. They landed back at Middleton St. George at 0418 hours and turned their kite over to the "erks" (ground crew) for an engine change. It would be ready for the next trip.

The Pathfinders' aerial light display provided signposts in the sky for the bomb-aimers crouched in their nose compartments, and 729 aircraft dropped 2,326 tons of bombs. It took merely five minutes from the release of the first marker to the hail of high explosives and incendiaries to tear the heart from Hamburg and produce an inferno of such gigantic proportions that the city's defences became immediately impotent. Most of the damage was done by fire, started by four-pound incendiaries landing on roofs. The larger thirty-pound firebombs smashed through ceilings to set off fires inside the buildings. While the high explosives blew out windows, doors, and walls to help spread the fires and disrupt the work of rescue crews by wrecking streets, water mains, and power plants.

Most of Hamburg's fire vehicles were still in the western part of the city damping down the smouldering fires from the raid three nights before. Very few vehicles were able to pass through streets blocked by the rubble of destroyed buildings.

That night in Hamburg, the attackers' plans worked with horrific efficiency. The concentrated bombing set off scores of fires in the Hammerbrook district, competing with each other for oxygen causing a terrible new phenomenon to visit the earth—the firestorm! Suddenly the entire area was like a blast furnace run amok, sucking all air into it. And the bombing continued for another thirty minutes! It was estimated that 550 to 600 bomb loads were dropped on an area only two miles by one mile. Blazing timbers went spinning into the flames. Ferocious winds swept people into burning buildings. Those who fell on the streets were instantly burned to death and turned into charcoal. The wind screamed between blazing buildings. Roofs were ripped away and torn to shreds. Trees were uprooted and flung into the inferno. The air became supersaturated; buildings, vehicles, and even people burst suddenly into flame.

In later waves of bombers, crews could smell the fires. Bomb-aimers in their plexiglass-enclosed nose positions felt the heat wafting up while soot smeared the aircraft windows. Below, people hid in cellars and ditches or plunged into the Fleet Canal of the Elbe River to escape the flames. Sparks flew everywhere, setting new fires that added to the terror and despair of the population. Bomber Command had unleashed a truly cataclysmic blow against a major German city.

The firestorm raged for almost three hours and stopped only when there was nothing left to burn. Five hundred public buildings and more than 2,000 commercial enterprises were destroyed. Over half the private residences were in ruins. There were few survivors. Estimates of the dead were later put at 30,000 to 40,000. Most died in their basement shelters from carbon monoxide poisoning when all air was sucked out of their hiding places. Nearly a million people were homeless and a further 1.2 million (two-thirds the population) fled the city in fear of further raids. Extensive damage had been done to the shipyards and U-boats under construction, and some 18,000 tons of shipping lay at the bottom of the harbour.

Clandestine reports told of SS troops patrolling the city to keep order, but Hamburg rebounded rapidly; devastating air raids seemed to bolster rather than wreck the people's morale, which the planners of the raids could have known by observing the indomitable spirit of Londoners under siege. Five months later, by the end of the year, eighty per cent of Hamburg's productivity had been restored[6].

On the night of July 29–30, the crew found themselves back in aircraft DT 789 for the third time, making their third trip to Hamburg.

Due to the success of Window, the Luftwaffe was forced to adjust its night-fighter tactics. No longer could it rely solely on the bond between a ground-based radar controller and the fighter pilot. Significantly it introduced the Focke-Wulfe 190 and the Messerschmitt 109 into the night-fighter role. Tactically, senior air officers gave a much freer reign to twin-engine radar-equipped fighters to pursue potential victims.

The Pathfinders used H2S to find the Hamburg marking points. The targets were the northern and northeastern districts, which had escaped the previous bombings. However, the Pathfinders marked more than two miles too far east, just south of the devastated area, and the main bombing force crept back about four miles, through the devastated area. This resulted in heavy bombing of the residential districts of Wandsbek, Barmbek, Uhlenhorst, and Winterhude; 707 aircraft dropped 2,318 tons of bombs. No firestorm developed, but fire was widespread which the exhausted fire fighters could do little to combat.

After Stewart's crew landed at 0414 hours, they reported: "Successful. No cloud but much haze and smoke from target. Bombed on markers. Attack not

⁶ Much of the information on the raid on Hamburg came from Spencer Dunmore's Above and Beyond, (Toronto, McClelland & Stewart, 1996) pp. 261/262, and Martin Middlebrook, and Chris Everitt, The Bomber Command War Diaries. (Leicester, England: Midland Counties Publications (Aerophile) Limited, 1996) pp. 410 to 415.

so heavy as previous ones. Lots of scattered fire seen and one large explosion in centre of target." The squadron then went on a seven-day standdown, until August 7, exempting them from the fourth and final attack on beleaguered Hamburg.

On the night of August 9–10, Garland's crew went back into the fray, joining a force of 457 aircraft, 171 of them Halifaxes, headed for Mannheim. The night's operation was a medium-sized raid described by Bomber Command as "scattered." The crew was assigned to a different aircraft, JD 163, and they were airborne at 2217 hours, trundling towards the target.

Over blacked-out Mannheim the skies were cloud-covered. The Pathfinders marking was not accurate, and although the bombing appeared very scattered, the crew still considered their attack successful. On arrival over the target area, a very large explosion on the ground greeted them, and by the time they were on their bombing run, the city was well alight.

Although Bomber Command considered the raid modest it caused considerable damage: 1,316 buildings were totally destroyed and 42 large factories put out of production; 269 people were killed and 1,210 injured; and 144 farm animals perished.

After completing their run, pilot Stewart turned for home. The return trip was uneventful; they avoided any attack and landed safely at 0548 hours, just as the sun peeked over the horizon. But after eight exhausting hours in the air, all the crews enjoyed their bunks more than the bright August day.

The next night, August 10–11, they were airborne again in Halifax JD 163, this time heading for Nuremberg. Bomber Command was beginning its march on Berlin. In doing so they were launching raids all over Germany. Stewart's aircraft tucked its wheels in the well at 2113 hours and turned towards the continent; their target was the central and southern parts of the city. Although the Pathfinders' attempts to mark the target were hampered by cloud, the attack was still useful. There was a large fire area in the Wöhrd district causing serious property damage to industrial and residential regions and killing 577 people. The Lorenzkirche, the largest of the city's old churches, was badly damaged and about fifty houses in the preserved *Altstadt* (Old City) were destroyed.

Garland's crew posted another successful sortie. They found the weather conditions good, but were unable to observe their own bombing, although on run-up to, and leaving, the target, they did see other bombs bursting. When they arrived back over England they were advised that another aircraft at Middleton St. George had landed wheels up and was obstructing the runway. Therefore Pilot Stewart turned to their alternate aerodrome, Topcliffe, and touched down there at 0625 hours after nine hours and fifteen minutes flying.

The next afternoon, they took off for the short flight home to be briefed for their next flight on the night of August 12–13.

The capitulation of Italy was imminent at this time as the Canadians fought up the east coast and the Americans raced for Rome. To hasten the process, Bomber Command was called upon to renew visits to northern Italian cities, and Stewart's crew, in aircraft JD 163, was sent to Milan. Because of the distance, they took off about an hour earlier than usual, at 2040 hours, so it was just dusk when they rumbled down the runway into the air and turned south to cross the English Channel and the French Alps, joining a stream of 321 Lancasters and 183 Halifaxes. Losses were very light; only two Halifaxes and one Lancaster did not return.

The visibility was good under a bright moon. In the rear turret, Joe Garland had a spectacular view of the Alps. But as they neared Milan, they were racing a storm twenty miles away containing multiple lightning bolts drifting from the northeast towards the target. They identified the target by the green Pathfinder Force flares and with the help of the "commentator."[7] They reported that they did see their own bombs burst on the green markers and that there were many fires concentrated around the markers.

Four factories, including the Alfa Romeo motor works and the Caprioni aircraft factory, the main railway station, and the La Scala opera house all received major damage; 1,174 people died in the August air raids. Garland and his crew were back on the ground in Britain at 0645 hours after spending just over ten hours airborne, mostly at very high altitudes. The rapid advance of ground troops ensured Italy was out of the war within a few weeks.

Twenty-four hours after the bombers crossed the Alps, a decision was made to carry out a precision raid on Peenemünde. The RAF had clear evidence that Germany's experimental V-2 rockets were nearing operational readiness[8]. This was an entirely different type of raid for Bomber Command. It had to be a precision attack on a relatively small target, and it required the services of a master bomber to control the approach and drop of the raiders.

On the night of August 17–18, in a different Halifax, JD 459, Garland's crew was airborne at 2129 hours and heading east for Peenemünde on the Baltic coast. Above 10,000 feet they encountered only three-tenths cloud

[7] The commentator was a Master Bomber, a senior Pathfinder and usually a navigator, who "talked" the bombers in over the target and to their aiming points. While orbiting over the target he talked on radio/telegraph giving headings and distances for them to fly to an accurate release point. The final run-in and drop remained in the eyes and estimation of the aircraft's own bombaimer. The commentator assisted those aircraft whose H2S screens could not be read since they showed only completely lit-up screens indicating they were over a dense built-up area; or those crews who, virtually blinded by scores of searchlights, were unable to map-read.

[8] The first V-1 pilot-less bombs had fallen on London during the night of June 12, 1944. The Fiesler Fi 103, known to the Germans as the Vergeltungwaffe 1, Reprisal Weapon 1, was a simple, gyroscopically controlled aircraft packed with a ton or more explosives. Twenty-seven feet long with a seventeen-foot wingspan they were powered by an Argus As 014 pulse jet engine. Before take-off a timing device was set that would stop the engine at a predetermined time. The nose dropped, shutting off the fuel supply. Known in London as "doodlebugs," they caused much damage and killed thousands of Londoners. Spencer Dunmore, Above and Beyond, Toronto: McClelland and Stewart, 1996. p 308

cover in slight haze, which was good. This special raid had been scheduled for a moonlit night to increase the chances of success. It was the first raid on which No. 6 (Canadian) Group used Lancasters, flown by 426 Squadron.

There were other new methods employed this night. This was the only raid in the latter part of the war in which the whole of Bomber Command (596 aircraft) was used for a precision raid at night on such a small target. Plus, for the first time, a master bomber controlled a full-scale raid.

There were three separate targets in the German research establishment: the scientists' and workers' living quarters, the rocket factory itself, and the experimental station. The Pathfinders used a special plan for marking each of the three aiming points individually as the raid progressed. Bombers from No. 5 Group had practised a "time and distance" run-in as an alternative method of flying accurately to the drop point.

The initial marking and bombing fell on a labour camp for forced workers, one-and-a-half miles south of the first aiming point. The master bomber's control of the entire raid was successful as he and the Pathfinders quickly brought the bombing back to the main targets. All drops were successful; 560 bombers dropped 1,800 tons of high explosives. Germany's rocket programme was seriously delayed, and there was no need for a second attack.

Approximately 180 Germans were killed in the workers' housing and 500 to 600 Polish labourers perished in their flimsy wooden barracks. They had no air raid shelters.

Bomber Command lost forty aircraft, judged an acceptable cost for a successful attack against an important target on a moonlit night. Six bombers on their way home were lost to the German Messerschmitt 110s fitted with *schräge Musik* weapons (twin cockpit mounted cannons angled to fire upwards). This allowed the night fighters to stalk their prey from below and behind with virtual certainty that they would not be detected.[9]

Garland's crew reported at debriefing that they saw several fires all over the target area and one large explosion. The raid on Peenemünde marked the pinnacle of Bomber Command's successes in 1943, and the crew was taken off operations for the next four days. The time also gave their ground crew an opportunity to perform much needed maintenance, including painting on the left side under the pilot's window eight white bombs signifying their eight successful bombing missions. This was in addition to the one swastika marking the confirmed night-fighter kill they made on mission number three.

With summer fading, the chill winds of autumn began to blow over England bringing a change in focus. Bomber Command was directed against

[9] This was very reminiscent of the Great War tactics of fighter pilots who angled their guns upward to fire at their enemy from below and behind; especially before interrupters were invented to keep them from blowing off their own propellers.

Berlin. Goebbels had once boasted that no Allied aircraft would ever fly over the country's capital, and Harris took great glee in proving the error of the claim. During the last week of August and the first week of September, more than 1,600 sorties were flown in three raids, but with staggering losses: 125 crews failed to return. The Luftwaffe had gained its second breath and inflicted such a rate of attrition on Halifax and Stirling bombers during the second raid that these squadrons could not fly on the third. A meagre 316 Lancasters carried it out with a quartet of Mosquito Pathfinders.

Meanwhile, pressure was maintained on the industrial Ruhr area. The night of August 22–23 was a significant night for Carleton Place, but it is doubtful that those involved knew it. That night, two 419 aircraft carried two Carleton Place boys over Germany. Armour Garland flew his ninth trip, and Russell James flew his first. Both were scheduled for bombing runs on Leverkusen.

Garland was in the air at 2009 hours in Halifax JD 459, "Q for Quebec." Their target was the I. G. Farben factory, but thick cloud and Oboe failure scattered the bomber stream. Only superficial damage was caused and the raid was deemed unsuccessful. Neither Garland nor James made it to the target, both returning with unserviceable aircraft. Garland was back first, at 2150 hours with an unserviceable wireless set. They had flown out to sea to safely jettison their bomb-load then returned to land.

The next night the crew was briefed for the "really big" trip. They were going to Berlin! 710 bombers were ordered into the air (335 Lancasters, 251 Halifaxes, 124 Stirlings), with seventeen Mosquitoes marking various points along the route to keep the main force on track. This was the first of three planned attacks on the German capital. The master bomber was a Canadian, Wing Commander J. E. "Johnny" Fauquier, commanding officer of 405 Squadron; however, the raid was only partly successful. Fifty-six planes were lost that night, Bomber Command's greatest one-night loss.

Because they were carrying high explosives and incendiaries, Garland's crew, in bomber JD 459, took off in the second wave[10], becoming airborne at 2053 hours. Their load was one 2,000-pound bomb, 32 thirty-pound bombs, and 360 four-pound incendiaries. En route to the target there was no cloud, but visibility was minimally reduced in haze, and in the clear cold air, crystalline ice formed on the leading edges of the wings, over the gun turrets, and on the windscreen, The front gun froze and was rendered completely useless, and the control surfaces on the wings were jammed with ice. Their only recourse was to descend to warmer air and let the ice melt and break off (wing de-icing systems had yet to be developed), causing them to be five minutes late on the bomb run. Inside the fuselage, crewmembers had to flex fingers, toes, and limbs to ward off frostbite.

[10] The first wave dropped only high explosives damaging buildings to make the job of the incendiaries easier.

A tail gunner is helped into his unwieldy electrically heated flying suit. The rear turret was the coldest spot in the aircraft with temperatures reaching -40°C. Frostbite was a common occupational hazard. Credit "The Lancaster at War," p. 47.

The Pathfinders were not able to identify city centre by H2S and marked, in error, an area on the southern edge of Berlin. The main force was late, and both flak and night fighters were extremely fierce. Many bombs fell in open country and the sparsely populated southern suburbs. In spite of this, Berlin reported the attack to have been the most serious air raid to date; 2,611 industrial, public, and residential buildings were destroyed or severely damaged. The worst occurred well south of the centre of the city, in the residential areas of Lankwitz and Lichterfelde and the industrial districts of Mariendorf and Marienfelde. Industrial Tempelhof, nearer the centre, was hit, as well as some government buildings, almost by chance. The Wilhelmstrasse reported not a single building left unscathed. Twenty ships were sunk in the city's canals.

City officials reported 854 people killed, among them two prisoners of war. They were of the opinion that the high death rate was because many people had not taken to their allocated shelters when ordered to do so.

Stewart's crew considered their mission to have been successful. They reported one very large orange explosion seen at 2350 hours, and returned to base at 0327 hours, their tenth mission completed.

The crew was now one-third through their first tour. In May 1943, the Air Ministry, in keeping with a recommendation from Sir Arthur "Bomber" Harris, had laid down the rules for Bomber Command. The first tour by aircrew was to be thirty sorties, the second not more than twenty sorties. Between the two, aircrew would be posted to OTU training duties. Pathfinders were to complete a single continuous tour of forty-five sorties. At the end of the first tour, the flyers were entitled to wear the silver Operations Wing on their left chest pocket flap. It is interesting to note that all aircrew looked hungrily towards the end of their first tour, but their operational flying was not finished then. Aircrews were expected to complete at least two tours of thirty operations each[11].

The next sortie was set for August 27–28 and the target was Nuremberg. JD 464 was airborne at 2041 hours. Rear gunner Garland watched the airplane behind, JD 456, carrying second gunner Russell James, follow them

[11] John Terraine, The Right of the Line (London: Hodder and Strougton, 1985) p. 527.

into the air at 2042 hours. Garland's crew reported visibility hazy in two-tenths cloud while James' crew called the visibility "perfectly clear." The official version was that the target area was free of cloud, but it was very dark.

The initial Pathfinder markers were accurate but creep-back quickly developed because so many Pathfinder aircraft had difficulty with their H2S sets. The master bomber could do little to move the bombing forward as few of the crews could hear his broadcasts. Most of the bombs fell in open country with a few scattered across the southeastern and eastern suburbs of Nuremberg. Several bombs hit the zoo, killing sixty-five people. Garland's crew identified the target by the red and green markers and they could also see buildings. After they left the target area, they observed a few large fires well under way. Both they and the James crew landed at the same time, 0452 hours, but James had to use an alternate aerodrome, Tangmere.

The night of August 31–September 1 was set for the second raid on Berlin. Halifax II, JD 464 "N for November," carrying rear gunner Sergeant A. D. H. Garland, took off at 1952 hours with a full bomb load and headed east. It was never heard from again. 419 Squadron had had no losses on the previous four operations, but lost three crews returning from this raid on Berlin.

It was during this raid that the Luftwaffe used a new tactic. Their fighters over-flew the bomber stream dropping hundreds of flares. The flares lit the sky as if it were day, and forty-seven of the 622 aircraft sent to Berlin this night never returned; about two-thirds of those lost were shot down over the target by German fighters. Commonwealth aircrew would remember this night as being particularly long. Fighters could be seen in the pools of light dashing about firing at any bomber that flew into their sights. The carnage was considerable. The entire sky above the Nazi capital was filled with death. The raid was deemed unsuccessful. Armour and the members of his crew were listed as missing in action.

On September 11, the commanding officer of 419 Squadron penned the following letter to Vivien Garland:

> I regret to inform you that your husband, Sergeant Armour Douglas Haig Garland, is missing from operations on the night of August 31st, 1943. The operation was a very heavy attack on one of the main German targets and was very successful, but unfortunately your husband's plane failed to return and its loss can only be attributed to enemy action. There is quite a possibility that all or part of the crew may be prisoners of war but this would not be known for some weeks yet.

Your husband was with us for two months and during that time he had taken part in ten attacks on the enemy, including some of the recent heavy raids on Berlin, Hamburg and Milan. During these operations he had five successful combats with enemy fighters, two being severely damaged and the other three being forced to break off the engagement. He was a very good shot and his crew had full confidence in his ability. In his off hours your husband took quite a prominent part in our recreational activities, being particularly interested in our ball team. Your husband's cheery determined personality and enjoyment of operational flying made him one of the most popular men on the Squadron and I can assure you we miss him badly.

If any further news comes to hand, you may rest assured you will be notified immediately.

Sergeant Garland's kit and personal effects have been collected and forwarded to the Central Depository, Colinbrook, Slought, Bucks., who, after completion of necessary details, will communicate with you as to their disposal.

May I express my sincere sympathy with you in your great loss and hope with you that better news may follow.

Unfortunately better news was not forthcoming. In October, the Minister of Defence sent a card of condolence. Then, a letter from Flight Sergeant Embley, now a prisoner of war, arrived at the Rochdale, England, home of his mother:

You probably know by now that Joe is gone, anyway I will try and explain, even if it gets censored, I would like his people to know. He was wounded badly and his parachute was almost destroyed, so I had to bring him down on my back, but unfortunately, he fell off at approximately 3000 feet, into the Black Forest, so if you can get it through the Red Cross please do so . . .

Flight Sergeant. Embley's mother did get the information through to Vivien. She replied in a letter dated February 13, 1944:

Rec. your letter sometime before Xmas and really I am sorry for not having answered sooner, but I just seem to fall down on my corresponding until I get in a good mood. Right now truthfully speaking I have 15 letters to ans. so I'll be kept out of mischief for a while eh?

I am quite well, also the children are fine. I do hope you are all doing good over there.

I am so glad Bert is well and safe, really it must be a great relief to know where they are.

Mrs. Embly, I have every hope of my darling "Joe" but its just the suspense of waiting. He will be officially presumed dead the end of this month if no word comes before, but that wont knock the wind out of my sails because there isn't anything can bring me to believe those other three boys aren't safe somewhere. I don't be in the habit of fortune telling or card reading, but some of my friends along with myself have been going to a few of these persons and they all give us about the same picture. They have all told me my husband will return in late summer or autumn and that he is safe in a country where he cannot communicate with us.

Vince's mother [bomb-aimer Vince Cleveland] and I have become friendly through letters although we have never met I know she is a wonderful woman. I am looking forward to going to Toronto in the spring to see her. I have had letters from Bob's wife [pilot Flight Officer Robert Stewart] over there and she sent me a picture of the wedding. Our "Joe" looks very nice on it and so does Bert. Armour wrote and told me how he liked to go to your home on leave. He said you were a grand family and let him call you Mom and Pop.

I am so sorry there is nothing I can tell you that could relieve Bert's suspense of "Joe" I got the cable of missing on Sept. 3rd and have had no official word since. The Air Ministry & Casualties Officer keep in constant touch with me but cannot tell me anything only to still hope.

My one thought is no news is good news and as Bob's wife says they couldn't go so completely missing unless they were alive which I am a sure of . . .

Mrs. Garland ("Joe's Mom") wants to write you also, so I will send her your address. I was so glad you wrote Me and really believed when I say I am sorry for not having answered sooner.

My little Garry was two yrs old on December 5th, and Jackie one on February 1st so they are growing up.

Well my dears I will have to close for now and please write me soon.

I had a letter from the Airforce a few weeks back stating "I regret that since my letter of December 2nd no further information has been received on the whereabouts of your husband, Sergeant Douglas Haig Armour Garland.

Every effort is still being made to trace your husband, although owing to the lapse of time it is now felt there is less hope in locating them . . ."

I gathered by this they were trying to prepare me for when the presumption come up. If and when he does come back, I guess he'll have to get back to England first give him one of the biggest hugs and kisses, that you have ever given your own boys just for little me.

Well again I will say God Bless you all and let me know the news of Bert. Your friend's wife

Vivien, Garry and Jackie Garland.

On February 6, 1945, Vivien received a message of condolence from the king and queen, and both she and her mother-in-law were presented with the Memorial Cross. That spring, the wait, the realization of Armour's death, and the responsibility for two little boys caused Vivien to be hospitalized with a "nervous breakdown." She was granted a government pension of $87 a month, and she moved to North Bay to live with her mother. She also received Armour's War Service Gratuity of $305.46 for 784 days' service, 216 of them overseas.

The RCAF made a Casualty Enquiry to the Casualty Officer in the Russian Zone of Germany on October 11, 1946, requesting that an investigation be made to locate the burial place of the three missing crewmembers. Along with specific details of the aircraft and its crew they provided the following information:

F/O James, W/O1 Northcliffe, F/S Embley and Sgt. Tenny parachuted and have since been repatriated. F/O James, the navigator, gives the location of the crash as Magdeburg. W/O1 Northcliffe, the second gunner gives the location as Logonburg, the map reference for which cannot be found.

F/S Embley stated that F/S Garland, the rear gunner, was wounded when three Ju 88's attacked the aircraft. The aircraft caught fire and the order was given to abandon the aircraft. Before leaving the aircraft his attention was drawn, by W/O1 Northcliffe, to F/S Garland who was immediately behind him and was wounded and bleeding profusely from wounds on the right side of the head. F/S Embley went back to the rear turret for Garland's parachute but on arrival found it burning and almost blown to pieces by cannon fire. He returned to the exit, attached his parachute and told F/S Garland they would have to go it together whereupon Garland put his arms through the padding on the back of Embley's parachute, wrapping his legs around Embley's waist, whereupon the latter jumped. Garland spoke to Embley two or three times on the way down but later at about 2,000 feet he began to slip away and despite Embley's efforts he fell away completely.

F/S Embley states that he landed in the Black Forest near Weisenburg and searched for approximately two hours in a futile effort to locate F/S Garland's body. Weisenburg cannot be located in the Gazetteers and it is assumed that the Black Forest referred to is a forest near Magdeburg. No additional information is available.

Flight Sergeant Tenny, the flight engineer, was taken prisoner. He believed the crash location was Medewitch-Weisenberg, and when he was repatriated, he made the following statement regarding the fate of his crew:

Before I baled out we heard the Rear Gunner telling us he had been hit and did not know how badly. —I saw Sgt. Northcliffe go and chute open and I followed him. I saw no more come out but later saw P/O James at Dulag Luft and also Sgt. Embley and Northcliffe with whom I proceeded to next Camp. Sgt. Embley baled out after me it seems and took Sgt. Garland pick-a-back but Garland fell off and must definitely have died. I do not know the fate of F/Sgt. Stewart or Sgt. Cleveland as I lost sight of the aircraft from then on . . .

Sgt. Embley[12] and Northcliffe attempted to make their own way home from Muklberg when the Russians took over. I do not know whether they were successful.

Flight Sergeant Garland's name is engraved on the Runnymede Memorial overlooking the River Thames on Cooper's Hill in Surrey, near Windsor. The Canadian published his last memorial on August 29, 1946:

The Runnymede Air Forces Memorial.

[12] Embley survived the war, was repatriated and lived out his life in England.

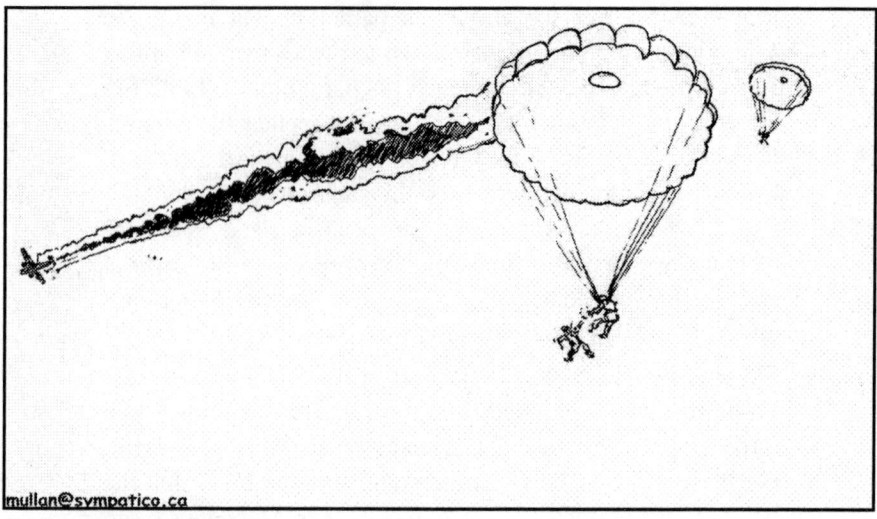

F/Sgt. Garland's fall to earth.

GARLAND—In fond and loving memory of our loving son, Flt. Sgt. Armour D. H. Garland, who was killed over Germany with two of his gallant crew on the 31st of August, 1943.

Little more than a happy schoolboy,
When called away to war;
Now he lies in a warrior's grave
On a far-off foreign shore.
When I see the Welcome Home signs
And I feel so all alone;
Its then I wish with all my heart
That he only could come home.
If all the world were mine to give,
I'd give it, yes, and more,
If I could hear his cheery voice
Call 'Hello Mom' once more.
We miss him most
who loved him best.

Mom and Dad

The Canadian Bomber Group was unique and became renowned. Officially known as No. 6 (RCAF) Bomber Group, it grew from eight squadrons at formation on January 1, 1943, to fourteen squadrons by war's end. It was formed in Yorkshire and its badge had a maple leaf superimposed upon a York rose to symbolize this association. It adopted the motto *Sollertia et ingenium* (Initiative and Skill).

Upon formation, the RAF handed over six stations with RCAF squadrons already established on them: Leeming (408 and 424), Middleton St. George (419 and 420), Dishforth (425 and 426), Croft (427), Dalton (428), and Skipton-on-Swale, which was still under construction. The Group had control of 405 Squadron, serving in Coastal Command and later with No. 8 Group (Pathfinder Force), and No. 1659 HCU. All squadrons were flying Wellingtons except Nos. 405, 408 and 419, which had Halifax II's or V's.

The only squadron to remain at a single station for the duration of the war was 419 Squadron at Middleton St. George. 419 also took delivery of the first Canadian-built Lancaster (Mark X), KB 700, the famous "Ruhr Express." It had flown three operational Pathfinder sorties with 405 Squadron before it was handed over. As "VR-Z" it flew forty-six more operational missions with the Moose Squadron before it was destroyed in a crash on landing at Middleton St. George, after returning from a raid on Nuremberg on the night of January 2–3, 1945.

Lancaster Mk. X KB700 was the first Canadian-manufactured Lancaster. Nick-named the "Ruhr Express," and coded LQ-Q, it served with 405 (B) Squadron and, coded VR-Z, with 419 Squadron.

R 188839 Sergeant Russell George James
Air Gunner
Royal Canadian Air Force

Sergeant Russell James, Air Gunner

On September 5, 1943, No. 419 RCAF Squadron reported that Halifax aircraft JD 210 "S for Sugar," with a crew of seven, failed to return from an operational attack on Mannheim. There had been no news of the aircraft or its crew since it took off from Middleton St. George. The crew had been on squadron one month, and this was their fourth operational sortie. Flying as rear gunner was Sergeant R. G. James.

William Thomas James, born in Renfrew, and Florence Elizabeth Belford, born in Pakenham, were married in Pakenham on December 29, 1920. Their first child was a daughter, Blanche (who married Ross Dezell and moved to Carleton Place). She was followed by three boys (Russell, Malcolm [Mack], and Robert) and another two girls (May and Irene).

Russell was born in Hyndford, Gratton Township, Renfrew County, on January 7, 1923. When he was one year old, the family moved to Ramsay Township where the children grew up on the family farm. Each Sunday they travelled to town to worship in the Anglican Church.

Russell received his education at Appleton public school and Almonte High School. He completed first form before turning his full attention to farming with his father. He had little time for sports, but while in school, he liked to skate, play hockey, and occasionally play softball. He also enjoyed animal husbandry and while quite young joined the Almonte calf club, with which he exhibited Hereford calves and won honours for his club at many showings. A friendly, hard-working lad, he also helped his father exhibit at many agricultural fairs, including Ottawa's, and was a favourite with the other exhibitors. Then, in 1940, at age seventeen, he obtained employment at the Collies' Woolen Mill in Appleton where he became proficient as a weaver and spinner. He stayed at this job until 1942 when he joined the air force.

At Russell's enlistment medical examination, in Ottawa on September 22, 1942, he was described as 5' 10" tall and only 126 pounds. He reported that his tonsils and adenoids had been removed in 1936, that he smoked fifteen cigarettes a day, and that he only occasionally drank alcohol. He was given a category of A1B A3B, fit for flying duties anywhere, and was promptly dispatched to No. 1 Manning Depot in Toronto for basic training with the rank of aircraftsman second class and the following recommendation: "Applicant anxious to get in aircrew. Should brighten up with training. Recommend Air Gunner."

Six weeks later, somewhat fattened up on air force food and looking every inch the airman in his new blue uniform, Russell arrived in Hagersville, Ontario, on November 23, 1942, to attend No. 16 SFTS and be introduced to flying and the art of air-to-air and air-to-ground gunnery. Apart from Christmas leave and the occasional weekend off, he was there until spring. Two weeks into his training, on December 15, he went to the Medical Inspection Room to have a irritating wart removed from his right thumb, as it appeared to be growing larger, and was interfering with his operation of the guns. Two days later, he was admitted to hospital for a two-day stay until a bad case of scabies that covered his arms, legs, and body was cleared up.

Russell progressed to the No. 1 AGTS in Quebec and then to the No. 9 B&G School in Mont Joli where he attended Course No. 52 from March 8 to May 28, 1943.

When war came, the RAF leaders discovered, much to their dismay, that tight formations of bombers with air gunners bringing dozens of guns to bear on any target seldom hit anything. The gunners were not trained as such, but were instead ground crew pressed to fill a slot. German fighters carried 20-mm cannons while the bombers were armed with .303 Brownings. It didn't take the fighters long to determine the limited range of the Brownings and stand off outside it to blaze away with their cannon. A few months into the war the Air Ministry introduced proper training, the air gunner's brevet[13], and decreed that air crew gunners would be sergeants or better.

Gunnery accuracy required skilled aircraft recognition. Knowledge of the target's wing span and fuselage length allowed the gunner to effectively use his ring-and-bead sight. At 200 yards, a Messerschmitt 109 flying parallel would just fill the ring. Every third round was a tracer so the student could gauge his deflection. Skeet shooting was the best practice for gunners to learn the art of leading a target and calculating in a split second the required deflection. In 1942, Fairey Battle aircraft were fitted with turrets in place of the open gunner's position. Later, Bolingbrokes came on line at gunnery schools with power-operated gun turrets. Gunners honed their skills by firing at twenty-foot sleeve targets dragged through the sky by other aircraft. At least once during each pass at the target, just to relieve the monotony, the gunner's pilot would pull a turn that either lifted the gunner three feet in the air or drove him to his knees. Inevitably it occurred just as the student had his target perfectly lined up in the gunsight.

---

[13] The original air gunners' half-wing was sketched with thirteen feathers. To avoid superstitious reaction one feather disappeared before the wing came into use.

Russell was promoted to leading aircraftsman on April 17, 1943, a month into his gunnery course. During the course he flew twenty-seven hours and ten minutes, before graduating seventy-fifth out of seventy-seven students. His course report read: "Neat routine worker, has to be checked up occasionally." On May 28, Russell was presented with his air gunner wing and simultaneous promotion to sergeant. He was given embarkation leave and told to report to the "Y" Depot in Halifax on June 11 for transfer overseas. Russell embarked on June 16[14] and arrived in England on the 24th, when he was immediately sent to No. 1664 HCU at Croft, Yorkshire, reporting on July 6, 1943.

At the HCU, Russell converted his skills to the guns of the Halifax bomber. To complete the course required three weeks flying for forty hours with a crew, all of whom were new to bombers. The exercises were very similar to those performed at OTUs. In the air, in case of emergency, each crewmember familiarized himself with the others' tasks. Particularly exciting for nineteen-year-old Russell was piloting the aircraft, which was driven by four powerful Rolls-Royce Merlins.

At the HCU, Russell joined his crew: Flying Officer J. A. Studer (pilot/captain), RCAF; Sergeant A. W. Hallworth (flight engineer), RAF; Flying Officer Harry A. Danninger (bomb-aimer), an American serving with the RCAF[15]; Sergeant R. D. Hayes (wireless operator/air gunner), RCAF; Flying Officer George A. Shannon of Arnprior (navigator), RCAF; and Sergeant G. A. Usher (rear gunner), RCAF. Russell was initially crewed as the second gunner, but air gunners usually rotated their positions unless a particular gunner claimed a turret.

The crew arrived at Middleton St. George for flying duties with 419 Squadron on July 31, 1943. From August 1 to 7, the squadron was stood down from flying operations because they had been very busy on the raids to Hamburg. Therefore, the crew spent most of the rest of August familiarizing themselves with squadron aircraft and procedures. Finally they were ready for their first operational mission, to Leverkusen, on the night of August 22–23.

Once an operation had been agreed upon at RCAF headquarters, a "may fly" message was issued. to each squadron, detailing the aircraft and crews necessary for the mission and sending the entire squadron into a hive of activity. Pilots consulted with the technicians regarding the serviceability and habits of the aircraft to which his crew had been assigned, gunners checked their guns and polished the perspex, and all crewmembers busied

[14] The day before he left Canada, the 15th, Russell made a pay allotment of $35. per month to his mother.
[15] At the end of 1941 6,129 Americans were serving in the RCAF, half of them as aircrew. The U.S. government treated such men as part of its aid policy and exempted them from its own draft. Americans made up about 10% of the BCATP intake. Many were employed as staff pilots and EFTS instructors. When the United States entered the war almost one-quarter of those serving in the RCAF chose to transfer to the USAAF.

themselves with pre-flight duties. After a night-flying test for a last minute check of all equipment, the airplane was taxied to a dispersal area, and long caterpillars of bombs were towed by tractors from the bomb dump to the aircraft, where armourers loaded and prepared the bombs for live drops.

Meanwhile, the crews detailed to fly, and standby crews, assembled in the briefing room. Each skipper answered the roll call to confirm that his entire crew was present and prepared. A large map of the British Isles and Europe was unveiled and all eyes followed the tapes marking the route from their aerodrome to the target. The squadron commander spoke first, outlining general tactics, flying altitudes, turning points, arrival times, time over target, and exact details of their squadron's aiming point. The meteorologist outlined the weather en route, including amount and types of cloud, temperatures and expected precipitation, and the possibility of icing conditions.

After briefing they went for their "night ops meal" with its highly prized real egg. All left the mess with flying rations (a jug of coffee and a sandwich), for it would be a long trip in sub-zero temperatures. They boarded the crew tender (an open stake truck) and were driven to their aircraft, usually a trip of at least a mile, but often further. At the dispersal point, they stood around, sucking all the strength they could from a final cigarette before boarding. Engines started, equipment checked, the crew waited for the appointed time to taxi onto the runway in line with other squadron kites. Time ticked by slowly. Finally, through the dusk, a green Aldis winked at them from the checker-board-painted flying-control truck.

The pilot moved the throttles forward, his hand covered by that of the engineer to ensure a smooth and steady movement. Four Merlins hummed with increased power, the brake was held as power increased, then released, and the huge machine surged into its roll, gathering speed until the wings took the weight and the wheels left the earth. Into the darkness sailed their winking navigation lights as they climbed for a rendezvous with other squadron crews at 12,000 to 14,000 feet. Soon, too soon, the navigator called, "Dutch coast crossing," and the entire crew braced as nerves tightened. Most crewmembers would welcome a "nervous pee," but it was prohibited by the fumbling required to open their many layers of clothing.

But this night, Flying Officer Studer's crew only got as far as the enemy's coast. On their maiden flight, all of the preparations, all of the tension of flying into battle for the first time was for naught. Airborne at 2042 hours, in aircraft BB 376 "G for George," they turned back because the starboard outer engine sputtered and died just as they approached Holland. They had also lost their compass earlier, but had pressed on. After jettisoning their bomb load into the sea, they arrived back at base at 2358 hours.

Coincidentally, Armour Garland, on his ninth trip, also returned early with a sick airplane.

Their target that night was to have been Leverkusen, but the entire raid was deemed unsuccessful as the raiders' bombs fell over a wide area far from target. Düsseldorf was hardest hit with 132 buildings destroyed, while Solingen reported forty people killed and sixty-five injured.

The next target for James' crew was Nuremberg, scheduled for the night of August 27–28. In Halifax JD 456, having followed the identical pre-flight routine as before, they trundled off into the darkness, with Russell James flying in the mid-upper turret as second gunner. They were airborne at 2042 hours, one minute behind Garland's crew who was in the aircraft directly before them.

En route, the visibility was perfectly clear but the night was very dark, and all held their breath as they approached the enemy coast. A million stars twinkled brightly over James' head. Their airplane stayed healthy, and they proceeded to target. Searchlights filled the sky with long white fingers probing for droning demons. Caught in a cone, pilot Studer used all the tricks he was taught. He corkscrewed the aircraft, first right, then left, jinking all over the sky and trying to avoid the flight paths of his squadron mates. Suddenly they were free, driving back into merciful darkness.

Aircraft JD 456 arrived over target exactly on time. They saw the Pathfinders' red markers, but had to orbit to await the green markers signifying their target. Finally, bomb-aimer Danninger's American-accented voice called, "Bombs gone! Bomb doors closed!" Navigator Shannon quickly responded, "Now, let's get the hell out of here!"

Falling in a flat arc, the four sticks of bombs were scattered over a wide area. Incendiaries dotted the black landscape, their magnesium fires spreading quickly. A brilliant display of reds, yellows, and oranges caught the corner of their eyes as the airplane wheeled for home. White flashes lit up the fuselage. Red and green dots of tracers shot up towards them, above them, and curved downwards to disappear in the blue-black night.

Both James' and Garland's crews landed at exactly the same time, 0452 hours, but at different aerodromes. James' crew was forced to land at the alternate airdrome, Tangmere.

Russell's third trip was to Berlin. In aircraft JD 456 again, they took off at 2005 hours, thirteen minutes behind Armour Garland. While the crew reported their mission as successful, the raid as a whole was not. Of 622 bombers dispatched, forty-seven were lost (twenty Halifaxes, seventeen Stirlings, and ten Lancasters). Night-fighters, using "fighter flares" dropped above the bomber stream to mark its progress in, and exit out of, the target area, shot down two-thirds of them. Fortunately the flares were vulnerable to high winds and most were soon blown away. The cloud over the target was not substantial, but difficulty with RAF radar and the ferocity of the city's defences caused Pathfinders to drop their markers well away from the city centre. Main force bombing was even further away. Eventually the bombs dropped thirty miles back along the approach route.

Flying Officer Studer's crew, with Russell James manning a side gun, identified their target by following the red and green Pathfinder flares. Just as they dropped their load, bomb-aimer Danninger identified the large lake in Berlin. They saw many large fires at the target area and observed bombs bursting in the fires. For one hundred miles on their return journey, they could still see the glow of the flames.

Eighty-five dwellings were destroyed, but industrial buildings were classified as only damaged. The state police hospital and Berlin inland canal and harbour system headquarters were hit, sixty-six civilians and two soldiers were killed, and 2,784 were bombed out. Following this attack, Goebbels ordered all children and adults not engaged in war work evacuated to the country or eastern German towns less likely to be bombed.

Russell's Halifax landed at 0532 hours on September 1 after flying for nine hours and twenty-seven minutes. Armour Garland and his crew did not return. Because of the high losses, especially among the Stirlings, only Lancasters were sent on the fourth and final raid on Berlin.

On September 1, Bomber Command ordered the squadron to stand down for a day, but the squadron did not get back into action until September 5–6. 605 bombers, 195 of them Halifaxes, were sent to Mannheim-Ludwigshafen; Moose Squadron detailed fourteen aircraft for the strike. The evening started most inauspiciously. During the marshalling of the aircraft into line, aircraft "A" was hit by aircraft "U", damaging the wingtips of both. Flying aircraft JD 210, "S for Sugar," with Sergeant James riding for the first time as rear gunner, the crew was airborne at 1941 hours. Two returned early: "R" with electrical equipment failure and "T" with an unserviceable intercom system. Two aircraft went missing:"S" and "V."

All night a friend of Russell's, Flight Sergeant C. Ramsdell, waited in the operations room, close by the radios for any word from "S for Sugar." Frustratingly, only static emanated from the radio sets. He had also flown on the raid and confirmed that he saw Russell's airplane over the target at 2330 hours.

In clear weather the Pathfinder Force plan worked perfectly. The Pathfinders dropped markers on the east side of Mannheim so that any creep back by the bombers, approaching from the west, would be across the city and into Ludwigshafen on the opposite side of the Rhine River. Both targets received severe damage. The Mannheim reporting system completely broke down, and Ludwigshafen reported the south and central parts of the town "devastated": 1,993 fires were recorded by the fire department, three described as "fire areas"; the I. G. Farben works suffered significant damage; and 127 people were killed with ten of the dead flak troops. The relatively small number of casualties may have been due in part to the fact that German cities, after Hamburg's firestorm, were evacuating parts of their population.

In Appleton, Russell's parents were informed that:

> No. 419 RCAF Squadron reported that Halifax aircraft, JD 210, with a crew of 7, failed to return from an operational attack on Mannheim. It left base at 1941 hours, on the 5th September 1943, after which no further news was received. The aircraft was due to return to base at approximately 02.56 hours on the 6th September.

The squadron commander sent a letter stating that, "The attack was successful. (Russell) was on squadron one month and had taken part in three attacks including two of the heavy raids on Berlin. He was a quiet lad, determined to do his part to bring the war to a successful conclusion."

A Halifax II of 419 Squadron sits in the open at Middleton St. George. These aircraft served from November 1942 to March 1944. (Photo—Canada's Air Force, Vol II, p.5)

On November 14, his parents were informed that Russell was "Missing, presumed dead," and were provided with Air Force Pamphlet No.10, entitled "Notes For The Information And Guidance Of The Next-Of-Kin Or Other Relatives Of Airmen Reported Missing, Deceased, Prisoners Of War Or Interned." It included eight pages of instructions regarding pay, pensions, and personal effects.

At the Ontario Hereford Breeders' meeting in Toronto on February 1, 1944, a minute's silence was observed in Russell's memory. A similar tribute was made on February 7 at the Dominion Hereford Breeders' meeting in Winnipeg.

In May, German authorities, via the International Red Cross, advised Mr. and Mrs. James that their son's body had been found in a British airplane crashed near Altrhein. He was buried in Huttenheim, a town nineteen miles south of Mannheim in the district of Baden.

In 1946, some of Russell's effects found their way home. On January 17, a package arrived from the RCAF Casualties Officer containing a gold identification bracelet that had been recovered when the bodies were exhumed from the communal grave alongside the north wall of Huttenheim Cemetery. They were re-interred in separate graves in the British Military Cemetery at Bad Tolz.

On March 12, bomb-aimer Harry Danninger's sister, Mrs. Carroll Lewis, wrote from Hollywood, California, to the James family. Danninger's uncle, serving as a major in the U.S. Army, had visited the graves. Mrs. Lewis wrote:

Dear Mrs. James:

> I am Flying Officer Harry Danninger's sister and I am sending you a copy of a letter we received from our uncle, Major Harwood, from Germany. I knew you would be as interested as we were to know exactly where your son was buried and the circumstances surrounding it. I also received a picture and you can see where they have planted flowers, etc. It has made us happier knowing exactly how everything was over there.

Russell's ops wing was sent to his mother on September 25.

Durnbach War Cemetery in Bavaria serves as the British Military cemetery. Durnbach is a village sixteen kilometres east of Bad Tolz, a town forty-eight kilometres south of Munich. The site was chosen, shortly after hostilities ceased, by British Army, RAF, and American Occupation Force officers. Durnbach was in the American zone of occupation. The vast majority are graves of airmen shot down over Bavaria, Wurtemberg, Austria, Hessen, and Thuringa, and the Army Graves Service brought them from graves scattered elsewhere. The remainder contains men who were killed while escaping from prisoner of war camps or who died near the end of the war on forced marches.

CHAPTER TWENTY-ONE—FIRE AND SWORD

The Battle of Berlin, from November 18, 1943, to the end of March 1944, was not an assault on a single city, but merely a convenient name for air raids on targets all over Germany. During this period, Bomber Command sent 9,111 sorties against Berlin and 11,113 against Mannheim, Stuttgart, Frankfurt, Nuremberg, Leipzig, Brunswick, and Schweinfurt; 1,047 bombers never returned and 1,682 were damaged, most never to fly again. With the Stirlings and most Halifaxes withdrawn from the order of battle, Lancasters, supported by Mosquitoes, carried the war into deepest Germany.

For the crews it was a nightmare. Northern Germany seldom experiences decent weather in winter, and 1943–44 was exceptionally bad. Every night Lancasters took to the air laden to capacity with bombs and fuel for the 1,150-mile trip, through rain and snow into high-altitude freak winds and sudden icing. To gain height and speed, crews dumped their largest bomb, the 4,000-pound "cookie," into the North Sea, until the bomb-release circuits were wired to a photoflash that popped automatically when the bomb was released.

Psychological damage was pervasive. Crews lost confidence in their aircraft and some, who otherwise would never hesitate to fly to the centre of a target, began orbiting over the fringes. Mother Nature's forces tested the best of aircrew. Long hours at sub-zero temperature dulled the brain and reflexes. Mistakes were made; frozen gunners missed the shadows slipping up on them and lost that split-second required for survival. In the cockpit, pilots and navigators suffered frostbite, and in the rest of the fuselage the crew's affliction was worse.

On the last hundred miles coming in from the west, the airmen could not conceal the fact that their target was Berlin, meaning ground defences and independently operating night-fighters had more than adequate time to prepare. If they successfully reached the city, the bombers then encountered a thick cloud obscuring any chance of accurate bombing.

Berlin's catchment area exceeded 883 square miles. The operation exceeded Bomber Command's capabilities. It was simply impossible to cover this area with bombs, in winter, against Germany's most formidable defences. Damage was done to the Siemens electrical factories and the Allkett tank construction plants, but Berlin's war production was scarcely diminished.

In February 1944 at the insistence of the Americans, Air Marshall Sir Arthur Harris grudgingly assigned Bomber Command to fairly successful precision attacks on the German aircraft industry. But he would not be swayed from directing the weight of Britain's effort, and that of the Commonwealth air forces, towards an area offensive.

J 19011 Pilot Officer James Gordon Bennett
Air Gunner
Royal Canadian Air Force

James Gordon Bennett was a Carleton Place boy, born and raised. He was the second child of James Henry Bennett, who worked at the Parliamentary Library, and Annie Myrtle Boyle. He had an older brother (John Henry), three younger sisters (Elizabeth, Mary Eileen, and Annie Doris), and a younger brother (William Albert). Jimmy was born on August 13, 1915, and attended Carleton Place schools, matriculating from CPHS in 1932. The family lived on Flora Street and belonged to the Church of England.

Although he was remembered in later years as a boy whose health was none too good, Jimmy was quite an athlete. He played football and baseball during his school years, and enjoyed shooting. He was also active in the Boy Scouts, eventually becoming an assistant leader.

Jim Bennett with the prop on his sleeve indicating the rank of LAC and the white flash in his cap indicating that he was training for aircrew. (Family photo)

But paddling was his first love, participating in most events at the Carleton Place Canoe Club. On July 11, 1940, Jim teamed up with John Muff in the Dominion Junior Tandem event at the annual regatta and won the Fulford trophy. The *Canadian* reported: "After paddling a nice course these two lads came in at the head of the field leading by about eight lengths. It was an easy walk away." In fact, his prowess was such that when he left for the air force, the Canoe Club announced that it had decided to call off its 1941 regatta because the "ranks of the regular paddlers have been much depleted owing to enlistments."

Upon leaving high school, Jim went to work as a driller for the Department of Highways. He stayed three years, until 1935, then began delivering for the Carleton Place Dairy. He remained with the dairy until he visited the air force recruiting centre on July 17, 1941.

At the recruiting centre, Jim was given a medical examination. He was described as having a medium complexion, blue eyes, and brown hair, and weighing 145 pounds. His short stature (5' 3") determined that he could only get an A3B medical category instead of A1B, thereby limiting his aircrew opportunities. He insisted that he wanted to be a pilot, but the interviewer allowed that he would need to be checked-out in an RCAF plane before he could be accepted for pilot training. Jim claimed to have no hobbies, a smoking habit of ten cigarettes a day, and that he consumed only three to four quarts of beer a month. Within a few days, he was sent to Montreal and RCAF Station St. Hubert for basic training at the Auxiliary Manning Depot.

Following the usual month of drill, uniform and kit inspections, Jim was sent off for the obligatory guard duties at No. 8 SFTS in Moncton, New Brunswick, arriving on August 28, 1941. He left the Manning Depot to enrol in Course No. 30 at No. 1 WTS in Montreal to be trained as a wireless air gunner. Jim reported on November 8.

Training in Canada, most likely at the WTS. Note the differences in uniforms. The airman on the left is not aircrew (no white flash in cap), but both he and Jim are wearing summer dress. The airman on the right is aircrew in training and wearing a winter uniform. The photo was probably taken in the spring of 1942 just as they were changing uniforms. (family photo)

Jim had a difficult time at wireless school. He mastered the academic subjects, but just could not get his brain and hand co-ordinated for Morse code. In order to give him more practice, he was sent to Course No. 34, which began on January 15, 1942. But his inability to send and receive Morse code continued to plague him. He needed 200 marks to graduate and the best he could attain was thirty-five. Clearly he could not achieve the required speed and was "ceased training" on June 8, 1942. Although it was suggested that he could possibly remuster to pilot, he was assigned to standard (general duties) and sent to Trenton on June 20 to the KTS.

In Trenton, the No. 1 Re-Selection Centre took control of his destiny. It was at this unit that aircrew trainees who found aircrew training programs too strenuous or too difficult were redirected into other areas. Jimmy managed to stay aircrew and left the wireless trade to become an air gunner.

Nor was discipline his strong suit. He went AWL for two hours on November 3, for which he was admonished, and again for a day on December 13–14, 1942. This time it cost him one day's pay. But these minor indiscretions did not interfere with his career. From aircraftsman second class in July he was promoted to leading aircraftsman on December 9, 1941.

While at Trenton, Jim often found time to get home. He was pleased that the Canoe Club had announced in April that, in spite of many of the previous year's paddlers having enlisted for active service, the club would carry on for the 1942 season.

Jim, like most Canadian airmen, purchased a $1,000 life insurance policy from Mutual Life shortly after enlistment. He made his mother his beneficiary and also assigned to her $40 a month from his pay.

Jim persisted in his quest to be aircrew and on July 20, 1942, he was sent No. 4 B&G School at Fingal for air-gunner training. This quiet town was host to wireless operators, air gunners, air bombers, and observers until it closed in February 1945. Gunners received four to six weeks training, and Jim was on Course No. 36A from July 20 to August 8, 1942.

Jim on leave at home with two of his young sisters (family photo)

While there, he flew six hours and forty-five minutes on the Fairey Battle and seven hours and forty-five minutes on the Bolingbroke. (The gunners were always glad to leave the open turret of the Battle for the enclosed power-operated turret of the Bolingbroke.) Jim completed the course fifteenth out of nineteen students with a course report that he was, "Just fair in the class room, but good on practical work and in the air."

On Sunday, August 28, Jim received his air-gunner's brevet and his sergeant's chevrons. He was granted embarkation leave until September 12 when he had to report to the "Y" Depot in Halifax for shipment overseas. Sergeant Air Gunner Jimmy Bennett proudly returned to Carleton Place

Jim wearing his new air gunner's wings. (National Archives C148181)

before leaving "for an eastern port." His older brother, Jack, had been overseas for two and a half years.

In Halifax, while waiting for a ship, he was put through the decompression chamber to test his altitude tolerance. On September 16 he endured three two-hour tests at 35,000 feet, and he must have had some trouble clearing his ears as it was recommended that he fly to only 25,000 feet. This was a ridiculous recommendation in that pressure changes occur mainly below 10,000 feet and he would have little control over the altitude of his aircraft. Even the pilots had little control and in transit flew at altitudes and speeds assigned at briefing.

Jim boarded his ship on October 26 and arrived in the U.K. on November 5. He cabled his parents of his safe arrival and waited at the PRC until December 8 when he went to the OTU.

After training on their first "real" bomber, the twin-engine Wellington, affectionately known as the "Wimpy," and crewing up, Jim and his new crew went to No. 1659 HCU on March 25, 1943, four months ahead of Armour Garland. His all-Canadian, all-Ontario crew was made up of Squadron Leader C. W. "Woody" Smith of Windsor, Ontario, pilot and captain of the crew; Flying Officer H. R. Wilson, co-pilot; Flying Officer Denis M. Sims, of Toronto, navigator; Flying Officer John D. Teskey of Kingston, bomb-aimer; Flying Officer T. Kenneth Canning of Toronto, wireless operator / air gunner; and Flight Sergeant Jimmy Bennett, rear gunner.

RAF Station Topcliffe, Yorkshire, was home to No. 1659 HCU. The crew went there for training on the larger, faster, four-engine Handley Page Halifax. They found many differences from the Wellington and gained two additional crewmembers: Pilot Officer Al Dutton of Brantford, flight engineer, and Sergeant Elmes, mid-upper-gunner for the top turret. Since pilot Woody now had four throttles, four mixture controls, pitch controls, four temperature gauges and many more fuel tanks, each with their own gauges and tank-switching handles, an engineer was a necessity.

All trades had to take courses on the new equipment. Jim Bennett and Ken Canning joined Bill Frauts for training on the Boulton-Paul gun turret. This was an electric-hydraulic turret, as compared to the Fraser-Nash hydraulic turrets used in the Wellingtons. The Boulton-Pauls were equipped with the same four Browning .303 machine guns in the tail turret and two in the mid-upper position. The same electronic ring and bead sight was used, but the gunners had to get used to the new control column. They trained in a turret mounted on a wheeled stand in a darkened room. A very dim moving light was their target. Every time they fired, everything stopped and the lights came on so their hits and misses could be tallied. But the gunners were warned; this turret did not move in as in real life, and no one was shooting back at them.

Ten days into the course they started flying. The first day the crew rode without duties as the pilots stayed within the airport circuit practising take-offs and landings. Then they practised three-engine flying and three-engine landings, flew air-firing exercises and two-engine flying and more air-firing exercises. They flew fighter-affiliation exercises to get used to having them dart about in their airspace.

After two five-and-a-half-hour cross-country trips in daylight, their final trip was a night-time cross-country flight. Only after all this was completed to the instructors' satisfaction were they sent to an operational squadron.

On April 11, 1943, Squadron Leader Smith's crew reported to RCAF Station Leeming and 408 "Goose" Squadron, which had been formed on June 24, 1941, as part of the all-Canadian No. 6 Group. They flew Hampdens from RAF Syerston as a night-bombing unit, and in October 1942, the squadron converted to Halifaxes and flew them for a year until taking delivery of Lancaster II's. In July 1944 they reverted to Halifax III's and VII's. The Squadron badge depicted a Canada goose "volant" (flying) and the motto was "For Freedom."

One can only imagine the gunners' dismay to discover that the guns on the Lancaster were the Nash and Thompson (FN20); they thought they had left them behind on the Wellington. However, gunnery leaders had made a few modifications. An armoured shield was provided and the gunner had a clear-vision panel. But the main improvement was the supply of ammunition. Large capacity boxes were fitted to the rear fuselage, and ammunition belts were fed along tracks and through booster units (because they were so heavy) to the breeches of the guns. Provision was made for observing the angle of drift to assist the navigator, and a more efficient

oxygen delivery system was incorporated. The gunner could abandon the aircraft by opening the doors behind him, grabbing and clipping on his parachute, traversing the turret, and falling out backwards.

The Bennett boys were certainly making their mark in England. Naturally gregarious, they had no difficulty making friends out of strangers. An unsolicited testimonial arrived at *The Canadian* office from Englishman John B. Turner of "The Birches," Winchmore Hill, London, telling of an evening spent with three Carleton Place boys in a small English home:

> Two essentially Canadian products were recently received into this house— a tin of 'Corn on Cob' and a copy of *The Carleton Place Canadian*. They formed the advance guard sent ahead by one of your townsmen now in this country as one of many thousands of Canadian forces overseas . . .
>
> The night of Friday, 9th July, was noteworthy not only for the invasion of Sicily, but also because it marked probably the first occasion upon which three citizens of Carleton Place have gathered together in an English home during the present hostilities. They were Signalman John H. Bennett, R.C.C.S.; Flight Sergeant James G. Bennett, R.C.A.F. [he had been promoted on February 28, 1943], and Sergeant-Major John (Strawberry) McCann, R.C.O.C. Bed was reached at 2:30 a.m. . . .
>
> My wife and I have known Jack Bennett since Christmas, 1940, and his brother since his first arrival in this country. What we now don't know about the virtues of Carleton Place I guess is not worth knowing! . . .
>
> I remember reading in our newspapers at the time of the tour of the Dominion by the King and Queen that previously Canadians had tended to regard themselves as 'forgotten' by the Home Country. I think that was probably a justified complaint at the time, but it can certainly be true no longer. Valuable as have been the contributions of other parts of the Empire, Canada by her magnificent efforts has impressed even the 'man in the street' over here, and thousands of Canadian soldiers and airmen in many parts of the country-but especially in London-bear witness to Canada's greatest contribution of all. It will not be forgotten[16].

---

[16] It is very interesting that as I write this section (April 2002) I turn to the television to watch funeral and Memorial services for the four PPCLI soldiers killed in Afghanistan. Appearing in the Sunday Telegraph in London, England, and re-printed in The National Post, is an editorial titled **"The Country the World Forgot-Again**

It seems that Canada's historic mission is to come to the selfless aid of both of its friends and of complete strangers, and then, once the crisis is over, to be well and truly ignored. Canada is the perpetual wall flower that stands on the edge of the hall. Waiting for someone to come and ask her for a dance. A fire breaks out, she risks life and limb to rescue her fellow dance-goers, and suffers serious injuries. But when the hall is repaired and the dancing resumes, there is Canada, the wallflower still, while those she once helped glamorously cavort across the floor, blithely neglecting her yet again."

Perhaps I may also mention that there was in England at the beginning of the war a popular delusion that Canadian troops were 'tough guys' ('tough' in this instance being better translated by 'rough' or 'rowdy') compared with the representatives of other Dominions. Those like ourselves, who have had the pleasure of giving hospitality to Canadians know now how absurd that notion was. The several friends in Jack Bennett's Section whom we have met, for example, come from all parts of Canada, but are among the finest fellows imaginable, and they are all looking forward to joining the First Division in real action.

So, greetings from one small English home to Canada and to Carleton Place in particular.

After being checked out on the squadron's Halifax II's, the crew's first mission was slated for the night of April 27–28, 1943. It was to be a short trip, only about two hours. Their mission was part of operation "Gardening Nectarines X," and Halifax squadrons provided fifty-eight aircraft to join the total of 160 in the largest minelaying operation in the war to date. Jimmy's crew was flying Halifax BB 375, "P for Papa," and they took off at 0135 hours on the 28th in good visibility and climbed to transit altitude. Navigator Sim got a good fix over the island of Terschelling and they descended to 2,000 feet, their drop altitude. They were carrying two 300 Mark IV and one 100 Mark IV mines. At 0321 hours, they made their drop, saw the parachutes open, and believed they had dropped in the allotted position. Almost fifteen minutes later they were back at base, landing at 0334 hours after a successful "first op."

Although this flight was really only the last training mission for Jimmy's crew, the first op was a never-to-be-forgotten experience for any crew. Even as mundane a trip as minelaying heightened the adrenaline of each crewmember. None of the lectures, handbooks, or advice from experienced crew really prepared men for the realities of flying with loaded guns and bomb bays into enemy air where any shadow may be a fighter intent upon taking them down. Every man knew his job and had proved it numerous times during training exercises. But the "real thing" was the real thing.

That night, 123 of the 160 aircraft were successful in laying 458 mines. They sowed the waters off the Frisian Islands and the approaches to the Biscay and Brittany ports. Only one Lancaster was lost.

Jimmy's crew got their first taste of a maximum effort raid on their second trip during the night of May 13–14. Their target was Bochum and they would be joining a stream of 442 bombers led by 135 Halifaxes. Squadron

Leader Smith's crew was assigned Halifax JB 968 "R for Robert,[17]" and they were airborne from Leeming at 2346 hours. The raid started well but after fifteen minutes, German decoy markers led the mainstream bombers away from the target. At 0240 hours on the 14th, at 18,000 feet, bomb-aimer Tesky called "Bombs gone!"

German information indicated that 394 buildings were destroyed and 302 people were killed; twenty-four of the raiders did not return.

As Smith turned for home, the aircraft was caught in a cone of searchlights, hit by flak, and corkscrewed down to about 200 feet before the pilot regained control. At 0255 hours, they finally evaded the searchlights. During their precipitous fall, flight engineer Dutton noticed the mid-upper gunner opening the escape hatch. After control of the aircraft was regained wireless operator Canning informed the captain that Sergeant Elmes was not in his turret. Pilot Officer Dutton was sent to look. He found the escape hatch open and an oxygen hose hanging out in the opening. Both Sergeant Elmes and his parachute were missing. The crew landed at 0532 hours, but Sergeant Elmes was never seen again.

After a nine-day break in operations, 826 aircraft were dispatched on May 23–24 to Dortmund in the largest raid in the Battle of the Ruhr. The force included 199 Halifaxes.

Jim, second from the left, and some of his 408 Squadron crew. Note the usual wartime mode of transportation, the bicycle, lower right.

[17] This identification system for aircraft is based on the phonetic alphabet as used at the time. The serial number (JB 968) is not prominent on the fuselage. Rather, the squadron identifying letters, in 408's case "EQ" are painted before the RCAF roundel and after it is the aircraft identifier, in this case "R." Radio transmissions intended for this aircraft and crew would begin "R for Robert this is ... etc."

Flying aircraft HR 658 "V for Victor," Jimmy's crew was airborne at 2310 hours on the 23rd. Their new mid-upper gunner was Pilot Officer G. W. "Bill" Frauts of Trenton, who kept the crew all-Ontario and also made it an all-officer crew, both circumstances quite unusual.

It was a very successful raid. In clear weather, the Pathfinders marked the target well and bombing went according to plan. Nearly 2,000 buildings were completely destroyed, including the large Hoesch steel works, which consequently ceased production and never came back on line during the war; 599 people were killed, 1,275 injured, and 25 were never found. Thirty-eight aircraft were lost. Dortmund was not attacked again for a year to the day.

The night of May 27–28, the crew was in the air heading again for the Ruhr, to Essen. They were flying aircraft JB 968 and were airborne at 2310 hours along with 518 other bombers flying in cloudy weather that extended all the way to the target. Sky marking had to be used, and the bombing was very scattered, causing limited damage to central and northern Essen. Bombs fell on ten surrounding towns killing 196 people and destroying 488 buildings.

A day's rest and they were called for action again in Halifax "R" along with 719 bombers that were aimed at the Barmen, half of the long and narrow town of Wüppertal. This attack was the outstanding success of the Battle of the Ruhr. Both Pathfinder marking and Main Force bombing were particularly accurate. The fire became so severe that the first, small firestorm developed. It was a Saturday night and most of the town's fire and air raid officials had gone to their country homes for the weekend. In this, their first raid, the fire service was not able to control the blaze.

About eighty per cent of Barmen's built-up area (1,000 acres) was levelled by fire. Property damage was twice as severe as any previous raid on a German city, and the number of people killed was five times greater. Five of the six largest factories, 211 other industrial buildings, and nearly 4,000 homes were completely destroyed. Approximately 3,400 people killed was the best "guestimate."

Jim's crew was over the target at 19,000 feet and released their bombs at 0119 hours on the 30th. They saw a "good concentration of fires and a column of black smoke rising to 14,000 feet on the western side of the town." They were back at base at 0426 hours, their fifth mission completed.

On June 19, 1943, the squadron entertained the High Commissioner for Canada, the Honourable Vincent Massey, and his wife, the same night the squadron sent their Halifaxes against the Schneider heavy arms factory and the Breuil steelworks at Le Creusot. Jim's crew was airborne in aircraft JB 893 "U for Uniform" at 2209 hours. The Pathfinders only dropped flares, instead of coloured markers, and each crew was tasked with finding its target by the light of these flares. The bombers made two runs over the target dropping a short stick of bombs on each run from between 5,000 and 10,000 feet.

The visibility was clear and unlimited. At debriefing, Jim's crew reported the Pathfinders were "bang on track" in from the coast. They made their run-in and could clearly see rail sidings and factories well lit by the white flares. They bombed from 6,500 feet, releasing their load at 0201 hours on the 20th. They saw one bomb explode on their primary target, the Schneider armaments works, and another hit a building. Just as their bombs were dropped, heavy flak bursts were seen just below them but they were not hit.

Another industrial city in the Ruhr, Krefeld, was Bomber Command's next target, but the raid had to be carried out before the full moon had passed. On the night of June 21–22, 705 aircraft left British air stations for the continent, and Jimmy's crew, back flying JB 968, was airborne at 2337 hours. Although there was three- to four-tenths alto-stratus cloud cover over the target, the Pathfinders did a good job of ground marking: 619 aircraft dropped 2,306 tons of bombs on the markers and later photographs showed them all to be within three miles of the city centre. Bomb-Aimer Tesky dropped his load from 20,000 feet at 0159 hours on the 22nd. They considered their load fell close to the aiming point.

Fire raged out of control, destroying the city centre: 5,517 houses were destroyed and 1,056 people killed; 72,000 people lost their homes; 20,000 were billeted with families in the suburbs, 30,000 moved in with friends and family, and 20,000 were evacuated to other towns.

The very next night, aboard JB 972 "W for Whiskey," the crew took off at 2340 hours bound for Mulheim, but they were back an hour later with their full load of bombs and an unserviceable airplane. Their airspeed indicator had refused to work and without it an accurate run-in to the aiming point could not be made.

Back in aircraft JB 968 (they would fly this aircraft for the next seven trips), they were up at 2321 hours on June 24 bound again for Wüppertal. Having devastated the Barmen half of the city in May, this attack was aimed at the Elberfeld half. Creep-back became more pronounced than usual, and thirty bombers hit targets in the western part of the Ruhr. Wüppertal was in the eastern end.

Pilot Smith reported good visibility through the smoke haze of that night's earlier bombing and about two-tenths alto-stratus cloud. They were at 19,000 feet when they bombed at 0132 hours on the 25th and saw a mass of large and well-established fires in the target area with smoke rising to 12,000 feet. In the rear turret, Jimmy Bennett could still see the glow of flames when they crossed back over the Belgian coast.

The next night, they were headed for Gelsenkirchen, a town just twenty miles north of Wüppertal. This was the first raid on Gelsenkirchen since 1941, but situated as it was in the middle of the Ruhr, bombs intended for other targets had often hit it. The city was obscured in ten-tenths cloud that topped at 10,000 feet, and Smith's crew dropped from 20,000 feet at 0129 hours on June 26, but they observed no results. They could see flashes below the clouds, but the effectiveness of the attack was not visible. The raid could not be considered a success. Düsseldorf reported twenty-four destroyed buildings, but mainly superficial blast damage, and loss of production lasted less than two weeks. Solingen, thirty miles away from Gelsenkirchen, reported twenty-one people killed. The crew landed at 0400 hours.

There was a lull in the air war during which German targets were still hit, but there were no major bombing raids. The squadrons were all preparing for Air Marshall Harris' next offensive against Hamburg. He ordered four raids over the space of ten nights, beginning the night of July 24–25, 1943.

There were 791 bombers ordered into the air that night. Window was used by Bomber Command for the first time and it so confused the German radar controllers that they were completely incapable of vectoring their fighters to real targets. Over the Channel at RCAF Station Middleton St. George, Armour Garland took off at 2203 hours for his first operational mission in a 419 Squadron Halifax II. Exactly one half-hour later, from Leeming, Jim Bennett was airborne in his Halifax II for his tenth mission. The night was clear with only a gentle wind and most of the markers fell at or near the city centre. Jim's crew arrived over the aiming point at 0133 hours on July 25 and dropped from 19,000 feet.

Jim saw a heavy, oily pall of smoke drifting south and rising through fragmentary clouds to a height of 17,000 feet. Bomb-Aimer Teskey reported that he clearly saw the aiming point identified by green markers at the instant he released their load. All crewmembers reported smoke and haze partially obstructing their view and a bright red glow under the smoke. They thought the Pathfinders had done a great job and it seemed like a good attack. Ground defences were considered to be disorganized and the searchlights were feeble and only on the outskirts of the city. They landed at 0438 hours, twenty minutes before Garland.

During the assault on Hamburg the crews got no rest, and they were airborne again on the night of July 25–26. However, due to the heavy smoke still obliterating Hamburg, their target was Essen. This raid was particularly successful, inflicting the most serious damage to the Krupp factories of the entire war. Again two Carleton Place aviators were in the air, unknown to each other. Garland went airborne at 2201 hours and Jim Bennett was up at 2225 hours.

Bennett's crew reported that, by the time they got to the target, 0102 hours on the 26th, it was hazy and ground details were obscured by smoke. They were unable to see their own bombs explode and thought they may have overshot the bombing point. They did witness a pillar of black smoke rising to 18,000 feet with many fires on the target area. The crew considered Window to be very effective since the searchlights were wandering aimlessly in two lanes. They told the debriefers, after landing at 0305 hours,. that the route was well chosen and quite free of flak. They were six minutes behind Garland's crew which touched down at 0259 hours.

Both Carleton Place men were in the air for the next two raids on Hamburg. The second, on the night of July 27–28, was the night of the infamous "firestorm," a phenomenon not previously witnessed in the history of modern warfare. All the elements were perfect. It was an extremely hot, dry day and it remained so that night. Fire-fighters were off working the fires from the previous raid, and in any event, could not get through to the heart of the city as every street was blocked by rubble. The fires killed by burning and by sucking all available oxygen out of the air much like a flame-thrower. Fires raged for three hours and only abated when all combustible material was consumed.

Jimmy's crew was off the runway at 2227 hours. They found only a very small amount of stratus cloud en route and over the target, which resulted in them arriving over Hamburg at 0122 hours at 19,500 feet when they made their drop. There was only moderate visibility so they were not able to observe their results. Scattered incendiaries were seen burning on the outskirts of the city and the column of smoke reached 20,000 feet. An explosion and big red fire was seen at 0135 hours, so extraordinary that the navigator marked the time. They were home at 0404 hours.

The last raid in this series of attacks on Hamburg happened on the night of July 29–30 when 777 aircraft thundered into the night with their loads of death and destruction. Again a widespread fire area resulted, but there was no firestorm this night. One of the worst incidents happened when a large department store in the Wandsbek district collapsed, killing 370 people in its basement bomb shelter. The exits were blocked and carbon monoxide fumes from a nearby burning coke (a type of coal) store poisoned them.

Jim Bennett was aloft at 2220 hours. Their bombing altitude was again 19,500 feet and at 0112 hours they dropped. There was only scattered cloud and the visibility was good, but they still failed to see their own bombs explode. They thought that perhaps they might have bombed slightly short. They saw many well-concentrated fires but considered the raid not to be very effective. They also noted that the city's defences appeared to have been greatly increased. They were home at 0349 hours.

There was no rest for Jimmy Bennett's crew, and they flew again on the night of July 30–31 on their fifteenth mission. It was also the last time they would fly Halifax JB 968 "R." Their target was Remscheid, a previously unbombed town on the southern edge of the Ruhr; 273 aircraft flew on this raid that marked the true end of the Battle of the Ruhr. The ground marking by Oboe-equipped Mosquitoes was particularly accurate. Fifteen aircraft were lost and only 871 tons of bombs dropped, but about eighty-three per cent of the town was destroyed and 1,120 people were killed. The town's industry lost three months production and never fully regained previous levels.

The crew was airborne at 2201 hours carrying a load of one 2,000-pound high explosive, 56 thirty-pound and 510 four-pound bombs with 30 four-pound incendiaries. They found visibility over the target very good and released their bombs at 0120 hours from 20,000 feet. At the same time, they saw a large orange-coloured explosion billowing oily black smoke. Many incendiaries undershot the target. Because the defences at Cologne and Düsseldorf were so strong they were unable to use that area as a route into their bomb run. They landed at 0408 hours on August 31. Later that day, Russell James and his crew reported to 419 Squadron at Middleton St. George.

In August, 408 Squadron began converting to the Lancaster II bombers, and to do so, they moved to Linton-on-Ouse. But Squadron Leader White's crew had one more mission in the Handley Page Halifax II. They were scheduled to take aircraft JD 278 "O for Oboe" for one last fling at Hamburg.

The bombing force encountered a large and vicious thunderstorm en route and many aircraft had to turn back early. The raid was a failure. But Jim's crew did not even make it that far.

Shortly after take off at 2301 hours, their port inner engine began leaking oil. Then telltale puffs of white began emerging from the cowling of the starboard outer engine, and as soon as it hit the slipstream, it turned to a misty steam. No question—it was glycol. In a moment the engine lost all its coolant, and Smith watched the temperature gauge's needle climb into the red. Flight engineer Pilot Officer Dutton began to shut the engine down before it blew up, burst into flames, or seized, and with one engine out and another leaking oil, they jettisoned their bombs at seventeen minutes after midnight and turned for home. They were back at 0107 hours. Their last two hours flying in a Halifax had certainly been memorable.

Throughout the rest of August and September, the crew rested and trained as the squadron converted to Lancasters and completed the move to its new station. On August 13, the crew gathered in the sergeants' mess to celebrate Jimmy's twenty-eighth birthday[18]. Celebrations consisted of presenting the "birthday boy" with a tankard filled with beer, or other spirits as seen fitting by the crew captain, then singing: "So, drink chug-a-lug, chug-a-lug . . ." Jimmy drank down the tankard in a single gulp, then placed it upside down on his head.[19]

On August 28, 1943, Jim's promotion to warrant officer II came through—another reason to celebrate!

In October, Jim and his mates were back on operations, and flying from an alternate aerodrome, East Moor, they were briefed for a raid on Stuttgart during the night of October 7–8. They were now fully up-to-speed on the Lancaster II, a decided improvement over the Halifax, although the crew

A Lancaster from 408 Squadron being loaded with bombs.

[18] Fraternization in the RAF, and hence the RCAF, was severely frowned on. Since Jim was still a Flight Sergeant and all the rest of the crew were officers, it was to his mess they went, although even that was frowned upon. But Canadians had a knack for thumbing their noses at British traditions and this special event was just another reason for a crew party. They had completed fifteen missions, when the average was six before a crew "bought the farm." They were a very experienced crew. Few disciplinarians would interfere.

[19] The RAF had the attitude, adopted by the RCAF which had no problem taking on "good" RAF habits, that if you were old enough to fight you were old enough to drink. The Americans, on the other hand, brought prohibition with them, restricting their soldiers, and airmen, from drinking until they reached the age of majority. United States Navy ships, to this day, are completely dry.

regarded it fondly as a reliable, comfortable aircraft. 343 Lancasters were sent to the area, which was cloud covered, and the H2S Pathfinder marked two sites.

Jim and his crew were airborne in Lancaster DS 718 "R for Robert" from East Moor at 2036 hours. It was still daylight as they took to the air, carrying a full load of bombs and incendiaries. The target was overcast with 10/10 cloud, meaning they had good horizontal visibility but could not see the ground. At 0024 hours and 20,000 feet, they tried to drop. The electrical circuit malfunctioned and the bomb-aimer had to drop the bombs manually. Still the 340 four-pound bombs, 20 four-pound "X"-type bombs, and 16 thirty-pound incendiaries hung up and would not drop. They could not get rid of them. They had to take them home and risk their dropping on the runway on the jolt of landing.

Stuttgart lost 344 buildings, mostly dwellings in the outskirts, and in the city centre, four hospitals, the Lindenmuseum, and the garrison church. In the main railway station underground shelter, thirty-four people drowned when a water main burst. A total of 104 were killed or declared missing. The secondary target, the town of Böbington ten miles to the southwest, had 350 houses hit and sixty people killed.

The winter months of 1944–45 in England brought the worst weather anyone had experienced for years. There were heavy snowfalls and no equipment to remove it, extreme cold, heavy fogs and rains. Aircraft, if airborne, were often diverted to alternate aerodromes and didn't get back for several days until the fog cleared. In any event, operations became considerably more dependent on weather forecasts, both for home and over the continent.

Night raiders had to take off earlier. On October 18–19, Jim's crew was airborne at 1721 hours bound for Hanover in "R for Robert." Again they flew through 10/10 overcast conditions, but the cloud topped out at 10,000 to 12,000 feet with good visibility above them. The Pathfinders could not mark the position accurately, and bombs were scattered all over the country. When Jim's crew arrived they could see from 20,000 feet the fires from previous bombs. That coincided with their ETA[20] (2025 hours), so they dropped their bombs and reported large explosions and a glow from the fires visible on the cloud from fifty miles away from the target.

This raid concluded that series on Hanover. Eighteen Lancasters were lost this night, including the five-thousandth Bomber lost on operations since the start of the war.[21]

[20] Estimated Time of Arrival.

[21] By the end of this night Bomber Command had flown 144,500 sorties – 90% at night – and lost 5,004 air craft. The average number of sorties flown in each 24-hour period was 96 and the average loss rate was3.5%. Each loss represented the lives of a crew of from five to eight airmen, many of them Canadian. Bomber Command War Diaries p.439

Kassel was the next object of Bomber Command's attention. On the night of October 22–23 it suffered the most devastating attack on a German city since the firestorm raid on Hamburg. The Pathfinders' visual markers were accurate and correctly identified the city centre. Jim and his crew were airborne at 1757 hours, and as they left the English coast, they encountered icing, and by the time they crossed the Dutch coast, they had lost both time and altitude. The warmer weather over land broke up most of the ice, but they encountered similar conditions for the rest of the run, making them too late to carry out their mission. They returned at 2239 hours with their full load of bombs.

The fires in Kassel were so concentrated that another firestorm occurred, but not as extensive as the one in Hamburg. The main raid was exceptionally accurate and concentrated, and the results at Kassel would not be exceeded until well into 1944. The damage was impossible to tally accurately: more than sixty-three per cent of all living accommodation was unusable and approximately 120,000 people had to leave their homes. Destroyed or badly damaged were 155 industrial buildings, 78 public buildings, 38 schools, 25 churches, 16 police and military buildings (including the local Gestapo), and 11 hospitals. The railway system and all three Henschel aircraft factories were seriously damaged. This was very important because they were making V-1 flying bombs at the time. Consequently, this had a major deleterious effect on the opening and eventual scale of the V-1 campaign. By the end of November the German "Missing Department" recorded 5,599 people dead and a further 3,300 still untraced.

On October 26, the squadron diary recorded that the "weather again very foggy, so dense that the birds were walking."

The main battle for Berlin began on the night of November 18–19, 1944, and went on until the end of March. Air Marshall Harris was given a free hand and he mounted thirty-two major raids on Germany during this period. Bomber crews had to contend with long flights in wintry weather and a succession of fierce battles against a reorganized night-fighter force. Lancasters carried the brunt of the fighting, as the Stirlings were withdrawn from frontline operations, as were the Mark II and Mark V Halifax bombers due to inferior performance.

The opening attack included Warrant Officer II Jim Bennett and his crew flying Lancaster DS 729 "D for Dog." They were in the air at 1728 hours. The weather was completely overcast from 8,000 to 10,000 feet, and marking and bombing were carried out blindly. However they found horizontal visibility above the cloud over Berlin to be good and they released at 2107 hours from 22,000 feet. They were unable to judge any of their results because of the thick carpet of cloud.

The crew was home at 0204 hours on the 19th to a very pleasant surprise for Jim. He had been appointed to commissioned rank, pilot officer, effective November 18. Now this all-Canadian crew had the further distinction of each member being from Ontario and each being a commissioned officer.

They were to be back in the air on the night of November 22–23, and during the afternoon, gathered in the briefing room. The target was Berlin again. The crews groaned, stomachs lurching at the news. The Bloody Big City again! How many wouldn't make it back this time? What would go wrong? Bad weather, equipment failure, human failure? Or all three? Nothing had been going right recently.[22]

But on this raid everything worked. Jim's crew joined 763 other aircraft in the greatest force ever sent to the German capital. Berlin was completely cloud-covered again, the lower layer with tops to 12,000 to 14,000 feet and another layer of stratus above that at 22,000 feet. The bad weather kept the fighters on the ground, but Bomber Command still lost twenty-six aircraft.

Jim flew off at 1712 hours in Lancaster DS 723 "B for Baker." Over the city the crew saw flares at 2019 hours, and one-and-a-half minutes later dropped their bombs from 22,000 feet. The results were obscured by cloud, but one minute after their bomb release, they saw a large explosion. The glow of fires reflected very brightly on the cloud base. This was the most effective raid on Berlin. The vast area of destruction spread from the central districts west across the mainly residential suburbs of Tiergarten, Charlottenburg, and Spandau. At least 3,000 houses and twenty-three industrial sites were destroyed, 175,000 people were bombed out and soldiers from as far as 100 kilometres away had to be brought in to help.

Destroyed or severely damaged were the Kaiser-Wilhelm-Gedächtniskirche (the Kaiser Wilhelm Memorial Church which, half-restored, half-ruined, remains a major attraction in Berlin), the Charlottenburg Castle, the Berlin Zoo, much of Unter den Linden, the British, French, Italian and Japanese embassies, the Waffen S.S. Administrative College, and the Imperial Guard Barracks at Spandau. Five factories of the Siemens electrical group and the Alkett tank works, both of which had recently moved from the Ruhr, were destroyed. Bomber Command lost eleven Lancasters, ten Halifaxes, and five Stirlings. This was the last raid in which Stirlings were sent to Germany.

Jim's crew was home at 2354 hours on the 22nd, one of the only times they took off and landed on the same day.

On December 3, they took off at 0025 hours for a raid on Liepzig. The bombers were to fly a direct route to Berlin before turning to attack Leipzig; however, it was a short trip for the crew in aircraft DS 790. They were forced to abandon the mission and return to base when the starboard inner engine

[22] Spencer Dunmore, Reap The Whirlwind, ibid, p.178.

went unserviceable. At 0115 hours, they jettisoned their main bomb, a 4,000-pound nose-armed high explosive from 13,000 feet, and the rest of the load returned to base with them. They were home at 0203 hours on the 4th.

Frankfurt was next. The night of December 20–21, 650 bombers crossed the Channel with German ground control tracking the force as soon as it left the English coast, all the way to the target. There were many encounters with night-fighters en route. The return flight was much quieter, but forty-one air-craft didn't make it.

Smith urged Lancaster DS 790 "B" into the air at 1701 hours. The fore-caster had called for clear weather and the ground-marking plan was based on that. But six- to eight-tenths of cloud covered Frankfurt at 6,000 feet. The Germans lit decoy fires five miles southeast of the city and some bombing fell on the decoys.

Bomb-Aimer Tesky released his bombs at 1943 hours from 21,000 feet on a timed run. They had one 8,000-pound high explosive, 150 four-pound, and 30 four-pound "X"-type incendiaries. After dropping they saw one large orange fire spring up and the smoke rise above the clouds. They reported to the intelligence officer that the picture of the target was confusing because of the numerous fires burning on the route of their run-in. Red spot fires were seen on the homeward journey. They felt the attack was not very con-centrated, nor very effective, but when they landed at 2248 hours, they had completed their twentieth mission. Ten to go for completion of their tour!

On December 24, the squadron was stood down from flying ops, and on Christmas Day, eighty officers paraded to the men's mess to serve the air-men their traditional Christmas dinner of turkey, creamed and baked pota-toes, buttered carrots, the ever-present Brussels sprouts, the customary Christmas pudding, and mince pies. Beer and minerals were also available to all. The youngest airman and the base commander traded tunics, and sym-bolically traded positions, for the evening.

On the 26th they were still stood down and on the 27th all aircrew were scheduled for flying training and lectures in air-sea rescue.

German airmen who "ditched" had a fairly good chance of survival. Their aircraft carried inflatable dinghies, far better than the simple "Mae Wests" carried by British aircrew. The Luftwaffe's safety equipment also included a chemical that spread a green dye in the water that was much more easily seen from the air. They had also organized an efficient air-sea rescue service with about thirty aircraft and high-speed launches spread along the English Channel and North Sea.

Mollie McGee, the London correspondent for *The Globe and Mail* wrote the following article that was re-printed on December 23 in *The Canadian*:

London—Once upon a time there was a bomber pilot who slept peacefully as his plane travelled over the flak of Berlin. Sounds like a fairy story, doesn't it? But it happens to be true, though the nap was fortunately not of very long duration.

Sqdn. Ldr. Woodward Smith, of Windsor, Ont., has this unique exploit to his credit and blames it on the lack of oxygen. "I just dropped off I guess, and didn't realize it until the boys caught on when an enemy plane made for us and I didn't respond to the first warning at once. Then the engineer shook me, yelling 'There's a kite on our tail,' and I came to and automatically edged over."

In Recent Big Shows

Woody Smith and his all-Ontario bomber crew have several Berlin flights to their credit and they were in the recent 'big shows,' but Woody says he gets all the real news of his big raids out of the newspapers.

"From what I can see up there the whole show looks like a log fire seen through half-closed eyes. It's funny, too, how sometimes we will get a pretty rough trip and the other crews will tell us they had 'a piece of cake;' then we'll all have an easy do, and then they'll have trouble. You can never tell," he said.

Bomb bursts seen from above look like the sparks from a wood fire and even great columns of smoke which cameras catch closer to the ground after raids are over, are mere blobs seen by the men who start them. The latest Berlin raiders noticed one difference during their stay over the city. "It was so light it was like flying around in daylight, even when we were just approaching the target. The boys ahead certainly lit the way," Woody said.

Woody's Ontario crew are: Navigator, FO Denis Sims, Toronto; bombaimer FO John Tesky, Kingston; wireless operator FO Ken Canning, Toronto; engineer, PO Al Dutton, Brantford; rear gunner, PO Jimmy Bennett, Carleton Place; mid upper gunner, Sgt Bill Frants, [sic] Trenton.

One Spot of Trouble

"We had one spot of trouble together," Woody told me. "One time over Bochum, in the Ruhr, we were coned for 18 minutes, blown on our back by flak and finally finished 200 feet up over Dortmund. We hit a balloon cable and cut it in half, but got away all right, though it was pretty grim and shook the boys a bit,"

When I asked him if they got a 'rest-up' after that, he looked surprised. 'No, that wasn't really much,' he replied. 'We went through what the other lads are taking, but we managed to get away with it, that's all.'

Woody and the boys have made four trips over Hamburg and believe "it is finished for a while, though Hamburg was a good party." They don't mind Ruhr "dos," but they have several places they would like to go and bomb on their own, "real hot trouble spots," as Woody described them.

When I left him he was hunting for an afternoon paper to "read up" what he had helped accomplish. "That's what you get for sleeping through the best part," I chided. He grinned, "I guess I'll just have to cure myself of the habit."

Editor's Note—Jim Bennett is a son of Harry Bennett, Carleton Place, and is well known to the younger people of the town.

A month later they would all be dead.

In the New Year, the raids on Berlin continued. During the night of January 27–28, 1944, 515 Lancasters and fifteen Mosquitoes droned east to the German capital; Jimmy Bennett and his crew left Linton-on-Ouse at 1747 hours on the 27th. They climbed to altitude and the crew settled in for their twenty-first sortie, flying Lancaster DS 710 "A for Able," the first time they had flown this machine. The gunners were very surprised to see their first fighter attacking when they were still some seventy-five miles off the Dutch coast over the North Sea. This was unusually early for fighter interception.

The target was cloud-covered again, and sky marking had to be used. Local reports later revealed that the bombing was spread over a wide area. Some fell in the southern half of Berlin, but sixty-one small towns and villages were also hit and twenty-eight people killed. In the city, 567 people were killed, 132 of them foreign workers, and at least 20,000 were bombed out of their homes.

Thirty-three Lancasters were also lost, and one of the aircraft that did not return was "A for Able." Following the war, investigators learned that DS 710 had been attacked by a night-fighter in the vicinity of the town of Wollseifen. During the fight, the two aircraft collided and the Lancaster broke up in the air. It left a trail of components one-and-a-half miles long, and the main fuselage came down at Walbich Tal, about one mile south of the town of Urftalsperre (Eifel). The Luftwaffe salvaged most of the parts.

Within two days, Mr. and Mrs. Harry Bennett received a telegram from the RCAF casualties officer advising that "Pilot Officer James Gordon Bennett, J19011 former number R11836[23], is reported missing after air operations January 28. Letter follows."

It appears that none of the crew bailed out. Villagers from Wollseifen collected seven bodies from the wreckage and took them to the local cemetery. Herr J. Brull of 104 Dorfstrasse, Wollseifen, took part in the actual internment. He said that seven bodies, as well as part of a skull, were buried on January 29 in a communal grave. Coffins were not available so the corpses were wrapped in heavy paper. A report was made to the *stadt obersekretar* (town mayor), Herr Dr. Putzer of the nearby town of Gemund, but it was destroyed when the town hall burned during later land fighting. Dr. Putzer, however, vividly recalls that it mentioned seven fliers.

Another body identified as that of John D. Tesky was found several months later in the woods near the crash site. It was buried on April 22 in a separate grave adjoining the communal grave. Herr Brull stated that all of the bodies (except Tesky's) were placed in a single grave and that two crosses were put up. Only one flier was identified from papers recovered by the Luftwaffe at Hangelar Station, and his name went on one of the crosses:

ENGL.
C. W. SMITH
X
27.1.44

The other cross bore the inscription:

ENGL.
UNBEKANNTE SOLDATEN
X
27.1.44

A third cross was erected over Tesky's grave:

ENGL.
JOHN D. TESKY
X
27.1.44

The graves were in Field IV of the Gemeindefriedhof (Communal Cemetery) at Wollseifen and were well kept and supplied with flowers. When Flight Lieutenant Hirth, No. 15 Search Section, RAF, investigated the site in September 1946, he was satisfied that the entire crew had perished in the

---

[23] The first number is his officer's service number, the next is the number assigned to him when serving in the ranks.

crash. He wrote that an exhumation might be advisable to establish individual identification, but since Rheinberg Cemetery was closed, only the Graves Commission Unit was doing exhumations at isolated cemeteries. He felt that there should be no reason to delay informing the relatives of the fallen.

The list of dead crewmembers contained the name of Sergeant M. F. R. Sorton, RAF, as the flight engineer. It is not known what happened to Pilot Officer Dutton, whether he was ill and was replaced just for this trip or whether he had been transferred.

On January 30, Wing Commander D. S. Jacobs, officer commanding 408 Squadron, wrote the following to Mr. and Mrs. Bennett:

> At approximately 5:45 P.M. on the night of the 27th instant, "Jimmie" (as he was known to the boys) and members of his crew took off from this Aerodrome to carry out bombing operations over Berlin, Germany, but, unfortunately, failed to return. He and his crew were due back at this Aerodrome at approximately 1:30 A.M. the following morning, but no news has been received from either the aircraft or any members of the crew since the time of take-off.
>
> It is with regret that I have to write to you this date to convey to you the feelings of my entire Squadron. The loss of your son and other members of the crew is greatly felt by everyone and he was very popular with the boys on the Squadron.
>
> We lost one of our best aircrews when this aircraft did not return for it had already been mapped out for a great future with my Squadron. Your son had 20 operational trips to his credit and a total of 135 operational hours over enemy territory, and was fast becoming an 'Ace[24]' Air Gunner.
>
> There is always the possibility that your son may be a prisoner of war, in which case, you will either hear from him direct or through the Air Ministry who will receive advice from the international Red Cross Society. To be a prisoner of war is not the happiest thought in one's mind, particularly for you who were so fond of your son, but on the other hand, I hope you will bear with me that it carries a certain gratifying thought in knowing that our loved ones are alive and well and will, some day, return home safely.
>
> This war has caused grief to millions of people all over the world, and, it is a sorrowful state to know that so many fine young men must make great sacrifices in order to crush and erase from the face of the earth an infuriated enemy whose

[24] An "Ace" was a gunner who had been credited with at least five kills.

jealousy and hatred of our spirit and strength will eventually crush him and the members of his clique. . . .

Your son's effects have been gathered together and forwarded to the Central Depository, Royal Air Force, where they
will be held until further news is received, or in any event,
for a period of at least six months before being forwarded to
you through the Administrator of Estates, Ottawa.

May I offer my most sincere sympathies as well as those of
my Officers and men in your anxiety.

The International Red Cross Committee could not provide comforting
information. They advised the Air Ministry that Pilot Officer Bennett and four
members of his crew, along with three "unknown," were buried on January 29,
1944, in Comrades Grave Number One, Field Four, Wollseifen, Germany.
Wollseifen is approximately thirty-four miles southwest of Cologne.

While the Bennett family was awaiting definite news regarding Jimmy's
fate, they exercised some political influence. On July 11, 1944, Stanley H.
Knowles, MP for Winnipeg North Centre, wrote the Director of Records
seeking information on Pilot Officer Bennett.

On July 15, 1947, the bodies of this crew were exhumed from the cemetery at Wollseifen, kreis Schleiden, gemeinde Dreiborn, and re-interred in
Rheinberg British Military Cemetery. Jimmy Bennett was the only pilot officer on the crew at the time, and his body was identified by the rank braid, air
gunner's brevet, and Canada shoulder flashes on his service blouse (tunic).
He was clothed in trousers, an officer's shirt, long underwear, white flying
pullover, airman's vest, and an electrically heated flying suit.

In settling Jim's estate, his parents were paid his War Service Gratuity of
$476.08 for 913 days' service, 446 days overseas. That amount was before
£2.13s.9d ($12.01) was deducted to pay his outstanding mess bill. Wing
Commander Jacobs sent an ops wing to Jim's mother, explaining that it was
"indicative of operations against the enemy, will be a treasured memento of a
young life offered on the altar of freedom in defence of his Home and Country."

Twenty-four kilometres north of Krefeld and thirteen kilometres south of
Wesel lies the Rheinberg War Cemetery. The initial crossing of the Rhine in
Western Europe was near Rhineberg, and the site was chosen in April 1946
by the Army Graves Service for the assembly of British and Commonwealth
graves recovered from numerous German cemeteries in the area. The majority are graves of airmen, and there are more than 3,300 World War II graves
here. Thirty-nine special memorials inscribed "Buried near this spot" have
been erected to the memory of men known to have been re-buried in the
cemetery, but whose graves cannot now be precisely located.

At the bottom of the regulation stone marking Jim Bennett's grave is inscribed:

From Carleton Place, Ontario
He Came
Tranquil may you sleep
Dear Son

In *The Canadian* of January 24, 1946, appeared the following:

In Memoriam—Bennett—In loving memory of our dear son and brother, Pilot Officer James Gordon Bennett, who was killed Jan. 27, 1944, overseas.

He sleeps not in his native land,

But 'neath some foreign skies,

Far from those who love him,

In a hero's grave he lies.

Father, Mother, Sisters and Brothers.

R 95843 Leading Aircraftsman Boyne Hogan Dunphy
Electrical/Radio Mechanic
Royal Canadian Air Force

Boyne Dunphy should not have been aboard the Cessna Crane that crashed twenty miles north of RCAF Station Trenton, near Marmora.

Two pilots were flying cross-country training exercises and needed a crewman to carry out various duties in the fuselage of the aircraft. Groundcrewmen of all trades were urged to volunteer for flying duties as a crewman on board training aircraft, and if they accumulated the required number of hours airborne each month, they would be paid a small flying allowance.

Leading Aircraftsman Boyne Dunphy was an electrician and radio mechanic who volunteered for crewman duties, and the extra pay, on February 17, 1944. Also volunteering was Eldon Gibson, so the two airmen decided to flip a coin. Boyne lost the toss and the opportunity for the flight.

The Cessna Crane training aircraft used at Trenton.

Born on October 10, 1922, in New Glasgow, Nova Scotia, Boyne was the oldest child of Richard Patrick Dunphy and Ethel Mary Hogan. The Dunphys were Maritimers from New Brunswick; Richard was born in Woodstock and Ethel in Charlo N.B. Richard was employed as an express agent for the Canadian Pacific Railway. He was often transferred and was in New Glasgow in 1921 when he married Ethel, a talented young musician and actress in amateur dramatic and musical entertainments. Ethel had moved from Charlo to Campbellton, a very short distance, and became the first, and only, woman employed as a secretary to an urban school board in Canada.

Upon her marriage Ethel moved to New Glasgow with her groom. A year later their first son, Boyne, was born. Two years later, the young family moved to Chapleau, Ontario, to Richard's new post. While they were in northern Ontario, Ethel's health began to fail, and by 1930, when Richard took the position of manager of the Carleton Place express office, she had given up all stage appearances. However, she still devoted much time to encouraging young people in music and drama, but she restricted her performances to providing piano accompaniment for three of her sons who played violin.

Richard and Ethel produced six children: sons Boyne, Kerry, Wayne and Garth, and daughters Ilene and Brenda. In Carleton Place they lived at 51 Lake Avenue; it was there that the children grew and thrived. All were excellent students and were raised as devout Catholics in St. Mary's congregation. Boyne and Kerry inherited their mother's special talent for music. As well as the violin, Boyne played euphonium and Kerry played trumpet. The town band, CPHS Band and orchestra, and the Veteran's Guard band were the eager recipients of these boys' musical expertise.

Boyne attended Carleton Place public school from 1929 to 1936. He then went to Carleton Place High School from 1936 to 1940, attaining his junior matriculation. While in school he became interested in building model airplanes that actually flew, and participated in such team sports as baseball, basketball, and rugby and individual sports like cycling and skiing.

Boyne Dunphy in the Carleton Place Citizen's Brass Band. (Photo "Founded Upon A Rock")

Early in 1939, Ethel suffered a debilitating relapse of her cancer. She had undergone surgery a few years before, but this time, after several weeks' treatment in hospital in Ottawa, she was brought home. Ethel was confined to bed until noon on Tuesday, November 28 death released her from a long period of suffering. Two days later Richard comforted his six young children as they buried their mother in St. Mary's cemetery.

Boyne in High School.
(Photo courtesy sister Ilene)

The summer that he graduated from high school, July 1940, Boyne and his brother Kerry travelled to visit family and friends in New Brunswick. Boyne returned to his employment as a clerk at G. M. Williams Pharmacy. He had worked there after school and holidays since September 1939 and now began full time employment. In November 1940 Boyne took a new job, as a serviceman for Beatty Bros. On April 9, 1941, Boyne presented himself to the RCAF Recruiting Centre in Ottawa.

He was medically examined to determine his fitness for service. During the interview he claimed his only previous medical incident was a broken nose at about age three. Boyne was a very lean and lanky lad. He stood 5' 8" but only weighed 111 pounds. However, the examiner concluded his development was good and he was deemed fit for service. He described the young man as having hazel eyes and black hair. Boyne was told he would be enlisted as an Aircraftsman Second Class and to go home and wait for a call to go to basic training.

Boyne just prior to joining the RCAF. (Photo courtesy sister Ilene)

The call came three weeks later, and on April 29, 1941, Boyne boarded a train bound for Toronto and No. 1 Manning Depot. Boyne was selected to train as a radio mechanic, and after passing the three-week basic training course, he was sent home on leave until the end of May.

On May 24, Boyne travelled back to Toronto to the RCAF detachment at the University of Toronto where he was enrolled in electronics, radio theory, and transmission and basic electricity. Boyne graduated on September 16, 1941, and after a week's leave at home, he was sent back to the Manning Depot where he was held in reserve until November 22, when he was sent to St. Thomas, Ontario, to No. 22 SST.

In mid-February, half way through his course, Boyne again got leave to return home. Then, on March 28, 1942, Boyne was promoted to Aircraftsman First Class; he reported to RCAF Station Trenton on April 2.

Trenton was the first permanent RCAF Station that many airmen saw, and most were very impressed with its beautiful setting on the Bay of Quinte.

There were seaplane ramps running up to the hangars and a lovely little island only a short swim away. The barrack blocks were built of cement and all buildings were painted a dazzling white. Roads were paved and wide, and Highway No. 2, running from Windsor, Ontario, to Halifax, Nova Scotia, went arrow-straight through the centre of the base, separating the hangar line from the administrative section of the station. The parade square in front of headquarters was gigantic, and the RCAF crest was everywhere! Inlaid in floors, over building entrances, on the dishes and cutlery, and even woven into the blankets, many provided by Carleton Place woollen mills.

RCAF Station Trenton was by far the largest BCATP base. At its peak, it had 3,200 air force personnel and 500 civilians working on base. Boyne's posting was to the Maintenance Wing of the Central Flying School (CFS). This unit, more than any other, made Trenton known as The Hub of the BCATP. Originally named the Flying Instructors' School (FIS), it was transferred from Borden to Trenton in January 1940 and was soon working and flying at full capacity, training flying instructors for all the BCATP training schools. By the end of July 1942, the CFS had trained 2,622 flying instructors.

There were three bands at Trenton: a brass band that quickly welcomed Boyne's euphonium skills, a pipe band, and a bugle band. With the exception of a professional RCAF musician for bandmaster, all three were composed of talented airmen drawn from among the tradesmen, administration clerks, cooks, mechanics, and military policemen on base. Commanding Officer's inspections often put a thousand men on parade and employed all the bands for a march past.

In August, three more separate flying instructor schools were formed enabling the CFS to concentrate on post-graduate courses for senior instructors and to give more effective supervision to the pilot training and testing programme of the BCATP. No. 1 FIS specialized in training instructors for twin-engine service flying training schools. It flew Avro Ansons, Airspeed Oxfords, and Cessna Cranes. The courses lasted eight weeks with an intake of fifty-one instructor candidates every two weeks.

Boyne's job at Trenton was to keep the radios and other electronic equipment functional in any of the airplanes CFS was flying. Like all members of the servicing crews, he was expected to fly as a crewman whenever required so as to take care of the fuselage, close the door, ensure all equipment was secure and ready for take-off, and perform any other jobs the pilots needed. For this he could apply for a small flying allowance each month if he had flown the requisite number of hours.

Throughout 1942–43, Boyne enjoyed his posting to Trenton, primarily because it was so close to home that he could return on most weekends and holidays. Boyne got home for Easter the first weekend of April, but all this leave was not spent with family. Like most boys home on leave he visited his alma mater, CPHS, and enjoyed watching his brother Kerry and friends like David Findlay play hockey on the school team and in the school bugle band. Boyne was even known to pick up a bugle and play along. But the prime reason for Boyne's spending every free moment in Carleton Place was a comely teller at the Bank of Nova Scotia. Boyne had met, wooed, and won the heart of Miss Mary Cecelia McGregor, daughter of Mr. and Mrs. John McGregor of Appleton.

By October, Boyne was certified as an electrician and radio mechanic. With these qualifications, he was promoted to Leading Aircraftsman. During this time, his relationship with Mary matured and they announced their wedding for Christmas 1943.

Boyne on one of his visits home.

After obtaining special dispensation from the Catholic church to get married during the Christmas season, Boyne and Mary exchanged vows at 9:00 a.m. on December 24. It was a small pretty wedding, performed by the Reverend Father J. G. Clancy of St. Mary's. Standing with the bride and groom were Boyne's brother Kerry and Mary's sister Mary Elizabeth. Following their wedding, the couple moved into an apartment on Bridge Street and Mary returned to work at the bank and Boyne to Trenton.

Boyne spent the weekend of January 22–23, 1944, in Carleton Place with his new bride and his father and family. It was the last time they saw him alive.

On February 17, Boyne volunteered to fly with instructor pilot Flight Lieutenant Richard Long in Cessna Crane 1A 8842 on night cross-country training flights. Long had more than 2,100 hours total flying time with about 530 in the Cessna Crane, but he had only reported to the CFS Training Flight on January 13 and had no previous experience flying over eastern Ontario. He had also requested practice in radio range work, which suggested his proficiency in this area was less than satisfactory.

No formal pre-flight weather briefing took place for night flights. A forecast report at 1730 hours showed a cold front approaching from the northwest that was expected to reach Trenton by 2330 hours. The meteorological officer told the officer in charge of night flying that he did not think the last flight could be completed before the weather set in. The responsibility for whether the trip proceeded belonged solely to the captain of the aircraft.

On Long's first trip of the evening, with student instructor pilot Flight Lieutenant Redfern, he became disoriented between Stirling and Trenton, located himself over Tweed, and returned to base, making his the last aircraft of the flight to return. All captains had encountered the edge of a cold front coming in from Killaloe, and they had been warned of deteriorating weather before their second flights took off. But because he was last to land, Long was only twenty minutes on the ground between flights. He and Boyne quickly had the plane re-fuelled, took on the next student, Flight Lieutenant Thomas Schofield, and hurriedly took off for the second trip at 2200 hours, flying from Trenton to Renfrew to Killaloe to Stirling and back to Trenton, at an altitude of 3,000 feet. He was the last pilot to take off.

There were three Cranes airborne before Long's. The first aircraft had visual contact with the ground for the entire trip, and the pilot saw no snow and experienced no airframe icing. The second airplane ran into no icing[25], but entered heavy snow after Killaloe and had to complete the course on instruments. The third Crane encountered even heavier snow after Renfrew and was on instruments for the rest of the flight. He experienced severe icing both on the mainframe and in the carburetor, and on landing, the leading edge of the wings still had ice on them. It was expected that Long would encounter even poorer visibility and more severe icing than the previous pilots.

Nothing was heard from Cessna 8824 after take-off, which was not too surprising since none of the aircraft had two-way communication ability, only the AR2 receiving sets. Flight Lieutenant Redfern said that on the first flight they had good radio reception, but a court of inquiry into the accident concluded that the aircraft had run into very severe icing on the airframe and consequently crashed. When signing off the court report, the air officer commanding No. 1 Training Command, Air Vice-Marshall A. T. Cowley, noted that flights along or across civil airways at the heights indicated (3,000 feet) were unlawful. In the February 24 issue of *The Canadian* was the following story:

---

[25] Icing occurs when the aircraft encounters precipitation that freezes to the wings and fuselage. As layers of ice build up on the wings it destroys the aerodynamics of the wing. It can no longer support the air craft and the pilot completely looses control. The result is that gravity takes over and the aircraft makes a violent return to earth.

Toronto, Feb 18. —A Royal Canadian Air Force training 'plane is missing on a night training flight from the air training station at Trenton to eastern Ontario, headquarters of No. 1 Training Command of the R.C.A.F. said today.

The 'plane, carrying three crewmembers, left Trenton last night at 10 o'clock on a scheduled 2-hour flight which was to take it to Renfrew, Killaloe and Coe Hill. Although equipped with radio, no word has been heard from the 'plane, and search planes are out today looking for it.

On Saturday morning last Mr. Richard Dunphy C.P.R. expressman, received official notice that his son, Boyne Dunphy, was a member of the crew aboard the lost plane. To date no further word has been received by Mr. Dunphy nor the young man's wife, who was the former Miss Mary McGregor, daughter of Mr. and Mrs. John McGregor of Appleton. The young couple were married here at St. Mary's church just two months ago.

RCAF searchers found nothing and after they had several times crisscrossed the intended route of the lost aircraft they had to abandon their search.

On April 20, 1944, two deer hunters, brothers Kenneth and Dorland Harten of the village of Malone, near Marmora, were trudging through the bush when the glint of sun on yellow metal beckoned them to the wrecked Crane. Inside were the remains of three airmen, and an ambulance from RCAF Station Trenton was dispatched to retrieve the bodies. A medical examination determined that death had been instantaneous.

Boyne's body showed multiple contusions and lacerations, fractures to the sixth and seventh ribs, and a fractured left ankle. The probable cause of death was listed as shock due to multiple injuries.

Comrades from the Maintenance Wing took Boyne's body home to Carleton Place and provided the escort, firing party, and a trumpeter from the band in which Boyne played, for a funeral with full military honours and internment in the family plot in St. Mary's Cemetery. On May 3, 1944, the Minister of Defence sent a condolence card, and in August, a Memorial Cross was sent to the family for Boyne's mother and in September the king sent a message. On September 7, Mary Cecilia received the Memorial Cross for her lost husband.

The Carleton Place Canadian published the following tribute from a grieving father:

Among his treasured papers we will find newspaper clippings, consisting for the most part of tributes I had written in memory of treasured friends who had been called by death[26]. Most of them were men whom I have known from boyhood. Some had gone far and had achieved high place, but had retained a lovely humility, which permitted them to consider me worthy of their fine friendship. Others were men on whom success had never smiled, but who held in their hearts something of the fineness, which in boyhood days had held my admiration. Two of them were boyhood friends of Boyne's for whom he and I had affection. Boyne was proud of these tributes, and proud of the fact that his friends were among those in whose behalf my feeble powers of expression were employed.

And it is a comfort to me now to feel in my heart that Boyne always knew that if he should go I would feel that he too was worthy of a place in my gallery of fine people. For he was my first-born son.

He would not have me say he was heroic. I dare to think that in that awful moment preceding his death that he felt a lonely and painful fear. That thought cradles him all the more securely in my heart, as being more truly my son, for I too have known the agony of awful fear.

For Boyne, I can claim the lovely attribute of quiet and undemonstrative loyalty. A sweet, boyish love and loyalty to the young wife who was to so soon be bereft of his companionship. A flaming loyalty to the memory of the sweet mother whom he loved with innocent idolatry. A loyalty to his brothers and sisters. And a dear affection for a loyalty to me, the least of his loved ones. Loyalty to his country, to whose service he surrendered his youth, his youthful dreams of peaceful achievement, and, in the end, his very life. And loyalty to his God, to whose keeping he has returned, and to whose tender mercy and compassion I plead that happiness and rest may be granted to my little son for all eternity.

Boyne Dunphy died at age twenty-one. His War Service Gratuity was paid for 1,026 days service.

In December 1944, brother Kerry joined the RCN, followed by brother Wayne. They both survived World War II.

[26] See also Chapter One, the tribute written by Richard Dunphy for Horace Stark

R 161591 Warrant Officer Class II Lloyd George Scott
Air Bomber
Royal Canadian Air Force

The bodies of Lloyd George Scott and Russell George James lie in the same hallowed ground, the British Commonwealth Durnbach War Cemetery in Bavaria, Germany. Russell James is in grave number 7, plot C, row 21, while Lloyd's body rests in grave 11, plot C, row 1. Both men were originally from the Renfrew area, and when they died, Russell was twenty years, seven months old, and Lloyd was twenty years six months old.

Their shoulders held the sky suspended;
They stood, and earth's foundations stay.

—A. E. Housman, *Last Poems*

Lloyd Scott was born on September 11, 1923, to Joshua Scott and Millie Mabel Pretty in Renfrew. The family eventually moved to 72 Albert Street in Carleton Place, where his father worked as a "warper"(weaver) in the local mills. Lloyd attained his junior matriculation at CPHS and the family regularly attended the Church of England. His older brother, James Oswald, died of unrecorded causes on August 8, 1934, leaving Lloyd with four sisters: Mary Agnes (Termarsch), Grace Isobel (Hickey), Mabel Irene, and Marjorie Laney.

For five months after leaving school, from July to December 1941, Lloyd worked on Mr. W. J. Giles' farm. His family then returned to Renfrew, and he took a job at the Renfrew Woolen Mills working as a chain builder before going to Ottawa in April 1942 to enlist in the RCAF. He was eighteen years old. His interviewing officer reported Lloyd to have a "Rather slim build—on the shy side. Retiring nature. Still young and will adjust himself as he goes along. Good middle class stock." Lloyd was recommended for training as a pilot or an observer.

The results of his enlistment medical examination, however, dashed his hopes of becoming a pilot. He had undergone an appendectomy in 1940, drank no alcohol and guessed he smoked eight cigarettes a day, but he was described as "wiry" and was deemed ineligible for an A1B medical category. He was given an A3B category for an "eye muscle imbalance." No further elaboration was given, and that decision allowed him to train for any aircrew trade except pilot.

While most RCAF volunteers wanted to become pilots, many would not realize their dream. And the majority who were selected to be pilots would not become fighter pilots. From 1942 on, the need was for bomber crews, and a two- or three-officer selection board decided each recruit's destiny. The board wasted no time, and if the boy failed to impress his examiners, he did not get a second chance.

On April 20, Lloyd reported to No. 5 Manning Depot at Lachine, Quebec. The first two weeks were spent in a segregated area while they went through indoctrination. One of the very first stops was the barber who cut all hair the same length—short! Clothing stores issued uniforms and all the accoutrements that went with them. From then on their nights were taken up with polishing brass buttons and badges with Brasso, and boots and oxford shoes with Kiwi black shoe polish, spit, and a soft rag. The boys with girlfriends had a steady supply of scarce, because they were rationed, nylon stockings for the final shine, but the rest had to scrounge as best they could. Uniform tunics and trousers were ironed to a razor-sharp crease.

Many of the boys had never shaved before they went into the RCAF, but after their first inspection, it became a daily ritual. A favourite test by the disciplinarian corporal was to take a stiff piece of paper and scrape it upwards, against the grain of growth of a man's cheek. If he could hear a scratch, the hapless recruit needed a shave.

They also had to shave the fuzz off their new blue uniforms, but not with the same razor one used on one's face! Many thought the uniforms were made from the same material as horse blankets, as next to the skin they scratched unmercifully. The blues were of heavier wool for winter wear, or for dress wear in any season. Parades in July and August were to be avoided at all cost, but hardly ever were. Summer dress was khaki twill that looked quite good with the blue badges. They were washable, the blues were not, but the khakis would not hold a crease, wilting seconds after being removed from a hanger. They also turned a pale shade of pink if caught in the rain.

After finishing training at the Manning Depot, recruits were held in reserve until posted to an airbase for general duties. This was the air force method of warehousing the bodies until they were needed for further training. Guard duties required the men to stand sentry duty in shifts of two hours on and two hours off. They were also used as labourers for almost anything, specifically for KP (kitchen patrol), moving 100-pound sacks of potatoes, washing mountains of dirty dishes, and cutting weeds with hand scythes. Washing and waxing floors was a particular hardship because most had never ventured near such a task at home.

On June 3, Lloyd was sent to No. 4 Manning Depot in Quebec City, and then on July 18, back to Lachine. While in Quebec, from July 9 to 11, Lloyd was hospitalized with a severe red rash and itching on his right arm and leg. It turned out to be scabies and was easily treated.

Finally, after dreaming and talking about going to a training station, Lloyd was sent to Belleville, Ontario, to No. 5 ITS. There he was given desk instruction in such subjects as mathematics and navigation and spent uncounted hours on the drill square, learning on every move to raise his left foot about six inches off the ground and then slam it down seven inches. As the recruits' synchronization improved, the noise of boots on pavement became one large "crash." They were not allowed near an aircraft, but some lucky students did get a chance to sit in a Link trainer.

Lloyd attended ITS Course No. 60 from August 17 to October 10, and when he departed, his evaluation stated that he was, "Quiet, lacks force but is reliable and steady."

Finally, he was off to a flying station. On October 25 he reported to No. 1 B&G School at Jarvis, Ontario. In the 1930s, American Airlines built Jarvis field for emergency landings, but it had fallen into disuse; however, the existing runways and isolated location made it ideal for a BCATP bombing school. It was officially opened in August 1940 to accommodate 130 students, and by 1942, it had been expanded to handle 400. The main training aircraft were Ansons, Fairey Battles, and Bolingbrokes, and the airfield had six hangars, a drill hall, messes, barracks, a hospital, offices, and lecture huts. The parade ground was called Utopia Square and the roads had such names as Raid Avenue, Sleepy Hollow, and Rotten Row.

Air observers took bombing training in a course lasting twelve weeks, and Lloyd was on Course No. 66 from October 26 to December 23, 1942. The proximity of Lake Erie was useful as bombing practice could be carried out on raft targets (wooden pyramids floating on oil drums) moored a mile offshore. Both day and nighttime exercises were flown.

In 1942, the air-bomber and the navigator-bomber replaced the observer. Lloyd was on one of the first courses for the new air-bomber designation.

On October 10, Lloyd was promoted to leading aircraftsman, which made him the equivalent rank of a lance corporal in the army. In addition to the propeller on his sleeve midway between the elbow and the shoulder, he also sported a white flash in the front of his wedge cap that told one and all that he was in aircrew training.

Fledgling bombers trained using the Mark IV course-setting bombsight. They flew about twenty-three hours and dropped eighty practice bombs. Their average error was 113 yards during daylight and 136 yards at night, and the practice bombs, filled with titanium tetrachloride, emitted a puff of smoke when they burst. Two observers on shore plotted the spots of smoke. In the unlikely event of a direct hit, only minor damage was done to the target; major damage occurred to the student's pocketbook as he anted up for beer for everyone in the mess that night.

The student air bomber depended on many factors beyond his control including inaccurate wind forecasts and bored, inexperienced, and inept staff pilots. Still, the first bombing exercises were exciting for the students because for most it was their first time in an airplane. And they got to arm

the aircraft. They had to lie on their backs under the Anson and attach the eleven-pound bombs to the rack by forcing metal loops into the latches. Then they had to untwist a wire in the nose of each bomb to arm it. Once over the lake, they had to set up the bombsight with myriad finicky adjustments for height, temperature, and airspeed. The bomber did all this while lying in the close confines of the nose compartment below the pilot's feet. It had a small downward looking window that more often than not was so scratched and dirty that he couldn't see through it. Therefore, he would slide it out of the way while a hundred-mile-an-hour wind blew on his bare hands and face. In the Canadian winter this proved downright dangerous[27].

Lloyd went home for Christmas with his initial flying training behind him. At Jarvis he had flown in the Anson for thirteen hours daytime and

twelve hours night. He then racked up eleven hours and thirty-five minutes, all day-time, airborne in the Bolingbroke.

He then moved on to No. 1 AOS at Malton for the final phase of his training in Canada, and reported for Course No. 66, training from December 28, 1942, to February 5, 1943. Lloyd's wings parade was scheduled for the last week in January, and as the new air-bomber's brevet was not ready, he and his classmates were presented with air observer's wings. *The Canadian* reported, on January 23, that, "Lloyd Scott

Lloyd wearing his new Observer's Wing. (Photo NAC C148177)

of Renfrew, formerly of CPHS, received his bombardier's badge at Malton last week." His promotion to sergeant was made effective the last day of the course, and Lloyd left Malton with more flying time in the Anson. He flew twenty-four hours and ten minutes daytime and thirteen hours and fifteen minutes night. His assessment read that he "works well and is quite co-operative, but lacks leadership."

With the raise to sergeant's pay, Lloyd increased his assignment to his mother from $20 a month to $25. He was given embarkation leave then sent to the "Y" Depot in Halifax to await a ship bound for England. He arrived on

[27] Spencer Dunmore, The Other Trades Wings for Victory (Toronto: McClelland and Stewart, 1994) pp. 189-192

the east coast on February 20 only to be sent by rail to New York City to meet his ship. He left New York on March 8 and arrived in England on March 17.

Lloyd proceeded to No. 3 PRC in Bournemouth where he was billeted for two months in one of the seaside hotels that had been taken over by the military while he waited for a course at the RAF AOS.

On June 15, Lloyd was posted to No. 19 OTU, where he flew Whitleys and Ansons and learned about the latest British bombsight, the wonderfully efficient Mark XIV. It took essential data (wind direction and speed, terminal velocity of the bombs, the aircraft's speed, course and height, and the target's height and sighting angle), and computed the moment at which the bombs should be dropped. In addition, Lloyd learned to assist the navigator by reading maps and operating various pieces of radar equipment.

Lloyd also crewed up at the OTU: Flight Sergeant R. "Goldie" Golding of Bangor, Wales (pilot); Sergeant W. "Bill" N. Hedges of Southhampton, England (navigator); Flight Sergeant Lloyd G. Scott of Carleton Place (air

Lloyd Scott, third from left, and his crew by their Halifax Mk I bomber. (Photo courtesy Art Evoy)

bomber); Pilot Officer A. "Al" Jones of Dunnville, Ontario (wireless opera-tor/air gunner); J. "Johnny" R. Quicke of London, England (flight engineer); and Sergeant W. C. "Robbie" Robson and Sergeant D "Davy" A. Bean both of London, England (air gunners). The crew referred to themselves as "Jones' Flak Boys" after the only officer on the crew, Al Jones.

Course No. 66 trained at the OTU from June 18 to August 26, 1943, after which Lloyd's crew was posted to No. 1663 HCU. They had accumulated thirty-seven hours and thirty-five minutes day flying and thirty-five hours and forty minutes night. Lloyd left with the assessment: "An average bomb aimer who has shown little keenness for his duties and who has required considerable supervision and driving to obtain the required result. Pin point-ing [finding the aircraft's location from a map] is good and log keeping fair."

Their conversion to Halifax bombers began on September 6, 1943. Lloyd's learning was mainly confined to the instruments and equipment in the bomb-aimer's position located in the nose, and the type and destructive power of the bombs he would be dropping. The "light case" bombs had been introduced, 4,000-pound mild steel tubes into which molten RDX explosive was poured. This "cookie" became a major Bomber Command weapon, and it was noted for its tremendous blast. Bigger and more powerful cookies would appear later in the war, but these bombs were ideal for area bombing and perfect partners for incendiaries.

Many high explosives contained time-delay fuses set anywhere for an hour up to a week. However, bombs could be as dangerous to the crews as they were to the targets. Investigators learned that 2,000- or 4,000-pound "heavy case" bombs released from the forward bomb racks could collide with 500-pound bombs released from the rear-centre racks. After travelling two or three hundred feet, the lighter bombs became armed and would explode if touched, thus detonating the heavier bomb just below the aircraft.

On October 9, Lloyd's crew reported to No. 76 (RAF) Squadron of No. 4 Group at Holme-in-Spalding Moor. 76 Squadron had to leave Linton-on-Ouse to make room for the squadrons of No. 6 (Canadian) Bomber Group. By the time Lloyd and his crew arrived, 76 Squadron was flying the Halifax B.V. and, as well as Commonwealth aviators, it also had a complete flight of Norwegian aircrew. The squadron motto was "Resolute," and its badge a lion passant in front of a white rose. The rose commemorated the squadron's association with Yorkshire, and the lion, in its guardant attitude, indicated readiness to attack or defend at all times. Squadron aircraft tail fins were painted white with the RAF red, white, and blue vertical stripes two-thirds the way up on the forward part of the fin. Painted on the fuselage were the squadron identifying letters "MP" followed by the RAF roundel and the air-craft-identifying letter.

A Halifax Mk. III wearing the colours of 76 Squadron.

No. 76 Squadron had the distinction of flying more bombing raids than any other Halifax squadron. It was also the first squadron, on April 10–11, 1942, over Essen, to drop the new 8,000-pound bomb. Other highlights of early operations included the squadron's three attacks on the *Tirpitz* in Trondheim, Norway, the *Scharnhorst* at La Pallice, France, and the heavy raid on Peenemünde in August 1943.

Lloyd flew twenty-eight successful missions with 76 Squadron; he was killed on his twenty-ninth, one short of completing his first tour with its expected transfer home or to a training unit.

Luck played an enormous part in deciding who survived their operational tours. Many crewmen came to rely on charms and rituals. They looked after the crew and the airplane when the flak and cannon fire came uncomfortably close. A pilot would walk around his aircraft and ensure that each propeller had one blade pointing straight to the ground. Men carried particular items from their boyhood, from home, from wives, or girlfriends. Navigators and wireless ops laid out their tools and instruments in a particular pattern on their desks. Gunners wiped and polished the perspex in their turrets, even when they were perfectly clean. Lloyd Scott carried a rabbit's foot, except on his last mission. It was found amongst his effects after he went missing.

During the fall, the English weather turned from bad to atrocious. The squadron flew less and less, grounded by fog, storms, rain, and snow. Adding to the squadron's woes was the fact that Halifax aircraft were being used less and less as the Lancasters came on stream. Lancaster squadrons would often carry out raids alone.

During the winter months, Holme-in-Spalding Moor was a very bleak place. It was flat with no trees of any consequence and the aircrew NCO's lived in Nissen huts that had their ends blocked with bricks into which was set a single door. The uninsulated, half-round, steel buildings were painted dull black, which absorbed all the sun and heat in the summer, and were set over a concrete floor covered with linoleum, which in winter made them "colder than a witch's heart!" The floor area was about 40' by 15', which was impossible to heat with one small coal stove. Plus, the small ration of allotted coal only lasted a few days so raids on other hut's supplies occurred regularly. The most junior men slept furthest from the stove and worked their way closer as crews "went for the chop." A man's inventory of bedding also grew in direct relation to the number of men who did not return to base.

English crewmen usually adopted the Canadians and often invited them to visit their homes. The Canadians got to know most people in the community, especially the children, who eagerly awaited the gifts of concentrated orange juice, chocolates, chewing gum, and candies that came from either packages from Canada or from their flight rations. In return, the children taught the Canadians such amazing games as skittles and cricket and how to appreciate such delicacies as rabbit stew and the local hard apple cider.

The first raid made by Halifax aircraft after Lloyd's arrival on squadron was on the night of October 22–23 against Kassel; 569 bombers, 247 of them Halifaxes, executed an exceptionally accurate and concentrated bombing of the city, making sixty-three per cent of the city's housing uninhabitable. The railway system and three aircraft factories were also seriously damaged, and 5, 599 people were killed.

Thereafter the crew's targets sound like an air tour of Europe. But the tourists only saw the same things: above them the sky, below them the ground, both shades of deep black velvet. The bombaimer called "bombs gone!" and for several seconds, nothing; the incendiaries burst first and sprinkled the dense black with thousands of glittering diamonds. Within seconds the display turned to reds and pinks, yellows and oranges, as everything began to burn; the twinkling starbursts amongst the swirling mass of flickering colour was very beautiful. As long as one was watching from 20,000 feet above the fireworks. Even then the scene was only momentary as the perpetrators dodged flak and night fighters and falling bombs from the aircraft above them.[28] Beauty remains in the eye of the beholder, depending upon perspective.

The fireworks continued: Düsseldorf (November 3–4) Mannheim–Ludwigshafen (November 18–19), Leverkusen (November 19–20), Berlin (November 22–23, the same night Will Valley was killed, and December 2–3), Leipzig (December 3–4), Frankfurt (December 20–21), and between Abbeville and Amiens (December 22–23). Lloyd's crew was approaching the halfway mark in its Bomber Command tour when they were sent to Magdeburg on January 21–22, 1944. This was followed by two more attacks on Berlin (January 28–29 and 30–31) and on Le Mans (March 13–14) when they severe-

[28] On December 15, 1944, the prominent American bandleader, Glenn Miller, took off in a Noorduyn Norseman from southeast England enroute for Paris to entertain U.S. soldiers. His plane disappeared into the murk and Miller was never seen again. Wild theories surrounded the incident. London's Guardian news paper reported, in December 2001, their belief that a 139 Lancaster raid that night dumped their load into the English Channel when their attack was aborted. One of the Lancaster navigators, in an obscure and disregarded interview in the early 1950s, reported that he watched his bombs fall on a high-wing monoplane, a Noorduyn Norseman. His claim was dismissed until the newspaper researched Miller's flight path and time, which left little doubt but that his aircraft was the one hit with the blizzard of bombs from the returning bombers, a victim of "friendly fire.

ly disabled the railway system. Many lines were cut and fifteen locomotives and 800 railway wagons were destroyed. Many Germans were killed along with forty-eight French civilians.

On the night of March 15–16, Flight Sergeant Scott[29] and his crew took off for their twenty-ninth mission, the next to last to complete their tour. Flying in a Halifax III, LW 657, MP "G for George," they were part of a huge raid on Stuttgart, with their target the railway yards at Amiens. Adverse high winds caused the Pathfinders' marking, and the subsequent early bombing, to fall well short of the target. As they approached their aiming point, Lloyd could pick out the Pathfinder's many-coloured indicators amidst the clear blue master searchlight and its white following searchlights. Heavy flak exploded in flaming onions all around them.

Lloyd saw the first bomber drop quite a bit short, its load falling in a flat arc. Incendiaries hurtled down to dot the darkness with small magnesium fires, and a crimson rosebud coming to full bloom marked each bomb[30]. The flames spread as Lloyd called for the bomb-bay doors to be opened. Suddenly a gunner shrieked, "Fighter!" and the adrenaline flowed. There was no time to drop as they took evasive action. Machine-gun fire pierced the fuselage and wings. A cannon shell started a fire, and the crew worked madly to extinguish it as the pilot hurled the aircraft around the sky. Acrid black smoke from electrical and hydraulic systems assaulted their breathing as the metal monster bruised bodies in its tumble through the air. Flames enveloped a wing and the fuselage, when Pilot Golding suddenly realized the trees were rushing up to meet them. They were too low and too late to bail out. Against a wooded hillside, a ball of flame crunched to earth and exploded. A few minutes later the flames flickered out, darkness and silence returned to the forest, and another bomber crew was not returning home.

Aircraft "G for George" came down near the village of Heslach, two kilometres south of Stuttgart. There were no eyewitnesses, and the village records were destroyed in later fighting. Herr Klein, a clerk in the police station at Heslach, later told investigators that he remembered the crash and took RAF personnel to the site. Polizei Obermeister Hilbert remembered the police record that the aircraft was shot down by a night fighter and crashed in flames. The Wehrmacht recovered an unknown number of bodies.

The next day, March 16, the wing commander of 76 Squadron wrote to Lloyd's mother at 140 Moore Street in Renfrew:

> It is with the utmost regret that I had to telegraph Air
> Ministry that your son, Flight Sgt. Lloyd George Scott, is

[29] Lloyd had been promoted to Warrant Officer II effective February 5, 1944, but the promotion had not caught up with him.
[30] Much of this description is from The RCAF Overseas. The First Four Years. (Toronto: Oxford University Press, 1944) p. 17.

reported missing from air operations against the enemy on the night of 15th/16th instant. The target against which he and his crew were detailed was Stuttgart. . .

Your son had been on the Squadron for just over five months, and during the whole of that time, never once failed to give satisfaction in any job he undertook to do. His ability as an Air Bomber was without question, and his sense of duty both in the air and on the ground was of a very high order. The news of his loss has been received with the greatest sorrow. . .

I am enclosing a list of names and addresses of the next of kin of the crew, in case you might wish to write them.

Please accept on behalf of myself and the entire Squadron, my sincerest sympathy in these anxious days of waiting.

The wing commander also sent Lloyd's ops wings to his mother, on December 2, 1946, but this time to the address on Albert Street in Carleton Place. On December 7, 1944, the CPHS column in *The Canadian*, "The Torch," reported, "We regret to report that Flight Sergeant Lloyd Scott, a former student at CPHS, who was listed as missing in March, has been officially reported killed in action."

On March 17, 1947, an RAF investigating officer, Flying Officer E. F. Nicholas, travelled to the village of Heslach. Herr Klein escorted him to the crash site where he found a mass of scattered wreckage. A number of objects had identifiable markings: an engine cowling, an exhaust pipe, and a piece of a radio/radar receiver. He also found two yellow-painted bomb fins, apparently from 2,000-pound bombs. They confirmed the crew was shot down before they had the opportunity to release their load.

Nicholas discovered that the crew had been buried in the Steinhalde Friehof at Bad Canstatt near Stuttgart. "8 unbekannte engklishe Fleiger" (eight unidentified English fliers) were buried in four coffins, and a fifth coffin contained the remains of Sergeant Davy Bean, one of the air gunners. They were buried in three graves with full military honours and white wooden crosses erected to mark the spot. The investigator advised that exhumation was necessary to provide separate identities.

The bodies were re-buried in the Durnbach War Cemetery near Bad Tolz, a town forty-eight kilometres southeast of Munich. The exhumation report read:

F/Sgt. Scott was identified by his discs and the second body in the same coffin as that of Sgt. Robson by his A/G's brevet and electrically heated flying suit, being the only other gunner in this crew. Scott and Robson were re-buried next to each other in the same grave and the bodies labeled with their respective names. Clothing found-tunic battle-dress with AG brevet and Sgt chevrons, sweater white aircrew (also civilian pullover), Mae West, electrically heated flying suit and a sheaf [*sic*] knife in belt.

Lloyd Scott shares a cemetery with Russell James. The majority of men in these graves are airmen shot down over southern Germany, and one of the graves contains the ashes of an unknown number of unidentified war casualties recovered from Flossenburg. Within the Indian section is a memorial commemorating twenty-three, non-commissioned officers and men of the army of undivided India who died while prisoners of war in France and Germany. They were accorded the last rites required by their religion—committal to fire.

J 86119 Pilot Officer Ross Edward MacFarlane
Air Gunner
Royal Canadian Air Force

Gunners' Gremlin[31]

---

[31] This cartoon was found in a scrapbook kept by Ross MacFarlane during his overseas service. A gremlin is an imaginary mischievous sprite, held responsible by most aircrew for any mechanical faults in the air craft's equipment. An identical drawing, along with his name and service number, was found on the boot top that was used to identify Ross' body

"DAWN"

The immortal spirit hath no bars
To circumscribe it's dwelling place;
My soul hath pastured with the stars
Upon the meadow-lands of space.

My mind and ear at times have caught,
From realms beyond our mortal reach,
The utterance of Eternal Thought
Of which all nature is the speech.

And high above the seas and lands,
On peaks just tipped with morning light,
My dauntless spirit mutely stands
With eagle wings outspread for flight."[32]

In the quiet, pretty, French farming village of Breuvery-sur-Coole, fourteen kilometres southwest of Chalons-sur-Marne, near Reims, is the peaceful, communal cemetery of Breuvery-sur-Coole. Here, where crimson poppies blow, close to the east wall of the church, lie the only two Commonwealth War Graves in the churchyard. A bomber exploded and disintegrated in the early hours of May 4, 1944, and pieces crashed to earth over a wide area in the pinewoods close by the village. The citizens of Breuvery collected two bodies, but found no remains of the rest of the crew.

Reverently laid to rest beside their church is Pilot Officer D. S. Jackson, DFC, RAFVR, bomber pilot, and Flight Sergeant R. E. MacFarlane, RCAF, tail gunner. Two wooden crosses were hammered into place at the head of each grave.

Ross Edward MacFarlane, his older brother Ronald (Ronnie) Martin, and sister Audrey Aileen were the children of George Edwin MacFarlane and Clara May Jenkins. George MacFarlane worked as a driller for Findlay's Foundry until pneumonia took his life at a young age, leaving Clara with the three children. The family resided at 7 Moffatt Street.

Ross was born on January 6, 1923. He had scarlet fever at age two, the usual case of measles, and when he was three, he was kept in bed suffering pleurisy with effusion (a chest inflammation). At age five he broke his nose.

Ross attended Carleton Place Public School from 1928 to 1937, then CPHS until 1940, when he left to go work, at age seventeen, as a checker in the moulding department of Findlay's Foundry.

---

[32] This poem was found on the last page of Ross MacFarlane's uncompleted "Operations" scrapbook. It was written there by the RCAF padre after Ross's death.

Ross and his dog on a winter's morning in Carleton Place circa 1937.

Both Ross and his brother Ronnie were interested in the military from young ages. Ronald, three years older than Ross, was one of the originals in the re-organized Lanark and Renfrew Scottish Militia, while Ross was active in the CPHS Cadet Corps, a member of No. 2 Platoon with Ross Stanzel and Earl Lancaster at the May 1939 annual inspection. That October, Ronnie, then a sergeant in the militia, joined the Royal Canadian Artillery and was soon overseas in England and quickly promoted to sergeant. But Ross was keen to fly. He wanted to be aircrew and he visited the recruiting unit in Ottawa several times before his dream came true. Although he was told repeatedly that he did not have sufficient education to make aircrew, he did have a letter of recommendation from Wing Commander D. D. Findlay[33], so he was given the option of going to Hamilton to take the Dominion Provincial Youth Training Course[34] to qualify for training as a pilot.

First he had to pass the medical examination[35], which he did on July 9, 1941, and was found to be physically fit for A1B A3B category. He reported that he smoked seven cigarettes a day, but drank no alcohol. He also described his job at Findlay's as a timekeeper and stated his hobbies were playing the guitar and collecting records. He enjoyed rugby and hockey and was an enthusiastic paddler and member of the Carleton Place Canoe Club. His 125 pounds on a 5' 7½" frame was described as "wiry." He was recorded as having brown hair, hazel eyes, and a medium complexion, and he sported a large scar from an empyema[36] operation on the outside of his left knee.

Ross jumped at his only chance for aircrew. He left Findlay's in October 1941 and travelled to Hamilton to begin his course on December 29. He

[33] In June 1940, Mr. Findlay, a pilot in the RAF in the Great War had been called to Ottawa to serve again in the RCAF. For more on Findlay's First World War career, see the "Epilogue" of Larry Gray's We Are The Dead, General Store Publishing, Burnstown, 2000.

[34] Until September 1941 the recruiting process was based exclusively on actual rather than potential academic performance. At first all applicants had to have junior matriculation standing. Too many potential aircrew were being lost because of this academic requirement, however, so in October 1941 special provision was made for suitable applicants who lacked the necessary education. Candidates signed an agreement to enlist for aircrew duties and received a small weekly living allowance while taking pre-air crew academic training under the aegis of the Dominion Provincial Youth Training Programme to bring them up to the desired academic standard. Starting in1942, candidates were actually enrolled in the RCAF, and in August they were given air force pay and allowances while undergoing academic training.
W.A.B. Douglas, "The British Commonwealth Air Training Plan" The creation of a National Air Force, University of Toronto Press, 1986. p 240.

[35] When he was examined by the RCAF dentist he was told that he had only twenty eight-teeth instead of the required normal thirty-two. His wisdom teeth had not yet grown in. Rather than take a chance on being rejected, Ross spoke with his own dentist, Dr. Forbes Baird, who made artificial wisdom teeth for him. Ross was allowed to pay Dr. Baird a littler payment each week to cover the cost. As soon as Ross passed the medical he discarded the appliance and in due course his own teeth did grow and develop.

[36] A large collection of pus in a body part.

remained there until March 7, 1942, studying all the required high school subjects in order to gain his junior matriculation so as to qualify for further training. There was more than usual emphasis placed on mathematics, algebra, and geometry, since a basic understanding of these was fundamental for aircrew trainees. Some theory of flight was also included.

At the end of this program, Ross was evaluated as, "Average intelligence. Fair at school. Timid, quiet, introverted type, had not many friends, little social activity. Prefers water sports. Slight inferiority complex with respect to older brother 'he has all the brains.' Somewhat immature but appears stable. Wants to pilot. Not impressive. Motives fair." It was certainly not a very impressive evaluation. Then a medical examination on March 5, two days before the end of his course, revealed he had "heavy and persistent albuminuria," (a symptom of kidney disease) which would make him unfit for further service. However, Ross was sent to the air force medical examiners at No. 1 ITS in Toronto for a final assessment, where he was found to have orthostatic (only present when standing) albuminuria and, consequently, was fit for service[37].

Ross enlisted at Hamilton on March 7, 1942, was made an aircraftsman second class, and was sent to No. 1 Manning Depot for basic training.

After two weeks, the trainees were allowed to go into Toronto to savour its delights, but after nine o'clock, most were back in barracks. Toronto had "rolled up its streets"! Sunnyside, a nearby amusement park with roller coasters, a Quickee Donut Shoppe and a first class dance hall, was the only attraction.

Once training was complete, the men were held in reserve until they could be posted to some station, preferably a flying unit, for general duties. Ross spent this time enjoying the comforts of the Manning Depot medical facilities, being treated for acute tonsillitis. Then, on May 24, Ross was sent to RCAF Station Mountain View, in Prince Edward County near Trenton, where he endured five weeks of guard duty interspersed with lawn cutting and floor mopping, all the while taking more drill classes. For two days, June 11 to 13, he was in the station hospital with pleurodynia (pain in the left costal margin of the chest).

On July 5, Ross began his aircrew training when he reported for Air Bomber Course No. 58 at No. 6 ITS in Toronto. The course ran from July 20 to September 11. At the end of his ITS course Ross was assessed as, "Sincere, quiet, a hard worker, inclined to belittle himself. Will apply himself diligently," was promoted to leading aircraftsman, and was posted to No. 1 B&G School at Jarvis.

---

[37] Ross was also operating on only one lung. Early in life one lung had collapsed, but apparently this was not detected by the medical examiners.

Air gunners usually took a six-week-long course in which gunnery was practised both day and night at the twenty-five-yard range on the ground and at twenty-foot drogues pulled by other aircraft in the air. However, most of their time was spent at ground school, learning the workings of the outdated Vickers gun and mastering a new vocabulary: sears[38], sear releases, sear release levers, sear release lever covers, and sear release lever cover pins. Before flying, the budding gunners also had to be specially fitted out in canvas coveralls with one leg zippered from ankle to neck. They were warned to urinate before "kitting up" because it would be impossible afterwards once wrapped up in the strangle-hold of parachute harness, flying suit, heavy-duty six-button fly, and long johns.

Ross (left) and his bombaimer, F/S Jack Liebscher from Silverton, B.C., kitted up for flying with 626 Squadron.

On their heads was a World War I flying helmet from which dangled a Gosport tube. This apparatus closely resembled a stethoscope at one end and a siphon at the other. It was the only means of communication between the gunners' position and the pilot in the cockpit. Usually, however, the air surging around the gunners made any intelligent conversation impossible.

Going to the aircraft they carried their parachutes and round panniers containing sixty rounds each of .303 ammunition. The aircraft was usually already running up and the student, with all this paraphernalia flopping about his head and dangling between his knees, had a difficult time just getting up the slippery aluminum retractable steps.

Ross had a great deal of difficulty at No. 1 B&G School. He reported in on September 13 to attend Course No. 65, but on September 28, with major respiratory problems, he was admitted to the station hospital. After a number of tests, Ross was diagnosed with bronchitis and told that he needed a long hospital stay in order to recover. He was there until November 2, which meant he was held over to Course No. 66. Ross's recovery was still slow and his academic performance suffered. He had trouble with his compass exams and was held over once more to Course No. 67, which he started on November 9. He also started some flying: five hours and five minutes day-

[38] The catch of a gunlock holding the hammer at half or full cock; the "safety."

time and two hours nighttime in the Anson, plus three hours and forty minutes daytime air gunnery in the Bolingbroke. Then the hammer fell! Ross
failed, with the comment that he "has lacked interest, failed to apply himself, posted to Trenton."

On January 13, 1943, he arrived at RCAF Station Trenton and the No. 1
KTS. Originally a School of Administration set up to train people in the
wide variety of trades that kept the BCATP functioning, it was also home to
No. 1 Re-Selection Centre to which aircrew trainees were posted when they
found aircrew training too difficult. Normally a posting here was the death
knell for any aircrew ambitions.

But Ross was not to be put off. He appealed the decision to terminate his
aircrew training and managed to convince a selection board of three officers.
That board ruled, on February 29, 1943, that Ross "Seems a good type.
Board considers that he should have been set back a course because of seven
weeks spent in hospital. Board does not believe that he ought to have been
washed out in view of circumstances." The next day, with a light heart and
a new spring in his step, Ross boarded a train bound for No. 9 B&G School
at Mont Joli, Quebec.

This time Ross applied himself to every facet of the course. He excelled
in the classroom and flew fifteen hours and five minutes of excellent gunnery
exercises in the Fairey Battle.

Ross was on Course No. 51 from February 22 to May 14, 1943, and was
assessed as, "Neat, keen, reliable, mentally smart." His training problems

Ross, far left top row, with the graduates of Class 28, Course 51 Air Gunners on May 14, 1943 at #
9 Bombing and Gunnery School, Mont Joli, Quebec.

were all behind him, and he passed eighth out of fifty-four students. On his wings parade on May 14, his air gunner brevet was pinned on his chest and his three sergeant chevrons on his arm. Ross was given two weeks embarkation leave, which he spent in Carleton Place, before reporting to the "Y" Depot in Halifax for shipment overseas. While he was home, news arrived from England that his brother, Ronnie, had been awarded the Member of the Order of the British Empire (MBE.) for valour.

Ross left Canada on June 15 and arrived in Liverpool on June 24. One of his last sights of Canada was the Salvation Army handing out coffee and doughnuts to the departing servicemen on the docks.

After the ship docked, the men were unloaded and marched to the train station for the trip to Bournemouth and No. 3 PRC for indoctrination to wartime England, English customs and habits, and the decorum and duties expected of them. Ross there for only two weeks when he was sent, on July 7, to No. 81 OTU.

All summer, Ross was on Course No. 16 being introduced to heavy bombers and the Whitley V. He crewed up with Pilot Officer Dave S. Jackson DFC, of Bristol, England, (RAF), pilot and the captain of the crew; Pilot Officer H. A. "Jim" Riddle of London, RAF, navigator; Pilot Officer (RAAF) R. H. "Dick" Watts of Toowoomba, Queensland, Australia, wireless operator / air gunner; Sergeant J. M. B. "Jack" Liebscher a Canadian native Indian from Silverston, B.C., RCAF, air bomber; Sergeant J. A. I. "Skin" Sutton of London, RAF, flight engineer; and Sergeant A. G. "Taffy" Brooks of Swansea, Wales, mid-upper gunner. Ross was given the position of tail or rear gunner.

The first crew gathered beside a Whitley bomber. From L to R: Jack Liebscher, age 31, bombaimer, Ross MacFarlane, 20, tail gunner, Dave Jackson, 20, pilot, Jim Riddle, 28, navigator, Dick Watts, 20, Wireless/air gunner. The photo was taken in August 1943 at 81 OTU in Whitchurch, Shropshire.

The crew accumulated forty-four hours and fifteen minutes daytime and forty hours nighttime flying before they were declared fit for operations and posted, on September 18, to No. 1656 HCU at Lindholme, Yorkshire, where they met the Wellington.

Ronnie and Ross had a happy reunion that summer. The two managed to get leave at the same time and met for the first time since Ronnie left Carleton Place for overseas some three years before.

After the Whitley, the Wellington was a comfortable aircraft. The geodetic design made it strong, and its twin engines were more than powerful enough to pull it at decent speed. The big drawback for training Ross's crew was that the "Wimpy" had only one turret, at the rear. The gunners took turns, but it was Ross's turret and the other two were usually flying as observers. These advanced crews were often used on minor operations to either create a dummy bomber stream or to drop Window or propaganda leaflets on missions called "nickle" raids. They were also used for

Ross and his brother Ron, wearing the ribbon of his M.B.E., on leave together somewhere in England.

mine laying in the Frisians from Texel to St. Nazaire. One mine-laying operation using training Wellingtons was flown on the night of October 24–25,

Ross at 1656 Conversion Unit taken in November 1943.

followed by Wellingtons dropping leaflets over France on October 27–28. There were no losses on either mission, and all crews did at least one of these trips before moving on. Ross flew his trip in Whitley "N for November," dropping leaflets over Casquets Island, France, on the night of August 30–31. The crew were credited with ½ a mission for this flight.

On November 8, 1943, Ross's crew was sent to RAF Station Wickenby, Lincolnshire, to join 626 Squadron. When they arrived, all was in shambles as the squadron had only been formed the day before from "C" Flight of No. 12 Squadron. They were to take part in the strategic bombing offensive and were to fly the Lancaster I. The crew had barely even seen a Lancaster before their arrival at Wickenby, but they were quickly converted and sent to fly operationally. The main battle for Berlin was on, and Harris needed every aircraft he could lay his hands on.

626 was one of No. 1 Group's squadrons which had itself only been formed in the autumn of 1943. The squadron flew 2,728 Lancaster sorties and lost only 49 aircraft in 187 bombing and 18 minelaying raids. A further eleven Lancs were destroyed in crashes. The squadron adopted the motto "To strive and not to yield," and depicted on its badge the waves of the sea, an ancient ship with its sails furled and charged on the bow with an eye. In the ship are seven oarsmen symbolizing the seven crewmembers of a Lancaster bomber.

The crew's first operational sortie was against Berlin, November 18–19, 1943 They were airborne at 1720 to join 440 Lancasters making the long cold trip via Texel Island to Berlin and Bremen into Germany's heartland. The city was completely cloud-covered so both marking and bombing was done blindly. German authorities recorded that bombs fell in most parts of the urban area, but there appeared to be no concentration. It was not a very auspicious beginning to a Bomber Command objective. . After leaving the target Ross' crew was forced to take evasive action to ward off the attention of a night fighter, estimated to be a JU (Junkers) 88.

Air Marshall Harris became almost obsessed with Berlin, capital of the Third Reich. It was a perfect target, a major industrial area and the second largest city in Europe. Berlin had a population of four million, iron and steel works, chemical factories, and plants that manufactured machine tools, engines, and electrical equipment. But it was almost impossible to hit. Deep inside Germany, it was about as far from the English airfields as a target could be. En route, tens of thousands flak guns, thousands of searchlights, and a reinvigorated night-fighter force were poised to impede the Bomber Command's progress.

It was also impossible to gauge a crew's reaction to their first operational sortie. The first couple of flights were totally bewildering, but the stresses and strains were masked by a large dose of adrenaline, so they tended to become spectators rather than participants. In the case of Ross's crew, they never even saw the target. Any trip to Berlin was an ordeal of plugging through a long and dangerous flight, hundreds of miles into enemy territory. Still the impressions were fantastic: flak so thick one could walk on it, searchlights stabbing up to criss-cross their path, and fighters spewing red tracers everywhere zipping through the only parts of sky not filled with bombers.

On the night of November 22–23, Ross's crew were part of the second raid on Berlin, with 764 aircraft the largest force sent to Berlin so far. Cloud

Ross' 626 Squadron crew standing under the nose of their Lancaster.

covered the target again, and bad weather kept most of the enemy fighters on the ground. Marking and bombing again were only estimates, but it still turned out to be the most effective raid of the war. Vast areas of the central city were destroyed, several firestorms broke out, 175,000 people were bombed out, and 50,000 soldiers, equivalent to three army divisions, were taken from their regular duties to help the civilians. Only twenty-six bombers were lost, eleven of them Lancasters.

During the night of November 26–27 they flew again against Berlin. Searchlight activity was active; Ross counted eight cones of sixty lights. On the way home Ross' oxygen mask froze and over Bremen they were held in a searchlight for about two minutes during which flak was very accurate. They managed their escape but had to make an emergency landing at Skipton because their "Wheels Locked" light failed to come on indicating that their wheels were not "down and locked." The only unservicability was the indicator light and the landing was uneventful although all crew had assumed crash positions.

After his second sortie, Ross reported to the station hospital on December 2 with a rarely reported malady of "frequency of nervous origin." He gave a history of his childhood empyema and scarlet fever, which made it difficult for him to hold water. During operational missions, he could not leave the rear turret and had been incontinent on two occasions on both trips. The doctors pried and prodded and subjected Ross to every test they could imagine. In the end they supplied him with a rubber thigh urinal for use when flying and released him back to duty on December 14.

This put Ross back in the tail turret for another trip to Berlin on December 16–17. The bombaimer saw three rockets fired at them this night. It was the first time rockets had been used against the British bombers. They avoided much of the defensive fire by cutting across Denmark and the North Sea to home. The next sortie was the raid on Frankfurt on December 20–21. The crew went back to Berlin the night of December 23–24 then was stood down for Christmas day[39]. They had a quiet trip back over Berlin on December 29–30. They were late taking off as Ross' guns needed the hydraulic system bled and re-filled. He tried them over the North Sea but only two guns fired and those only intermittently. During the raid their aircraft was hit by flak, but only lightly.

On January 2, 1944, they were sent to 156 Squadron at nearby RAF Station Warboys. This squadron was one of the original Pathfinder squadrons, and Ross's crew was sent to learn their craft. However, during training, it was decided that Pathfinding was not for them and three weeks later, they returned to 626 Squadron. They repeated their bombing of Berlin on January 20–21, 28–29, and 30–31. Ross recorded in his scrapbook that the trips were getting rather monotonous, in spite of the searchlights, the flak and the night fighters.

Ross was promoted to the rank of flight sergeant on February 14, and the next night, celebrated by flying to Berlin.

No. 1 Group sent 139 Lancasters in the heaviest attack made on the city, and concentrated bombing through cloud caused extensive damage. . On March 24–25 Ross's crew flew their "shakiest trip yet!" In his scrapbook he wrote:

> From Denmark until we crossed the French coast coming out there was heavy, accurate flak all about. There was a northerly wind of over 100 mph & we overshot the target. It took 20 min. to get back and we were the last kite to bomb. As we were 20 min. behind the main force, we cut off a hunk coming back to catch up and ran into the Ruhr defences. We were coned for 7½ min. & shot at but got out O.K. The M/U (mid-upper) turret was holed & also the pilot's windscreen. There was a hole in the elevators near my turret, some in the bomb doors and the main-plane and s/o (starboard outer) engine.
> We diverted to a Yankee Lib. (Liberator) 'drome and stayed overnight. (near Cambridge)

Twenty-one aircraft failed to return from the raid against Nuremberg on the last day of March. The last four flights recorded by Ross were:

> April 10–11 – Aulnoye (France), 900 Lancs. Most France trips are only counted as ½ of a sortie.

---

[39] King George had personally requested there be no operational air attacks by RAF and USAAF bombers. Allied aircraft stayed on the ground and so did the Luftwaffe. Britain, too, had a raid free night.

We did it in almost full moonlight. There was no cloud and the target was well marked. We circled for a couple times waiting for an accurate marker but none went so we bombed the backing-up marker. On the way back we were coned (6 min.) and shot at and were hit quite a lot. The B/A fired at the searchlights & we shot off a colour cartridge with no effect. ... Some of the hydraulics were shot away so we used emergency air & prepared for crash landing at Woodbridge but wheels came down O.K. Stayed there overnight.

April 20, 1944–Cologne, 320 Lancs. Just after take-off, Jerry's P.F.F. markers went down on Grimsby and we had to climb with our nav lights off which was none too comforting. Some Lancs were coned for a while but not shot at. It was so quiet over the Continent that we were at the target almost before I realized we were in enemy territory. The only active searchlights were at and around Cologne but a front was just passing over the place so we had good cloud cover. On the way out the S/L were active east of us at Rotterdam but we came out on track and avoided them. Flak was only moderate. A chandelier burst just behind us at the target on our track but I didn't see any fighters. What probably accounted for that was that there were dispersed attacks on northern France as well whose zero hour was prior to ours.

April 22–23 – Dusseldorf, 640 Lancs. I had a very quiet but tiring trip. It was fairly bright and all the kites were leaving contrails. (They were at 20,000 feet at −35 temperature) ...We were a bit early so we did a five-minute dog-leg to waste time which wasn't so easy on the nerves. The first markers went down when we were running up on the target, and by the time I got a look at it, the ground was pretty well covered with fires. ... I think they were the most intense fires I've seen in all my trips. On leaving the coast coming out we could still see them. It was a real good prang. A bullet came from somewhere, went through my ammo-box on the stbd side, richotchet (sic) off something and lodges itself in one of my bullets further down the tracks. It looked like a .303.

April 24–25 – Karlsruhe. 604 Lancs & Hallys. The attacking force went in two routes; we took the Northern one. A front expected over the coast was further inland and gave cloud conditions above and below 21,000' from Dussledorf (sic) to the target. On arrival at the target we didn't see any T.I.'s (target indicators) so we bombed a concentration of fires. S/L (searchlights) weren't very active on any part of the route as the cloud made it difficult. Flak wasn't very intense for that part of the country going in and over the target it was practically nil. The France route out was quiet except when the cloud ended about 40 mins. from the coast when fighter activity was pretty strong. The broadcast winds weren't very accurate and we left the coast 100 miles off track near Ostend. A Flak ship took a few shots at us in the North Sea coming back and I believe it hit us once or twice. There were intruders over this country on return. No moon.

This flight completed twenty-one and one-third missions for Ross MacFarlane's crew.

Years later, a pilot who had flown on 626 Squadron at the time, Pilot Officer David Oliver, wrote on the subject of morale:

Morale was high throughout the period that I was at Wickenby. An efficiently run station and intelligent leadership, including inspiration from a few whose exploits were legendary, helped a lot. Some other factors predisposed to high morale. The average age of aircrew was twenty or twenty-one and very few had the close attachments and responsibilities of wife and children, We were just as well educated academically as the young men of today but we were less socially and politically aware. We had nor experienced the clamorous debate in the media on every conceivable subject, nor the continuous dissection of authority that goes on today. In the event, we were united in our belief in the cause and in giving unquestioning support to those in authority.

We were intensely preoccupied with our own crew and very strongly motivated not to let it down. Apart from our commanders and three or four other crews that were close contemporaries, we knew few other aircrew on the station as more than passing acquaintances. The effect on morale is less severe if casualties are not known to one personally. By far the highest casualty rate occurred amongst the very inexperienced crews, whom established crews were unlikely to know personally.

In May and June, No. 1 Group had heavy commitments to smashing V-sites, gun emplacements, and rail centres and weakening German resistance generally. This was not without losses. On the night of May 3–4, the military centre at Mailly-le-Camp was the target. In bright moonlight, 346 Lancasters and 14 Mosquitoes dropped 1,500 tons of bombs with great accuracy. The main attack started late, and night-fighters arrived during the delay. 626 Squadron sent out thirteen Lancasters; one aborted the flight, nine bombed the target, and three went missing.

In the German camp, 114 barracks, 47 transport sheds, and some ammunition buildings were hit; 102 vehicles, including 37 tanks were destroyed; and 218 German soldiers were killed and 156 were severely wounded. Most of the casualties were Panzer NCO's. Dogfights with the night fighters continued as the bombers left the target for their return. No. 1 Group squadrons, which flew the second wave of the attack, suffered the most casualties: twenty-eight of the 173 Lancasters dispatched.

At home, Ross's mother received a cable that her son was missing in action. She had just received a letter from him, dated April 19, in which he wrote that he was well and glad to have been recommended for his commission. He sent regards to Ronnie who was serving in Italy. The Casualties Officer wrote to Mrs. MacFarlane:

> It is regretted that no further information has been received regarding your son since he was reported missing on May 4th and I wish to extend to you and the members of your family my sincere sympathy in this trying time.

On May 4, the day following the raid, Wing Commander G. F. Rodney of 626 Squadron wrote to Ross's mother:

> By the time you receive this letter you will have been notified that your son Flight Sergeant Ross McFarlane has been reported missing from air operations and I write to offer you my deepest sympathy.

> Your son was the Rear Gunner of one of our aircraft which left this country last night on a mission against the enemy, but unhappily since the time of take off we have had no news of the aircraft or its gallant crew. There is always a possibility in cases such as this that the crew may have escaped with their lives and are safe even as Prisoners of War. I sincerely hope that this will prove to be so in the case of your son. I might add that it usually takes the International Red Cross Society at least six weeks to obtain any news. . .

Flight Sergeant McFarlane had earned the admiration of all his colleagues for the cheerful but determined way in which he set about any task which was allotted to him. In his many sorties against the enemy he had shown the courage and complete disregard of danger that was noticeably the mark of all his crew. I can assure you that their loss came as a great shock to the Squadron.

Your son was immensely popular with his colleagues and they will all miss him in the Mess. His many friends have asked me to convey to you on their behalf their most heart-felt sympathy for you during this anxious time of waiting and hope that our hopes of his safety will not be frustrated.

When Ross's effects were collected, it was found he had truly eclectic tastes in reading. He owned such books as *The Spell of the Yukon and Other Verses, The Scottish Clans and Their Tartans, Billiards and Snooker, The Game of Patience, Tramping Holidays in Scotland, Logarithms and Other Tables, Burns Cottage Alloway, Pathfinders*, and *Global War*. He also had a pocket atlas and maps of England and Wales.

Ross's mother knew that he had a girlfriend in London. Many thousands of marriages resulted from wartime liaisons, but official policy dictated that RCAF ground personnel had to have six months' service before they could marry. Oddly enough, this restriction did not apply to those serving overseas. However, Canadian authorities insisted that the prospective bride produce a certificate attesting to her good character and that the bridegroom sign a form declaring that he was not married.[40] In disposing of Ross's effects, his mother sent his Hercules three-speed bicycle, with a padlock on the saddle, to Miss Vera Mickleburgh in London, England.

A ministerial card of condolence arrived on May 10, 1944, and Clara MacFarlane received a Memorial Cross on September 10; a message from the King was sent on September 13.

On May 28, 1945, a casualty investigation was completed and the following report filed:

I carried out an investigation at Breuvery-sur-Coole about 14 Kms., S.S.W. of Chalons-sur-Marne.

The Cure of Nuisement-sur-Coole took me to the scene of an aircraft which crashed in flames and exploded

40 Spencer Dunmore and William Carter Ph.D., Reap The Whirlwind (Toronto: McClelland and Stewart Inc., 1991.

on the night of 3–4th, May 1944. The wreckage of this machine is spread over a large area in some pinewoods.

Only two bodies were recovered and were buried in separate graves in the Parish Cemetery at Breuvery. Each grave is marked by a plain wooden cross. The body of P/O D.S. Jackson who was identified by a letter found on his body addressed to P/O D.S. JACKSON, R.A.F. Station, Wickenby Nr Lincoln. In grave number 2 is R.156954[41] F/S R.E. McFARLANE who was identified by a mess bill found in his tunic also by his number and name on his boots. . .

I searched in the vicinity of the crash and found several odd bits of identifiable clothing etc. I consider it most likely that the bodies of the unaccounted for members of this crew were completely destroyed by the explosion.

The enclosed identity disc marked 425389 WATTS, R.H. R.A.A.F., C of E, was found amongst the wreckage.

The following items found amongst the wreckage were handed by the Mayor of Breuvery to the Etat Civil at Chalons-sur-Marne who in turn forwarded them to the authorities in Paris.

1. A leather Wallet found about 12 metres away from the body of McFarlane R.E. 156954 containing:—A Hotel card, 2 photographs, remains of two calendars; Five £1 notes, one 10/- note, two group Photos (one torn), inside of a boot from which the identity was taken.

2. A partially burnt map of France, Belgium, Holland, Germany. Maps of Germany, Portugal and Spain. Various denominations of Belgas, Dutch and French currency.

In the July 5, 1945, issue of *The Canadian* a letter from Paul Horguelin, the mayor of a French village near Reims, to Mrs. Clara MacFarlane was published:

This letter comes from a stranger to you. I learned your address from Mr. H. G. Jackson of Bristol whose son, David, was pilot officer of the Lancaster in which your son was serving too. You have been writing to Mr. Jackson and probably have received the official letter of the loss of the plane and of all its crew-as he received it himself.

I am very sorry, madame, to have to write you under such painful circumstances, but I hope my English will be good enough to allow me to express to you all my sympathy and to take part in your sorrow.

I am the mayor of a small village, somewhere in France, near Chalons, Marne, not far from Reims. The plane of your son crashed there in flames at one o'clock on the night of the 4th of May, last year.

Describes Raid

And I am sure you will prefer knowing details about the tragedy, rather than wondering and making despairing suppositions. It was on a raid on Mailly le Camp, the biggest German tank centre in France, and there were heavy losses for all. The camp was entirely destroyed, the Germans had several thousand soldiers killed, the French villages around the camp, whose anti-aircraft batteries were in action, were shaved to the ground and most of the civilian population was killed. The R.A.F. lost 45 to 47 big bombers. For us, it was a night of Apocalypse and we thought our last moment had come too.[42]

The Lancaster was in a very bad state, completely destroyed and of a crew of seven, we only found two poor bodies that we could identify with certainty. PO Jackson was lying a little by the side of the wreckage, and your son, a little further away. They must have jumped at the last moment[43].

Of the others, nothing definite was found, except the identity disc of the Australian, Watts, who, I learned later, was the radio operator. I have written to Mr. Jackson about his son as we have managed to hide and keep away from the Germans everything that was found near the plane.

The identity of Flt. Sgt. McFarlane was made sure by a Mess note which bore his name and number, written inside his boots. There is no doubt about him. He was piously taken, in a coffin, to church, where a service took place

---

[42] Comparison should be made between the mayor's account of the damage and deaths from this raid to that "official" record made by British authorities (above).

[43] It is significant that the only bodies found were those of the pilot and the rear gunner, whose positions were at opposite ends of the airplane. From that one could conclude that the crew still had their bomb load on board when they were hit by flak or fighter fire; their own bombs exploded with the catastrophic result of tearing their aircraft and the men in the main fuselage, to shreds

attended by the young men and population of the villages. He is buried near the church, in the cemetery of Brewery Coole, in the territory where the plane fell.

The grave is well taken care of and an anniversary church service has been held lately. I am at your entire disposal, poor madame, to do anything you may wish for that grave, and may send you a photo and one of the wrecked plane if you wish. If your son is of Roman Catholic religion, our priest may say mass for the resting of his soul. And the young men and inhabitants are taking great care of those two graves.

In your great pain and sufferings, I am sure that it will be a relief to you and your family to know that your dear son is resting quietly somewhere in France, a sister country so far away from Canada—his duty done—in a friendly ground.

French People Thankful

We French people are very thankful to those brave and gallant young men that gave us courage in our bad time, passing over us, night after night, boldly facing their fate, working on for that so long hoped for victory.

Many of us have paid with our lives, or have been deported to those camps of death in Germany, for having hidden those who were lucky enough to be able to use parachutes or simply for having given them a decent burial.

Near the body was found a leather wallet containing two post card photos of a group of airmen, two small photos of the owner, a card of a K. of C. hotel in London, and a sum of money, but nothing concerning the identity of the owner. I am enclosing two of the photos and if it is not right, you will be kind enough to send them back to the R.C.A.F. Headquarters office in London, casualty section, with all explanations.

As for the wallet and contents, it was handed over, as soon as the Germans went away, to the French bureau of Etat Civil. They send them on to the British office in Paris and you will certainly receive them by the official way.

May Live In Canada

When things become easier and travelling possible again, there may be some chance you will receive my visit to

Ottawa. I had been in Canada in 1936 and passed through Toronto, going to Montreal and Quebec, and my great desire is to be able to go again as soon as possible. My intention is even to go to Canada for good and settle there with my family.

We had such a dreadful life in those two last wars; we wish for a better future for them that I would leave this country for another where French is well spoken. I may be writing to you later to get more information about life in Canada, if you will allow me to do so.

I hope, dear madame, Sergeant McFarlane was not your only son and that you have other children to receive his part of affection and to give you consolation.

My best wishes for courage, to you and your family.

The Jackson and MacFarlane graves in Breuvery. The photo was taken in September 2000 by Aileen after her daughter, Ross's neice, Carleen had affixed the poppy stickers to the stones.

Ten days after this letter was published, on July 15, 1945, Clara May MacFarlane died of chronic nephritis and arterial hypertension leading to myocardial failure, only a few days before Ron's arrival home.. She had been totally blind for some time. By Christmas 1945, Ronnie MacFarlane was back attending CPHS, pursuing his dream to become a lawyer. Along with other returning boys—Keith Craig, Kenneth Lowe, William Buse, Elwin Pretty and Donald Dunlop— they were sitting in classrooms to continue an education that had been so abruptly interrupted. Ronald MacFarlane did make the law his life, and he became a prominent lawyer and respected jurist after his appointment to the bench.

CHAPTER TWENTY-TWO—A VICTORY OF SORTS

*Two of the most unbelievable manifestations of human courage and
endurance in the history of war-the infantry of 1914–1918 and the
bomber crews of 1939–1945.*

—Sir John Slessor, *The Central Blue*

In the final months of operations, Bomber Command's official priority
was to attack oil and communications targets, with the secondary priority
being the transportation system. Air Marshall Harris devoted great effort to
these targets, but he still sent massive raids to attack German cities, some of
which had industrial importance. This insistence upon area bombing so late
in the war led to the post-war sidelining of Bomber Command's achieve-
ments. It also caused the RAF to reluctantly acknowledge the years of effort,
suffering, and sacrifice made by the airmen of Bomber Command. Instead,
the RAF preferred to honour the men who fought in the Battle of Britain, but
fewer airmen died in that scrap than in a single Bomber Command raid on
Nuremberg in March 1944.

Atrocious weather remained a constant problem for Bomber Command.
January 1944 was a quiet month because of the weather, until Bomber
Command and the USAAF were ordered to attack precise targets, such as
German jet aircraft manufacturers and the docks constructing the new
Schnorkel-equipped U-boats. Then, in February and March, flying opera-
tions rose to a crescendo. In March, night and day attackers dropped 67,637
tons of bombs—more than in any previous month of the war.

Their targets then changed. New cities were visited and various types of
oil refineries, many well inside eastern Germany, were bombed. Railway
yards, canals, and bridges were hit, and most German cities near the battle-
front on the ground were reduced to ruins. German defences declined, but
night-fighters still caused many losses. It was almost over by the end of
March, and Bomber Command's targets for the next five weeks were mostly all military. The strategic bomber offensive was over.

J 42702 Flying Officer Ross Samuel Stanzel
Air Bomber
Royal Canadian Air Force

Ross Stanzel was one of the many well-
rounded Carleton Place boys destined to excel
at whatever endeavour he tackled. He enjoyed
Boy Scouts, and he was a good athlete, playing
hockey, softball, rugby, and basketball at

school. However, his passion was paddling with the Canoe Club, and in June 1939, he was a competitor on the war canoe crew. Also while attending CPHS, he participated in the Cadet Corps, and in the May 1939 annual inspection, he was a cadet in Platoon No. 2, marching with Earl Lancaster and Ross MacFarlane, and for the April 1942 inspection, he was the cadet sergeant for the same platoon, which included Ray White in the ranks. The entire cadet corps was under the training and direction of Mr. J. S. Stark, "physical culture specialist" on the high school staff.

Ross Samuel Stanzel was born on April 24, 1924, to Oscar Milburn Stanzel and Ethel Sarah Jane Saunders. He was their second child; a girl, Ruth Olivia, was born a year earlier. At age nine, he had his tonsils and adenoids removed, and in 1938, he was hospitalized for a week with bronchitis.

The family lived in an apartment on Chapel Street in Ottawa, and Ross attended Devonshire (1930–31, 1935–37)) and Connaught Schools (1931–35), before the family moved to Carleton Place in 1937 when Oscar began working at a mill as a cloth inspector. Ross enrolled in CPHS, studied for four years and earned his junior matriculation. In July 1941, he "entered the service" of the local branch of the Bank of Nova Scotia as a junior clerk, was transferred to Avonmore that fall, and Martintown, near Cornwall, the following spring. In June 1942, he found that the reading and "close work" at the bank were bothering his eyes, so his doctor prescribed reading glasses.

On October 29, 1942, Ross presented himself to the air force recruiting officer in Ottawa, who summarized: "Applicant seems to be alert, well set up and keen to fly. Suitable material air crew. Anxious to be pilot." Ross was then told to go home and wait for a call for basic training, which came on November 19. Ross was enrolled in the rank of aircraftsman second class and given a train ticket for Montreal and Lachine, Quebec, where he spent the next weeks at No. 5 Manning Depot taking basic training. As February 1942 recorded the coldest temperatures in years (-40°F), most of the training that normally was held outdoors was re-scheduled inside.

At the end of basic, Ross went home on leave, and in March 1943, visited CPHS and his friends who were still in school. On April 21, he went to Toronto to take six weeks pre-aircrew training as the aircrew selection board had determined that he needed to improve his knowledge of science and skills in mathematics. Normally a junior matriculation was sufficient, but in 1942, the air force elected to use educational achievement tests rather than rely on formal education records. Ross achieved marks of 68% in English, 74% in science, and 87% in mathematics, and after completing the course on July 1, 1943, he was kept in Toronto to attend No. 1 ITS.

Before attending ITS, however, Ross underwent an aircrew medial examination. On June 24, the medical officer found an eighteen-year-old man of fair development, standing 5' 6½" tall, weighing 127 pounds. He was a good-looking young fellow with a fair complexion, blue eyes, and auburn hair. He had a scar on the back of his left thigh, a visible mole before his right ear, and a brown birthmark in the centre of his back. He was classified fit for aircrew with a category of A1B A3B. The medical officer's review stated that Ross was, "Physically fit. Athletic build. Intelligent and alert.

Ross as an RCAF recuit.

Aggressive type. Seems quite capable. Good morale. Wants pilot. Good aircrew material."

Ross attended ITS Course No. 82 from June 27 to September 4, 1943. He worked very hard and was found to be, "A pleasant and keen airman who is self-confident and aggressive." Ross was selected to train as an air bomber, and his second choice, air gunner, was duly noted in his records. With successful completion of this course came a promotion to leading aircraftsman.

Ross's next posting was to Jarvis, Ontario, for Course No. 94 at No. 1 B&G School. By this time Jarvis was a base of some 1,400 people, with a ratio of one staff member for every six students. From November 1, 1943, to January 28, 1944, Ross trained as an air gunner, and at the end of the gunnery phase of his training, Ross had flown nineteen hours and fifty-five minutes on bombing exercises and eleven hours and fifteen minutes as a gunner, all daytime and all on Bolingbroke aircraft. He also got in seven hours night flying in the Anson. He was assessed as "Overconfident, but very clever."

While Ross was home on Christmas leave, the Service Police picked him up at the corner of Dalhousie and Rideau Streets in Ottawa. A report went to his commander that, on December 30, 1943, he was improperly dressed on the street. He was wearing a white shirt instead of his blue service shirt. His defence: "All his issue shirts were being laundered while he was home on leave." After receiving a lecture in the Commanding Officer's office, he was dismissed back to duty.

The Commanding Officer's office was not far from Wallis House, where Elsie M. Shold a WREN with the Women's Royal Canadian Naval Service worked. Ross and Elsie had dated for a few months and were now engaged. He amended his records to list her as his secondary next of kin.

From January 31 to March 10, 1944, Ross concentrated on air-bomber training at No. 4 AOS in London, Ontario. For these twelve weeks, he flew out over Lake Erie to bomb targets mounted on rafts a mile offshore. His performance was considered, "easy going-somewhat overconfident." As an air bomber, he flew twenty-three hours and fifty minutes daytime and twenty hours and fifty minutes at night in the Anson. At the end of this course, Ross was qualified to wear the air-bomber badge and sergeant chevrons. But instead, he was discharged from the RCAF as an airman and commissioned into the service with the rank of pilot officer. As an officer and an air bomber, he was sent directly to an operational posting.

Pilot Officer Stanzel wearing his officer's uniform and his new Bombaimer wings. (NAC– C148179)

On April 29, Ross embarked from Canada, landed in England on May 7, and headed to No. 3 PRC before proceeded to No. 10 Advanced Flying Unit on July 18. His initial wartime training included flying thirty-five hours and twenty minutes daytime and fourteen hours nighttime on the Anson, an aircraft he thought he had left behind in Canada.

On August 22, he was posted to No. 19 OTU in Kinloss, Scotland, with the assessment that he was, "Self-centred and over-confident, understands his work but is inclined to be careless, by exercising a little more care he can become a valuable member."

Ross was crewed up at No. 19 OTU with Canadians Flight Lieutenant C. R. Mills (pilot and captain); Flying Officer L. A. MacDonald (navigator); Flight Sergeant J. H. Wilson (mid-upper gunner); and Sergeant C. J. A. Caryi (rear gunner). Rounding out the crew were two RAF airmen, Sergeant J. J. O. Heady (second pilot/engineer), and Sergeant W. H. Wicks (waist gunner). They were on Course No. 96, which ended on October 30. Ross's course report read: "Bombing results slightly above average with no particular tendency shown. Ground knowledge quite sound and navigational air work good." The crew flew fifty-one hours daytime and thirty-one hours forty-five minutes nighttime on operational exercises testing the proficiency of each crewmember.

Ross's crew was posted to 71 Base for flying duties on November 17. About three weeks later, Elsie received her overseas posting and, on December 8, reported for duty in Greenock, Scotland, to HMCS *Niobe*. Ross was promoted to flying officer, and on January 30, 1945, the crew was posted for operational duties with No. 153 Squadron.

After flying night coastal patrols from Northern Ireland, Algeria, and southern France, where they covered the Allied landings in August 1944, No. 153 Squadron gave up its Spitfires and Hurricanes and disbanded in Algeria on September 5. Re-formed on October 7, as part of 1 Group, it was equipped with Lancasters and twenty-seven crews from 166 Squadron who flew their first mission that same night. The squadron flew briefly from Kirmington then moved to Scampton, Lincoln, until the end of the war. For the year that it was operational, it carried out attacks on enemy targets as part of the Bomber Command main force. The squadron badge showed a bat (a nocturnal predatory animal indigenous to North Africa to symbolize their night fighting activities) in front of a six-pointed star (taken from the arms of Northern Ireland) and they adopted the motto *Noctividus* (Seeing by Night). They flew 1,042 wartime sorties and lost twenty-two aircraft.

F/O Ross Stanzel (Photo courtesy Mrs. Ruth Thomas)

Their first mission was a raid on Ludwigshafen during the night of February 1–2, 1945. The bombers dropped their loads on the Pathfinders' sky markers causing much property damage, including the railway yards and one of the Rhine road bridges, which was subsequently closed. On the night of February 2–3, Bomber Command carried out its only large raid on this city. Above complete cloud cover, most of the bombing hit the town, but war industries along the Rhine were untouched. On February 3–4, they hit the Prosper benzol plant in Bottrop in an accurate raid that resulted in severe damage.

Kleve was their target on February 7–8; 285 bombers hit the city, but casualties were light since most of the civilian population had been evacuated. Hours later, the British 15th Scottish Division started a successful ground attack, but had to halt due to flooded roads and blockages caused by the bombing. The next night, squadron aircraft flew in the second wave of the attack on Pölitz. Clear weather helped both waves make accurate attacks causing such severe damage to the synthetic oil plant that it was put out of production for the remainder of the war.

The Air Ministry devised Operation Thunderclap, a series of raids on Dresden that it hoped would cause the war machine and the civil administration to break down. Dresden was a vital communications centre and supply depot for the Eastern Front, packed with German refugees and the wounded from areas captured by the advancing Russians. The campaign should have begun with an American raid on February 13, but bad weather over Europe prevented any flying. It fell then to Bomber Command to carry out the initial attack that night.

In the raid's second wave, three hours following the first wave, 529 Lancasters of 1, 3, 6 and 8 Groups dropped more than 1,800 tons of bombs with great accuracy. A firestorm developed and large areas of the city were burnt out. No accurate numbers have been tallied, but it is accepted that more people were lost in Dresden than the 40,000 killed in Hamburg. It is assumed that the number exceeded 50,000. Bomber Command lost six Lancasters plus two more that crashed in France and one on return to England.

The next night, Mills and his crew took off at 2005 hours from Scrampton, one of nine Lancasters from the squadron sent to Chemnitz, and one of the 499 Lancasters and 218 Wellingtons that flew in two phases, three hours apart. Cloud covered the targeted area, so most bombs fell in open country, although many hit parts of the city. Flak was rated as slight to moderate in barrage augmented by moderate fighter activity; however, eight Lancasters and five Halifaxes were still lost, including Lancaster I, serial number NN 803, taking Ross down with it.

Ross had flown 280 hours, 40 minutes with 153 Squadron and was rated, "A reliable air bomber and member of aircrew." Following the crew's disappearance Wing Commander F. S. Powley wrote to Mrs. Stanzel:

> Although your son was a comparatively new member of the Squadron, he had already proved himself to be a keen and efficient Air Bomber, and I had every confidence in his courage and ability. The loss of such a man as he is always keenly felt, and he will be missed by all.

When Ethel responded, she directed that Ross's officer's uniforms, almost never worn, be donated to the Officers' Benevolent Department of the British Legion. A condolence card from the Minister of Defence arrived by post on February 26, 1945, and a message from the king on December 10. A Memorial Cross was presented to Ross's mother two days later and his ops wings on February 13, 1947. Ross's War Service Gratuity covered 716 days service with 292 overseas[44].

The Berlin Detachment of the Missing Research and Enquiry Service sent Flight Lieutenant C. F. Drysdale to investigate the crash site and determine the disposition of the crew's bodies. On April 14, 1948, he visited the two vil-

[44] Further information about Elsie did not become available to the writer.

lages of Grumbach and Arnsfeld. A four-engine bomber had crashed between Arnsfeld, twenty miles south- southeast of Chemnitz, and Grumbach, two-and-a-half miles from Arnsfeld, at about 2300 hours on the night of February 24, 1945. Drysdale found the graves of Flight Lieutenant Wilson, middle-upper gunner, and Sergeant Caryi, rear gunner, in the Grumbach cemetery. Wilson had been picked up the morning following the crash and Caryi a few days later. In the Arnsfeld cemetery he found the graves of Flying Officer MacDonald, navigator, and two other unidentified bodies. Extensive search in the two villages and surrounding district revealed no further graves. Those found

Ross wearing battledress at Scampton early in 1945. (Photo Ruth Thomas)

accounted for five, assuming the two unidentified were of this crew, of the seven crewmembers. The investigator suggested that the two missing be accepted as having perished in the crash and their bodies were never found.

In Drysdale's presence, Captain Fitzgerald of the Graves Registry Unit exhumed the graves. In Arnsfeld two bodies had remnants of RCAF battledress on them and the third had an RAF officer's battledress shirt. In Grumbach, one grave had Canadian battledress and in the second was a shirt collar with Sergeant Caryi's service number stencilled on it. From the evidence available, Drysdale identified the RAF officer's body at Arnsfeld as that of Flying Officer MacDonald; one remained totally unknown and the third was identified only as a, "25 year old Canadian student from Montreal." The graves at Grumbach contained Flight Sergeant Wilson and Sergeant Caryi.

Local villagers also insisted that the police had taken a badly injured member of this crew to Mildenau, and the records there show that the injured British flyer, name unknown to anyone in the district, had been taken away by military ambulance to an unknown destination. Drysdale concluded that one of the crew may have completely disappeared in the explosion and that any further investigation for the one badly injured who had been taken away could not be done without approval by the Russian authorities in whose zone the site now lay.

The three identified and the two unidentified bodies were re-interred in individual graves in the British Military Cemetery, Heerstrasse, Berlin. Wing Commander W. R. Gunn of RCAF headquarters in Ottawa explained the investigation results in a letter to Ethel Stanzel on May 4, 1949:

> There are, therefore, four members of the crew who do not
> have 'known' graves—your son; Flight Lieutenant C. R.

Mills (Pilot); Sergeant J. J. O. Heady, R.A.F. (Second Pilot); and Sergeant W. F. Wicks, R.A.F. (Wireless Operator), and their names will be commemorated on a general memorial which will be erected in England by the Imperial War Graves Commission (of which Canada is a member). Four of these general memorials will be erected in different parts of the world, for due to the extreme hazards which attended air operations, there are, like your son, many thousands of aircrew boys who do not have a 'Known' grave.

I realize that this is an extremely distressing letter, and that there is no manner of conveying such news to you which would not add to your heartaches, and I am fully aware that nothing I may say will lessen your great sorrow, but I would like to take this opportunity of expressing to you and the members of your family my deepest sympathy in the loss of your gallant son.

Ethel, by this time, had returned to Chapel Street in Ottawa.

Ross Samuel Stanzel's name is engraved on Panel 280 of the Runnymede Memorial in Surrey. It is situated in Cooper's Hill at Englefield Green overlooking the River Thames running between Windsor and Egham.

They flew by day and night

And gave their lives to keep forever bright

That precious light

Freedom

Air Force Memorial inscription

R 274514 Flight Sergeant William Cyril Jeffrey Reynolds
Air Gunner
Royal Canadian Air Force

Durnbach War Cemetery, located sixteen kilometres east of Bad Tolz, a town forty-eight kilometres south of Munich, holds the bodies of three Carleton Place airmen: Air Gunner Russell James, Air Bomber Lloyd Scott, and Flight Sergeant William Reynolds.

Billy Reynolds was born to Thomas John Reynolds and Margaret Pearl McDougall in Carleton Place on January 22, 1925. His father had been born in England and his mother in Almonte. Although Billy listed his religious affiliation as United Church, his father was a member of, and was sometimes employed by, the Salvation Army. His primary occupation, however, was with the Findlay Foundry, until he moved to Toronto around 1940. Billy's mother died at age forty, leaving sons James Gordon, Thomas Arthur and William Cyril, and daughters Dorothy Irene, Laura Isobel, and Mary Elizabeth.

Billy quit school in 1938 after passing Grade 8 at Carleton Place Public School, and at age fifteen, he went to work as a farm hand for Mr. H. McArton. He stayed on the farm for a little over three years, then worked as a delivery boy for Dan Cameron's butcher shop. In April 1943, he began work as a wool-washer in the Bates and Innes mill, and less than six months later, he appeared at the Ottawa recruiting centre for the RCAF. At eighteen years of age, he very much wanted to be an aviator.

Bill's two brothers were already in the army and overseas in England. One drove ambulances in 23rd Field Ambulance and the other was in the Royal Canadian Corps of Signals.

At his pre-enlistment medical examination, Bill's aspirations to be a pilot were rudely dashed. Standing 5' 2½" tall and weighing 104 pounds, his leg length of 37½" was too short to reach the rudders in most aircraft. However, none of the other jobs in an aircraft had such physical requirements, and pre-war medical standards had been relaxed somewhat to allow for greater aircrew enrolment. Bill was athletic, a keen skater and swimmer, enjoyed playing softball, drank no alcohol and smoked fifteen cigarettes a day. He also knew how to drive. But there was still one remaining hurdle to becoming aircrew. He had only a Grade 8 education and aircrew required junior matriculation.

The recruiter offered a solution. The air force had made provision to offer pre-aircrew training to suitable applicants who lacked the necessary academic qualifications. Bill passed aptitude and ability-to-learn tests and was offered a spot in the WETP School in Truro, Nova Scotia. Under WETP, Bill agreed to enlist for aircrew duties, be enrolled in the service with appropriate pay and allowances, and attend school to bring him up to the desired academic standard. But first he had to get through basic training to establish his suitability to be an airman.

Bill went to No. 5 Manning Depot at Lachine, Quebec, and just at the end of his course, he suffered a minor infection and was hospitalized on October 29. He went home on sick leave from November 3 to 8, which gave him a few extra days in Carleton Place before reporting to Brantford, Ontario, for guard duties.

For two weeks, Bill stood guard at No. 5 SFTS, for which he received $40 a month (most under-training aircrews sent $20 home to mom). Not that he posed much of a threat to any intruder. Most rifles issued to these interim guards had no firing pins, so could not accommodate ammunition. On November 22, he was posted for administrative purposes to Debert, Nova Scotia, but in fact he went to Truro to the WETP School and enrolled in Course No. 29 from November 23 to December 23, 1943. He passed and was accepted into aircrew training as an air gunner.

After Christmas leave at home, Bill travelled by train to Prince Edward Island to attend No. 10 B&G School at the Mount Pleasant BCATP airfield, which had been built on a low stretch of flat land about half way between Summerside and Tignish.

Travelling by train for three or four days in wartime was anything but luxurious. The airmen travelled the entire distance sitting up. They had been issued food chits, but the selection in the dining cars was Spartan at best. A highlight of the trip was crossing the Northumberland Strait on the ferry, *MV Abegweit*. The sinking of the Newfoundland ferry *SS Caribou*, forty miles off Port aux Basques on October 14, 1942, had brought the war home to Canada and put East Coast ferry crossings on a wartime footing. A night crossing occurred under blackout conditions; no one was allowed outside, least of all for a smoke. Daytime however could be quite pleasant as inlanders found a stroll on deck to be very entertaining.

Bill began his air gunner training on Course No. 74, starting on January 17, 1944. He began to learn the art of air-to-air firing, especially deflection shooting, aircraft recognition, navigation, Morse code using the Aldis lamp, and the complexities of turrets and guns. In order to train for night operations, he also had to learn how to strip and reassemble his Browning .303 machine guns while blindfolded and to clear stoppages with his gloves on and in very little light. There are many parts to a Browning .303, a great many of them extremely small. Scrambling on the metal floor of a bouncing aircraft in the dark while searching for a tiny spring is no fun. But being attacked by a night fighter when the guns were inoperable would not be pleasant either.

After a couple of weeks, Course No. 74 was suspended and all students were recoursed to Course No. 75. Shortly afterward, on March 13, Bill was promoted to leading aircraftsman.

At Mount Pleasant, they began training on the Bolingbroke aircraft, which had enclosed turrets, a tremendous advantage for gunners. Winter on the East Coast was not as cold as at some of the western stations, but it sure was wet and snowy! The snow accumulated half way up the telephone poles along the roads, and it was always a struggle to keep the runways clear enough for landings and take-offs. Prince Edward Island is always blessed with a good breeze, so snow does not fall straight down, and the young airmen learned to walk leaning into the wind as they made their way from barracks to mess halls to hangars, an exhausting proposition when carrying flying gear, parachutes, and ammunition panniers.

While at No. 10 B&G School, Bill flew a total of twenty-three hours and fifty-five minutes on the Bolingbroke.

As the snow melted and drained into the Gulf of St. Lawrence, flying over the Island was especially scenic. The fields shone a dull red bordered by a bright blue sea, and as the season progressed, the potato fields appeared, heaped row upon heaped row, their white flowers resembled a chenille quilt set in a particularly pretty shade of green. Then the roads turned rusty red with a red dust settling over everything. The airfield was somewhat isolated but a stake-truckload of airmen would motor to Summerside each weekend for day trips. The only attraction was a movie theatre, a dance hall, and the bootleggers.

Bill and his classmates completed their gunnery course on April 21 and proudly sewed the air gunner's badge over their left breast pocket and sergeant's chevrons to their sleeves before going off to AGTS in Valleyfield, Quebec, and overseas. Bill, like the oth-

Bill Reynolds wearing his new sergeant's chevrons and AG wings. (NAC photo C148180)

ers, returned home between April 21 and May 6 for embarkation leave as there would be no time after their course. The advanced course ran from May 6 to June 3, and Bill's instructors recorded that, "He had some difficulty in making course, should make a good AG though as he has worked hard." He was posted to 1 "Y" Depot in Lachine on June 4 and embarked from Montreal on June 15. The ship landed in Gauroch, Scotland, on June 24 and he reported in to No. 3 PRC at Bournemouth on June 25.

Three weeks later, on July 18, Sergeant William Reynolds, Air Gunner, reported to RAF Station Finningley to take his OTU instruction on Wellingtons. He was assigned to crew 332 on Course No. 33, and they were given a couple of weeks together before they started their operational flying training. The crew was made up of all RAF fliers except Bill Reynolds: Flying Officer Kevin P. Muncer, captain and pilot; Sergeant Victor Jones, flight engineer; Flight Sergeant James Patterson, air bomber; Flying Officer W. H. Gerrard, navigator; Flying Officer R. G. Buckland, wireless operator; Flying Officer JohannVincent Gardner, mid-upper gunner; and Sergeant William Cyril Jeffrey Reynolds (RCAF), rear gunner.

By the time they got to No. 18 OTU, all crew members were glad to see the "real" bomber, the Wellington III's and X's, which were still being used on many raids to Europe. Their geodetic construction left a fuselage of nice lines. Its twin engines were powerful, and even sitting on the tarmac, the aircraft looked fast and lethal. The training aircraft only had one turret, and fortunately for Bill, it was in the tail. While it was "his" turret, the gunners took turns riding in it.

The crew still went to classes every day, and each morning at ten o'clock, the NAAFI[45] truck came by to sell tea and cakes to the students. As their training progressed, the advanced crews flew missions to create dummy bomber streams, and their night cross-country exercises were made realistic by having night fighters "bounce" them so as to demonstrate their vulnerability if they were less than vigilant. The Wellingtons approached a target from a different angle than the attacking bombers, spewing out Window as fast as they could to confuse German radar operators. A training crew always made at least one specific trip, the "nickle" operation, dropping propaganda leaflets over the target. It introduced the crews to the hazards of flak and night fighters.

The course ended on October 12, 1944, during which the crew had flown fifty hours and five minutes daytime and thirty-two hours and fifty-five minutes nighttime. Bill's assessment described him as an, "Average air gunner. Made a poor start and required much supervision." However, he was allowed

[45] The Navy, Army and Air Force Institute ran various teashops, fixed and in mobile vans, and commissaries to sell the troops notions, snacks and toiletries. Each base, station and dockyard had their NAAFI stores. It was a private enterprise.

Wellington under fire. (. . . of Men And Planes, Vol III, p. 78)

to proceed to squadron, No. 166 RAF Squadron with his crew, but first they had to convert to the Lancaster, which they did, from October 28 to December 12, flying from No. 11 Base.

166 Squadron was located at RAF Station Kirmington on No. 13 Base near Elsham Wolds. The aerodrome was built on farm-land in 1942, close to the tiny village of Kirmington. It was a collection of small wooden huts and hangars scattered amongst clumps of trees. There was mud everywhere, and cutting winds made it piercingly cold under grey, drizzly skies.

The station was typically isolated and the only ground transportation available to most aircrew was the ever-reliable bicycle. Bill bought a Raleigh three-speed bike to travel to and from the village where there was a pub. Bicycles were considered vehicles, and after dark had to have "properly trimmed lamps" according to the *Transport Lighting Act* of 1927. However, batteries were few and far between, due to wartime shortages, and many bikes went without. Most aircrew could see in the dark like cats, there was little traffic on the roads, and in the summer, Britain had double-wartime-daylight-saving time so it did not get dark until about eleven p.m.

During the war, when threat of German invasion was very real, all road signs were taken down. Commonwealth servicemen often didn't know where they were, but it didn't stop their sense of adventure, exploring the nearby towns and villages. When it came time to return to barracks, explicit instructions were required and some Canadians were quite surprise to discover how far afield they had travelled.

No. 166 Squadron was formed on January 27, 1943, as a night-bomber squadron in 1 Group. It flew Wellington III's and X's until September 1943 when the squadron converted to Lancaster I's and III's. Its motto was "Tenacity," and its badge showed a bulldog affrontée (full face on). Its Lancasters flew 4,279 sorties, on 20 bombing, and 13 minelaying missions, with 114 losses.

Bill's crew flew their first mission against Bonn on the night of December 21–22, 1944. Thick cloud cover thwarted the intended attack on railway areas and the target was not hit and no aircraft were lost. The next night, they were airborne again aiming for the Mosel railway yards at Koblenz. Again clouds affected the bombing accuracy. The main weight of the raid fell two to four kilometres west on the villages of Güls and Rübenach, and some bombs fell on the rail yards, several main lines, and at least two important road bridges. Again no bombers were lost.

A Lancaster III painted in 166 Squadron colours.

On Christmas Eve, 1944, the crew flew to Cologne-Nippes where they made an extremely accurate attack on the Oboe marking by Pathfinders. Railway tracks were severely damaged and an ammunition train was blown up at a cost of five Lancasters. Railway yards were their main target for the rest of December, on the 27th they attacked Rheydt in a daylight raid and on the night of December 28–29, they were over Mönchengladbach. The next night, the squadron flew to Scholven-Buer and caused severe damage to the oil refinery, piping, and storage tanks. On New Year's Eve they were back to bombing railway yards, this time at Osterfeld with disappointing results; only thirty-five per cent of the sidings were hit and twenty per cent of the buildings.

In 1945 Bomber Command took a different tack. As Allied armies moved northwest, it flew more raids in support of the land forces and to cripple transportation, oil, and supply line targets. The Ardennes area was stabilized by the end of January, but it was not until late March that Allied soldiers crossed the Rhine in strength. No. 1 Group maintained its night operations with all squadrons, and its crews flew against the city of Nuremberg (January 2–3), the German garrison at Royan (January 4–5), the city of Hanover (January 5–6), the railway systems at Hanau and Neuss (January 6–7), and the last major raid on Munich's industrial area (January 7–8).

Bill's squadron was given a week's rest from January 7 to 14, then their targets were changed to the synthetic oil plants in Leuna (January 14–15), Zeitz near Leipzig and Brüx in western Czechoslovakia (January 16–17), Duisburg (January 22–23), and the Stuttgart area (January 28–29), where the first wave also hit the railway yards at Kornwestheim and the second hit the Hirth aero-engine factory in the suburb of Zuffenhausen. This was the last large RAF raid on Stuttgart; the city had endured fifty-three major attacks. One Wehrmacht flak lieutenant, at a battery in Vaihingen, thought all the bombs falling around his position meant that they were the primary target. Ignoring regulations about conserving ammunition, he fired his entire stock at the radar echoes of approaching bombers. To his relief, two Lancasters and a Halifax crashed near him, for otherwise he would have been court-martialled for such a prodigious use of ammunition.

Most of Bomber Command's targets were now well into German territory. Resistance on the ground was beginning to crumble, but air defences remained fairly strong. Night-fighters continued to fly in droves, but the weather, especially cloud cover, reduced the bombers' accuracy significantly and the ever-present flak never lessened.

The only way to defend against anti-aircraft fire was to fly a sloppy corkscrew that the German gunners could not follow. A conventional corkscrew consisted of the following: turn 30° off course, dive 500 feet, turn 30° in the opposite direction and climb 500 feet. However, this only guaranteed that at the end of the manoeuvre, only about ten 88mm shells would be waiting. Kevin Muncer, Bill's pilot, was often obliged to throw their bomber through this aerobatic exercise for miles until they were out of range. The rest of the crew could only hold on and hope for the best. Bomber operations were physically and psychologically draining on each member of the crew. They really were in it as a crew together, alone, even though there were hundreds of other aircraft in the surrounding sky.

Many photographs of bomber crews show young, smiling faces, but all were taken *before* the crew went flying, none afterwards. After six to ten gut-wrenching hours in the cramped fuselage, few resembled in any way the Brylcreem-ad figures on recruiting posters. Sweating in a snug leather flying helmet left everyone's hair plastered like wet fur to his head and an imprint etched across the forehead and around the ears, matched only by the mark left by the oxygen mask around thinly bearded faces and noses. Bleary eyes peered through a wreath of cigarette smoke and their shoulders sagged from weariness and tension, while the stench of sweat, smoke, oil, aviation gasoline, vomit, and urine leaked through the many layers of protective clothing. Most also suffered a tremendous buzzing roar in their ears for hours after a flight due to the incredible noise produced by the four unmuffled engines.

Even in level flight, every piece of equipment rattled so as to make one believe the whole was just a bunch of spare parts flying in formation. Wrung out like old wash rags, these boys got enough adventure in a single flight to last a lifetime.

February found the bombers searching for great German cities. Area bombing was carried out in good and not-so-good weather and on some targets of little industrial significance. No. 1 Group was sent to the railway yards and Rhine road bridges of Ludwigshafen (February 1–2), the only large raid of the war on Wiesbaden (February 2–3), the town of Bottrop (February 3–4), Kleve, a few hours before the 15th Scottish Division advance (February 7–8), Pölitz' important synthetic oil plant causing a tremendous setback to the war effort (February 8–9) and then Dresden.

Operation Thunderclap was planned as a series of heavy area raids to be implemented when the German military situation appeared critical. The night of February 13–14 was the chosen time. The Russians had raced across Poland and crossed the eastern German frontier, forcing the Germans to fight hard inside their own country on two fronts. The Russians wanted raids to assist their ground troops, and Dresden, Berlin, Leipzig, and Chemnitz were chosen as suitable targets.

No. 1 Group flew to Dresden in the second wave of 529 Lancasters, dropping more than 1,800 tons of bombs with great accuracy in clear weather. A firestorm, similar to that of Hamburg in July 1943, levelled large areas of the city, and 311 American B-17s dropped 771 tons of bombs the next day, principally on the railway yards. But the RAF night raids caused the most serious damage. Bomber Command lost six Lancasters one night, one of them carrying Ross Stanzel.

Dresden burned, and was a beacon for bomber crews for several days afterwards. Many aircraft had carried only magnesium incendiary bombs, hexagon-shaped pieces of metal eighteen inches long and three inches across, packed in containers made of strap steel with a set of fins on the tail. When dropped, they spun and then the container broke apart at a predetermined height, spraying bombs all over the target area. As each hit the ground the explosion looked like a diamond glittering in the velvet night.

After a week out of the line, No. 1 Group returned to bomb the industrial southern half of Dortmund (Feburary 20–21), the last major raid on Duisberg (February 21–22) and then to Pforzheim (February 23–24); 367 Lancasters dropped 1,825 tons of bombs from 8,000 feet in 22 minutes. The city was completely engulfed in fire and more than 17,000 met their death, making it the third heaviest air-raid death toll after Hamburg and Dresden. A South African flying with the RAF won Bomber Command's last Victoria Cross this night.

With twenty-five missions under their belt, Bill Jeffrey's crew began looking forward to the end of their tour. Then the Air Ministry, in its wisdom, decided that since resistance was weakening, a tour of operations would depend upon the accumulation of points as determined by some staff officer's estimation of the complexity and danger of flying to certain targets. No one took into consideration that as the Germans retreated, they could concentrate their air defences. Some aircraft returned to base with such flak damage it was a miracle they made the trip. Unfit for future flights, they were cannibalized for parts. Aircrew luck was being pressed to its limits.

The air gunners, from their domes at various positions in the machine, were the aircraft's eyes. Under normal nighttime conditions (starlight and no moon), the gunner could identify an aircraft at about 300 yards; with moonlight the range was greatly extended. It was not unusual for a gunner to identify fighter aircraft one kilometre away.

Inside a bomber stream, there were heavy Lancasters and Wellingtons all around them, But there was no sense in worrying about a collision. Crews could only hope that if they collided they would blow up and be killed instantly. After the bomb drop was the most perilous time, when they turned sharply 90° to leave the area. Thus they were flying directly across the path of other incoming attackers, often hidden in the cloud. When the aircraft started to suddenly bounce they knew they had just flown through the slipstream of another bomber. There would be no other clue.

Air gunners were expressly forbidden to load or clear their guns on take-off or landing, as the aircraft usually bounced on the runway, as did the air gunners (they were not strapped in). So, the chances of a stray round whistling across the flight line were not to be ignored. The gunners had to load their guns by pulling the breechblock back with the cocking toggle so that one round would be on the face of the block. The guns were recoil-operated and always had a round on the face until all ammunition was expended or until the gunner removed the round. This all had to be done in a safe area once airborne or, once the Luftwaffe was cleared from British skies, on crossing the coast on return.

No. 1 Group carried out two raids: Mannheim on March 1 and Cologne on March 2. Mannheim, and nearby Ludwigshafen, received considerable damage but the efficient German record-keeping was starting to break down and no specific reports survived. On March 2 there were two raids on Cologne. No. 1 Group was in the first wave of 703 aircraft, which scattered a carpet of bombs across the main part of the city on the west bank of the Rhine. The air raid warning sirens started only two minutes before the attack so many people were caught in the high explosive hail. This was the last RAF raid on Cologne; American troops captured the city four days later.

What set these two raids apart for Bill and his squadron mates was that they were daylight attacks. For the first time they could see what was going on. As they neared the rendezvous point, usually over Reading, they could see bombers rising from all over England heading for continental Europe. On night raids the feeling of loneliness was intense, but in daytime, crews had a real sense of being part of a united front. The Americans flew in formation with one navigator per squadron while the RAF flew in a loose stream, each aircraft operating self-sufficiently. Flying straight and level on the bomb run in formation gave the German gunners a much better target than a group of bombers stooging all over the sky.

After a week off the operation's list, No. 1 Group returned to night flying. Its first devastating raid was on another new target, the residential, industrial, and railway areas of Dessau, deep in eastern Germany (March 7–8). The next night was the first large raid on Kassel since October 1943, then two more daylight attacks followed, both returning to the Ruhr. March 11 was the last RAF raid on Essen when 4,661 tons of bombs were dropped by 1,079 aircraft, paralysing the ruined city until American troops entered some time later. Three Lancasters were lost. On March 12 a record number of bombers, 1,108, dropped a record tonnage of bombs, 4,851, on the hapless city of Dortmund. In this final raid, production was halted so effectively that it would be many months before any recovery could occur. Two Lancasters were lost. Clearly the RAF and the USAAF owned the air space night and day and ground defences were losing heart.

On the night of March 13–14, No. 1 Group attacked benzol plants at Herne and Gelsenkirchen. The raid was successful and only one Lancaster did not return. The Deurag refinery at Misburg, on the outskirts of Hanover was the target on March 15-16, and the main bomb load was dropped south of the target. Four Lancasters were lost.

At about 1930 hours on March 16, Flying Officer Muncer urged Lancaster I, number PA 234, off the runway at Kirmington. Upon reaching altitude at the rendezvous point, navigator Gerrard passed the heading for Nuremberg and they joined 231 other No. 1 Group Lancasters for the last heavy raid on the city.

At 2130 hours, a four-engine British bomber crashed into a field about ten kilometres north of Nuremberg, and two parachutes fluttered through the dark nearby. Dangling from the risers of one was the unhurt navigator, Flying Officer W. H. Gerrard, and from the other was the pilot, Flying Officer Kevin P. Muncer, whose left arm hung useless, torn, shattered by plexiglas when he had exited the cockpit window and barely attached to his shoulder. They were the only two of the crew to escape.

A French prisoner of war, M. Leon Planade, and a friend working in an agricultural camp in the village of Winsdorf, Kreis Forth, Regierung, saw the airplane and the parachutes land. They hurried to the drop spot where Planade's friend gave what first aid he could to Muncer. German soldiers were right behind them, and they took custody of the navigator and sent the pilot to hospital at Brucksburg. The Germans also removed four bodies from the wreckage and took them to the somewhat larger village of Gross-Haberdorf, where they turned them over to the village priest, Father Remohard, and a civilian villager, M. Georges Meyer. Gerrard saw the men and was able to identify the body of rear gunner Sergeant Bill Reynolds.

The crash site was one kilometre northwest of the village of Buerglein. Villagers reported that they witnessed the airplane circling the village in flames before it came down.

The bodies of the four fliers were not searched for personal effects and their identification tags were buried with them in the Gross-Habersdorf cemetery. The bodies were lowered into graves on March 19 and wooden crosses were raised with the following names:

PATERSON. JAMES.	1682300
SGT JONES. VICTOR.	1045917
GARDNER. JOHANN VINCENT.	172025
REYNOLDS. W.G. I.	374514

A day earlier, the body of another British airman was found in a field one-and-a-half kilometres south of the neighbouring village of Buerglein. Policemen from Heilbronn brought the body to the village cemetery and handed it over to the gravedigger, Herrn Holbeck. The policemen reported that the body wore the uniform of an English officer, was very tall and had blond hair. They removed all papers from the corpse, but found nothing to positively identify it. Everything was handed over to the Luftwaffe at Katterbach where it was eventually destroyed. The body was found two kilometres from the crash site and on the line of flight of the aircraft. No other bodies or graves were later found by investigators so it is assumed that the last body was that of the wireless operator, Flying Officer R. G. Buckland. Herrn Holbeck buried him on March 20.

A Missing and Recovery Unit investigation was completed in December 1946 after the pilot, Muncer, wrote to the Casualty Branch requesting an investigation into the disposition of his crews' remains. Muncer had been in touch with the Frenchman, Planade, who had found the pilot's watch in a field two days after the crash. It was engraved with Muncer's name and number, which led contact between the two men. Muncer wrote to the

Ministry in January 1946 while he was on indefinite leave from the RAF awaiting an artificial left arm. At the time his five crewmembers were only listed as missing. Bill Reynolds body was eventually exhumed and re-buried in the Durnbach war cemetery at Bad Tolz, Bavaria, 48 km. south of Munich.

PART SIX—ACROSS THE CHANNEL

CHAPTER TWENTY-THREE—WAITING AND WATCHING

r.mullan@sympatico.ca

The boys of summer 1939 were fit young men, most of them athletes, whose fathers had fought in the "War to end all Wars!" Most couldn't have been less concerned about the goings on in Europe that was soon to envelop them in clouds of destruction and death. Those who survived are now, six decades later, in their late seventies. They gather in Legion halls, at regimental, ship and squadron reunions to recall "their" war and those who did not come home. Many years have passed, but still their wounds, physical and mental, hurt. But the greatest hurt of all is that so few Canadians remember those deeds of valour from so long ago.

In September 1939, 58,337 Canadian men and women enlisted into the Active Service Force, and serious difficulties arose due to shortages of such basics as clothing, boots, and blankets. The government informed Canada House in London, on September 16, that it was considering sending one division overseas. The British government warmly received this news. All persons already serving in the Active Force were re-attested to ensure that there was no doubt in their minds that they had enlisted voluntarily and in so doing had accepted the obligation of general service at home or abroad for the duration of the war. Supply of modern equipment in England was a limiting factor in the departure of the division. The War Office assured Canadian authorities that the Division would not be sent to the front with any less a scale of equipment than that being issued to the English Territorial formations.

Early in December, from bases all across Canada, troops boarded trains bound for Halifax. However, instead of the First Division going overseas in one great convoy, as was done in 1914, groups of 7,000 to 8,000 men were sent to lessen the risks of transit. The first 7,400 all-ranks sailed in convoy TC-1 at noon on December 10 aboard five ships: the *Aquitania*, the *Duchess of Bedford*, the *Empress of Britain*, the *Empress of Australia*, and the *Monarch of Bermuda*. The Halifax docks, streets, and bridges were crowded with well-wishers waving hats and handkerchiefs in farewell, while horns and sirens echoed across the harbour. The liners were still fitted out for peacetime, and the soldiers travelled in comfort unknown in later convoys. In subsequent years, stripped liners would frequently carry as many men in one ship as was carried by all five in this first sailing.

The Royal Navy provided an impressive escort: the battle cruiser *Repulse*, the battleship *Resolution*, the cruiser *Emerald*, and the aircraft carrier *Furious*. For the first part of the voyage, six destroyers, four of which were Royal Canadian Navy (HMCS *Fraser*, *Ottawa*, *Restigouche*, and *St. Laurent*), led the ships out of Bedford Basin into the Halifax approaches, and manning the radios aboard *Fraser* was Ordinary Telegrapher Horace G. Stark of Carleton Place. Aboard one of the liners was Private Fred Dray, RCASC, also of Carleton Place.

P 28106 Corporal Frederick Albert Dray
1st Canadian Parachute Battalion

Fred Dray was born to Archibald J. and Minnie Dray in Goldalming, Surrey, England, on May 28, 1914. He was only twenty-one months old when his father was killed in action on a World War I battlefield in Belgium while serving in the 9th Battalion of the Royal Sussex Regiment. Following her husband's death, Minnie brought her young son to Canada and to Carleton Place, where she married John (Jack) Ryan and settled at 12 Lake Avenue.

John and Minnie had four daughters (Ethel, Doris, Gladys, and Violet) and two sons (John and Ronald). The family was Roman Catholic, and all of the children received their schooling at Carleton Place public and high schools.

Fred completed Grade 10 at CPHS in 1930 then worked as a textile hand in a local mill. From 1934 to 1938, he apprenticed as a mechanic in Mr. M. J. O'Brien's garage in Carleton Place, and once he received his papers, he stayed on as an automobile mechanic, earning $18.50 a week, a very good salary at the time. Fred also liked to tinker with electricity and electrical motors, play tennis, and bowl. He played forward on the town hockey team and in the field for both the baseball and softball teams. He could produce a very good sound from the harmonica. Fred was fascinated by the military, and on June 27, 1938, he joined the active army; his ambition was to be a professional soldier. At his enlistment medical examination, Fred was found, at age twenty-four, to be 5' 7" tall and 125 pounds. He had a medium com-

LtoR–Fred Ryan, Wilson Costello and Wally Mace circa 1931. (Photo courtesy Wally Mace.)

plexion, blue eyes and light brown hair, and his only visible scar was a linear mark on the back of his left hand. He was found fit for medical category "A," and since he was trades-trained, he was enlisted as a motor mechanic and assigned to the RCASC. He was then sent to Camp Borden for basic and advanced trades training.

While under training, Fred was hospitalized three times, once for acute rhinitis (September 5–7) and once for tonsillitis (September 21–26), and and once for Vincent's angina, a mouth and throat infection not unlike tonsillitis (November 4–9). Then, on September 11, he was "AWL from tattoo. [1]" This absence cost him two days confined to barracks and one day's pay, a common punishment for minor infractions committed by those still in training and not yet completely indoctrinated into army life.

On December 19, Fred was classified as a motor transport driver Class III and assessed as a "(young), willing and good worker. A good MT driver. Intelligent, energetic and trustworthy." He was posted to No. 2 Detachment, RCASC, Toronto, reporting after taking Christmas and New Year's leave at home.

From Toronto, he went to the Army Trades School (ATS) in Hamilton to take further training. In Hamilton, soldier-apprentices learned the trades associated with new mechanized equipment. ATS trained about 1,300 students at a time in courses that lasted from three to five months, depending on the trade. More than 150 trades were taught, including artillery artificer, carpenter, electrician, motor-vehicle fitter, engine artificer, and instrument and wireless technicians.

Canada has never shown much inclination to prepare for war in times of peace. After the Great War, the country's fighting forces were reduced to the insignificant, and in 1939, her army consisted of 4,500 professional soldiers. Then, in 1938–39, the NPAM was re-organized and money was allotted to enhance the training programme. Mobilization plans were made, but the country was far from a state of readiness. Neither the Permanent Force nor

[1] He was away from his cot at bedcheck

the NPAM had any transport and all their arms were from World War I. It wasn't until 1938 that Canada received her first armoured vehicle, two light tanks sent from England. Canada was totally dependent upon British war industries.

As politics heated up in Europe, Canada, called out NPAM units, on August 25, to protect federal property. Service was purely voluntary, and 10,000 men responded[2] On September 1, the Department of National Defence issued a General Order authorizing organization of the Canadian Active Service Force, consisting of two divisions and appropriate ancillary forces. Again, enlistment was entirely voluntary, and nearly all officers and most other ranks came from the Active Militia.

The remaining civilian volunteers were acquired with relative ease. As early as March 1939, Prime Minister Mackenzie King and the Leader of the Opposition, Robert Manion, had committed their political parties to a policy of no conscription for overseas service in the event of a conflict.

Private Fred Dray knew he wanted to stay in the army so he re-attested into the Active Force without hesitation, and on September 19, he was given an Active Service medical examination. He had gained five pounds, and his hair was now described as dark brown. He was assigned category "A" and was kept on strength of the RCASC of the Canadian Army Special Force.

His assessment when he completed training helped him obtain appointment as the personal chauffeur to Major General A. G. L. McNaughton, Commander of the First Overseas Division. Fred was posted to Headquarters, 1st Infantry Brigade, in Toronto, on November 21, and took some leave to tell the news to his family and that he would be going overseas as soon as the First Division sailed. He also visited the paymaster and made an allotment to his mother of $35 per month.

Fred boarded his ship in Halifax on December 8, and it slipped away from the dock at noon on December 10 for an uneventful crossing. On December 16, the convoy rendezvoused with twelve Royal Navy destroyers and the following morning sailed up the River Clyde. "All along the narrow channel," wrote one unit diarist, "the Scots poked their heads out of windows and doors, waved flags and bunting, and shouted a welcome to us.[3]" By noon the convoy reached Greenock. Fred's ship docked at Garish and he disembarked on December 17. The troops were immediately put aboard trains and arrived in Aldershot the next day. The entire First Division was in the United Kingdom by the end of the year.

---

[2] At the height of the Depression a guaranteed paycheck was a great incentive.
[3] Col. C.P. Stacey, The Canadian Army 1939-45 (Ottawa: King's's Printer, 1948) p. 6.

The Canadians were billeted in permanent barracks during the winter of 1939 and spent "the coldest conditions since 1894" in buildings that were not built for such extreme weather. Fred, and most other soldiers, received passes from December 23 to 28 to spend their first Christmas overseas on their own. The English around Aldershot were very hospitable to the young Canadians, but they were too used to having soldiers around to make undue fuss over them. That and a lack of activity caused morale to plummet.

It was estimated that the Canadian troops would require four months of further training in England before they would be considered battle-ready. Most had only completed elementary training and were dreadfully ill equipped. They had personal equipment, rifles and respirators, but no steel helmets. They carried the obsolete Lewis gun, instead of the new Bren gun, and artillery left over from the Great War. It was not until March 1940 that the first vehicles from Canadian factories began to arrive.

Throughout the winter, the division trained vigorously, hampered little by the severe weather and equipment shortages. Meanwhile, the Germans began expanding their aggression. On April 9,1940, they overran Denmark and took a firm grip on Norway. A Canadian assault force left Aldershot on April 18 for the Scottish port of Dunfermline, but by April 26, they were back. The fruitlessness of any frontal attack precluded their use. Then, on the morning of May 10, the Germans "blitzkreiged" two more neutral nations, The Netherlands and Belgium, which crumpled before the German war machine. The British Expeditionary Force (BEF) and the French army fell back before the German army, isolating them in the area around Dunkirk, their last remaining port of escape.

On May 23, Fred drove General McNaughton to Dover where the general boarded a destroyer to Dunkirk. He had been ordered to take command of the remaining forces on the continent and prepare for reinforcements. He was back in England the following night convinced that reinforcements would be to no avail. On May 27, the Belgians sought an armistice and evacuation of the BEF began.

Hitler's personal intervention contributed in no small measure to the BEF's escape. His tanks had overrun the north of France and were prepared to pounce on Dunkirk when he halted them for three days. Nothing else could have saved the British, many of whom were still miles away from the docks. His motives for this order, which ultimately produced his downfall, were never discovered. However, during that week, 338,000 British and Allied troops were withdrawn across the Channel in every conceivable type of vessel. But all their heavy equipment was left behind.

The Germans began to destroy what was left of the French army, and Britain committed herself to sustaining France at all costs. The troops realized the significance of this decision. They were headed for the fields of Europe.

With the 1st Infantry Brigade Group, Fred travelled to Plymouth by rail to cross the Channel, landing at Brest on June 11. Army headquarters had resolved to send two divisions, the 52nd (Lowland) and the 1st Canadian to France immediately. On June 8, George VI and Queen Elizabeth inspected the division under glorious summer skies; however, the main part of the brigade did not disembark until June 14.

The 1st Brigade Group was the only formation to get to France. They were expected to move to an assembly area near Brest, but instead were sent in-country to an area near Laval and Le Mans, about half way between Paris and Brest. Small groups of vehicles moved by road and larger units were placed on trains that carried them rapidly inland. By the night of June 14–15, the Canadian brigade was scattered along the roads between Brest and Le Mans. The 1st Field regiment, RCHA, was billeted in Parcé and three trains carrying the headquarters of the 1st Brigade, together with the 48th Highlanders, the Royal Canadian Regiment (RCR, to which Fred was attached) and the H&PE, were approaching the area.

Early on June 14, the Germans entered Paris. It was obvious that all movement of British troops had to be stopped and those in France turned back for home. The train carrying the Hasty Pees was turned around at Laval and that of the RCR near Châteaubriant. These troops were re-embarked at Brest and arrived at Plymouth on June 17. Fred had transferred to the head-quarters train, which reached its destination at Sablé-sur-Sarthe before receiving the order to return. After some delay, including an argument with the engineer, they headed back to Brest. Men and officers of the 48th rode the engine with two men equipped with Tommy guns on the tender. Every carriage bristled with assorted weapons as the train moved through the French countryside. However, because of a routing mistake, the train ended up at St. Malo instead of Brest. Luckily a British transport was at the dock and it sailed, overloaded with Canadians, for Southampton.

Only six Canadians were left behind: one killed in a motorcycle accident, four interned by the Germans in France (all of whom escaped and made their way back to England), and one who remained a prisoner of war until war's end. Almost all vehicles and equipment were ordered destroyed. The notable exceptions were a station wagon that the Hasty Pees loaded aboard a trawler and the guns of 1 RCHA. Their commander, Lieutenant Colonel J. H. Roberts, in spite of two orders to destroy his guns, managed to get permission to take as many as he could load aboard ship in two hours. He embarked all his own plus a dozen light anti-aircraft guns and a few special vehicles. This became an important cache of weapons for the defence of Britain.

Fred Dray disembarked in Falmouth on June 18, the same day that Winston Churchill delivered a speech to the House of Commons calling upon Britons to stand against the expected fury of Hitler. He concluded:

> Let us therefore brace ourselves to our duties, and so bear
> ourselves that, if the British Empire and its Commonwealth
> last for a thousand years, men will say 'This was their finest
> hour.'[4]

The Canadian force in England was now the strongest formation of a very weak army. By July 2, the division had moved through the Oxford area to the North Downs region of Surrey just south of the city of London. On July 21, the Anglo-Canadian 7th Corps was formed with McNaughton, promoted to lieutenant general, as its commander. He passed command of the 1st Division to Major General G. R. Pearkes, VC, and training emphasis now shifted to prepare for the defence of the Empire on British lands. However, as autumn approached, fears of invasion lessened and the 2nd Division from Canada arrived. The 1st Canadian Corps then replaced the 7th Corps.

At approximately 0900 hours on September 18, Fred was riding a motorcycle that slid out from under him on a turn that took him crashing into the ditch. He was whisked away to No. 5 Canadian General Hospital (CGH) at Brixham, where he was diagnosed with a fractured left clavicle (collar bone) and contusions (severe bruises) on his right leg and ankle and kept until October 11 for treatment and recovery. Fred joined an alarming number of Canadians who wiped themselves out on motorcycles. The frequency of this occurrence caused German officers to speculate, not entirely in jest, that to defeat the Canadians they need only issue a bottle of whiskey and a motorcycle to each man.

Upon release from hospital Fred was transferred, on October 29, from 1 Canadian Brigade to Canadian Military Headquarters in London. But first he went through a Canadian Infantry Holding Unit. These units were established to accommodate and further train reinforcements necessary to replace casualties in the field units.

During the months of June, July and August, 1940, 77,770 Canadians voluntarily enlisted. In May 1940, the Department of Defence began the formation of the 3rd Division. A Veterans Home Guard, later named the Veterans Guard of Canada, was also organized and a large number of Carleton Place men, many of whom had served in the Great War, signed up, as well as fathers or uncles of those who had volunteered for Active Service. Mr. W. R. McIlquham was the commanding officer with Mr. H. D. Gilmour

[4] Ibid. p.18

his second-in-command. In charge of No. 1 Platoon was Mr. G. W. Comba and commanding No. 2 Platoon was Mr. J. S. Stark.

In the summer of 1940, Parliament passed the *National Resources Mobilization Act*, which authorized compulsory military service so long as men were not obliged to serve overseas. (This proviso was removed in 1942, and in 1944, NRMA trainees were sent overseas). At first, men aged twenty-one to forty-five were called for training for thirty days. This was extended to four months, and eventually, it was announced that they would be kept in service indefinitely for home defence.

Meanwhile, Canadian troops reverted to the essential, but undeniably dull regimen of training.

The New Year started well for Fred Dray. On January 9, 1941, he was promoted to acting corporal and qualified as a group "A" fitter. This increased his pay to that of a corporal, $1.70 a day, plus the Class "A" trades pay of an additional 75¢ a day. In addition, he was among those local boys overseas to receive a package from the first shipment of 18,300 cigarettes from the Carleton Place *Canadian* Overseas Cigarette Fund. On April 9, Fred was confirmed in the rank of corporal.

In February and March, the division carried out large-scale exercises to practise marching to an attack and to tackle the difficult task of traffic control on English roads. In June, the Corps took part in manoeuvres based upon a German invasion, then in autumn they participated in a mock war which moved the largest force of soldiers to the field. The Canadians moved into the Chiltern Hills north west of London.

On August 11, Fred was hospitalized again in No. 5 CGH at Taplow for scabies and pyodermatitis, contagious skin infections. He was released on August 23 and returned to Headquarters in London.

In October, the Canadian Corps took on a new function: the direct defence of the Sussex coast. The Corps, with three infantry divisions and an army tank brigade, a very formidable military force, was now concentrated in Sussex. The troops were put to work reconstructing defences and improving positions along the beaches.

On February 2, 1942, Fred Dray was promoted to acting sergeant and his pay was increased to $2.20 a day. But since he was in a supervisory position, his trade grouping was dropped from "A" to "B," which reduced his trades pay by 25¢ a day to 50¢.

On Easter Monday, April 6, Lieutenant General McNaughton and his all-Canadian staff opened Headquarters, First Canadian Army, at Headley Court. The First Canadian Corps remained in Sussex under Major General Crerar.

In 1942, the German offensive reached its peak both in Europe and Africa, and in the Far East, the Japanese experienced their greatest triumph with the fall of Hong Kong. But the tide began to turn and by the end of the year both enemies had suffered significant defeats. Russia checked the Germans at Stalingrad, Rommel was driven from Egypt, and the Japanese suffered naval defeats as well as retreats on land in the face of Australian troops and the U.S. Marines.

Fred's promotion to sergeant was confirmed on May 2, 1942, and in August, as an NCO, he was allowed to move out of quarters into civilian accommodation. The army granted him a subsistence allowance of a dollar a day: 50¢ for food and 50¢ for housing. The first week in September Fred went on leave, and the first week in October, he was back in No. 5 CGH, diagnosed with acute tonsillitis complicated by the throat infection, Vincent's angina, and kept until October 13.

In 1942, the Canadians began to take part in raids against German-held positions across the Channel. The first attempt, by fifty trained men from the Carleton and York Regiments on the night of April 19–20, was thwarted by rough weather on the Channel. Their target was the village of Hardelot, just south of Boulogne, and they were to reconnoitre defensive positions, destroy a searchlight, and take prisoners. However, through a comedy of navigation errors, the Canadians did not get ashore before the recall rocket was fired.

The next planned raid was for a resort town on a good harbour—Dieppe. However, the planners seriously underrated the topography (the only gap in the unscalable cliffs was the mile of beach in front of the town itself), the effectiveness of the defensive works and the defenders, and even the fact that the fist-sized round stones comprising the beach were difficult to walk over in combat boots. After weeks of training and rehearsing, the 4th and 6th Infantry Brigades, 14th Tank Regiment (Calgary's), and the 1st Tank Brigade stormed ashore at dawn on August 19. Fred missed the operation because all engineers, artillery, medical, and other support units were taken from 2 Canadian Division; Fred was in 1 Division.

The *Canadian*, in its edition of September 3, 1942, trumpeted the Canadian landing in France with pictures showing the troops headed for the French coast over the caption, "The enemy attempted to stop them by coast gun barrages and dive bombing, but they went on and achieved their objective." Prominent was a photograph of "the men!" Tough, well-trained, hard-hitting and dogged fighters all. Strolling on the beach beside their invasion craft[5]. The men were all these things, but the planners seriously failed them! In spite of later evaluations that the Dieppe raid was "an indispensable preliminary to a full-scale operation," losses were disproportionately heavy. Canadian casualties numbered 3,369; fatalities numbered 56 officers and 851 other ranks.

[5] The pictures were photographs from an invasion exercise that the Public Relations people had released in anticipation of success.

384 FATHERS, BROTHERS AND SONS

On October 14, the day after his release from hospital, Sergeant Dray was before his commanding officer charged with, "Conduct to the prejudice of good order and discipline," a catch-all charge when no other specific charge can be laid. On September 23, 1942, Fred had failed to properly inspect a War Department vehicle before it was taken out on the road. The left rear wheel fell off and the vehicle was damaged. Sergeant Dray was found responsible for the damage and fined a stoppage of pay in the amount of £3-11-8, the cost of repairs. A severe reprimand was also placed on his record.

In 1943, one Allied success followed another. In May, the Germans were cleared from Africa; in July, Sicily was successfully invaded; and in September, the Allies crossed to the Italian mainland. The plan for the invasion of Europe, Operation Overlord, slowly developed. In March, Exercise Spartan gave the Canadian army the role of breaking out from an established beachhead. The 1st Canadian Corps departed for Italy leaving the 3rd Canadian Division to train for Overlord.

Fred was called in by his commanding officer in early 1943 to be told that he was being recommended for officer training. He was sent to the Army Service Corps Reinforcement Unit for preliminary tests where he was evaluated as an, "Athletic and well-trained soldier and mechanic. Seems very capable and ambitious. Has been recommended by OC [officer commanding] for OCTU [Officer Cadet Training Unit] and is anxious to get commission in CAC [Canadian Army Corps]. If able to pass tests should make an officer."

On March 21, Fred was attached to Canadian Military Headquarters in London while he attended the pre-OCTU course. He then spent the summer taking officer training. In reality it was like taking basic training all over again, but with considerably more emphasis on leadership problems and officer responsibilities. In order to keep his trades pay while under training, Fred had to be trade-tested to qualify as a motor-vehicle fitter, and in August, he was confirmed as a fitter, motor vehicle Class "B." But the writing was on the wall. Fred was not doing well in his academic courses, and on October 21, after several re-tests, he failed to qualify for a commission.

At that point, perhaps inspired by the Combined Operations' raids of the previous year, Fred applied for a transfer to "paratroopers." The 1st Canadian Parachute Battalion had been formed early that year. After training in Fort Benning, Georgia, the battalion arrived in Scotland that summer and made its home at Carter Barracks, Bulford, on Salisbury Plain in Wiltshire. The 650 men became one of three battalions in the 3rd Parachute Brigade of the 6th British Airborne Division. "Due to my extensive training in small arms and map reading I feel that I would be of more help to the service [in parachuting]" Fred pleaded. His commander endorsed the application: "Has taken extensive training in all types of small arms i.e. Bren Gun, Lewis Gun, Trench Mortar, Rifle, Pistol, etc. Also has passed "Q" [qualified] in anti-gas, map reading, unarmed combat, assault and also has extensive knowledge in mechanics."

6th Airborne Division

He was interviewed by three parachute officers. Fred convinced them of his sincerity in wanting to transfer to their elite unit. They found him suitable and commented that, "This Sgt is in the General Force and regrets having to revert to the ranks to join the paratroopers. However, he has decided to do so. He has the ability and should be able to obtain promotion in a short time if given the opportunity which he deserves."

The desired attributes for a paratrooper were quite the opposite of any regular soldier. Paratroopers had to be decisive and to think on their feet. As they discovered in their first combat jump on D-Day and became widely separated, they had to remain calm when things did not go as planned. Many paras were former athletes, having physical agility and excellent co-ordination. No one was considered who weighed more than 220 pounds and was under eighteen or over thirty-two. Motivation was essential. Every candidate appeared before a selection board of three officers from the battalion and underwent psychiatric assessment to detect any instability or alcohol dependency. These high-calibre troopers were without a doubt the finest, fittest soldiers in the Canadian army.

Training occurred in four stages. The first was a week of unrelenting physical training and long arduous route marches. The next week was a repetition of the first with judo lessons and hand-to-hand combat training added in. Week three they learned to tumble and roll on landing after jumping with a static line clipped to a cable from thirty feet, the height of a three-storey building. After falling twelve feet, they were jerked to a stop and lowered into a sawdust pit. Their moment of truth came, however, when they were raised in full gear, beneath an open parachute, to the top of a 250-foot tower and abruptly released.

They also spent sixty-four hours folding and packing their parachutes, the T5, a twenty-eight-foot silk canopy of twenty-eight panels and twenty-eight rigging lines. The lines were twenty-two-feet long attached to a harness fitting over the shoulders and around both legs.

The last stage of training was completed after five real jumps, and on January 4, 1944, after completing eight parajumps, Fred was awarded his

parachute badge and proudly placed the paratrooper's maroon beret over his closely cropped hair. Just five days before, on December 31, 1943, he had been awarded the Canadian Volunteer Service Medal and Clasp

The Canadian Parachute Corps wore distinctive badges. The cap badge was an open parachute between wings with maple leaves at the bottom of the parachute. The collar badge was a paratrooper's hand grasping an

unsheathed dagger dropping from a cloud, which was inscribed with the words *Ex Coelis* (Out of the Heavens). Every button on the uniform had a maple leaf suspended from a parachute with the word "Canada" at the bottom.

Fred's advanced training consisted of learning to drop into battle with a kit bag attached to his legs. At twenty feet above the ground, he dropped the bag which was attached to a twenty-foot rope. The bag would land first, and soften the landing by acting as a brake. If he dropped the kit bag too soon it would twist, spinning the jumper in circles. The bags, which contained various necessary personal and troop equipment, would be dragged away to the rendezvous point.

Fred also began to advance through the ranks. On February 1 he was appointed lance corporal and on March 1 acting corporal, the same day he was awarded the 1939–43 Star, for service in an operational theatre.

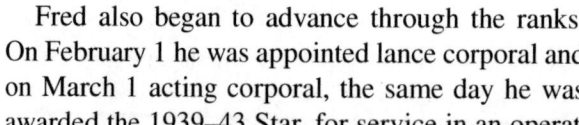

During April, training was speeded up. Special courses were given to various battalion companies that included a street-fighting course in Southampton and swimming courses in the Yeovill Baths. Under less than pleasant weather conditions, the entire battalion spent three days at Brighton doing field firing exercises. The conditions of light, moon and tide were most advantageous, and if necessary, a postponement of a day or two could be possible. When the king and queen visited the paras on May 19, 1944, each man knew without doubt that he was going into action soon. The brigade headquarters moved to the transit camp at Down Ampney in preparation for the invasion.

On May 30, the movement to marshalling areas commenced, camps near the south coast were sealed off, and all communication was halted. On June 1, Fred was promoted to corporal, and by June 3, the majority of the 3rd Canadian Division and the 2nd Canadian Armoured Brigade were aboard their ships around the Isle of Wight. Dubious weather conditions were forecast for June 4 and 5, so General Eisenhower, Supreme Commander, decided to delay Operation Overlord for twenty-four hours.

The 1st Canadian Parachute Battalion was picked to defend and hold a key objective, the crossroads of Le Mesnil. It sat on the high ground overlooking the beaches of a seaside holiday town, Ouistreham. "C" Company was to jump with the pathfinders of the 22nd Independent Parachute Company, making them the first Allied invaders.

Airborne "C" Company in 1944.

The 110 men had to dig in at the crossroads and secure the drop zone (DZ), and the Pathfinders were to set up navigational and homing devices for the main body of paratroopers who were to follow them in one hour. After the DZ was secure, they would move on to the hamlet of Varaville where an enemy artillery headquarters was located. After neutralizing the headquarters the company was to destroy a small radio and signals station en route to their final objective, the destruction of two bridges. The first was east of Varaville over a small tributary of the Dives River (the Divette), and the second was east of the village of Robehomme.

With the DZ secure in Canadian hands, the rest of the battalion, along with its sister battalion, the 9th of the 3rd Brigade, would come in. Their task was to take out the Merville battery of four guns perched on an enormous concrete bunker high above the invasion beaches. "A" Company was to protect the 9th Battalion's left flank and beat off any German assault. "B" Company had the final objective to blow up the key bridge at Robehomme, four miles southeast of Varaville. This bridge over the Dives River was most important because its destruction would deny the enemy a vital route needed to mount a counter-attack against the beaches. Success in storming the Merville battery assured safer landings for the seaborne troops who would be hitting the beaches just at daylight.

In England the weather turned extremely hot. From Carter Barracks, on June 3, the battalion travelled to Down Ampney airfield where they saw their aircraft for the first time. Squatting simmering on the tarmac was a host of C-47 Dakota transports and modified Albemarle bombers. The men were issued with their parachutes, and the next morning, in fine summer weather, the heat having abated somewhat, the battalion marched to church parade. That afternoon, the RAF aircrews came to the camp and were introduced to the "sticks"[6] of men they would be dropping. The men were greatly reassured by the airmen's confidence that they would drop the paras at the right time over the right spot. By then all participants knew that there was a twenty-four-hour delay on the operation.

On the morning of June 5, 1944, all ranks were ordered on enforced rest for the morning and afternoon[7]. They would be flying that night. At 1930 hours, the battalion was paraded in full kit. Each man's equipment was checked and his gear inspected to ensure that escape kits were well hidden and that they carried no incriminating documents. When all was ready, they proceeded to the airfield. The moment of truth was fast approaching. The air was thick with tension as they put on their parachutes and the battalion padre offered a short prayer for the mission's success.

Albemarle bomber painted with the three white invasion stripes. (Bombers 1939–45, p. 73)

"C" Company boarded their Albemarles at 2230 hours and the rest of the battalion boarded Dakotas at 2245. Their nerves were tight and their stomachs in their mouths as the aircraft started engines and began to taxi. No one had time to throw up before they were in the air fifteen minutes later.

[6] The paras did not drop singly from the aircraft, but in "sticks" of about five or six each. There was little time between sticks
[7] Most of the specific information regarding the D-Day drops was obtained from the 1 Canadian Parachute Battalion's's War Diary and Unit History held at the National Archives.

As darkness enveloped them, a watery moon arose. Approaching the DZ, "C" Company stood up and hooked their parachute static lines to a cable running along the roof of their Albemarles. The aircraft banked slightly to the right and they waited to drop through the exit hatch in the bomber's floor. When the red light flashed green, they plunged into the darkness. The roar of the engines, the blast of cold air, and the clang of equipment assailed their senses. Down they dropped. Fast. No one hesitated. All knew that the faster and closer together they jumped, the better their grouping on the ground.[8]

One trooper with the main battalion later wrote:

> During the run into the French coast and looking down in the dim moonlight, the fellows saw the Channel alive with ships of all sizes. As the green light came on to jump, it was very hard to reach the door of the C-47 Dakota as the plane bucked and swerved to avoid ack-ack fire. One of the crew stood at the door to help the heavily equipped paras make their exit and called out 'Good Luck' as each man stepped out into space to come to grips with the enemy. When my 'chute opened it became very quiet as the plane's engines faded away. You couldn't see the ground until you hit it or you landed in a tree or on the roof of a building.[9]

Paratroopers wore normal battledress underneath their parachute jacket, referred to as a smock, with a host of pockets bulging with personal gear. A crotch piece on the smock buttoned front and rear to keep it from riding up while hanging from a parachute. Over this was the web equipment, and dangling from it was the entrenching tool over the butt, a small pack on the chest and ammunition pouches on each side of the pack. Bandoliers of spare ammunition, rifles, and Bren guns were slung around the para's neck. The final piece of kit was the parachute jacket (a sleeveless vest), also with a crotch piece. It prevented all of the battle gear getting entangled in the parachute rigging lines.

Unfortunately the battalion was dropped over a wide area, some sticks landing as far as several miles from their targets. One reason for the scattered drops was that, although the Pathfinders had dropped accurately on the DZ, the radar beacons and responder units were all smashed and useless. The Pathfinders still had a green light for signalling, but it could not penetrate the great cloud of dust and debris thrown up by erroneously dropped RAF bombs. The bombers were supposed to drop on the Merville battery, but overshot it and unloaded their 4,000-pound high-explosive bombs on the DZ. Unable to see the green light, pilots were left to their own devices, usually dead reckoning, to get their paras over the DZ.

[8] Airborne, p.78
[9] ibid p.83

"C" Company was dropped west of the River Dives onto marshy ground. The defenders had flooded the area and many men fell into the water. At least three were never heard from again. A platoon, with the Royal Engineers, quickly took care of the bridge over the Divette and the remainder moved towards the château at Varaville. They attacked and cleared a gun position in the gatehouse, but then came under fire from a mortar and machine-gun position on the château grounds. A nearby pillbox, surrounded by wire, mines and weapon pits, had a 75-mm anti-tank gun aimed down the Varaville road.

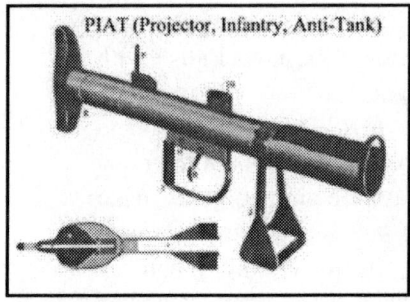

PIAT (Projector, Infantry, Anti-Tank)

The company commander, Major Murray MacLeod from the Maritimes, a lieutenant, and five men armed with a PIAT[10] gun ran to the top floor of the gatehouse overlooking the pillbox. The German gun crew spotted them and quickly aimed and fired two rounds into the gatehouse. One shell detonated the box of PIAT ammunition, instantly killing four men. MacLeod was grievously wounded and died shortly after being hit.

The rest of the company surrounded the pillbox, battling enemy soldiers trying to reach their comrades. The Canadians caused several casualties and the rest surrendered. They evacuated the château and left it as a dressing station. Later, an enemy patrol re-entered the building and took the wounded, the medical officer, and "B" Company sergeant major as prisoners. The paras counter-attacked, but the Germans escaped with their prisoners.

"A" Company dropped at about 0100 hours on June 6. Two officers and twenty-three ORs[11] reconnoitred the village of Gonneville-sur-Elville and encountered no opposition other than RAF bombing. They cleared an artillery battery then moved to the château and captured a German machine gun that had been firing at them. By 1530 hours, they had reached Le Mesnil Bavent crossroads.

Dropping with the paras was a number of para-dogs. These remarkable beasts, usually Alsatians, were left to one handler and were trained to detect enemy patrols and ferret out booby traps. They were trained, but never forced, to jump. Their handler started with familiarizing the animal with the inside of a Dakota aircraft. The dog was then coaxed to jump the six feet from the open door to the ground. It was then taken for rides around the field as the plane taxied and taught to jump from the moving aircraft when the

---

[10] Projector, Infantry, Anti-Tank was an anti-tank gun firing a two-and-a-half-pound hollow-charge projectile.
[11] Ordinary Ranks, any soldier below the rank of sergeant.

pilot throttled back and changed the pitch and sound of the propellers. Thus they were trained to leap into action at that sound, just like any of the other paratroopers[12].

"B" Company was dropped in marshy ground south and west of Robehomme[13]. A French woman guided one officer and twenty-nine ORs through the marsh and waited at the bridge for the Royal Engineers to show to blow it up. By 0630 hours, the engineers had not appeared so the paras gathered some explosives and blew the bridge up themselves. There were several skirmishes with enemy patrols and the company took some casualties, but no one was killed.

A mortar platoon detachment commander landed on top of the pillbox and was taken prisoner. He was in the pillbox during "C" Company's attack and until the Germans surrendered. The platoon had lost their mortars in the drop when their kit bags tore away and landed in marshy ground. The battalion endured heavy enemy mortar fire and sniping, but the local French populace was of great assistance. The women dressed wounds and the men acted as lookouts, messengers, and pack mules. One man was given a red paratrooper's beret and a rifle and distinguished himself by hunting and killing three German snipers and guiding the brigade commander to Le Mesnil. He was later killed in a bombing attack.

The Le Mesnil crossroads are in the centre of a long sloping ridge that gently rises near Merville and ends at Troan. To the west and north are the Caen Canal and the Orne River; beyond is the English Channel at Ouistreham. Those occupying the ridge would determine the fate of those arriving by sea. Thus the remnants of "C" Company and the stragglers of the rest of the battalion, by holding the ridge, ensured the success of the eastern flank of the invasion force.

Early in the morning of June 7, the German 857th and 858th Grenadier Regiments, supported by Mark IV tanks and self-propelled guns, began the first of many attacks on the Canadian positions. The Germans advanced in the open, but were stopped when the paras inflicted heavy casualties with their mortars and PIAT guns. One tank got to within 100 yards of the Canadians before being driven off by a PIAT gun.

The bayonets of "B" Company stopped the German's' last charge. Although frontal attacks ceased, heavy sniper fire continued, and for the next eight days, the paras were under constant bombardment, engaged in hand-to-hand fighting. Only stealth and courage differentiated victory from defeat.

One of the most debilitating effects of war on a soldier, especially those under fire for the first time, is the sound of incoming shells. There is an abid-

[12] Airborne, p.90.
[13] Airborne, p. 67

ing helplessness lying crouched in a slit trench or an underground bunker listening to the thunderous roar and feeling the ground twitch. There is no more terrifying sound than a shell on its way down. The soldier has no idea where it's going to land, and when it does, it is like a freight car dropped from the top of the CN tower. Hot, jagged fragments of steel explode everywhere, ripping into all bodies within range. Nerves of steel snap wondering where the "next one" is going to land.

Strafing was equally terrifying. Watching the plane bank and turn towards you, little flames of fire sprouting from the wings, raised emotions of despair. An RAF roundel on the wings invoked serious anger.

At 1200 hours on June 7, "B" Company found the road to battalion headquarters clear, and at 2330, all 150 troopers began to move. The wounded were carried in a car given to them by the curé and a horse and cart donated by a farmer. Near Briqueville, enemy sentries challenged the lead platoon. They opened fire, killing seven and taking one prisoner.

Hidden in a hedgerow in front of a farmhouse, "B" Company found six to eight enemy machine guns. They attacked and the enemy withdrew to behind the house. "A small number of enemy were found in the house and adequately dealt with.[14]" The Germans launched a counter-attack, but were caught in the assault party's crossfire. Privates Geddes and Naval, with a Bren gun and sniper's rifle, killed approximately twenty-five of the enemy. The Company estimated total German casualties at about fifty dead and an unknown number of wounded. They did not reach battalion headquarters until 0330 hours on June 8.

That day, under heavy shelling, Corporal Fred Dray was struck in the stomach by shrapnel. He was rushed to the Aid Station and at 0430 hours on June 9, he was administered ether in preparation for surgery. His abdomen was opened and a resection of four inches of small intestine was completed, another perforation was sutured, and the wound was closed.

On June 9, the bulk of the battalion had their first opportunity to rest. The weather was fine, and the snipers in the trees and hedgerows were only a nuisance factor. The next day, June 10, the weather continued pleasant. Battalion positions were shelled and machine-gunned intermittently throughout the day. On June 11, probing attacks by the enemy were driven back. "C" Company entered the village of Bavent, laid some booby traps, then withdrew without encountering any Germans.

Battalion headquarters moved into the nearby brickworks on June 12. The Germans mounted a do-or-die attack at the crossroads where the Canadians were dug in and nearly broke the line on the ridge. "C" Company, in reserve,

---

[14] War Diary, 1 Canadian Parachute Battalion. National Archives.

provided powerful reinforcements who drove the enemy back. "A" Company, the headquarters standing patrol, captured an enemy artillery outpost and ambushed a German staff car carrying a high-ranking propaganda officer, a Gestapo officer, a sergeant, and the driver. The propaganda officer was brought to headquarters alive, but the other three were killed.

There was no let up by the determined Germans. During the night of June 12–13, a platoon from "B" Company ambushed a Volkswagen car, killing all four occupants, all officers. When they searched the vehicle, they found one of the officers was a paymaster with 38,000 francs in his briefcase. They also found a complete day's rations for one of the enemy's forward companies.

The weather remained fine on June 14, and there was very little shelling by either side on this day. The battalion maintained patrols along the front, but made few contact with the enemy.

Drab morning light under overcast skies welcomed June 15. A light rain began to fall and continued all day through heavy enemy artillery and mortar fire. This was followed by a tank-supported enemy attack, which was driven off after intense fighting. That morning Corporal Fred Dray took his last painful breath. The cause of death was listed as "ASW [artillery shell wound] Abdomen Penetrating." He was eighteen days past his thirtieth birthday.

June 17 was a beautiful sunny warm day in Normandy. The 5th Parachute Brigade relieved the 3rd, and the 1st Canadian Parachute Battalion retired to Rainville where the only enemy activity was the occasional plane at night. Five hundred and forty-three officers and men had jumped into France on June 6; 367 had been killed in action, were listed as missing, or had been taken as prisoners of war.

Airborne soldiers interred their own before moving on. (Photo: 1canpara website)

Corporal Frederick Albert Dray's body was eventually interred in the Hermanville War Cemetery in Calvados, France. Hermanville-sur-Mer lies thirteen kilometres north of Caen, and Hermanville beach was the eastern flank of the disembarkation of the British army in June 1944. There are more than 1,000 World War II casualties in the site.

The *Canadian* reported on July 20 that Carleton Place had lost three boys in recent actions: Fred Dray on June 15, Gerald Lewis (Italy) and William Gerald Whyte (France), both on July 4. Fred's surviving siblings were listed as four sisters: Ethel (Mrs. Charles Morrow) of Sault Ste. Marie, Doris (Mrs. Borden Austin) of Metis Beach, Quebec, Gladys (Mrs. Clarence Dowdall) of Appleton, and Miss Violet Ryan of Carleton Place; and two bothers: Jack, with the RCOC Mobile Unit in France and Ronald of Carleton Place.

In August, Fred's mother, Minnie, received the following message from Buckingham Palace:

> The Queen and I offer you our heartfelt sympathy in your great sorrow.
>
> We pray that your country's gratitude for a life so nobly given in its service may bring you some measure of consolation.
>
> George R.I.

After the army informed Minnie that Fred had been killed in action and that she would be receiving his gratuity (which, she told them, she would use to help purchase a house), she heard nothing further. Finally, on January 31, 1945, she wrote to army headquarters in Ottawa:

> I am writing on behalf of my dear son who died of his wounds on June 15th/44 as I would like to know if he was buried in France or in England and also his personal belongings as I think it is nearly time. I heard nothing about him and also his deferred pay and I know he had quite a lot of money in his pay book as he wrote and told me as he was over there five years last Dec as you know he was in the regular army, he would have been in the army six years in June if he had lived so I do hope I will get some news about him as I would very much like to have something belonging to him and about his gratuity money do I have to fill in a form for it as I think they must have some record of him as he died in hospital so please if I am not asking to much will you kindly let me know as I am broken hearted in losing him I never stated his name on front page.

P.28106 Cpl. Frederick Albert Dray 1st Bn. Paratrooper but he was in R.C.A.S.C. when he first joined up as he transferred to the Paratroops as I am his mother so I would be very pleased if you would kindly do something for me trusting to hear from you in the near future.

If I do not get any word I will have to come down to Ottawa to see about it as I cannot wait much longer as it is bad enough to lose them after being over there so long and nearly eight months dead so please let me know as soon as you can.

On June 14, 1945, a small notice appeared in the Carleton Place *Canadian*:

In memoriam to Dear Fred

The late Corporal Fred Ryan,[15] who died of his wounds in Normandy, France, June 15th, 1944.

RYAN, In fond and loving memory of our dearly beloved son and brother,

> The midnight stars are shining
>
> On a grave we cannot see,
>
> Where sleeping without dreaming,
>
> Lies the one so dear to us.
>
> This warfare o'er, his battle fought,
>
> This victory won, though dearly bought,
>
> His fresh young life could not be saved,
>
> He slumbers now in a soldier's grave.

Sadly missed by Mother, Father, Sisters and Brothers.

---

[15] Ryan was his step-father's last name.

Chapter Twenty-Four—. . . For Overlord

From the disaster at Dieppe on August 19, 1942, there were many lessons learned. Allied planners now recognized the extreme danger in attempting to seize a defended harbour. A massive and intense naval and air bombardment was essential to cover the invading force, and special vessels, such as special-purpose landing ships (e.g. rockets, tanks, infantry, and assault) needed to be devised and employed. The landing in Sicily in July 1943 provided the opportunity to test the new landing craft.

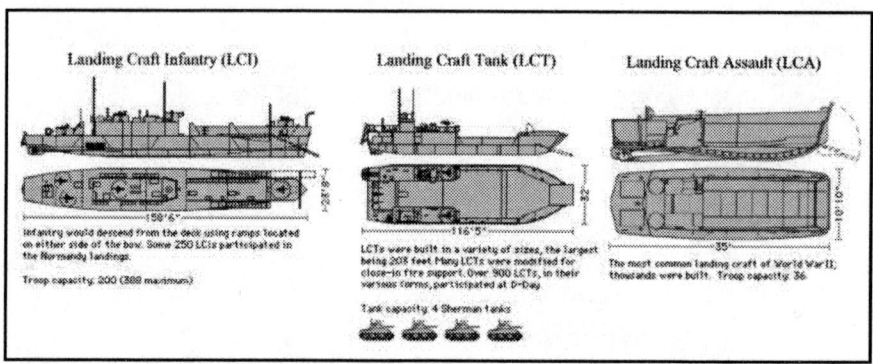

Of major concern was the problem of safely unloading thousands of tons of necessary supplies and equipment, vehicles, ammunition, and food where no port facilities would be available. The answer came in the design of huge artificial harbours (i.e. floating docks) that could be towed across the Channel and sunk. Code-named "mulberries," they proved durable enough to take the weight of re-supply until major port facilities could be captured.

The 3rd Canadian Division, backed up by the 2nd Canadian Armoured Brigade, would assault the Normandy shores under the direction of the 1st I British Corps. The Canadians' target was Juno Beach between the British landings on Gold and Sword Beaches. To get the troops to shore and to provide covering firepower was the task of 7,016 ships of the Allied navies, including a large number of RCN destroyers, minesweepers, corvettes, and motor-torpedo boats. The entire invasion fleet numbered 6 battleships, 2 monitors, 22 cruisers, 93 destroyers, 71 corvettes and thousands of landing craft of all description. Overhead flew 171 squadrons of fighters and fighter-bombers.

The Canadian attack was to go in on a two-brigade front. The 7th Brigade in Mike sector on the right (looking towards shore) and the 8th Brigade in Nan sector on the left. The 8th had the Queen's Own Rifles, the North Shore Regiment from New Brunswick, and Le Régiment de la Chaudière in reserve. Tanks of the Fort Garry Horse were to support the 8th Brigade.

EASTERN FLANK
OF THE
NORMANDY BRIDGEHEAD
JUNE–JULY, 1944

Stacey, The Canadian Army 1939-45.

Following the 8th would be the 9th Brigade with infantry highland battalions: the North Nova Scotia Highlanders (NNSH), the Highland Light Infantry (HLI), and the Stormont, Dundas and Glengarry Highlanders (SD&G) supported by the tanks of the Sherbrooke Fusiliers.

Defending Juno Beach was the 716th Infantry Division, comprising a little over 7,700 men including two *Ostbataillone*, battalions of captured Soviet, and sometimes Polish, prisoners of war. These "third-rate troops" proved strong enough behind their concrete fortifications. As well, the area commander, General Rommel, had placed elements of the 21st Panzer Division with the 716th, and only five miles inland waited two panzer-grenadier battalions and an anti-tank battalion.

The first landing craft, carrying Toronto's Queen's Own Rifles, ground ashore at 0812 hours, twenty-seven minutes late, onto a beach littered with obstacles and anti-tank mines. Still shaking with seasickness, the Queen's Own charged out of the boat and began a 200-yard dash to the seawall. Withering fire thudded into bodies every foot of the way. Due to rough seas, The amphibious DD (Duplex Drive) tanks, due to rough seas, had to be taken closer to shore because they could not swim in five-foot waves. The tanks landed after and not before the infantry.

The 8th Brigade's reserve regiment, the Chaudières, touched land at 0830 hours, with many of its landing craft foundering before reaching the shoreline. The French civilians were totally surprised to hear French almost identical to that spoken by the Normans, and by late afternoon, supported by the Fort Garry Horse, the Chaudières had taken Beny-sur-Mer. They had help from HMCS *Algonquin* which placed thirteen out of fifteen shells directly on a targeted battery of three German 88mm guns that was holding up the advance.

Just before noon, the reserve brigade, the 9th, with the SD&G, HLI, and NNSH supported by the tanks of the Sherbrooke Fusiliers, rode the surf onto the sand. Tetrahedral obstacles and mines were, for the most part, avoided. By late afternoon, they were moving towards Beny-sur-Mer and dug in for the night around Anisy.

Lieutenant Harold Murfitt
Stormont, Dundas and Glengarry Highlanders

Harold "Duke" Murfitt spent several years in Carleton Place working as a weaver with the Hawthorn Woolen Mills after emigrating from England in 1930. While in Carleton Place, he became active and well-liked in the Scouting movement for many years. Scoutmaster Murfitt and his assistant, Jimmy Bennett, were especially interested in ensuring that the scouts had a firm grasp of the basics of first aid. Scoutmaster Murfitt also taught the boys semaphore.

In 1936, he joined the militia, the 1st Battalion of the Lanark and Renfrew Scottish, spending his summers training in Petawawa, and in 1938, he was commissioned as a second lieutenant.

After a few years working at the mill, Murfitt took a job with the Carleton Place Dairy. In 1934, he went to Toronto to become the manager of the Eglington Dairy pasteurizing plant and moved in with his sister, Inez Cruise, who, with her husband, lived at 42 Fairleigh Crescent in Forest Hill. He stayed there only a short while before returning to Carleton Place and the local dairy.

Harold was born in Renishaw, Derbyshire, England on November 11, 1911. His father, Joseph Gibbons Murfitt, died when Harold was but a baby, and his mother, Lucy Ann, continued to reside in the family home at Broomhill, Sheffield. The family members were Church of England adherants. In 1926,

at the age of fifteen, Harold went to work for Thomas Firth & Sons, Research Laboratories, as a pyrometrics section assistant. However, his thirst for learning to better his situation was never quenched. He attended night school at Central School in Sheffield, receiving his diploma in 1928, and after two more years of night school at Sheffield University, Harold was qualified in metallurgy in 1930.

In the Lanark and Renfrew Scottish, NPAM, Harold had risen through the ranks of private, corporal and sergeant[16] before gaining his commission, in 1938, to second lieutenant (although the effective date was backdated to July 1937). Militia units, the only real source of experienced people, provided good officer material. Harold's militia experiences, added to his academic and technical qualifications, were sufficient for his acceptance as an officer.

As a second lieutenant, Harold was paid $4.25 a day, compared to the $1.30 a day privates received after reaching age eighteen. Overall, Canadians were the highest paid soldiers in the Allied forces. The Canadian private averaged $39 a month, a U.S. Army draftee averaged $35, a British Tommy $23.55, a French conscript a minimum of $1.05 (which was reduced to nothing after France's fall to Germany), a Russian the equivalent of $11.77, and Hitler's famed Wehrmacht soldiers an average of $6.

As an experienced militia second lieutenant, Harold was appointed recruiting officer and, on September 7, 1939, opened a recruiting office for the Lanark and Renfrew Scottish Regiment in the Carleton Place Legion rooms on Bridge Street. Britain had already declared war and it was only a matter of time before Canada would follow suit, meaning the militia would be called out very soon. The regiment wanted to fill its ranks as quickly as possible for that eventuality. Many of the young Ottawa Valley men, "with the fire of the Scottish clans in their blood," wanted to join a highland regiment immediately. Most were sent to the Cameron Highlanders in Ottawa who were recruiting for their Active Force machine-gun battalion.

Harold was twenty-eight years old when he enlisted in the Active Force on September 4, 1940. His medical examiner described him as a man of good development, 5' 8" tall, weighing 143 pounds. He had brown eyes and

---

[16] On November 15, 1940, the Minister, Col. Ralston, announced that "every candidate for a commission must first pass through the ranks." The time spent in the ranks had to be four months for Active units and one year (or the 30-day annual training period) for the reserves.

brown hair, was of a medium complexion, and had an upper denture. Harold said his hobbies were sports and first aid.

Although he was transferred on paper to the Canadian Military Training Centre in Brockville, Harold remained in Petawawa on training duties for the militia. On March 17, 1941, "Duke" transferred to the Canadian Army Regular Force and was sent on furlough until an opening occurred on officer training course.

Effective leadership of the new army depended heavily upon the proper training of all officers. Even after experience in the ranks, special knowledge and skills were required. Intense training also served to determine the candidate's fitness for a king's commission. In the spring of 1941, two Officer Training Centres were opened, one at Brockville for eastern Canada and one at Gordon Head, near Victoria, for western Canada. Harold arrived at Brockville on July 15, 1941.

The syllabus included four weeks spent on basic subjects common to all arms, six weeks devoted to elementary subjects special to the (candidate's) arm, and a two-week course in platoon tactics, designed to ensure that every officer would be able to take command of men performing duties in an area defence scheme.[17]

Second Lieutenant Murfitt took his basic training at Brockville then moved to No. 32 Basic Training Centre in Peterborough on September 3 for the six weeks of elementary infantry training. After a further two weeks of platoon tactics training at No. 22 Educational (Basic) Training Centre North Bay,[18] "Duke" qualified and was posted to the Advanced Training Centre (Infantry) at Camp Borden. On December 26, the chairman of an officers' examining board concluded that Murfitt: "Appears to be a good officer with plenty of experience. His men work well for him, and while his manner is quiet, I believe the results will be good. Is not afraid of work, and is interested in his men after hours."

After Christmas leave with his sister in Toronto, he reported to Camp Borden on December 31, 1941. Upon completion of his advanced infantry training, Harold was promoted to lieutenant, backdated to November 1, and remained at the training centre as an instructor. In April 1942, he took and passed course A10 (driver tracked vehicles) at the Canadian Infantry Training Centre in Camp Borden, qualified as a Class III driver.

[17] Col. C.P. Stacey, Six Years of War, Volume I (Ottawa: Queen's Printer, 1955), p.138.
[18] Many colds and sore throats interrupted his training. From November 26 to December 1 he was in St. Joseph's's hospital for investigation and treatment of his sore throat.

On March 5, 1942, the Lanark and Renfrew Scottish Regiment mobilized for home defence[19]. The formation of these home-defence units created an even greater demand for officers, so fully qualified Lieutenant Harold Murfitt was sent to his home regiment on May 1, 1942. That summer he went to Vernon, British Columbia, to take the A31 Battle Drill course at the Canadian Battle Drill Training Centre (later to become the Canadian School of Infantry). It now became obvious that the Lanark and Renfrew were not going overseas, at least not as a unit. Lieutenant Murfitt transferred to the 2nd Battalion, Royal Highland Regiment of Canada, on September 5, and on September 24 boarded a ship in Montreal bound for a River Clyde port.

Lieutenant Murfitt arrived in Scotland on October 7 and travelled south to England immediately to 3 Canadian Division Reinforcement Unit (CDRU). Originally known as Holding Groups, these reinforcement pools were tasked with training the basic-trained recruits from Canada. By 1941, each infantry division had its own reinforcement unit, and all men destined for the 3rd Division were held at 3 CDRU. Harold only spent one month there when he was sent, on November 20, as a replacement officer to the SD&G.

The SD&G was in the 9th Infantry Brigade of the 3rd Division, along with the HLI from the Galt-Waterloo area and the NNSH of the 3rd Division. The Glengarrys were originally formed in 1868 as six independent companies of the 59th Stormont and Glengarry Battalion of Infantry. Mobilized on May 24, 1940, it went to England on July 19, 1941, and after landing on the Normandy beaches fought with the 9th Brigade throughout the northwest European campaign.

Dorothy Sarah Jones, of Avenue Road, Southgate, London, became a major factor in Harold's life after his arrival in England. It is not known whether he knew her prior to emigrating and or whether he corresponded with her during his years in Canada. His army records reveal only that, with army permission, Harold married her at Christ Church on February 20, 1943. Harold changed the pay allotment of $25 a month he was sending to his mother, to $35 a month to be sent directly to his wife. They had a son, Michael David, born around Christmas 1943.

While Harold spent as much time as he could with his young wife, most of his attention was taken up with intense training. From April 7 to May 13, he led his platoon on a small-arms weapons course at the Special Air Services facility in Hyde, and in July, he was appointed commander of No. 6 Rifle Platoon.

[19] The Regiment never got overseas and was disbanded on October 13, 1943. The First Light Anti-Aircraft Regiment, after service in Sicily and Italy was redesignated The Lanark and Renfrew Scottish Regiment on July 13, 1944. It moved to NorthWest Europe on March 5, 1945 and on March 15 was redesignated as 1st Light Anti-Aircraft Regiment (Lanark and Renfrew Scottish Regiment). It was disbanded overseas on June 29, 1945. At home the regiment was redesignated ""59th Light Anti-Aircraft Regiment (Lanark and Renfrew Scottish), Royal Canadian Artillery". On December 1, 1959 it was reconverted to infantry and redesignated "The Lanark and Renfrew Scottish Regiment [The Regiments and Corps of the Canadian Army, Volume I of the Canadian Army List (Ottawa: Queen's's Printer, 1964), p. 163]

No. 5 Canadian Training School (CTS) conducted a series of night-fighting courses for officers in the summer; Harold attended from July 23 to August 7, 1943.

To the Canadian soldier, it seemed that 1943 was just a string of exercises, one after another. There were artillery and infantry units exercising together for advanced co-operative training; there were wireless exercises without troops; there were exercises for commanders and their staff; in the field, there were exercises at brigade and divisional levels; and when the troops returned to garrison, their battalions had exercises to implement the lessons learned on larger excursions.

Harold's battalion entrained at Worthing Station for their second trip to Scotland and went to Wemyss Bay to participate in combined operations training with the navy. On arrival at Rothesay, the YMCA fed them hot tea and cookies before starting a rigorous training syllabus that included assault landings with live ammunition.

In September, they participated in Exercise Strone Point, which trained the troops for beach landings from landing craft. On September 17, Major Gemmill, officer commanding "B" Company, ordered Lieutenant Murfitt to load No. 11 Platoon aboard landing craft No. 886 of No. 571 Motor Boat Company of the Royal Army Service Corps (RASC) and to have his Bren gunner open fire through the slit in the boat's ramp at a given signal from the exercise-control boat.

It was an unusually bright day, and the boats bounced out to sea on fairly calm water. They rode the waves until all were co-ordinated, then they turned for shore and the beach landing point. Army platoons are subdivided into sections, each with a section leader, usually a corporal, and twenty to thirty soldiers, and three sections clambered into the boat in single file and sat three across facing the ramp that lowered to splash ashore. Lieutenant Murfitt was standing front and centre at the bow. To his right, and slightly behind, was Lance Corporal Barton, leader of No. 4 Section, to his left was Private Jeffrey, the Bren gunner from No. 5 Section, and immediately behind him was Corporal Puffer, No. 5 Section Leader. Jeffrey, a short man, was

Bren Machine Gun

struggling to raise his Bren gun into the slit that was fairly high. He had been a Bren gunner for eight months but had only been in a landing craft three times, and he had never fired from a moving boat before. He had difficulty keeping the gun in place due to the bounce and sway of the boat.

As the boat neared the beach, Lieutenant Murfitt ordered his men to ready themselves to run ashore as soon as the ramp was down.

"Jeffrey," he yelled over the noise of the boat's engine and the slapping waves. "Prepare to fire on my signal. Automatic. Fire in short bursts. Three magazines."

It was 1430 hours. Private MacPherson, of the boat's crew, moved up to remove disengage the safety catch from the ramp. Suddenly the craft lurched as Sergeant Durman, the coxswain, decreased power to run up onto the beach. The bow dropped and the ramp clattered down as the boat beached. MacPherson then felt a "sting" on his hand and foot before he heard the explosion of the Bren gun firing.

"I've been shot! I've been shot," screamed Murfitt as Puffer moved to his side. The lieutenant's hand was bleeding and he told Puffer, "My legs are all shot up. Take over as platoon commander." Puffer and the boat crew moved Murfitt to the stern and laid him on the motor cover. Murfitt gave Puffer the Verey pistol and flares and ordered the platoon ashore. "Carry on with the exercise, Puffer!"

When the boat reduced speed for landing, it surged, causing Jeffrey, the Bren gunner, to lose his balance and jolt backwards. He was finishing his second magazine, and as the gun came back into the boat, five shots were fired inside before he could release the trigger. Three went through the armour-plated ramp and two ricocheted downward. All sprayed metal fragments, hitting MacPherson and Murfitt. MacPherson's wounds were only scratches, but Murfitt had shrapnel embedded in his right leg, and a field dressing was slapped on his leg to staunch the blood flow.

As soon as the troops had disembarked, Durman moved his boat alongside the Landing Craft Medical (LCM) that was carrying an ambulance and a medical officer. Murfitt made the transfer without assistance. Captain Jung, of 23rd Field Ambulance, (Wilson Costello's unit), was the Canadian doctor on board the LCM, and he noted that Murfitt was in no acute distress and could walk. The doctor applied first-aid dressings to the many penetrating wounds on Murfitt's right hand, lower thigh, right knee and right toe, and authorized the patient to be sent back to his unit regimental aid post[20].

At 1530 hours, Captain Fraleigh, medical officer for the NNSH, was called to the SD&G aid post. He re-dressed Murfitt's wounds and sent him to the nearby Royal Canadian Naval Hospital, HMCS *Niobe*, because "(metallic) foreign bodies" were still embedded. Murfitt could walk into the hospital, but did not remember the operation to remove the shrapnel, which included a pea-sized shard from the inner lower third of his thigh, minute fragments from the inner side of his right knee, a jagged U-shaped piece

---

[20] That same morning Lt. A.F. Stirland was killed while working with a pole charge.

from the terminal phalanx (last bone) of his right ring finger, many minute pieces from the back of his hand, and a pea-sized metal foreign body from the first metacarpal (small bone in the back of the hand). After the operation, the doctor gave him the small bits of steel taken from his hand and foot as souvenirs. Murfitt was released from the hospital on September 22.

The Canadians, after years of waiting in England, were considered a lead element for any attack across the English Channel. Plans for Operation Overlord had begun in 1943 with a target date of May 1, 1944. On Christmas Eve 1943, U.S. General Eisenhower was appointed Supreme Allied Commander, and the popular General Montgomery became Commander-in-Chief of the 21st Group of Armies, the British component of the ground forces.

When the First Canadian Corps departed in July 1943 for Italy, they left behind the 3rd Canadian Division. It had been earmarked for the assault on Normandy, and for operational direction and training, it passed to the 1st British Corps. The division trained in combined operations at their own bases in southern England, then went north for advanced training in Scotland. By autumn 1943, it had returned to the Channel coast for exercises with the Royal Navy and the RAF, and consequently, became intimately familiar with the Royal Navy and Imperial Army combined assault force. This explains why the LCV in which Harold was wounded on September 17 was crewed by an RASC crew.

No. 6 Platoon was one of three platoons in "C" Company, and on January 10, 1944, it was relieved of all other duties in order to represent the battalion in divisional endurance tests. The day the endurance contest started, January 18, was also the day the battalion received their last typhus inoculation. Thus, the company began the physically challenging twenty-four-hour endurance test with sore right arms.

On February 1, "C" and "B" Companies hiked out of camp on a ten-mile march. It was a cloudy morning but quite mild. On February 8, "C" Company was initiated to the folding bicycles they would be carrying to Europe with an uneventful fourteen-mile trip. This went so well that the next day, the company left Rochecourt camp on a three-day trek. March came in like a lion with very cold temperatures and high winds. Still, the rifle companies trudged about on ten-mile marches. The month went out like a lamb in warm, wet, spring-like weather.

April rains brought mud, so on the 4th, the battalion moved to Rookesbury Camp, and on the 25th, marched to Fareham Common to join the 9th Brigade on parade for inspection by George VI. Tension filled the air, as a royal inspection usually meant a regiment was being sent to France.

In May, Allied air forces pounded strategic German targets and the rail network all over northwest Europe, with airfields and tactical targets near the intended assault area receiving special attention. The Germans retaliated with flying bombs and long-range rockets. During May, Supreme Headquarters fixed June 5 as the most auspicious time for D-Day and Operation Overlord, although postponement to June 6 or 7 remained possible. By May 30, the 3rd Division and 2nd Canadian Armoured Brigade began to move, and by June 3, they were all embarked on their ships and landing craft. However, during the transit and marshalling for embarkation, the troops were kept behind barbed wire, along with endless rows of vehicles, guns, and equipment. They offered a tantalizing target for the Luftwaffe, but the skies over Portsmouth–Southampton clearly belonged to the RAF.

On June 2, Lieutenant R. R. Dixon, battalion intelligence officer, record-ed in the SD&G war diary that the day was cool, with slight rain, enough that the men wore tunics. Popular activities included getting an "assault" haircut (a short brush cut), sleeping, eating, playing cards, and throwing stones at targets. Most were in their bunks at sundown because they would be awakened at 0200 hours the next day. On June 1, they had been issued with two, twenty-four-hour ration packs containing two tins of chocolate, bully beef, biscuits, chewing gum, cigarettes, and water sterilizing kits.

At 0200 hours on June 3, waking to a mild morning, the battalion was roused, fed breakfast, and under a slight overcast, moved to Stokes Bay. The rest of the day was spent standing around waiting to board one of the seven landing craft, which carried the infantry, their bicycles, and wheeled and tracked vehicles. The ships set sail to take up their assigned positions with the invasion fleet.

Personal equipment had been checked and stowed in pockets or attached to web harnesses. Each man wore a leather jerkin, leather jump boots, antivermin- and antigas- treated battledress, a special assault helmet, and a canvas assault jacket. These jackets had many pockets in which some carried two Bren gun magazines, two No. 36 grenades, a No. 75 anti-tank grenade, and a No. 69 smoke grenade.

Lieutenant "Hal"[21] Murfitt received a message telling him that his wife was seriously ill in hospital. She had developed blood poisoning from a wart that had been accidentally scratched. He applied for compassionate leave, but since all ranks had been given highly secret information regarding the invasion, divisional headquarters was obliged to refuse the request. Therefore, he went to the Normandy beachhead with his battalion.

Sunday, June 4 found the battalion headquarters aboard Craft No. 636 rid-ing comfortably in Southampton Roads off the Isle of Wight. After breakfast

[21] Known as Duke in Carleton Place, he was called Hal by his army friends.

at 0800 hours, the men crowded the decks to see ships of every conceivable shape and size streaming down the navigation channel to their allotted spots. Their ship's skipper, described as "a mere boy," told the soldiers that 4,000 ships, not including landing craft, were to take part. The magnitude of the operation was obvious.

By the morning of June 5, the wind had increased, but the skies were still cloudy. The battalion commanding officer gathered his officers early and crept up on a sleeping Captain Forman, who was rudely awoken by the singing of "Happy Birthday." Deck games and physical exercises were the order of the day, although card games also broke out in various nooks and crannies. At 1500 hours, the ship's captain announced that the invasion was "on!" An electric thrill swept everyone on board, along with a last check of weapons: rifles with three ban-doliers of ammunition and bayo-nets and, for some, PIAT 2-inch mortars, light Bren machine guns, Sten guns, and commando or folding knives. First-aid field dressings were attached to hel-mets and some soldiers were issued vials of morphine. All wore Mae West life preservers and carried blankets, mess tins, mugs, extra socks, and gas capes. Some were also equipped with compasses, map cases, binoculars, and portable radios. Not counting the bicycle, steel helmet and ration packs, the equipment weighed seventy-eight pounds.

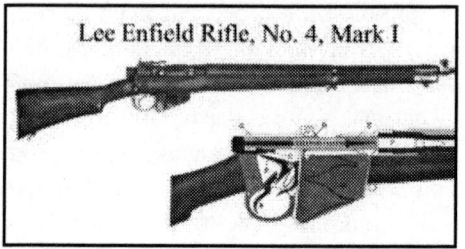
Lee Enfield Rifle, No. 4, Mark I

On D-Day, Allied troops numbering 150,000, of which 14,000 were Canadian, poured ashore along an eighty-kilometre front. The RCN provid-ed 110 warships and the RCAF had fifteen squadrons in the air. Ultimately, Canada suffered 1,074 casualties, of which 359 died.

Most men were wide-awake at 0600 hours on June 6 as their ship approached the beach at Bernières-sur-Mer. Those that weren't were soon lured on deck by the drone of large numbers of aircraft passing overhead. They could hear bombs exploding and could see large fires at Bernières and St Aubin-sur-Mer. Surprisingly, the sky was completely devoid of German aircraft.

The beach ahead was covered in dense smoke as the destroyers poured shellfire onto the defenders, and water erupted all around as the German artillerymen returned the favour. At 1100 hours, battalion officers received the signal for the 9th Canadian Infantry Brigade to land in NAN sector behind the 7th and 8th Brigades. At 1220 hours, their boat touched shore. The infantry charged into waist-deep water to swim/wade onto White Beach in front of Bernières-sur-Mer, directly in the centre of the British front.

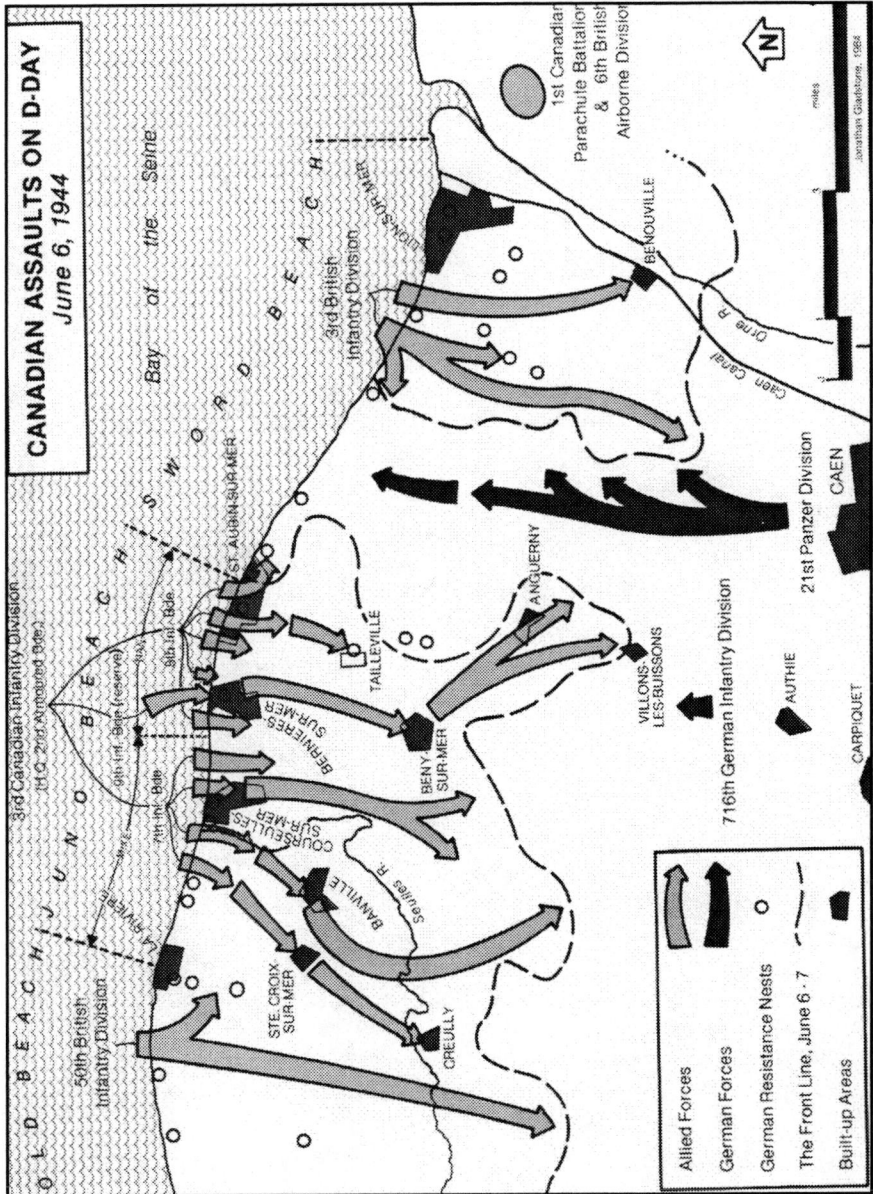

CANADIAN ASSAULTS ON D-DAY
June 6, 1944

Just before he led his platoon onto the beach, Harold Murfitt could have had the following poem running through his mind. It was written by Major Alex R. Campbell during the Great War while waiting in the trenches to lead his men into battle with the enemy:

When 'neath the rumble of the guns,

I lead my men against the Huns,

'Tis then I feel so all alone and weak and scared,
And oft I wonder how I dared
Accept the task of leading men.

I wonder, worry, fret and then I pray,
Oh God! Who promised oft
To humble men, a listening ear,
Now, in my spirit's troubled state
Draw near, dear God, draw near, draw near.

Make me more willing to obey,
Help me top merit my command,
And, if this be my fatal day,
Reach out, Oh God, Thy Guiding Hand,
And lead me down that deep, dark vale.

These men of mine must never know
How much afraid I really am,
Help me to lead them in the fight
So they will say, 'He was a man.'

SD&G land on Juno Beach. (Photo www.SDG_BRGD.HTM/Regimental History)

The SD&G were about four hours behind the first assault by the 7th and 8th Brigades, which had landed at about 0800 hours. They could see the first waves of 3 Division slowly moving off the beach toward their assigned targets, leaving behind in the shallow water legs, arms, and other body parts washing onto the shore. It was the first time into combat for these men, and the sights and smells and sounds were foreign to their senses. Abandoned equipment and burning vehicles were everywhere. There was very little enemy sniping, but mortar and artillery shells dropped in the water and on the beach as they ran across 300 yards of shingle[22] and along a single railroad track into the village. But the 9th Brigade encountered no resistance on the beaches as the previous assault brigades had cleared them and made it inland as far as the nearest villages.

At 1530 hours, the SD&G were still in Bernières-sur-Mer. A German stronghold in St. Aubin-sur-Mer, one mile to the east, was still in action. Ahead of them, about two miles south, the Queen's Own Rifles reported that they were attacking enemy positions, and the SD&G soldiers were surprised to see that Bernières was not as devastated as they had imagined. Civilians, contemptuous of the danger, were in the streets making friends with their Canadian liberators. The first enemy plane to be spotted roared low overhead with two Spitfires "hot on its tail." On the roads, small groups of enemy prisoners were being taken back to the beach.

The 8th Brigade ran into stiff resistance that held up the advance of the NNSH and the 27th Canadian Armoured Regiment (Sherbrooke Fusiliers). It was not until late afternoon that the SD&G (the Glens) were able to pass through and begin moving south. They, too, were delayed by stubborn machine guns and had to halt for the night some four miles north of Caen, near Beny-sur-Mer, with the rest of the brigade behind them. The battalion hunkered down for the night in slit trenches dug around the church under skies lit with explosions of heavy shellfire and rent with the constant clatter of small-arms fire.

During the night, "A" Company bumped into an enemy infantry and armoured patrol of the 21st Panzer Division. One private was killed and a lieutenant and ten soldiers were wounded.

14,500 Canadian soldiers were reported to have made the D-Day landing. They persevered in an extraordinary military endeavour. Their success was not cheap, nor was victory easy. Losses were fewer than expected, as the men of 1944 owed their success to the Canadians of 1942 who raided the small French port of Dieppe. Yet, of the ground forces, not counting the airborne, 335 officers and men were killed in action or died of wounds. Another 611 suffered wounds that took them out of action but were not fatal.

---

[22] A beach composed of mostly stony sandloose rounded pebbles.

At their first opportunity, the men discarded their collapsible bicycles in a dump at Beny-sur-Mer and started on foot for Basly, and the first of the Glens reached Villons-Les-Buissons at 1000 hours. Burned-out enemy half-tracks, assessed as light and inferior to Allied equipment, blocked their road, while Italians and Russians, as well as Germans from 716 Division deemed to be "very poor quality,"[23] were taken prisoner. Around noon, they witnessed two enemy aircraft shot from the skies above them.

Badge of the 12th Schutzstaffen Division.

At 1400 hours, "A" and "B"[24] Companies were deployed to the grounds of the Château Les Buisons. One of their slit trenches was close to the corner of the road to Buron and the driveway to the château. Enemy pressure rapidly increased, and the battalion dubbed the area as "Hell's Corners." The NNSH, who had been fighting the 12th SS Panzer Division (*Hitlerjugend*) at Authie and Buron, joined the SD&G. The Glens moved right, in the vicinity of the château, and "B" Company occupied the village of Les Buissons. They were advised that aircraft would be bombing the airfield, so the commanding officer was grateful for the support while acknowledging that the RAF was doing a great job of keeping the skies clear.

Later in the day, about 1730 hours, the battalion had a very hectic time as enemy resistance began to stiffen. There was considerable confusion on the battlefield as a phoney radio station was talking over the armoured regiment's net. The Glens heard considerable tank gunfire to their rear and thought that they had enemy behind them. It transpired that the tanks were Canadian, but the HLI mistook them for German, and the tankers mistook the HLI for German paratroopers. They started to blaze away at each other before the brigade major went back and sorted them both out. The tanks of the Sherbrooke Fusiliers, supporting the SD&G, ran into some heavy Panzer VI "Tiger" tanks and had to withdraw to cover.

At 2040 hours, the North Novas, moving ahead with the Sherbrookes, bore the brunt of a counter-attack by the 12th SS Panzer Division. German bayonets drove two companies of the NNSH back to the lines of the SD&G. The battalion intelligence officer wrote in the war diary:

> Very bloody mess indeed. Very fierce fire from armour up here now grimly returning enemy fire. The NNS and 27th launch the counterattack. Magnificent!!!!
>
> Words cannot express such courage and determination! It seems they only have about 100 men left in action ["D" Company NNSH was wiped out with the bayonet], yet the

remainder take BURON. They doubt if they have the strength to hold the position, however.

In this engagement, the 27th lost twenty-five tanks and the NNSH lost 250 killed, wounded or missing.

This left the Glens, with the decimated NNSH, as the spearhead for the brigade. The Fort Garry Horse, who arrived shooting at everybody and everything in sight, relieved the 27th Armoured. Mortar and shellfire became more intense and snipers more numerous. The brigadier ordered no withdrawal from their positions, to which the SD&G radioed back: "Up the Glens!"[25]

The next morning, the battalion was just 1,000 yards south of the village of Villons-les-Buissons. For breakfast they chewed on a piece of hardtack and opened a tin of sardines or bully beef, depending upon the eater's taste. They were pushing towards the village of Vieux Cairon, but the enemy was too strong to dislodge. The Germans tried a direct frontal attack, but the Glens held the position with terrific fire from tanks, machine guns and mortars, and called for artillery support. Three field regiments, a medium artillery regiment, and the cruiser HMS *Belfast*, just offshore, poured masses of fire and death on the attackers.

The Germans continued fanatical attacks causing many tank and artillery duels throughout the day of June 9, but the Canadians put up a stubborn, desperate fight to halt any push towards the English Channel. On June 10, there was a brief respite. As the men relaxed and cleaned weapons and equipment, they still had to bat off spasmodic attacks. During the afternoon of the 11th, the Glens took the village of Vieux Cairon after a short intense fight. The next day, mail arrived; little delights a soldier so much as news from home.

The Glens had trained in England until they were satisfied they could meet the enemy, but there is nothing so terrifying as the first "face-to-face" contact when he starts shooting, knowing that the other fellow is returning fire. The Glens had undergone a change, a change that only comes to men who have experienced combat. They had been tested and knew that they had proved their worth. They could meet, and beat, the enemy. And now they would meet the worst—the 12th SS Hitler Youth Division, a band of fanatics, who took no prisoners, commanded by Major General Kurt Meyer.

The next week or two was a time of watchful waiting. Many of the SD&G were skilled snipers, crack shots who had been trained at a Canadian snipers' school in England. The sniper section was operating very effectively, and while they had few kills, it was providing a great deal of information

---

[25] This battle cry originated in an English tavern before the unit sailed for France. The Colonel was having a beer one evening with Major Fred Lander of Kingston when the barmaid remarked "There surely are a lot of you Glens around here." The unit had been called the Glengarrians, but this was a new one! The Colonel and the Major liked the name and raised their glasses in a toast **The Glens**. It caught on through out the battalion and upon their blazing baptism in Normandy and the bitter fighting at Hell's Corners the men would pop their heads from the slit trenches and send the wild shout ringing "**The Glens!**" W. Boss, Up The Glens (Cornwall: The Old Book Store, 1995), p. 104n.

through daily patrols, in return, for which they suffered heavy casualties from enemy mines and traps. On June 16, "C" Company sent out a patrol of one officer and five enlisted men, but they returned with little information and no sign of the enemy facing them. Shelling, mostly from 88mm guns, took a few casualties every night.

On June 20, the battalion celebrated its fourth anniversary at a ruined and abandoned farmhouse in Vieux Cairon. The men took turns attending the "banquet" of inch-thick steaks, the result of a curious cow that had investigated a booby-trap left by retreating Germans, and maple syrup for dessert, sent from their reserve battalion in Cornwall. The officers gathered before the farmhouse for a photograph, which shows Hal sitting in the foreground,

a cigarette in his left hand while his right raises one of the three single-malt Scotches he and each officer enjoyed that day. Judged the best tale of the day was that of a poor old duck wandering about a village with a tag on its neck, on which were the scrawled words: "Do Not Destroy. I am sitting on eggs!"

A message came for Lieutenant Murfitt finally approving his leave. He immediately packed up and headed for England, and with a fair amount of envy, his friends and fellow officers wished him well and

Lieutenant Murfitt toasting the battalion's success.

"God speed." However, he was too late. He arrived in Southgate to find his wife had died the day before. But fate was even yet more unkind. The day after her funeral, July 1, there was an air raid. However, before the family could reach shelter, a robot V1 flying bomb scored a direct hit. Murfitt and his infant son, Michael David, his wife's parents and her sister (who was also married to a Glens' officer) were killed instantly.

The same comrades that envied Hal's leave to London were thunderstruck to learn of his death. They faced death in France every minute of every day; they never considered the prospect of death at home.

Lieutenant Reg Dixon, the SD&G's intelligence officer, summed up the month in the battalion's war diary with these words:

> The men feel that their mettle was tested (at Hell's Corner) and as a result of the experience, face the future with confidence. Thus ends the month, and not without mixed feelings for all of us. We are proud to have participated in this, the greatest of military operations, proud to have been in the vanguard of the Divs. following us. Not without sorrow have we laid away many of our comrades, but our casualties have been lighter than we had reason to expect. We are confident,

in our leadership and in our weapons and look forward to the next months when the enemy can and will be dealt a decisive and mortal blow.

Lieutenant Harold Murfitt was laid to rest with his baby son in Southgate Cemetery on Waterfall Road, 200 yards west of Christ Church where short months before he had been married. It is an ancient ground, opened by the Southgate borough council in 1880. Harold Murfitt was thirty-three years old.

Hal's medals were sent to his mother at Broomhill, but were returned as undeliverable. Finally, in April 1951, they and the Memorial Cross were delivered to her home in Lincolnshire.

C 39208 Private Wilson Adison Costello
23 Field Ambulance
Royal Canadian Army Medical Corps

Wilson Costello was born on March 18, 1922, in Westmeath, near Pembroke, Ontario, to Simon and Jean (Jenny) Costello, the second youngest of five children. He had one brother, Albert Hacker and three sisters: Donalda (Mrs. Clyde Taman), Laurel (Mrs. Cecil McCann), and Charlotte. Simon died in 1941 when Wilson was nineteen years old. Simon was working for the John Brown Woolen Mills on Mill Street and was razing a disused building when part of the roof fell and struck Simon on the head.

Wilson was just a toddler when the family moved to Carleton Place, where he went to the United Church and attended Carleton Place schools. Growing up on Nelson Street he was a good friend with his neighbour, Wally Mace[26], who lived behind him on Antrim Street, a friendship that continued even after both joined the army and went to England. Wally was with the artillery and both went to France on D-Day. Wally recalls Wilson as a quiet, very serious fellow, and they often would hang out together at the coffee shop run by "Clicker" Peden. Joe Borland would drop in from time to time, and although he was considerably older than Wally and Wilson, he always took the time to chat with them.

After graduation from CPHS, Wilson went to work as a labourer for the Carleton Place Dairy. He missed working with Harold Murfitt by just one year.

Three-and-a-half months after his father died, Wilson joined the

Costello (centre) and friends. (Photo courtesy Wally Mace.)

[26] Wally served in an artillery regiment commanded by the legendary Conn Smythe of N.H.L. fame. He recruited Wally in Petawawa in the forties to play hockey with the National Army team. Other legends serving in Wally's crew were Ted Reeves, a sports writer from the Toronto Telegram and Ralph Allen who became a war correspondent for the Globe & Mail and after the war took over as editor of Macleans magazine.

army. Since Albert was still at home helping to support the family, it was agreed that Wilson could go to war. On September 18, 1941, he travelled to Ottawa to join the Royal Canadian Army Medical Corps (RCAMC). At his medical examination he reported having had measles and mumps as a child and was found to be in excellent condition, standing 5' 10½" tall and weighing a slight 137 pounds. He was described as having a medium complexion, brown hair, and hazel eyes, and his only visible mark was a scar above his right knee. He explained that he had injured his knee while playing sports at school.

The RCAMC's training centre was in Ottawa, so Wilson did his basic training close to home. At the end of basic training, in December, he had progressed so well that he was promoted to the acting rank of lance corporal and sent home for Christmas leave before going on advanced training. With the promotion, Wilson's pay increased from $1.30 to $1.50 a day; he was already assigning $20 a month to his mother to help her and his sister Charlotte at home.

In January 1942, Wilson went to Camp Borden for eight weeks training at the RCAMC's advanced training centre. Except for a cold that put him in hospital for one day in February, Wilson completed the training on schedule. At the end of the course, he was assessed as: "Good NCO material. (Recommended as a) Hospital orderly." He was also warned that he was going overseas immediately to be employed as a stretcher-bearer. However, to get to England, he had to relinquish his acting lance corporal rank and revert to private.

On March 19, 1922, the day following his twentieth birthday, Wilson Costello sailed from Halifax and landed in England ten days later. After combat familiarization training, Wilson was assigned, on May 7, 1942, to the 23rd Field Ambulance of the Medical Corps. Each division had three infantry brigades and each brigade had one field ambulance unit. The 23rd Field Ambulance was assigned to the 9th Brigade of the 3rd Division. Thus they were supporting the HLI, SD&G, and NNSH. They also provided a detachment to the armoured corps, the 17th Duke of York's Royal Canadian Hussars. It was a doctor from the 23rd Field Ambulance, taking part in the 9th Brigade's combined operations exercise on September 17, 1943, who treated Lieutenant Hal Murfitt for his wounds.

Costello's field ambulance unit joined the brigade on every exercise. Medical emergencies happened during training, and medical personnel needed to be aware of the hazards infantrymen would be facing. Contrary to the riflemen, however, their job was to save lives. But everywhere the infantry brigade went, so too went the field ambulance. In fact, during one exercise in November 1942, Wilson jumped from his moving jeep and had to be treated for a sprained left foot.

Medics were not exempt from combat training, as it was expected that under fire they could defend themselves and their unit. During 1943 and early 1944, medical personnel on large exercises acquitted themselves well. They gained expertise and the capacity to organize and conduct their operations to the satisfaction of the corps and army commanders. Early in 1944, the 3rd Division and 2nd Armoured Brigade, with all ancillary troops, were placed under command of the 1st British Corps to prepare for the assault on German-held Europe.

On June 1, 1944, the 23rd Field Ambulance moved into a marshalling area at Chanderford. The men were somewhat mollified with their new quarters in that they reported the food to be better than what they were used to. For the next three days, under a bright sun, they spent the hot days quietly until word came on June 3 that they would probably move out during the night. The unit had been separated according to the landing craft that they would ride to France, and all were issued with rations for twenty-four hours, an emergency ration, a vomit bag, and seasick pills. The men for the first craft left at 0130 hours on June 4, while the remaining loads moved to Southampton at various times during the day. All were aboard their ships in time for their evening meal and they spent the night swinging at anchor in the harbour.

All day on June 5, their ship remained at anchor. At 2330 hours, the unmistakable sound of the anchor chain rattling warned the medics of their imminent departure. The men on deck, eager to be ashore either because of seasickness or anticipation, spotted the coast of France at 0500 hours. At 1100 hours, "B" Company of the Field Ambulance followed the HLI to the beach and on to Bernières-sur-Mer where they established an advance dressing station. They worked there until 1600 hours, then moved to Beny-sur-Mer to set up in a church in the village centre. The ambulances brought in casualties all night.

The next day, June 7, dawned clear and cool. "B" Company moved forward to Basly to set up their aid post in the village school. Close to the front lines, they were very busy, and in spite of having considerable trouble from snipers, did a good job all night. The medical units were collecting casualties from the regimental aid posts just behind the lines, while jeep ambulance drivers elected speed to ensure some safety of the wounded who then endured an agonizingly rough ride.

Army doctors now had plenty of penicillin to control infection and plasma to help save dying soldiers. But in many cases, it was not enough for those torn apart by artillery and mortar blasts and burned inside their armoured vehicles. By the end of June, some 3,000 wounded had been sent back to England while many more with lesser wounds stayed in France to be treated in hospital tents at Secqueville-en-Bessin and near Bayeaux.

After the original onslaught (the Canadians lost 340 men killed and 574 wounded on D-Day alone), the fighting intensified as the Canadians moved south. The 9th Brigade angled slightly west towards the airfield at Carpiquet. It was very dangerous work, as they now faced the 21st Panzer Division, which had been rushed in to fill the breach left by the 716th moving back. When the NNSH and the Sherbrooke Fusiliers reached Buron, they ran headlong into the Panzer defence; however, suddenly to their dismay, they realized they had outrun their own artillery and were facing the 12th SS Panzer Division, a tough and experienced group, veterans of the Russian front. These fanatics firmly believed in the German master race.

Panzer Silver Assault Badge.

The brigade moved on to Authie, and the 23rd Field Ambulance, having set up shop at Basly, was getting many casualties. At Authie the Canadians bore the brunt of a German counter-attack by the 12th SS. Three battalions of the 25th SS Panzer-Grenadier Regiment, commanded by Colonel Kurt Meyer, had been ordered to take back the beaches, but first they had to re-take Buron and Authie. The *Hitlerjugend* proved a formidable foe and the fight degenerated into brutal hand-to-hand combat. The North Novas were already weakened and had no choice but to pull back. Many surrendered. That night, the 12th SS Panzer Division shot twenty-three prisoners; but it was not the last time that this division carried out similar atrocities against the Canadians[27].

In Basly, June 9 ground on through scattered showers. The nights at the field ambulance were very noisy as ack-ack batteries surrounded their location. There were no casualties except for two jeep ambulances that were hit by shrapnel, each suffering a flat tire. The rain and low cloud continued for several days, and on June 12, the first mail arrived at unit headquarters since they had left England. Then on June 13, the medics took their first casualty when an SD&G guard wounded Private Ashie of 5 Section. By the 15th, fighting seemed to have reached a lull, so the men took the time to go swimming and bathing in the Seulles River.

On June 19, an Atlantic storm battered the Channel, with high winds and waves damaging the Brits' artificial harbour and completely destroying the

---

[27] After the war the Canadian war trial sentenced Meyer to death but later commuted his sentence to life imprisonment.

one feeding the American beaches. There was few days' respite from action, allowed time for reinforcements to arrive and fill depleted ranks. On July 3, a jeep ambulance with a driver and an orderly were directed to the SD&G regimental aid post to relieve the members of the 22nd Field Ambulance.

The Canadians were only partly rested when the commander of the 3rd Division, Major General Rod Keller, was given the order to capture the Carpiquet airport. It was held by only 250 "boys" of Meyer's 12th SS, but the Canadians had learned their lessons well and were quite aware of the enemy's ferocity and fanaticism. At dawn on July 4, they rose to walk through waist-high wheat, pausing only to mark the location of the wounded and the dead—a rifle with its bayonet stabbed into the dirt. The wheat field was soon littered with the bodies of Canadian boys, many

Panzer Beret Badge

with their white faces turned upwards, unseeing blind eyes staring towards the heavens. There was no cover. Pitiless warfare raged in the ruins of Carpiquet village, and the North Novas suffered their bloodiest day: forty-six dead and eighty-six wounded.

On July 5, the 23rd Field Ambulance Advanced Dressing station was in full operation at Beny-sur-Mer, although reported casualties were relatively light. In contrast, the War Diary records that Major Holmes attended a child-birth case in the village, and with tongue-in-cheek, noted that "Mother, child and Major Holmes all doing well."

The savage fight at Carpiquet was deemed a failure and the 3rd Division was pressured to take the initiative and take Caen. Plans for the upcoming offence were shared with the Field Ambulance officers so they could take appropriate action in anticipation of the expected increase in casualties.

During the morning of July 7, the troops watched overhead as waves of bombers arrived from England. A total of 467 aircraft dropped 2,561 tons of bombs on the stricken city of Caen. It was a great confidence builder for the men on the ground as they were convinced that most of their battle had been won by the air force. But there were few Germans in Caen. Most were sheltered in fortified villages outside the city.

During the day, the 23rd Field Ambulance prepared to move to a new location: Villons les Buisson. A section of seven medics and transport moved to the village at 1900 hours to establish a car post, while the rest of the unit prepared all medical supplies and equipment for the imminent battle.

The 9th Brigade pushed south and ran up against a familiar enemy, Kurt Meyer's 12th SS. In a daylong battle, the HLI lost 262 men and their colonel.

In the early hours of July 8, the medics in the aid station were moderately busy, but the remaining two sections were able to move to les Buisson by 0800 hours. However, they barely had time to get established when ambulances began to arrive at about 1300 and unload patients. From 1500 hours on, the ambulances poured patients of all types into the station. This was the first major trial of the unit and all ranks performed smoothly and efficiently.

By midnight, the dressing station had processed 265 patients, most of them wounded who were treated and then evacuated to No. 86 or 88 General Hospital or No. 16 or 32 Casualty Clearing Station. Ten ambulances and a Bren-gun carrier attended to the transportation needs of the evacuated. The five doctors at the station worked almost non-stop treating the wounded. One ambulance driver took a shrapnel hit in the shoulder, but after treatment and rest, he refused to go back off the line and stayed on duty.

Men from the Highland Brigade (the 9th) worked their way very cautiously into Caen. Mines, booby traps, and snipers hindered their advance even though the main body of Meyer's troops had left. Urged forward to seize the bridges across the Orne River, reconnaissance units were halted by the rubble in the streets left by the indiscriminate bombers. With Caen captured, Montgomery was happy, but the Americans were far from it. The city was supposed to have been taken shortly after D-Day. Hedgerows and flooded marshes had bogged down their offensive, but it was easier to blame the "arrogant little [British] general" and his Canadian troops for being too slow.

The Advanced Dressing Station worked around the clock treating the tremendous number of wounded. By 0600 hours on the 9th, it was clear that the worst was over. Small bunches of injured men arrived throughout the day, but it was possible for those who had worked all night to snatch bits of sleep. A total of forty-five men remained in the station's wards, thirty-nine of them "battle exhaustion" cases. That night the men were treated to the movie, *So Proudly We Hail*, in the recreation barn. It provided a couple of hours escape other than retreating into a bottle of booze.

July 10 was crucial. The exhausted Americans needed help—just ten days to re-supply and re-build shattered units—and a British attack would give them just that. It was planned to send three armoured divisions through the narrow bridgehead over the Orne that had been secured by the parachutists on D-Day. They could then drive for Falaise. The 2nd Canadian Division arrived in the field early in July, and on July 11, II Canadian Corps became operational. The 2nd Division moved into the line along the Orne River to the right of the 3rd Division.

On July 10, a German Luftwaffe raider swept over the 23rd Field Ambulance, machine-gunning everything in sight; however, the only casualty was a wounded horse, which was quickly dispatched by one of the Ambulance NCO's. The soldiers suspected that the fighter's real target was the airstrip beside them, which was a temporary home to a Spitfire squadron. During this lull in the ground war, the padre took the opportunity to properly bury Canadian dead in the Beny-sur-Mer Canadian cemetery. In two days, more than 300 Canadian lads were laid to rest.

The first bread the men had seen since D-Day arrived with the rations on July 12. It amounted to one slice per man. Medical activity had dropped off considerably, but still German fighters continued to cause havoc and slight casualties. Their indiscriminate bullets hit a four-and-a-half year old French girl on July 14. She died after being admitted to the aid station, the first casualty to die after being admitted. During the night, three bombs dropped close enough to break the windows in the houses billeting the medics. While men were put to work cleaning up the glass next morning, a detail was dispatched on the very necessary mission of picking up the liquor ration for the officers and sergeants and the beer ration for the men.

After the capture of Caen, the objective was to cross the Orne. The RAF planned a more precise bombing plan that would concentrate on anti-personnel bombs. They hoped to avoid creating the large craters that stopped tanks and armoured vehicles in their tracks. The offensive began on the morning of July 18, and tanks of the British 11th Armoured Division rumbled across bridges to meet a ready and waiting 1st Leibstandarte Adolf Hitler. By noon they were in trouble. Meanwhile, the 8th and 9th Brigades crossed the Orne just below Caen and set about clearing Colombelles and neighbouring villages. The fighting was bitter and confused.

At 1330 hours, "B" Company, under the command of Captain Handford, moved to a position in the 9th Brigade headquarters area near Anisy[28]. From here they participated in the rapid advance. Wilson and Private Hughes, his jeep ambulance driver, were sent to the NNSH's regimental aid post to clear casualties from the regimental post back to the Field Ambulance.

At 0900 hours on the 18th, "B" Company of the Field Ambulance crossed the Orne and set up a casualty clearing post at Ranville. Headquarters and "A" Company moved to Couvre-Chef and set up the advanced dressing station. At noon they took delivery of "Dukw" vehicles (amphibious light armoured vehicles with a front-loading ramp). They tried using these Dukws

[28] Pte. Costello served in "B" Company under Capt. Handford.

A jeep ambulance in action with the 3rd Division in Normandy 1944.

to cross the river, but they were driven back by intense enemy artillery. All afternoon "B" Company evacuated patients to the 86th British General Hospital and by 1900 hours, the engineers had erected a pontoon bridge over the Orne beside a "normal," bombed-out bridge. Casualties could now cross, and the Ambulance began receiving a steady flow of wounded. No. 5 Field Dressing Station set up beside the ADS to treat the more serious cases.

The weather remained fair and warm, and the flow of casualties continued at a steady, but not overly heavy, pace all day, including many German prisoners. At 1400 hours, "B" Company moved to Colombelles, and a car-post made up of two heavy ambulances and four nursing orderlies was established at Benouville. During the day, the post was enlarged by adding four more heavy ambulances.

For the next couple of days, the heavens opened and rain flooded the battlefield. The number of casualties began to ease, so "B" Company closed the casualty clearing post and moved to DeVaucelles. The unit was allowed to rest, but stayed ready to move on a moment's notice. The field they had set the dressing station in was now a sea of mud due to the heavy rainfall.

The North Nova's aid post was in Bourguebus. On July 24, Wilson was at the post with a medical officer when it took a direct mortar hit killing Private Costello and one of the regiment's stretcher-bearers instantly, while the medical officer and another medic were wounded slightly. Private Hughes' wounds were so severe that he died a few hours later.

On a bright and warm July 26, Regimental Sergeant Major Ward made the sad trip by ambulance jeep to the North Novas and picked up the body of the first fatality in "B" Company, Wilson Costello. Twelve men and Captain Handford attended Costello's interment in the Beny-sur-Mer Canadian Army Cemetery. Private Hughes had still not been located.

Beny-sur-Mer Cemetery lies on the north side of the main road one kilometre east of the village of Reviers, eighteen kilometres east of Bayeaux, fifteen kilometres northwest of Caen, and four kilometres south of Courseulles-sur-Mer. It contains the graves of those Canadians who gave their lives during the landings at Normandy and in the early stages of the subsequent campaign. There are over 2,000 World War II dead commemorated at this site.

Wilson's mother received his War Service Gratuity of $554.50 for his 1,041 days service, including 837 days overseas. In November 1944, she was sent the Memorial Cross. When the casualties officer was gathering Wilson's effects in England, he found a pawn ticket from Messrs. Walter Bull & Son in Horsham, Sussex. It was for a gold signet ring that Wilson had pawned for ten shillings.

The officer commanding the 23rd Canadian Field Ambulance RCAMC summed up the month of July in his war diary thusly:

> . . . the unit has been called upon to do considerable work. From the results gained, it has been proven that the unit can do the work for which it has been trained and do it well. Much experience has been gained during the past month . . . Morale of the men is extremely high and discipline is excellent. Relatively few casualties have been suffered and the general health of the unit is good.

In November 1944, Captain H. L. Handford of Renfrew wrote to Wilson's mother at 41 Lake Avenue explaining how Wilson lost his life. The letter was printed in *The Canadian*:

> This is a most difficult letter for me to write and it is a long time coming to you. For that, I must apologize. But, really, for me it is difficult to sit down and write about these things.

> I have been Wilson's company commander for a long time and knew him

Private Wilson Costello, RCAMC.

better than any other officer. I've played ball with him and worked with him. He was a grand boy, the best in our unit, and for some reason he had to be the first one of the 23rd killed in action. One thing I can assure you of, is that he did not suffer a moment. He was killed immediately and never knew what hit him. Let me tell you about him.

We arrived together on D-Day and he did a good job for the next two days that no one else could have equalled. He was tireless and kept his mates in the game all the time. He was worth his weight in more than gold to me and to the Canadian Army. Unfortunately we do one of those jobs in war, which is just taken for granted, and we don't make headlines when a good job is done.

After D-2, he went out for a rest as none of my section had had a wink of sleep since D-1. We then took on a fairly easy job for a month but had plenty to do.

On July 17, we went up forward again and were in on a fairly rapid advance. We finished the first phase without any trouble. Wilson was riding as ambulance orderly in a jeep ambulance. His job was to keep contact with and clear casualties from the regimental aid post of the North Nova Scotia Regiment.

The aid post was in Bourguebus at the time he was killed. This evening when he was with their medical officer, the R.A.P. was hit directly with a mortar bomb. Wilson and one of the N.N.S.R. stretcher-bearers were killed instantly. The medical officer and one other were wounded slightly and the driver of the jeep ambulance, Pte. Hughes, died a few hours later of wounds.

There is nothing more I can say. That is the story and I thought it might help if you knew just exactly what happened. Dear knows how many stories you have heard already. I wanted you to know that Wilson was in the midst of doing his duty when he was hit and that it was (not) an accidental shot while he was off duty or resting.

As far as I am concerned, it was just like losing a younger brother. He was so full of life. I was in the process of making a left-handed baseball pitcher out of him and he had everything.

On three occasions I tried to make an N.C.O. out of him but he wouldn't take the stripes. The last time, I had him paraded to the colonel to see if he couldn't persuade him to take the job. The main reason he refused was that he was sure he would leave his company and his friends.

In closing, let me mention that Wilson was a real soldier and you have every reason to be extremely proud. He had done his duty, he never had anything but praise from his senior N.C.O.'s and officers and he has been a gentleman in every respect since he came to our unit in 1942.

All his company have been down to see his grave. He is buried in the Canadian Army cemetery at 'Beny Sur Mer,' Normandy, which overlooks the sea and points toward the west.

Some day when this is over, I will call in and see you in Carleton Place. My home is in Renfrew and Wilson and I had a great deal in common.

Please accept my deepest sympathy. You and your family can be extremely proud of having a real soldier and an unsung hero.

C 21008 Corporal William Melville Loney, MiD
Cameron Highlanders of Ottawa (MG)

On Sunday, September 10, 1939, the *Canada Gazette* proclaimed, "that a State of War with the German Reich exists." The next day, William Melville Loney presented himself to the Smiths Falls' recruiting officer of the Cameron Highlanders of Ottawa (Machine Gun), and by day's end, he had sworn to be faithful to His Majesty and to serve in the Canadian Active Service Force, "so long as an emergency exists." He was nineteen years old.

It was the waning years of the Depression, and since 1936, when Bill finished school, he had held odd jobs around town, as a carpenter's helper and farm labourer, and working in the bush, generally for small logging operations. In his off hours, he played hockey and enjoyed fishing and swimming in the Mississippi.

Recruiting totals that September exceeded the rate of enlistment for the Great War. Some regiments, like the Cameron Highlanders of Ottawa, filled their ranks very quickly. Units that were being mobilized were responsible for recruiting, administering medical exams, and training their own men. To be found "fit for general service," a man had to be "perfectly fit, mentally and physically, for all active service conditions of actual warfare in any climate, (be) able to march, see to shoot, and hear well." The minimum age was eighteen, the maximum forty-five. Chest measurement had to be at least thirty-four inches and the minimum height was five feet, four inches (Bill stood 5' 8" tall and weighed 135 pounds).

Although he had worn glasses growing up, Bill Loney passed the vision test with 20/20 in both eyes, could hear a whispered voice at twenty feet, and had a chest of $36\frac{1}{2}$", which expanded to $38\frac{1}{2}$" with a deep breath. He was nervous during the examination so his blood pressure was first recorded at 154/84; however, when resting, it was a respectable 140/76. He reported that he had suffered measles and whooping cough as a child. The medical officer recorded his physical development as good and described him as having a fair complexion, hazel eyes, and brown hair. Bill Loney was passed into active service with medical category "A."

Bill was born on March 19, 1920, to George and Margaret Ann Loney at 42 Morphy Street, Carleton Place.

Bill was enrolled into "B" Company of the Camerons and stayed at the armouries in Ottawa for his basic training. The battalion had to mobilize, including "first reinforcements" to a war establishment of twenty-six officers and 774 other ranks. Most Canadian Active Service Force (CASF) enlistments came from the militia battalion, but far more were required from the general population to augment the undermanned NPAM unit. Accommodation for the newly mobilized Camerons was to be at their armouries and the exhibition grounds at Landsdowne Park, although a few recruits were allowed to live at home and report for daily parades. They were given what few uniforms were left over from the Great War, as new uniforms were not available until the end of October.

Needless to say, what kit was available was inadequate, as were stocks of blankets, socks, and underwear. As civilian footwear fell to pieces, some men had to be excused from parades until proper boots could be obtained (on September 21, commanding officers were authorized to make local purchases of whatever boots were available). Rifles issued were the short magazine Lee-Enfield No. 1, last used in 1918.

Basic training involved instruction in first aid, rifle and bayonet drill, squad drill, gas protection, anti-aircraft rifle and light machine gun training, fieldcraft, and map reading. In December, Bill was allowed weekends home; he was also allowed home leave over the Christmas holidays. Then, from February 18 to 20, Bill went missing and was declared AWL, so the commanding officer

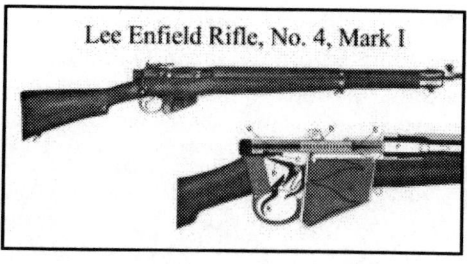

Lee Enfield Rifle, No. 4, Mark I

ordered the forfeiture of three days' pay. Prior to going to Camp Borden for advanced infantry training, he was given ten days leave from March 24 to April 3. Bill spent most of his leave in Carleton Place, but he also visited friends in Toronto and elsewhere in Ontario.

Camp Borden was home to the armoured corps schools, and a motor machine-gun company trained with motorcycles, reconnaissance cars, universal weapons carriers, and utility trucks. With an apparent wealth of weapons they learned to provide covering machine-gun fire to troops sent to occupy a position and to use machine guns, rifles, and smoke bombs to cover an advance in a hail of bullets. Their intensive training devoted two months to the use of vehicles and machine guns that would be their stock-in-trade.

In June, Bill was given a lesson in anger management, especially in regard to his NCO's, after being sent for fourteen days to the Camp Borden detention barracks and forfeiting fourteen days' pay. At $1.30 a day this cost him $18.20, a considerable sum. A sergeant had charged him with, "Conduct to the prejudice of good discipline," in that he had struck one of his sergeants. The details of the altercation remain unknown.

The men enlisted into the CASF in 1939 and early 1940 could not be required to serve in the field for longer than one year. Thus, the men of both 1 Canadian Division and 2 Canadian Division destined for overseas service had to be re-enlisted, "for overseas service." Bill was taken on strength of the overseas force on June 30, 1940, and at the same time, his battalion was assigned to the "Z" Force for service in Iceland.

Had the Germans occupied Iceland, they could have threatened the valuable convoy routes from North America to Britain; thus, British troops occupied the island in May 1940. The Canadian War Cabinet advised Britain that they were expediting the movement of the 2nd Division overseas to join the 1st, and that a Canadian battalion was being sent to the West Indies to replace British troops. Authorities in England then suggested that Canadian forces might be useful in garrisoning Iceland. Canada promised an infantry brigade, close to 2,700 men, led by the RCR. Les Fusiliers Mont-Royal and the Cameron Highlanders of Ottawa machine-gun battalion arrived in

Iceland on July 7. Later it was agreed that all of the 2nd Division should be concentrated in England, and on October 31 the brigade, with the exception of the Cameron Highlanders, sailed for the U.K.

CHofO men at mail call in Iceland. Note the accommodation in tents. (Photos courtesy the Cameron Highlanders of Ottawa Foundation.)

The Camerons stayed in Iceland all winter, enduring rain and high winds and considerable discomfort in their inadequate accommodations. One bright spot for Bill during the dreary winter was the arrival of cigarettes from the first consignment sent overseas by the *The Carleton Place Canadian* cigarette fund.

The battalion was earmarked to join the 3rd Division, then forming in Canada. During training on the old Vickers machine gun, the only machine gun available at the time, Bill qualified as the No. 2. This meant that he would feed ammunition in adequate quantities to match the gunner's shooting.

On April 27, 1941, the Camerons embarked at Reykjavik, and on May 1 they landed in Greenock, Scotland. Simultaneously the battalion was transferred from the "Z" Force to the Canadian Army (Overseas). On May 5, all battalion members were given seven days' landing leave. Bill sent a telegram to his mother advising her of his safe

Vickers .303 Machine Gun

arrival in England and then immediately left to visit his grandmother and other relatives that he had never met.

He was back in camp only a few days when the company quartermaster sergeant put Bill on charge for failing to report after being warned for duty, thereby causing another man to do duty. Consequently, the company commander sentenced Bill to seven days confined to barracks and the loss of one day's pay. He had been AWL for one hour and fifteen minutes. In July 1942, Bill was before his commander charged with "using language unbecoming a Pte. [private] while speaking to his platoon sergeant." This cost him three days confined to barracks. Then a month later, he "showed a willful defiance of authority, failed to appear on P.T. [physical training] parade." For this infraction, the battalion commander threw Bill in the "digger" (jail) for seven days and relieved him of seven days' pay.

On January 1, 1943, Bill was awarded a raise to $1.40 a day as proficiency pay, and on April 30, he was transferred to the 3 Division Support Battalion, the 8th Battalion Support Group. At the same time, he was appointed acting corporal and received another pay hike to $1.50 a day. Bill's only visit for medical attention occurred on March 2, 1943, when he reported sick with gastroenteritis.

On August 24, he was given permission to marry Joan Yvonne Martin of the Womens' Auxiliary Air Force[29]. In his marriage application, he stated that he would seek a position with Findlay's Foundry in Carleton Place upon his return to Canada. They were married on a pretty autumn day, September 25, 1943, at the Barcombe Parish church.

Organizing a wedding in wartime England was an exercise in frustration. Only two people in love would put themselves through the hassle. First, they had to submit themselves to questions from inquisitive administrative officers, padres, and medical officers, have blood tests taken, and supply written references from prominent citizens of their communities. Once written permission was granted, a three-month waiting period followed during which the authorities checked in Canada for any "forgotten" wives tucked away. In Bill and Joan's case, they managed to convince authorities to intercede and allow their wedding after only a one-month waiting period.

Although rationing of all goods was strictly enforced, and the law stated that no wedding cake could have icing, neighbourhood ladies conjured up a real wedding cake for Joan, complete with currants, fruit peel, icing sugar, and eggs.

Joan's father was dead, so her grandfather gave her away. She made a lovely sight in a floor-length, white-satin gown, with a round neckline and long sleeves. Her veil was three-quarter length falling from a halo of silk net. In her hands rested a bouquet of red carnations and trailing fern. After a reception in the Barcombe Assembly Room, the bride and groom departed for a honeymoon in London. Joan then returned to her posting in Bentley Priory near Stanmore, Middlesex, where she served with No. 1 Flight, No. 2 Squadron as aircraftswoman first class. Shortly afterwards, she took her release from the RAF and moved home with her mother. Bill went back to barracks.

On August 31, Bill was posted to the No. 5 Canadian Infantry Reinforcement Unit (CIRU), and from November 28 to December 23, he attended an NCO course at Canadian Military Headquarters in London. While there, he was awarded his Canadian Volunteer Service Medal and

[29] 2144629 ACW1 Joan Martin, was stationed with #1 Flight, #2 Squadron, at RAF Station Bently Priory, Stanmore, Middlesex.

Clasp (CSVM). The CVSM was authorized in 1943 for men and women of all ranks who volunteered for service and had honourably completed eighteen months. Those who served abroad got the clasp, which was a silver maple leaf, attached to the ribbon.

At the end of February 1944, Bill Loney was sent back to his battalion with the 8th Brigade of the 3rd Division. The Cameron Highlanders of Ottawa were making intensive preparations for the invasion of France. On March 1, Loney was confirmed as corporal, which meant he would lead his platoon into battle.

D-DAY (CANADIAN AREA OF OPERATIONS)
JUNO BEACH, BERNIERES-SUR MER, 6 JUN 44

FRANCE

DIRECTOR IMAGERY EXPLOITATION
DIRECTEUR - EXPLOITATION PHOTOGRAPHIQUE
OTTAWA, CANADA

0492800N/0003200W

ELMS OF
7 CDN INF BDE
MOVING OFF THE BEACH

N

On June 3, Bill Loney boarded his landing craft in England. At 1910 hours on June 5, the battalion sailed out of Southampton to the wail of pipes from the unit's pipe major. In dawn's early light on June 6, he led his section of No. 6 Platoon into chest-deep water and scrambled up Juno Beach under the Red Ensign, the first time Canadian troops had not gone into battle under the Union Jack. The Camerons were the 3rd Division's machine-gun battalion operating with the 7th, 8th, and 9th Brigades. Corporal Loney was in the unit attached to the 8th Brigade; they were assigned Nan Sector and were tasked with overwhelming the beach defences and proceeding inland to capture Bernières. Their reserve infantry regiment was Le Régiment de la Chaudière, landing two-and-a-half hours behind them.

The brigade ran into stiff opposition. The supporting tanks of the Fort Garry Horse could not land as planned due to high waves, and much confusion ensued. Only thirteen of their tanks got ashore intact and they were behind rather than in front of the infantry.

A battery of German 88mm guns held up the advance until the scream of shells from HMCS *Algonquin* roared over the Canadians' heads to silence the enemy artillery. By the evening of June 6,the invaders were well entrenched ashore and were moving inland at a good pace. However, beyond Bernières, the brigade slowed and it was not until evening that Bèny-sur-Mer, on the road to Caen, was taken.

Ahead lay more savage fighting as the Canadians continued, through June and July, to advance through Normandy. They experienced dreadfully fierce fighting with the Panzer divisions and it was not until July 10 that Caen fell. They were now ordered to break out of Caen across the Orne River to solidify the bridgehead and to take some pressure off the Americans trying to break out to the west. The Canadians faced some of Germany's best armoured units, suffering heavy losses. But with the Germans engaged here, the Americans were able to break out of Cherbourg and begin circling around the German army.

On a warm and clear July 25, a renewed offensive met with serious enemy opposition. . The NNSH were to take Tilly la Compagne, assisted by heavy machine-gun support from the Camerons, but the division was unable to make any advance. They took the town, but by early evening, were evicted by German counter-attacks. During this fighting, Bill Loney's force was counter-attacked and he found his platoon standing alone against the enemy. Bill held fast at his gun, pouring fire at the advancing tank of the Panzer squadron leader. He finally hit a vulnerable spot, completely disabling the tank and its gun. Bill then captured the tank commander and his comrades.

The next day, under scattered showers, the companies retained their defensive positions. Picks and shovels were put to good use improving slit trenches when a few enemy artillery and mortar shells landed in their lines. The soldiers sat tight and watched Allied Typhoons strafe and rocket-bomb Tilly. One Typhoon was hit and crashed, and infantrymen ran out to save the pilot who turned out to be the brother of a former member of "B" Company. At night, enemy aircraft flew over the Canadians' heads, and slight breezes dispelled the multitude of flies that attacked the men on the ground.

CAMERON HIGHLANDERS MEMBERS EAT BREAKFAST DURING A BREAK IN BATTLE IN CARPIQUET, FRANCE IN 1944

July 28 was a warm and fair day, and after surviving the intense fighting from D-Day and during the fierce attacks against crack Panzer brigades, Bill Loney's luck ran out. Enemy aircraft attacked and bomb fragments filled the air, wounding Bill severely in both legs. He was evacuated to the Régiment de la Chaudiére's aid post where the medical officers decided his only hope lay in a double amputation. So, while the surgeons did the deed, Bill's platoon was still at work.

In the misty pre-dawn darkness, No. 6 Platoon heard a three-man patrol approaching their gun position. They lay in wait and as a lad of eighteen reached for the Canadian PIAT gun, they shot him. A second German, nineteen years old, wounded one of the Canadian privates before being taken into custody. The third took off in a blur along the hedgerow with a hail of bullets chasing him into the darkness. "B" Company also captured a Chevrolet touring car, which they presented to their commander, Lieutenant Colonel Klaehn.

The battalion endured heavy shelling, but in return, inflicted many casualties when the enemy ran away from bombed buildings. Most of the day was devoted to harassing enemy positions near the wood at La Hogue and Hubert Folie. A couple of the platoons lost personnel carriers to incoming artillery fire.

Meanwhile, Corporal William Melville Loney succumbed to his wounds and drew his last breath. He was twenty-four.

The division was moved into a rest area at Villons Les Buissons-sur-Thaon, and on July 30, the Camerons moved into the beautiful château and grounds of the Baron D' Gronier, mayor of Villons. It was an ideal spot for a rest cure. The padre, Major Forth, had hurriedly buried Corporal Loney according to the rites of the Church of England on July 28 at St. Germain La Blanche Herbe. His body was later exhumed and re-interred in the new Beny-sur-Mer Canadian War Cemetery, which was opened on July 6, 1944. He lies not far from another soldier from Carleton Place, Wilson Costello. Recovered from Bill's body was one dried rose, a gold ring, and an RAF pin.

Bill's son, Terence (Terry) William, was born on the night of October 30, 1944. As well as his wife, Bill left behind younger sisters, Margaret Drenda (Mrs. William Jackson of Truro, Nova Scotia), Annie Doreen, and Pauline Joyce (both at home). Also surviving was a twelve-year-old brother, George Lindon. As he had changed his next-of-kin to his wife in England, it became her sad duty to inform his mother of Bill's death. Only days before she had received a letter that her son had been responsible for the capture of four Germans.

Joan applied to emigrate to Canada with her son as the wife of a Canadian soldier killed overseas. The application was granted, partly because she planned to go to her mother-in-law's house in Carleton Place. It was described as a six-room home with plenty of space for the newcomers. Before she left England, Joan received two letters, both written on February 21, 1945. The first was from Acting Lieutenant Colonel R. M. Ross, Commanding Officer of the 1st Battalion Cameron Highlanders of Ottawa:

> The King has been graciously pleased to approve that your husband, the late Corporal Wm. M. Loney be mentioned in recognition of gallant and distinguished services in North West Europe.
>
> The bronze Oak Leaf which I am enclosing is the symbol of the award.

Oak Leaf for Mentions in Despatches

> I would like you to know that your husband was held in the highest regard by myself and my Battalion both for his personality and for the exemplary manner in which he carried out his assignments. His death was a great loss, not only to his family, but also to the Cameron Highlanders of Ottawa. Please accept my sincere condolences.

The next letter was written by a J. C. Woodword and contained details of Bill's death:

> I am so glad to know that Bill has received recognition for his gallantry and outstanding good service. The Oak Leaf which we are forwarding should enrich the memories of yourself and 'The Nipper,' [their son] particularly the latter.
>
> The particular action for which Bill was cited was at [undecipherable] when we were almost overrun and counterattacked and at one time 6 platoon stood alone against the enemy. We were attacked by Panther tanks and Bill, manning his gun, got the squadron leader for a start.
>
> I trust that young Bill is progressing favourably.

Joan received a certificate from King George VI on June 25, 1946. The covering letter read:

> . . . to denote that your husband was Mentioned in Despatches for distinguished service and that His Majesty the King has recorded his high appreciation of the services rendered.
>
> The Honourable the Minister of National Defense expresses his sincere regrets that your husband did not survive to receive the award so gallantly earned.

Beny-Sur-Mer War Cemetery is in the pastoral village of Reviers, fifteen kilometres northwest of Caen. To the north is Juno Beach where the 3rd Canadian Division landed on June 6. It holds the graves of Canadians who were killed or died of wounds during the landings in Normandy and the early stages of the subsequent campaign. There are over 2,000 casualties commemorated at this site.

CHAPTER TWENTY-FIVE—THROUGH NORMANDY

Approximately 14,000 Canadian soldiers landed in Normandy on June 6, 1944. Once the beachhead was secure, at considerable cost to Canada, the force swung northeast along the coast. The assault caused 1,074 Canadian casualties, 359 of them fatalities. In front of them was some of their hardest fighting against experienced and powerful Panzer troops.

After the capture of Caen on July 10, the headquarters of the 2nd Canadian Corps entered the theatre. The Corps was directed to cross the Orne River on a breakout from Caen. The fighting was violent and bloody. At Verrières Ridge, Canadian soldiers were executed by the Panzer Grenadiers of Kurt Meyer's force, earning him undying hatred and the only post-war trial for war crimes held in Canada. On July 25, the Canadians attacked some of Germany's best-armoured forces on either side of the Caen–Falaise road. Casualties were heavy as the Germans held their ground, but the enemy had to move some of their armour away from this sector to meet the American threat near St. Lô. As the Americans swept in, surrounding the Germans in a large pocket, General Crerar, commanding the First Canadian Army[30], was ordered to Falaise. It was essential that Falaise be taken without delay for the army to link with the American forces, trapping the enemy in the Falaise pocket.

Lieutenant General Guy Simonds, commanding the 2nd Canadian Corps, planned a night attack using personnel carriers to move his troops forward, with tanks ahead and behind the infantry. Just before midnight on August 7, after a very heavy air bombardment, the attackers surged forward. Initially they were successful, and the defensive lines on the ridge at Verrières were overrun. But then resistance stiffened and, after an Allied navigation error caused bombers to drop on their own troops, the momentum faltered and stopped.

The second attack was carried out in daylight, aided by new smokescreen tactics. Again, Allied bombers erred and bombed their own men on the ground, but this time the assault succeeded, and by August 16, Falaise was in Allied hands and many German forces were caught in the rapidly shrinking pocket. Their only exit was a narrow gap between Falaise and Argentan, which the First Canadian Army was sent to close. By August 19, the gap was loosely closed, but a desperate enemy continued counter-attacks. They took heavy losses, but a great number managed to escape; the German armies were weakened but still intact. Then Paris was liberated on August 25, and the German armies retreated to their own borders to make their last stand.

---

[30] The First Canadian Army was formed in the European Theatre on July 23.

C79100 Private Earl Ernest Porteous
Calgary Highlanders

On March 5, 1942, the Lanark and Renfrew Scottish Regiment mobilized for home defence.[31] The formation of these home-defence units created an even greater demand for recruits, and a month later, on April 3, eighteen-year-old Earl Porteous travelled from Carleton Place to Perth for a medical examination in order to enlist.

Since leaving school after Grade 8, Earl had worked as a weaver in the Bates and Innes Mill. Although he was a thin, wiry young man (5' 11" and 133 pounds), he was physically fit and had no problem with the medical; he was awarded a category "A." His only distinguish-

ing mark was a scar on the outside of his left knee, but he could not recall the incident that had caused it. However, because he was so thin his develop-ment was listed as only "fair." He had a light com-plexion and intensely blue eyes under a shock of brown hair that had more than a trace of blond in it.

Earl was a single man, still living with his par-ents, Ernest and Martha Emeline, on Napoleon

Street. He was born on April 15, 1923, and celebrated his nineteenth birthday shortly after enrolling in the Lanark and Renfrew Scottish. Growing up, Earl had been an infrequent attendee at the United Church in Carleton Place.

The last year Earl was in elementary school, he was hired to start the stove on winter mornings. He was very excited to get this position, which paid him a grand total of $13 for the season. This was in the days when men worked a week for a dollar.

Earl spent the summer of 1942 doing his basic training with the regiment at the Connaught Ranges outside Ottawa. Over the next eight weeks, Earl was given the

[31] The Regiment never got overseas and was disbanded on October 13, 1943. The First Light Anti-Aircraft Regiment, after service in Sicily and Italy was redesignated The Lanark and Renfrew Scottish Regiment on July 13, 1944. It moved to NorthWest Europe on March 5, 1945 and on March 15 was redesignated as 1st Light Anti-Aircraft Regiment (Lanark and Renfrew Scottish Regiment). It was disbanded overseas on June 29, 1945. At home the regiment was redesignated "59th Light Anti-Aircraft Regiment (Lanark and Renfrew Scottish), Royal Canadian Artillery". On December 1, 1959 it was reconverted to infantry and redesignated "The Lanark and Renfrew Scottish Regiment [The Regiments and Corps of the Canadian Army, Volume I of the Canadian Army List (Ottawa: Queen's's Printer, 1964), p. 163]

usual inoculations and qualified in all the basic training: drill, physical fitness, first aid, marching, small arms training, gas training, fieldcraft, and basic map reading. On June 26, he fell and cut his left knee badly enough that he was sent for medical treatment. Then on July 6, he was back at the hospital, having torn off his toenail. At the end of July, he was examined again, declared still fit for category "A," and passed on for advanced training.

The usual nine weeks of advanced training was packed into a month at the camp in Sussex, New Brunswick. Marching and physical fitness were augmented with additional courses in bayonet training, distance judging, and

---

The Amazing Sten

Sten Gun Mark II

The Sten was a deadly little rapid-firing, lightweight weapon that dismantled easily and could be stowed away in the pockets of a soldier's battle dress.

When Britain's Expeditionary Force fled France in 1940, it left behind most of its equipment, weaponry, and ammunition, meaning improvisation became the order of the day. The first Sten was a crude weapon, lacking the finish of the U.S. Thompson sub-machine gun and the weight and solidity of the German Schmeisser. Only the absolutely essential parts of the Sten were machined to fine limits. The rest remaining parts were very rough.

Two men had developed this gun: Major Sheppard and a civil servant named Turpin. They named it STEN, with the S and T standing for Sheppard and Turpin and the EN for England. It fired at a rate of 550 rounds a minute using standard 9mm ammunition. That was almost as fast as the Thompson and faster than the Schmeisser. It could be fired from either the hip or the shoulder. The earliest guns cost about $12 each, but mass production reduced that to $8 or less.

The Sten was the simplest of sub-machine guns. It had only forty-five parts and any infantryman could handle and carry the Sten with eight magazines, each holding thirty-two rounds. It weighed exactly six-and-three-quarter pounds.

During the war, Britain was desperately short of tools, machines, and workshops. Old stables, derelict barns, coach inn lofts, disused laundries, and garages were commandeered for this purpose. Workers included wives, sweethearts, brothers, and fathers of those in military service. Machines that were too inaccurate for fine work were used for producing rough parts, and as parts became available, they were shipped to army ordnance factories for assembly.

The Sten was, like all sub-machine guns, not accurate beyond sixty yards. Instead, it was a hose for spraying lead and could kill at up to 200 yards and wound at up to 600. It was meant to be used as a surprise weapon, ideal for ambushing jittery enemy soldiers and for street and house-to-house fighting. Thousands of Stens ended up in the hands of vengeful resistance fighters making for outright unpleasant surprises for the German occupiers.

grenade digging, as well as use of the pistol, rifle, mortar, and the light sub-machine gun (the newly issued Sten Gun).

Earl was sent to Dartmouth, Nova Scotia, on September 8 to await shipment overseas. Two days later, he was given embarkation leave until midnight on September 19. He embarked on a troopship on September 24 (together with another Carleton Place man, Lieutenant Hal Murfitt) and disembarked in the England on October 7, designated as reinforcement for the SD&G. He was sent immediately to the holding group, 3 Canadian Division Infantry Reinforcement Unit.

Each division had its own reinforcement group, and each was tasked with operational training of the basic-trained recruits. While waiting assignment, Earl took the regimental motorcycle course, No. 8, receiving his Class "C" qualifications on January 27, 1943. He then received nine days' leave and promptly hied himself off to London. Things were more enjoyable in this great metropolitan city now, as the RAF had taken control of the skies by 1943, and London, while submitting to black-out regulations, had come alive once more.

In February, Earl was transferred from the divisional holding unit to 5 CIRU. On the morning of the 14th, Earl lingered ninety minutes too long in bed, which resulted in an AWL charge and confinement to barracks for five days. On February 24 he was AWL again for one hour and fifteen minutes and was assessed a fine of one day's pay, and on April 8, his corporal, charged him again for being AWL, this time for three hours during the evening. This cost him another five days confined to barracks.

From the CIRU he was posted, on April 15, 1943, as reinforcement to the SD&G. Ten days before, the battalion had moved from wet and muddy Rochecourt Camp into Rookesbury. The regiment formed one of three infantry battalions in the 9th Brigade of the 3rd Canadian Division, and its members were mostly farm boys from the three eastern Ontario counties. They had landed in England on July 19, 1941, and were training for the invasion of France.

The SD&G trained hard all during 1943. They practised tactics with artillery units and undertook infantry exercises at brigade and divisional levels. Meanwhile, each battalion honed the skills of individual platoons and sections with aggressive exercises practising the lessons learned in the larger schemes. The battalion travelled by train to Scotland on two occasions: to Wemyss Bay to where it joined a combined operations and rigorous training exercise in making beach landings from landing craft while live ammunition whizzed overhead.

In July, the Canadian Corps left for Sicily, but the 3rd Division, earmarked for the European invasion, was left behind in England under British command. They moved to the English Channel coast where they trained with the British army and the Royal Navy.

In mid September, the battalion practised more beach landings from landing craft. Originally these boats had no ramps, meaning the men had to jump up on deck and then leap over the side, three to four feet above the surface, into water of unknown depth. Many sprained and fractured ankles later, steel ramps were added, which also provided additional protection.

After dinner on September 28,Earl had something better to do than army duties. He was absent for seventeen hours, returning at lunchtime the next day. Because of his earlier infractions, he was awarded a forfeiture of sixteen days' pay; a substantial sum of $24.

On January 1, 1944, Earl changed his next-of-kin to his mother, Mrs. Martha Porteous, who was now living at RR 3, Ashton. He was sending her $20 a month from his pay.

A kit inspection was ordered for January 11. No. 10 Platoon Commander, Lieutenant W. R. Grant, entered the hut, and as he anticipated being there all morning, removed his web belt and holstered Smith and Wesson .38 calibre sidearm and laid them on an empty upper bunk. The pistol had been loaded a few days previously during an exercise, but the lieutenant had taken all the cartridges out, except one. It had been left in the cylinder so that the first pull would fire the weapon. Earl and a buddy, Private Lehman, passed the bunk, noticed the revolver, and decided to take a closer look.

Lehman picked up the holster, removed the pistol, and looked in the cylinder, but saw no rounds. He pointed it upwards and squeezed the trigger, intending only to observe the action of the hammer. His only experience had been with .45-calibre handguns, and he expected much stronger pressure to be required. The weapon fired, and Porteous reeled back holding his chest exclaiming increduously, "You've shot me!" Lehman threw the pistol on the bed and ran out the door to get the first-aid man at company headquarters. By the time he returned with the company sergeant major, a stretcher and two sergeants, Porteous had already been taken to the regimental aid post.

The medical officer noted that the bullet had entered Earl's lower left chest just lateral to and below the nipple. He could not determine the extent of internal injuries, so had the soldier admitted to the Royal Portsmouth Hospital. Investigation showed that Earl's paybook and other items in his breast pocket had provided some protection from the full extent of the gunshot blast. The wound was cleaned and sutured, and on January 13, he was transferred by ambulance to No. 2 CGH.

On admission, Earl had limited movement of his chest due to the pain and a great deal of distress when coughing. The good news was that no lung or abdominal injury could be detected, and for five days he was treated with sulfa drugs applied to the wound to ward off infection[32] The doctors finally decided that the bullet had been deflected downwards, lodging in the lateral wall of the abdomen and causing no specific symptoms. On the eleventh day, the sutures were removed and the incision was opened, extensively cleaned, and covered with a dry dressing. Earl was convalescing rapidly, generally well and active. However, never to overlook an opportunity, the surgeons removed two small lumps on Earl's right eyelid; they had healed before he was transferred to No. 2 Convalescent Depot at Alton on February 3, 1944.

On March 22, Earl was sent back to his battalion. However, he apparently was not ready to resume soldiering and he went AWL at 0900 hours on the 27th. He did not return until almost midnight on April 3. This almost constituted desertion, and for this absence, he spent fifteen days doing field punishment and lost a total of twenty-nine days' pay and an additional fine of £1.12.1. One of his buddies quipped that he hoped "she was worth it!"

During the month of May, Allied air forces struck at enemy targets in France and the rail network all over northwest Europe, with airfields and tactical targets along the Normandy coast receiving special attention. The Germans retaliated with flying bombs and rockets. Earl missed this and most of the preparations his battalion made to assault Fortress Europe due to his confinement.

On May 10, he was admitted to No. 11 General Hospital complaining of a continuous sharp pain in the left side of his chest and below his shoulder blade, the same area he was shot. He was admitted for further testing and evaluation of the damage done by the gunshot wound, and on May 16, an X-ray revealed the bullet lying immediately under the ribs. However, the radiologist found that the "metallic foreign body" caused no impairment to the movement of the diaphragm. It was fixed to the chest wall, and was apparently causing no obvious problem, but surgery was undertaken to remove it.

Earl was discharged from the hospital on May 18 to a medical holding list. He was carried on the strength of the reinforcement unit until a medical board could be held to determine his fitness for full duties. Meanwhile, his battalion had completed all practice and preparations possible and had been moved into secure camps to await a decision to invade. Supreme Headquarters had decided on June 5 as the most auspicious time, in regards to moon and weather conditions. However, a postponement to June 6 or 7 was still possible. By May 30, the 3rd Division began to move, and by June 3, they were all waiting aboard a variety of ships and landing craft to set sail for France.

On May 25, a medical board sat and determined that Earl had no appreciable disease and was fit for full combat service. He was called in to the

[32] This was long before the use of antibiotics. Penicillin was the new drug of choice during the 40's.

hospital for overnight on May 30–31 to learn the board's results and to undergo a last medical examination. But he could not be released from the medical holding unit until the results were signed off, which did not happen until June 16. By then, D-Day was history, and Earl's battalion had long been in France.

Earl was, therefore, sent then went to 11 Battalion of the Canadian Base Reinforcement Group to await the first opportunity to go to Europe to join a fighting unit. It was common practice that if a man had joined a highland battalion, he was kept in another highland battalion if he had been lost from his original unit. This was to keep men with the same motivation together.

Headquarters of No. 2 Canadian Corps arrived in France shortly after Caen was taken on July 10. On July 22, Earl left England as part of the Corps' defensive company, and as the Calgary Highlanders were in need of reinforcements, on July 27, he was sent to them. The Calgarys were in the 5th Infantry Brigade of the 2nd Division. Four days later Earl Porteous was dead.

The Calgary Highlanders had sailed for France with the Régiment de Maisonneuve and The Black Watch on July 6. In fair weather they crossed a calm channel and landed on one of the temporary "mulberry" harbours. Everything was serene as they walked ashore and began the trek to divisional concentration points. However, the stony roads and day's heat ensured the march was no "walk in the park."

On July 18–19, the battalion marched through Caen and into action at Fauberge de Vaucelles and Fleury-sur-Orne. Their first contact with the enemy, on July 25, was vicious and frightening. The regimental War Diary records:

> . . . attack on St. André Sur Orne to May sur Orne. The Hun
> played many very dirty tricks on us during the day, such as
> 88mm sniping at Red Cross sites and the machine gunning
> of their own men who had been taken prisoners by us. He
> would not even hold fire to allow plainly identified stretch-
> er-bearers the chance to evacuate casualties from the field of
> battle. He absolutely mowed our (Regimental Aid Post) per-
> sonnel down as they attempted evacuation. It was noticeable
> that the Hun was pushing in fresh troops to our front
> because opposition was gradually becoming heavier.
>
> Unofficially we have 5 officers and 172 (other ranks) casu-
> alties in killed, wounded, missing. This number is being
> whittled down as some missing men are straggling back.
> Another battle and another 'win' for us. We have at least
> managed to draw all of Herr Hitler's famous SS troops to

our point and this relieves the other fronts for this very important hour in the battle of Freedom[33].

The Highlanders had delivered their attack, and although twice some got into the village during that morning, they were pushed back out both times.

Earl had barely missed a "down and dirty" fight, and activity was at a minimum for the next few days. The chaplain even managed to hold a well-attended church service in the caves below Fleury on Sunday the 30th. Then they were warned that at 0230 hours on August 1 that they would be attacking Tilley des Compagnes in relief of the Essex Scottish.

East of the River Orne it was also essential to keep the enemy pinned down so they could not turn and attack the Americans closing in on the German western flank.

At 2315 hours on July 31, marching troops from The Calgary Highlanders started the long trek to Tilly-la-Campagne to form up in the Essex Scottish area. Battalion headquarters was set up in the basement of a pump house as soldiers waited behind the start line for the 0230 H-Hour. Prior to the start time, battalion scouts, forward with a section of carriers[34], advised that the "coast was clear" for the battalion advance.

At 0230 hours, all hell let loose as the guns of Nos. 4, 5, and 6 Field Regiments pounded the ground ahead on targets identified by the infantry commanders. The Calgary Highlanders advanced. Two minutes later, "D" Company crossed the start line and the other companies followed. Immediately, the "B" Company wireless failed and they had to rely on runners and other companies to get their messages back to battalion headquarters. However, progress appeared to be quite normal as the infantrymen moved behind their artillery bursts at a rate of 100 yards in five minutes. The noise was terrific, and the Hun improved the din and clamour by laying down a terrific mortar and artillery barrage of their own. Headquarters resembled a buzz saw with messages going hither and thither, runners coming and going, and the odd casualty being steered in. Yet, the Regimental Aid Post and medical evacuation system were not working. Wounded were attended by one and all in headquarters using all available means of transportation for evacuation. At 0252 hours, "D" Company reported passing a check line closely followed by the other companies reporting their crossing.

Shortly afterwards, the forward troops reported that they were under terrific shellfire from their own artillery. This caused more than a furled brow on the forehead of Lieutenant Colonel D. G. MacLaughlin, the commanding officer. He had ordered artillery targets nowhere near his advancing soldiers.

[33] National Archives of Canada. The Calgary Highlanders CA(O) War Diary, Volume 15020.
[34] An innovation in this battle was the use of armoured personnel carriers for the first time. Some were half-track vehicles but most were improvised "Priest" self-propelled guns that had been withdrawn from 3rd Canadian Division. – Col. C.P. Stacey, The Canadian Army 1939–1945 (Ottawa: King's Printer, 1948), p.196.

He told them it must be German artillery, but the advancing companies insisted it was from their own guns. MacLaughlin ordered his guns to cease fire and still the infantry reported themselves under fire. It then became clear that the Hun was up to his old trick of firing into the Allied barrage. Many casualties were caused by this tactic.

Several setbacks occurred over the next anxious hours. Some troops managed to get into the outskirts of Tilly, but were immediately pinned down by concentrated machine-gun and mortar fire. "B" Company knocked out two tanks with their PIAT gun, but could not possibly get into Tilly itself, so they dug in close to the railroad tracks under terrific counter-fire. Tanks from the 14th Canadian Hussars went in and assisted the infantry in crossing the tracks into the village towards their original objective. 88's knocked out two of the tanks and the third withdrew.

The Highlanders were forced back by greatly superior firepower. At 1000 hours, with very few men left, the troops withdrew to their original start line. An RCR company came up to assist, but they too were unceremoniously thrown back to the start point. The Canadians dug in and prepared for a counter-attack that fortunately did not happen as they had no automatic weapons nor PIAT guns. German 88 gunners could hear the Canadian carriers, but could not target them through the heavy fog. Then rations arrived, and all the men had hot tea while they licked their wounds and counted their losses. Among the missing was Private Earl Porteous. Later in the day, he was confirmed as killed in action.

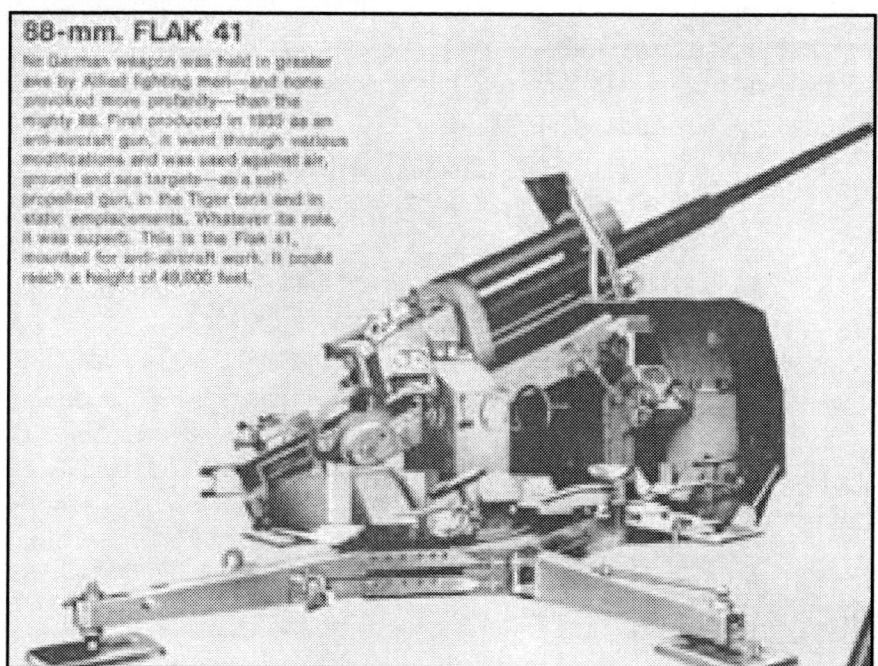

88-mm. FLAK 41

No German weapon was held in greater awe by Allied fighting men—and none provoked more profanity—than the mighty 88. First produced in 1933 as an anti-aircraft gun, it went through various modifications and was used against air, ground and sea targets—as a self-propelled gun, in the Tiger tank and in static emplacements. Whatever its role, it was superb. This is the Flak 41, mounted for anti-aircraft work. It could reach a height of 48,000 feet.

The Essex Scottish relieved the Calgary Highlanders on August 2, but before they left, they buried their dead where they had fallen. Earl Porteous was buried west of the Tilly-la-Campagne railroad tracks.

The only personal effect found on Earl's body was his identity disc. As well as his father and mother, Earl left his brothers: Kenneth in Carleton Place, age twenty-three; Percy, age twenty-two, somewhere overseas; and Emerson, eighteen, Lawrence, sixteen, and Gerald, thirteen, all of Ashton.

On September 30, 1944, the Minister of Defence sent his condolences, and on October 27, Earl's mother, Martha, received the Memorial Cross. Earl's War Service Gratuity of $412.63, minus an earlier overpayment of $20 to his mother, was paid. It represented 806 days of active service.

Martha was told in 1945 that none of Earl's personal effects had been recovered, so on June 11, she fired a missive at Army Headquarters: "Sorry to say," she wrote, "but do you mean to tell me that the Discs which they wear on the neck were not recovered? If not I feel there's nothing to show of my son's death. If they were recovered would you please forward same." On September 21 a package arrived with Earl's identity discs.

The body of Private Earl Porteous, Calgary Highlanders, was exhumed along with the other bodies buried near Tilly and re-buried in the Bretteville-sur-Laize War Cemetery in Calvados. It is on the west side of the main road from Caen to Falaise, just north of the village of Cintheaux. The village of Bretteville lies three kilometres southwest of the cemetery.

The cemetery contains those who were killed during the latter stages of the Battle of Normandy. Almost every unit of the 2nd Canadian Corps is represented, and nearly 3,000 war casualties are commemorated in this site.

Buried close by Earl is Tippy White.

C103111 Private Raymond Wilbert White
Essex Scottish Regiment

Ray "Tippy" White was nineteen when he was killed, and his army service closely parallels Earl's in that he only served in the Essex Scottish a mat-

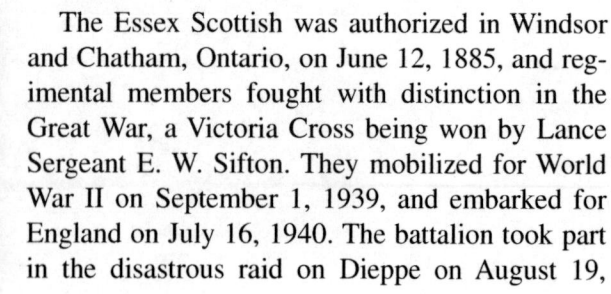

ter of days before meeting his death.

The Essex Scottish was authorized in Windsor and Chatham, Ontario, on June 12, 1885, and regimental members fought with distinction in the Great War, a Victoria Cross being won by Lance Sergeant E. W. Sifton. They mobilized for World War II on September 1, 1939, and embarked for England on July 16, 1940. The battalion took part in the disastrous raid on Dieppe on August 19,

1942, losing a great majority of its seasoned troops before a rebuilt and re-equipped, but totally inexperienced, battalion, landed in Normandy on July 5, 1944, with the 4th Infantry Brigade of the 2nd Canadian Division.

Ray White was born to William Milton and Hannah White in Carleton Place on January 25, 1925. He started school at age six and went on to high school, but he spent two years completing Grade 9 and then left school to go to work. He was employed first as a mill worker with Bates and Innes Woolen Mill and then he apprenticed as a spinner. About five weeks after he turned eighteen, he left the mill to enlist in the army. His older brother Lloyd had already joined the RCN. Behind him were brothers Carl,

Private Raymond White

Ivan, Ritchie, David, and Kenneth, and sisters Reta, Roberta, Edith, and Frances, all living at home on the corner of William and Bain Streets.

Ray, known to his friends in Carleton Place as "Tippy," went into Ottawa on March 15, 1943, to enlist. His only previous military exposure was two years in high school cadets. He was sent to Ottawa Military Hospital for X-rays and a medical examination, where he reported that he had suffered measles and mumps as a child, but had no ill effects from either. He had had a tonsillectomy in 1942, his vision was perfect, as was his hearing, and although he was slight (5' 5$\frac{1}{2}$", 124 pounds), he was pronounced Category A1.

Ray was interviewed and determined to have a good attitude towards military service. He was also found to be in good health, alert, stable, and co-operative, and to have a pleasant manner. He tested at average learning ability.

Ray was taken on strength of No. 3 Military District, Ottawa, and was given all his inoculations on March 24. Sent to clothing stores, Ray was issued with boots, web belt, and uniform, and told to report back on April 1 for Canadian Army Basic Training, Course No. 33, at Lansdowne Park.

On June 2, 1943, Ray was transferred to Camp Borden, Ontario, to A-11 Advanced Infantry (Rifle) Training Centre. Here he honed his military education to become a barely competent rifleman. This included nine weeks of foot-slogging, rifle drill, classroom, and in-the-field instruction, after which, he was given fourteen days furlough before reporting to Prince Rupert, British Columbia.

Ray had no experience or aptitude for any particular trade in the infantry. He was suitable for overseas service on general duties in a rifle company, but he had to be held on an operational unit in Canada until he became of age to go abroad. Ray had no regimental affiliation, so he was attached to the Midland Regiment (Northumberland and Durham) and was employed as part of the Prince Rupert defences on the Pacific coast. Ray stayed with the Midland Regiment for eight months before he started for overseas.

Ray was attached to No. 1 Transit Camp in Windsor, Nova Scotia, from April 3 until April 13 when he went to Debert, Nova Scotia, to await shipment to England. At last, he went to Halifax and embarked on April 30 and disembarked in the U.K. seven days later.

An average daily routine aboard ship was rising about eight, for breakfast at nine. A brief turn about the open deck when the weather permitted, then a chat in cabins until boat drill, held only during good weather. One could sleep until three or four then chat with his chums, have dinner, and go to bed. The program varied when movies were shown at the captain's pleasure on certain days. All too often it was not his pleasure as it was dangerous to have so many people congregated in one area.

On June 1, 1944, Ray was sent to 12 Battalion, 2 Canadian Brigade Reinforcement Group. Then he was passed along to 10 Battalion, Lorne Scots[35], for duties with 4 Infantry Brigade Defensive Platoon. On June 8, Ray shipped out for France, and on August 7, was sent as a reinforcement to 1 Battalion, Essex Scottish, then fighting with 2nd Division, 4th Brigade.

The Essex Scottish had been fighting close to the 5th Brigade and the Calgary Highlanders throughout the Normandy campaign. At Tilly-la-Campagne on July 29, the Scottish were occupying the château of Baron de Gronier, the mayor of Villons les Buissons. It was a lovely estate, and the Scottish had a grand view of the Calgary Highlanders' fight on July 27. The Scottish witnessed the Highlanders firing on about fifty Boche and were able to confirm German casualties. On the 30th, the Highlanders replaced the Scottish in the château.

On August 2, in very hot and dusty conditions, the Scottish saw their first "doodle bug," a mobile mine about the size of a universal carrier[36] that exploded with terrific noise and blast. In this case, the German driver either

---

[35] The Lorne Scots (Peel, Dufferin and Halton Regiment) provided seventeen platoons to the 1st Corps Defence Company. They were used in the defence of or employed as required at army, divisional and brigade headquarters.

[36] A lightly armoured open tracked vehicle for carrying men and/or equipment.

left just before it exploded or the machine was driven by remote control. Four appeared on the "B" Company front, killing four Canadians and wounding four more.

Just after midnight on August 5, the Scottish were relieved and retired to Louvigny Woods for a rest. Most of the battalion slept until noon, then the men spent the afternoon cleaning weapons, writing letters, and getting more sleep. Ray joined the battalion on August 7, just as they were told their rest was cut short and ordered to move into an assembly area by 1500 hours. Their job was to capture and hold the high ground in front of them, including the village of Caillouet. H-Hour was set for 2330 that night[37].

Introduced in Europe in 1944, the universal carrier finally took the walking out of infantry.

West of the Falaise Road, the 2nd Canadian Infantry Division and the 2nd Canadian Armoured Division were to lead the charge, with self-propelled guns and tanks supporting the night attack. They were ordered to bypass the villages at the front line and push far beyond them before the infantry would alight from their carriers. At 2300 hours, thirty minutes before the infantry started to move, Bomber Command aircraft began hitting the villages on the flanks of the attack: May-sur-Orne, Fontenay-le-Marmion, Secqueville-la-Compagne, and La Hogue.

At 2345 hours, the supporting artillery shattered the silence with a deafening roar.

There is no sound more terrifying than incoming artillery. The soldier hears the shell on the way down, but has no idea where it may be aimed. When it does land, fragments explode everywhere in a deafening roar to propel as many pieces of hot, jagged steel into as many enemy soldiers as possible.

Having never been in, or even near, combat before, Ray's heart must have been pounding as the adrenaline flowed. The heat, the dust, and the noise could only be compared to Dante's inferno. Two troops of Sherman tanks, followed by two troops of tanks with flails to explode any mines, followed by one troop of AVRE (Assault Vehicles, Royal Marines[38]) were to breach the German defensive positions. The night's objective was a position some

---

[37] War Diary of the 1st Battalion Essex Scottish, National Archives, Ottawa.
[38] These armoured vehicles were first used on D-Day. They were converted Churchill tanks with a stubby gun that fired a huge and heavy projectile to demolish concrete defensive bunkers.

5,000 yards behind the enemy's forward defensive line. The breaching group was to lay tape and light the route.

The main body consisted of two troops of Sherman tanks from the 2nd Division's 8th Reconnaissance Regiment (14th Canadian Hussars) from Swift Current, Saskatchewan, tanks followed by rifle companies riding in  half-tracks, plus the attached supporting arms from the Toronto Scottish Machine-Gun Battalion, artillery (the 2nd Anti-Tank Regiment) and Service Corps' truckers. The order of march for the Scottish was "A," "B," "C," and "D" Companies followed by battalion headquarters. Ray was one of the first soldiers across the start line with "A" Company, riding into the darkness in a Bren-gun carrier. The move forward was planned to take fifty-five minutes, moving behind an artillery barrage at the rate of 100 yards a minute. The barrage was to lift 200 yards every two minutes. In spite of this slow speed, a dense cloud of dust enveloped the column, which, together with thick

The 25-pounder was the usual gun used by the Canadian Field Artillery in close support of the infantry.

ground mist and enemy smoke, reduced visibility to almost zero. The column closed up as frequent halts were made because of enemy mortar and small arms fire.

In the total lack of visibility, the lead company, "A" Company, was soon a casualty, their column cut in half. A German 88mm gun had fired on the leading tanks and some vehicles, including half-tracks, had been set ablaze. Then some tanks turned around and collided with the half-tracks behind, throwing the entire column into a state of utter confusion.

The 88mm gun and light machine guns held the Scottish column at bay. The 12th SS and the newly arrived 89th German Infantry Division fought hard and delayed some units until well into the afternoon. The Essex's commanding officer was wounded in the bloodstained village of Rocquancourt and evacuated to the South Saskatchewan Regiment's command post. The column re-grouped, but there were no tanks left, and they had lost fourteen half-tracks.

From 0800 hours until noon, no information came from brigade headquarters whether any troops had made the objective. Only nineteen radios were working and those only sporadically. The only opposing fire dwindled to light and medium machine guns and mortars, and the infantry covered the open space to the objective in tracked and half-tracked vehicles in order to utilize their speed for advance. Finally, the pathetic ruins of the hamlets and Verrières Ridge, where the bodies of the Black Watch had lain since the battle of July 25, passed into Canadian hands. The Essex Scottish pounded their target with mortar fire from 1215 to 1330 hours, when they entered and searched the building to find it free from enemy. The ground gained was never lost again. The casualties were considered to have been light, and Private Raymond White had survived his first encounter with the enemy.

That afternoon, while the 4th Division Armoured Brigade was fighting a furious tank battle to the east of 2nd Division, the 2nd Division swung somewhat southwest and took the village of Bretteville-sur-Laize and the bridge crossing the Laize River. On August 9 and 10, the battalion dug in to a reserve defensive position and only minor mortaring and shelling disturbed the dusty air. After a third dry hot day, the Scottish started to move forward at 2215 hours on the 11th to take up a position near the hamlet of Moulines.

The infantry were on foot again. The Essex had taken up defensive positions in fields on either side of the road leading to Barbery, and an attack by the other two battalions of the 4th brigade was successful. The Royal Hamilton Light Infantry moved ahead fairly quickly, but the RCR from Toronto passing through the Royal Hamilton Light Infantry (RHLI) met more opposition. At 2000 hours the Essex Scottish advanced, tasked to seize the high ground. During the night and the early morning of the 13th, their attack was successful, their carriers distinguishing themselves by taking a field that was completely surrounded by a ditch with twelve machine-gun posts, two "stovepipe" bazookas, and three other bazooka crews. Into the bag went seventy-five prisoners-of-war. The Division then swung further southeast towards Falaise.

The Germans were falling back out of Normandy, and as the British and Canadians squeezed from the west, the U.S. 12th Army Group was rushing northward to pinch off a huge concentration of the enemy in a pocket just past Falaise. The objective was to bring the Canadians and Americans together near Argentan, completely cutting off the German forces around Mortain.

When the Scottish started to move on August 11, it was in response to an order from General Montgomery that the Canadians were to capture Falaise. The 2nd Division crossed the River Laize on August 12, and for the next two days, fought its way southward in the face of stiff enemy opposition. By nightfall on the 13th, they had re-crossed the river at Clair Tizon and were threatening the German line. On August 14, the battalion moved back through waving fields of golden grain to the area of Urville. Ray found the march most annoying as husks from the grain and the dust kicked up by feet and tracked vehicles clung to his face and neck working its way under his collar. The heat and dust were beginning to be oppressive.

Slightly north of them marched an infantry brigade of the 1st Polish Armoured Division. At 1400 hours, RAF and RCAF heavy bombers droned overhead to provide the second phase of air support. However, several waves of following bombers went astray and dropped their bombs on their own lines for well over an hour, causing 165 casualties and heavy losses in transportation and guns to the Canadian and Polish armies. The battalion reached Urville that afternoon and was allowed to rest for the night.

On the morning of the 15th, the Scottish resumed their advance from the west. Canadians advancing further north ran into formidable resistance from tanks and anti-tank guns, but the 4th Brigade seemed completely unopposed. As he marched along the road to Falaise, Ray witnessed a most desolate sight. The aftermath of severe fighting was everywhere. Most of the houses lay in complete ruins, but the farm inhabitants greeted the Canadians warmly and offered them fresh milk. The drink was much appreciated by the troops and many learned then what they were fighting for.

The Essex were leading the brigade, and as darkness fell, weariness, tension, and excitement all curdled in their stomachs. They were exhilarated at the thought of being the spearhead of the attack that would finally break German defences in Normandy.

During the afternoon of August 16, Canadian troops entered Falaise, but the 4th Brigade was stopped and held on the high ground just southwest of the town. Allied bombing had totally destroyed the centre of town, but the rearguard and snipers fought savagely among the ruins. It was generally cleared by noon on the 17th, except for survivors of a *Hitlerjugend* division that held out until midnight. For the next four days, the battalion remained in position. Enemy sniping and mortar shelling caused a few casualties and on the night of August 17–18, the Luftwaffe flew over in strength and bombed Falaise. The flood of refugees fleeing the city greatly increased as the night wore on, and Ray and his comrades evacuated 100 of them that had spent a thoroughly miserable few days in the cellar of a farmhouse.

The weather then turned miserable with continuous rain and cold winds. The only good news was that patrols reported no enemy activity in the Essex's area. On August 21, the brigade started to move towards Livarot, a town some twenty miles distant. The Essex Scottish was in the lead, its companies strung out along each side of the road, and they met no opposition in the rain-washed fields until the hamlet of Tortisambert. The lead company had barely entered the area of destroyed buildings when they were fired upon from the remains of the only church. Most sought shelter where they could, but several men on the point were hit. Mopping up scattered enemy resistance took some time and the battalion did not reach Livarot until 1600 hours on the 22nd. They took up defensive positions on the grounds of a local château whose occupants were not particularly glad to see them digging trenches and fortifying defences.

The troops were barely dug in when they were ordered to move again towards LaChapelle Yvon. The Canadians were now moving frequently and fast, their only contact with the fleeing enemy being minor skirmishes. The bridge over the river had been blown so the battalion had to use its own ingenuity and resources to get across. They took up positions in an orchard on the reverse slope, where French citizens told them that the enemy had passed through only the day before, appearing footsore and weary and heading in all directions. The Scottish picked up a few prisoners who proved to be from every service of the German forces, all fighting as infantry. There was even a Japanese soldier with them. From August 19 to 21, as the Germans pressed through the gap at the top of the pocket, the Canadian army captured 12,000 prisoners. The Canadians suffered a few casualties from the ever-present 88's and from rifle fire, but generally the enemy was not active.

Although fighting had almost ceased, the remnants of war were everywhere. As he marched along, Ray could sometimes hardly believe his eyes. Bodies of German soldiers carpeted the ground. Tanks, trucks, and cars blocked the roads and filled the ditches. Some 8,000 horses lay slaughtered and rotting in the August heat. Eight German divisions had been destroyed and more than sixteen suffered crippling losses. One armoured division fought to annihilation, and the remains of Meyer's 12th SS Panzer Division, only sixty troops, were finally overrun west of Trun. Meyer escaped on foot, but was subsequently captured, brought to Canada, tried, and sentenced to death for his role in the murder of Canadians at Verrières Ridge. His sentence was later commuted to life imprisonment.

Montgomery now issued a new directive. The British and Canadians were to mop up what was left of the enemy and then push for the Seine River. They would cross the river then clear the Havre peninsula between the Seine and the English Channel.

On August 24, the day dawned clear and bright. The battalion remained in position until just after suppertime when they boarded their half-tracks and set out down the road for Elboeuf on the River Seine. They encountered no opposition and stayed overnight in another orchard by the town of Lemesnil. The next day the weather was again fair and they moved out at 1215 hours. The RCR led followed by the RHLI and the Essex Scottish bringing up the rear. Their route was through Brionne where they found the bridge destroyed. With two battalions having crossed before them, the Essex encountered a sea of ruts and mud, but got all their vehicles to high ground at Bosrobert-Auxpoulets where they found a Tiger tank that had been clumsily booby-trapped and was easily circumvented. The night was quiet except when the Luftwaffe made a brief attack on the Brionne bridge.

On August 26, the weather gods smiled again on the Allied armies. The leading Canadian troops reached the river and took over Elboeuf from the Americans. Canadian forces were then close to Rouen, but its occupation was delayed for several days as the Germans exacted a heavy toll. The 4th Brigade moved off at 2000 hours with the Essex Scottish in the lead. On the outskirts of Bourgtheroulde, the Scottish came under heavy machine-gun and mortar fire, but they eventually ran the gauntlet through the centre of town. On the far side, they found the Black Watch, who had taken a beating, but had fought off several counter-attacks, while the Essex suffered a few casualties taking up a position just beyond the RHR. Everything quieted down, but at 2350 hours, the Essex were again on the move. They raced down the road again, passed through Elboeuf, and proceeded along the road to Port de Gravier.

Just as the Scottish were approaching the village, at 0300 on the 27th, they started to take fire from high ground between the fork in the road ahead. "B" Company was challenged to "halt" by an excited enemy machine gunner. Instead, they all dove for cover, while the enemy opened fire and brought their mortars to bear upon the troops and transport. Deployment under fire is an exciting time, but fortunately the fire was not accurate and the mortars were of the light variety.

"A" and "B" Companies were along railway tracks to the right front; battalion headquarters was well forward in the midst of ruined houses at the road fork, fairly well protected by the railway embankment; and "C" and "D" Companies were back along the road to Elboeuf but were moved forward to cover the left flank.

The RHLI and the RCR were positioned on the battalion's left and the river was to the right. At daybreak it became obvious that the Germans held extremely favourable positions on the cliffs to the front of the battalion. They had ample cover and could seek cover in the numerous caves that dotted the cliffs. Enemy positions dominated both forks of the road making entry into battalion headquarters a matter of running a hazardous gauntlet for 200 yards then swinging quickly into the courtyard. The RCR made an attack on the left, followed by "C" and "D" Companies, but neither made any progress due to the nature of the ground. Intermittent enemy mortar fire caused many casualties in the two companies.

Rouen stands at the apex on one of the many loops in the Seine. Ten miles south lies the Forêt de la Londe, "a rugged piece of country that would do credit to the Canadian Laurentians." On this range of thickly timbered hills, the Germans made their resolute stand. When the 2nd Canadian Division moved into the forest on the morning of August 27, they encountered a well-equipped enemy. During the next three days, the 4th and 6th Canadian Infantry Brigades sustained heavy losses in nasty forest fighting without making much progress.

During the night of August 28, another attack was mounted by the RCR and "C" and "D" Companies of the Essex. Ray White was now fighting with "C" Company. They tried to push around on high ground to the battalion's left in order to outflank the enemy machine guns that were dominating the road. Preceding their attack at 1330 hours was intensive artillery and mounted machine gun barrage. Once the attackers reached the area from which they believed the enemy fire had originated, they found a steep slope that they had to slide down to cross the left branch of the road to get to the high ground where the enemy was. "C" and "D" Companies went down this slope with great gallantry, under heavy fire, but could proceed no further. After sustaining many casualties, they dug in along the left branch of the road. Nothing further could be done. Harried by snipers and mortar fire they held the position and only after darkness could they withdraw to their original area. Private White was left on the slope.

Only on August 29 did the Germans withdraw[39]. Evidence before the Essex Scottish was that the enemy had indeed pulled back. The Battle of Normandy was over. For the 2nd Canadian Division, the climax came on August 31 when they returned to Dieppe where they had lost so many in that disastrous raid in August 1942. Thus, they honoured the graves of their dead and enjoyed a ceremonial march through the town of wildly exuberant citizens.

That same day, Ray White's body was buried near Orvial, on the east side of the high railway embankment, just below train level. Later, his body was exhumed and re-interred in accordance with the rites of the Roman Catholic Church in the Bretteville War Cemetery, a mute memorial to the struggle to relieve Europe.

Meanwhile at home, his sister Roberta had been trying to get Ray's mail delivered in a timely fashion. If he got anything at all, it was months late. She enlisted the help of the local branch of the Legion of the British Empire Services League, but they were no more successful than she. The army replied that they were doing their best, but Ray was "moving around a lot."

Ray left behind his father and mother, six brothers and four sisters, all at home.

[39] Col. C.P. Stacey, The Canadian Army 1939–45 (Ottawa: King's Printer, 1948), p.208.

"Tippy's" parents received the telegram notifying them of his death on September 7, 1944, and that was the last they heard from the army for almost a year and a half! Finally, Ray's dad wrote to the Department of National Defence:

> Dear Sirs
>
> Could you please let me know where I could find or to whom I should write for Gratuits [*sic*] for my son who was killed in action if France in Aug/44. . .
>
> We have received a bond and what pay he had coming. Nothing else. No personal belongings. He had made a will in his mothers favor . . . But I understand there should be gratuities for his time in Canada also for services overseas. It is over 18 months now since he was killed and not a word from anybody yet. We don't even know where he was killed other than somewhere in France . . . Would appreciate it very much if you could help me to get things fixed up.
>
> Thank you his Dad

Ray's War Service Gratuity of $144.87 for 513 days service, 120 of them overseas, was eventually paid. His mother, Hannah, also received the Memorial Cross, which was delivered to their William and Bain Street address.

The Canadian published the news of both "Tippy" White and Earl Porteous' deaths in the same edition—September 21, 1944.

PART SEVEN—THE END IS NEAR

CHAPTER TWENTY-SIX—CHANNEL PORTS

Broken and disorganized, the German armies streamed back through France. Resistance to the Allied pursuers was often fierce, but only local and temporary.

However, the Allied advance depended upon timely provision of supplies to the fighters, and the Canadians and British could no longer sustain the long supply line from a base in the Caen area. Every mile east increased the strain on Allied supply and communication lines. The solution was to use ports closer to the new front. The only problem was the Germans still controlled them.

After crossing the Seine, personnel carriers and trucks rushed forward over miles of cobbled streets and dusty roads. The civilians welcomed the liberators with cheers, flags, flowers, food, and drink. A pinnacle for the 2nd Division was Dieppe. They had sent men to the beaches during the disastrous raid in 1942 and now expected the Germans to fight for this important port. But on September 1, 1944, when the 8th Reconnaissance Regiment (14th Canadian Hussars) reached the outskirts of the city, the only barrier to their progress was dense crowds of citizens, delirious with liberation fever.

The Germans had mysteriously left Dieppe without a fight and had even left the port facilities mostly intact. Dieppe received its first British ships on September 6.

The small port of Le Tréport fell to the 3rd Division on September 1, but a German garrison occupied every harbour of any importance north of the Seine. Even after the city of Antwerp was liberated, the Germans held both banks of the River Scheldt leading from the city to the sea, so the Allies could not use this port.

Le Havre fell on September 12, yielding more than 11,000 prisoners, but the port was badly damaged and would not be useful for a month.

General Crerar's army was now dispersed over a 200-mile stretch. His 2 Canadian Corps' armoured divisions swept on in pursuit of the Germans, leaving the infantry to contain the ports. The 1st Polish and 4th Canadian Armoured Divisions crossed the Somme and charged into Belgium. At Bruges they collided with enemy defences along the river approaches to Antwerp. Resistance was stiff, as the Germans had no intentions of giving up their positions until forced to. The 2nd Division was moving on Dunkirk and the 3rd Division attacked Calais and Boulogne.

Major General D. C. Spry's 3rd Division occupied Pas de Calais and chased the Germans from the nearby V-1 flying bomb launching sites. No other achievement gave the Canadian soldiers—not to mention the citizens of London—such satisfaction. After the 3rd Division had dealt with Boulogne, it moved on to Calais. Its attack on Boulogne was held up until September 17, when the 8th and 9th Brigades, veterans of the D-Day landings and the fighting around Caen and Falaise, advanced against the German defences. Support was strong. Bomber Command sent 690 aircraft, both heavy and medium bombers, over the battlefield, while special armoured assault vehicles and two artillery divisions poured fire on the defenders. Huge guns stationed on the English coast near Dover fired repeatedly on German artillery batteries at a range of about forty-two kilometres, including one direct hit.

Cyril Hughes of Carleton Place had landed in France on July 3, 1944, temporarily assigned to the Black Watch (RHR of Canada) as a reinforcement. On July 9, he was sent to the NNSH, of the 9th Brigade of the 3rd Canadian Division. With them was the HLI and the SD&G. The day Cyril joined the battalion, the 9th Brigade had just taken the towns of Buron and Authie and was advancing into Caen.

D136195 Private Cyril Garnet Strong Hughes
North Nova Scotia Highlanders

Cyril Hughes was attending Taber's Business College in Carleton Place when his brother Bob, flying with 412 Squadron, was killed in an aircraft collision over England. Cyril, known to most of his friends as "Cy," was learning shorthand and typing so as to pursue a career in business (he had been offered a position with the Upper Ottawa Improvement Company upon completion of the course).

Bob's death was the second personal loss that Cyril experienced that year. On April 24, 1941, he had been a pallbearer at the funeral of eighteen-year-old Donald Fee, who had been accidentally shot by a friend while on a hunting expedition.

Born on January 28, 1922, Cyril was the third child of four of William James Hughes and Mable Vaughn Strong of Carleton Place. William was the druggist at the local Rexall Store. Cyril was a good student at both Carleton Place Public School and CPHS. He particularly enjoyed history, chemistry and physics, remaining in high school to complete his fifth year (senior matriculation) in order to attend business college.

At school, Cy enjoyed most sports, being a member of the track and field team, as well as skating and swimming. At six feet tall and weighing only 120 pounds, he played centre for the basketball team. In November 1940, he and Donnie Knox were recognized at a banquet held in the Mississippi Hotel, as they had both attended the Ontario Athletic Commission summer camp at Lake Couchiching in Muskoka.

Cy held his job as a clerk-stenographer with the Upper Canada Improvement Company for six months before he left to join the armed forces.

Cyril claimed good health but he looked rather frail, so, for whatever reason, he thought his chances to get into the army would be better if he went to Montreal to enlist. It obviously worked, because on June 19, 1942, he was medically examined for enrolment and awarded a medical category of "A." The examiner noted Cy's medium complexion, blue eyes and brown hair, plus a vaccination scar on his left arm and a "sports scar" on his right leg. His right eye was perfect, but he wore spectacles due to some problems with the vision in his left. In spite of being underweight and having a tachycardia (systolic murmur in the left second and third interspace of the heart), he was considered to have good development.

During that same summer, the youngest Hughes brother, Morley, joined the RCAF.

Since Cy already had a trade, he was taken on strength of No. 4 District Depot and was absorbed into the Home War Establishment staff to work as a clerk. He stayed in Montreal South, with the RCASC in Longueuil, and was supplied with basic army skills. He did well in the forces and within four months, on October 27, was promoted to acting lance corporal. The very next weekend he came home sporting a new single chevron on his sleeve.

For Christmas 1942, both Cyril and Morley made it home to celebrate the holiday with their parents. Also home was their sister Freda, married to a Navy paymaster, Lieutenant F. J. Lovett serving on HMCS *Saskatchewan*. Cy went back to the Depot in Montreal but then got another two weeks leave, from January 23 to February 7, 1943.

Being a clerk on the General List was starting to pale for Cyril as his friends at home and in the army made their ways overseas. In June 1943, he requested a transfer to the infantry, even offering to take a reduction in rank to private. He told the officer that he wanted a change in employment and that he wanted to go overseas. His interviewer felt that Cyril should be trade-tested in his present trade due to his army and civilian experience as a clerk, skills the army needed.

Although he had clerked in the army for more than a year, Cyril had not passed any trade tests. The officer assessed Cyril as "intelligent and educated and has 18 months service in the army. He is stable, has an excellent attitude—should do well." He was also rated as being "NCO material." However, because his only army training was in administration, on June 3, 1943, Cyril was sent to Canadian Army Basic Training Infantry Course No. 48 at St. John's, Quebec, to receive training as an infantry rifleman. In the past year he had also gained weight and now tipped the scales at 136 pounds.

Cyril did well at the basic training centre. He had been sent to the school to see if he could handle infantry training. He proved himself reliable and trustworthy and got along very well with the other students. He expressed a desire to continue to advanced training and ultimately overseas. Accordingly, on July 10, he was officially remustered to private and reallocated to the infantry. His next step was to the Advanced Infantry Training School A-12 at Farnham, Quebec. He was given the daily rate of pay of $1.40, which was increased to $1.50 in September. During this training Cyril was given fourteen days furlough, which he spent at home in Carleton Place. Italy had just surrendered on September 8, which took some worry from his father's brow.

On October 4, Cyril completed advanced training and qualified as a rifleman. He was sent to No. 1 Transit Camp in Windsor, Nova Scotia, to await shipment to England. There he was put through more tests and was declared "Suitable for Overseas Service," before boarding a troop ship on November 25. He was now wearing the CVSM ribbon, awarded to volunteers with eighteen months service.

Cyril's group disembarked in the United Kingdom on December 2, and one of his first actions was to notify his parents by cable of his safe arrival overseas before reporting to No. 5 CIRU.

Cyril spent the rest of the winter and following spring on general duties around various headquarters units. He was transferred to No. 4 CIRU in March 1944 and then, on April 13, to the 1st Battalion, RHR, for duties at the 1st Canadian Army headquarters. The headquarters troops watched and waited while the divisions assaulted Normandy on D-Day, frustrated with their own inaction. Then, on July 2, Cyril gathered up his combat equipment and spent the night on a ship headed for France. On landing he was ordered as a reinforcement to the NNSH and caught up with the regiment shortly after they entered Caen.

The Canadians had to fight their way to Falaise, an old Norman town twenty-one miles southeast of Caen. The ground rises steadily from sea level at Caen to about 200 metres at Falaise. Along this smooth dangerous slope, through open wheat fields, the 3rd Division fought for many weeks. Any small woodland along their route was full of anti-tank guns, which the Germans used to good purpose. The 8th and 9th Brigades crossed the Orne just below Caen and began clearing Colombelles and surrounding towns. After a bitter fight they cleared the area on the 19th, and the next day, the rains started. The advancing soldiers went forward through a sea of mud that only their fathers from the Great War would recognize.

On July 25, the Canadians began a new offensive against the six enemy armoured divisions in the sector east of the Orne. The 3rd Division, east of the road to Falaise, was to take Tilly-la-Compagne. At 0330 hours the NNSH moved out from Bourgébus to lead the attack. It went well at first, with the leading troops getting into Tilly. But the 1st SS (Liebstandarte Adolf Hitler) Panzer Division had no thoughts of giving up the town and counter-attacked with armour and infantry. The Highlanders' supporting Sherman tanks, from the 17th Duke of York's Royal Canadian Hussars, were almost wiped out and the infantry platoons were cut off. After dark, many survivors, including Cy Hughes in his first major battle, escaped back to Bourgébus. Many more fought on for hours until they were overwhelmed.

On the night of July 30–31, the 4th Canadian Armoured Division relieved the 3rd Division, and after fifty-six days in the line, the division withdrew for a short rest.

Montgomery wanted Falaise and he wanted the Gap closed. However, the soonest the Canadian Army could attack was August 14. Two columns, each led by an armoured brigade followed by two infantry brigades, thrust forward. The 8th Brigade was loaned to the 4th Armoured Division for the attack in the left column and the rest of the 3rd Division formed a column on the right. The armour was to cross the River Laize and drive south to the high ground above Falaise, while the infantry were left to mop up the river valley. Other infantry brigades, riding in trucks, were to push forward to hold the ground overrun by tanks.

Smoke and dust made it difficult to see where they were going, but the armoured divisions, in spite of the confusion, broke through the German line and pressed the advance forward. The leading infantry, including the 9th Brigade mounted in Kangaroos[1], jumped from their armoured carriers and cleaned up the valley with little difficulty, taking many prisoners in the process. By evening, it was clear that the operation had been successful; the infantry were within three miles of Falaise.

Unfortunately, for the second time, RAF and RCAF (No. 6 Bomber Group) bombers missed their targets on the haze-covered ground, and for more than an hour, seventy-seven aircraft (out of a total force of more than 800) bombed their own lines, resulting in many casualties and heavy losses in transport and guns. However, those bombs that did find their mark contributed a great deal to the Canadian success. On August 16, the 2nd Division entered an almost totally bomb-destroyed Falaise.

The NNSH had been tasked to mop up any enemy on the high ground immediately north of the river. They completed their job late in the afternoon, contributing to a very successful day for the 3rd Division. It had started to move just before noon with parade-ground precision. Tanks churned the ground with flails, followed by Sherman tanks, half-tracks, and armoured carriers. Interspersed were the British Engineers in Churchill tanks with bundles of fascines to help bridge the river. Behind was the infantry in Kangaroos and more infantry in unarmoured trucks. Various anti-aircraft and anti-tank vehicles, trucks, water wagons, and jeeps completed the divisional column.

At the same time, medium bombers roared overhead to strike selected targets, then the guns opened up to provide a smoke-screen and to bring down known or suspected enemy positions. The roar of aircraft, the thunder of the

[1] A Kangaroos was a 105-mm self-propelled howitzer that had its gun removed and was converted to carry infantrymen into battle behind the protection of armour plating. It resembled a tank without a turret. These armoured personnel carriers could carry a driver and ten or eleven infantrymen, the greater part of a section.

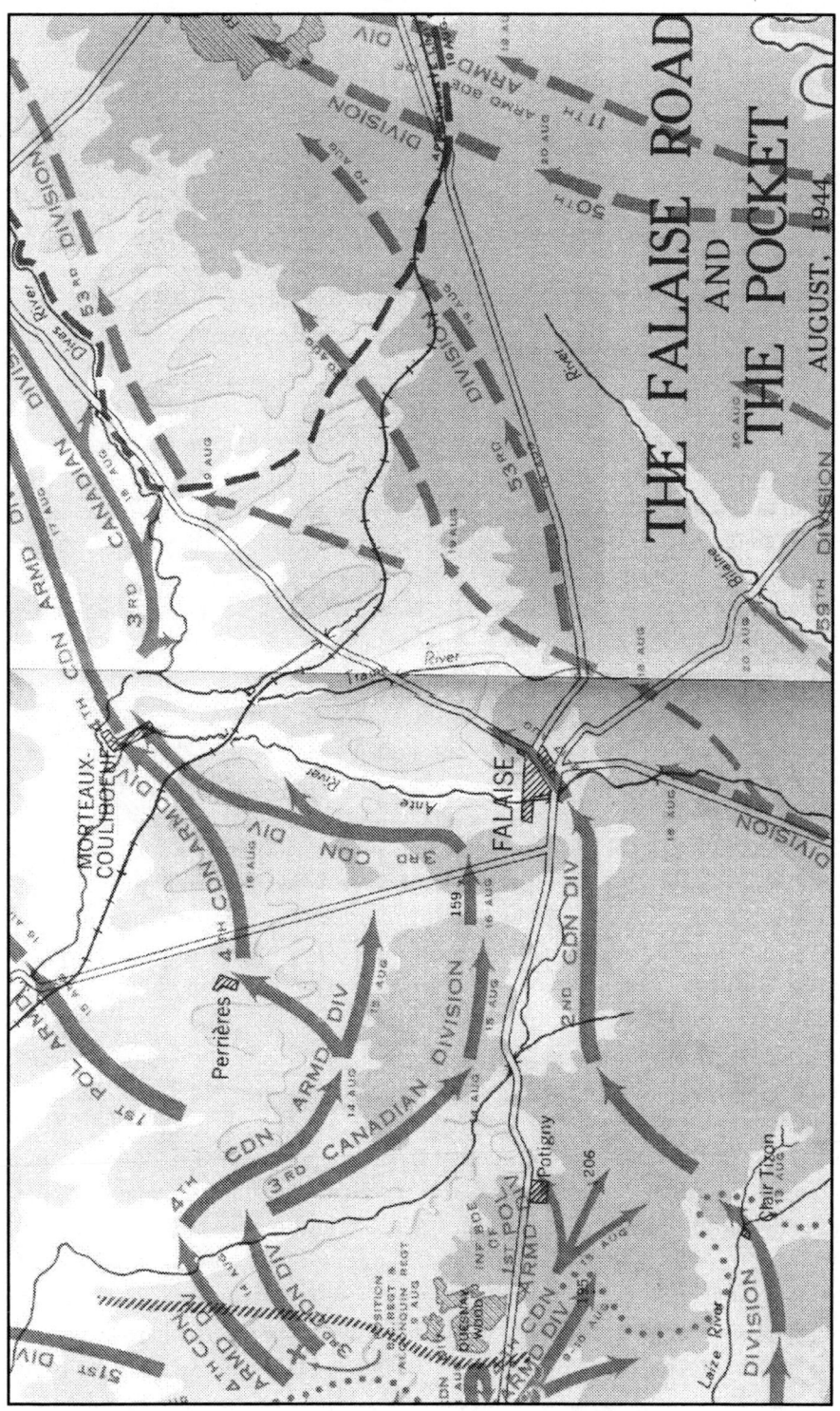

THE FALAISE ROAD AND THE POCKET — AUGUST, 1944

guns, and the noise of moving vehicles almost made the men's whooping and yelling inaudible. The noise died down in the air after the battle, but many men suffered the noise ringing in their ears for years afterwards.

On July 31, General Harry Crerar's Canadian Army Headquarters took command of the Canadian Corps, comprising the 2nd and 3rd Canadian Infantry Divisions and the 4th Canadian Armoured Division. It was the first time in the war that the Canadians had had an operational command in the field.

Early in August, a new infantry division, the 85th, arrived to add depth to the German line, and on August 10–11, the 3rd Canadian Division launched the 8th Brigade at Quesnoy Wood, which yielded nothing but heavy Canadian casualties. The Americans, under General Patton, continued their drive from Argentan to the northeast while the Canadians and Polish pressed in from the north to close what small gap remained for Germans to flee through. Still, a good many of the enemy escaped to stand and fight all the way back to the Fatherland. On August 19, at 1900 hours, the Poles and the Americans met when the Polish Mounted Rifle Regiment captured Chambois.

Canadian progress through the hilly, wooded countryside remained slow. While many enemy were glad to put "finish" to their war, there were more fanatical Germans who, like the 12th SS Panzers, fought until their units were annihilated. The Canadian advance was rapid but the enemy continued to fight stubbornly and skilfully at many points as they retreated across the Seine. A strong, well-equipped German force held the thickly treed woods around Rouen. However, pressed to the extreme by the 2nd Division, they withdrew on August 29, and the next day, troops from the 3rd Division entered Rouen. The Battle of Normandy was over, but eight months of hard fighting still lay ahead in northwest Europe.

While the 2nd Canadian Division headed for Dieppe, the 3rd headed further east to the port of Le Treport, en route up the coast for Calais. But first they would have to deal with Boulogne. On September 1, a warm day under clear skies, the NNSH left Rouen at 0700 hours mounted on all available vehicles. Going through the town, they received a warm welcome from the populace, but the young boys from Canada could hardly believe their eyes when a woman collaborator was paraded before them. Her hair was shaved off and a bright swastika was painted on her forehead.

They stopped in a town for the night and were surprised when a German officer and an enlisted man rode in on a motorcycle. The Germans were even more surprised, as they did not expect to find Allied troops there. They carried orders for delivery to the next town for those troops to withdraw. An hour later, two trucks with about forty Germans loaded aboard arrived and started shooting. They quickly learned their error when the Canadians opened fire in return.

The attack on Boulogne was held up while they waited for special assault equipment, and the North Novas waited, in pouring rain, for several days in the small town of Tinghem. Then, under Boche artillery airbursts, they moved closer to the city. On September 10, the RAF bombed Boulogne but the troops on the ground could not observe the extent of damage due to a heavy thunderstorm. They sent out patrols to pass out leaflets to the civilians ordering them to evacuate their homes.

The Germans had fortified the old forts of Boulogne with new concrete, plus the high hills just outside the city afforded good defensive positions and the enemy had plenty of artillery. However, morale in the 10,000-man garrison was not high, and during the night of September 12, the NNSH moved into positions held by the Queen's Own Rifles.

Their immediate concern was the civilians streaming out of Boulogne with carts, wheelbarrows, carriages, and prams. They told the Canadians that the German soldiers were ready to surrender, but a few of the officers and NCOs were prepared to fight "to the last man."

For the next three days, the Canadians waited in their lines. On the 14th, aircraft dropped more leaflets, but it seemed all the civilians had left. The next day was very quiet and, on the 16th, they had the usual artillery shells thrown at them in the morning. During the afternoon, they trained on another new weapon, the "lifebuoy," which was a flame-thrower that spewed jellied gasoline which lit on firing. Throughout the day they received no more shelling but observed the Typhoon aircraft bombing Boulogne's defences.

During the night, the NNSH received heavier than usual artillery fire. The house where battalion headquarters was billeted took a direct hit, but fortunately there were no casualties. At 0800 hours on September 17, another clear warm day, the battalion lined up to attack the city, and at 0825 hours, 690 heavy bombers began their lethal drops with great effect. Very little anti-aircraft fire went up to meet them. The bombs raised tremendous clouds of brown and black smoke that, at times, covered the high ground around the targets. The men on the ground thought it hard to believe that anyone could survive such a blasting. In fact, the German commandant, Lieutenant General Heim, later said that the bombs caused few casualties and had little effect on the defences.

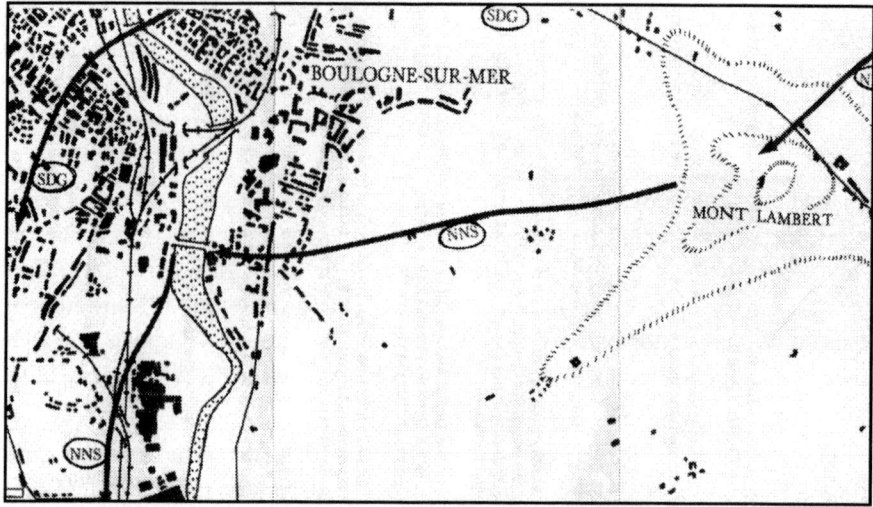

When the last bomb fell, on the fortified height of Mont Lambert, east of Boulogne, the infantry started forward, with the NNSH moving across the start line at 0958 hours. Cyril Hughes was marching with "D" Company. The enemy positions immediately opened fire and the artillery sent in air-bursts. "D" and "A" Companies were held up at the foot of a hill when they were pinned down by machine-gun fire from a pillbox. "C" Company continued forward, but only after considerable trouble were "A" and "D" Companies able to bypass the machine gun and get up the hill. Finally an Avery got in close and knocked out this pillbox and two others further up the left side of the rise.

The battalion pushed on and took up a position along the lower side of the road. "A" Company was on the left, "D" in the centre, and "C" on the right. "B" Company remained in the valley on reserve. "D" and "A" Companies suffered quite a few artillery shells and mortars, but held their positions. Headquarters was trying to arrange an attack supported by the Averys, Crocs[2], and gun tanks, but "D" Company was heavily mortared during the night[3]. "B" Company moved along the edge of the hill to cover the battalion's rear.

It rained all that night but stopped before first light. The battalion had taken approximately fifty-eight casualties. Reported missing was Private Cyril Hughes.

"Cy" Hughes was found on September 23 and buried where he fell, in front of the village church in Mont Lambert close by Boulogne. Cyril's parents were notified by telegram on October 7, who in turn informed Cyril's

---

[2] "Crocodiles" were flame-throwing tanks

[3] The mortar was a unique affair. It came up out of the pillbox, fired and was then lowered to safety. With only the barrel protruding it made a very difficult target. "D" Company took the Command Post on the top of the hill and then the German Regimental Aid Post, which yielded many "bottles of various vintages." (War Diary).

sister Freda in Leaside (Toronto) and his brother Morley in England, who was at the RCAF No. 3 PRC. On November 29, his parents received the traditional message from the monarch. For 819 days in the army, 297 of them overseas, Mabel Hughes received a War Service Gratuity of $305.74. His "estate" also included an identity bracelet, his red army identity disc, and information that he owned fifty shares of Pickle Crow stock that had been bought for $2.60 a share.

Cyril Garnet Strong Hughes was exhumed and re-buried in the Calais Canadian War Cemetery Leubringhen near St. Inglevert, Pas de Calais, France. A temporary cross marked his grave until the permanent headstone, suitably engraved, was erected. The Hughes were asked to submit a short personal inscription if they so cared.

Leubringhen is a village half way between Calais and Boulogne, and the cemetery is on the east side of the road. There are more than 700 World War II war casualties, including more than thirty unidentified, that are commemorated at this site.

On February 7, 1945, the postman delivered a Memorial Cross and a Memorial Plaque to Mabel.

Chapter Twenty-Seven—To Holland and Beyond

The opening of Antwerp's port facilities became absolutely necessary in order to continue the advance into Europe. Allied troops occupied the city, but it was fifty miles inland from the sea. The connecting Scheldt River, the South Beveland peninsula, and Walcheren Island, which controlled the mouth of the waterway, were still in German hands. Therefore, in early October 1945, the 2nd Canadian Division started north of Antwerp to close the Beveland peninsula. They attacked over open flooded ground and ran into heavy opposition from enemy paratroopers. The 4th Armoured Division moved north, heading for Bergen-op-Zoom, and by October 31, the peninsula had fallen.

On the south shore of the Scheldt, the 3rd Canadian Infantry Division met tenacious German resistance to their attempts to cross the Leopold Canal. On October 9, the Canadians launched an amphibious assault that broke the enemy's hold, and on November 3, the Canadians freed the south shore of the Scheldt.

Walcheren Island was the last obstacle. After a grim struggle, the Canadians crossed the only causeway, then, in conjunction with waterborne attacks, continued their advance. By November 8 all resistance faded, the channel was cleared of mines, and on November 28, the first Allied convoy docked at the port of Antwerp.

The Canadians spent the rest of the winter in position along the Maas and in the Nijmegan sector, and in February 1945, they advanced southeastwards to clear the area between the Maas and the Rhine. Progress was hampered by mud and flooded ground that was three-feet deep in places. Regardless, the 3rd Division—the water rats"—made significant gains. They fought their way through the pine forest of the Reichswald and cracked the Siegfried Line to face the defences mounted in the Hochwald before they arrived at the Rhine. Resistance, however, continued until March 10, when the Germans blew up the bridges over the Wesel and departed to the east bank of the Rhine.

In the final days of the liberation of the Netherlands, the Canadian Army's role was to open a supply route through Arnhem and clear northeastern Holland, the coastal area of Germany to the Elbe River, and western Holland.

For the first time in history, the Canadian Army was completely Canadian. The 1st Canadian Corps that had fought so long in Italy had been transferred to northwestern Europe. The two corps would fight together.

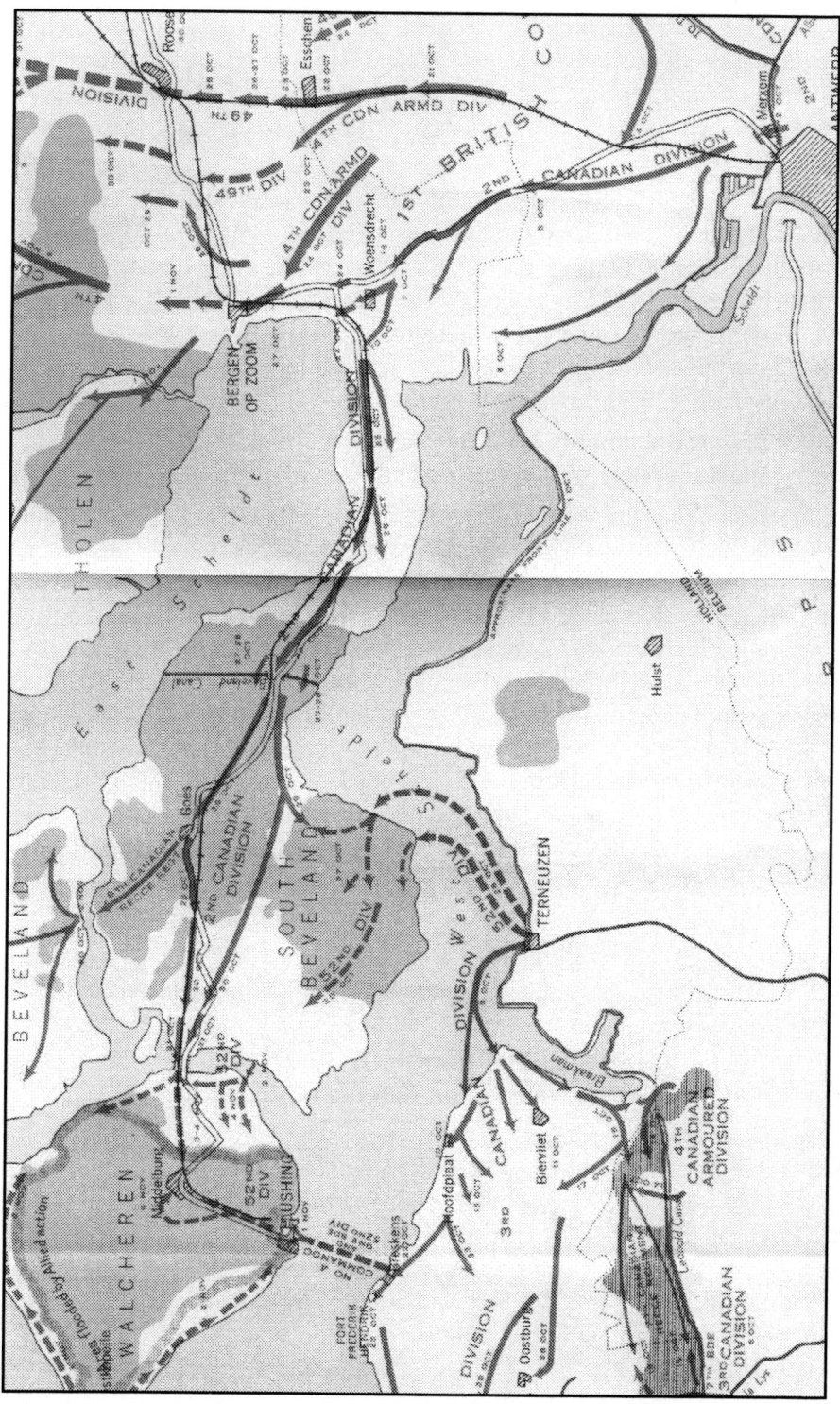

The 1st Canadian Infantry Division and the 5th Canadian Armoured Division liberated the area north of the Maas River, which included the cities of Amsterdam, Rotterdam, and The Hague. The citizens of these cities had exhausted their food and fuel supplies by this time, which had resulted in the deaths of thousands.

The Canadians began their assault on Arnhem on April 12, and after vicious house-to-house fighting, the town was cleared on the 14th. The 5th Armoured dashed thirty miles north to cut off the enemy at Ijsselmeer, which cleared the way for the 1st Division to occupy Apeldoorn on April 17. On April 28, the Canadians arranged a truce and for several days food supplies were moved in to the starving people of western Holland, who greeted the Canadians with cheers and great joy.

As they pushed towards war's end, casualties were, thankfully, light, but many veterans of Italy were killed, some the last to die in their regiment.

The 1st Canadian Infantry Brigade, composed of the RCR, the 48th Highlanders of Canada, and the Hasty Pees, left the Reichwald Forest near Zutphen heading towards Apeldoorn. The 3rd Brigade was working its way up from the south, and the First Hussars' tanks supported both brigades. By noon on April 13, the H&PE had been making good progress and was at the edge of the woods. "A" and "D" Companies were leading the battalion as they seized the crossroads west of Teuge, and the commanding officer was with "D" Company as they moved steadily towards the bridge crossing the canal. Most of the infantry were riding on tanks, shooting up small pockets of the enemy as they advanced, and a steady stream of prisoners (242 was their "bag" for the day) trudged towards the rear. The company suffered casualties of one officer and twenty-three other ranks wounded and the following killed: Privates McDonnell, Luard, Pindar, O'Meara, and Monsour.

O'Meara of Carleton Place had joined the regiment in Canada, trained in England, fought in Italy and now, within weeks of the cease-fire, had bought the farm.

C41329 Private Kenneth Orval O'Meara
Hastings and Prince Edward Regiment

Kenny O'Meara was born to John Joseph and Charlotte O'Meara on September 2, 1917. The family lived on Carleton Street in Carleton Place in an area known as "Happy Valley." Apparently this name was derived from the fact that so many of the town's bootlegging establishments operated there. Ken was the third of four boys: Robert James and William Benjamin who were older and Harold Wilbert, who was several years younger. William also joined the army. With three brothers, and living in Happy Valley, Ken became a scrapper. His small stature (5' 4" and 140 pounds) fooled many a boy who thought he could "take" Ken O'Meara. Most were soon surprised.

Ken was a mediocre student at best. He missed a great deal of school because he had to work at home on the farm, and finally, having completed Grade 8, he left school to help support his family. He took whatever jobs were available and never really learned any trade. The best regular weekly wage he made was $12, although he made anywhere from $15 to $35 a week slaughtering cattle for A. C. Bennett, a butcher. He worked for Bennett for two years, but the work was irregular. Before he enlisted in 1939, he worked for eighteen months, on and off, as a truck driver for various employers, which brought him $20 to $25 a week. He usually worked as a delivery boy for a local grocer.

On June 26, 1938, Ken joined "D" Company of the Lanark and Renfrew Scottish Militia. He swore his oath of allegiance before Lieutenant Harold Murfitt, and at his enlistment medical, he stood tall enough to be listed as 5' 6". He was recorded as having a fair complexion, blue eyes, and brown hair. His only visible scars were a vaccination mark on his left upper arm and a scar on his left knee.

Ken attended annual training during the summer of 1938, and the next year, he accepted the offer of being "called out" (full-time employment with the militia) and was assigned guard duties at Centre Lake internment camp, near Petawawa. Ken came home on leave early in December, and when he returned to his unit, he enlisted in the Lanark and Renfrew Active Force. He remained in the guard detachment until June 1940 when he transferred to the H&PE and reported to the regimental depot in Picton, Ontario, for basic infantry training.

With Ken's enlistment, and brother Bill already in the army, their mother displayed a service flag in the window of their home. It had two blue maple leaves on it, one for each family member in the service

Kenny O'Meara stands proud in his Lanark and Renfrew Scottish uniform.

Since he had already taken his training with the militia, within a week Ken was sent to Camp Borden to the Infantry Replacement Training Centre. Again he was only there a short time before departing for England to continue his infantry training at a holding unit. He arrived in the U.K. on July 17, 1940, and on September 19, he was sent to the H&PE in the field as part of the 1st Battalion.

The 1st Battalion had been in England since Christmas 1939 and had gone to France in June 1940 in the abortive attempt to rally a defence against the German "Blitzkrieg."

The 1st Brigade, composed of the RCR, the 48th Highlanders of Canada, and the H&PE, lost all their equipment, except for personal arms, and all their vehicles, except for one station wagon that the H&PE managed to load aboard a trawler, in their escape from France. This was an especially hard blow; the RCR was part of the Permanent Force and the 48th Highlanders was an old and socially prominent Toronto militia unit (a large number of their officers were lawyers). The city polish of these two battalions contrasted sharply with the country look of the H&PE, who with their ties to the central and eastern Ontario counties were known as "Plough Jockeys." The H&PE commander was a lawyer and former mayor of Trenton, Brigadier Howard Graham.

On September 19, 1940, Ken joined H&PE's "B" Company "in the field." The "field" turned out to be the Wal River valley in the rolling Sussex countryside. The companies were billeted in comfortable English homes and enjoyed a "lovely heated house with plenty of hot and cold water and a complete bathroom[4]." In a letter home on January 5, 1941, Ken wrote:

> We spent three weeks at the coast where we had a wonderful time and it just seemed as if we were on a picnic. We were on guard down there as the 1st Division took over from the English soldiers to let them go home for Christmas. We spent our Christmas there and had a very nice time . . . For our Christmas dinner we had turkey, pudding and everything else that could be given on that day. The Y.M.C.A. from Canada sent us each two packages of cigarettes and a small box containing one handkerchief, chocolate bars and gum and I think I am safe in saying that it was one of the best Christmases that many have had. The officers and sergeants served the men.
>
> We left the coast last Monday to come back where we were formerly stationed . . .

After Christmas, Ken took a seven-day leave and travelled to Glasgow. He had a great time enjoying Scottish hospitality over the holiday season and described it as "one of the best times I have ever had[5]." Early in January, Ken received a gift of cigarettes from the *Carleton Place Canadian* Overseas

[4] From a letter sent by Ken to Mrs. William Folkhard and published in The Canadian on February 6, 1941.
[5] Ibid.

Cigarette Fund, which provided smokes to the boys in uniform. The first consignment went out on January 9, 1941, and among the recipients were Fred Dray, Jock Findlay, Will Loney, and Kenny O'Meara.

Ken took leave again from March 12 to 18, and when returning to his base, he was involved in an altercation and was seriously injured with head and facial injuries, which also severely affected his hearing. Ken wrote to his parents stating that he was making improvement, but was still confined to hospital "somewhere in England."

From October 13 to November 2, 1941, Ken languished in No. 18 Canadian Field Ambulance Hospital recovering from the mumps, but he wasn't missing much. The winter of 1941–42 was a difficult period, and the Canadians were tired of all training and no action. Since the fall of France in 1940, they had been charged with repelling any attack on southeastern England. None came. In autumn 1941, the role changed to direct defence of the coast of Sussex. The 1st Division was now considered fully operational.

Every man in an infantry battalion became competent in a complex array of areas. The fighting soldier, the very essence of a regiment, was a member of a ten-man section led by a corporal. Three sections formed a platoon, usually led by a lieutenant, and three platoons became a rifle company commanded by a captain. Four companies made up the battalion led by a lieutenant colonel.

The soldier's sole function was to fight. He became proficient with his rifle (and its bayonet), the Bren gun (a light machine gun), the mortar, and the anti-tank rifle. He was also trained to use the Thompson submachine gun, the British Sten gun, and at least five types of hand grenades. These were his basic weapons and his basic needs. He learned tactics, battle drills and map reading, and trained in co-operation with tanks, artillery, and supporting aircraft. To assist him in staying alive, he learned field hygiene, patrol techniques and methods, and equipment that his enemy may employ.

In addition to the rifle companies were a support company and the headquarters company. The support company included the anti-aircraft platoon, signals platoon, mortar platoon, carrier platoon (equipped with ten armoured-tracked Bren-gun carriers), pioneer platoon (the battalion's engineers), and anti-tank platoon. Headquarters company had a transport section, quartermaster's section, mechanics, butchers, cooks, batmen, repairmen, postal clerks, water and sanitary men, and a host of administrators, all of whom were infantry-trained. The battalion headquarters held the executive officers to direct the force in battle, the intelligence section, the medical section, military police, and chaplain. By the fall of 1941, the Hasty Pees were regarded as fully trained and fully operational for deployment on the battlefield.

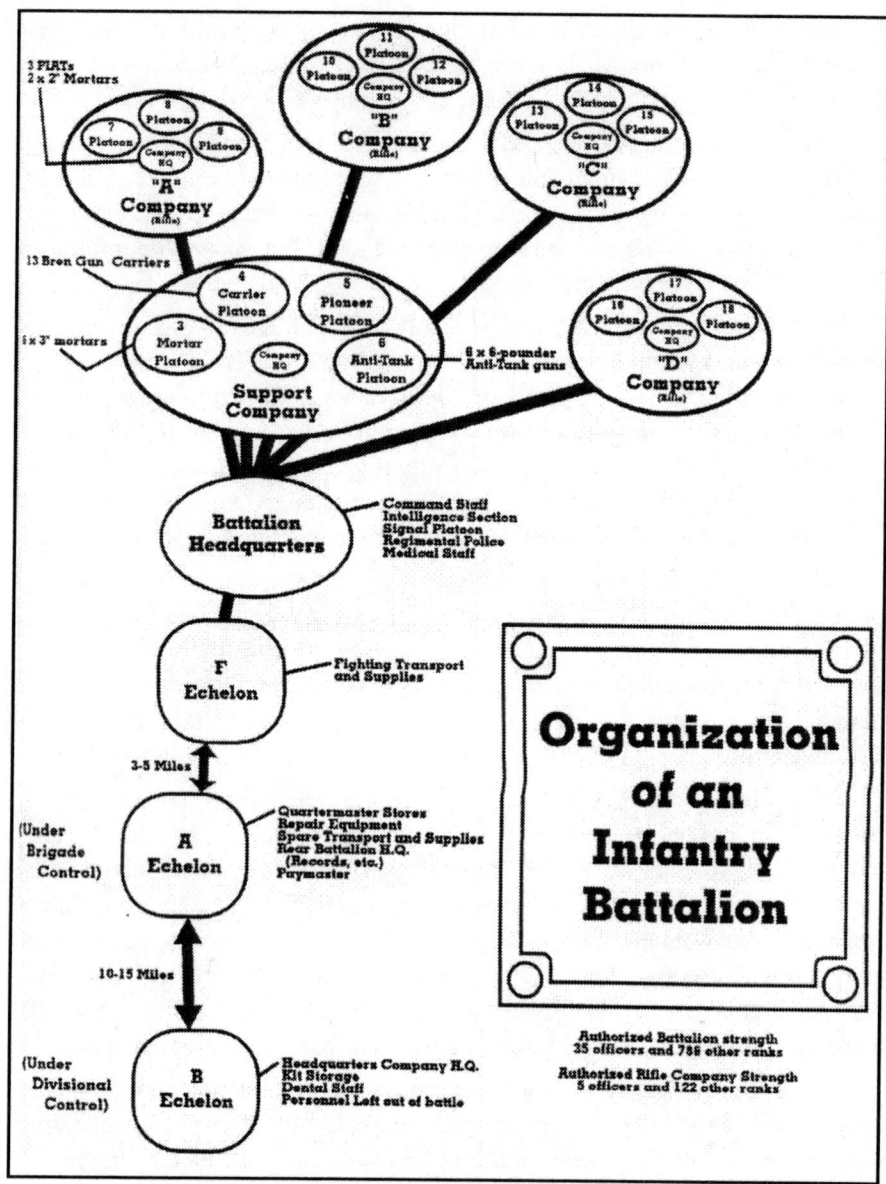

A Canadian's Guide to the Battlefields of Normandy, p. 167.

Ken went on leave from March 24 to 30, and on his return was admitted to No. 5 CGH. No reason for this admission can be found in his records, in spite of the fact that he was hospitalized for almost two months. He was released to the divisional infantry holding unit on May 22 where he stayed until being sent back to his battalion on August 3. In July, the battalion moved from Aldershot to Surrey and under canvas in the countryside. The nearby towns of Dorking, Reigate, and Redhill welcomed the Canadians, and within a few months, British families had adopted many of the men. Before the war ended there were more than a hundred marriages between local girls and Canadian soldiers. England was becoming like home.

In September, training became more intense and the Luftwaffe appeared overhead more often. The H&PE tent camp was on the German's direct route to London, and jettisoned bombs often fell within the battalion's perimeter. As the weather worsened in October, the camp became a quagmire, and finally the men were moved into billets near Betchworth. Ken checked into No. 4 Field Ambulance on September 14 and the next day was sent to 14 CGH. He was not discharged back to the reinforcement unit until October 10.

On December 8, the H&PE moved out of their comfortable billets to the area around Brighton for coastal defence. During foul winter weather they had the tedious employment of guarding minefields and manning pillbox defences. A sleepy summer passed and the battalion moved back to Sussex near the Saxon village of Horam. August 19 and the raid on Dieppe caused morale to plummet, but it bounced back with the rumours that the 1st Division would soon seek its destiny in battle. During the autumn, training began again but with a difference. They were now training for assault landings instead of coastal defences, and in November 1942, they were moved into a camp crowded with Nissen huts sinking into the muddy quagmire.

Just as the unit moved, Ken was doing very poorly in all his shooting tests. He said his eyes would get bleary, so he was sent to a specialist who tested his vision and prescribed glasses for him.

In mid-December, the battalion travelled north to Loch Fyne in Scotland to learn techniques for an assault on an enemy-held coast. For two weeks, they scrambled up and down nets perilously swaying from the sides of troop ships. Winter rains added to the misery of soldiers stumbling ashore. On Christmas Eve, they waded through freezing surf and battled a winter gale to participate in a seaborne assault on a coastal cliff. Upon reaching the top, the exhausted men were ordered to march through snow and up and down mountains to capture the town of Oban.

Their camp was on the Duke of Argyle's estate, whose deer filled many a platoon cooking pot. Trout fishermen, using hand grenades, added to the diet.

Ken went to No. 15 CGH on December 29 complaining of a right elbow and shoulder sprain, lacerations on his face, and multiple bruises. He said that he had been on the station platform at Guilford waiting to catch a train back to camp, when he got into a fight with a French Canadian. The next thing he remembered was that he was on the train. X-rays revealed a fractured right clavicle and right elbow. He stayed in hospital until January 14, 1943, then returned to the battalion for duties with "B" Company.

On January 1 his daily regimental rate of pay had increased to $1.50, which allowed him to send his mother $23 a month, up from the $20 he had been sending since 1940.

Also in January, the bone-weary regiment returned to Sussex, to Possingworth. Back on the coast, the men tore down the formidable defences that had been erected against German invasion. They were no longer needed, and the steel could be re-shaped into more useful weapons. In May the battalion moved back to Scotland, to the quiet lowland town of Darvel.

Meanwhile Ken was spending time in convalescent centres. From April 12 to 17 and from May 7 to 20 he was in No. 3 CMC.

On June 13, the H&PE embarked at Greenoch for Italy, but Ken O'Meara was left behind, attached to the headquarters battalion of the Canadian Base Overseas detachment of the reinforcement unit. On August 8, 1943, he was admitted to the British Isolation Hospital in Aldershot with diphtheria, and his parents were advised that he was dangerously ill. However, ten days later the army reported to them by telegram that Ken was progressing favourably and had been moved from the dangerously ill list to the seriously ill list. On September 18, Ken had improved enough to be sent to No. 2 Canadian Convalescent Depot.

By this time, the Hasty Pees had fought their way through the fiercest fighting in Sicily. Valguerna, Leonforte, Regalbuto, and Militello were all behind them as they made their way up the east coast past Catania towards Mount Etna and Messina.

Ken's diphtheria left him in a weakened condition and very susceptible to respiratory diseases. He was then found to have scabies, a contagious and extremely itchy skin disease, caused by a parasitic mite. In mid-October he complained of chest pains, and on October 26, he was sent to No. 17 CGH suffering from acute bronchitis and atypical pneumonia. On November 23, he went back to No. 3 CMC, and on January 4, 1944, he was admitted to No. 1 Special Hospital.

While in hospital, Ken complained of an ache in his right ear and hearing loss. He said that he couldn't hear well when on the parade square and that this had been a problem since 1941 when he "took a blow" behind the right ear. He was diagnosed as having an outer ear infection, and when he was discharged on February 22, he was attached, to the rear party of Headquarters 1st Canadian Army. Ken had recovered his health and was deemed fit to rejoin his battalion. On March 25 he sailed for Italy and landed on April 9. While aboard ship he was appointed acting lance corporal.

Before dawn on September 3, the H&PE boarded landing craft to cross the Straits of Messina to attack Reggio di Calabria on the toe of Italy. The Italian army had pretty much given up by this time, so the battalion chased the Germans through the Aspromonte mountains in steady rain. Then, on September 8, the announcement came that Italy had capitulated. The regiment continued north along the east coast of the peninsula riding in surrendered Italian trucks, then turned inland to climb the pine-forested mountains to Catanzano. Here they halted for the rest of the army to catch up. The fragments of the Italian army overrun by the Hasty Pees proved very amiable. So much so that some insisted an attaching themselves to the battalion.

The Canadians lost far fewer men in their advance to Campobasso during September, October, and November than they had in Sicily.

They were brought down from the mountains to relieve a mauled British division on November 29, and they crossed the Sangro River on December 1. On December 5, the battalion crossed the Moro River near its mouth, meeting heavy opposition that took one-third of their 400 men killed or wounded. After a particularly bloody fight for a gully leading to Ortona, while the 2nd Brigade took the city in fearsome house-to-house battles, the 1st was sent west of Ortona to cut off the enemy's communications. They got cut off themselves, and while holding their positions on Christmas Day, went hungry until a group from the Saskatoon Light Infantry got through with rations.

December's desperate fighting had exhausted the Canadian units. Their rifle companies had suffered particularly heavy battle casualties, and the offensive finally ground to a halt early in January 1944. For three miserable winter months they held their line in wretched muddy conditions, in constant contact with the enemy. On January 30–31, the H&PE made a limited offensive effort along the road leading to Tollo, but the paratroopers opposite them held, and after losing many men, the battalion withdrew to its original position. For five weeks the Canadian Corps remained in the Ortona sector. During this hiatus reinforcements arrived, among them, on April 18, 1944, was Acting Lance Corporal Ken O'Meara.

There were few faces Ken O'Meara recognized. Not more than 200 soldiers who had sailed from England remained in the battalion. Many replacements came from other regiments, full of resentment at being sent to join the "Plough Jockeys." With full acceptance by the wearied men of the Hasty Pees, this attitude soon changed.

The regiment left the Ortona lines on April 21, and Ken O'Mears encountered a myriad new sights and sounds. His truck rolled over tortured earth, past ruined buildings, and burned-out tanks. The sun shone and his nostrils

An editorial published by The Canadian on Thursday, January 6, 1944:

PRESERVE THE HOME FRONT

Reports from the war front suggest that while our men know what they're fighting against, there is some confusion as to what they're fighting for. However inarticulate their war aims may be, nine out of ten agree that one thing they are fighting for is their homes. What the average soldier wants most of all is to get it over with and come home.

Canadian boys are sacrificing for their homes. But meanwhile what is happening in their homes? The womenfolk they left behind are being called from their reside to the factories, to various war organizations, and to the armed services. Under these circumstances it becomes increasingly difficult to 'keep the home fires burning.'

A high school boy writes: 'Our home is greatly disrupted by the war. Before, I used to have all my meals at home. Now I only eat supper at home, and then sometimes I won't eat if I have to get it myself. It has become an overnight stopping place for the members of the family.'

This year's offensive overseas must be matched by an offensive at home to win the kind of home front the men are fighting for.

Homes are not home if they become just 'an overnight stopping place.' The real Canadian home from the pioneer days has been a place where the family draws strength from its unity and mutual caring.

A woman who works in a bomber factory on the day shift says: 'The unity we build at home is the only pattern for unity in our department at the plant.'

Housewives, whatever their occupation, can fight side by side with the women next door and the men at the front to protect Canadian home life. Home-making cannot be regarded as a non-priority activity, it is the heart-beat of democracy.

were filled with the sickly stench of rotting human flesh from thousands of bodies lying in shallow graves.

The H&PE spent a week at Campobasso then moved on to Lucera where they went under canvas to receive battle training in tank/infantry exercises. On May 5, they moved again, across the mountains and, for the first time, to the west side of the Italian boot. They stopped at the Volturno River, thirty miles short of Naples, and spent a week on exercises practising river crossings and investigating the delights of Naples, Avellino, and Caserta. The regiment was also re-equipped, primarily by their quartermasters scrounging through their own supplies and from the Americans who always seemed to have more of everything than they needed.

On May 11, the 8th Army launched an attack on Cassino and the Gustav Line, and the Hasty Pees moved to do battle against the Hitler Line in the Liri Valley on May 14. On May 16, they relieved the 8th Indian Division at the town of Pignataro and were ordered to strike north towards the Hitler Line. Looking down at the backs of the invaders were the German paratroopers holed up in the fortress-like monastery on the top of the mountain at Cassino. While the Poles engaged the troops on the mountaintop, the 1st Brigade advanced into a valley dominated by German observation posts. Contact with the enemy came almost at once.

The fight quickly degenerated into platoon and company battles, a savage melee of infantry versus infantry. "D" Company went forward on the left flank, got lost, and ended the day in a private war watched by the 48th Highlanders. "C" Company got so far up a covered lane that it was in grave danger of becoming cut off. Germans and Canadians intermingled, yet jeeps and stretcher-bearers evacuating wounded from deep in the enemy's lines emerged unscathed.

The Germans had a seemingly unlimited supply of artillery and mortars, and any movement by the Canadians drew a massive bombardment. In the first few hours, the H&PE lost forty men killed or seriously wounded, but by nightfall, the enemy had been driven off the wooded ridge behind Pignataro and was again in full flight[6].

On May 19, the Hasty Ps "bumped the Hitler Line," the final block on their path to Rome. Unable to positively determine the strength of the defences, albeit known to be formidable, there was a pause in the action until May 23, during which time the battalion was under a constant hail of mortar and artillery fire. It was also within range of the enemy's well-concealed machine-gun posts.

At 0500 hours on the 23rd, 800 guns belched fire and destruction towards the Germans. An hour later, the entire front line drove forward. The Plough Jockeys were ordered to relieve the 48th Highlanders who had been in serious trouble for two days, and "D" Company moved toward the 48th's positions at 1400 hours. Leapfrogging sections miraculously got through the "killing ground[7]" to the enemy's wire, alone inside of which, one platoon, firing rifles, Bren guns and tommy guns from the hip, had nowhere to go but ahead. In a savage fight, the Canadians took over the enemy's trenches, easing the pressure on the 48th. "B" Company supported by Churchill tanks attacked and took a row of strong points, and two hours later, the Hitler Line was broken, and "A" Company moved swiftly through "B" to occupy the high ground. The cost to the regiment was eight men killed and twenty-two wounded, while they had killed about 100 Germans and captured more than 300.

For a few days the regiment rested.

Then, on May 30, they joined the pursuit northwards, where their greatest enemy was heat, dust, and booby traps. On June 3, the battalion was in the hillside town of Anagni when the campaign ended, and three days later,

---

[6] _Farley Mowatt, "The Regiment" (Toronto, McClelland and Stewart Limited, 1955), p. 183.

[7] This was the area before the German line of defence that had been denuded of all buildings, trees and vineyards, providing unimpeded lines of crossfire for the machine gunners. It was designed to deny survival to any vehicle or soldier attempting to cross.

their comrades invaded France. On June 4, Ken O'Meara was made an acting corporal and section commander.

For almost two months the Canadians enjoyed their rest unnoticed by the rest of the world. The Americans got all the publicity when they entered Rome on June 4, and the Eternal City was immediately put out of bounds to Canadians. On June 9, they moved to barren landscape near the ancient village of Piedmonte d'Alife.

The regiment trained hard while "at rest," primarily because reinforcements were arriving from Canada with totally inadequate preparation, making them a danger to themselves and to their comrades. The men understood the need for this, but when saddled with ceremonial parades and other meaningless functions, they voted with their feet. After a year in battle, absenteeism became a problem.

On July 25, having removed all regimental and Canadian identifiers from their uniforms and vehicles, they began a slow trip northward to parts unknown. From the backs of their moving trucks they saw Rome, Perugia, Assisi, and Florence. In Florence, while they held the southern bank of the Arno, the Germans held the northern part of the city, and a separate war raged across the tiny muddy river. They were only in Florence a few days, but all agreed it was a lovely place.

On August 8, once again removing all identifying marks, they convoyed south and east.

Although the Allies had abandoned Italy as a major battleground, the Germans had built a new defence system, the Gothic Line, on the east coast. The 1st Division was moving into eight months of desperate battle. On August 23 they reached the valley of the Metaura River, and two days later, behind the barrage of 300 guns, the 1st Brigade forded the shallow river. The H&PE were in reserve and the next day moved forward to rejoin the leading RCR and 48th Highlanders. The enemy had withdrawn so the advance was quite easy. The Hasty Pees reached a gentle ridge topped with an old church tower. And as the sun was hot, they rested.

But the Germans had not retreated far. With such a tempting target, they collected about thirty guns, which opened fire on the unsuspecting battalion. The 48th, slightly ahead, had encountered heavy fire, which greeted any attempt to move forward or back. The Plough Jockeys were ordered to pass through the 48th and take the lead, and "D" Company, backed up by Churchill tanks, was ordered to the assault. Within an hour the men had scrambled up the slope and, with the tanks, wiped out the enemy strong point.

The next day's action was quite different.

By late afternoon, the battalion had advanced three miles with no serious opposition. Ahead lay the last ridge between them and the Foglia River and on the crest, three little villages-Monteciccardo, San Angelo, and Ginestreto—gleaming white in the afternoon sun. Backed by a British tank squadron, the men made their way down the slope to the ravine of the steep-sided Arzilla River. The tanks could not get across, but the infantry slogged on, and "D" Company scrambled up the opposite slope under intense mortar and artillery fire. Once again they were facing the toughest soldiers in the Wehrmacht, the 1st Paratroop Division. When they could go no further, they dug slit trenches for cover.

"A" Company's lead platoon was caught in an ambush. They called for artillery support, but the enemy was so close that many of the shells landed on their own positions. And just when it looked like the situation couldn't get worse, it did! Churchill tanks assumed the houses were held by the Germans and opened fire. Then two of 417 Squadron's Spitfires joined the fray. One of "A" Company's officers threw out a canister of yellow smoke, which both the tanks and aircraft recognized, causing them to break off their attacks.

The dark brought little relief. The RCR, mixed with "B" and "C" Companies, wandered in confusion. The 48th, off to the right, were thoroughly lost. During the night of August 28, the PPCLI cleared Ginestreto and the 1st Brigade moved in. On August 30, the brigade went into reserve for four days.

At 1600 hours on September 3, the H&PE was moved from along the coastal road to assault and clear the ridge at San Maria di Scacciano. Through hedges, vineyards, olive groves and orchards, "D" Company led the attack, its three platoons leapfrogging up the slope. They almost succeeded, coming to within 300 yards of the village before the paratroopers drove them to ground. Under heavy shellfire, the rest of the battalion moved forward, and by midnight, "B" Company scouts had penetrated the western edge of the village. In the early morning, "A" Company fought house-to-house, but only got to within 200 yards of the crest. The reserve company, "C," was thrown in. Behind three tanks and against German paratroopers occupied on three fronts, "C" advanced and soon was engaged in bitter battle. The fighting was hand-to-hand, kill or be killed, and both sides were completely exhausted when night fell. It was a stalemate. The Canadians withdrew to make way for an artillery barrage, and when the battalion attacked again at 0600 hours, following the artillery, the enemy withdrew. The battle for San Maria ridge was over. The Hasty Ps had suffered eighty-seven casualties.

For three more days they pursued the retreating enemy, dodging artillery fire as they went. On September 6, the weather broke in a tremendous downpour and two days later the battalion went to the seaside resort of Cattolica to rest. Each man was issued a bottle of beer, a package of gum, and three chocolate bars as a "comfort." But there was little comfort for Corporal Ken O'Meara. He had been admitted to No. 14 CGH with a severe case of impetigo on his face and arms, which at least got him out of the rain until September 15.

Rimini was fifteen miles to the north. On September 19, the H&PE was committed to assault the steep San Fortunato Ridge where the 1st Paratroop Division was prepared to make its final stand. With no reconnaissance, the men moved forward at 0400 hours, using maps and compasses.

The enemy had not expected a night attack, but by dawn their resistance was fanatical. The lead companies needed artillery support and went to cover to let the gunners do their job. The "D" and "C" companies attacked again and dug in to hold their position. The battalion was ordered to withdraw 300 yards for an artillery barrage, and under the shelling, night fell on a disheartened enemy. The companies returned to their abandoned positions and went forward into the night scarred by shell flashes. Before dawn, resistance was broken and victory belonged to the Canadians. They had killed forty paratroopers and taken 112 prisoners. The final battle for the Gothic Line was over. From August 25 to September 22, the 1st Division had taken 2,511 battle casualties, including 626 dead.

Major General Chris Vokes led his 1st Division up a narrow front to the north, while Brigadier Allan Calder's 1st Brigade led the advance. The H&PE was the first to cross the Fiumicino River on October 11. Following the railroad line to avoid some of the heavy muck in the drowned landscape, they reached the Scolo Rigossa drainage canal and pushed along the Via Emilia (Highway 9) to Bologna. Lieutenant Colonel Don Cameron found his Hasty Pees in a precarious position. They had plunged deep into enemy territory. Ahead was the village of Gambettola joined by a rail line to the hamlet of Bulgaria, which the Hasty Pees were ordered to capture.

After an artillery and aerial bombardment, they attacked at dawn on a sunny Saturday, October 14. Sherman tanks from the Lord Strathcona's Horse lumbered up behind them. The infantry was able to wade the canal, but the tanks would have sunk in the ooze. Not to be left out, they gambled on a partly demolished bridge that the engineers had ruled would not support a Sherman. They won the risk and got across to help the H&PE. All day the tanks blasted buildings in Bulgaria with high-explosive shells and machine guns while the infantry completed the job through door-to-door fighting with grenades, Tommy guns, and Lee-Enfields. By 1630 hours, the ruins belonged to the Canadians, and the Germans were forced to withdraw along most of the corps' front.

The Germans left fifty-five prisoners and many more dead. The Canadians suffered thirty casualties, among them Huron Brant, an aboriginal from Ontario who had won the Military Medal in Sicily. He and his entire section were wiped out when they were caught by machine-gun fire in a shallow trench.

On October 18, the battalion withdrew to rest under canvas in soaking fields near the town of Santarcangelo as the autumn rains returned with a vengeance.

Ken O'Meara reverted to private on October 29, but on November 10, he was reappointed to lance corporal. The reason for these rank changes is not apparent in his records.

The rains continued without pause until early in November, and hardly a man in the Hasty Pees remembered what it was like to be dry, mud-free, and totally warm. The first week of the month, the battalion moved into abandoned villas in Miramare and received the first real furloughs since they had landed in Sicily. Fifty men at a time left in trucks for the delights of Florence, and five days later, they returned with their fill of "bargains, booze, and broads." A scheme for Home Leave was announced that would permit long-service men to be home by Christmas, but the troops could not retain their hostility and rage when it was finally announced that only three men from the H&PE would be picked for thirty days leave in Canada before being returned overseas to active service. Insensitive politicians delivered the ultimate stab in the back to an army, most of whom had not seen wives and children for five years.

Adding to the woeful news from Canada was the conscription crisis. After the invasion of Normandy, reinforcements for Italy became almost non-existent. Defence Minister Colonel Ralston had visited Italy and returned with the demand for conscription at once. The prime minister's solution was to sack Ralston and replace him with General Andy McNaughton, who was convinced he could fill the ranks with volunteers. He was sadly mistaken in his naïveté, and very few National Resources Mobilization Men volunteered for overseas service. Finally, to avoid a Cabinet revolt, MacKenzie King implemented overseas conscription.

The first men sailed from Halifax on January 3, 1945. A total of 12,908 were sent, 2,463 actually joining combat units; 331 became casualties and 69 were killed. Not a single man went to the Italian theatre. The lack of infantry soldiers in the front lines was obvious to the front-line troops, and companies, platoons, and sections were all well below their minimum strength. Any reinforcements that did arrive were painfully poorly trained. Morale suffered commensurately.

Winter brought no respite to the Allied forces in Italy. On December 1–2, the 1st Canadian Corps returned to the line stretching from the Montone River to the Fiumi Uniti. The 1st Division was assigned an assault role, attacking northwest to cross the Lamogne River just east of Lugo. The 3rd Brigade reached the Lamone on the morning of December 4 where the 1st Brigade took over. Early on the 5th, the H&PE and the RCR held a bridge-head of five companies on the western shore, but fierce German counter-attacks drove them back across the water.

Both battalion commanders of the H&PE and the RCR had warned Division that the planned assault could not succeed. Nevertheless they were ordered forward into the greatest debacle ever suffered by the battalions. German tanks and mortar and artillery fire ravaged the attackers, and many men had to abandon their equipment in order to get back across the swollen and swift-running river. "For the first time the unit had been severely beaten in the field, and for the first time its spirit had been broken.[8]"

The 3rd Brigade crossed again on the night of December 10–11. The 1st Brigade followed, passed through the 3rd, and crossed the Vecchio the night of the 11th. The next day, the Hasty Pees and the Carleton and York Regiments, in bitter fighting, forced a crossing of the Naviglio, and before dawn on the 13th, held a bridgehead 1,000 yards deep, which they were ordered to hold at all costs. And hold they did, against no fewer than thirteen counter-attacks.

That night, the Germans withdrew beyond the banks of the Naviglio Canal. The Westminster Regiment passed through this foothold on the 14th, and that night, the Lanark and Renfrew Scottish made a successful attack. During the morning, the H&PE was withdrawn behind the Vecchio, and by late afternoon on the 15th, the Canadians were firmly established on the west bank of the canal.

But the victory brought little joy to the Hasty Pees. As almost all suffered from battle exhaustion, the men were devoid of any emotion except desper-ate weariness. More than a hundred men had been lost at the Vecchio and the Naviglio alone. "B" Company had been reduced to a handful of soldiers culled from the starved ranks of the remaining companies, while "A", "C," and "D" Companies were hardly above the fighting strength of platoons. Spiritually, the wastage had been even greater.

On December 16 the regiment was returned to action[9].

The 1st Brigade was ordered to shift westwards and again cross both the Vecchio and the Naviglio, pushing towards the Senio River and the town of Bagnacavalo. They were again fighting with the RCR, a battalion that was a

[8] Farley Mowatt, The Regiment (Toronto: McClelland and Stewart Limited, 1955) p. 266.
[9] ibid. p. 281.

mere shadow of its former self; only nine officers and twenty-four men remained of those who had landed in Sicily in July 1943. The Hasty Pees were similarly burned out, every company weak, with one composed entirely of batmen, cooks, and drivers. Things went wrong right from the start.

On the night of December 16–17, the battalion were in close support of the 48th Highlanders trying to cross the Vecchio. The attack failed in frozen mud that trapped the feet of the advancing troops. The next night, the RCR on the right and the Hasty Pees on the left were ordered in for another assault. At 0400 hours on December 18, the shattered companies moved toward the Vecchio dikes, but the conclusion was foregone. The RCR got over the canal, but at 0615 hours were heavily counter-attacked. "D" Company, with only eighteen men, reached the dikes with the ghost of "B" Company following. "C" Company arrived to find the RCR thrown back across the canal. Enemy artillery intensified its barrage, and the sleeping infantry lay inert beneath the explosions.

That night, the three battalions of the 1st Brigade were treated to a new tactic. In order to cover preparations for an attack by the 2nd Brigade, far to the east, high-powered amplifiers broadcast recorded noises of moving vehicles, tanks, and troops towards the Germans. They reacted by directing a violent barrage of guns into the 1st Brigade's area. From December 21 to 23, the battalion laboured on, too weak to be effective but still in the line. By the morning of the 21st, the Germans had been driven back, or had retreated, and Bagnacavallo had been occupied with little resistance. In the last days before Christmas, "B" Company had arrived on the banks of the Senio.

On December 23, they were withdrawn for a forty-eight hour relief to the town of Cattolica. In the line on Christmas Day, a wary truce of sorts kept the area quiet. Although staying under cover, soldiers sent wishes of "Merry Christmas" and "Fröhliche Weinacht" across the frozen land between them. For twenty-four hours men became human again[10]. On the 26th the Hasty Pees moved back to a reserve position near Bagnacavallo.

The unit was thoroughly reorganized. "A" Company, devoid of all officers save one lieutenant, was broken up and its handful of survivors sent to strengthen the other three companies. From Support and HQ companies, drivers, mechanics, runners, administrative personnel, and every man who could still handle a rifle were gathered together into what was called "X" company and given a combatant role. Drawing on the last of its own inner resources, the regiment was at least able to assume the semblance of a fighting battalion once again[11].

In order to fan the flame of any unit morale that was left, the commanding officer introduced a Spartan regime during the battalion's stay near

---

[10] Col. C.P. Stacey, The Canadian Army 1939–1945 (Ottawa: King's Printer, 1948) p. 162.
[11] Mowat, op cit. p. 286.

Bagnacavallo. Each day at dawn, the soldiers were rousted from their billets to participate in physical training and "hardening exercises." Parade drill spit and polish returned after a two-year absence. The men were worked hard and most grumbled. But the old face of the battalion started to return. They won a competitive brigade PIAT shoot and celebrated the victory. The gap between officers and men narrowed.

The soldiers formed a strong attachment with the Italian civilians. Taking advantage of this, Lance Corporal K. O'Meara disappeared at 2200 hours on the night of January 4. He returned much the worse for wear at 1130 hours on January 14. His excursion to parts unknown cost him thirty-one days' pay at $1.50 per day. He also relinquished his appointment as a lance corporal effective January 4, the day he left.

Two days after Ken went AWL, a draft of Cape Breton men arrived. They were hard men from a hard land and soon proved their worth to the eastern Ontario battalion. On January 11, the Hasty Pees returned to the Senio dikes near Cotignola, and throughout heavy snow, frosts and freezing rain, both sides held their positions on the Winter Line with a minimum number of troops. Such stagnation could have lead to apathy, but the Plough Jockeys' officers kept them busy. Patrols and platoon or section operations were planned and executed with care and uniform success. Sniping was encouraged, and sentries were wound up to exceptional vigilance. Slowly the H&PE recovered its physical and emotional strength.

At the end of January, the battalion enjoyed a week's rest then moved, on February 3, into the marshes beyond Ravenna. Their position was near Mezzano where the frozen slush still gripped the bodies of dead Germans. Thaws and freezes turned the roads into deep quagmires, and boats, not vehicles, provided a supply line. Men still died—from artillery shelling, sniper fire, and illness—and once again, men from all branches of the army were drafted into the infantry.

At the beginning of February, the Combined Chiefs of Staff met in Malta and decided to divert five British and Canadian divisions from Italy to northwest Europe, a hope long cherished by Canadian commanders and politicians. Movement came quickly. The first Canadians sailed from Livorno for Marseilles on February 15, and the 1st Canadian Division continued to hold the Senio line until relieved by the 8th Indian Division on February 23 to 27. But before moving, the Hasty Pees were treated to the delights of the town of Ripratransone in the Adriatic coastal mountains.

There were endless spaghetti dinner parties in Italian homes and endless escapades when the *vino* flowed a mite too freely. There were expeditions into the lovely mounded hills and green valleys, and there was a plethora of eggs, fresh meat, chickens, and those simple things that mean so much to a fighting man. There were even women—those improbable beings whose very existence had seemed mythical for so long.

Ripratransone was noon-day festival after the long night. Men breathed deeply and without fear, and there was a contentment over them that they had not known before[12].

On March 2, a Canadian convoy left the people of Ripratransone, wound down the spine of Italy into the Arno valley, and through Florence and Pisa to a transit point called Harrod's Camp. On March 10, the men climbed the gangplanks of American landing ships at Leghorn (Livorno), where the lavish generosity of their well-fed hosts provided unaccustomed and almost forgotten treats, like white bread and ice cream. Standing on the trembling decks they stared across the widening water towards the fading Italian shore. There were no regrets!

Canadians who served in Italy numbered 92,757. Still lying in Italian soil are 5,799.

The battalion enjoyed crossing the Tyrrhenian Sea in bright sunny weather. Disembarking on March 12, in Marseilles, they boarded trucks for the ride north up the Rhône Valley, rolling past Valence, Lyon, Cambrai, and the cemeteries of World War I. They arrived in Belgium on March 20 and took up quarters in a Trappist monastery near the little village of Westmalle, a monastery, incidentally, renowned for the brewing of beer.

Passes to Brussels were handed out and leave to Britain was available. Groups of fifty to one hundred men took the ferry *Canterbury Belle* to England. There was sweet irony in that this ferry had taken the battalion from Brest to England during the collapse of France in 1940. Thirteen of the oldest serving men left for Canada on April 1, while others were issued with the "plumber's nightmare" (the Sten gun), and most of their equipment was replaced. The 8th Army's famous Crusader Cross disappeared from their left shoulders to be replaced by a meaningless flash of the 1st Canadian Army, and men were ordered to wear the CVSM that was disdained in Italy[13]. Uniforms dictating each article of dress, even to a shirt and tie, replaced garish outfits collected and worn in Italy.

Reorganization was instituted to meld the "D-Day Dodgers" into the 1st Canadian Army in northwest Europe; however, a severe blow was dealt the Lanark and Renfrew Scottish when they reverted to the role of anti-aircraft gunners. The Italian minimum of reserves, minimum of ammunition, and minimum of support was replaced by more than enough aviation and artillery support and no shortage of troops and equipment. When they went into action early in April, their assignment was to deal with 120,000 heavily armed and

[12] Ibid p. 293
[13] In Italy the medal was referred to as the "EGBO" – "Every Bastard's Got One."

desperate Germans holed up in a pocket of the western Netherlands. The starving civilian population delineated their race against time.

At 0900 hours on April 1, the advance party left the comforts of Brussels for the desolation of the Reichswald Forest, inside Germany. It was a very cool day with periodic light rain, and Ken O'Meara attended Easter services at the Abbey Church with the other Roman Catholics. The U.S. 30th General Hospital held services for the Protestants. For the next two days the battalion trained in house and woods clearing, and loaded their vehicles getting ready to move. Shortly after noon on the 3rd, the H&PE moved off towards Germany. They arrived at 2330 hours in a dark, brooding Reichwald Forest dripping from incessant rain.

The war had become a process of liquidating the enemy piece by piece. The 2nd British Army was moving east into Germany, and the Russians were moving west at a frightening pace. The Canadian Corps were to push west from Zutphen, cross the Ijssel River, and cut the German 25th Army Group in two. On April 7, the weather turned agreeably warm and sunny, and on the 9th, the Hasty Pees reached their area near Zutphen at 1615 hours. On April 12, the men from Italy tasted their first combat in northwest Europe.

Roused from their "hootchies" (two-man tents) at 0430 and fed breakfast at 0500, the battalion was ready to move on fifteen minutes' notice at 0700. They moved forward at 0930 and rested until 1215 when the first section of "C" Company and the Tactical Company crossed the Ijssel in Buffaloes[14]. The entire battalion quickly followed and at 1730 hours was ordered into the cleared but battered town of Hoven. In half an hour, Tactical HQ was set up in the town, and all of the companies had taken up defensive positions in and around the built-up area. Each man was fed his first hot meal of the day.

That night orders came for the battalion to pass through the positions of the 48th and strike for Apeldoorn. At 0500 hours, the commanding officer and the intelligence officer went forward to reconnoitre the railway station in the town of Twello. A platoon of "C" Company went out on carriers into the new battlefield, a crossroad a few miles to the west. The commanding officer joined the patrol, and just before reaching the crossroad, they ran into remnants of SS, Jaeger, Luftwaffe, and many other troops. The enemy posed a problem in that they were divided into two factions: those who fought savagely and those who dropped their weapons and walked out to safety. There was no way of telling which the Canadians would encounter. In fact they met both. "C" Company, and a squadron of tanks belonging to the 1st Hussars from London, Ontario, took an hour to clear the crossroads.

[14] Buffalos were a species of amphibious tanks that took water obstacles in stride. The Plough Jockeys had no such equipment in Italy. They marveled at the effortless crossing. There were many surprises: an end less stream of aircraft overhead instead of a few war-weary Kittyhawks; instead of worn Sherman tanks there were armoured troop carriers, fighting tanks, flame-throwing tanks, bridging tanks and bulldozer tanks; there were self-propelled guns and no shortage of ammunition. (Mowatt, ibid, p. 300)

By noon, "C" Company had advanced several miles to the edge of the woods and had taken sixty prisoners. The regimental diary records that they "put the fear of the Lord into the Hun in this area." At 1300 hours, "A" and "D" Companies went forward through "C" Company and seized a cross-roads just west of Tuege in a thick pine forest. In warm bright weather, they carried the assault steadily forward towards a bridge over the great canal that ran east of Apeldoorn. The commanding officer moved with "D" Company, the infantry riding on the backs of tanks and shooting up any pocket of resistance as they advanced. A steady stream of prisoners were passed back; the battalion took 242 that day. But the battalion also suffered: thirty men were dead or wounded. The official War Diary records: "Casualties were: 1 officer and 23 ORs wounded and the following killed: Ptes McDonnell, Luard, Pindar, O'Meara and Monsour."

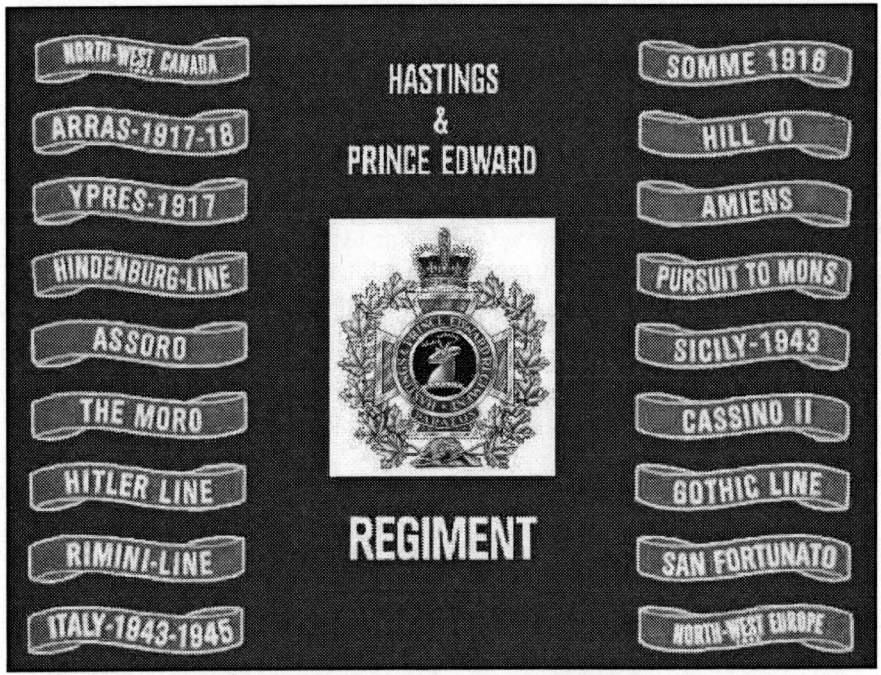

O'Meara was one of the last originals, having joined in 1939, suffered training for three years in England, and fighting through the muck and dust of Italy, he answered his last roll call with his beloved Hasty Pees in Holland.

The battle continued through the night, and by daybreak, "D" and "B" Companies were engaged in house-to-house fighting. On the night of April 16–17, the RCR and the 48th crossed the canal into Apeldoorn. The Hasty Pees climbed aboard their tanks and moved past the 48th into a city waiting for liberation.

It was tough going due to the cheering of the thousands of liberated Dutch who crowded the streets and showered bouquets of flowers on the troops. A good-looking soldier had to use his weapon to beat off the girls and many a fair maiden's kiss.

The battalion made for Queen Wilhelmina's Royal Palace and got there without firing a shot, except for the CO who fired three shots in the air to clear some of the people away to get through[15].

The war still lay just beyond the next row of trees, in the Nieuwmilligen woods. Each soldier learned that he had to fight alone against an enemy vicious to the end. They were up against Nazi SS troopers, many of whom were Dutch. The Germans were well aware of their fate, and the Dutch traitors knew their future was even grimmer. They fought with special savagery and received no mercy.

On April 23, 1945, the H&PE went out of action. In the early days of May, when flowers bloomed and the air smelled spring-fresh, Germany surrendered.

Private Ken O'Meara and his four comrades were originally buried in the H&PE temporary burial ground at Teuge. After war's end, their bodies were moved to the Holten Canadian War Cemetery, a village twenty kilometres east of Deventer on the main road from Amsterdam to Bremen. The cemetery lies at the end of a dirt track named Willenbergweg. Most Canadians buried here died during the last stages of the war in Holland and during the advance into Germany of the 2nd Canadian Corps.

The France and Germany Star, awarded for operational service in France, Belgium, Holland and Germany.

The 1939-45 Star, awarded for service in operations during the Second World War.

Ken's parents received a message of condolence from the king on May 29, 1945, and his mother was given the Memorial Cross. Ken's war service gratuity of $1,100.19 was paid on the basis of 1,960 days service, with 1,732 days overseas. His effects (a ring, a sports medal, a prayer book, and a pair of glasses in a case) were packaged up and sent home. In January 1946, his estate had still not been settled and letters were written to the Department of Defence seeking resolution. His father was unable to work and they were in dire need of financial assistance.

---

[15] The Hastings and Prince Edward Regiment War Diary, 17.4.45, National Archives of Canada.

C 70268 Lance Bombardier Joseph Borland
14th Field Regiment, Royal Canadian Artillery

Also in Holten Canadian War Cemetery, is the body of another Carleton Place man, Joe Borland.

Joe left his wife and daughter behind when he joined the army in 1941. He had worked many years as a "bushman" in the forested lots around Carleton Place, so when he enlisted, it was natural that he be assigned to the Canadian Forestry Corps. His wife, Lavina, was mollified with this choice, because she hoped it would keep him out of the main action. However, in 1943, flushed with patriotism and a desire to be in the midst of things, Joe transferred to the Royal Canadian Artillery (RCA). He was killed eleven days before the end of the war, in Holland, while his battery was returning fire from a German 20-mm gun that was peppering his position with shellfire.

In May 1940, the Canadian Forestry Corps (CFC) came into being. Repeating the important work it performed during the Great War, the CFC provided much-needed lumber for various war purposes. This valuable, and characteristically Canadian, contribution to the war effort was considerable.

In the summer of 1940, Britain asked Canada to provide as many as eight companies for service in Britain and on the continent. When France collapsed, service in Europe was no longer a factor, but foresters were still needed urgently in Great Britain to meet essential requirements.

Twenty forestry companies, each with 200 men, were mobilized, given an appropriate amount of training as soldiers, and sent to England. The first men arrived in October 1940, and by Christmas, were joined by a headquarters unit and an entire company. They were assigned to work in the timbered areas of Scotland, and by July 1941, all twenty companies had arrived. Still, Britain requested more forestry companies (there wasn't the space to ship timber from North America), so ten more were raised and were in Scotland by October 1942. Overall, the Corps had 6,000 men overseas.

Joe Borland, born on May 24, 1908, was fifteen when, in 1923, he left his father's home at Seacon Cottage, Ballymoney, County Antrim, Ireland. His mother was dead, leaving his father, a local labourer, with two other sons

(Samuel and William), and two girls (Annie and Margaret). However, as the youngest, Joseph felt his chances of success were better in Canada. He landed in Halifax, cleared immigration at Pier 11, and took the first available train heading west. Joe carried the name of an aunt in the United States and it was to her home that he was headed.

The train stopped often, and one of those stops was Almonte. Joe and his travelling companions climbed down from the train to stretch their legs and take deep breaths of fresh, clean air. On the platform, they met Clifford Sadler, who was offering jobs on his farm in nearby Appleton, and as Joe had had enough travelling, he accepted[16]. It was hard work, but Joe revelled in it. He liked to drive the team of large horses used to plough, till, thresh, and even transport goods and people to the closest town, Carleton Place.

But it wasn't all work, and at a dance following a threshing "bee," Joe met Lavina Shail. Her mother, Marion, had brought her to help with cooking and serving meals to the workers. Lavina took an immediate liking to Joe. His Irish brogue, dark hair, and smiling grey eyes entranced the young lady, and after a suitable courtship, they were married on February 29, 1932, at the Anglican Church in Carleton Place. Joe left the farm to reside in town with his bride and took a job with Tommy Miller who operated a horse stable across the street from Findlay's Foundry. It was Joe's job to take the truck to pick up horses to bring back to the livery barn. Later, he spent six years working for Clyde Construction as a "cat driver." Joe loved tramping through the Ontario woods and took employment whenever he could as a bushman, doing whatever was required to get timber from the woods to the mills.

One of the popular hangouts in Carleton Place at the time was a coffee shop run by "Clicker" Peden. Wally Mace recalled Joe Borland being there much

of the time, and although he was older than most of the boys, Joe was friends with all the younger people. Wally described him as a "real, nice guy."[17]

On April 21, 1935, Lavina gave birth to their only child, a daughter. She was named Marion Lenore, after her maternal grandmother Marion Shail.[18] That summer, the young couple and their new baby would often be seen strolling Bridge Street or picnicking in the town parks by the Mississippi River.

[16] From an interview with Borland's daughter Marion LeClair and his granddaughter, Janice Gibson, on April 6, 2001
[17] E-mail from Wally Mace dated December 12, 2002.
[18] Marion was a Hamilton from Huntley. After marrying George they farmed the family homestead in Tennyson.

The winter of 1940–41 came early and stayed late. Regardless, work in the woods usually halted for the winter, and Joe got employment as a labourer on the highway. Then, on February 6, he travelled to Ottawa to the recruiting office, and because of his previous experience, was enlisted by the Canadian Forestry Corps. Plus, at 5' 9" tall and 155 pounds, Joe was in top physical condition.

Lavina was less than happy, but conceded that the Forestry Corps was reasonably safe and that they could certainly use the guaranteed income. The recruiters told Joe that the government paid allowances for dependents and that he could expect to get the daily rate of $1.30 plus a monthly allowance of $35 for his wife and $12 for his daughter. Of his monthly pay of $39, he assigned Lavina $20 in addition to the dependents' allowance.

Although the money paid the rent and bought groceries, Lavina went to work at Findlay's, which had stopped making stoves in favour of ammunition boxes and had an entire floor of women workers who had been hired to replace the men gone to war. Each morning, Lavina, like most other women working in the plant, would don her overalls, tie her hair in a kerchief, and carry her heavy gloves to her station at the degreaser tank. Her job was to clean the ammunition boxes so they could be spray painted.

On February 15, Joe left Lavina and Marion, and his dog Teddy, to ride the train to Three Rivers, Quebec, for basic training at the CFC Machine-Gun Training Centre. At his earliest opportunity, on March 6, he took the first of many trips home to spend the weekend with his wife and daughter. On April 28, he was transferred to No. 10 Company of the CFC, quartered in Cove Field Barracks at Quebec City, and on June 8–9, he spent his last leave with his wife and daughter before sailing to England on June 20.

On board ship, Joe was put to such duties as "fire piquet," where he had to ensure that doors were kept closed to guard against the spread of fire and to close bulkhead doors if the ship was torpedoed and in danger of sinking. A fire piquet also peeled potatoes and washed dishes. Plus, Joe carried supplies, such as wine, beer and soft drinks, up from the storage hold to the officers' and men's canteens where they were sold at quite reasonable prices (a soft drink—4¢, a pint of beer—18¢, and a chocolate bar—5¢).

Joe, daughter Marion, and dog Teddy before Joe's departure for England. (Photo courtesy Marion LeClair.)

Any soldier with machine-gun training, as Joe had, was detailed to man the "ack ack" (anti-aircraft) defences on board the troop ship. These were Lewis Guns, Great War equipment still being used, issued just before the ship left Halifax. The larger three-inch guns were usually manned by RCN gunners posted to DEMS for just that purpose.

Joe's ship docked at Gourah (Inverness) on July 2, 1941, and he walked directly to a cable office to send Lavina news that he had landed safely. He could hardly believe his good luck in being back in the "Old Country" and able to visit with friends and family he had not seen in eighteen years. He took landing leave a week after disembarking, returning to No. 10 Company at Dockfour Camp on July 16.

For the rest of the war, the Scottish Highlands rang to the crash of Canadian axes and the shriek of Canadian chain saws. No. 10 Company worked in two sections: one would be in the woods, felling and bringing out the timber; the other worked in the company mill, with Canadian mechanical equipment, sawing the logs into lumber. Each company maintained the logging practices of the area from which it was raised. For instance, the men from western Canada preferred "high rigging" techniques and wire ropes. The eastern companies felled the trees and dragged them out of the bush harnessed to teams of huge horses.

Each section was a self-contained community, and each man was capable of turning his hand to any task, not the least of which was clearing snow from Highland roads in the Scottish winter. Regular intervals were spent in military drill; uniform, barracks and kit inspection; weapons handling; guard duty; coastal patrols; and defensive exercises.

Joe trained to improve his knowledge of forestry, and in September 1942, he became qualified as a log canter (Forestry) Group "C," which resulted in a meagre increase in trade's pay. Lavina's allowance also increased such that by the end of 1942 she was receiving $72.60 a month for herself and Marion. This compared favourably to other Allied dependents: an American wife with one child received $62 and British dependents received the equivalent of $33.22.

Then, early in 1943, Joe's pay was increased to $1.40 a day, about the same time he got it into his head to transfer to the Artillery. He gave up his trade's pay, and on February 23, was transferred to No. 1 Canadian Artillery Reinforcement Unit (CARU) for three-month's training as a gunner. But before he left the Forestry Corps, he was granted his first Good Conduct Badge, a gold stripe worn on his lower right sleeve.

At No.1 CARU, Joe was introduced to the Norton motorcycle, a machine that was standard issue for all line units. The rider was taught off-road techniques such as cross-country riding; how to cross shallow, stony streams without the bike stalling halfway; "walking" the tough, smoke-belching machine through gorse, deep sand, and up steep rock ledges; and how to ride sitting and standing up, especially when climbing or descending the incredibly steep cliff walls.

Joe was also sent to "battle school" where he learned unarmed combat, how to assault over nasty obstacles and under even nastier ones, and how to recognize and avoid booby-traps. He was exposed to real bullets whizzing overhead as he crawled and cut through barbed wire. Instructors tossed "thunder flashes" at them and buried gun cotton to explode near them. Both provided great blast effects without the usual fragmentation that grenades and incoming shells would during actual combat.

On April 29, 1943, Joe was granted a pay increase to $1.50 per day and seven days' leave to mark the end of his training, which he spent in London, as did most Canadians. Upon graduation as a gunner, Joe was sent to the 7th Army Field Regiment, and on May 23, he began the specialized training to operate as part of a gun's team. That summer, however, was spent either overstaying his leave or in the "digger" (military jail), infractions for which he was penalized seven days confined to barracks and one day's pay.

On December 7 he was AWL for nearly six days. This absence cost him twenty-eight days' pay, and for good measure he was sent to No.1 Canadian Field Punishment Camp for twenty-seven days. While in confinement he was awarded the Canadian Volunteer Service Medal and Clasp and attached to the 7th Medium Regiment of the 2nd Army Group.

Joe was sent back to the CARU on January 21, 1944, where he waited until August 1 when he was transferred to his operational unit, the 14th Field Regiment, which was already in France.

The 14th was formed in Petawawa in August 1940. It was one of three field regiments in the 3rd Canadian Infantry Division that languished in the U.K. from 1941 to 1944 then landed in Normandy on D-Day in the first wave in the centre of the British front. They fought through Caen and along the Route Nationale No. 158, the Falaise Road, in support of infantry and armoured advances to Tilly-la-Campagne[19]. The Division had spent fifty-six days in the line, when, on July 30–31 it was withdrawn for a short rest. Joe Borland sailed from

[19] George G. Blackburn, Where the Hell Are the Guns? A Soldier's Eye View of the Anxious Years, 1939—44 (Toronto, McClelland and Stewart Inc., 1997. P383.

The 25-Pounder Field Gun

A Field Regiment is equipped with guns to support the infantry. It must be able to move forward quickly behind an advancing front and could well decide the outcome of a particular battle. For the gunners to sustain a high, uninterrupted rate of fire for long periods, the projectile should weigh no more than twenty-five or thirty pounds.

In determining artillery strategy, there is also the choice of a gun or a howitzer. A gun has a powerful propellant charge producing high muzzle velocity for long ranges and a high degree of accuracy. Its trajectory is relatively flat. A lighter propellant charge used in a howitzer produces shorter range and less accuracy. But a howitzer can lob its shells on high trajectories at targets sheltering behind steep hills or in deep valleys.

The gun chosen for the field regiments was inspired. The British 25-pounder of 1938 was both a gun and a howitzer, and it was possible to lay the gun at widely varying elevations. As well, a low, medium, or high charge could be used to propel the shell by separating the cartridge case from the shell. The gun crew could remove one or two of the three (red, white and blue)

bags of cordite to reduce the propellant charge and increase the looping effect of the shell.

The vertical breechblock, when dropped open, provided a shelf for ramming the shell, greatly easing loading. When the shell and cartridge case were loaded, springs helped to close the heavy breech. The "intense" rate of fire for 25-pounders was officially listed as five rounds a minute, but experienced crews could get off ten to twelve rounds per minute.

Getting a 25-pounder ready to fire was easier than any other gun in the world. There was no need to construct a level platform since it carried its own under its trail. Dropped from its carrying position the gun's quad tractor hauled the wheels onto the platform, while claws on the bottom dug into the ground, or even a roadway, which were aided by the gun's 4,032 pounds. One gunner could swing the gun in a complete circle, an accomplishment no other gun could do.

Moving after action was even simpler. The gun trail was hooked to the ammunition limber, which was hooked to the quad. The quad rolled backwards a few feet to push the gun off the platform so it could be raised and secured to the trail and they were on the road in seconds.

The maximum range for a high explosive shell was 13,400 yards and for a smoke shell, 11,000 yards. In 1943, the gun was fitted with a "muzzle brake" to reduce wear and tear on the recoil system, particularly when the "super charge" was used. It had a muzzle velocity of 2,000 feet per second to fire armour-piercing solid-shot against tanks.

England on July 29, landed in France the next day, and caught up with the 14th Field Regiment to join his gun crew.

The 3rd Division was back in action on August 7, and Operation Totalize began at 2300 hours with Bomber Command dropping on the four villages of May-sur-Orne, Fontenay-le-Marmion, Secqueville-la-Compagne, and La Hogue. The armour rolled across the start line at 2330, and at 2345, all guns in the Corps shattered the night silence with an ear-splitting roar. Firing as one, they laid down a barrage of steel in front of the attackers. The enemy line was smashed.

Then things began to go wrong. That afternoon, the 8th USAAF dropped by mistake on the Canadians' rear causing many casualties. The gunners could only cower near their weapons since they had no time to hook them to the vehicles and disappear.

The German line was held by, among others, General Kurt Meyer's 12th SS, which had massacred men of the Black Watch on Verrières Ridge on July 25, and a new infantry division—the 85th. On the night of August 10–11, the 3rd Division used their guns to screen an attack by the 8th Brigade at Quesnay Wood. The only result was heavy Canadian casualties.

A new operation, "Tractable," commenced on August 12 in an effort to capture Falaise. This operation began in daylight and used a smoke screen on the flanks and in front of the advancing infantry laid down by the artillery for cover. There was no preliminary bombardment in order to create maximum surprise for the enemy. The day ended with the infantry well established within three miles of Falaise, but once again, "friendly fire" from RAF and RCAF heavy bombers hit the Canadian and Polish lines for well over an hour. The attack went on successfully, but many vehicles and the guns suffered heavy losses even though the Falaise Gap was closed. During August 19–21, more than 12,000 Germans surrendered and uncounted others lay dead.

The 2nd Division headed for Dieppe as the 3rd charged up the coast. On September 1, the 3rd took the small port of Le Tréport and then headed for Calais and Boulogne, both held by enemy garrisons. On September 6, Major General Dan C. Spry led the 3rd Division in chasing the Germans from their flying bomb-launching sites, and the Canadian Army took great satisfaction in denying the enemy the ability to launch bombs against cities such as London. In each action, the 12th, 13th, and 14th Field Regiments were instrumental in silencing the opposing 75- and 88mm German guns. Often the infantry were only able to move forward under the protective umbrella of an artillery barrage.

On the morning of September 17, 3rd Division's 8th and 9th Brigades advanced against the solid defences forward of Boulogne. They had plenty of support, from bombers in the air to the artillery of two divisions, their own and the 51st British. The complete reduction of the position took six days.

Calais and its batteries were next. Following a shattering bombing and artillery bombardment on September 25, the armour and infantry began their assault. Two days later, after 342 bombers raided the inner port and the Cap Gris Nez defences, the 14th Field Regiment subjected the German guns to an eighty-minute bombardment, which silenced all three enemy batteries. On September 28, the German commandant surrendered the city to the tired, dirty, and grateful 3rd Division.

In the Battle of the Scheldt, it fell to the 3rd Division to clear the little port of Breskens of Germans from behind the Leopold Canal. Operation "Switchback" began in the early morning of October 6.

The Leopold Canal is not wide, but the high dikes, topped with lines of trees, made it a formidable obstacle, especially since the enemy was known to be well dug in on the opposite side.

The infantry flung assault boats into the water and furiously paddled across. The wave of fire from the Wasps[20] initially demoralized the enemy's 64th Infantry Division, but their recovery was quick. The Canadians were under heavy fire from small arms, mortar and machine guns, but they established a bridgehead by October 9, and Bailey bridges were quickly erected over the canal. By October 14, tanks were rolling across, and after a heavy artillery bombardment, the port of Breskens fell on October 22.

By November 9, the 1st Canadian Army front ran from near the German frontier south of Nijmegan through the Dutch islands to Dunkirk, a distance of over 200 miles. For the next three months they would carry out no major operations, the only down time the Canadians would know during the northwest European campaign. However, planning continued for the army to strike southeastward from Nijmegan driving between the Maas and the Rhine. In the meantime, vigilance and unending patrols in wretched weather over flooded fields continued unabated during the main thrust, which was called Operation "Veritable."

Gunner Borland was promoted to lance bombardier on December 9. This was equivalent to the infantry rank of lance corporal and put him second-in-command of one of the guns.

The build-up for Veritable was enormous, and the weight of artillery was particularly impressive. More than a thousand guns, one-third of which were mediums, heavies or super-heavies, were to bring down a volume of fire

---

[20] Flame-throwing Bren gun carriers with large fuel tanks

equal to, if not greater than that supporting any British army during the war[21]. The attack began on February 8. The night before, at 2230 hours, the first wave of bombers attacked the first major town in the army's path—Cleve, home of Henry VIII's fourth wife, Anne.

At 0500 hours, 9,000 gunners "stood to" as the lanyards of 1,034 guns and twelve rocket-launchers were pulled. It was a cold and miserable morning, and the gun crews had been at their positions for many hours in drizzling rain before the firing began. Stumbling through mud in incredibly deep ruts left by trucks they prepared for the big shoot. Shells were removed from their cases, safety caps taken off, and stacked close to the guns.

In the opening salvoes of the Battle of the Rhineland, the 25-pounders alone dumped more than 5,000 tons of high explosives on the Germans in the Reichswald. No fewer than forty "Heavies" (7.2-inch howitzers on their great rubber tires) belched 200-pound shells up to 16,000 yards away. Two 8-inch guns with a range of 18,000 yards unloaded 240-pound shells on the Reich, while the strongest concrete emplacements of the Siegfried Line received the attention of four superheavy 240-mm (9.5-inch) howitzers capable of throwing their howling 360-pound missiles up to 25,225 yards. During the course of the firing that morning, each great monster fired eighty rounds for a total of 320 shells, adding more than fifty-seven tons of high explosive to the hellish cauldron[22].

After two-and-half hours of artillery, a sudden silence fell over the front. It lasted ten minutes, then the artillery began again, accompanied by the rumble of forward-moving tanks. At 1030 hours, the infantry advanced. The German troops had been stunned by the bombardment, but it was the weather rather than the enemy that proved the larger obstacle. A sudden thaw had reduced roads to muddy tracks and armoured vehicles became bogged down. Tanks, Kangaroos[23], and Flails[24] all bottomed-out in the mud. Thankfully, they, and the equipment working to free them, were obscured by smoke from the artillery barrage, burning buildings, and a smoke-screen laid down on the left flank by the guns of the 13th and 14th Field Regiments.

With the assistance of bombers and artillery, the 3rd Division advanced to clear the flooded area between the Nijmegan–Cleves road and the Waal. From the beaches of Normandy and the shores of the Scheldt and to Nijmegan, the division accumulated a unique experience in amphibious warfare. The nickname "Water Rats" was well earned. At times they fought forward through water three feet deep.

[21] Col. C.P. Stacey, The Canadian Army, 1939—1945, An Official Historical Summary (Ottawa, King's Printer) 1948. P 238.
[22] George G. Blackburn, The Guns of Victory (Toronto, McClelland and Stewart Inc.) 1996. P243.
[23] Armoured personnel carriers
[24] Tanks with a revolving drum in front with pieces of logging chain welded to it. As the drum rotated the chain beat the ground exploding any mines.

On February 10, the 14th Field supported a break by the 9th Brigade of the northern tip of the Siegfried Line. Despite losing vehicles in rising water and forward battalions becoming marooned, the Canadians' determination carried them forward. They encountered particularly severe fighting at Rindern when German paratroops counter-attacked from fortified houses and pillboxes. However, using Buffaloes, they reached the Spoy Canal north of Cleve. Maintaining artillery support for units sailing in Buffaloes or wading through three feet of water was a very trying business, and they found little left of the mediaeval town. By February 13, the Reichswald was finally cleared.

Moyland Wood was a strip of forest midway between Cleve and Calcar and the centre of the Panzer Lehr Division's stubborn resistance. On February 16, the 3rd Division began clearing it, but after three days of struggle, the Germans still had a toehold in the wood. By the 21st, after some of the fiercest fighting of the war, the enemy lost control of the vital road and the Royal Winnipeg Rifles cleared the remainder of the Moyland.

Doug MacFarlane was a captain posted to the 14th Field from the 4th Field and was on his first duty as a forward observation officer with the 14th on February 25. He had gone forward with the Highland Light Infantry to call in predawn artillery fire on the crossroads hamlet of Ebben. As the sky lightened, an enemy self-propelled gun about 600 yards distant fired upon his outpost. Its first shot killed his signaller, wounded him about the face and eyes, and put his radio out of service. More mortar fire cut the landline he had just laid leaving him with no means to call in fire from the 14th. MacFarlane crawled back, found the break, fixed it, and returned to the OP, still under mortar fire. He contacted the 14th gunners and they shelled the German position until the gun went silent.

Doug MacFarlane would later be awarded the Military Cross for his bravery under fire.

The gunners had little rest from their exhausting routine and were constantly called upon to provide intense shelling to beat back enemy counter-attacks. The firing continued unabated throughout the night to keep the Germans on edge, and each shell had to be carried by weary gunners from trucks hundreds of yards away across thick mud. Often the trucks and the quads pulling the guns into position had to winch themselves out of the muck by using whatever ground anchors they could find.

A new offensive was launched early on February 26 against the forested high ground south of Calcar. Under heavy artillery bombardment, the 2nd and 3rd Divisions assaulted a determined enemy. The bitter fighting for this ridge moved back and forth through the Hochwald and Balberger Wald, but the 3rd Division pushed into the Balberger on March 2, fighting through this last barrier in their drive to the Rhine. By March 6, they had secured the town of Sonsbeck.

The German failure to withdraw across the Rhine after their defeat in the Ardennes was a major blunder. The troops that may have opposed the Allied crossing and prolonged the defence of Germany were badly mauled. From February 6 to March 14, it was estimated that Germany suffered 210,000 casualties and a further 343,000 were taken prisoner[25].

April was very busy for the regiment[26]. The period of slogging through mud came pretty well to an end and the gunners were able to employ the principle of fire and movement. In the early hours of April 2, the 14th Field crossed the Rhine at Emmerich, and the subsequent rapid advance north into Holland consisted of a series of one-day deployments. The enemy was retreating and rapidly losing the initiative. Only at Zutphen and Deventer did they resist with any determination. On April 7, Zutphen fell, and by April 10, the Water Rats had cleaned up Deventer. The clearing of the east bank of the Issjel River took the guns back into Holland.

On April 12, the regiment came under the command of the 9th Canadian Infantry Brigade, which advanced straight north in Holland. When resistance was met, usually one battery (four guns) deployed for a few hours practising all the principles of fire and movement. By April 14, the 14th Field was at Steenwijk, and by midnight of April 15, they established regimental headquarters in the railway station at Leeuwarden. The main holdup to their advance had been craters, blown bridges, and mines.

The batteries fanned out from Leeuwarden in support of their respective infantry battalions to finish cleaning up the peninsula. Leeuwarden gave the regiment a wonderful welcome, considering the unit as their liberator. Harlingen gave a little trouble, but was cleaned up in short order. The gunners then spent a day or so resting and refitting on the outskirts of Leeuwarden waiting to be relieved by the 17th Field Regiment of the 5th Canadian Division.

The 3rd Division was given the job of cleaning up the peninsula south of Emden, and eventually assaulted Emden from the north and east. On April 22, the 4th Field gunners crossed back into Germany just west of Winschoten, but the weather failed them once again, and for the last week of April, they wallowed in mud and water in one of the lowest and flattest parts of Germany they had the misfortune to find.

In the Emden sector, the enemy resisted quite vigorously with artillery. Regimental headquarters was shelled heavily several times, but fortunately with no casualties. Their position just west of Jemgum was considered one of the hottest they had endured since D-Day.

On April 26, the regiment was on the move and firing as they moved:

0930—enemy guns firing. (Our) shoot successful.

1000—engaged Scale III (3 batteries firing).

1100—Division Headquarters moving

1345—P Battery moving. Reports (arriving) that our new area is being heavily shelled—ordered to stay off position (and remain) on the road while Air OP [an observer in an aircraft] looks over situation. Rest of regiment on wheels stopped.

1700—on move.

1820—RHQ, P, Q, R Batteries in position. We have a clear view of Emden—barrage balloons and dock installations. Very flat country.

1935—targets engaged by all four batteries. Enemy retreating from this area.

2045—engaged—enemy retreating.

2130—engaged—assault boats Scale I

2215—engaged—Scale I.

2305—engaged (target) enemy transportation. Full moon—cloudy—little activity. Ammunition expended last 24 hours—13 rounds per gun.

27 April:

JEMGUM 0025—Dyke down at north of peninsula—water may be coming into this Area. The Régiment de la Chaudière has reached this area (and) may be able to check the flow of water.

0125—on hour notice to move because of possible flooding.

0130—RCASC ammunition being dumped on position.

0210—Stand down on hour notice to move.

0645—(enemy) 20-mm firing into locality from house.

0730—drawing of ammunition continued (500 rounds per gun)

0800—10 (German) officers and 160 other ranks surrendered to QOR & RdeChaud. Peninsula now completely cleared—QOR & RdeChaud holding northern portion.

1320—Engaged in returning fire. Also at 1345/1351 and 1400.

1805—Engaged in firing. (enemy) 20-mm active.

2300—Gun area under shellfire—several fell close to RHQ.
Rest of night very quiet. Weather—overcast and raining heavy
at times. Visibility fair. Ammunition expended last 24 hours—
41 rounds per gun.

The division began crossing the Ems and arrived in Leer on April 28, and by
the end of the month had cleared the town and was well on their way to the
north.

Casualties suffered during the month were: Lance Bombardier Borland
killed in action, April 27, 1945; three other gunners were wounded in action
the same day.

Nearby, Wally Mace was serving in Conn
Smythe's artillery regiment[27]. He never knew that
he had lost a friend so close to the end of the war
until he received a letter from his mother. In any
event, in combat conditions, he could not have left
his position to help bury his buddy.

Joe Borland's body was buried in the temporary
Canadian cemetery in Winschoten, Holland, on
April 28. It was later exhumed and reburied in a
permanent grave in the Holten Canadian War
Cemetery, twenty kilometres east of Deventer, on
the main road from Amsterdam to Bremen. The
cemetery contains the bodies of most of the
Canadians who died in the last stages of the war in
Holland and the advance into northern Germany. After hostilities ended, the
bodies were gathered and brought to this cemetery.

Days later the war ended. In Carleton Place, Lavina's heart felt a great
weight lifted. Her daughter's father and her lover would be soon home to
restart their life. The town was having a great parade on Bridge Street to
mark the end of the war, and Lavina dressed both herself and her daughter
carefully to go downtown to watch. However, without warning, Lavina's sister arrived and inexplicably stalled their departure. Soon afterwards the
Anglican minister arrived and within minutes came the official telegram.
Marion could not understand her mother's anguish and the sudden reversal
from happiness to the flowing tears of sorrow.

The official royal message arrived on June 8, but by that time Lavina had
received a letter from one of Joe's comrades who had been present when the
shell landed just behind the gun crew. He never knew what hit him.

In due course, Lavina received Joe's effects: a small box containing two
rings and three trinkets.

[27] Smythe had picked Wally, serving in Petawawa in the 40's, to play hockey on the National Army Team.

CHAPTER TWENTY-EIGHT—JOURNEY'S END

Joe Borland was the last man from Carleton Place to be killed in action. But he was not the last to die as a result of World War II.

By 1945, the Canadian Army was, for the first time in history, completely Canadian. There were no British troops under its command. The 1st Canadian Corps had arrived in northern Europe from Italy, and also for the first time, two Canadian army corps would face the enemy side by side. The First Canadian Army would, however, take no part in the crossing of the Rhine. Instead, they were tasked to hold the line of the Rhine and the Maas from Emmerich to the sea.

The 1st Canadian Parachute Battalion, serving with the British 6th Airborne Division, dropped northwest of Wesel during the morning of March 24, and the 9th (Highland) Brigade, under the 51st (Highland) Division became the first Canadian infantry brigade across the Rhine. On April 1, the engineers completed a bridge across the river at Emmerich; the 2nd Canadian Corps started over and gathered momentum in their drive north. The Canadians were now fighting on the north German plain on low lands just as flat and wet as Holland had been. German resistance was collapsing on the western front but pockets still fought bitterly.

On May 1, the 3rd Canadian Division, having cleared Leer, was nearing Emden and Aurich. On May 4, the 2nd Canadian Corps was still pushing northward against constant opposition, and shortly after noon, Montgomery informed Crerar that negotiations were underway for unconditional surrender by the Germans. Simonds immediately called off attacks by the 3rd Division against Aurich. The surrender was signed and became effective the next day at 0800 hours. For the Canadians in Europe, the war was over. They had served in action up to the last minute.

Ernie Morris's war ended on Thursday, August 24, 1944, in the Soldiers' Pavilion of the Ottawa Civic Hospital.

C 12548 Corporal George Ernest Morris
Royal Canadian Army Service Corps

Ernie Morris was born in Scotch Corners on September 12, 1904. Growing up, he spent little time in school and never graduated from high school. As a young man, he went west on the railroad harvest excursions, and, when home in Carleton Place, worked variously at the Hawthorne Woolen Mills and in the enamel shop of Findlay's Foundry.

Ernie eventually married Margaret Edna Drummond and they had one child, Floyd Erwin. When Floyd (known as "Tex") was only eight months old, Edna suddenly died on New Year's Day, 1928. Edna's aunt, Clara Idene Ferguson (later Mrs. Archie Porteous), who was the same age as Edna, became the only mother Tex ever knew.

Partly to escape his grief, but mostly because he was just restless, Ernie went to the United States, near Syracuse, New York, to find work. A few years later he returned to Carleton Place and moved in with Clara and Archie, around 1936. That way he could be with his son and also help out the family as a labourer since Archie was very ill and died soon after. Tex would later recall that his dad and his uncle would augment their incomes by fishing[28]. They would catch "mickeys" (catfish) at night and would spear frogs during the day. Tex denies ever eating either, but the men would peddle them around Carleton Place to make a little money.

When war broke out, Ernie was one of the first to enlist. He was working in the Foundry at the time and convinced his friends, Cy Townend, Harold Briscoe and Roy Collins, to enlist with him. The problem of how to get to Ottawa was solved when they convinced Jack Turner, owner of a butcher shop (and more importantly, a car) to go with them. Ernie must have been inspired by the moment, for although he had never worked in a butcher shop in his life, when the recruiter asked his occupation, Ernie said "butcher." He figured the army would train him and that was as good a job as any.

The men joined on September 9, 1939, three days before Ernie's thirty-fifth birthday, and they were all sent to Lansdowne Park for basic training. Ernie was appointed to the Royal Canadian Army Service Corps (RCASC) and scheduled to be assigned to a Supply Column.

During his enlistment examination, Ernie was found to be in good health, except that he had limited flex in the middle and ring fingers of his right hand. He couldn't recall any injury that could have caused this. Ultimately, he was given medical category "A" as completely fit for service. While he was training at Lansdowne Park, Ernie moved his son and Clara to Glen Avenue in Ottawa, and whenever Ernie got leave, they returned to Carleton Place to visit.

Ernie had never been sick in his life except for having measles when he was a child. However, at Lansdowne he began having trouble with sore throats. The medical officers admitted him to the camp hospital for investigation on January 22, 1940, and found he had tonsillitis and scheduled him for surgery. On March 5 he was admitted to the Ottawa Civic, discharged as

[28] Interview with Floyd "Tex" Morris in his home during the autumn of 2002.

cured on March 24, and returned to his unit fit for duty. Ernie was smoking forty cigarettes a day then and the doctors strongly advised him to quit. He didn't, and from December 6 to 9, he was a guest of 23 Field Ambulance with another throat infection.

After completing basic training and enjoying a week's leave, Ernie was assigned to the advanced training centre for the RCASC at Camp Borden. He knew that he would be going to the 3rd Canadian Infantry Division as a member of the Divisional Supply Column. On June 20, because he was doing so well on his training and his age, Ernie was made an acting corporal. He was not a very imposing man at 5' 6½" tall and 143 pounds, but he had the maturity to make a good leader. He did not suffer fools gladly, but he curbed his sarcasm when dealing with his fellow recruits.

From Camp Borden, Ernie was sent to the new training base at Debert, Nova Scotia. On April 15, 1941, having gained permission from the army, Ernie married Clara in the United Church near Lansdowne in Ottawa. He

Ernie and Clara on their wedding day. (All Photos courtesy Tex Morris.)

returned to Debert and in June was posted to the 3rd Division Composite Company, RCASC, at Sussex, New Brunswick. He only spent a month there when he was sent back to Debert and the Divisional Supply Column to await posting overseas. He was given embarkation leave and in July went back to Carleton Place before shipping out to England. On July 19, Ernie took the train directly to Halifax, and on July 20, was aboard ship headed for the Canadian Army Overseas. He landed at Gourah, Scotland, on July 30.

Ernie was granted landing leave from August 15 to 19, which he used to explore Scotland. He became so enamoured of the land that whenever he got leave while in the U.K. he headed north for Scotland.

On September 19, Ernie was confirmed in the rank of corporal with the appropriate pay of $1.70 a day. He was assigned to No. 9 Company of the 3rd Division Supply Column.

Ernie was just back off a week's leave when he was in a motorcycle accident. On April 28, he was travelling by motorcycle with the Supply Column from Chilgrove to Horsham. The column was travelling at night under black-out conditions, and approaching the first inter-section into Broadbridge Heath, Ernie prepared to overtake the truck in front of him. He blew his horn to pass and was just beside the cab door when the truck driver suddenly made a right turn with no signal or warning (in England vehicles travel in the left lane). The motorcycle crashed into the truck's right front fender send-ing it and the rider careening down the road.

The medical officer on the scene found Ernie suffering from a moderate degree of shock with a probable depressed fracture of the skull in the right parietal-occipital region. He was semi-conscious, moving about, and feeling pain, but not speaking. He was also bleeding from both ears, especially the right. After first aid on the

Corporal Ernie Morris some-where in England in 1943.

road the doctor sent him by ambulance to No. 1 Neurological Hospital at Basingstoke, which they reached about two hours later.

At the hospital, Ernie was diagnosed with the following: a compound fracture of the skull with the fracture line going through the right petrous temporal bone; depression of the lower posterior fragment; laceration of the temporal lobe; leakage of brain tissue from the right external auditory canal; and left subdural haematoma. Although his back and right leg were injured, they were not life-threatening, so his head wounds received immediate atten-tion. The prognosis was not good. The medical officers assessed his condi-tion as, "Serious permanent disability is certain with impairment of mental process."

Clara was sent an official telegram informing her that her husband was "dangerously ill" overseas. She and Floyd had moved back to Carleton Place to a home on Woodward Avenue.

Ernie was posted, on paper, to the RCASC Reinforcement Unit while he was in hospital. Then, on June 16, 1942, a medical board re-categorized Ernie to "E," unfit for service, and decided to send him home by hospital ship to Halifax and medical train car to Ottawa for admittance to the Rideau Military Hospital. Upon arrival, Ernie complained of frequent headaches, eye trouble, and pain in his back and both knees.

By now officially diagnosed with a "cranio-cerebral injury," Ernie was considered ambulatory, although still far from well. The specialist at Rideau Military found "a man who appears somewhat older than his given age. His face is lined and yet there is an emotionless, blank expression except when he is laughing and talking with friends. Healed scars are present over both parieto-temporal areas of the scalp. There is a small depression palpable in the left posterior parietal region."

His eyes showed the onset of bilateral optic atrophy and his right eardrum showed scarring. There was a healed scar on the back of his right leg just above his knee, and his back had discolouration over the lower back area that was tender to the touch. He had no limitation of movement in his knees or back, but his mid-upper spine was slightly curved to the left.

Ernie's medical condition continued to be monitored at the Rideau, while specialist attention and physiotherapy were provided by the Ottawa Civic. The doctors thought that he would improve over several months and could return to part-time duty, but would forever have a partial permanent disability.

On August 25, a medical board concluded that Ernie was improving very slowly, but he would be incapacitated for a very long time. His medical category of "E" was made permanent, and army officials began the paper work to release him. In the meantime, he remained at Rideau Military and Ottawa Civic Hospitals for continuing treatment and therapy.

In September, Clara fell in her home and broke her arm. Fortunately, the breadman was making a delivery and heard her calls for help. He splinted Clara's arm with a shingle and took her to the doctor. Ernie was allowed home for weekends to help his wife. He had learned that his release would be effective in October and that he would be eligible for a meagre disability pension of $40. a month.

Ernie Morris somewhere in the U.K. prior to the motorcycle accident.

In his last army medical examination, Ernie complained of a constant headache on his left side, sore eyes with impaired vision in his right eye, and aches and pains in his back and legs. He knew that his memory was impaired, and he was finding it difficult to think about anything. His examiner found he was slower than average with his answers, but he remembered his army number, date of birth, and when he went overseas. Ernie was able to do light jobs around the hospital and did not ask for sedatives for discomfort. Optic atrophy was present, but incomplete in his right eye. The examining doctor had known

Ernie since his return from overseas and concluded that, "He is essentially honest and if properly handled will improve to the point where he will be a useful citizen, although he will have permanent disability of some magnitude." Almost as a warning to the army disability pension adjudicators, the doctor wrote: "He could readily be made a psychoneurotic individual, by sympathy, delayed or unfair settlement, etc."

Ernie was released from the army on October 8, 1942, and sent home. He received his War Service Gratuity of $472.21 for 1,125 days in uniform, and was also given a lapel button, War Service Badge, Class B, showing he had served overseas.

By this time, Tex had decided to quit school to go to work to help the family. His father went back to his old job in the enamel shop at the Foundry. However, Ernie simply could not endure the heat and noise of the open ovens in the enamel shop. His head never stopped aching, and he had difficulty sleeping. He would go to bed about midnight, but be awake and up two hours later. Ernie was not a well-educated man so his job prospects were limited.

The War Service Badge was awarded to those who were on active service in Britain or at the front, and were discharged on account of age, wound or sickness.

On Monday February 1, 1943, the Town of Carleton Place paid tribute to six returned men with a civic reception at the Town Hall. There was a capacity audience to honour Private Adelarde Bell, CFC; Private Mansel Hamilton, Cameron Highlanders; Private Alan Purdy, SD&G; Private Gordon McLaughlin, RCOC; Corporal Ernest Morris, RCASC; and Flight Sergeant Thomas Oswald McIlquham, DFM, RCAF. Major W. H. Hooper introduced the men and Mayor C. J. Taber read an address commending them for their early enrolment and devotion to duty for their country.

Finally, in the summer of 1944, Ernie secured work as a conductor on the streetcars for the Ottawa Electric Railway, but on August 18, he fell ill with difficulty breathing. Clara phoned the doctor who sent a military ambulance, and Ernie was taken to the Soldiers' Pavilion of the Ottawa Civic. Five days later he lapsed into unconsciousness and died the next morning. He courageously bore the extent of his injuries until the very end.

Ernie's coffin, draped with the Canadian Red Ensign, was lowered into its grave in the Pine Grove section of the United Cemeteries of Carleton Place. Clara's silver Memorial Cross was not delivered until May 14, 1949.

C100106 Private Harold Allan Stokes
Royal Canadian Electrical and Mechanical Engineers

The Second World War was over.

The Canadian Army's role in the waning days had been to open a supply route north through Arnhem. The 1st Canadian Corps, after distinguishing itself fighting in Italy, had joined the 2nd in northwestern Europe, which cleared the northeastern Netherlands and the German coast, while the 1st dealt with the Germans in western Holland north of the Maas (also known as the Meuse) River. This area contained the cities of Amsterdam, Rotterdam, and The Hague. Food supplies had been exhausted, fuel had almost completely run out, and transport was non-existent. The people had virtually reached the end of their endurance from misery and starvation, but not before thousands of men, women, and children had died.

The assault on Arnhem began on April 12, 1945, and after house-to-house fighting, the city was cleared two days later. Dashing northwards, the 5th Division drove thirty miles to capture Ijsselmeer and cut off the Germans opposing the 1st Division at Apeldoorn. They occupied the town on April 17.

On April 28, a truce was arranged to move food supplies to the starving people, and fighting ceased in western Holland at a vital moment. The next day, Allied bombers dropped 510 tons of food into the area, and by May 2, the 1st Canadian Corps was trucking 1,000 tons a day behind enemy lines. Dutch civil authorities distributed the supplies with trucks and fuel provided by the Canadians. Pending the enemy's final collapse, the immediate needs of the people of the Netherlands were met.

On May 5, Lieutenant General Charles Foulkes, in a small, battered hotel in the village of Wageningen, accepted the surrender of German troops in Holland from General Johannes Blaskowitz. On May 7, at Rheims, France, the Germans formally surrendered. More than a million Canadians served, about one-tenth of the population, and more than 45,000 gave their lives. The army played a proud role in many theatres around the globe, but most significant, at least in which the most number of troops served, were the European theatres of Central Mediterranean and Northwest Europe. Private Harold Allan Stokes survived both and was on his way home when he died.

Allan Stokes was born on November 8, 1914, to Lawrence Newton Stokes and Effie Heddleston. When Allan was four years old, his father died of influenza, and he went to live with his grandparents, Mr. and Mrs. James

Heddleston of Frank Street in Carleton Place. His mother remarried when he was eighteen. He attended Carleton Place public school, completing Grade 8, and he went to work at age fifteen as a clerk in the CPR yard office in Ottawa. He stayed with the railroad for seven years, making $25 a week, then, in 1935, moved to the Renfrew Woolen Mills in Carleton Place, where he accepted the position of foreman at $35 a week.

In 1940, Allan became an inspector of textiles with the Inspection Board of the United Kingdom and Canada. This meant a move for him and his new wife, Mildred Irene Smithson of Almonte, to Ottawa, where they lived with Allan's older sister, Mrs. Marjorie Mahoney, at 525 Albert Street. His new position was paid at the same rate ($35 a week), and he was with the Inspection Board only a year and a half when he joined the army on April 14, 1942.

From October 14, 1936, until he enlisted, Allan served in the militia with the Princess Louise Dragoon Guards. When he joined the Active Force, Allan was a fit twenty-seven year old, and reasonably tall at 5' 11¼" and 160½ pounds. He had a sallow complexion with brown eyes and wore his dark brown hair neatly groomed. He admitted to having had measles as a child and pleurisy at age twenty-two, but he was totally healthy and fit for category "A." His only visible marks were a scar on the back of his left arm and on the palm of his right hand, both acquired from handling material in the mill.

Allan spent a month in basic training in Ottawa at Lansdowne Park, and on May 15, 1942, was sent to No. 31 Basic Training Centre at Cornwall. He was trained as a general-duty soldier, but at the end of basic training, he elected to go to the RCOC as a supply clerk, a trade he already had some skill in from his duties with Renfrew Woolen Mills. And because he was already trained, he was immediately sent to St. John to await posting overseas. On July 28, he reported to the RCOC Holding Unit; on August 8, he boarded a troop ship, and on August 18 landed in England.

The RCOC increased from 300 all ranks to more than 25,000 during World War II. It was a rapid expansion of both infrastructure and personnel. In December 1939, when the 1st Canadian Division sailed for Scotland, elements of the Ordnance Corps and the RCASC sailed with them. In 1941, the RCOC was designated a combatant corps. Ordnance soldiers served in supply depots, the Canadian Mobile Ammunition Repair Units, and Canadian Forward Ammunition Maintenance Sections, and roadhead and railhead ordnance companies advising and assisting in pushing forward spare parts and ammunition stocks to the front.

The day after Allan landed in Britain, Canadian troops went into their first action at Dieppe. The ill-fated participants in the operation included Ordnance and Service Corps' soldiers.

Private H. A. Stokes was first sent to the Canadian Divisional Reinforcement Unit until October 9 when he went to the Canadian Ordnance Reinforcement Unit. At the Ordnance Unit, he was trained and tested and was granted 25¢ a day trades pay by qualifying as a storeman grade "C." The same day he was posted to the Supply Group at 5 Canadian Armoured Division.

Stokes was fortunate to be included in a demonstration of Canadian military might that occurred on December 17, 1942, the third anniversary of the arrival of the 1st Division in Britain. Thirty units, representing every arm and service, rolled past a saluting base near Sussex, and the fruit of Canadian factories was showcased. Almost all of the equipment on display had been made in Canada, sometimes of British design but not exclusively. From home came the infantryman's No. 4 rifles, Sten guns and Bren guns, and the 2-pounder anti-tank gun. The artillery's 25-pounders and the armoured corp's Ram tanks rolled past, plus a variety of special equipment and vehicles. The most notable weapon, developed in Canada, was the Sexton, a self-propelled 25-pounder on a Ram chassis.

On January 1, 1943, Ordnance Corps field corps, supply and transport companies, were tasked to support individual infantry brigades. On January 30, Allan was transferred from the Division supply group to the Workshop Company of No. 11 Canadian Infantry Brigade, which was the infantry element of the 5th Canadian Armoured Division of the 1st Canadian Corps. It included the 11th Independent Machine Gun Company (The Princess Louise Fusiliers), The Perth Regiment, The Cape Breton Highlanders, The Irish Regiment of Canada, and The Westminster Regiment (Motor). The motor battalion in fact formed part of the division's armoured brigade.

Allan's first brush with army discipline came when his corporal put him on charge for drunkenness. He was brought before the unit commander who, because it was Private Stokes' first offence, let him go with an admonishment. On May 15, he was charged with neglect to the prejudice of good order in that he was riding in a War Department vehicle with the full knowledge that it was on an unauthorized journey. He and some friends had "borrowed" a jeep for their own use. For this infraction he was confined to barracks for fourteen days, except to go to and from meals.

The 1st Canadian Infantry Division and the 1st Canadian Army Tank Brigade made the assault on Sicily in July 1943. By September 3, the Canadians were poised on the shores of the Strait of Messina to begin their invasion of the mainland. Earlier it was considered that, after the campaign in Sicily was completed, the Canadians would be brought back to England to share their combat experience with the rest of the Canadian Army. However, early in October, the decision was taken to keep the Canadians in Italy and the headquarters units of the 1st Canadian Corps and the 5th Canadian Armoured Division were moved to the Mediterranean theatre.

On October 26, the 11th Infantry Brigade Workshops boarded a ship in England; Allan Stokes went ashore in Italy on November 8. There, they faced significant problems. The Division had been forced, due to a lack of ships, to leave its heavy equipment in England and have it replaced by that of the 7th British Armoured Division, which was moving from Italy to England. But vehicles and equipment belonging to the "Desert Rats" was ancient and much worn, and the Workshop was swamped with repair orders from units that painfully recalled the new equipment they had left behind. Re-equipping the Canadian division proved a slow process so it was just as well that they saw no action for a long time. The only good news was that General G. Simonds moved from commanding the 1st Division to leading the 5th.

Shortly after his arrival in Italy, Allan was awarded the Canadian Volunteer Service Medal and Clasp. However, the soldiers in Italy thought so little of this medal that few of them ever wore it or the ribbon.

Before offensive operations were completely abandoned in the most wretched winter conditions imaginable, Brigadier George Kitching's 11th Canadian Infantry Brigade, which had arrived with the 5th Canadian Armoured Division in November, was considered ready for action. Accordingly it was brought forward, and on the night of January 13–14, relieved the 3rd Brigade on the right sector of the Ortona salient. On the morning of January 17, the Brigade made a limited attack against the opposing paratroops that was quite unsuccessful. The Perth Regiment made some progress, but then ran into heavy fire, took substantial losses, and could proceed no further. The Cape Breton Highlanders followed but they also accomplished very little, and that night were withdrawn. In its first operation, the brigade suffered about 200 casualties and the front lines remained unchanged.

The 5th Armoured Division, under Major General E. L. M. Burns, on the night January 31–February 1, relieved the 4th Indian Division in the Orsogna area and entered the line as a division eighty-five days after arriving in Italy. There were no offensive operations for the next five weeks when the division was withdrawn for training and planning. During the winter of 1943–44, the heavy workshop function of the Ordnance Corps was combined with elements of the Service Corps to form the new Royal Canadian Electrical and Mechanical Engineers (RCEME), so as to provide better support and greatly increase repair capabilities for the modern, more mechanized army. On May 15, Allan rebadged to the new corps but remained posted to the workshop of the 11th Infantry Brigade.

To keep the enemy off balance concerning Allied intentions, a great deception was planned that had the Germans believing an assault along the coast was imminent. Elaborate measures were taken to conceal the movement of forces, and a skilful camouflage program masked the transfer of Canadian formations from their training areas. All travel was by night, and men and machines lay hidden during the day. In the maintenance areas, tremendous reserves of ammunition, fuel, and engineer equipment, along with a great variety of stores required for the coming battle, were expertly concealed in olive groves and along roadways.

By May 11, unbeknownst to the enemy, the 5th Division was at Capua. At 2300 hours, approximately 1,000 guns thundered a violent bombardment on the Gustav Line defences. The 5th Armoured waited in reserve. The Line was broken after four days of fighting and the Germans withdrew to the fortified positions of the Hitler Line.

The 1st Canadian Division was ordered to break through the Hitler Line and seize the high ground about 1,000 yards behind it, while the 5th Armoured was to drive forward through the gap and secure crossings over the River Melfa to push on towards Ceprano. On May 25, the 11th Brigade's Irish Regiment attacked across the river, and by noon, a bridgehead for the 5th Armoured was established. This marked the end of the battle for the Liri Valley and the Division could concentrate on the Hitler Line, which became a pursuit to Ceprano. The town was reached on the 27th, and a race developed between the two brigades (armoured and infantry) to re-establish contact with the retreating enemy going up the Sacco Valley towards Frosinone. On the afternoon of the 30th, the 2nd Infantry Brigade relieved the 11th Brigade and entered Frosinone unopposed the following day.

The 5th Division was withdrawn into reserve.

The war in Italy was an infantryman's campaign rather than a tankman's, and the single infantry brigade of the 5th Division was seriously overworked in difficult terrain. During July, the division was authorized to increase its infantry component to two brigades. The 12th Canadian Infantry Brigade was organized by using the Westminster Regiment (Motor) and converting into infantry battalions the 4th Canadian Reconnaissance Regiment (4th Princess Louis Dragoon Guards) and the 1st Light Anti-Aircraft Regiment (designated the Lanark and Renfrew Scottish Regiment).

Allan stayed with the 11th Brigade and during the period in reserve managed to go afoul of army rules a couple of times. On June 5, he failed to show up for a parade and was awarded seven days' field punishment and lost seven days' pay. Then on July 21 he was charged with neglect again for failing to maintain a vehicle to the standard required by unit maintenance orders. This cost him fourteen days' pay.

The 5th Armoured went back into action late in August in a drive across the Foglia. The 11th Brigade was heavily counter-attacked north of Montecchio on August 31, and in the early hours of September 1, the Princess Louis Dragoon Guards of the 12th Brigade fought their first battle as infantry against the Tomba ridge. They suffered 129 casualties, but the Gothic Line was broken.

The hot Italian summer now turned to a steady rain, and dusty roads became impassable muddy quagmires. The offensive slowed to a standstill. Then, on September 12, the 11th Brigade augmented with the Westminster Regiment attacked the northeastern end of Coriano Ridge. This successful operation cost the enemy many killed and the Canadians took over 1,000 prisoners. The 5th Division went back to relieve the 4th British Infantry Division, although the 5th had taken 1,500 casualties. The Allies had beaten eleven German Divisions and broken through to the Po Valley. But movement north from the San Fortunato Ridge was not to be an easy ride.

The plain before them was laced with rivers, canals, and drainage ditches. The rains began again and water flowed over the reclaimed swamplands. The 5th Canadian Armoured Division, using both infantry brigades, crossed the Uso under heavy shelling and mortaring, and by the end of September, had reached the Fiumicino River. But ten days of heavy rain made tank operations impossible.

During any combat operation, the workshops were busy repairing vehicles, tanks, and heavy equipment, as well as keeping ammunition and supplies moving forward. As tanks and trucks bogged down in the mud, the Engineers used special vehicles to go forward to recover the fighting armour.

Winter brought the Allies no respite from operations. In December, the 12th Brigade broke out of the Montone bridgehead and continued northeast past Ravenna. Heading northwest, the 11th Brigade reached the Lamone River at Mezzano. Ahead lay thickly concentrated water obstacles, including many smaller drainage canals flanking the stongly diked Canale Naviglio. Further ahead was the Senio River. The Princess Louise Dragoon Guards and the Lanark and Renfrew Scottish fought over the high dikes against increasing machine-gun and mortar fire.

Ahead of the 5th Division lay the enemy-occupied town of Bagnacavallo, and German troops defending the nearby Fosso Munio had the unpleasant experience of being the first in Italy to be on the receiving end of Canadian flame-throwers. On December 16, a company of the Westminsters, using "wasps" spurting long jets of shrivelling flame that both burned the target and robbed the air of all oxygen, broke the machine-gun positions on the far bank, crossed the canal, and gained a foothold from which to launch further operations. The 11th Brigade began its advance to the Senio on December 19, occupied Bagnacavallo on the 21st. They were mopping up with their Wasps flaming enemy outposts into submission by Christmas Eve.

Allan's wife Mildred spent this Christmas at home in Almonte with her parents. She had moved into their Martin Street residence around December 5 to await her army husband's return from overseas. She was receiving a $25 pay assignment from Allan, which qualified her for a $35 a month dependent's allowance[29].

In a three-day operation beginning on January 2, 1945, the 5th Canadian Armoured Division hit the 114th Jaeger Division with the speed and precision of a whirlwind. The 11th Brigade beat off a counter attack by the 16th SS Panzer Grenadiers on January 3–4 and advanced to a line running along the Senio and Reno Rivers to the south edge of Valli di Comacchio. This was to be the Canadians' final position in Italy. An Italian formation of bold and active partisans took over the 5th Armoured Division's static positions, and it went into Corps reserve at Cervia.

In May 1944, General Crerar had been made aware that the government wanted the Canadian troops in Italy to go to northwest Europe to the First Canadian Army. In February 1945, the first to move were those in Corps Reserve, the 5th Division.

The infantry brigades and their support units moved by truck to the Italian port of Leghorn, then by sea to Marseilles and again by road up the Rhone Valley into the Low Countries. The tanks were moved by rail both in Italy and in France. On February 26, Private Stokes, with his workshop, boarded a ship in Italy and landed in Marseilles after a two-day sail. The speed was striking testimony to the Canadians' efficiency. On March 31, the 5th Canadian Division went into the line in northwest Europe, but before leaving Italy, Allan had one more brush with military law. On February 16, he was fined fourteen days' loss of pay for absenting himself without permission from his unit on February 13.

For the Canadians in Europe, their main task became to clear northeastern Holland and the coastal belt of Germany instead of moving against the Germans in the west. The 1st Canadian Corps, under General Foulkes, captured Arnhem and was threatening Apeldoorn by April 14. This allowed Foulkes to use the 5th Division in a bold manoeuvre to dash north from Arnhem thirty miles to the shores of the Ijsselmeer. This stroke cut off the

[29] The dependent's allowance was paid only if the soldier assigned to his wife at least 15 days' pay per month.

enemy still resisting in Apeldoorn. On April 15, they cut the main road and railway connecting Apeldoorn to the rest of the Netherlands, causing the Germans to beat a hasty retreat. One group attempted to break through the 5th Division's line.

On April 17, they blundered into the Division's headquarters protected by the guns of the 17th Field Regiment. With only the Irish Regiment close by, "staff officers, clerks, runners, signalers, drivers, batmen, cooks"[30] and the craftsmen of the RCEME Workshops all turned their hands to fighting. They beat off the attackers and took about 200 prisoners. The 5th Division's drive ended on April 18.

Information was coming from behind enemy lines that the food situation in Holland was getting desperate. Something had to be done, and a decline in the German's fighting spirit made it possible for a temporary truce. The Canadians were ordered to cease fire at 0800 hours on April 28, unless fired upon. Allied bombers dropped 510 tons of food on April 29, and on May 1, food began to move in by road. Every thirty minutes, convoys of food rolled down safe corridors through the lines. There was no more fighting of any importance in western Holland .

Some Nazis resisted to the bitter end. The Cape Breton Highlanders of the 5th Canadian Armoured Division fought its last battle on May 1 and 2 in the North Sea peninsula west of the Ems estuary. They attacked and cleared a pocket of fanatical Germans around the port city of Delfzijl, taking over 3,000 prisoners. By the evening of the 2nd, the Dutch mainland was free of the enemy; yet twenty Canadians had died and fifty-three were wounded in liberating this town. It was the same day that Hitler and his mistress, Eva Braun, took their lives in a Berlin bunker, along with that of his faithful dog.

The Third Reich was falling into sudden ruin and could no longer terrify the world.

The war ended for the Canadians in the Netherlands at 0800 hours on May 5, and the formal surrender of all German forces was signed at Rheims on May 7. The staid Dutch went giddy with gratitude, embarrassing many a Canadian soldier by treating him like a conquering hero. The Canadians were tired, physically and emotionally, and many felt nothing of the joy of the Dutch. Death, dirt, and destruction had become the common denominator. Young men from across the Atlantic Ocean had fought and died to liberate the Netherlands. The Dutch would never forget them.

The 11th Canadian Infantry Brigade's RCEME Workshops ended the war occupying the Ennam Chevrolet garage on Heereweg Street in Groningen. Their work in recovering and repairing battered combat vehicles went on for some months.

[30] Stacey, op cit. P. 266

The process of repatriation and demobilization began at once, and a system of point-scores was put into effect. Each month's service in Canada was worth two points and each month's service overseas counted three, while the scores of married men, widowers, or divorced men with dependent children were increased by twenty per cent. The majority of men returned in accordance with their individual scores. The men with longest service, who could be spared, were released from their units and sent home in drafts. Some major units, with low-point men filling their gaps, returned as units and once more marched the streets of cities and towns whose names they bore.

On November 17, 1945, Private Allan Stokes was ordered to the MIR for examination prior to returning to Canada. He was found medically fit, requiring no medical treatment before going home, and to the personnel selection interviewer, he indicated that he would like to take up motor mechanics. He was noted to have extensive experience in the manufacture of textiles and it was considered he would have no trouble obtaining employment in that field. He also indicated that he had a good knowledge of rehabilitation legislation.

On November 19, Allan went to Nijmegan to join Repatriation Draft No. 665. That morning, however, he awoke with a headache, fever, chills, and a sore throat, but there was no way he was going to report sick and jeopardize his trip home. On November 26, he had written a letter home telling his wife that he was on his way and was in both good health and spirits. He was transferred from the 11th Brigade to the 5th Canadian Repatriation Depot in the U.K. when his condition became worse. He couldn't sleep, lost his appetite, and suffered constipation. He still had his frontal headache and sore throat. On November 27, he vomited twice and reported to the sick bay medical officer who promptly had him admitted to No. 4 CGH. He was found to have brachycardia, he was sleepy with photo-phobismus (double vision), but had no special pain on palpation of the chest and stomach. It was first thought he was to be suffering from influenza. Two days later, Allan developed numbness on both sides of his face. He had difficulty swallowing and took choking spells when he tried to swallow. This caused fluid to regurgitate through his nose. As the day progressed his headache got somewhat better but the numbness and difficulty swallowing got much worse.

The doctor came in to examine him and found Allan to be fully co-operative and mentally coherent. His vision remained the same, and he had difficulty turning his eye left and right. His voice had a marked nasal quality and his palate moved only slightly. His throat was full of thick fluid. He had been medicated with sulfathiazate, but then treatment was increased to include a duodenal tube for feeding, intravenous fluids, and penicillin. But biceps, triceps, and patellar reflexes gradually disappeared.

His condition further deteriorated and at approximately 2130 hours, cyanosis was present. No relief could be effected with oxygen therapy. Allan lapsed into a coma with very irregular, shallow, and slow breathing. At 2350 hours on November 30, 1945, Allan Stokes was found dead in his hospital bed. The diagnosis was written as "Bulbar Palsy" of unknown etiology, which means the medical people had no idea what had caused it. A post-mortem examination concluded with the examiner's opinion: "I remember that the cause of death was put as Respiratory Paralysis secondary to Poliomyelitis and that no tumour was found in his throat."

At 1500 hours on December 5, an army officer and nine other ranks gathered in Brookwood Military Cemetery about thirty miles from London. The cemetery is an extensive burial ground near Woking in the northwest corner of Surrey. In earlier times oak trees from the forest here were used to build many sailing ships. It is the largest Commonwealth cemetery in the United Kingdom. The land was set aside in 1917 for the burial of men and women of the Commonwealth and American forces who had died, mainly of battle wounds, in the London district. It was extended in World War II and contains the bodies of Allied soldiers as well as those of German and Italian prisoners of war.

The small burial party carried Allan Stokes' coffin, draped with the Canadian Red Ensign to his grave. He was interred according to the rites of the Presbyterian Church, with the haunting notes of "Taps" stirring the leaves of nearby trees and a volley of three rifle shots signalling the end of the service.

The officer gathered Allan's personal effects: a Kodak camera, a pipe and lighter, a "Simmons 15 jewel" wristwatch, and a tire gauge. They were packed up and sent to Mildred. In January 1946, she also received a message of condolence from the king, but it was not until February 1952 that Allan's mother received the Memorial Cross. Mildred's Cross was sent to her new address and name, Mrs. Mildred Keteley, in Winnipeg.

The Canadian printed an article stating that Allan had suffered a critical illness prior to boarding ship for home and had died in England. It mentioned that his brother, Lawrence "Sonny" Stokes, a flight sergeant in the RCAF at Arnprior, and his sister, Mrs. W. Mahoney of Ottawa, survived him. It reported that his grandparents Mr. and Mrs. James Heddleston of Frank Street in Carleton Place raised him, but no mention was made of his wife.

POSTSCRIPT

As with the list of names from World War I on the Carleton Place ceno-taph, there is one in the list of World War II names that eludes discovery: G. A. Elliott. No person of that name can be found as a resident of Carleton Place. Military records have been scoured, as well as the Commonwealth War Graves Commission Web site, but there is no register of a person fitting this name killed in World War II, or World War I.

The only hint was found in *The Canadian* of December 21, 1944, where a short piece notes that an Ordinary Seaman Gordon Elliott was serving on HMCS *Carlplace* and that he had connections to the town. He was the son of Mr. George Elliott of northern Ontario and Mrs. Elliott of Moose Jaw, Saskatchewan. His father was well known in Carleton Place, having attend-ed school here and teaching for many years at the 11th Line School after graduating from CPHS. George, in turn, was the son of Mr. J. C. Elliott and the late Mrs. Elliott on the Franktown Road.

Young Gordon, when he was nineteen, visited Carleton Place in December 1944 with his grandfather and an aunt and uncle, Mr. and Mrs. James W. Murray on Judson Street. He had enlisted in Moose Jaw the end of January 1944, trained in Regina and Cornwallis, and went to Halifax in July 1944. He served on HMCS *Carlplace* from December 14, 1944, to October 25, 1945. The ship's records confirm his service under the name Gordon Alexander Elliott.

Mystery solved!?! Not quite! There is no record that this Gordon Alexander Elliott died during the war; in fact there is no record that he is dead at all! In the National Library and National Archives records, there is no record of any other G. A. Elliott. So while it is quite likely that Gordon Alexander is the man, how did he get on the Carleton Place War Memorial, and where is he now?

CODA

This book was written for the people of Carleton Place, in particular the young people who have few or no sources from which to learn of the con-tribution made to freedom by their forebears. A faded picture of a uniformed stranger in a dusty photograph album is usually all that is left.

We must learn and remember these stories; Canadian soldiers, airmen, sailors and female members of the forces fought a genuine evil. Today's world would be a grimmer, vastly different place if they had refused to go.

42,042 men and women of that generation died, and their sacrifice gave us the freedom we enjoy to live in peace in God's country. We should all be grateful.

On March 22, 1944, the Active Army reached its peak strength of 495,804. During the war, 1,086,771 Canadians and Newfoundlanders served. Almost 700,000 were under twenty-one years of age. The Active Army comprised 630,052, of which 25,251 were women. All were volunteers. Another 100,573 men were called up under the NRMA. A total of 249,624 men and women served in the RCAF and 106,522 in the Canadian naval forces.

For all three services, fatalities numbered 41,992, with the RCAF suffering particularly heavy losses with 17,047 dead. In comparison, the Great War cost Canada 60,661 dead. The difference is attributed to the mobile nature of the second war compared to the singularly lethal static warfare on the Western Front of 1914–1918.

The Canadian Army in both world wars was a civilian army. The tiny Permanent Force of 1939 provided a nucleus of soldiers with professional abilities and skills. The rest were very good soldiers, but they were citizen soldiers. At the time of surrender, the German Army commanders suffered the ultimate blow to their dignity upon learning that most Canadian commanders were many years younger than themselves (General Simonds was forty-one). They were shaken further upon learning that most senior officers were not even regular army. The Canadian fighting men and women were volunteers. They came forward of their own free will to do their duty for their country. They gave up their civilian lives, with varying degrees of reluctance, and were quick and happy to return to them.

The army owed much of its effectiveness to the fact that it was Canadian; but one cannot assume that any Canadian citizen can be clothed in military dress and instantly become a first-class soldier. However, by the time it went into action, it was the best-trained force ever assembled. Commanders soon found that there was no better school than the battlefield, and many lessons were reinforced when the bullets began to fly. The men and women that came home were proud of their **Canadian** identities; there were few hyphenated Canadians in action. Language barriers were surmounted, and comradeship on the battlefield overcame most parochial attitudes. Therefore, it often came as a shock to discover that the people at home still harboured an abiding localism. From this aspect, the Canadian nation was strengthened.

No civilian experience compares to the what can be experienced on the battlefield: the fear, the din of battle, and the smell of smoke, cordite and dead bodies, to expect sudden death from the next bend in the road or from the bushes bordering the ditch. War sharpens experience and focuses perception. A soldier becomes acutely aware of his own existence.

Among the veterans' memories, daily miseries stand side by side with hilarious incidents and enduring comradeship. You had to have been there. And so the Royal Canadian Legion has fostered this spirit by providing a meeting place for those who claim this special kinship.

What kept a soldier's nerves from cracking? A man dodging lethal steel while cowering in a muddy pit can only hope. Hope that he gets out alive. And realization that he probably won't be performing heroic actions. That epiphany usually comes in the first minutes of one's first battle. The soldier only wants it all to end.

After war, there is general disillusionment that victory changes little. The returning soldier often finds that home differs from the dream he cherished while on the battlefield.

But war changes a soldier and a soldier's life. There is a void in the heart of a man returning from war that sometimes even he cannot see. It rarely appears as he comes down a gangplank to his native soil; usually it will be five to ten years before it begins to take its toll. That is what war does. Therefore, it behooves governments to take care of their veterans; to support them, not just at their homecoming, but for years afterwards as they struggle with war's aftereffects. Governments must treat veterans with honour and respect, and not leave them resorting to the courts to secure benefits earned with flesh and blood. Whatever patriotism evidenced today is the fruit of their sacrifice. Never, never forget our fighting men and women.

World War II is now a distant memory. Jack Granatstein asks in his book of the same name, *Who Killed History?* The armed forces that did our nation so proud in two world wars and Korea is a shadow of its former self. A government that has neither memory nor vision has decimated it. Canadians boast of the best legislated benefits for veterans in the world, yet anomalies remain. Some illegal immigrants fare better in this state than the veterans who guaranteed the state's existence.

Canadians need to venerate the remarkable volunteer fighting force that was sent to ward off desperate crises. Learn! Remember!

Lest We Forget.

Stanley Bridge, Prince Edward Island

May 1, 2003.

GLOSSARY

AB	Able Seaman
AC1	Aircraftsman First Class
AC2	Aircraftsman Second Class
ADS	Advanced Dressing Station
AFU	Air Fighting Unit
AGTS	Air Gunnery Training School
ANS	Air Navigation School
AOS	Air Observer School
AWL	absent without leave (also AWOL)
ATS	Army Trades School
B&G	Bombing and Gunnery
BCATP	British Commonwealth Air Training Plan
BEF	British Expeditionary Force
BEM	British Empire Medal
BR	Bombing and Reconnaissance
CAC	Canadian Army Corps
CAMC	Canadian Army Medical Corps
CARU	Canadian Artillery Reinforcement Unit
CASF	Canadian Active Service Force
CBE	Commander of the Order of the British Empire
CBI	China-Burma-India
CDRU	Canadian Division Reinforcement Unit
CFC	Canadian Forestry Corps
CMC	Canadian Medical Center
CFS	Central Flying School
CGH	Canadian General Hospital
ChofO (MG)	Cameron Highlanders of Ottawa (Machine Gun)
CIRU	Canadian Infantry Reinforcement Unit
CMSC	Corps of Military Staff Clerks
CNR	Canadian National Railway
CNE	Canadian National Exhibition
CPHS	Carleton Place High School
CPR	Canadian Pacific Railway

CTS	Canadian Training School
CU	Conversion Unit
CVSM	Canadian Volunteer Service Medal
DEMS	Defensive Equipped Merchant Ships
DFC	Distinguished Flying Cross
DFM	Distinguished Flying Medal
DoInj	died of injuries
DoW	died of wounds
DR	dead reckoning
DSC	Distinguished Service Cross
DSO	Distinguished Service Order
DZ	drop zone
EEG	electroencephalogram
EFTS	Elementary Flying Training School
EOSSAA	Eastern Ontario Secondary School Athletic Association
ERA	Engine Room Artificer
ETA	estimated time of arrival
FIS	Flying Instructors' School
F/L	Flight Lieutenant
F/O	Flying Officer
GGFG	Governor General's Foot Guards
GOC	General Officer Commanding
HAI	high altitude indoctrination
HCU	Heavy Conversion Unit
HLI	Highland Light Infantry
HMCS	His Majesty's Canadian Ship
HMS	His Majesty's Ship
HMT	His Majesty's Troopship
H&PE	Hastings and Prince Edward Regiment
IODE	Imperial Order of the Daughters of the Empire
ITS	Initial Training School
KC	King's Counsel
KIA	killed in action
KTS	Composite Training School
LAC	Leading Aircraftsman
LAD	Light Aid Detachment

LCM	Landing Craft Medical
MBE	Member of the Order of the British Empire
MC	Military Cross
MiD	Mentioned in Despatches
MIR	Medical Inspection Room
MM	Military Medal
mph	miles per hour
MV	motor vessel
NAAFI	Navy, Army and Air Force Institute
NCO	non-commissioned officer
NNSH	North Nova Scotia Highlanders
NPAM	Non-Permanent Active Militia
NRMA	National Resources Mobilization Act
OBE	Officer of the Order of the British Empire
OCTU	Officer Cadet Training Unit
OSS	Office of Strategic Services
OTU	Operational Training Unit
OR	ordinary ranks
PIAT	projector infantry anti-tank
P/O	Pilot Officer
PPCLI	Princess Patricia's Canadian Light Infantry
PRC	Personnel Reception Centre
PT	physical training
R22eR	Royal 22nd Regiment
RAF	Royal Air Force
RAAF	Royal Australian Air Force
RASC	Royal Army Service Corps
RAFVR	Royal Air Force Volunteer Reserve
RCA	Royal Canadian Artillery
RCAF	Royal Canadian Air Force
RCAFSR	Royal Canadian Air Force Special Reserve
RCAMC	Royal Canadian Army Medical Corps
RCASC	Royal Canadian Army Service Corps
RCCS	Royal Canadian Corps of Signals
RCE	Royal Canadian Engineers
RCEME	Royal Canadian Electrical and Mechanical Engineers

RCHA	Royal Canadian Horse Artillery
RCMP	Royal Canadian Mounted Police
RCN	Royal Canadian Navy
RCNR	Royal Canadian Navy Reserve
RCNVR	Royal Canadian Navy Volunteer Reserve
RCOC	Royal Canadian Ordnance Corps
RCR	Royal Canadian Regiment
RHLI	Royal Hamilton Light Infantry
RHR	Royal Highland Regiment (Black Watch)
RNZAF	Royal New Zealand Air Force
RRC	Royal Regiment of Canada
SD&G	Stormont, Dundas and Glengarry Highlanders
SEAC	Southeast Asia Command
SFTS	Service Flying Training School
S/L	Squadron Leader
SOS	struck off strength
SS	Steam Ship
TOS	taken on strength
TTS	Technical Training School
USAAF	United States Army Air Force
USN	United States Navy
USS	United States Ship
VC	Victoria Cross
VD	Volunteer Officers' Decoration (now obsolete)
VLR	very long range
WAG	Wireless Operator/Air Gunners
W/C	Wing Commander
WETP	War Emergency Training Program
WOP or WoP	Wireless Operator
WREN	Women's Royal Naval Service
WTS	Wireless Training School

APPENDIX I

Honours and Awards bestowed upon Carleton Place
residents during the Wars

WORLD WAR I

Breadner, Air Chief Marshall Lloyd Samuel. Chief of the Air Staff in WWII
DSC (1917); Commander, Legion of Merit (U.S.) (1946); Order of Polonia
Restituta (Poland) (1946); Military Cross (Belgium) (1943); Order of the
White Lion (Czechoslovakia) (1946)

Brown, Captain A. Roy. RAF. DSC + Bar. Died: 9 March 1944.

Edwards, Captain Stearne Tighe. RAF. DSC. DoInj: 22 Nov 1918.

Galbraith, Captain Daniel Murray Bayne. RAF. DSC + Bar, Croix de Guerre
(France). Died: 29 March 1921.

† Murphy, Lieutenant Francis Michael.15th Battalion (Central Ontario
Regiment). MiD. DoW: 2 September 1918.

Poynter, Henry Richard. MM

Rawding, Dean Evans. MM

Wilson, Matron Evelyn Martha. Nursing Sister, CAMC. Royal Red Cross
1st Class & Bar, MiD. Born: 5 October 1878; Died: 6 July 1969. buried in
Auld Kirk Cemetery

WORLD WAR II

Barker, Corporal Alan, MiD

Duncan, Captain W. M. MiD. Son of Mr. and Mrs. E. Duncan.

Evoy, Sergeant Elmer Milton, Regina Rifles, MM won 18 July 1943 (won
second MM in Korea).

Houston, Flying Officer James T. Wireless Operator / Air Gunner. DFC. Son
of Mrs. William Houston.

Kellough, Captain Margaret Helen. Nursing Sister. Royal Red Cross.

† Loney, Corporal William M. CHofO, MiD (called Bronze Oak Leaf in
local papers), in recognition of gallantry and distinguished service rendered on the field of battle. KIA 28 July 1944.

Mallory, Sublieutenant Gordon Ewart. MBE

McFarlane, Regimental Sergeant Major Ronald Martin. RCA. BEM

McFarlane, Colonel J. A. Surgeon with No. 15 CGH, OBE

524 FATHERS, BROTHERS AND SONS

McIlquhan, Flight Sergeant Thomas Oswald. Tail-gunner. DFM (downed two fighters).

Miller, Private Ernest Morris. S.D.& G. MM. Awarded April 14, 1945.

Muff, Flying Officer John. Pilot. MiD. Son of Mr. and Mrs. Frank Muff.

Nicol, Corporal Fred James. Order of the Bronze Lion (Netherlands).

Patterson, Flying Officer Elmer. Air Gunner, DFC , son of Mr. & Mrs. D.P. Patterson

Prime, Pilot Officer Harry. Air Gunner. DFM

Saunders, Warrant Officer I Edgar Ferguson. RCOC. MiD and Meritorious Conduct Cross (Netherlands). Son of Mr. and Mrs. W. J. Saunders.

Stewart, Signalman Neil H. RCCS. MiD, son of D. W. Stewart

Taber, Brigadier Harold E. CBE.

Vallee, Bombadier Leo. G. RCA. MM (& Bar?) for courageous work in bringing a fire under control at an ammunition dump, on 18 July 1944 near Bienville, France.

KOREA

Dunphy, Corporal Kerry John, MM

Legend: BEM – British Empire Medal

CBE – Commander of the Order of the British Empire

DSC – Distinguished Service Cross

DFC – Distinguished Flying Cross

DFM – Distinguished Flying Medal

MBE – Member of the Order of the British Emoire

MiD – Mentioned in Despatches

MM – Military Medal

OBE – Officer of the Order of the British Empire

APPENDIX II—SERVING SIBLINGS

Beach, Corporal Garnet, RCAF; Privates Alvin and Leonard, RCASC; Privates Orville, Cecil J., Frederick, Lanark and Renfrew Scottish. Six sons of Mrs. William Beach of Park Avenue, Carleton Place.

Bennett, Pilot Officer James Gordon † and Signalman John "Jack" H.

Brown, Margaret and Barbara, RCAF. Daughters of Captain and Mrs. Roy A. Brown

Brown, Thomas and Dalton, CFC.

Buffam, Earl, Meredith, Reginald, Fred, RCA; Lynwood and Norman, Lanark and Renfrew Scottish. Six sons of Mr. and Mrs. Ernest Buffam, Napoleon Street, Carleton Place.

Cameron, LAC Cedric, RCAF †; Byron, RCASC; Victor, RCAF; Robert, army. Sons of Mr. and Mrs. Stewart Cameron

Crawford, Lance Corporal Wallace H. and Sergeant Lorne. Sons of Mrs. Nesbitt Crawford, Franklin Street, Carleton Place.

Dunlop, Corporal John Barron and Signalman Earl Warren, Canadian Railway Troops. Served together for entire war.

Dunphy, LAC Boyne, RCAF †, Kerry, RCN and Wayne, RCAF, Richard (father), Veterans Guard

Findlay, Flying Officer H. Jock. Pilot, † and D.D., RCAF.

Giles, Corporal Alfred Giles, Veterans Guard of Canada; Private Arthur, RCOC; Leading Aircraftsman Earl (Musty), RCAF; Private Wilbert (Wibs), RCAMC; Private Merrill, Lanark and Renfrew Scottish; Air Crew Eric, RCAF. Grandsons Gunner Eddie Parsons, RCA; Signalman Donald Thompson, RCCS. Six sons and two grandsons of Mr. and Mrs. George Giles, Moore Street, Carleton Place.

Gilmour, Sublieutenant Ronald, Pilot; Flight Sergeant Dawson L., Air Gunner; Victor, CMSC. Sons of Mr. and Mrs. Harry Gilmour, Judson Street, Carleton Place.

Haley, Arnold (army); Bill, RCASC.

Hamilton, Mansel (Jack), Nelson Hamilton and Alex Hamilton, Veteran's Guard.

Hooper, Lieutenant Marjorie E., Nursing Sister; Audrey, CWAC. Daughters of Major and Mrs. William Hooper.

Hughes, Pilot Officer Robert (Bob) Hughes †; Private Cyril Hughes †; Morley Hughes, RCAF. Sons of Mr. and Mrs. W. J. Hughes (plus son-in-law Lieutenant F. Lovett, Paymaster, RCNVR).

Lancaster, Able Seaman Earl Franklin Lancaster †, Douglas, Ordinary Seaman Stewart, RCN. Sons of Mr and Mrs Frank G. Lancaster

Lesway, Ronald and Raymond, CHofO

MacRae, Warrant Officer II W. P. F. (Bill) and Private Cornell B., RCASC

McIlquham, Flight Sergeant Oswald, RCAF, Walter, RCAMC.

McKittrick, Corporal Wallace (Wally) D., 1st Army Tank; A. W. S., RCOC; Trooper Edward (Eddie) R., "A" Squadron, 11th Army Tank Battalion; Sergeant Roy N., CHofO (MG); Corporal Harry, RCASC; Leading Aircraftsman Kenneth (Bob), RCAF; Private James (Jimmy), Seaforth Highlanders †; Stanley of Toronto. Seven sons of Mr. and Mrs. John McKittrick.

Neron, Leo (father); sons Rene (Raney), Romeo (both CHofO) and Roger (RCAF).

O'Leary, Sergeant Robert J. (Bob) RCAF †, Edward, RCAF, Frank GGFG

Patterson, Flying Officer Elmer, F/L Lorne, Wop/AG †, Grant, and James, RCAF.

Paul, Leading Aircraftsman Kenneth, Corporal Leslie, RCAF.

Porteous, Private Fred, Private John, Carl, and Gordon, CHofO; W. L., GGFG; Lance Corporal Basil, No. 2 Provost Company, Private Russell P., GGFG; Arthur Borden and Clarence, Lanark and Renfrew Scottish. Sons of Mrs. Mina Porteous (also spelled Portieous), Ramsay Street, Carleton Place.

Prendergast, Aircraftsman 2 Wilfred F. F., Flight Sergeant Albert "Bert"E. †, Wireless Operator / Air Gunner, RCAF.

Pye, Corporal Bernard, RCE, and Private James †.

Reynolds, T. J. and William, RCAF.

Saunders, S. G. and P. R., RCASC, and Edgar, RCOC.

Southwell, Mark, Thomas, and James.

Townend, Cecil, Orville and Herbert, RCASC; Jerry Townend, RCAF.

Turner, Allan (Jo) and Flight Sergeant Arnold, Air Gunner, RCAF †. Sons of Mr. and Mrs. John S. Turner

Valley, Warrant Officer II William, navigator, † and Corporal Cameron, RCAF.

Wallace, C. Howard, RCA; G.C. Anti-tank Battery

Walsh, L. B., RCHA, and Valerie, RCOC.

Walters, Orville and George, CHofO.

Warren, Sergeant James, Air Observer †, Arthur and Carman, RCAF.

Welsh, Corporal Jack D., RCAMC; Vincent, RCN; and Pilot Officer Thomas E., RCAF. Sons of Mr. and Mrs. Emmett Welsh, of Ottawa, but at one time of Carleton Place.

West, Wilfred, CHofO; George, RCE; Stanley, RCE; and Eric, RCOC. Sons of Mr and Mrs Fred West, Napoleon Street.

Whyte, Cecil (White), RCR, and Garfield, RCOC.

Williams, Privates Gerald and Charles.

Wright, Sergeant Arnold and Edward, RCAF, Private Austin

APPENDIX III

The Carleton Place Canadian, Thursday, July 20, 1944
Watty McIlquham Writes Interesting Letter From Front
Italy, June 14, 1944

Dear Davie:—

I guess you will be surprised to hear from your old friend but after reading your April 27th edition of the *Carleton Place Canadian* from cover to cover, at least twice, I thought I would drop you a line and let you know how I was getting along. I do not think anyone ever read your paper with as much interest as I did that issue. Of course I would have also read the *Herald* with as much vim and vigor if I had been fortunate to receive a copy of it along with yours. Funny, we always subscribed to the *Canadian* and never to the *Herald*. I really used to like the hockey write-ups in the *Herald* though I generally went over to **Bunny Bond's** to read it. I'm really Scotch anyway, Davie.

When I came to that thirty year column and read about my grandmother getting ready to go to California to see her sick brother, I began to think how the world has changed since then. I just wrote her a couple of weeks ago and told her I would take her on a motor trip as soon as I arrived home. In the same column I read the item about "Lead Kindly Light." I memorized this song when I was going to school and many nights through all the fireworks I have repeated it to myself. It really makes a nice little prayer. When you pray here you pray in earnest and are not thinking if the oil in your car should be changed or not. I was never more than the average for religion but over here amid death and destruction you sometimes get a different slant on life.

In a way it is going to be awfully hard to get used to living in Canada again where the only worry people have is looking for a bigger apartment or whether you get a raise in pay or not.

Davie, your paper was in a parcel sent by mother and I read it through before I looked to see what she had sent to me. A fellow shouted over to me *"any comics there, Mac"* and I told him no, that I came from a very conservative town and they had neither comics nor crossword puzzles in either of their papers. I also told him that it was not contaminated by either a liquor store or hotels selling beer. All he said after was, *"Say, what a heck of a town you live in."* All I said was *"yes, I guess you are right at that."* He comes form Vancouver and has been overseas since 1939. Gee, Davie, that is a long time to be away from your loved ones. These fellows have climbed the beaches of Sicily and have been under shellfire so long that nothing can surprise them. I did show the Major padre, who gave me communion, that letter to the Ladies' Temperance Union from the ministers in Pembroke. Oh, I see it is the Women's Christian Temperance Union. Are there no ladies attached to it? Well anyway there is one soldier in Italy that they never helped very much although I am glad they are sort of making up for it now. I wonder though if the boys would rather have a glass of beer than the magazines. I know some of them would anyway. We are just the opposite here, we have wines and cherry brandy but the magazines are worn out before anybody sees them.

I am sending a copy of our newspaper along with this letter. One time I noticed an article with **Ernie Foote** as a byline. I cut the piece out and sent it to brother **Gillie**. I also wrote this chap in care of the *Maple Leaf* but so far have not received any reply.

I was not in England very long but I did go to visit **Dr. Kellough**, in London. I had been there once before in 1937 and had no trouble getting around. London, 1937, and London, 1943, were two vastly different cities although things looked the same when riding the buses. The doctor and I had one swell Sunday together, even going to his golf club and then visiting some patients. He is very well known around the Holland Park residential section of London, and rated as one of the finest doctors. I was taking infantry medical training at the time so I gave him my R.C.A.M.C. patches. The first day in England we were told to take off our Christmas tree decorations. I put one on each side of his fireplace and I suppose they are still there. I will certainly call on him again if I am fortunate to ever get back to England.

Say, Davie, who is this **Anne Allan** and does she know how to make bully beef and dehydrated potato taste any better? She writes about sewing being an agreeable job and about turning the frayed collar of a white shirt. I guess its ok when you are not shaking and able to put your mind to it. I'd sure like to wear a white shirt again for a change. I'm lucky to have a pair of scissors anyway. Oh well as long as you have a spoon and a mess tin you won't starve over here. You do not have to worry about the juice from those powdered eggs getting on your vest either.

Chief Irvine's son is in the Provost over here and somehow got the word around that I was in Italy and as a result **Bill Phillips**, his father works for **"Dutchie,"** looked me up. Bill and I really had a swell time together. He is in the R.C.M.P. and knows all the tricks. I was afterwards told that a fellow by the name of **Whyte** was looking for me but he never came back. I'll bet a dollar to a doughnut that it was **Cecil**. I came out to the field a few days later, reverting to private in order to do so. My rank was confirmed so I did it at my own request. I joined one of the best units in the Canadian Army, medical or otherwise. **Major Hooper** and I do not see eye to eye on certain business transactions but I think he will vouch for this statement. I never did see young **Irvine** but I hope to run into him sometime in the future. It is wise to stay as far from these provosts as possible.

Leaving all jokes aside it is really swell to meet a chap from your hometown or even from Ottawa for that matter. I met **Taffy Williams** and young **Clark** while I was in England and we sure had a long chat together. I also met **"Dedum" Sinclair** a few days before I sailed for Italy. He gave me a few cigs that **Ella** and **Jim McIlquham** had sent him. They surely tasted grand after smoking the English bands for so long.

One day, just after I arrived in England, I attended a padre hour with a few hundred other troops and the padre turned out to be a **Captain Scott**, who used to be minister in Zion church. He recognized me at once and we became great friends during my stay in England. We drank tea and ate cake together and told each other our troubles. He said he had not been feeling so well lately and had been up for a medical reboard. I worked in medical headquarters in Ottawa and from what I know of medical boards I think he will get his discharge and be sent back to Canada. I made him promise that he would call in at the hotel and see the folk.

In the short time I was in southern Italy I ran into **"Biddy" Williams**, a **Lewis** fellow and young **McKittrick**. I was also instrumental in getting **George Walton** a meal one day. I happened to be orderly corporal at the time and arranged for the battalion meals. He just happened to be passing through this town and was pretty hungry. He was a sergeant in rank but that was one time he had to eat in the men's mess. I hope I run into him again some day.

Carleton Place sure gets the old raking over when some of the natives get together but deep down we are all proud to say we came from there. We were told one time that for the sum of 400 lire you could send flowers home for Mother's Day. They took the money out of our pay book ($4.47) and I don't think the flowers were ever sent.

The Canadians have lost a good many men in the last few weeks and it would be ironical if flowers and telegrams were delivered the same day. In the medicals every wounded soldier, Allied or German, is treated the same and gets every chance to live. The surgeons work night and day in the field and when a human life is at stake war is forgotten. Even the padres, both R.C. and C. of E. help care for the wounded and are right there to ease a man's soul and help him make his peace with God. This blood plasma really saves many lives that were doomed ...

You cannot sleep for the rain in your face or your own boom booms and the other moaning minnies. The skies are lighted up like day and you don't know whether to run for your slit trench or lie there in your blankets and pray. Sometimes it's hard to tell which is shaking the most, the ground or yourself. Boy, oh boy, would I often have liked a quart of rye and no temperance society would stop me from drinking it either. Funny thing is they bury you in these blankets and then charge you for them afterwards. I often wonder who pays for the ones we wrap the dead Germans up in. I saw one Jerry paratrooper wrapped up in one of **Bates & Innes'** good woollen blankets. Wish I had a couple instead of these two American ones.

I remember one trip I had in a small boxcar with thirty-seven other fellows. I was corporal in charge of the car and I was supposed to see that everybody had a place. Of course there were many other cars on the train, also packed with men and equipment. Well it took about fourteen hours to arrive at our destination and when we got there it was pitch black and rain was coming down in torrents. I had a small flashlight that I bought in England and by the time we had gathered our equipment the light was about as good as the end of a cigar would be. I still have the flashlight, but alas, no batteries. I was the last one out of the car and when I lit a match I was surprised to see a respirator in one corner, a helmet and tin cup in another. In the Canadian army you are supposed to carry your equipment a certain way so it was not hard to find out who owned the respirator and helmet. By looking at each man's web I soon found out but I never found the owner of that cup so I gave it to an Italian standing by the tracks. We walked for about three miles in the rain with everything we owned on our back and I was never so tired or hungry in my life. When we arrived at the barracks they had a meal of stew, bread and tea all ready for us. Honest, it tasted like a Christmas dinner. We were so cold we ate it with our overcoats and gloves on and then lay on our blankets the same way and I went to sleep.

Italy seems to be extreme one way or another, very hot or very cold, no happy medium. The same applies to their liquor or wine; it is either good or knocks you out altogether. Good stuff to stay away from, the same can be said of the girls, ha! ha! ...

I sure wish the old Mississippi could get a beer license but I guess those days are gone forever in every town. I stayed at a swell hotel in Berlin and had beer with my meals. I hope they don't shoot holes in the barrels like they did with the wines over here.

I have a swell camp here under a big tree and you can see for miles around. I have a couple of blankets, gas cape, ground sheet and mosquito netting. The rear party have brought up our large packs and kit bags so that I now have all my equipment with me. We move mighty quick at times and only carry our small pack, water bottle and trench tools. I was lucky to receive the parcel when I have a place to keep the stuff. I can only carry so much in my pockets and small pack so unless you have other packs with you most of the stuff has to be given to the Italians. Of course the rear party always looks after the equipment you leave behind but sometimes you don't see them for a couple of weeks. The one thing you are pretty sure of though is your mail which is delivered right up to the front and sometimes get killed doing so. Mail is the most important thing in a soldier's life in the field. Sometimes though it acts the other way. A fellow has lots of time to cry after he tucks himself in his blankets. Memory is a funny thing and I don't know what a fellow would do without it. I sure have lived life over again and I have had a lot of nice trips concerned they can give it back to the Italians. I hope France is in better condition. I guess it won't be when the Allies are through with it either.

I started this letter about two weeks ago and in the meantime I have had a chance to visit the Eternal city and also found out that my grandmother received her flowers. Better late than never.

Davie, this city has not been damaged by war, thanks to the Pope and is a sight for sore eyes. I guess the Germans were sorry to leave, although I do not think Hitler wanted them to.

I received a clipping from the *Canadian* telling about cousin Walter's funeral. **Ernie Foote** also answered my letter and informed me he was attached to the *Maple Leaf*. I always liked **Ernie** and I know you did too.

I wrote and told Mother to send more copies of the Canadian.

An old pal

Wattie

P.S. We handled three famous infantry regiments but on those fateful days in May we did not have any Carleton Place boys among the wounded. You can assure their parents that they would get the best of care from our fellow field ambulances. Best of luck to all in Carleton Place.

Walter "Watty" McIlquham, son of Mr. and Mrs. Clyde McIlquaham, joined the RCAMC in 1942 and served in Field Ambulance units. He was a well-known athlete in the Valley, playing championship senior hockey and baseball. A younger brother, Oswald McIlquham, completed a tour of operations with the RCAF overseas, winning the Distinguished Flying Medal.

MEMORIALS

Agira Canadian War Cemetery (near Regalbuto, Sicily)
Wilmer Camelon – p. 141

Air Forces Memorial Runnymede (on Cooper's Hill, Surrey,)
Arthur Prime – p. 219
Armie Garland – p. 283
Ross Stanzel – p. 362

Beny-sur-Mer Canadian War Cemetery (Riviers, France)
Winston Costello – p. 412
William Loney – p. 432

Bretteville-sur-Laize War Cemetery (Calvados, France)
Earl Porteous – p. 442
Raymond White – p. 451

Brookwood Military Cemetery (Woking, Surrey, U.K.)
Earl Rathwell – p. 117
Alan Stokes – p. 515

Calais Canadian War Cemetery (Leubringhen, France)
Cyril Hughes – p. 463
Ken O'Meara – p. 486

Cambrai Communal Cemetery (Cambrai, France)
Arnie Turner – p. 238

Canadian War Cemetery Bergen-op-Zoom (Netherlands)
Chester Maxwell – p. 231

Carleton Place St. James Anglican Cemetery
Earl Lancaster – p. 52

St. Mary's Cemetery
Boyne Dunphy – p. 324

United Cemeteries (Pine Grove)
Cedric Cameron – p. 59
Ernie Morris – p. 505

(St. Filans)
Robert Cavers – p. 211

Caserta War Cemetery (near Royal Palace at Caserta)
Bob Irvine – p. 178

Chevington Cemetery (Chevington, U.K.)
Jock Findlay – p. 100

BIBLIOGRAPHY

Allison, Les. *Canadians in the Royal Air Force*. Roland, Manitoba: Les Allison, 1978.

Ashworth, Chris. *RAF Coastal Command 1936–1969*, Sparkford, England: Patrick Stevens Limited, 1992.

Barker, Ralph and The Editors of Time-Life Books. *The RAF at War, The Epic of Flight*. Alexandria, Virginia: Time-Life Books, 1981.

Barris, Ted. *Behind the Glory, The Plan that Won the Allied Air War*. Toronto: Macmillan Canada, 1992.

Barris, Ted and Alex Barris. *Days of Victory. Canadians Remember: 1939–1945*. Toronto: Macmillan Canada, 1995.

Bell, Major G. K. *Curtain Call*. Toronto: Intaglio Gravure Limited.

Benedict, Michael. *Canada At War, from the archives of Maclean's*. Toronto: Penguin Books Canada Ltd., 1997.

Bercuson, David J. and Holger H. Herwig, *Deadly Seas: The Story of the St. Croix, the U305 and the Battle of the Atlantic*. Toronto: Random House of Canada Limited, 1997.

Berton, Pierre. *Marching as to War: Canada's Turbulent Years, 1899–1953*. Toronto: Doubleday Canada, 2001.

Blackburn, George G. *Where the Hell Are the Guns? A Soldier's Eye View of the Anxious Years*, 1939–44. Toronto: McClelland and Stewart Inc., 1997.

Boss, Lt. Col. W. and Brig. Gen. W. J. Patterson. *Up The Glens, Stormont, Dundas and Glengarry Highlanders, 1783–1994*. Cornwall, Ontario: The Old Book Store, 1995.

Bowyer, Chas. *Bomber Group at War*. Shepperton, Surrey: Ian Allen Ltd.,1991.

Bryant, Arthur. *The Turn of the Tide*. London: Collins, 1957.

Chorley, W. R. *Royal Air Force Bomber Command Losses of the Second World War*. Leicester, England: Midland Counties Publications, 1996.

Clarke, R. Wallace. *British Aircraft Armament, Volume 1: RAF Gun Turrets from 1914 to the Present Day*. Somerset, England: Haynes Publishing Group PLC, 1993.

Copp, Terry. *A Canadian's Guide to the Battlefields of Normandy*. Waterloo: the Laurier Centre for Military Strategic and Disarmament Studies, 1994.

Copp, Terry, ed. *Canadian Military History*, Waterloo: Wilfred Laurier University, 1999–2001.

Copp, Terry and Robert Vogel. *Maple Leaf Route: Antwerp*. Alma, Ontario, Maple Leaf Route, 1984.

Copp, Terry and Robert Vogel. *Maple Leaf Route: Scheldt*. Alma, Ontario, Maple Leaf Route, 1985.

Copp, Terry and Robert Vogel. *Maple Leaf Route: Victory*. Alma, Ontario, Maple Leaf Route, 1988.

Daikens, Don. *Against All Odds, Those Horrible Little Men*. Unpublished.

Dancocks, Daniel G. *The D-Day Dodgers, The Canadians in Italy, 1943–1945*. Toronto: McClelland and Stewart Inc., 1991.

Dewar, Jane, ed. *True Canadian War Stories. From Legion Magazine*. Toronto: Lester & Orpen Dennys Limited, 1986.

Douglas, W. A. B. *The Creation of a National Air Force—The Official History of the Royal Canadian Air Force, Volume II*. Toronto: University of Toronto Press,1986.

Dunmore, Spencer. *Above and Beyond, The Canadians' War in the Air, 1939–45*. Toronto: McClelland and Stewart Inc., 1996.

Dunmore, Spencer. *Wings for Victory, The Remarkable Story of the British Commonwealth Air Training Plan in Canada*. Toronto: McClelland and Stewart Inc., 1994.

Dunmore, Spencer and William Carter, PhD. *Reap The Whirlwind, The Untold Story of 6 Group, Canada's Bomber Force of World War II*. Toronto: McClelland and Stewart Inc., 1991.

Fairlie Wood, Herbert and Swettenham, John, Silent Witnesses. Ottawa: Canadian War Museum Publications, 1974.

Findlay, David K. *The Search for Amelia*. Philadelphia: J. B. Lippincott Co., 1958.

Fisher, William. "The End of HMCS St. Croix," *Canadian Military History*, Vol. 8, No. 3, Summer 1999. Waterloo: Wilfred Laurier University, 1999.

Forchuk, Stephen M., *Metal Canvas, Canadians and World War II Aircraft Nose Art*. St. Catherines: Vanwell Pub. Ltd., 1999.

Fraser, Donald A. *Live to Look Again*. Belleville: Mika Publishing Company, 1984.

Frost, Col. C. Sydney. *Once A Patricia (Memoirs of a Junior Infantry Officer in World War II)*. St. Catharines: Vanwell Publishing Limited, 1988.

Garbutt, Mike and Brian Goulding. *The Lancaster at War 1*, Shepperton, Surrey: Ian Allen Ltd., 1971.

Garbutt, Mike and Brian Goulding. *The Lancaster at War 2*, London: Charles Scribner's Sons, 1979.

Gardam, John, OMM, CD. *Fifty Years After.* Burnstown: General Store Publishing House Inc., 1990.

German, Tony. *The Sea is at Our Gates.* Toronto: McLelland & Stewart Inc., 1990.

Geisler, Patricia. *Valour at Sea—Canada's Merchant Navy.* Ottawa: Queen's Printer, 1998.

Giesler, Patricia. *Valour Remembered—Canada and the Second World War 1939–1945.* Ottawa: Queen's Printer, 1981.

Goodspeed, Lt. Col. D. J., CD, *The Armed Forces of Canada 1867–1967.* Ottawa: Queen's Printer, 1967.

Gordon, John. . . . *Of Men and Planes.* Volumes 1, 2 and 3. Ottawa: Love Printing, 1968.

Granatstein, J. L. and Desmond Morton. *Bloody Victory: Canadians and the D-Day Campaign 1944.* Toronto: Lester & Orpen Dennys Limited, 1984.

Greenhous, Brereton, Stephen J. Harris, William C. Johnston, and Wm. G. P. Rawling. *The Crucible of War 1939–1945, The Official History of the Royal Canadian Air Force, Vol. III.* University of Toronto Press and Department of National Defence, 1994.

Griffin, Anthony. *A Naval Officer's War.* www.naval.ca/article. Ottawa: Vol. VII, No. 8, Autumn 1999 issue of *Starshell*, Naval officers Association of Canada.

Gwyne-Timothy, John R. W., *Burma Liberators, RCAF in SEAC, Vols I & II.* Toronto: Next Level Press, 1991.

Halliday, Hugh A. *DISPATCHES—Canada's Air Force in War and Peace.* Ottawa: Canadian War Museum, 1999.

Hammerton, Sir John, ed. *ABC of the RAF.* London: The Amalgamated Press Ltd., 1942.

Harris, Sir Arthur, Marshall of the RAF, GCB, OBE, AFC. *Bomber Offensive.* London: Collins, 1947.

Hart, B. H. Liddell. *History of the Second World War.* New York: G. P. Putnam's Sons, 1970.

Harvey, J. Douglas. *The Tumbling Mirth: Remembering the Air Force.* Toronto: McClelland and Stewart, 1983.

Hastings, Max. *Bomber Command,* London: Book Club Associates, 1980.

Heathcote, Blake. *Testaments of Honour: Personal Histories of Canada's War Veterans.* Toronto: Doubleday Canada, 2002.

Heide, Rachel Lea. *The British Commonwealth Air Training Plan.* Ottawa: Veterans Affairs Canada, 2000.

Heide, Rachel Lea. *The Politics of British Commonwealth Air Training Plan Base Selection in Western Canada.* Ottawa: an unpublished Master's thesis submitted to Carleton University, 2000.

Jackson, Robert. *Before the Storm—The Story of the Royal Air Force Bomber Command, 1939–1942.* London: Arthur Baker Ltd., 1972.

Johnston, Mac, ed. *Legion Magazine.* Ottawa: Canvet Publications Ltd.

Kinlock, Dave. *First Canadian Corps—Italian Tour—September 1997.* Unpublished: Whizbang Association.

Kostenuk, Samuel and John Griffin. *R.C.A.F. Squadron Histories and Aircraft, 1924–1968.* Toronto: Samuel Stevens & Co., 1977.

Lawrence, W. J. *No. 5 Bomber Group RAF (1939–1945).* London: Faber and Faber Ltd. 1951.

Lewis, Peter. *Squadron Histories, RFC, RNAS & RAF since 1912.* London: Putnam & Company, 1959.

Lotz, Jim. *Canadians At War.* London: Bison Books Ltd. 1990.

Marteinson, John. *We Stand On Guard. An Illustrated History Of The Canadian Army.* Montreal: Ovale Publications, 1992.

Mason, Francis K. *The Avro Lancaster.* Bourne End, Bucks: Aston Publications Ltd, 1989.

McAndrew, Bill. *Canadians and the Italian Campaign, 1943–1945.* Montreal: Éditions Art Global Inc., 1996.

McAndrew, Bill, Bill Rawling and Michael Whitby. *LIBERATION, The Canadians in Europe.* Montreal: Éditions Art Global Inc., 1995.

McKee, Fraser and Robert Darlington. *The Canadian Naval Chronicle 1939–1945.* St. Catharines: Vanwell Publishing Limited, 1996

Middlebrook, Martin. *The Berlin Raids, R.A.F. Bomber Command Winter 1943–44.* London: Penquin Group, 1988.

Middlebrook, Martin and Chris Everitt. *The Bomber Command War Diaries.* Leicester, England: Midland Counties Publications (Aerophile) Limited, 1996.

Milberry, Larry. *Canada's Air Force at War and Peace, Volume One.* Toronto: CANAV Books, 2000.

Milberry, Larry. *Canada's Air Force at War and Peace, Volume Two.* Toronto: CANAV Books, 2000.

Milner, Marc. *The U-Boat Hunters: The Royal Canadian Navy and the Offensive Against Germany's Submarines.* Toronto: University of Toronto Press, 1994.

Minister of National Defence. *The Regiments and Corps of The Canadian Army.* Ottawa: Queen's Printer, 1964.

Monks, Noel. *Squadrons Up!* London England: Victor Gollance Ltd., 1940.

Montemaggi, Amedeo and Bill McAndrew. *The Gothic Line, The Canadian Breaching at Tavullia, Key of the Italian Campaign.* Commune di Tavullia, Provincia di Pesaro e Urbino, Italy: Amedeo Montemaggi, 1997.

Mowatt, Farley. *And No Birds Sang.* Toronto: McClelland and Stewart Limited, 1979.

Mowatt, Farley. *The Regiment.* Toronto: McClelland and Stewart Limited, 1955.

Moyes, Phillip J. R. *Bomber Squadrons of the Royal Air Force and Their Aircraft.* London: Macdonald & Co. (Publishers) Ltd., 1964.

Munson, Kenneth. *Bombers, Patrol and Transport Aircraft, 1939–45.* Poole, Dorset, England: Blandford Press, 1969.

Munson, Kenneth. *Fighters, Attack and Training Aircraft, 1939–45.* Poole, Dorset, England: Blandford Press, 1969.

Nolan, Brian. *Airborne—The Heroic Story of the 1st Canadian Parachute Battalion in the Second World War.* Toronto: Lester Publishing Limited, 1995.

Normand, Marion, ed. *Camp Borden, Birthplace of the RCAF, 1917 to 1999.* Borden: 16 Wing, 1999.

Ozorak, Paul. *Abandoned Military Installations in Canada, Vol I: Ontario.* Privately published, 1991.

Peden, Murray. *A Thousand Shall Fall.* Stittsville: Canada's Wings, 1979.

Reader's Digest, *The Canadians at War 1939/45.* Volumes 1 & 2. Montreal: The Reader's Digest Association, 1969.

Roberts, Leslie. *There Shall Be Wings—A History of the Royal Canadian Air Force.* Toronto: Clarke, Irwin & Company Limited, 1959.

Rohwer, Jürgen. *Axis Submarine Successes of World War Two.* London: Greenhill Books, 1999.

Roy, Reginald H. *1944: The Canadians in Normandy.* Toronto: Macmillan of Canada, 1984.

Russell, E. C. *Customs and Traditions of the Canadian Armed Forces.* Ottawa: Deneau & Greenberg Publishing Ltd., 1980.

Sarty, Roger. *DISPATCHES—The Royal Canadian Navy and the Battle of the Atlantic, 1939–1945.* Ottawa: Canadian War Museum, 1999.

Schull, Joseph. *The Far Distant Ships.* Ottawa: King's Printer, 1950.

Stacey, Col. C. P. *Six Years of War, Volume 1.* Ottawa: Queen's Printer, 1955.

Stacey, Col. C. P. *The Canadian Army 1939–45.* Ottawa: King's Printer, 1948.

Sturtivant, Ray, ISO, John Hamlin and James. J. Halley. *RAF Flying Training and Support Units.* Tunbridge Wells, Kent: AirBritains (Historians) Ltd., 1997.

Sweetman, Bill and Watanabe Rikyu. *Avro Lancaster*, Tokyo: Zokeisha Publications Ltd., 1982.

Taylor, Scott R., pub. *Esprit de Corps, CANADIAN MILITARY*. Ottawa: Esprit de Corps, Taylor, Scott R., Editor-in-Chief. *Canada At War and Peace, II, a millennium of military heritage*. Ottawa: Esprit de Corps Books, 2000.

Terraine, John. *The Right of the Line, The Royal Air Force in the European War, 1939– 1945*. New York: MacMillan Publishing Company, 1985.

The Editors of Time-Life Books. *The Luftwaffe, The Epic of Flight*. Alexandria, Virginia: Time-Life Books, 1982.

Thomas, David A. *The Atlantic Star 1939–45*. London: W. H. Allen & Co Plc, 1990.

Tracy, Bob, pub. *Airforce Magazine*. Ottawa: The Magazine of Canada's Air Force Heritage.

Velleman, Alexander. *The RCAF as Seen From the Ground*. Stittsville: Canada's Wings Inc., 1986.

Verrier, Anthony. *The Bomber Offensive*. London: BT Batsford Ltd., 1968.

Williams, Jeffery. *Princess Patricia's Canadian Light Infantry*. London: Leo Cooper,1972.

Willis, D. & B. R. Holliss. *Military Airfields in the British Isles, 1939–1945*. Sherington, U.K: Enthusiasts Publications, 1987.

_____. "Bomber Command Salute," *Flypast*. Stamford, Lincolnshire: Key Publications Limited, July 2001.

_____. *Canada in World War II, Post-War Possibilities*. Montreal: William S. Boas & Company, 1945

_____. *The RCAF Overseas. The Fifth Year.* Toronto: Oxford University Press, 1945.

_____. *The RCAF Overseas. The First Four Years.* Toronto: Oxford University Press, 1944.

INDEX

Photo by Rick Bardawill

ABOUT THE AUTHOR

Larry Gray served twenty-four years in the Royal Canadian Air Force as a navigator. He went on to serve veterans as an advocate and adjudicator of disability pension claims.

This is Larry's second book on the war dead of the Ottawa valley town of Carleton Place. The first, *We Are The Dead*, related the lives of those men, and one woman, who lost their lives in World War I and whose names are engraved on the town's cenotaph. This book completes that project, called Faces to Names, by narrating the lives and times of those lost in World War II. Over half were sacrificed to the Air war; some perished at sea, some in Italy and many in North West Europe.

Larry and his wife and inspiration, Gloria, live in Carleton Place and Stanley Bridge, PEI. They have three grown sons.

ISBN 141201901-X